Every Decker book is accompanied by a CD-ROM.

The disk appears in the front of each copy, in its own sealed jacket. Affixed to the front of the book will be a distinctive Bc̄D sticker **"Book *cum* disk".**

The disk contains the complete text and illustrations of the book, in fully searchable PDF files. As an added feature, most chapters feature problem-solving cases to allow for testing and reinforcing of the material as it applies to clinical situations. The book and disk will be sold *only* as a package; neither will be available independently, and no prices will be available for the items individually.

BC Decker Inc is committed to providing high quality electronic publications that will compliment traditional information and learning methods.

We trust you will find the Book/CD Package invaluable and invite your comments and suggestions.

Brian C. Decker
CEO and Publisher

Essentials of
Oral Medicine

Sol Silverman, Jr, MA, DDS
Professor
Division of Oral Medicine
Department of Stomatology
University of California School of Dentistry
San Francisco, California

L. Roy Eversole, DDS, MSD, MA
Professor
Department of Pathology and Medicine
University of the Pacific School of Dentistry
San Francisco, California

Edmond L. Truelove, DDS, MSD
Professor and Chairperson
Department of Oral Medicine
University of Washington
University of Washington Medical Center
Seattle, Washington

2001
BC Decker Inc
Hamilton • London

BC Decker Inc
20 Hughson Street South
P.O. Box 620, LCD 1
Hamilton, Ontario L8N 3K7
Tel: 905-522-7017; 1-800-568-7281
Fax: 905-522-7839; 1-888-311-4987
e-mail: info@bcdecker.com
website: http://www.bcdecker.com

02 03 04 05 / UTP / 9 8 7 6 5 4 3 2 1

ISBN 1-55009-146-8

Printed in Canada

Sales and Distribution

United States
BC Decker Inc
P.O. Box 785
Lewiston, NY 14092-0785
Tel: 905-522-7017; 1-800-568-7281
Fax: 905-522-7839; 1-888-311-4987
e-mail: info@bcdecker.com
website: www.bcdecker.com

Canada
BC Decker Inc
20 Hughson Street South
P.O. Box 620, LCD 1
Hamilton, Ontario L8N 3K7
Tel: 905-522-7017; 1-800-568-7281
Fax: 905-522-7839; 1-888-311-4987
e-mail: info@bcdecker.com
website: www.bcdecker.com

Japan
Igaku-Shoin Ltd.
Foreign Publications Department
3-24-17 Hongo, Bunkyo-ku
Tokyo 113-8719, Japan
Tel: 81 3 3817 5680
Fax: 81 3 3815 6776
e-mail: fd@igaku-shoin.co.jp

U.K., Europe, Scandinavia, Middle East
Harcourt Publishers Limited
Customer Service Department
Foots Cray High Street
Sidcup, Kent
DA14 5HP, UK
Tel: 44 (0) 208 308 5760
Fax: 44 (0) 181 308 5702
e-mail: cservice@harcourt_brace.com

**Singapore, Malaysia, Thailand,
Philippines, Indonesia, Vietnam,
Pacific Rim, Korea**
Harcourt Asia Pte Limited
583 Orchard Road
#09/01, Forum
Singapore 238884
Tel: 65-737-3593
Fax: 65-753-2145

Australia, New Zealand
Harcourt Australia Pty Limited
Customer Service Department
STM Division
Locked Bag 16
St. Peters, New South Wales, 2044
Australia
Tel: 61 02 9517-8999
Fax: 61 02 9517-2249
e-mail: stmp@harcourt.com.au
website: www.harcourt.com.au

Foreign Rights
John Scott & Co.
International Publishers' Agency
P.O. Box 878
Kimberton, PA 19442
Tel: 610-827-1640
Fax: 610-827-1671
email: jsco@voicenet.com

Notice: The authors and publisher have made every effort to ensure that the patient care recommended herein, including choice of drugs and drug dosages, is in accord with the accepted standard and practice at the time of publication. However, since research and regulation constantly change clinical standards, the reader is urged to check the product information sheet included in the package of each drug, which includes recommended doses, warnings, and contraindications. This is particularly important with new or infrequently used drugs.

Contributors

BRUCE BLASBERG, DMD, FRCD(C)
Associate Professor and Division Head
Division of Oral Medicine and Pathology
Department of Oral Biological and Medical Sciences
University of British Columbia Faculty of Dentistry
Vancouver, British Columbia
Atypical Facial Pain

WILLIAM M. CARPENTER, DDS, MS
Professor and Chairman
Department of Pathology and Medicine
University of the Pacific School of Dentistry
San Francisco, California
Infection Control

ELISA M. CHÁVEZ, DDS
Clinical Assistant Professor
Department of Removable Prosthodontics
University of the Pacific School of Dentistry
University of the Pacific On Lok Senior
    Health Center
San Francisco, California
Special Senses: Disorders of Taste and Smell

EVE CUNY, MS
Director
Environmental Health and Safety
University of the Pacific School of Dentistry
San Francisco, California
Infection Control

JOEL B. EPSTEIN, DMD, MSD, FRCD(C)
Professor
Department of Oral Medicine
University of Washington
Seattle, Washington
Medical Dental Staff
British Columbia Cancer Agency
Vancouver Hospital
Vancouver, British Columbia
Oral Fungal Infections
Burning Mouth Syndrome
Orofacial Pain in Patients with Cancer

L. ROY EVERSOLE, DDS, MSD, MA
Professor
Department of Pathology and Medicine
University of the Pacific School of Dentistry
San Francisco, California

JACOB FLEISCHMANN, MD
Clinical Professor
University of California School of Medicine
    and Dentistry
Greater Los Angeles VA Medical Center
Los Angeles, California
Oral Fungal Infections

PHILIP C. FOX, DDS
Biomedical Consultant
Cabin John, Maryland
Diseases of the Salivary Glands

MICHAEL GLICK, DMD
Professor
Department of Oral Medicine
University of Pennsylvania School of Dental Medicine
Director
Programs for Medically Complex Patients
Philadelphia, Pennsylvania
Human Immunodeficiency Virus Disease

MIRIAM GRUSHKA, DDS, PhD
Active Staff
Etobicoke Campus
William Osler Health Centre
Toronto, Ontario
Burning Mouth Syndrome

PETER L. JACOBSEN, PhD, DDS
Professor
Department of Pathology and Medicine
Director
Oral Medicine Clinic
University of the Pacific School of Dentistry
San Francisco, California
Adverse Drug Reactions

JED J. JACOBSON, DDS, MS, MPH
Assistant Dean
Department of Oral Medicine, Pathology,
    and Oncology
University of Michigan School of Dentistry
Ann Arbor, Michigan
Bacterial Infections

JILL S. KAWALEC, PhD
Director of Research
Ohio College of Podiatric Medicine
Cleveland, Ohio
Burning Mouth Syndrome

CRAIG S. MILLER, DMD, MS
Professor
Department of Oral Medicine
University of Kentucky College of Dentistry
Lexington, Kentucky
Hepatitis B and Hepatitis C Virus Infections

DOUGLAS E. PETERSON, DMD, PhD
Professor and Department Head
Department of Oral Diagnosis
University of Connecticut School of Dental Medicine
Associate Director
Cancer Program
University of Connecticut Health Center
Farmington, Connecticut
Blood Dyscrasias

MARK M. SCHUBERT, DDS, MSD
Professor
Department of Oral Medicine
University of Washington
Director of Oral Medicine
Seattle Cancer Care Alliance
Seattle, Washington
Blood Dyscrasias

JONATHAN A. SHIP, DMD
Professor
Department of Oral Medicine
Director
Bluestone Center for Clinical Research
New York University College of Dentistry
New York University Medical Center
New York, New York
Special Senses: Disorders of Taste and Smell

SOL SILVERMAN, JR, MA, DDS
Professor
Division of Oral Medicine
Department of Stomatology
University of California School of Dentistry
San Francisco, California

DAVID A. SIROIS, DMD, PhD
Associate Professor and Chairman
Department of Oral Medicine
New York University College of Dentistry
Adjunct Associate Professor
Department of Neurology
New York University School of Medicine
New York, New York
Orofacial Neuralgias and Neuropathic Pain

CAROL M. STEWART, DDS, MS
Associate Dean for Clinical Affairs
Department of Oral and Maxillofacial Surgery and
    Diagnostic Sciences
University of Florida College of Dentistry
Gainesville, Florida
Endocrine Diseases

EDMOND L. TRUELOVE, DDS, MSD
Professor and Chairperson
Department of Oral Medicine
University of Washington
University of Washington Medical Center
Seattle, Washington

Contents

SOFT TISSUE DISEASE

FACIAL PAIN AND NEUROLOGY

Preface

Oral medicine is a diverse and dynamic specialty that requires a clinician to have a background in the dental, medical, and basic sciences in order to manage the myriad of diseases and conditions that affect the head and neck area. These disorders may reflect local disease processes, oral manifestations of systemic diseases, or oral conditions that can affect other organ systems.

While a structured training program is required to attain a fundamental knowledge of oral medicine, varying degrees of expertise are essential to incorporating the principles of oral medicine into general practice. Since oral medicine integrates basic elements of pathology, diagnosis, prevention, and treatment, reference texts are needed; continuing education in this field never ends. Having experience in differential diagnosis, becoming knowledgeable about and proficient in diagnostic testing, and keeping abreast of therapeutics are all essential components of optimal patient care.

With this in mind, we have organized *Essentials of Oral Medicine* into five sections: The Patient Workup, The Medically Compromised Patient, Infectious Disease, Soft Tissue Disease, and Facial Pain and Neurology. These sections describe and illustrate a large number of oral diseases and conditions, including pathologic and molecular correlates. Our objective is to enable both students and practitioners to attain a final diagnosis and initiate the appropriate treatments.

The essential procedures of history taking, and oral or head and neck examinations, are discussed and illustrated. These are the critical first steps in correlating patient complaints and findings with abnormalities and disease entities (differential diagnosis). A brief overview of the important organ systems adds to an understanding of the interactions between oral findings and overall patient health. The text has an abundance of colored illustrations to aid a clinician in defining and classifying deviations from normal as well as disease entities. An accompanying CD-ROM contains the full text and illustrations plus problem-solving cases that accompany most chapters. This addition not only allows for testing but also reinforces the material as it applies to clinical situations.

We have prepared this text in oral medicine to simplify patient evaluation and treatment, improve patient care, and prevent complications. We hope the work will help you achieve these goals.

Sol Silverman Jr
L. Roy Eversole
Edmond L. Truelove

June 2001

Acknowledgments

We would like to express our appreciation of our students and patients, who have constantly challenged our diagnostic acumen. Special thanks is extended to Ms. Heather Kidd at BC Decker for her support and efforts in keeping us focused on the overall mission for this text, and for engineering all the aspects of this book and accompanying CD with regard to organization, the myriad of details, and formatting.

The editors also wish to extend their gratitude to Drs. Rasika Naran, Perry T. Francis, Don Fowkes, and to Mrs. Maria Co-Viray for serving as examiners and patients in the chapter on physical diagnosis. The expertise and cooperation of the contributing authors is recognized and their substantive additions to *Essentials of Oral Medicine* are greatly appreciated.

This book is dedicated to the patients that the three principal authors have examined, diagnosed, and treated in their clinics throughout more than a century of collective oral medicine practice. These patients have endured pain, loss of function, disfigurement, and lowered quality of life from the many neoplastic, infectious, inflammatory, and neurologic diseases from which they have suffered. We hope that we have contributed to their healing and comfort.

1 Procurement of the History

L. Roy Eversole, DDS, MSD, MA, and Sol Silverman, Jr, MA, DDS

An effective approach to the patient who requires dental care entails the following steps: (1) establishing rapport, (2) learning the chief complaint, (3) recording the history of the present illness, (4) procuring the medical history, and (5) conducting a thorough physical examination (Figure 1–1). Completion of these five steps provides details that collectively are known as the history and physical database, which may suggest a number of diagnostic possibilities. The database may be compatible with a variety of disease processes, which constitute the differential diagnosis. Once a differential diagnosis has been established, a process of elimination is pursued by further questioning into the history and procuring clinical laboratory tests, cytology, biopsy, imaging studies, and other diagnostic aids. Once all necessary data have been accumulated, sufficient information should be present to determine a definitive diagnosis. In some instances, when a definitive diagnosis is not readily apparent, therapeutic drug trials can be instituted to determine if any pharmacologic benefit is obtained.

Patient approach

The establishment of rapport is perhaps the most important part of the patient workup. A favorable doctor–patient relationship ensures honesty and trust and places the patient in the role of a cooperative participant in his or her oral health care rather than a passive bystander. The patient undergoing an oral medicine workup is often apprehensive, possibly suspecting that he or she suffers from a serious disease such as cancer or acquired immunodeficiency disease (AIDS). The patient who is in pain also may be apprehensive and irritable, owing to weeks or months of chronic pain with no effective treatment in sight. Kindness, reassurance, a caring approach, and honesty need to be exercised at the outset. The patient must be made to feel that he or she is the most important person on your schedule, at least for the private time you have together. Some patients will be accompanied by a spouse, friend, or relative. In general, it is prudent to explain that you need to engage in a private discussion and will inform the accompanying person of everything that transpires, if disclosure of such information is not detrimental to the patient. Of course children require the presence of their parent or guardian.

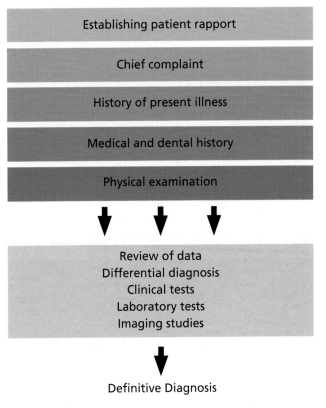

Establishing patient rapport

Chief complaint

History of present illness

Medical and dental history

Physical examination

Review of data
Differential diagnosis
Clinical tests
Laboratory tests
Imaging studies

Definitive Diagnosis

Figure 1–1 The patient workup.

In this day of litigation in the health care setting and particularly in light of sexual harassment issues, it is wise to leave a door open or have an assistant in the same examination room, particularly when doctor and patient are of the opposite sex. Jokes and idle banter are insulting to many people and should be avoided in the professional setting.

Procurement of the database is approached in one of two ways.

1. A patient-generated history may be completed prior to the visit. Then, during the appointment the clinician reviews the history and enters additional notations that are gleaned during the patient interview.
2. The doctor generates the history by direct interview, making appropriate notations throughout the one-on-one discourse.

The overall format for both methods is the same. *Symptoms* are subjective musings on the part of the patient. Pain, discomfort, burning, numbness, roughness, and swelling are all examples of symptoms. These are usually the first aspects of the history to be recorded. *Signs* are objective findings discovered by the examining clinician. The pulse, blood pressure, a mass, ulcer, erosion, white lesion, blister, pigmentation, and red lesion are all examples of signs. Signs are usually observed in the physical examination segment of the database. Signs of disease are detected by visualization, listening (auscultation), smelling, and palpation of the tissues.

Chief complaint

The first segment of the database procurement is the recording of the *chief complaint*. At this time the patient is asked the reason for reporting to the office; all responses represent symptoms. Table 1–1 lists the elements of the chief complaint. In the oral medicine clinic setting, there may not be a chief complaint if in fact a

Table 1–1   Chief Complaint and History of the Present Illness

Characterization of the Chief Complaint	Symptoms
Onset	Pain
Duration	Burning
Periodicity	Soreness
Nature or character	Dry mouth
Severity	Paresthesia
Triggers and associations	Hypesthesia
	Swelling
	Roughness
	Visualized change in tissue

general practitioner or a hygienist had detected the lesion. Once the symptom is noted, the clinician must further characterize this subjective finding by asking the patient to describe the onset of the symptom; its duration; whether the symptom is acute, chronic, or cyclic; the nature of the complaint; and how severe the patient believes the symptom or symptoms may be. Note the plural here; there may be more than a single complaint. This questioning constitutes that part of the history referred to as the *history of the present illness*. For example, a patient may complain of pain and swelling of the gingiva and may relate that the pain was first noticed 1 week earlier and the swelling has been present for 3 days. He or she may describe the pain as constant and aching with sharp stabbing episodes that are triggered by cold; the steady-state level of pain is mild to moderate, whereas the acute episodes are severe. Another example that characterizes the chief complaint is as follows: a patient states that his or her mouth is becoming progressively dry. This dryness was first noticed about 9 months ago and within the past 2 months it has become much more noticeable. The dryness is more problematic in the earlier part of the day, and the patient wonders if the problem could be associated with the use of an antidepressant drug that was first administered just prior to the onset of the symptoms. All of these symptomatic complaints should be recorded in the chart. As these data are being documented, the clinician may be thinking of possible diagnoses that conform to the subjective findings; however, a differential diagnosis should not be constructed until the entire database has been completed.

Medical history

The next segment of the history and physical examination is the procurement of the medical history. This can be noncontributory, or there may be systemic conditions that are associated with the chief complaint. Table 1–2 lists the elements of the medical history, which, by the way, includes the dental history. The usual childhood exanthems and infectious diseases, such as mumps, measles, rubella, varicella, and so on, are noted with verification of vaccinations, both in childhood and later, in adult years.

A record of hospitalizations is recorded, obtaining information on the nature of the hospital stay and any surgical procedures that the patient has undergone. This is followed by recording the patient's drug history both current and past, noting any adverse or allergic reactions. Each drug should be listed along with dosage and daily intake. Unfamiliar drugs should be investigated, using the Physician's Desk Reference (PDR) or similar reference, prior to rendering any treatment.

Dental history

The dental history includes an assessment of past caries experience, restorative dental procedures, periodontal disease, prosthetics, and past oral surgical procedures. Patient home care status is recorded and any habits,

Table 1–2 Medical History

Category	Parameter
Childhood exanthems and other diseases	
Vaccinations	
Hospitalizations and prior surgeries	
Current medical care	
Last physical examination	
Medications	Current drugs
	Drugs taken in the past 6 months
	Drug, dosage, and duration of use
	Adverse reactions and allergies
Dental history	Caries
	Periodontal disease
	Oral surgery
	Need for premedication
	Previous problems during dental care
Oral habits	Flossing
	Brushing
	Mouthrinses
	Use of tobacco products
	Use of alcohol
	Tooth grinding or clenching
Psychological profile	Phobias
	Anxiety
	Depression
	Hostility
	Psychosis
	Mental ability
	Recreational drug use
Socioeconomic profile	Nutrition, obesity, weight loss
	Home environment
	Insurance, income
	Marital status
	Work status
Review of systems	Cardiovascular
	Renal
	Pulmonary
	Endocrine
	Nervous
	Musculoskeletal
	Eyes, ears, nose, and throat (EENT)
	Gastrointestinal
	Hepatobiliary
	Hematopoietic
	Genitourinary
	Dermal
	Immune (include allergies)

such as smoking, smokeless tobacco use, bruxing or clenching, and mouthrinse use should be noted.

An overview of psychosocial issues is germane to dental care, oral mucosal diseases, and facial pain conditions. Anxiety and dental phobias must be noted and addressed, perhaps with psychological referral and intervention. Careful observation during the interview may lead one to suspect that more serious psychological problems are present. The use of illicit drugs should be investigated with direct, unabashed questioning, reassuring the patient that such information may impact the treatment that you will ultimately recommend. This is particularly true for patients with a chief compliant of pain. Some individuals may be malingerers, seeking narcotic or mind-altering drugs, others may be recovering addicts who do not want to be exposed to narcotic analgesics. Drug interactions are of significance in illicit-drug users. Alcohol consumption should be recorded. Heavy alcohol consumption may herald chronic liver disease with a potential for hemorrhage. A patient's nutritional status should be assessed, although nutritional deficiencies are uncommon in industrialized countries. Sugar intake in the caries-prone individual and in patients with xerostomia is of significance. Socioeconomic considerations should be discussed at the outset. Who will be responsible for remitting payment for services rendered? The treatment plan and economic alternatives should be openly discussed between doctor and patient. In addition, it should be explained that many oral medicine procedures, such as examination, biopsy, cytology, and orthotics may be covered under medical insurance programs.

Review of systems

The final aspect of the medical history is a review of systems. Questions must be posed so as to reveal any diagnosed as well as undetected systemic diseases. Many patients seek dental care, yet have not seen a physician in years. It is important, as health care providers, that dentists be familiar with signs and symptoms of systemic diseases so that timely referral to a physician can occur or that precautions may be taken for patient protection. Pertinent questions are posed for each of the major organ systems. Beginning with the cardiovascular system, the oral medicine clinician should address congenital as well as acquired cardiovascular diseases. Patients should be questioned about valvular, septal, and large vessel congenital defects, particularly those that manifest with a heart murmur. Inquiries regarding acquired valvular insufficiency and stenosis should be made, particularly in light of potential oral microbial bacteremias. In this respect, rheumatic heart disease is the primary culprit. Atherosclerotic vascular occlusive disease, bypass surgery, coronary angioplasty, aneurysm, and hypertension history are all germane to dental procedures. Asking how easily the patient develops dyspnea after walking up a flight of stairs or whether he or she needs three or more pillows to sleep should assess congestive heart failure. During the interview, ankle edema can be noted, and later in the physical examination, jugular vein distention can be assessed, both being signs of congestive heart failure. Carotid atherosclerotic lesions can often be detected on panoramic radiographs, provided aneurysms with calcifications are dense enough to be visualized radiographically. Further assessment of cardiac status takes place while vital signs are being taken.

Renal diseases include congenital defects, glomerulonephritis, pyelonephritis, and urolithiasis, all of which can culminate in end-stage renal disease with filtration failure. Patients in the later phases of renal disease will be on peritoneal or hemodialysis. Hematuria, polyurea, and anuria are all signs of urinary tract disease. Low flank pain is a common finding in urolithiasis. Any of these signs or symptoms should be recorded and followed-up if the patient has not seen a physician for some time. Renal transplantation is common practice today, and kidney recipients are generally placed on immunosuppressive drugs, such as prednisone and cyclosporine for the first year after their surgery.

A history of pulmonary system diseases, including upper airway lesions, may have an impact on dental care, particularly if the airway is compromised. Upper airway diseases (larynx and sinonasal tract) are marked by eye, ear, nose, and throat lesions. Patients undergoing inhalation anesthesia or even conscious sedation for dental procedures may be at risk if they have asthma or chronic obstructive pulmonary disease. Asthmatic patients are often taking bronchodilator drugs and using inhalers. A history of pulmonary tract infections, particularly tuberculosis, mycotic infections, and pneumonia poses infection control risks and also compromises the airway, owing to pulmonary granulomas or post-infection fibrosis, chronic cough, dyspnea, and history of hemoptysis.

Diabetes mellitus is the most common endocrine system disease to affect humans. Undiagnosed cases may present with oral manifestations or early signs that include polydipsia, polyurea, and hyperventilation. Diabetes may occur at an early age and be insulin-dependent, or it may be of adult onset and most often is noninsulin-dependent. Attending complications include angiopathy, neuropathy, ketoacidosis, and delayed wound healing. Hyper- and hypofunctioning of the thyroid and adrenal glands can also have an impact on dental care. Patients with hyperfunctioning thyroid are nervous and anxious and often manifest exophthalmia, whereas hypothyroidism is characterized by lethargy and facial edema. Hypoadrenalcorticism is characterized by diffuse hyperpigmentation of the skin, low blood pressure, and low blood sugar, whereas patients with hyperadrenalcorticism show moon facies and increased adipose tissue on the upper back. Endocrinopathies of the parathyroid can have oral and jaw manifestations. In hyperparathyroidism, radiologic changes are seen and patients complain of abdominal cramping, bone deformities, and kidney stones caused by hyercalcemia.

Neurologic disorders involve peripheral nerves, the spinal cord, and the brain. Diseases of this system result in such neurologic deficits as paralysis, spastic movement, numbness, paresthesias, forgetfulness, and other disorders of thought and emotions. Many of the diseases that affect neural functioning are infectious, others are degenerative. Loss of muscle contractility may be of neural origin or may be the consequence of primary muscular diseases, such as the muscular dystrophy group disorders. Diseases of the bones and joints cause structural deformities of the limbs, vertebrae, and even the jaws. The arthritides affect all joints and may sometimes cause symptoms in the temporomandibular joint.

Diseases of the head and neck, outside the oral cavity proper include disorders of the sinonasal tract, larynx, hypopharynx, nasopharynx, eyes, ears, and nasal passages. Signs and symptoms indicative of disorders of the eyes include loss of vision, diplopia, visual field defects, ophthalmoplegia, and mucosal diseases of the conjunctiva. Aural diseases include cancers of the external ear, infections and tumors of the middle ear with damage to the tympanic membrane, and inner ear disorders that involve balance, hearing acuity, and auditory tinnitus. Symptoms referable to upper airway lesions include epistaxis, nasal congestion, nasal speech, hoarseness, and numbness of facial tissues. Pain and lymphadenopthy may occur as well.

The gastrointestinal system includes the esophagus, stomach, gut, and accessory digestive organs. Symptoms that indicate diseases of the intestinal tract include substernal and abdominal pain, diarrhea, constipation, hematemesis, pale stools, melena, and distention. Liver diseases are characterized by upper right quadrant enlargement (hepatomegaly) and jaundice, with or without fever. Biliary tract diseases cause upper abdominal pain and cramping, jaundice, and malabsorption-related symptoms.

The hematologic system comprises the blood-forming tissues, subsuming diseases of the red and white blood cells and platelets. Hemostasis is also included under this system. A history of anemia, polycythemia, leukemia, lymphoma, myeloma, leukopenia, and thrombocytopenia should be noted, as should any acquired or inherited bleeding disorders. Signs of hematologic disease include petechia, ecchymosis, gingival bleeding, pallor, hemarthrosis, bone pain, and lethargy.

The review of the genitourinary system for history of disease is, of course, different for males and females. Among females, urinary tract infections are common. Symptoms relative to the female genital tract include sexually transmitted diseases as well as cervical, uterine, and ovarian diseases. Common symptoms include dysmenorrhea, amenorrhea, vaginal discharge, genital pain, masculinization, and lower abdominal signs or symptoms. Inquiry should be made as to whether the patient is pregnant and if so how far along. Diseases of the male genitourinary tract focus on prostatic disease, characterized by urinary retention, sexually transmitted diseases, pain, discharge, "sores," and testicular diseases. Upper urinary tract diseases, such as urolithiasis, pyelonephritis, and glomerulonephritis, will have been reviewed in relation to renal diseases. Pain, urethral discharge, and lesions of the external genitalia can be seen.

Many skin diseases have oral manifestations (mucocutaneous disease). A record should be made of any past treatments for skin carcinoma and melanoma. Chronic dermatologic diseases that are scaly or bullous should be noted, as should instances of acne, particularly if long-term tetracycline therapy was instituted. The breast is a skin appendage, and any diseases, including cancer, should be noted in this portion of the history. When undiagnosed skin lesions are observed, the patient should be referred to a dermatologist.

The immune system may be compromised by a variety of diseases, including leukemia and lymphoma, by chemotherapy for systemic cancers, by organ transplantation, through infection with the human immunodeficiency virus (HIV), and by aging. Regarding HIV infection, the patient should be questioned about risk factors and, if he or she is known to be HIV-positive, immune status markers, such as CD4 lymphocyte counts. Earlier in the gathering of information for the database, allergies to medications will have been noted; this can be reviewed, and newly identified allergies to other substances can be added. Any history of an autoimmune disease, such as lupus erythematosus, should be noted in this section of the database.

If the patient has a significant health history with a compromised status, consultation with that individual's physician is often needed. Such consultations can be made by telephone or by written requests. Before information can be obtained from another health care worker or facility, the patient must sign a written consent and release. This may be important if one desires to order clinical, laboratory, or imaging data resources from another practitioner or health care institution.

Once the medical history has been completed, the salient details should be summarized and any significant treatment precautions that are found should also be noted, beginning with those that constitute a medical alert or could lead to a medical emergency. The next phase of database procurement is the physical examination.

2 Physical Diagnosis of the Head and Neck

L. Roy Eversole, DDS, MSD, MA, and Sol Silverman, Jr, MA, DDS

Upon completion of the history, a physical examination is conducted for the assessment of patients with complaints relevant to oral medicine problems. This examination involves assessment of vital signs and clinical evaluation of the tissues in the head and neck region, including the anatomic areas listed in Table 2–1. Visual inspection, palpation, and auscultation assessments of the head and neck tissues are made in a sequential manner. During this procedure, various anomalies or lesions are recorded in the patient's chart. Recording of abnormalities can also be assisted by procurement of clinical photographs and other forms of imaging, including radiographs, computed tomography (CT), magnetic resonance imaging (MRI), sonography, and use of electronic devices for nerve conduction and hearing.

Table 2–2 lists the categories of disease that may be detected during the physical examination. Surface lesions of skin, hair, scalp, and mucous membranes of the eyes, oral cavity, nasal cavity, and larynx are usually visible. Visualization can be direct or indirect, using a

Table 2–1 Head and Neck Physical Examination

Vital signs
Hair and facial skin
External eyes (lids, conjunctiva, iris)
Ear (external, tympanic membrane)
Oral cavity and oropharynx
Dental and periodontal tissues
Temporomandibular joint
Facial muscles
Nasal cavity and nasopharynx (endoscopy)
Larynx (endoscopy)
Major salivary glands
Anterior neck (thyroid)
Lateral neck
Posterior neck
Supraclavicular notch
Cranial nerve function

Table 2–2 Lesions That May Be Encountered during the Physical Examination

Physical Examination	Finding
Hair	Loss, fineness, scalp lesions
Skin	White scales, erythema, petechiae, telangiectasia, pigmentation, scar, ulceration, bulla, vesicle, tumor
Mucosa	White, red, or pigmented mucosa, petechiae, telangiectasia, ulceration, scar, vesicle, desquamation, tumor
Deep tissue	Soft fluctuant masses, firm movable masses, fixed indurated masses, bruit, pulsation, crepitis
Craniofacial	Asymmetry, osseous expansion, atrophy, clefts
TMJ	Path of opening, restricted opening, clicking, crepitis
Tympanic membrane	Red, white, convexity, perforation, mass
Neurologic	Pain, hypesthesia, paresthesia, motor deficit, special sense deficit

TMJ = temporomandibular joint.

Table 2–3 Standard and Specialized Physical Examination Procedures

Standard physical examination
  Vital signs
  Facial skin
  Major salivary glands and neck
  Oral soft tissues
  Dental hard tissues
  Periodontal examination
The patient in pain (TMJ and jaws)
  Cranial nerves
  Otologic examination
  Muscle palpation
The patient with salivary enlargement or pain
  Cranial nerves
  Salivary flow
Comprehensive head and neck cancer screening
  Oral cavity
  Salivary glands and neck
  Nasal cavity, nasopharynx
  Larynx
The patient with a history of bleeding or purpura
  Bleeding time
  Clotting time

mirror. Visualization of sequestered areas requires special instruments, such as the otoscope, ophthalmoscope, nasopharyngoscope, or fiber optic laryngoscope. Masses of the deeper tissue are usually detected by palpation. The stethoscope can be used with auscultation to assess the carotid artery, temporomandibular joint (TMJ), and larynx.

The primary elements of the physical diagnosis in dentistry are the following:

1. Testing and recording of vital signs
2. Facial skin assessment
3. Major salivary glands and neck examination
4. Oral soft tissues
5. Dental evaluation
6. Periodontal examination (See also CD-ROM.)

The other examination procedures included in this chapter are for special purposes. Table 2–3 outlines the indications for more specialized physical examination procedures.

Certain tray setups are used for the physical examination. The basic examination tray, head and neck examination tray, and biopsy setup are shown in Figure 2–1.

Vital signs

The first phase of the physical examination is the evaluation of a patient's vital signs, which include respiratory rate, heart rate, and blood pressure. Height,

weight, and body temperature may also be obtained at the outset. It is important to establish rapport with the patient and to take time to discuss what the examination entails.

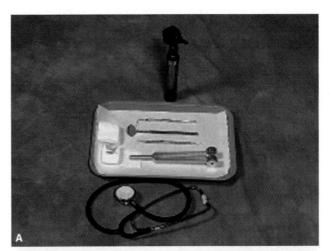

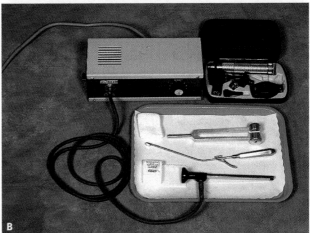

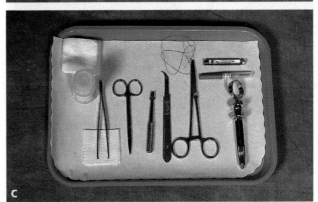

Figure 2–1 *A,* Basic examination tray with otoscope, stethoscope, tuning fork, gauze, mirror, explorer, and periodontal probe; *B,* head and neck examination tray with fiber optic light source, laryngoscope, otoscope or ophthalmoscope, tuning fork, and nasopharyngeal mirror; *C,* basic biospy tray setup with anesthetic syringe, punch instrument, scalpel, scissors, forceps, and suture.

Respiration

Respiration rate is determined by sitting next to or standing behind the patient seated in the dental chair and looking down at the patient's chest. Count the number of times the chest rises and falls for 30 seconds and then multiply by 2. A normal respiratory rate is 12 to 15 respirations per minute. Hyperpnea occurs in acidosis when an increase in carbon dioxide exhalation occurs as a physiologic compensatory process to increase blood pH. Increased shallow respirations, tachypnea, may be encountered in anxious patients. Metabolic alkalosis results in a decreased rate of respiration.

Pulse

Cardiac rate, rhythm, and strength are assessed by taking the radial or carotid artery pulse. The first two measures are objective and easy to learn; a measure of pulse strength is subjective and is learned after evaluating the pulse of numerous subjects. To undertake these measures of cardiac function, one uses digital means. For the carotid pulse, the first two fingers are placed just anterior to the sternomastoid muscle, posterior to the larynx, and below the angle of the mandible in the region of the carotid bulb (Figure 2–2). Only light pressure is applied until pulsations are readily detectable. Excess adipose tissue of the lateral and anterior neck in obese patients may preclude a reliable examination, and it may be more prudent to attempt to take a radial

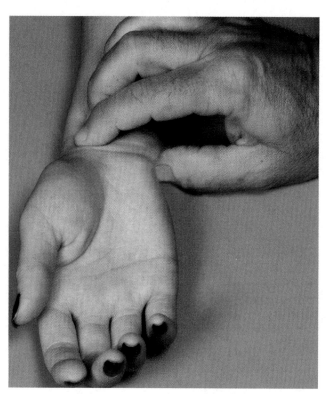

Figure 2–3 Finger placement for detection of the radial pulse.

pulse. This is accomplished by placing the first two fingers in the slight trough produced by a tissue depression between the radius and the flexor tendons located on the ventral wrist just proximal to the thumb's thenar eminence (Figure 2–3). Only light pressure is exerted until pulsations are perceived.

The cardiac rate is determined by counting the number of beats during 15 seconds and multiplying by 4. Normal heart rate is 60 to 80 beats per minute. Bradycardia occurs in dedicated athletes yet can also be pathologic. Tachycardia occurs in anxious subjects and in a variety of metabolic and cardiac diseases. The rhythm is assessed after or while taking the pulse rate. A normal pulse should be steady with equal intervals between pulsations. Rapid beats followed by delayed intervals are indicative of cardiac conduction disturbances, as may occur in myocardial ischemia and myocarditis or from various metabolic disorders. Pulse strength, as mentioned previously, is a subjective measure and is learned after repeated palpation of the carotid or radial artery on many patients. A strong pulse is indicative of high cardiac output, whereas a weak pulse occurs during low contractility.

Blood pressure and body temperature

Measuring blood pressure assesses pressure within the arteries during cardiac contraction (systole) and pres-

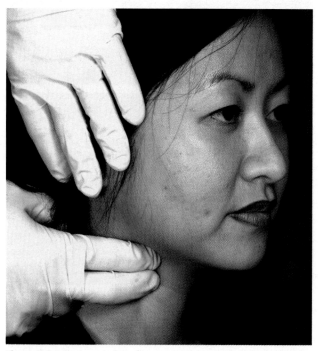

Figure 2–2 Placement of the fingers over the carotid artery, just anterior to the sternomastoid muscle to assess cardiac rate, rhythm, and strength.

sure during cardiac pause (diastole). To obtain these values, one must generate an external pressure that exceeds that within the artery then slowly lower that pressure until the intra-arterial pressure exceeds the externally applied pressure, thereby opening the arteries and being able to detect the pulse as blood is again pumped through. The pressure at which the first evidence of a pulse can be detected is the upper, or systolic pressure, which normally is about 110 to 130 mm Hg. After detecting the systolic pressure, the externally

applied pressure continues to be decreased until pulsations are no longer detected. This level of pressure, the diastolic, varies normally from 70 to 90 mm Hg.

To measure blood pressure, an inflatable sphygmomanometer cuff is placed around the upper arm (Figure 2–4). For children there are small cuffs and for adults with large arms there are oversized cuffs. A stethoscope with a flat diaphragm is placed in the antecubital notch. The precise location of the brachial artery varies somewhat, so it might be advisable to first palpate the area

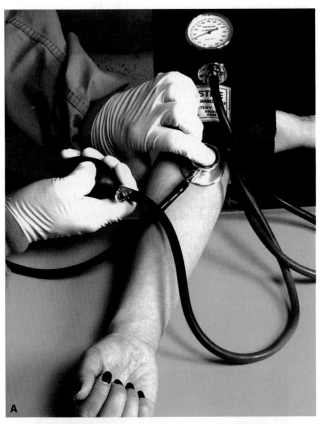

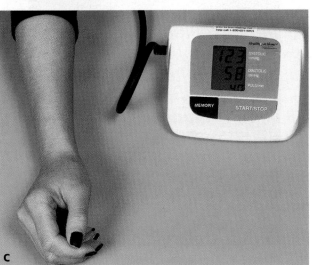

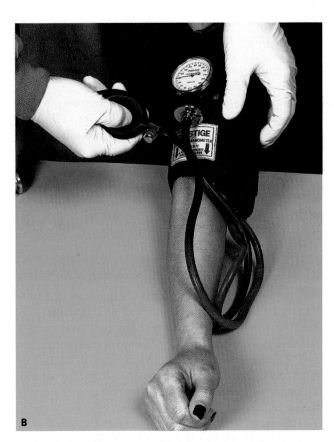

Figure 2–4   Blood pressure measurement. *A*, Pressure cuff with stethoscope over the antecubital fossa; *B*, sphygmomanometer showing a high diastolic pressure reading; *C*, digital readout gives systolic and diastolic pressures as well as heart rate. Elevated diastolic pressure is a sign of increased peripheral resistance ("hardening" of the arteries or arteriosclerosis). High systolic pressure is also indicative of hypertension.

and attempt to detect a pulse. With the stethoscope in place, the cuff is inflated to about 150 mm Hg by pumping the rubber bulb on the sphygmomanometer. The air release screw under the bulb must be screwed tight to the closed position (turning clockwise). If pulsations are detected immediately, the pressure in the cuff must be pumped up higher until no sounds are auscultated. Turning the air release set screw below the bulb counterclockwise slowly deflates the cuff. If the screw is turned too far, the cuff will deflate rapidly and the two pressure levels will be inaccurate. Let the needle fall about 5 mm Hg every second to obtain an accurate reading. On some patients, during the interval between systolic and diastolic, pulsations cease only to resume after the pressure falls 5 to 15 mm. This is normal. Therefore, one should continue to auscultate for the diastolic endpoint until the pressure reaches 60 mm Hg.

Temperature is recorded using a thermometer or temperature sensitive disposable oral strips. Either of these recording devices should be inserted orally, with the tip placed under the tongue, and left in place for 1.5 to 2.0 minutes. Recall that normal body temperature is 37°C (98.6°F). Elevation in body temperature (febrile state) equates with fever most often associated with microbial infection.

Hair and facial skin

The hair is assessed for thickness (or thinness) and loss. Pattern baldness in men is normal and hereditary. A focal region of hair loss is termed alopecia areata and is pathologic. Fine curly hair or lanugo is encountered in some diseases and syndromes. Diffuse loss of hair occurs in patients taking chemotherapeutic drugs for cancer. Radiation can induce temporary or permanent damage to hair follicles.

The facial skin is sun-exposed, and a variety of ultraviolet radiation or so-called actinic lesions occur on the face. These include erythematous lesions with scaly keratosis, nodules, tumors, ulcers, and pigmentation. Maculopapular and vesicular eruptions also occur on the face. The examiner easily visualizes all of these lesions. Survey the forehead, eyebrows, eyelids, nasal bridge and alae, malar region, vermilion of the lips, and chin; also, inspect the submental, anterior, lateral, and posterior neck skin as well as the external ear region.

External eyes

Visual acuity, peripheral vision, visual fields, pupillary reflex, and retinal integrity (funduscopy) can be tested when conducting the cranial nerve assessment. At this point in the physical examination, only the external aspects of the eye are observed. The eyebrows are first examined followed by the skin surfaces of the upper and lower lids and then the eyelashes. The inner mucosal surfaces of the eyelids (palpebral conjunctivae) are examined by inverting the lids. The lower lid is easily inverted by placing the thumb or forefinger on the center of the lid skin and sliding it inferiorly. The upper lid does not retract as easily, and to clearly visualize the mucosa, a match stick or blunted toothpick can be placed longitudinally along the upper lid and with light pressure of the finger, the lid can be rolled back over the stick. The white portion of the globe of the eye, the sclera, is covered by bulbar conjunctiva, a mucosal membrane with fine vascular channels (Figure 2–5). The conjunctivae are examined for dryness, erosions, telangiectasias, scars, and nodules. A scar band that traverses the bulbar and palpebral conjunctivae is referred to as a symblepharon. A slit-like defect in the eyelid is termed coloboma. The iris, or pigmented ring, surrounds the black pupil and is covered by a convex transparent cornea. A slit in the iris, giving a keyhole appearance, is termed iridial coloboma. The iris can dilate and constrict, varying the diameter of the pupil, depending upon the focal distance of the eye and the amount of light. In neurologic disorders and drug overdose, the papillary diameter is altered. An overly dilated pupil (over 6 mm) is termed mydriasis whereas an overly contracted pupil (less than 2 mm) is called miosis. The pupillary reflex is checked during the cranial nerve function assessment. The cornea is examined for opacifications, which usually represent cataracts.

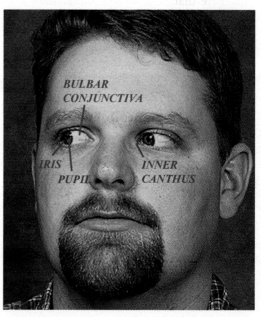

Figure 2–5 Anatomic components of the external eye.

Ears

Cartilage gives shape to the external ear (Figure 2–6). Its structure helps to funnel sound waves into the external auditory meatus. The outer curvature is the helix, which terminates inferiorly as the lobe. The cartilage flap just anterior to the external canal is the tragus. Skin cancers can arise on any of these sun-exposed areas, especially the superior helix or pinna.

Examination of the tympanic membranes (TM) or eardrums requires the use of an otoscope (Figure 2–7). This visualization instrument consists of a battery-containing handle, a light source, a magnification lens, and a funnel-shaped speculum. Since individuals have external ear canals of varying diameters, the ear speculums vary in size. To allow visualization of the TM the external auditory meatus must be free of cerumin (earwax). A Q-tip will usually suffice, although in some patients, small ear curettes must be employed to clear the canal of wax. To examine the TM, the pinna should be grasped with the thumb and forefinger and pulled up and back. The speculum is inserted slowly and gently into the canal with a slight anterior angulation. The canal does not extend straight at a perpendicular angle to the side of the head. The speculum is inserted just short of the hub, and at this point, the examiner looks through the lens. If the TM is not readily visualized, the speculum can be rotated and angulated slightly while the examiner continues to gaze through the lens. The membrane is whitish and taut, like the head of a drum (Figure 2–8). The upper region is opaque and referred to as the pars flaccida, whereas the lower portion, the pars tensa is translucent. Fine vascular markings may be present over the surface. At the junction of the two regions is an inferiorly directed linear structure that represents attachment of a middle ear ossicle, the malleus, on the opposite (middle ear) side of the membrane. During the examination, one should check for telangiectasia, bulging, and erythema, surface white plaques, and perforations.

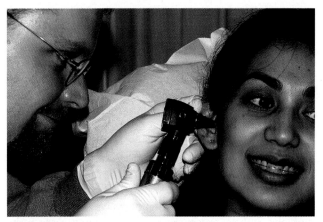

Figure 2–7 Placement of the otoscope into the external auditory meatus.

Oral cavity and oropharynx

Examination of the oral cavity involves visual inspection and palpation. It is prudent to develop a specific sequence and to follow it consistently so as not to overlook any areas. The entire examination should be done visually at first (Figures 2–9, 2–10, and 2–11). The same tissues should subsequently be reevaluated by palpation (Figures 2–12 and 2–13). The examination begins with the facial compartment, that region of the mouth anterior to the facial or buccal surfaces of the teeth.

Begin the inspection by examining the right maxillary tuberosity, using mirror-assisted indirect vision. The patient's head can be turned and tilted as the examination proceeds, to use the lamp source to advantage and employ direct vision whenever possible. After checking the right tuberosity, directly inspect the maxillary buccal gingiva, vesibule, and frenal attachments. The cheek and lips can be reflected with the fingers and mirror face. Proceed all the way around to the left side, examining the buccal gingiva and ending with the left tuberosity (see Figure 2–9, *A* and *B*). Next, drop down to the retromolar pad and observe the retromolar trigone, that triangular region extending from the retromolar pad up the ptery-gomandibular raphe. Continue inspection of the left mandibular facial gingiva and sulcus, reflecting the cheek and lips and completing the circuit to the right retromolar trigone. The right buccal mucosa is then inspected from sulcus to sulcus superiorly and inferiorly and from the pterygomandibular raphe to the commissure of the lips posterior to anterior (see Figure 2–9, *C*). Reflect the lower then the upper lips to assess the mucosal surfaces (see Figure 2–9, *D* and *E*). Notice that the lip mucosa is slightly bumpy, owing to the presence of a minor salivary gland located in the submucosa. Continue the examination in a like manner for the left buccal mucosa.

The next step is to visually inspect the lingual compartment of the oral cavity (see Figure 2–10). The lin-

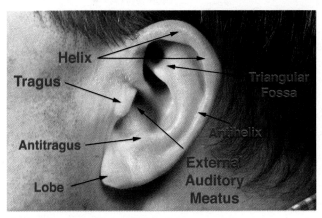

Figure 2–6 Anatomic landmarks of the external ear.

gual compartment includes the palate, tongue, and floor of the mouth. Start with your mirror at the right palatal gingiva opposite the tuberosity and continue around the palatal gingiva to the opposite side, then drop down and examine the mandibular lingual gingiva, moving along from left to right and ending at the right retromolar region. Follow by examining the anterior regions of the mouth and by looking at the hard palate either directly or with the dental mirror (see Figure 2–10, *A*). Subsequently have the patient protrude the tongue and examine the dorsal surface from the tongue-base between the epiglottis and the ridge of circumvallate papillae anteriorly to the tongue tip. Next open a gauze pad and lightly grasp the anterior tongue. Move the tongue to the left to see the tongue-base attachment, foliate papillae (lingual tonsil), lateral border and lateroventral aspect of the tongue, and floor of the mouth (see Figure 2–10, *B–D*). Repeat this procedure on the opposite side by moving the tongue to the right. Release the tongue and ask the patient to place the tongue tip up to contact the palate. In this position the anterior ventral tongue, floor of the mouth, and lingual carunculae can be easily visualized.

Lastly, the oropharynx is visually inspected, beginning with the right anterior and posterior tonsillar pillars (fauces). The pharyngeal tonsils are interposed between these mucosal columns that arch onto the soft palate (see Figure 2–11). Check the soft palate and uvula, then observe the left tonsillar region. The posterior wall of the oropharynx is viewed by placing an inverted mirror face on the posterior tongue, depressing gently, and having the patient say "ahh." The adenoids can be seen on the oropharyngeal wall.

Individuals may choose different sequences for their examinations. The important points are an organized methodology and understanding the finding and significance of deviations from normal. Obviously, all of these examinations will not be performed routinely.

Upon completion of the visual examination of the oral cavity, return to the facial compartment and conduct the palpation aspect of the examination. Whenever possible, use bimanual or bidigital palpation methods. The forefinger is placed into the right cheek area buccal to the teeth until the tip of the finger contacts the pterygomandibular raphe area. With the opposite hand placed on the side of the face, move the finger up and down across the buccal mucosa, compressing the soft tissues between the hand and finger (see Figure 2–12). Repeat this on the opposite side. The upper and lower lips can be palpated in the same manner or can be examined keeping the index finger positioned against the mucosa with the thumb of the same hand over the skin side of the lips.

Palpation of the lingual compartment begins by palpating the lateral and anterior movable parts of the tongue between the thumb and forefinger. The oral floor contents include connective tissues, the sublingual gland, submandibular gland, and associated lymph nodes (submental and submandibular node groups). To palpate these structures, the forefinger is placed in the floor of the mouth, sliding back along and below the lateral aspect of the tongue. The opposite hand is placed along the submental region medial to the inferior border of the mandible (see Figure 2–13). In these positions the oral floor contents can be

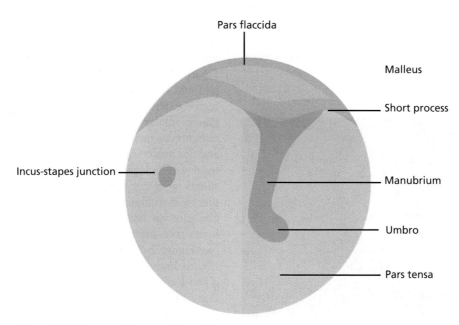

Figure 2–8 Diagram of the tympanic membrane.

bidigitally compressed and palpated. After palpating the opposite side, run a finger over the soft palate from the right fauces to the left. At this time, the pterygoid muscles can be palpated to assess for tenderness, a finding among patients who habitually clench their teeth and develop headaches. The forefinger is placed against the lateral pharyngeal wall at the arch with the soft palate. The finger is gently advanced superiorly and laterally, compressing the pterygoid muscles against the medial mandibular ramus. A salivary tumor in the deep lobe of the parotid gland can be detected by this procedure as well.

Salivary glands

While still gloved from the oral examination, the practitioner can assess salivary function. Milking the glands will give a crude estimate of salivary flow, and one can determine whether an obstruction of the duct is present (Figure 2–14). For the parotid glands, a gauze square is used to dry the buccal mucosa over the parotid papilla (see Figure 2–14, A). The mouth must be wide open with the cheek stretched taut. All four fingers are placed flat on the face, over the parotid gland, which is found in the preauricular region. The gland is milked by plac-

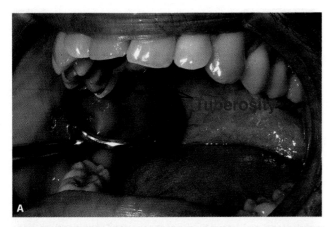

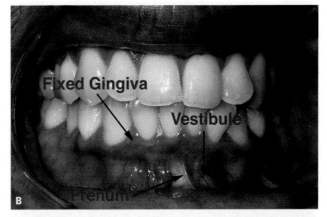

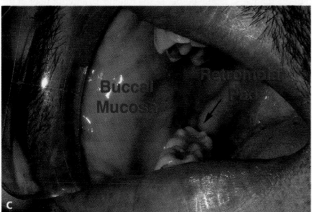

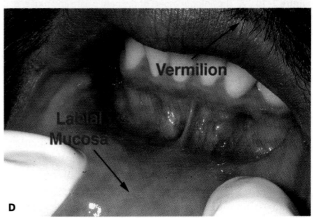

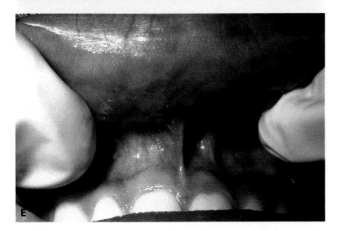

Figure 2–9 Visual examination of, *A*, the tuberosity with the dental mirror; *B*, the anterior mandibular gingiva; *C*, the buccal mucosa; *D*, the everted lower lip, showing the mucosal surface and the sulcus; *E*, retracted upper lip showing the gingiva, lip mucosa, and vestibule.

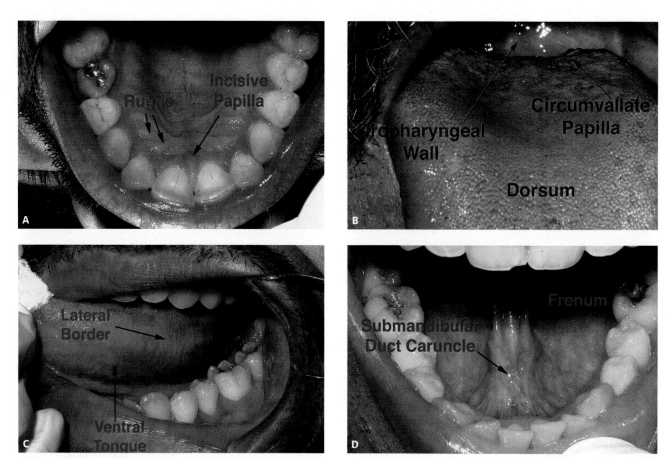

Figure 2–10 *A*, The anterior aspect of the hard palate and rugae; *B*, dorsum of the tongue; *C*, lateral border of the tongue; *D*, anterior floor of the mouth, lingual frenum, and carunculae.

ing digital pressure, compressing the gland against the masseter or ramus area. The fingers, in a closed group, are dragged anteriorly across the face while the parotid papilla is observed to detect the flow of saliva from the duct (see Figure 2–14, *B*). A sialolith, mucous plug, or occluding tumor can prevent the flow of saliva. Purulent material coming out the duct orifice is indicative of parotitis. Various drugs and herbs as well as some diseases can markedly alter salivary flow.

The submandibular gland flow is checked by drying the lingual carunculae in the floor of the mouth, then placing one or two outstretched fingers under the chin and along side the inferior mandible. Upward pressure directed to the submandibular gland area should produce flow from Wharton's duct orifice. The submandibular glands were palpated to detect abnormal masses during the oral examination. At this point the parotid glands can be palpated by compressing the preauricular tissues over the angle of the mandible.

When obstruction is encountered, patients usually experience pain or a drawing sensation when salivary flow is stimulated (ie, at mealtimes). An obstructed duct can be cannulated and dilated with progressively thicker diameter lacrimal probes. Stensen's or Wharton's ducts can be dilated beginning with a small blunted probe. The probe, moistened with the patient's saliva, is directed into the orifice and slowly advanced down the duct for about 4 to 5 cm. Once in place, the probe is twirled along with a back and forth motion. After 30

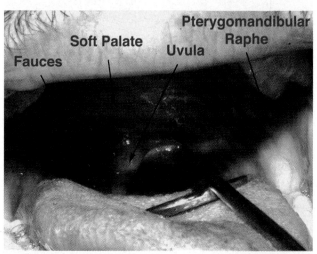

Figure 2–11 Visually inspect the oropharynx: soft palate, uvula, and fauces.

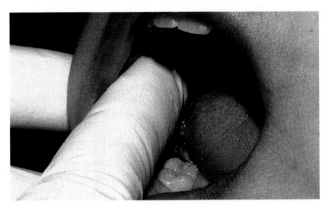

Figure 2–12 Bidigital palpation of the buccal mucosal soft tissues.

seconds, the probe is removed and larger probes are inserted, repeating the process. Wharton's duct has a larger diameter than Stensen's duct. Dilation will loosen mucous plugs and overcome strictures.

The dilation process is also used for sialography. If a sialogram is to be performed, following dilation, an angiocath sleeve can be advanced into the duct for a distance of 2 to 4 cm. A 5-mL syringe loaded with Renographin 40® or Hypaque® is then attached to the angiocath sleeve. (Note: This procedure is contraindicated in patients with allergies to iodine or radiographic contrast media.) Once the patient is positioned for the procurement of radiographs of the gland under study, the patient is instructed that upon injection of the dye, he or she will experience pressure and fullness. The patient is instructed to raise the hand as a signal when this fullness turns into a stinging pain sensation. Begin slowly filling the duct tree with radiopaque contrast media, never force the plunger (Figure 2–15). When the patient raises the hand, deliver an additional 0.5 to 1 mL, let go of the syringe and move out of the way so that a radiographic exposure can be made immediately. Take another backup film then remove the angiocath. A post-fill film should then be obtained 5 minutes later. Sialography is used sparingly and is not free from the risk of ductal perforations.

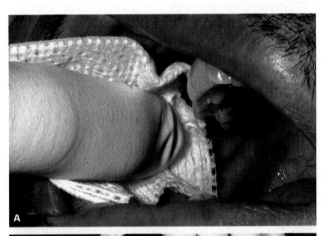

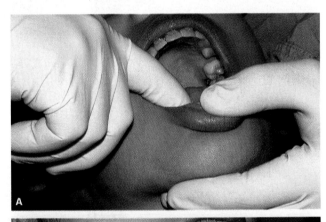

Figure 2–13 *A*, Bidigital palpation of the anterior floor of mouth contents. *B*, Palpation of posterior floor of the mouth.

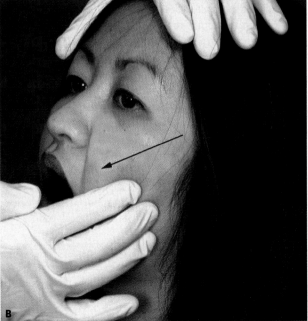

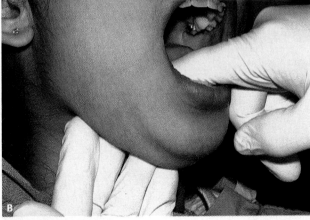

Figure 2–14 *A*, Wiping saliva away from Stensen's duct prior to milking the parotid gland. *B*, Milking saliva from the parotid gland.

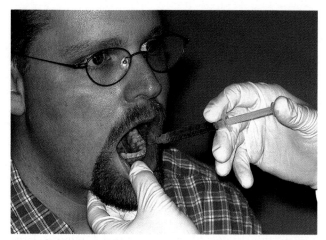

Figure 2–15 Injection of contrast media into predilated submandibular duct.

Nasal cavity and nasopharynx

Only the anterior aspect of the nasal cavity can be examined directly. A nasal speculum is placed in the nares and gently separated, with one blade resting against the lower aspect of the septum and the other against the ala. The mucocutaneous junction harbors nasal hairs. The septum is smooth on the medial surface, and as light is directed into the nostril, inspection of the lateral wall discloses the inferior and middle turbinate ridges. An otoscope may be used for anterior nasal cavity inspection using a special wide speculum (Figure 2–16).

A fiber optic nasopharyngoscope is used to examine the upper recesses of the nasal cavity to observe the olfactory region of the superior nasopharynx, the superior turbinate, posterior septum, and recess of Rosenmüller. This examination is often performed after applying topical vasoconstrictor to the mucous membranes. Cotton balls soaked with aqueous constrictor and local anesthetic are inserted one by one into the nasal cavity, using long thin nasal tweezers. After 4 to 5 minutes, the cotton is removed; a thin fiber optic nasopharyngoscope is inserted into each side, and the tissues are viewed through the optics of the instrument. This fiber optic scope can also be attached to a video camera to allow viewing on a monitor screen. Nasal mucosa may be involved in some mucocutaneous diseases or may be erythematous because of irritation, dryness, or infection.

Larynx

Examination of the supraglottic larynx is performed with either a rigid or a flexible laryngoscope. The vocal structures can also be viewed indirectly using a headlamp and a laryngeal mirror, but gagging is problematic, and fiber optic endoscopes are much easier on both examiner and

patient. Sitting up straight, the patient should open the mouth wide and jut the chin forward. Topical lidocaine can be sprayed onto the tongue base and soft palate to help minimize gagging. The tongue is then grasped by the tip using an opened gauze square and gently pulled forward, making sure not to catch the lingual frenum between the lower incisors. The scope is inserted back until it touches the posterior pharyngeal wall (Figure 2–17). The secret for minimizing the gag reflex is never to contact the tongue. The instrument is advanced along the soft palate, while elevating it slightly and directing the end of the scope just to the right of the uvula. Once the scope is placed in this location, peer into the ocular. Have the patient phonate "eee" alternating with "ahh" and rotate the scope handle until the true cords are easily observed. The voice structures that are visible include the true cords, false vocal cords, pyriform sinus, aryepiglottic fold, arytenoids, anterior commissure, and laryngeal wall bounded anterosuperiorly by the epiglottis (Figure 2–18).

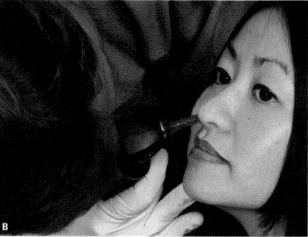

Figure 2–16 *A* and *B,* Otoscope used to examine anterior nasal cavity.

As with the nasopharyngoscope, the laryngoscopic equipment can be attached to a video system. This allows for procurement of a permanent record.

Neck

The neck should be initially examined by visualization, searching for any masses, surface skin lesions, jugular vein distention, and asymmetry. Palpation of the neck proceeds from the anterior to the posterior triangles. Beginning with the anterior triangle, the body of the larynx is grasped between the thumb and forefinger. A stethoscope is placed anteriorly, and the trachea is moved from side to side. Audible crepitus should be noted. Next, the stethoscope is placed over the carotid bulb just anterior to the sternomastoid and below the angle of the mandible (Figure 2–19). The patient is asked to take and hold a breath while the clinician auscultates both sides, listening for a bruit or thrill (a chugging or slush sound), which can be indicative of aneurysm.

The thyroid is not normally palpable. To examine for enlargement, place the grouped fingers on one side of the larynx and push laterally while palpating the opposite side. Next, bidigitally palpate down the course of the anterior sternomastoid, burying the fingers into the trough between the muscle and the anterolateral neck (Figure 2–20). The area is palpated from the carotid bulb where carotid-body tumors can arise, down to the clavicle, along the cervical lymph node chain. End by pushing fingers into the supraclavicular notch, a region where upper intestinal tract malignancies may metastasize (signal node) (Figure 2–21). Repeat the palpation examination for the opposite lateral neck. Lastly, the postauricular, retrosternomastoid region should be palpated along with the back of the neck.

Muscle palpation for tenderness

Patients with clenching and tooth grinding habits may place their masticatory muscles in sustained contraction, which results in myalgic facial pain and headache. Trigger-point tenderness can often be detected. Finger palpation of the pterygoid muscles will have been performed during the oral examination. Extraoral muscle palpation is quickly done by pushing into the belly and insertion points of the temporalis, masseter, sternomastoid, and semispinalis muscles. Finger pressure is applied at right angles to the muscle and the patient is asked to report tender spots (Figure 2–22).

Temporomandibular joint

The temporomandibular joint (TMJ) is examined by palpation and auscultation. First, the interincisal maxi-

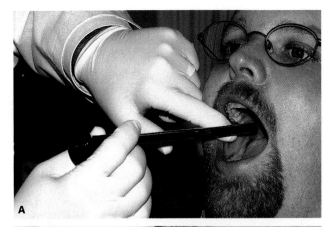

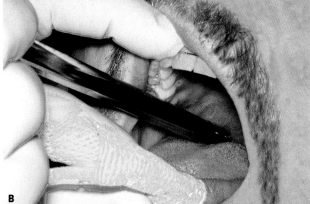

Figure 2–17 *A,* Insertion of fiber optic laryngoscope; *B,* scope is placed high, deflecting the soft palate superiorly. *C,* Once the scope is in place, the larynx is visualized through the ocular.

mal opening is measured in millimeters (about 45 mm for females, 55 mm for males) (Figure 2–23). The path of opening is also recorded and drawn in the chart. Joints with pathologic changes move to the side of pathosis since that condyle is restricted in its movement. When the meniscus is anteriorly displaced, the jaw deviates to the affected side, then, as the disc is reduced, the mandible returns to a midline position. If there are bilateral malposed discs, opening can be limited, so-called closed lock. Inflammatory and neoplastic lesions

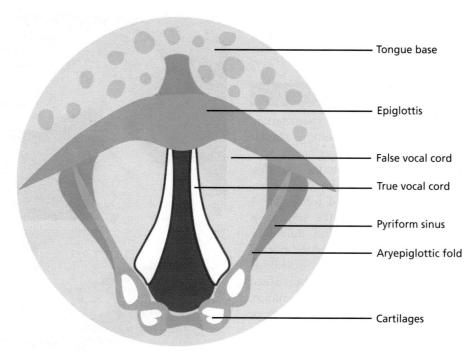

Figure 2–18 Diagram illustrating anatomic landmarks of the larynx.

of the TMJ region can also cause deviant opening as can myospasm in masticatory muscles.

The joint can then be palpated for tenderness. The little fingers can be inserted into the auditory meatuses bilaterally, while the patient is instructed to open and close the mouth. Misplacement of the meniscus can often be detected in this manner. As the condyle undergoes translation on opening, an abrupt movement of a reducing displaced disc can be felt. The final phase of the TMJ examination is auscultation. The diaphragm of the stethoscope is placed directly anterior to the tragus of the ear, overlying the condyle (Figure 2–24). The patient is asked to repeatedly open and close. A popping or clicking sound can be heard when anterior displaced discs reduce or pop back into place midway through opening, and a reciprocal click may be auscultated on closing. Because the facial bones are sound conductive, a joint sound emanating from one joint may be detected in the contralateral joint. Intra-aural finger palpation on opening and closing, as described above aids in determining whether the problem is unilateral or bilateral. In arthritic joint disease, when damage to both the meniscus and cartilaginous tissues is extant, crepitis will be heard during movement. Sonographic devices can be

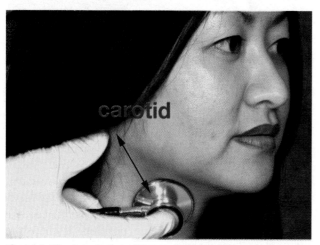

Figure 2–19 Auscultation of the carotid bulb region with the stethoscope.

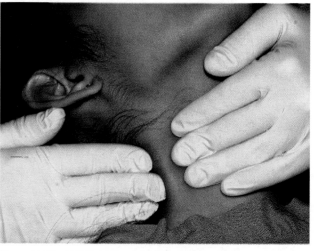

Figure 2–20 Bidigital palpation of the lateral neck.

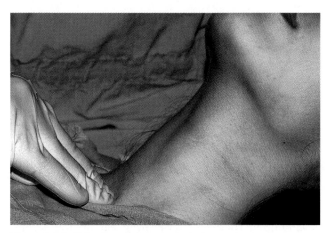

Figure 2–21 Palpation of the supraclavicular notch.

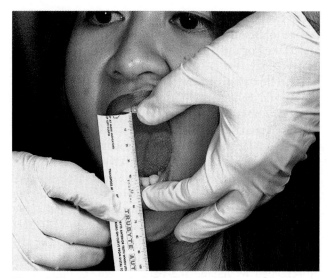

Figure 2–23 Measuring the interincisal opening.

used in place of a stethoscope to graphically record joint sounds. A variety of imaging modalities that include TMJ tomography, arthrography, CT, MRI, and sonography can be applied when physical findings are indicative of joint pathosis. Arthroscopic examination can also be performed, a procedure usually performed by the oral and maxillofacial surgeon.

Cranial nerves

The cranial nerves can be divided into three functional subgroups: (1) special senses, (2) somatic sensory, and (3) motor nerves (Table 2–4). Defects in neural signaling are referred to as deficits. Defective signaling by sensory nerves results in hypesthesia and paresthesia. Motor deficits manifest as paralysis. Both sensory and motor neurologic deficits occur when there are lesions of the

peripheral nerves or within the ganglia and nuclei of the central nervous system (CNS). Sensory and motor deficits of the cranial nerves are often serious signs. Both occur when nerve fibers are invaded by malignant tumors that arise adjacent to nerve trunks, or they may evolve secondary to cerebrovascular disease, neoplasms, degenerative processes, or inflammatory diseases of the CNS. Trauma to nerve trunks also results in neurologic deficits.

Special senses can be assessed objectively and subjectively. In oral medicine, subjective assessment is usually undertaken and, when an abnormality is uncovered, an objective test can then be performed. The subjective evaluation is done by simply asking whether the patient has noticed any change in smell, vision, hearing, or taste during the past 6 months and whether changes are cur-

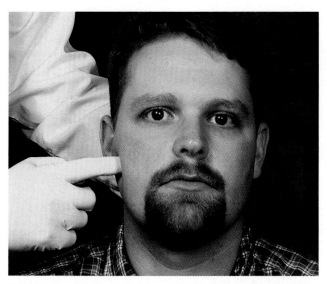

Figure 2–22 Muscle palpation tenderness assessment of the masseter.

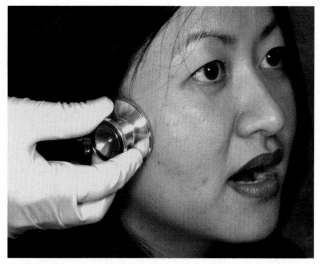

Figure 2–24 Auscultation of the TMJ for detection of pathologic joint sounds.

rently extant. If in fact the patient responds in the affirmative to any of these questions, objective assessment is undertaken or the patient may be referred to an internist or neurologist for in-depth examination.

The first cranial nerve (olfactory) can be tested by having the patient occlude one nostril while allowing specific aromas contained in liquid form within a vial to enter the open nostril. Commonly tested aromas include coffee, vanilla, perfumes, and hydrogen sulfide. Failure to detect odors is termed anosmia. Dysosmia is mistaking a common odor for something else. Nasal obstruction, trauma to the cribriform plate, or lesions of the olfactory tract may be present. The second cranial nerve (optic) can be tested objectively by using an eye chart for visual acuity and by examining visual fields. The latter is performed with an electronic view chamber or can be screened by having the patient gaze straight ahead while the examiner introduces an object or fingers around the periphery of the visual fields. One eye at a time is tested, beginning with placing the peripheral object above the forehead and progressively dropping it until it is perceived. This procedure is then repeated for the lateral, medial, and inferior aspects of peripheral vision, noting any restrictions. Rapid movement of the eyes is referred to as nystagmus; strabismus is a deviant position of one eye, usually either laterally or medially. Diplopia refers to double vision. Funduscopic examination is performed to assess the retina. Eyegrounds, or retinal vessel disease connote hypertension and diabetic microangiopathy. Retinal detachments, hemorrhages, and pigmentations are also visualized. In an oral medicine practice, a retinal examination is rarely performed, because the pupil must be dilated pharmacologically to achieve accurate observations.

The eighth cranial nerve (auditory) is examined by audiology, a test performed by an audiology technician. Screening tests for hearing are done with a tuning fork. The fork is held between the thumb and fingers, it is struck against the heel of the hand to start the ringing and is then placed at the vortex of the skull. The patient is asked whether he or she can hear the sound and then to determine whether the sound is more audible on one side compared to the other (Weber test) (Figure 2–25). This is termed lateralization and can be indicative of unilateral hearing loss secondary to a variety of causes. In conductive hearing loss, the sound is lateralized to the deaf ear whereas in sensorineural hearing loss the sound is lateralized to the better-hearing ear. In the second auditory test, the Rinne test (Figure 2–26), the base of the vibrating fork is placed over the mastoid. The patient is asked to indicate when the sound is no longer perceived, and at that time, the fork is immediately moved so that the vibrating ends are directly in front of the external auditory meatus. The sound should be audible; if not, this is an indication of conductive hearing loss.

Taste testing involves the seventh and ninth cranial nerves. A series of soluble recognizable flavors are placed in vials and individually applied to the lateral and dorsal aspects of the tongue. Flavors are perceived in the anterior tongue via nerve VII, whereas the posterior regions are innervated by nerve IX. The patient protrudes the tongue, and the flavors are applied with a cotton-tipped applicator to first one side and then the other. Taste perception should be equal on both left and right sides. Failure to detect these tastes usually occurs in CNS lesions involving these nerve pathways. Altered taste is termed dysgeusia.

Somatic sensory testing is done by using a cotton-tipped applicator for perception of light touch and with

Table 2–4 Cranial Nerves

Subgroup	Nerve	Cranial Nerve Designation	Function
Special senses			
Smell	Olfactory	1st	Nerves of smell
Seeing	Optic	2nd	Nerve of sight
Hearing	Vestibulocochlear	8th	Nerves of hearing
Taste	Facial, glossopharyngeal	7th, 9th	Taste fibers
Somatic sensory	Trigeminal	5th	Muscles of face and upper air passage sensations
	Facial, auricular	7th	Sensory component
	Glossopharyngeal	9th	Throat and tongue base sensations
Motor	Oculomotor	3rd	Moves eyes up, down, and medially; elevates lid, pupillary reflex
	Trochlear	4th	Moves eyes inferolaterally
	Trigeminal	5th	Muscles of mastication
	Abducens	6th	Moves eyes laterally
	Facial	7th	Muscles of facial expression
	Vagus	10th	Gag reflex, speech
	Spinal accessory	11th	Superior movement of shoulders
	Hypoglossal	12th	Tongue movements

a dental explorer for perception of pain (pin-prick sensation) (Figure 2–27). The cotton tip is pulled out to a thin whisp and is applied gently to the facial skin to test the sensory component of the fifth cranial nerve (trigeminal). For pin-prick testing, the examinar should first lightly touch the dental explorer to the back of the patient's hand, to orient him or her as to the sensation prior to using this sharp object on the face. Both light touch and pin-prick are tested over the forehead (V1), the malar region (V2), and the chin (V3) on each side of the face. Intraoral sensory perception can be assessed by using both light touch and pin-prick on the hard palate, maxillary gingiva, mandibular gingiva, and lateral tongue. Sensory fibers of the seventh cranial nerve (facial) innervate the tissues of the external ear that lie adjacent to the auditory meatus. This region is also tested by light touch and pin-prick. The ninth cranial nerve (glossopharyngeal) is sensory for the oropharynx and can be tested over the fauces and the posterior aspect of the soft palate. Altered sensations are paresthesias; loss of sensation is hypesthesia. These sensory deficits may be attributable to trauma, such as injury to the inferior alveolar nerve during third molar extraction or jaw fracture; however, when there is no history of injury, a malignancy must be considered.

Motor nerve testing involves observing movements. The three nerves that supply the extraocular muscles are tested by having the patient move the eyes in five directions: up, down, left, right, and down and out. The patient focuses on the examiner's finger as it is moved in various directions, and the examiner makes note of the patient's eye movements (Figure 2–28). The motor nerves that control eye movement are tested together by having

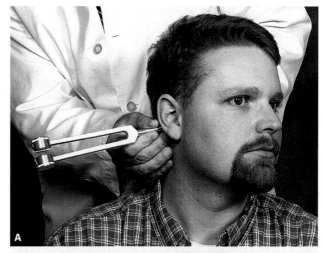

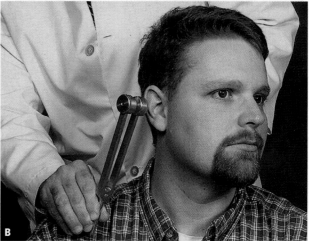

Figure 2–26 *A* and *B*, Rinne test for conductive versus sensorineural motor hearing loss.

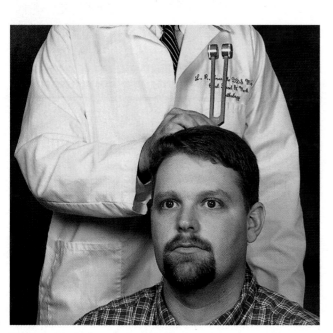

Figure 2–25 Weber test for lateralization.

the patient move his or her eyes up and down and side to side. The third cranial nerve (oculomotor) moves the eyes up and down and medially; the sixth cranial nerve (abducens) moves them laterally. The examiner then asks the subject to follow the finger as it is moved down and out for each eye, a test for the fourth cranial nerve (trochlear) function. Failure to complete these movements is referred to as ophthalmoplegia, a condition that can be caused by extraocular muscle injury or a neurologic lesion along the course of these motor nerves. The third cranial nerve also regulates in part, pupillary diameter. This is tested in two ways. First a light beam is directed at the pupil; this stimulus should cause pupillary constriction (Figure 2–29). When the light stimulus is directed into the right eye, the left pupil constricts as well, in consensual response. The pupils also respond to accommodation. The subject is asked to gaze across the room, then to focus on a card with lettering held 2 feet from the eye. The pupil will dilate if normal. Anisocoria represents constriction of a single pupil and may be a sign

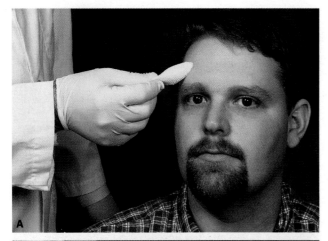

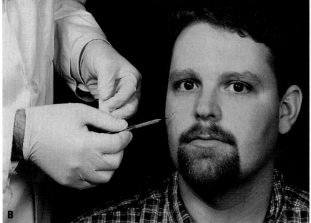

Figure 2–27 *A*, Soft touch sensory perception testing; *B*, pin-prick sensory perception testing.

parotid gland. Importantly, most parotid tumors with attending seventh nerve deficit are malignant. When the palsy is limited to the lower half of the face, a CNS lesion of the ipsilateral side is suspected because the upper branches cross over, whereas the lower branches do not. Alternatively, when the entire side of the face shows paresis, a peripheral nerve lesion is suspected. The eyelid deserves special consideration in a discussion

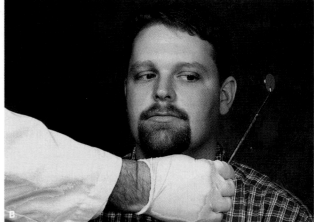

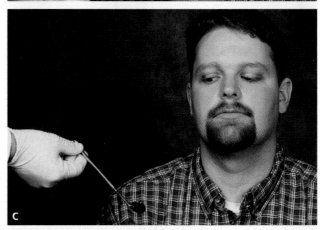

Figure 2–28 *A* and *B*, Testing the oculomotor (nerve III) and abducens (nerve VI) by lateral eye movement. *C*, Testing the trochlear (nerve IV) for down and out eye movement.

of apex lung cancer in the condition referred to as Horner syndrome. In this situation, the pupillary response is unrelated to nerve III; rather, the stellate ganglion is compressed by tumor, resulting in a sympathetic deficit to the pupil. When the eyes react normally, the term PERLA is recorded in the chart to indicate that the pupils are equal and react to light and accommodation.

The trigeminal motor branches innervate the muscles of mastication. The patient is asked to clench the teeth together while the examiner places two fingers on each masseter; as the clench is initiated, the muscles will bulge. Next, the pterygoid function is observed by having the patient move the jaw from side to side (Figure 2–30). The seventh cranial nerve (facial) motor function is evaluated by having the patient generate various facial expressions. The examiner requests the following: "wrinkle your forehead, raise your eyebrows, smile and show me your teeth, frown, purse your lips (whistle), close and open your eyes." Facial nerve palsy is often easily visualized and readily confirmed by these simple tests (Figure 2–31). Facial palsy may be caused by infections, trauma, surgery, or tumors, particularly of the

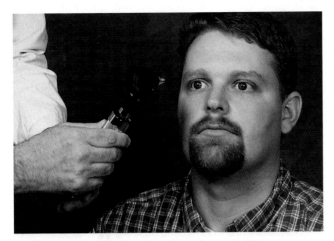

Figure 2–29 Pupillary constriction tested with a penlight.

needed and can be performed following completion of the physical examination. Venipuncture is needed for ordering laboratory blood tests to include hemograms, chemistries, and serologies. A phlebotomist in the clinical laboratory usually performs the procedure. In most cases, a prominent vein located in the vicinity of the antecubital fossa is selected and palpated. A tourniquet

of the facial nerve. Actually, the fibers from the facial nerve into the upper lid serve to close the lid; opening of the eye and raising of the upper lid are accomplished by oculomotor nerve (nerve III) innervation (Figure 2–32).

Motor function of the tenth cranial nerve (vagus) is tested by determining if an object, such as a dental mirror triggers a gag reflex when placed against the soft palate and tongue base. The spinal branch of the eleventh cranial nerve (accessory) is tested by placing a hand on each shoulder and requesting that the patient raise one shoulder and then the other (Figure 2–33). Lastly, the twelfth cranial nerve (hypoglossal) is assessed by having the patient protrude the tongue and determining whether it deviates to one side or the other (Figure 2–34). The patient is also asked to move the tongue from side to side or laterally push against a tongue blade. Deficits may be caused by a variety of lesions located in the periphery or centrally.

This completes the routine head and neck oral examination. There are other clinical tests that are often

Figure 2–31 Testing the seventh cranial nerve. *A,* Upper facial nerve: raising eyebrows and, *B,* closing eyes. *C,* Lower facial nerve: smiling, showing teeth.

Figure 2–30 Motor function of the fifth cranial nerve tested by moving jaw from side to side.

Third nerve supports and elevates upper lid

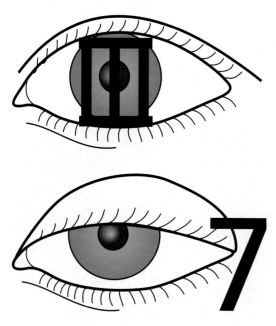

Seventh nerve closes upper lid

Figure 2–32   The oculomotor nerve, like a pillar, raises the upper lid; the facial nerve, like a hook, closes the lid.

Figure 2–34   Testing the twelfth cranial nerve (hypoglossal).

Another clinical test that is performed in the oral medicine clinic is allergy patch testing. In patients suspected of having an allergic stomatitis, particularly of the delayed type, or patients with lichenoid lesions, in whom heavy metal sensitivity is a consideration, the patch testing can be performed on the forearm skin. The test materials are mixed in a vehicle, usually petroleum

is placed around the upper arm and the patient is asked to make a fist (Figure 2–35, *A*). Contracting muscles in the forearm aids in distending the target vein. A venipuncture needle is inserted into the vein and advanced slightly until blood drops are seen, after which the collection vacuum tube is snapped over the needle face (Figure 2–35, *B*). The tourniquet is released as blood fills the tube. Various vacutainer tubes are available for obtaining plasma and serum.

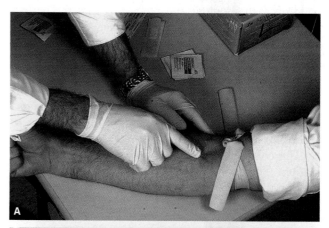

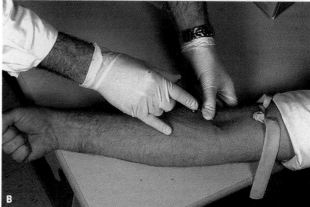

Figure 2–35   Venipuncture. *A*, Application of tourniquet; *B*, placement of needle into vein and compression of vacutainer tube.

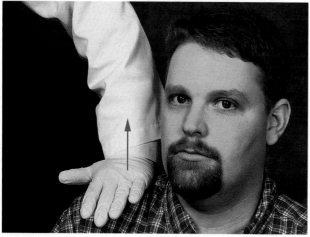

Figure 2–33   Testing the spinal branch of the eleventh cranial nerve (accessory nerve).

jelly, yet can also be applied directly. The materials are coded and paced on a nonallergenic adhesive tape. The tape is applied to the volar skin and left in place for 48 hours. If the patient harbors a T-cell response, a zone of erythema will appear at the site of contact (Figure 2–36).

Biopsy is a critical aspect of oral medicine practice. The three types of biopsies used most frequently are punch biopsy, incisional biopsy, and brush biopsy. Local anesthesia is used for punch and incisional biopsies. In most instances the tissue is covered with topical anesthetic for 2 to 3 minutes followed by injection of lidocaine with vasoconstrictor. Most biopsies require only one-half carpule, and the needle should be placed adjacent to the site of biopsy, inserted directly below the site, and dispensed. The punch biopsy can be done with a 5-mm disposable punch, cutting a core to 3 to 4 mm in depth (Figure 2–37). Tissue forceps are used to

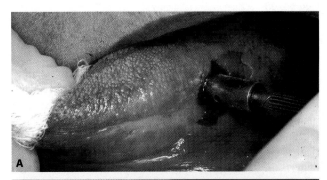

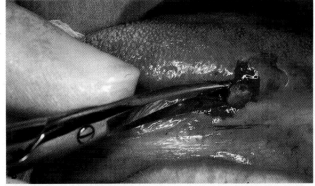

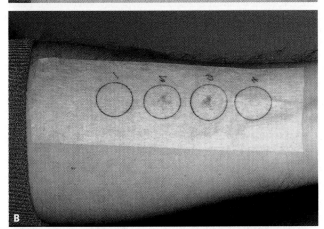

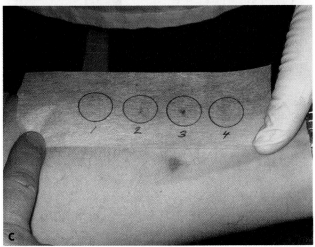

Figure 2–36 Patch test. *A*, Application of test materials to tape; *B*, placement of tape with allergens to skin; *C*, a zone of erythema indicates delayed-type hypersensitivity.

Figure 2–37 Punch biopsy. *A*, Obtaining a core with a 5-mm punch instrument; *B*, removing the punch biopsy tissue fragment with curved scissors; *C*, placing the tissue in formalin.

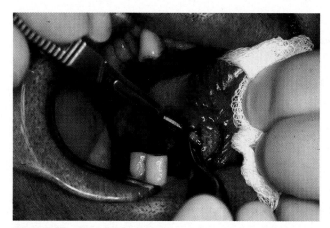

Figure 2–38 Scalpel incisional biopsy.

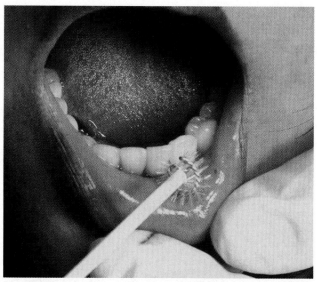

Figure 2–39 Brush biopsy. The brush is rotated or "twirled" over the area to be sampled.

grasp the specimen gently, avoiding crushing, and curved scissors are used to remove the core. These specimens can be hemisected for immunofluorscence; one sample should always be placed in formalin for routine histopathology. The incisional biopsy can also be made with a No. 15 blade scalpel. In most instances, an elliptical incision is made with the blade directed at a 45-degree angle (Figure 2–38). The wound can then be closed with two to three interrupted silk sutures. In both punch and sutured biopsies, gauze compression must be placed for a few minutes to achieve hemostasis. Patients should be instructed to avoid hard foods and to use warm saltwater rinses for the first day or two postoperatively. A wet tea bag can be applied to the wound should minor bleeding occur. The brush biopsy requires a special instrument with bristles that are able to retrieve cells from the spinous layer of the epithelium when firmly rotated over the mucosal lesion (Figure 2–39). The collected cells are transferred to a glass slide, fixed, and forwarded to a processing laboratory for interpretation.

Suggested reading

Alexander MM, Brown MS. Physical examination. Part 17: neurological examination. Nursing 1976;6:38–43.

Bates B. A guide to physical examination. 4th Ed. Philadelphia: Lippincott, 1987.

Hicks JL. Important landmarks of the orofacial complex. Emerg Med Clin North Am 2000;18:379–91.

Mulliken RA, Casner MJ. Oral manifestations of systemic disease. Emerg Med Clin North Am 2000;18:565–75.

Seidel HM, Ball JW, Dains JE, Benedict GW. Mosby's guide to physical examination. 2nd Ed. St. Louis: Mosby Year Book, 1991.

Tanaka TT. Recognition of the pain formula for head, neck, and TMJ disorders: the general physical examination. CDA J 1984;12:43–9.

3 Cardiovascular Diseases

L. Roy Eversole, DDS, MSD, MA

The diseases discussed in this chapter include developmental and congenital malformations of the heart, atherosclerotic thromboembolic vascular occlusive disease, acquired cardiac inflammatory and infectious diseases (rheumatic heart disease and endocarditis in particular), and congestive heart failure. These common conditions have significant impact on dental professionals and their patients. Dental implications include disease detection by cognizance of salient signs and symptoms, management of emergencies, treatment-plan alterations and prophylaxis owing to the patient's medically compromised status, and treatment considerations in the patient who is under pharmacologic management for cardiovascular disease.

The clinical tools used to ascertain the presence or absence of cardiovascular disease include the health history, vital sign assessment, electrocardiography, specific serum chemistries, echocardiography and other imaging techniques, and exercise tolerance testing. The findings that one encounters using these tests are detailed in the section on clinical features.

Pathophysiology

The heart is a four-chambered muscle that is lined by endothelium. This organ is often considered in the context of a double pump: a right heart and a left heart. The two pumps each have an upper chamber, the atrium, and a lower chamber, the ventricle. These two chambers are interfaced by a valve. The right atrium receives blood through large vessels draining the liver and systemic circulation, whereas the left atrium receives oxygenated blood from the lungs. Blood is pumped from the atria through the valves into the right and left ventricles. The two ventricles contract in unison, sending blood out into the circulation while the valves close, preventing regurgitation back into the atria. When the ventricles are at rest and the atria are pumping blood into them, the term diastole is used. When the atria are at rest and the ventricles are contracting, the term systole is used. The right ventricle pumps its blood through the pulmonic valve and pulmonary artery into the lungs and the left ventricle delivers blood to the systemic circulation through the aortic valve and into the aorta. It is the systolic contraction of the left ventricle that accounts for the higher recorded level of the blood pressure, whereas the lower level of pressure recorded is the resting pressure during diastole. If peripheral vessels are constricted, there is an increase in peripheral resistance to the outflow of blood through the circulation and the diastolic pressure is elevated (hypertension). In general, normal blood pressure is considered to be less than 130 systolic and less than 85 diastolic. When the diastolic pressure exceeds 90 mm, the patient is considered to be borderline hypertensive.

The contractions of the atria and ventricles are a biologic miracle. The heart has an innate capacity for muscular contraction that emanates from a focus in the right atrium known as the sinoatrial (SA) node. The impulse involves the movement of ions across the cardiac sarcolemmic membrane and specialized conduction fibers, an event termed depolarization. The impulse travels through the cell membranes switching from negativity to positivity. These migrating positive charges are detectable with an electrical recording instrument, the electrocardiograph. Positively charged electrodes are placed on the skin, and when a positive depolarization wave migrates toward the electrode, there is an upward (positive) deflection of the recording devise. When the positivity moves away from the positive electrode, there is a downward (negative) deflection of the record.

The electrocardiogram (EKG) is a graphic tracing of the heart's electrical activity over time (Figure 3–1). The recording paper strip moves at a constant rate and is calibrated longitudinally and vertically. The longitudi-

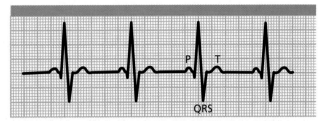

Figure 3-1 Electrocardiogram shows regularly spaced spikes indicative of a normal steady rhythm. The depolarization wave originates in the right auricular sinoatrial (SA) node, which is represented by the P wave; the impulse then reaches the atrioventricular (AV) node that triggers a depolarization wave down the bundle branches then out through the ventricular musculature via Purkinje fibers. The ventricular wave is represented by the QRS complex. The electrical wave of repolarization in the atria is obscured in the EKG by the QRS complex, whereas ventricular repolarization is represented by the T wave followed by a pause until the SA pacemaker fires again.

nal divisions allow one to calculate the heart rate, and the vertical dimensions are a measure of charge intensity. If an electrode is placed on the chest, directly over the anterior lower aspect of the left ventricle (so-called lead 5), a standard EKG pattern can be recorded. In this lead, the first wave one observes is the P wave. This is the passage of the depolarization impulse from the SA node through the atria. When the depolarization impulse reaches the atrial-ventricular (AV) node there is a slight pause followed by a small negative deflection, the Q wave. Immediately there is an abrupt positive spike with a downward deflection to the baseline, the R wave, then continuation of the negative component with an upward deflection back to baseline, the S wave. The QRS complex represents the electrical activity of the conduction of fibers of the ventricles. The impulse travels from the AV node down the interventricular septum through the right and left main bundle branches, then up through the ventricles via Purkinje fibers and on into the myocardial cells to induce contraction There is then a lull in electrical activity followed by a slight positive then negative deflection, the T wave, that represents repolarization of the ventricles. The interposed quiet period is the S-T interval. This, of course, is the normal pattern of polarization and depolarization of the heart. The atrial repolarization wave is masked by the ventricular QRS complex.

There are numerous other leads that the cardiologist can use to assess electrical activity in the heart. There are six limb leads and six chest leads. These leads allow one to pinpoint foci of cardiac pathology and also to assess the axis of the cardiac electrical conduction system. The electrocardiogram can be analyzed to assess rate, rhythm, conduction blocks, infarction, electrolyte imbalances, drug toxicity, and other organ-system pathology, particularly pulmonary dis-

ease. In the analysis of coronary ischemia and infarction, comparison of the various chest leads is essential to pinpoint the region of the left ventricle in which the vascular occlusive change has had its effects. An overview of EKG interpretation is given in the section on clinical features.

The opening and closing of valves during the cardiac cycle can be detected by placing a stethoscope on the chest, directly over the heart. Auscultation of specific areas on the chest discloses a major sound during systole, when the mitral and tricuspid valves snap shut, and during diastole when the aortic and pulmonic valves close (Figure 3–2). The mitral-tricuspid sound is designated S1; the aortic-pulmonic sound is termed S2. The aortic valve may close slightly ahead of the pulmonic valve, and when auscultated at the region of the base during inspiration, S2 is split into two closely sequenced sounds. The S2 split on inspiration is a normal finding. Some patients also manifest S3 or S4 sounds that are interposed between the two major "lub-dub" (S1-S2) sounds. During diastole ventricular filling is initially passive and then muscular contraction in the atria results in rapid ejection. During the passive phase, a vibration in the ventricles occurs and is perceived as faint extra sound, sounding like "Ken-tuck-y"; this is S3. During the muscular ejection phase another sound may be detected, sounding like "Tenn-e-see"; this is S4. The S3 and S4 sounds are often undetected and when present in a normal subject, they are usually quite faint. If they are pronounced, they are termed a gallop and cardiac pathology is likely to be present.

A murmur is an abnormal heart sound or a deviation from normal sounds, including physiologic splits of S2. Murmurs occur in patients with septal defects, patent ductus, valvular stenosis or insufficiency, and mitral valve prolapse with regurgitation. Murmurs may also occur in high cardiac output states, such as anemia, thyrotoxicosis, and pregnancy. Valvular diseases or deformities in which murmurs are detected are subdivided into two major groups: those that cause a nar-

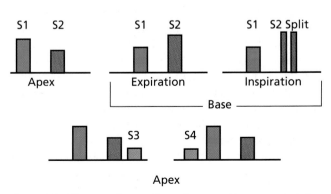

Figure 3-2 Electrocardiogram illustrating normal heart sounds during systole and diastole.

rowing of the valve aperature between the heart chambers at the exit of the great vessels and those that result in failure of valve closure. Narrowed valves are said to be stenotic, whereas valvular insufficiency is the terminology used to denote defects in closure. In many cases, valvular stenosis and insufficiency may coexist.

Before the discussion of the pathophysiology of various cardiac disease states, an overview of cardiac failure is presented (Figure 3–3). Heart failure simply means there is inadequacy of the heart as a pump and tissues can no longer be perfused. The heart fails as a consequence of (1) myocardial damage, as in myocardial infarction; (2) increased peripheral resistance; (3) compression of the heart, a process that occurs when the pericardium is filled with fluid or blood; (4) malfunction of the heart valves; and (5) pathologic shunts. Because the heart is a closed vascular system, what affects the left heart will in fact have implications for the right heart and vice versa. Nevertheless, it is convenient to consider the heart as two sided. Right-sided heart failure occurs when there are right valvular defects, pathologic shunts, pulmonary disease, or pericardial compression. When the right heart fails, blood returning from the venous hepatic and systemic circulations becomes congested, leading to distention and edema from increased venous hydrostatic pressure. When the left heart fails, congestion into the lungs occurs leading to pulmonary edema. Eventually, regardless of the source, congestive heart failure progresses to involve both systemic and pulmonary vasculature.

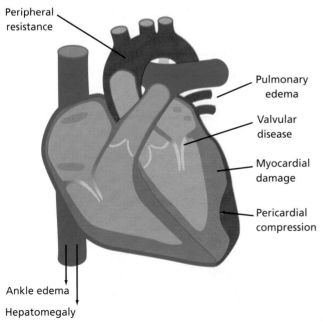

Figure 3–3 Mechanisms of congestive heart failure include increased peripheral resistance, valvular insufficiency or stenosis, myocardial damage, and cardiac compression.

Table 3–1 Cardiac Diseases That May Predispose to Endocarditis

Congenital heart defects
   Atrial septal communication
   Ventricular septal communication
   Patent ductus arteriosus
   Aortic stenosis
   Mitral stenosis
   Pulmonic stenosis
   Bicuspid valve stenosis
   Tetralogy of Fallot
   Eisenmenger complex
   Miscellaneous other combined deformities
Acquired heart defects
   Rheumatic valve disease
   Fenfluramine-dexfenfluramine valvulopathy
Prosthetic valves

Congenital deformities of the heart occur during the process of growth and development and are, therefore, evident as congenital malformations. Table 3–1 lists the more common congenital heart defects. Atrial and ventricular septal defects reflect an embryologic failure of septal closure. Patent ductus arteriosus is a shunt extending from the pulmonary artery to the aorta, an embryologic structure that normally closes to become the ligamentum arteriosum. Congenital valvular stenosis (narrowing of the valve orifice) involves primarily the aortic, mitral, and pulmonic valves. All of these defects, if severe enough, can culminate in congestive failure and may predispose to infection of the internal aspect of the heart (endocarditis). There are numerous combination defects or cardiac syndromes, the two more common of which are the tetralogy of Fallot and the Eisenmenger complex. In the tetralogy, there is a ventricular septal defect, a dextroposed aorta (such that the opening of the aorta directly overlies the septal defect), pulmonic valve stenosis, and a secondary right ventricular hypertrophy. Because unoxygenated blood can pass across the septal defect and enter the aorta, cyanosis is a classic feature. In the Eisenmenger complex, the defects mirror tetralogy, yet there is no pulmonic valve stenosis.

Rheumatic fever is a streptococcal systemic infection in which immunopathologic sequelae evolve. Following immune clearance of infectious organisms, streptococcal antigens remain in the circulation as immune complexes. These complexes filter into various tissues where they fix complement, and initiate inflammatory lesions that are host-tissue destructive. The three target tissues and organs affected by immune complex post-streptococcal events are the heart, kidneys, and synovial membranes. Rheumatic heart disease comprises sterile fibrotic lesions of the heart valves (mitral and aortic being the favored sites) and inflammatory lesions along conduction fiber pathways in the myocardium. Valvular stenosis and insufficiency are detected as cardiac murmurs, and myocardial lesions result in arrhythmias. Immune complex lesions in the glomerulus lead to glomerulonephritis, and synovial inflammatory lesions result in the formation of a pannus in rheumatoid arthritis. The cardiac lesions of rheumatic heart disease can cause congestive heart failure, and damaged valves can be colonized by pathogenic bacteria, a disease known as endocarditis (see Chapter 17).

Another form of acquired valvular deformation is attributed to a combination of two drugs that are used in diet control. Fenfluramine and dexfenfluramine, commonly known as fen/fen, are associated with cardiac valvulopathy but with variable differences in risk assessment. These valvular lesions are often associated with murmurs.

One of the most common diseases to affect mankind is atherosclerotic thromboembolic vascular occlusive dis-ease (Figure 3–4). Atherosclerosis evolves as a conse-quence of endothelial damage followed by accumulation of lipids within the intima of arteries and veins. The primary risk factors include genetic predisposition; hyper-lipidemia, particularly with very low density (VLDL) and low density lipoproteins (LDL); hypertension; sedentary life-style; male gender, and increasing age. Vascular adhesion molecules, such as selectins, cell adhesion molecules (CAMs), and integrins, are upregulated and facilitate the emigration of leukocytes into the atheroma. These complicated lesions may then develop tunneling fissures with erosion of the endothelial lining, resulting in activation of the intrinsic pathway of coagulation. In this manner, thrombi form within vessel lumens, leading to ischemia or infarction; thrombi may be dislodged to become emboli. Arterial emboli become lodged in lumens, whereas venous emboli break free, travel in the enlarging

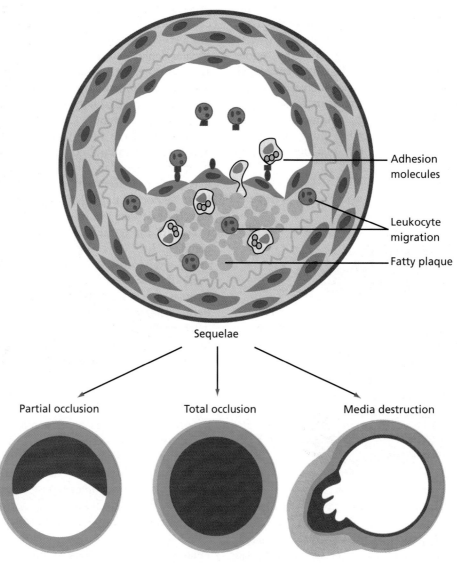

Adhesion molecules

Leukocyte migration

Fatty plaque

Sequelae

Partial occlusion   Total occlusion   Media destruction

Figure 3–4 Consequences of atherosclerosis with thrombosis.

veins to enter the right heart, into the pulmonary artery, and become lodged in the lung arteries (pulmonary embolism). The consequences of arterial vascular occlusion include ischemia and infarction, coronary heart disease, cerebrovascular accident, and aneurysm.

Coronary occlusion leads to ischemic heart disease that is often detectable on EKG. Complete vascular occlusion is responsible for coronary infarction or heart attack. Occlusion can result in small infarcts that may be inconsequential, whereas large vessel occlusion can result in massive necrosis and death. Sudden infarcts lead to myocardial necrosis with seepage of cardiac enzymes into the circulating blood. Elevated lactic dehydrogenase and creatinine phosphokinase enzymes are detected, and the EKG reveals specific conduction defects. Epidemiologic studies have shown a correlation between dental and periodontal infections and coronary heart disease. Even so, no causal relation can be documented.

Clinical features

The clinical manifestations of cardiovascular diseases are signs and symptoms of cardiac failure, arrhythmia, hypertension (see Chapter 4), angina, myocardial infarction, stroke, and risk of endocarditis. As has been mentioned previously, the signs of heart failure include ankle edema, jugular vein distension, and hepatomegaly if there are right heart lesions and dyspnea in left heart lesions. Syncope and fatigue are also signs and symptoms of cardiovascular disease. In ischemic heart disease, rheumatic heart disease, and selected drug toxicities, conduction disturbances occur and are detectable on the EKG (Figure 3–5). When the SA node fires rapidly, over 70 times per minute, the condition is referred to as sinus tachycardia. Reading cardiac rate on an EKG strip is fascilitated by the bold black vertical lines. If a QRS complex occurs at the first major subdivision, the rate is 300 per minute. If the depolarization occurs every two major divisions, the rate is 150; at three subdivisions, the rate is 100; at four it is 75, and at five subdivisions the rate is 60. Bradycardia is assessed by noting how many depolarizations occur during a 15-second segment and multiplying by 4.

When there are no coordinated depolarization waves originating in the SA node and multiple ectopic foci fire, the P waves disappear and the EKG pattern becomes highly erratic. Although irregularly spaced QRS complexes are evident as some of these ectopic foci trigger the ventricular node, such a pattern is termed atrial fibrillation, and in essence, there is no coordination of atrial contractions. Ventricular fibrillation is a dire medical emergency; it is characterized by a jagged EKG pattern with no identifiable normal depolarization waves. In ventricular fibrillation and flutter, pumping

action is no longer extant. In sinus arrhythmia, extra beats are identifiable on the EKG, and such ectopic beats are evident as early P waves followed by normal QRS complexes. Wandering pacemakers represent depolarizations emanating in the atria, outside the SA node, and under these conditions, the P waves are heterogeneous in shape.

Premature ventricular contractions (PCVs) are considered pathologic if there are more than five per minute (Figure 3–6). They are characterized by QRS intervals that are widened. Sinus arrest is characterized by a lengthy interval between the end of the P wave and the origin of the QRS complex. In AV arrest, there is a repeatable delay from P to QRS. Conduction system blocks are easily visualized on selected chest leads.

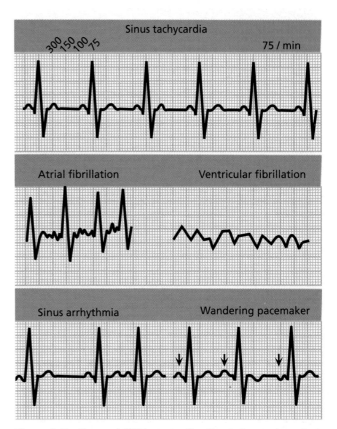

Figure 3–5 Abnormal EKG patterns. *Top Panel*, sinus tachycardia is portrayed by normal-appearing P waves followed by normal QRS and T waves occurring with a periodicity exceeding 70 beats per minute. *Middle panel*, atrial fibrillation is characterized by the firing of multiple pacemakers in the atria. No normal P waves are evident, rather there is a staccato pattern of P waves with occasional QRS, indicating that some of these ectopic pacemakers transmit to the AV node. Ventricular fibrillation evolves when multiple ectopic sites fire within the ventricles, yielding a sporadic irregular EKG pattern. During ventricular fibrillation, the heart has no effective pumping action. *Lower panel*, sinus tachycardia is represented by periods of nonactivity, indicating that the SA node is failing to fire in sequence, a sign of coronary artery disease. Wandering pacemaker signifies variable ectopic foci in the atria, replacing the normal SA node, and is characterized by P wave pattern heterogeneity.

Recall that the depolarization wave travels down the right and left main bundles and then back up through the ventricular walls and out into the musculature via Purkinje fibers. These impulses are portrayed by the QRS complex. Main bundle branch blocks are differentiated with chest leads V1, V2, V5, and V6, since the V1 and V2 leads overlie the right heart and the V5 and V6 leads overlie the septum and left ventricle. The peak of the S wave is bifurcated when depolarization is blocked and then resumes through the conduction fiber pathways. In right main bundle branch blocks, the bimodal peak in V1 and V2 is markedly accentuated, whereas in left bundle branch block, a dip is witnessed at the vertical peak of the R wave in leads V5 and V6.

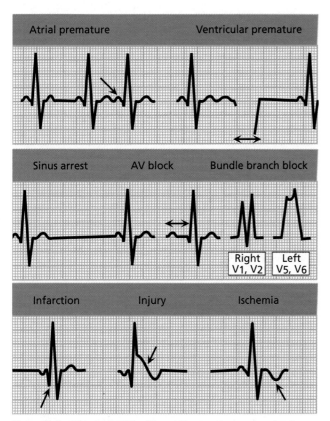

Figure 3–6 Abnormal EKG patterns. *Top panel*, premature beats may occur in the atria, where P waves follow on the heels of T waves, or in the ventricles, where the QRS complex is widened and accentuated, a phenomenon termed PVCs (premature ventricular contractions; over six per minute are pathologic). *Middle panel*, blocks in conduction pathways can occur anywhere in the heart. Sinus arrest is characterized by a flat line due to lack of SA node firing. In AV block the P wave interval is prolonged. Bundle branch blocks are evaluated in chest leads V1, V2, V5, and V6. In right bundle block, the R wave is bifurcated in V1 and V2, and in left bundle block, the bifurcation is witnessed in leads V5 and V6. *Bottom panel*, myocardial ischemia, injury, and infarction are represented in these EKG pattern. In myocardial infarction, a prominent Q wave is seen and the localization of the infarct can be determined by evaluating each of the chest leads. Myocardial injury is characterized by an elevated T wave. In coronary artery ischemia the T wave is inverted.

Myocardial injury, ischemia, and infarction all show characteristic EKG patterns. Recall that ischemia and infarction are mainly left ventricular events. Myocardial injury shows an elevated repolarization T wave, infarction may manifest with an accentuated Q wave downward deflection, and ischemia often reveals itself with an inverted T wave. There are many other characteristic patterns indicative of cardiac pathology. Cardiac hypertrophy, depolarization axis perturbations, certain drug toxicities, and various other disorders can be detected on the basis of EKG patterns.

Angina pectoris is chest pain that radiates into the left jaw or down the left arm as a consequence of coronary artery spasticity. Angina is a prelude to infarction and requires further workup that includes cardiac enzymes, EKG, and sonography. If these studies suggest coronary occlusion, cardiac catheterization is performed, to detect arterial narrowing or blockage by a thrombus or embolus. The consequences of coronary artery ischemia range from mild arrhythmia to cardiac arrest and death. Infarction invariably occurs in the left ventrical and ventricular septum, and its precise localization can be determined by assessment of the various chest leads on the EKG. Small infarcts may have no clinical significance, whereas larger foci may lead to papillary muscle collapse with resulting valvular insufficiency. Conduction pathway blocks occur in infarcted areas leading to significant arrhythmias. Coronary artery balloon angioplasty and bypass surgery are required when significant vascular occlusion is detected.

Cardiac disease diagnosis employs auscultation. Heart sounds are detected through the stethoscope, and in a normal heart, the sounds that are heard are those of valve closure. Valvular stenoses and insufficiencies create abnormal heart sounds, termed murmurs, that are referred to as splits and clicks. As mentioned previously, a split of S2 during inspiration is normal. When there is a delay between the two split sounds, cardiopathology is present, such as a bundle branch block. Many heart sounds are complex and subtle, requiring an experienced ear for adequate detection, classification, and interpretation. Chest radiographs disclose heart size, cardiomegaly being a sign of hypertrophy and compensation during congestive failure. Serum chemistries are particularly useful in the diagnosis of myocardial infarction. Lactic dehydrogenase and creatinine phosphokinase isoenzymes can be assessed when a patient reports chest pain or pressure and also in the emergency room when a patient is admitted unconscious.

Medical management involves surgical techniques and or medications to reduce morbidity and mortality. Drugs can be used as single agents or in combination. For coronary artery disease, balloon angioplasty and bypass surgery are the primary interventions. Open heart surgery is performed to repair congenital defects and place artificial valves. Heart transplant is reserved for instances of severe infarction leading to cardiac failure. Preventive interventions include low-fat, low-sodium diet, regular exercise, and smoking cessation. It follows then that dental care of the cardiac patient may require special precaution and understanding. These are discussed below and in Chapter 11, where drug interactions are discussed.

Dental management

The risk of endocarditis evolving as a consequence of bacteremia from oral microorganisms is a major concern in dental practice. Any patient with a history of organic murmur is at risk. Invasive dental procedures, such as exodontias and oral, periodontal, or endodontic surgery, are considered to increase the risk of endocarditis in patients with valvular disease, septal defects, patent ductus, and mitral valve prolapse with concomitant regurgitation. It matters not whether valve defects are congenital or acquired; in both instances turbulent flow occurs within the heart chambers, and in areas of flow voids, bacterial colonization can ensue. The protocols for prevention of endocarditis by antibiotic prophylaxis are detailed in Chapter 17. As discussed previously, the lesions at risk usually manifest as a cardiac murmur. When a patient indicates that he or she has been diagnosed with a murmur, it is recommended that the physician be contacted, to ascertain whether it is "organic" or "functional"; the former indicates cardiac damage, the latter is of no clinical consequence. Mitral valve prolapse is a common malady among females. If no regurgitation is detected, antibiotic coverage is unnecessary; if present, the valve is susceptible to bacterial colonization, and prophylaxis is required for invasive dental procedures. Recall from earlier discussion that the fen-fen diet regimen was found to be associated with or perhaps even to cause valvular lesions in which a murmur can be detected. If a patient indicates a history of taking this regimen, it is recommended that he or she consult their physician to determine if any valvular pathosis was incurred and whether antibiotic prophylaxis may be indicated for invasive dental procedures.

Some patients may indicate having had a detectable murmur as a child and that as an adult, it is no longer detectable. It would be prudent to pursue this in more detail with the patient's physician by telephone, electronic mail, or written consultation. When a patient indicates having been diagnosed with a murmur, yet is not aware of the necessity for antibiotic prophylaxis during invasive dental procedures, the prophylactic recommendations should be followed if a dental emergency is extant and there is no time to confirm the status of the murmur.

Coronary atherosclerosis is the commonest cause of cardiovascular disability and death in the industrialized world. The average age for males is 50 to 65 years and for females, 60 to 70 years. Atherosclerotic vascular occlusive disease is a common medical illness that requires attention when dental procedures are being performed. Coronary ischemia, myocardial infarction, and stroke are all complications of thromboembolic disease. Any of these complications may occur during the undertaking of dental procedures, and all of them are more likely to evolve during periods of anxiety and stress. These same concerns apply to hypertensive patients, since they are at increased risk for thromboembolic events. Among patients with a history of angina, myocardial infarction, or stroke, efforts must be made to reduce stress levels by achieving sound and profound anesthesia for dental and soft-tissue surgical procedures. In consultation with the patient's physician, the dentist may elect to prescribe an anxiolytic medication prior to dental procedures. Any of the diazepam group drugs can be used, such as 1.0 mg of lorazepam or 10 mg of benzodiazepam 1 hour prior to an office visit. When prescribing anxiolytics, it is important to realize that sedation and drowsiness occur, thereby precluding the driving of an automobile. Patients should be advised to arrange for transportation following completion of the dental procedure.

If during a dental procedure a patient complains of angina, the procedure should be stopped and a coronary vasodilator must be administered. A differential diagnosis is critically important, to ensure that the patient's symptoms are indeed indicative of angina. Recall that angina may arise as substernal pain, a severe pressure sensation, and may be confused by the patient as indigestion. When the pain radiates over the left arm or into the left jaw, coronary ischemia is the primary clinical diagnosis. Many patients with chronic angina wear nitroglycerin patches, and the dentist should be aware of this practice, emphasizing to the patient that the patch should be worn the day of their appointment. For those patients who take nitroglycerin sublingually, it is prudent to have them bring their medication with them when they are receiving dental care, and keeping the tablets within easy reach is important. During severe angina, cardiac arrest may evolve. If the patient slips into unconsciousness, 911 should be dialed, and the dental team should assess breathing and pulse. If a carotid pulse is detectable yet no respirations are perceived, assisted breathing by mouth-to-mouth or a bag device should be initiated. When neither pulse nor respirations are present, cardiopulmonary resuscitation must commence immediately. Automated external cardiac defibrillators are being placed in many public places and will eventually find their way into the dental office as a significant addition to the office emergency

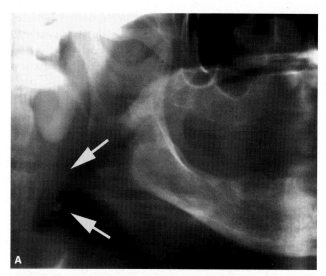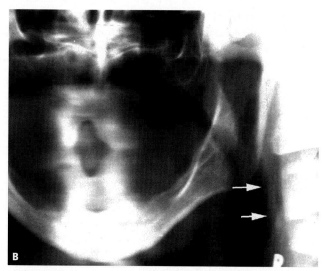

Figure 3–7 Carotid atheromatous calcifications as seen on panoramic radiographs. *A,* Focal opacities; *B,* longitudinal calcifications.

kit. In the event of sudden coronary arrest in a subject with no detectable pulse, defibrillation should be attempted. These automated devices are applied to the chest wall and activated. If repeated attempts fail, CPR should be performed until the mobile emergency care unit arrives. The American Heart Association's CPR Guidelines should be followed.

If the patient experiences signs of cerebrovascular accident while in the dental operatory, he or she should be reclined and oxygen should be administered. Impending stroke may be signaled by transient ischemic attacks manifested by sudden vision changes. In other cases, no warning signs appear and a patient loses consciousness. Unfortunately, there are no emergency interventions that will prevent cerebrovascular occlusion or rupture of aneurysms. Certain strokes are the consequence of emboli derived from carotid artery aneurysms. Calcified atheromatous plaques of the carotid artery can sometimes be seen on panoramic radiographs; the plaques appear as focal radiopacities or extend longitudinally up the course of the artery and appear just posterior and inferior to the mandible on the film (Figure 3–7). For patients who have not been diagnosed with carotid vascular occlusion or aneurysm, this finding on routine dental films should be noted and reported to the patient's physician. Vascular surgery and replacement of the diseased vessel can be a life-saving event. Administration of fibrinolytic enzymes within minutes of a stroke may remove thrombi.

Another important consideration for the patient with a history of stroke, coronary artery disease, or thrombophlebitis is the fact that such individuals may be medicated to reduce the risk of thrombosis. Anticoagulant regimens may be of no clinical consequence when the patient is taking a single preventive daily dose of aspirin;

alternatively, some high-risk patients are placed on Coumadin and have significantly depressed coagulative capability. The effects of Coumadin are monitored by the prothrombin time and the international normalized ratio (INR). In general, invasive surgical procedures should be avoided or undertaken with great caution in patients with a prothrombin time that is 50% of normal (or double the control time) or an INR exceeding 2.5 (see Chapter 7). When these markers of coagulation status are indicative of a potential for severe bleeding and the patient requires immediate dental intervention, the procedure should be performed in a hospital dental setting in consultation with an internist or hematologist. Expertise in coagulopathies is required in the event that factor supplementation may be needed. In nonemergency situations, the patient's physician should be consulted about the possibility of withdrawing Coumadin 3 to 4 days prior to the dental surgical procedure, to allow the INR to decrease. Importantly, the dentist should never alter the patient's anticoagulant regimen without consultation. If the coagulability is restored to normal levels, there is the possibility that the patient could experience a thromboembolic event.

Patients who are experiencing dental pain should be treated with analgesics that will not interfere with coagulation or platelet adhesion. In this context, aspirin, ibuprofen, ketorolac, and other nonsteroidal anti-inflammatory drugs (NSAIDs) with platelet adhesion inhibitory effects should be avoided. Codeine, oxycodone, and hydrocodone without aspirin can be used in pain management.

Other complications occurring in the patient with atherosclerosis involve medications that are prescribed to reduce edema in congestive failure, lower blood pressure, and treat arrhythmias. Diuretics and antihypertensives may render the patient prone to the development of orthostatic hypotension. Standing suddenly after residing for some time in a reclined dental chair may bring about such an episode. Calcium channel blockers reduce vascular tone, and these medications often induce gingival hyperplasia (see Chapter 23).

Many mild arrhythmias are managed medically, whereas more severe arrhythmic disease may be treated by placement of a pacemaker. Most pacemakers are shielded from external electrical and microwave radiation; nevertheless, ultrasonic devices, cleaners, and microwave ovens should not be operated within the immediate vicinity of a patient with a pacemaker until the patient's physician is contacted and reassurance is given that the specific device brand is safe under such circumstances. Specific management considerations for the hypertensive patient are detailed in Chapter 4.

Suggested reading

Alexander RE. The automated external cardiac defibrillator: lifesaving device for medical emergencies. J Am Dent Assoc 1999;130:837–45. (Published erratum: J Am Dent Assoc 1999;130:1162).

Blanchaert RH Jr. Ischemic heart disease. Oral Surg Oral Med Oral Pathol Oral Radiol Endod 1999;87:281–3.

Friedlander AH, Maeder LA. The prevalence of calcified carotid artery atheromas on the panoramic radiographs of patients with type 2 diabetes mellitus. Oral Surg Oral Med Oral Pathol Oral Radiol Endod 2000;89:420–4.

Lewis DA, Brooks SL. Cartoid artery calcification in a general dental population: a retrospective study of panoramic radiographs. Gen Dent 1999;47:98–103.

Mattila KJ, Asikainen S, Wolf J, et al. Age, dental infections, and coronary heart disease. J Dent Res 2000;79:756–60.

Montebugnoli L, Montanari G. Vasovagal syncope in heart transplant patients during dental surgery. Oral Surg Oral Med Oral Pathol Oral Radiol Endod 1999;87:666–9.

Moskowitz L. Cardiac disease and hypertension. Considerations for office treatment. Dent Clin North Am 1999;43:495–512.

Niwa H, Sato Y, Matsuura H. Safety of dental treatment in patients with previously diagnosed acute myocardial infarction or unstable angina pectoris. Oral Surg Oral Med Oral Pathol Oral Radiol Endod 2000;89:35–41.

Pallasch TJ. Current status of fenfluramine/dexfenfluramine-induced cardiac valvulopathy. J Calif Dent Assoc 1999;27:400–4.

Parry JA, Harrison VE, Barnard KM. Recognizing and caring for the medically compromised child: 1. Disorders of the cardiovascular and respiratory systems. Dent Update 1998;25:325–31.

Wynn RL. Atrial fibrillation: medications and dental considerations. Gen Dent 1999;47:548–51.

4 Renal Diseases and Hypertension

L. Roy Eversole, DDS, MSD, MA

Renal diseases have significant implications for dental practice. When kidney failure surfaces, patients are managed by either peritoneal dialysis or hemodialysis. Dialysis patients await the opportunity for a renal transplant, a procedure that requires tissue human leukocyte antigen (HLA) matching. The more prevalent renal diseases are glomerulonephritis and pyelonephritis. The former is an immunopathologic disease, the latter is an infectious disease. Both forms of inflammatory renal diseases predispose to hypertension. The dental implications revolve around metabolic disturbances that occur during renal failure, medications that affected patients are taking, and specific considerations that are required for renal transplant patients. Neoplasms of the kidney are uncommon, yet cases of renal cell carcinoma have been reported to metastasize to the oral cavity.

Pathophysiology

In both glomerulonephritis and pyelonephritis, inflammation of the kidney occurs and the glomerular vessels become narrowed. Luminal constriction of afferent arterioles with resultant ischemia triggers the release of renin by the juxtaglomerular apparatus (Figure 4–1). Elevated serum renin stimulates the release of angiotensin-converting enzyme (ACE) synthesized in lung tissues, an enzyme that cleaves angiotensinogen to angiotensin peptides. Angiotensin is a potent vasoconstrictor and also stimulates the release of aldosterone from the adrenal cortex, a hormone that acts on renal tubules to retain sodium. These pathophysiologic events lead to increased peripheral resistance and hypervolemia, the combination of which is manifested as hypertension.

The pathologic lesion of the afferent arterioles and glomerular vessels is termed microangiopathy or arteriolonephrosclerosis. As the vessel walls progressively thicken, the filtration of waste substances and ion exchange mechanisms become impaired. In some forms of glomerulonephritis, the glomerular basement membrane is damaged and becomes porous, allowing protein leaks (Figure 4–2). Albuminuria initiates an osmotic diuresis and hypoalbuminemia leads to ascitis and generalized edema. These changes constitute the nephrotic syndrome. In other forms of glomerulonephritis and in late stage pyelonephritis, glomerular basement membranes are markedly thickened and impervious to solutes. Nitrogenous wastes then accumulate with elevations of serum creatinine and urea nitrogen, a clinical syndrome termed uremia or azotemia. As azotemia worsens, biochemical toxicity effects, including metabolic acidosis, ensue and result in death if the blood is not dialyzed.

The various forms of glomerulonephritis evolve as a consequence of immune complex injury to the nephron (ie, rheumatic disease), antiglomerular basement membrane antibodies, and autoantibodies directed to podocyte antigens (Figure 4–3). These immunologic events fix, complement, and initiate inflammatory cell infiltration into the mesangium. Immune complexes and autoantibodies occlude and thicken the basement membrane, thereby accounting for the aforementioned glomerular lesions. An accompaniment, either primary or secondary in origin, is systemic arteriolosclerosis.

Pyelonephritis is caused by retrograde or ascending infections that reach the kidney, pelvis, and tubular regions from the lower urinary tract. Either vesiculo-urethral reflux or urinary obstruction from tumors or kidney stones (urolithiasis) will mitigate micturation, thereby abrogating the usual flushing that would eliminate bacteria. The microorganisms responsible for pyelonephritis are coliforms. Repeated infections cause both tubular and glomerular inflammatory disease that eventuates in glomerulosclerosis, uremia, and ultimately, renal failure.

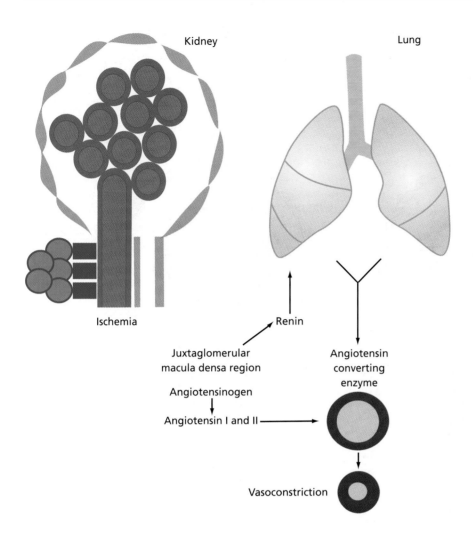

Kidney

Lung

Ischemia

Renin

Juxtaglomerular
macula densa region

Angiotensin
converting
enzyme

Angiotensinogen

Angiotensin I and II

Vasoconstriction

Figure 4–1 Renal mechanisms in hypertension. Vascular disease leads to luminal narrowing and ishemia at the level of the afferent arteriole, triggering the release of renin. Renin interacts with angiotensin-converting enzyme to release angiotensins, which in turn stimulate peripheral vessel constriction.

Tubulointerstitial disease of the lower nephron is the consequence of infection or ischemia secondary to microangiopathic lesions (arteriolosclerosis) involving the vasculature that supplies the renal tubular collecting system. Chemical toxins may also cause tubular degenerative changes, and such alterations culminate in a diminution in renal tubular cell transport mechanisms, leading to acidosis and electrolyte loss.

Congenital lesions of the kidneys include agenesis, horseshoe kidney, and polycystic kidney disease. There are numerous subtypes of polycystic kidney, some of which begin in childhood and rapidly eventuate in renal failure.

Clinical features

The chief clinical syndromes that evolve as a consequence of renovascular glomerular disease include hypertension, nephrosis, and uremia. Hypertension is one of the most common diseases to afflict individuals in the developed world, being less prevalent in underdeveloped countries. Some forms of hypertension are direct sequelae of renal arteriolar narrowing, and others arise independent from renal mechanisms. The major types of hypertension are listed in Table 4–1.

Essential hypertension is the most common form and begins to appear in the third to fourth decades of age. Risk factors include male gender, smoking, stressful life style, hyperlipidemia, and diabetes. Diastolic pressure between 90 and 95 is considered to be borderline; anything above 95 is bona fide hypertension. There is a sustained increase in vascular tone as a consequence of vasocontriction. Why vascular smooth muscle constriction evolves is unknown but, in part, has been attributed to release of vasopressor mediators as a consequence of anxiety and stressful life style. In this regard, hypertension among women has become more prevalent as more and more women have entered business and professional careers. The underlying concern with hypertension is the predisposition to atherosclerotic coronary heart disease and cerebral vascular accident (stroke). Clinical trials have confirmed that pharmacologic control of hypertension reduces the risk for these cardiovascular diseases. The more commonly employed medications are diuretics,

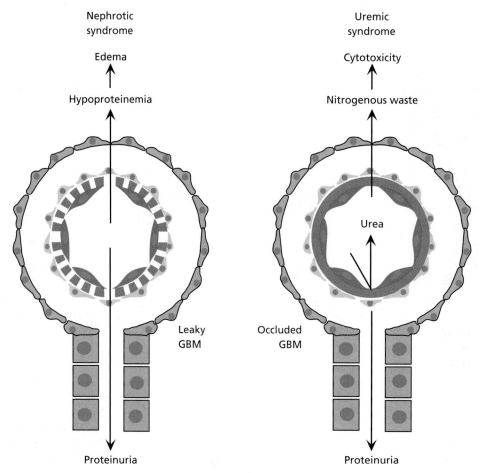

Figure 4–2   Nephrosis and uremia. GBM = glomerular basement membrane.

vasodilatory drugs, and ACE-inhibitors. Combinations are usually prescribed, particularly for more severe levels of hypertension. All of these medications have side effects that should be reviewed with the patient.

Malignant hypertension occurs primarily among males in their twenties and is far more prevalent among those of African descent. The diastolic pressure rises progressively and rapidly reaching 130 to 150 mm Hg with systolic pressure over 250. These subjects are at high risk for other cardiovascular events and may succumb to coronary infarction at an early age. Aggressive pharmacologic intervention is required.

Secondary hypertension occurs in glomerulonephritis and progressive pyelonephritis. As afferent arterioles become narrowed from arteriolonephrosclerosis, renin levels increase and initiate release of angiotensin II, a potent vasoconstrictor. Angiotensin-converting enzyme-inhibitor medication is effective in the control of hypertension secondary to renovascular disease. Other forms of secondary hypertension include aldosteronoma, adrenal hypercorticism, and pheochromocytoma; these rare forms of high blood pressure are attributable to neoplasms that secrete aldosterone and catacholamines.

Hyperaldosteronism is the consequence of an adrenal cortical adenoma that secretes aldosterone. Elevated serum aldosterone results in hypervolemia, owing to sodium retention. In the Cushing syndrome, a cortical tumor or adrenal cortical hyperplasia results in secretion of various corticoids, aldosterone included. The excess fluid causes the cushingoid swollen appearance, particularly the round or "moon" facies. Pheochromocytoma is a neoplasm, often a malignant one, that sporadically releases norepinephrine. Spiking blood pressures along with irritability and facial skin flushing are encountered. In all of these neoplasm-associated forms of hypertension, surgical excision can be curative.

The three clinical conditions associated with glomerular disease are nephritic, nephrotic, and uremic syndromes. The nephritic syndrome is characterized by oliguria, hematuria, and nitrogen retention. The nephrotic syndrome occurs when the glomerular basement membrane is damaged, with increased porosity allowing protein leaks. The outcomes are proteinuria (usually albuminuria) and hypoproteinemia, the latter of which results in decreased intravascular osmolarity with subsequent edema and ascitis. Urine protein is

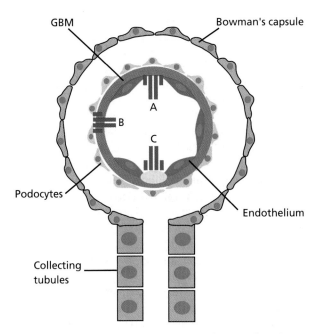

Figure 4–3 Immunopathologic mechanisms of glomerulonephritis. *A,* antibasement membrane autoantibodies; *B,* antipodocyte membrane antibodies; *C,* immune complex precipitation in glomerular basement membrane (GBM).

detectable and serum albumin is decreased, lowering the albumin:globulin (A:G) ratio. In uremia, glomerular filtration becomes progressively compromised with retention of nitrogenous wastes, a physiologic effect that is confirmed by observation of elevated blood urea nitrogen (BUN) and serum creatinine. Measures of glomerular filtration rate (GFR) are included in the workup, to ascertain the degree of renal failure. Fluid and electrolyte imbalances evolve along with acidosis. Hyperkalemia is a common consequence and leads to cardiac arrhythmias. Vitamin D absorption is impaired, and in conjunction with hypocalcemia, secondary renal hyperparathyroidism evolves (see Chapter 10). These irreversible changes can only be overcome by dialysis three times each week or renal transplantation.

As mentioned previously, the primary causes of these three renal malfunction syndromes are glomerulonephritis (GN) and pyelonephritis. There are many subtypes of GN, depending upon the immunopathologic mechanisms taking place. The renal workup usually includes needle biopsy of the kidney with immunofluorescence staining to identify the pattern of glomerular basement membrane (GBM) immunoreactant deposition (Table 4–2). Acute proliferative GN occurs in children as a post-streptococcal immune complex and planted antigen disease, whereby a foreign molecule becomes trapped or planted into the GBM and is then bound by specific antibody. The nephritic syndrome is typically seen in acute proliferative GN and in IgA nephropathy. Rapidly progressive or crescentic GN leads quickly to anuria and uremia. In Goodpasture syndrome, a common basement membrane antigen is present in both the kidney and lung, causing both GN and interstitial pneumonia.

The nephrotic syndrome is seen with membranous GN, an immune lesion with antigenic targets on podocyte membranes. Secondary membranous GN occurs in other autoimmune diseases, such as lupus erythematosus. Lipoid proteinosis, also termed minimal change GN, is the most common disease to manifest as the nephrotic syndrome. It begins in early life and progresses slowly. There are no immunoreactants seen with immunofluorescence staining of the glomerulus, yet most cases arise following an infection, particularly viral. Nephrosis also occurs in focal segmental GN, a lesion with IgM glomerular deposits. This form of GN may be seen in heroin addicts and human immunodeficiency virus (HIV)-infected subjects. Membranoproliferative GN occurs as two subtypes, both of which begin with signs of nephrosis. All of these lesions may progress to severe end-stage kidney disease with uremia. Monitoring of renal disease involves routine blood analyses, to observe electrolyte, nitrogen, and protein values.

Table 4–1 Classification of Hypertension

Benign "essential"
Malignant
Secondary
Renovascular
Aldosteronoma
Pheochromocytoma
Hyperadrenal corticism

Table 4–2 Glomerulonephritis

Disease Type	Immune Lesion	Clinical Syndrome
Proliferative GN	Post-streptococcal Immune complex	Nephritic
IgA nephropathy	ANCA Immune complex	Nephritic
Membranous GN	Anti-podocyte antigens	Nephrotic
Minimal change GN	No immune complexes	Nephrotic
Focal segmental GN	IgM anti-GBM	Nephrotic Hematuria
Goodpasture syndrome	Anti-collagen IV	Nephrotic Lung
Rapidly progressive (crescentic)	Immune complex	Uremia
Chronic GN	Various types	Uremia

GN = glomerulonephritis; ANCA = antineutrophil cytoplasmic antibodies; GBM = glomerular basement membrane.

Oral manifestations

In end-stage renal disease, the urea nitrogen levels are extremely high, resulting in secretion of ammonia into the saliva. The alkalinity of saliva is believed to cause stomatitis, although the precise mechanism is in question. Uremic stomatitis occurs only in severe uremia, just weeks preceding a fatal outcome if dialysis or transplantation are not initiated. The oral lesions consist of buccal mucosa erythema with a gray pseudomembrane or frank ulcerations of the gingival and buccal mucosa. Uremic patients also complain of dysgeusia, manifested as metallic or sour taste. Increased salivation is usually observed as well. Dysesthesia of the lips and tongue may also evolve, probably as a consequence of neuritis secondary to metabolic acidosis. The clinical manifestations of end-stage uremic stomatitis resemble those of acute necrotizing ulcerative gingivitis (ANUG), clinically and histologically, and both fusiform and pleomorphic bacteria can be isolated from the necrotic lesions. Such lesions can be treated, palliatively, by antihistaminic mouthrinses and antibiotics, particularly tetracyclines.

Oral and cutaneous purpura are accompaniments to end-stage kidney disease, since platelet adhesion is impaired because of accumulation in the blood of an inhibitory factor that can be removed by dialysis. The hemorrhagic diathesis is eliminated by renal dialysis or functional transplant.

As previously noted, renal osteodystrophy may occur in late-stage kidney disease secondary to either glomerulonephritis or pyelonephritis. Impaired tubular function leads to secondary hyperparathyroidism. Increased parathormone levels are associated with calcium transport out of osteoid matrix. Demineralization of bone is often observed in the skull as focal, well-circumscribed radiolucencies (osteoporosis circumscripta), loss of lamina dura around teeth, ground-glass opacification, and brown tumors. The ground-glass pattern of trabeculation is similar to that seen in fibrous dysplasia and osteitis deformans, and therefore, a bone biochemical panal, blood urea nitrogen, creatinine, and renal function tests should be ordered. The brown tumors appear as well-circumscribed uni- or multilocular radiolucencies of the jaws, and biopsy discloses the presence of giant cell granuloma. Serum parathormone levels and renal chemistries should be ordered.

Dental management

The hypertensive patient is of major concern to the dental practitioner. Most concerns surface when anesthetic solutions containing vasoconstrictors are to be used. First and foremost is the issue of profound anesthesia during dental procedures for operative dentistry and oral surgery. Vasoconstrictors afford optimal anesthesia by preventing venous clearance of the injected local anesthetic. If one selects an anesthetic without a vasoconstrictor, it will be unlikely that profound anesthesia will be obtained and the patient will experience pain. Clinical studies have revealed that avoidance of vasoconstrictor may actually serve to elevate blood pressure during dental procedures as a consequence of incomplete anesthesia. Pain and anxiety serve to increase the output of endogenous catecholamines from the adrenal medulla, with consequential increases in blood pressure. For all patients, not just the hypertensives, aspiration is essential when injecting a local anesthetic with vasoconstrictor. Intra-arterial injection can result in severe tachycardia and systolic hypertension, a response that could potentially trigger angina, myocardial infarction, or cerebrovascular accident.

Considering the foregoing, it is usually recommended that patients with mild or borderline hypertension (diastolic pressure under 100 mm Hg) receive injection anesthetics with a vasoconstrictor and that aspiration be undertaken routinely. Should a bloody aspirate be obtained, the needle must be withdrawn and reinserted, ensuring that no blood enters the Carpule. In patients with blood pressure levels exceeding 180 systolic and 100 diastolic, special considerations are in order. First, for routine dentistry, it is recommended that patients with this status be referred back to their physician for evaluation. Antihypertensive medication adjustments are required. For operative and prosthetic procedures, conservative endodontics and routine scaling and root planing, it is preferred that blood pressure be under control by way of medication or other medical and psychological interventions. Once the blood pressure is less than 180/100, routine dental procedures can be performed without untoward effects.

When emergency dental procedures are required and the subject is hypertensive, special modifications must be instituted. Oral or intravenous sedation should be considered and vasoconstrictors can be avoided in these circumstances. Such measures are reserved for trauma surgery or exodontia for odontalgia secondary to pulpitis or periodontitis in which the incriminating tooth is nonrestorable. For elective procedures, patients can be reappointed once their blood pressure is controlled.

Another major concern for the hypertensive patient is the use of retraction cord for ensuring accurate impressions of margins from inlay, onlay, and crown preparations. Some of the retraction cords available for these procedures are soaked with epinephrine to achieve hemostasis through microcapillary vasoconstriction. These cords are impregnated with 1:1000 epinephrine, a 100-fold increase over that of vasoconstrictors in local anesthetic solutions. The epinephrine can readily transfuse across the sulcular epithelium. Hypertensive crises have occurred when numerous crown preparations have been impacted with epinephrine cord. There are other salt-impregnated cords that offer similar vasoconstriction locally and do not elevate systemic blood pressure. Electrocautery and laser ablation of the superficial gingival epithelium are effective methods for achieving the same result without causing permanent damage to the periodontium.

Patients with renal disease come to the dental office setting with varying levels of renal failure. As the disease progresses, which invariably occurs, kidney function becomes impaired and dialysis is implemented. There are over 300,000 patients receiving hemodialysis in the United States and over 30,000 renal transplants being placed annually. The major concerns for dentistry are related to the patients' blood pressure status, drug metabolism, bleeding tendencies, and anemia. In the transplant subject, sepsis is a complication, since these patients are maintained on immunosuppressive medications.

The renal disease patient on hemodialysis requires specific attention. Most patients are dialyzed from two to three times weekly. During the process of hemodialysis, the patient is heparinized, to avoid coagulation at the needle insertion site. This site, incidently, is often grafted with a porcine vessel because it is pierced so frequently. The effects of heparin are no longer extant the following day. For this reason, dental procedures that cause bleeding should be performed the day after, not the day of hemodialysis. There is also a tendency for bleeding in patients with advanced kidney disease, and clinical laboratory indicators of hemostasis should be evaluated when oral surgery is to be undertaken (ie, international normalized ratio [INR], prothrombin time, partial thromboplastin time, platelet function).

The administration of local anesthetics is usually not problematic, although it should be recalled that both amide and ester anesthetics are cleared through the kidney. Consultation with the patient's physician is prudent regarding any drugs or medications that are contemplated for dental care. In addition to local anesthetics, concern would include potential drug interactions and medications metabolized by the kidney. Additionally, some of the diuretics used to control hypervolemia may secondarily cause xerostomia.

Suggested reading

Buller DL. Team approach to oral health treatment of pre and post renal transplant patients. J Hosp Dent Pract 1973;7: 144–8.

Lapointe HJ, Armstrong JE, Larocque B. Clinical criteria for the use of a decision-making framework for the medically compromised patient: hypertension and diabetes mellitus. J Can Dent Assoc 1998;64:704–9.

Massie BM. Systemic hypertension. In: Tierney LM, McPhee SJ, Papadakis MA, eds. Current medical diagnosis and treatment. New York: McGraw Hill, 2000:444–66.

Moskowitz L. Cardiac disease and hypertension. Considerations for office treatment. Dent Clin North Am 1999;43: 495–512.

Pyle MA, Sawyer DR, Jasinevicius TR, Ballard R. Blood pressure measurement by community dentists. Spec Care Dentist 1999;19:230–4.

Svirsky JA, Nunley J, Dent CD, Yeatts D. Dental and medical considerations of patients with renal disease. J Calif Dent Assoc 1998;26:761, 763–70.

5 Respiratory Diseases

L. Roy Eversole, DDS, MSD, MA

The respiratory system includes the nasal and oral cavities: the sinuses and larynx as the upper airway, and the trachea, bronchi, bronchioles, and alveoli as the lower airway. Many of the diseases that occur in the oral cavity are also found in the upper airway regions. Inflammatory lesions, both infectious and allergic are found in the nose, sinuses, nasopharynx, oropharynx, and larynx. Tumors of the upper air passages are similar to oral neoplasms, with a few lesions being unique to the sinonasal region. The respiratory mucosal lining overlies mucinous glands, and these glands can give rise to salivary type tumors. Since these tissues are in close proximity to the oral cavity, the dentist should be familiar with the basic disease processes that are diagnosed and treated by the otolaryngologist.

Diseases of the lower tract are typically referred to as pulmonary diseases. Acute and chronic pulmonary infections are of concern to the dental team since some of these infections are transmissible in the dental office. Pulmonary infections can compromise respiratory function and pose a risk during inhalation anesthesia. Allergic reactions of the airway, particularly anaphylactic shock, can be induced by a variety of drugs and may constitute a medical emergency. Asthma is also an immunopathologic condition that is characterized by airway constriction and can become an emergency when a severe attack develops. A group of chronic pulmonary diseases progressively lead to a loss of pulmonary function, a condition known as chronic obstructive pulmonary disease (COPD). Patients with COPD have difficulty breathing, particularly when reclined, and they also pose a risk during inhalation anesthesia. Chronic obstructive pulmonary disease is one of the major causes of death each year in the United States.

Pathophysiology

The upper air passages are lined by either stratified squamous or respiratory pseudostratified columnar epithelia. Respiratory epithelium is found throughout the sinonasal tract, whereas stratified squamous epithelium is found throughout the oral cavity, in certain regions of the oropharynx, and covering the vocal apparatus in the larynx. In all regions, minor mucus-secreting glands are found, and these glands transmit their secretions through ducts that empty onto the surface of the airway epithelium to form the moist mucosal surface.

Anatomically, the paranasal sinuses are located around the nasal cavity, and all of these sinuses have exit sites, or ostia, that allow mucous secretions to drain into the nasal cavity. The sinuses, being hollow cavities within the skull, reduce the bony mass and weight of the head while serving to moderate the temperature of inspired air. The connective tissues of the lateral nasal walls are traversed by a rich supply of blood vessels. Inflammatory diseases of the sinonasal region are common and are usually of an allergic nature, although bacterial and viral mucosal infections are also common in these regions.

Most of the sinonasal allergies are IgE-mediated immediate hypersensitivity reactions. Inspired allergens, such as pollens, dander, and various other particles, can stimulate a specific IgE response (Figure 5–1). These IgE antibodies (reagins) are bound to mast cell membranes by a specific receptor that binds to a ligand on the Fc region. When allergen passes into the mucous membrane and diffuses into the submucosa, binding to the IgE-mast cell complex causes bridging of two contiguous immunoglobulins, a conformational event that triggers internal signaling pathways that initiate degranulation and release of histamine. Histamine induces vasodilation and increased capillary permeability with leakage of proteins from serum, including kinins and other mediators that cause pruritus and sneezing. Protein leaks increase tissue osmotic pressure, culminating in edema and swelling of the mucous membranes. Prolonged exposure to allergens over many years may stimulate proliferation of the soft tissues, the result of which is the formation of nasal and antral polyps. Mucosal edema that develops in either infectious or allergic inflammations can lead to swelling and occlusion of the sinus ostea, with resulting pain and fluid retention. These changes are readily visualized on computed tomography (CT) scans and magnetic resonance imaging (MRI) of the sinus regions.

Neoplastic processes of the nose and sinuses are of both the benign and malignant varieties. There are three histologic variants of papillomas that occur in the nose, usually arising on the lateral wall and also extending into the antrum. Fungiform papillomas are innocuous, whereas inverting type papillomas are aggressive, causing osseous destruction. Inverting papillomas are associated with human papillomavirus (HPV), usually types 6, 11, and 16, although Epstein-Barr virus DNA has also been identified in the papilloma tissues. It is more probable that the HPVs are causative. About 5% of inverting papillomas undergo carcinomatous transformation. The cylindric cell papilloma is histologically unique and is rare.

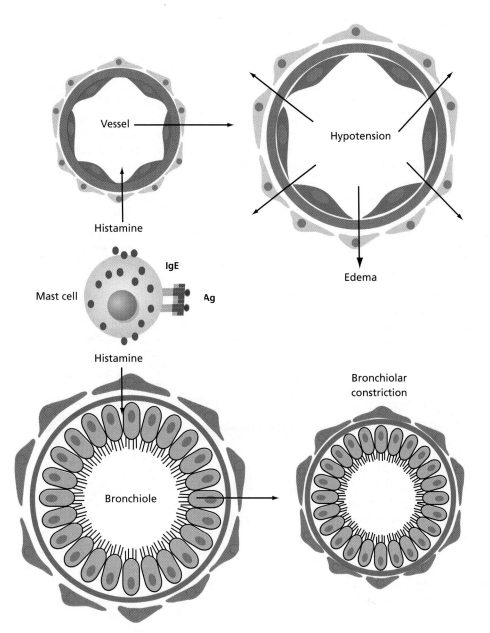

Figure 5–1 IgE-mediated reactions in allergic pulmonary inflammatory diseases. Allergens react with reagin (IgE) antibodies that are bound to receptors on mast cells. Histamine and leukotrienes are released and exert pharmacologic effects on endothelial cells, mucus-secreting epithelial cells, and smooth muscle. In anaphylactic shock, acute and severe vasodilation with bronchospasms occur following systemic introduction of allergen. In asthma, hypotensive reaction is lacking, since the allergen is introduced via the airway and only affects bronchiolar smooth muscle.

Squamous cell carcinoma is the most common cancer to arise in the sinuses. Adenocarcinomas are seen in the nasal cavity; hardwood saw dust is considered a risk factor for these adenocarcinomas, many of which microscopically have the appearance of intestinal epithelium. As stated previously, the presence of numerous salivary type glands accounts for the occurrence of salivary gland tumors in the airway. Certain neoplasms are unique to the sinonasal region. The olfactory neuroblastoma derives from neuroblasts in the olfactory bulb. Craniopharyngiomas arise in the pituitary gland and may invade the upper nasopharynx. A unique vascular tumor that arises in young boys is located in the posterior nasal cavity and apparently arises from the vascular tissues that are so plentiful in the lateral nasal wall. Carcinomas that are poorly differentiated or undifferentiated are also found in this region. The sinonasal undifferentiated carcinoma is a neoplasm with a poor prognosis that is encountered in the adult. Nonkeratinizing squamous cell carcinoma is a nasopharyngeal malignancy of teenage males that is often first detected as a neck metastasis.

The larynx is also a site of inflammatory disease. Both allergies and infections can cause laryngitis. Severe infections with marked edema can compromise the airway and even lead to death. Laryngospasm or bronchospasm secondary to anaphylactic shock can also be a fatal event. The same mechanisms described earlier are operational in anaphylactic shock. Allergen IgE reponses with histamine release can be systemic or local with profound hypotension and loss of consciousness. The effect of histamine release on bronchiolar smooth muscle is constriction, with airway stricture. A similar reaction is encountered in asthma. Leukoplakia of the larynx is relatively common, and squamous cell carcinomas of the larynx account for more than 1200 malignancies each year in the United States.

Inflammatory diseases of the lungs include allergies, as well as bacterial, viral, and fungal infections. These infections involve the bronchioles and the alveolar air sacs (Figure 5–2). Pneumonia is a wide-spread infection of the lung parenchyma in which a lobe or an entire lung becomes infected with either bacteria or virus, resulting in purulent exudate accumulation in the alveolar air sacs (Figure 5–3). Gaseous exchange can become severely compromised, leading to death. When the infection is multifocal throughout the lungs, the condition is referred to as bronchopneumonia. When the infection localizes to an entire lobe, the term lobar pneumonia is used.

Foreign bodies may be aspirated into the airway from the oral cavity. Endodontic files and reamers coated with pathogenic microorganisms can cause lung abscess. There are instances where crown castings and even partial dentures have been aspirated. Because the right main stem bronchus courses vertically, whereas the left bronchus is angled to the left, most foreign bodies lodge in the right lung. Many can be visualized radiographically; the majority can be retrieved during bronchoscopy.

There are a group of microorganisms that cause chronic granulomatous infections of the lung; tuberculosis is the most common. Certain fungi, including histoplasmosis, blastomycosis, and coccidioidomycosis cause chronic lung infections with granuloma formation. As these granulomas enlarge over time, they may erode vessels, causing hemoptysis, coalesce, and compromise pulmonary function. Organisms are subsequently seeded into other alveolar air sacs, thus disseminating the infection throughout both lungs. The granulomas are readily visualized radiographically if sufficiently large.

Tuberculosis (TB) is contracted by aerosol spread in close contact with an infected subject. The primary infection occurs at the periphery of the lung tissue, the Ghon focus, and via lymphatics, a hilar lymph node becomes infected and subsequently enlarged with granulomas, the Ghon complex (see Figure 5–3). This primary infection usually becomes quiescent. Reinfection or reactivation of the tubercle bacillus results in secondary TB. The secondary infection occurs in the face of an intact T-cell response and a positive tuberculin

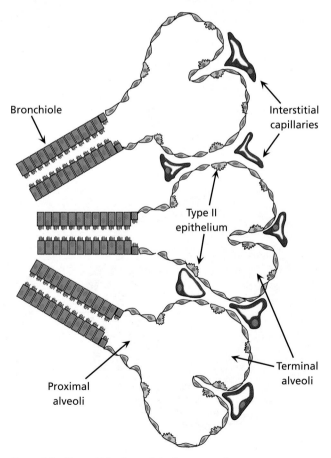

Figure 5–2 Normal histology of the lung parenchyma.

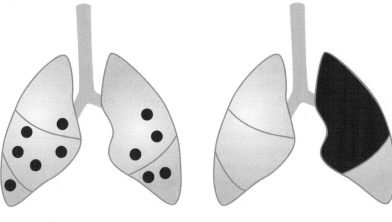

Bronchopneumonia   Lobar pneumonia

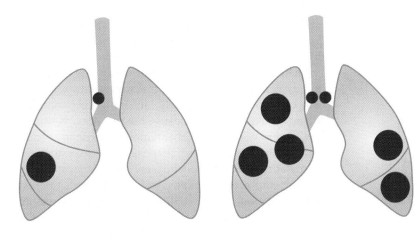

Primary tuberculosis   Secondary tuberculosis

Figure 5–3 Bronchopneumonia is a multifocal infection of the entire lung; lobar pneumonia is a consolidated infection affecting an entire lobe. In primary tuberculosis, the Ghon complex is characterized by peripheral granulomas and hilar lymph node granulomas. Multiple granulomas are seen within one or both lungs in reactivated or secondary tuberculosis.

skin test. Granulomas develop as a response to the organism, enlarge within the lungs, cavitate, and then can be disseminated systemically, a condition referred to as miliary TB. Tuberculosis is a major global cause of death, but is under control in the United States. Antibiotic-resistant mycobacterium is a considerable problem in controlling TB.

When the alveolar surface area available for gaseous exchange is damaged and reduced, pulmonary function is hampered. The diseases that result in this damage are collectively referred to as chronic obstructive pulmonary disease (COPD). The primary etiologic factor is tobacco smoke, and the two chief diseases are emphysema and bronchitis (Figure 5–4). In most instances of COPD, the patient suffers from both emphysema and bronchitis. In centrilobular emphysema the terminal bronchioles leading into the alveolar air sacs become dilatated and lose septation; in panacinar emphysema both terminal bronchioles and alveolar air sacs are damaged by chemical toxins, resulting in dilatation and loss

of septation. When the terminal alveoli along the pleural margin are dilated as blister-like sacuoles, the condition is referred to as bullous emphysema. In bronchitis, irritants cause mucinous secretions to accumulate in the bronchioles, with resulting chronic productive cough. Long-standing COPD shows classic clinical features, and affected patients are at risk for serious pulmonary infections and cor pulmonale (pulmonary artery hypertension).

Bronchiectasis is a lesion that occurs in the bronchioles after repeated bouts of influenza or other pulmonary infections. The bronchiolar walls become thin and aneurysmal. These focal dilatations accumulate mucins, leading to chronic productive cough and COPD. Brochiectasis is particularly problematic in cystic fibrosis. This childhood illness is an autosomal recessive disease that results from a mutation on chromosome 7, involving a gene that encodes a transmembrane chloride channel. In sweat ducts, excessive chloride is secreted, whereas in lung tissues chloride does not pass

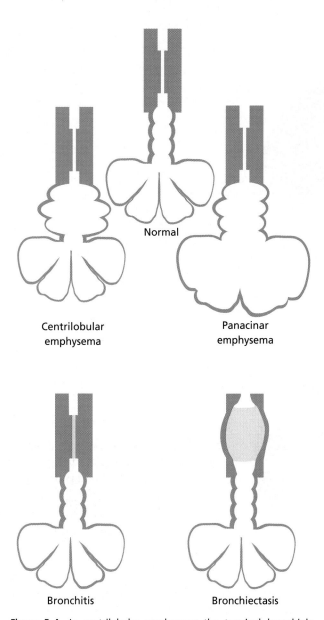

Normal

Centrilobular
emphysema

Panacinar
emphysema

Bronchitis

Bronchiectasis

Figure 5–4 In centrilobular emphysema the terminal bronchiole-proximal alveoli are dilatated, whereas in panlobular emphysema, both proximal and distal regions of the alveoli are dilatated with loss of septation. Mucus plugs accumulate in bronchitis and are retained within the lumens of aneurysmal-like dilatations of the airway in bronchiectasis.

from the epithelial lining cells into the lumen, and sodium is retained as well. The result is a dry airway with compensatory hyperplasia of the epithelial lining. This airway loses its mucinous wet layer, and ciliary action is impaired, leading to repeated pulmonary infections that progress to bronchiectasis.

Asthma is also considered a form of COPD. Unlike bronchitis, emphysema, and bronchiectasis, asthma begins at a young age and is an allergic disorder with a psychosomatic element and a genetic predisposition. The condition is equivalent to anaphylactic shock in that allergen binding in conjunction with emotional

stress leads to airway constriction. Severe attacks are known as status asthmaticus, an emergency situation in which the airway shuts down.

Restrictive pulmonary disease is a condition that evolves as a consequence of environmental exposure to toxic chemicals or to certain infections. Common to all of these diseases is interstitial fibrosis. The tissues between the alveoli and bronchioles are loose, areolar, and fibrovascular. In the restrictive lung diseases, this interstitial tissue becomes progressively scarified, and as it does, the alveolar air spaces become compressed. In pneumoconiosis, a group of fibrosing lesions evolve from prolonged exposure to inspired chemicals, such as coal dust (anthracosis), beryllium, asbestos, and silica. Certain infections with viruses and bacteria lead to interstitial pneumonitis, whereby the interstitial spaces are edematous and inflamed and heal by fibrosis.

Cancer of the lungs can arise from the bronchiolar epithelium, mucous glands, or the pleural cells. The most common form of lung cancer is bronchogenic carcinoma; 80% of cases are related to smoking tobacco. The bronchiolar epithelium undergoes squamous metaplasia and dysplasia and, ultimately, transforms into squamous cell carcinoma. Interestingly, in laboratory animals, forced smoking does not cause lung tumors. Nevertheless, a variety of potential carcinogens exist in tobacco smoke. Prolonged heavy exposure to asbestos also increases the risk for bronchogenic carcinoma, and when tobacco and asbestos exposure are combined, the relative risk for lung cancer is 90-fold. Adenocarcinomas are rare, as is mesothelioma, a cancer of the lung pleura that is typically encountered in asbestos mine workers.

The diseases that compromise pulmonary function, particularly COPD and restrictive lung disease, affect respiratory physiology. Pulmonary function tests can be used to assess various parameters that are diagnostically useful. The spirometer is an instrument that measures various inspiratory and expiratory volumes. In a normal individual without lung disease, the total lung capacity is over 5500 mL of air (Figure 5–5). Regular breathing involves a volume of about 500 mL of air with each inspiration and expiration, a measure referred to as the tidal volume. The amount of air that is able to be inspired maximally, in excess of inspired tidal volume level is called the inspiratory reserve volume. This represents the maximum amount of air that can possibly enter the lungs, about 3000 mL. After a normal exhalation during the tidal cycle, more air can be forcefully exhaled; this is the excretory reserve volume. Even after this maximal exhalation there is still residual air in the alveoli (the residual volume) that is not available for respiratory function. In pulmonary diseases, in which alveolar surface area is decreased, or in lesions that restrict gaseous exchange, perturbations in these volumes can be identified when testing with the spirometer (Figure 5–6).

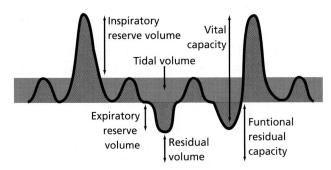

Figure 5–5 Normal spirometer tracing showing gas volume parameters. Upward deflections on the graph represent inspirations; downward deflections are expirations.

Clinical features

Upper airway diseases present with sinonasal symptoms. The inflammatory diseases typically manifest nasal stuffiness, sneezing, rhinorrhea, dysosmia, mucosal itchyness, nasal obstruction, or pain. The temperature should be taken in these situations; if elevated, infection is favored over allergy. Allergic rhinitis and sinusitis are typically seasonal. Some patients have had allergy testing and, therefore, are aware of the environmental allergens that trigger an immediate hypersensitivity response. Physical examination discloses a nasal discharge along with erythema of the mucous membranes. Long-standing allergic disease may result in polyp formation. Nasal polyps are a common cause of loss of smell. With a nasal speculum, the polyps appear as pink fleshy masses high in the nasal cavity, usually above the middle turbinate.

When the ostia become obstructed, sinus pain may develop and can mimic toothache. The sinuses may be tender to palpation over the malar eminence and the entire maxillary quadrant may manifest a chronic dull aching pressure sensation. All teeth in the quadrant are often percussion sensitive. The pain and pressure are exacerbated if the patient places his or her head below

the knees while seated. Transillumination of the sinuses in a dark room shows clouding. Radiography may disclose soft-tissue thickening of the sinus membranes or an air:fluid level may be seen on an anterior posterior skull radiogram, Waters' sinus projection, or computed tomography (CT) scan. When the patient is febrile, an infectious process is probable and may be of viral or bacterial origin. Acute pain symptoms in the sinus are most indicative of bacterial sinusitis, and culture of the nasal discharge is in order.

Sinonasal symptoms indicative of neoplasias include persistant nasal obstruction, nasal speech, dysosmia, and swelling in the lateral nasal wall or the palate. Infraorbital paresthesia or hypesthesia are suspicious signs for malignancy within the maxillary sinus, and epistaxis may occur with sinonasal malignancies. Imaging studies discloses soft-tissue, space-occupying lesions, bony wall expansion and osseous perforation or destruction (Figure 5–7). Biopsy is then required to derive a definitive diagnosis.

Nasopharyngeal carcinoma is characterized by pain, stuffiness, unilateral hearing loss, epistaxis, and cervical lymph node enlargement. It is not uncommon for an enlarged indurated node to be the first sign of nasopharyngeal carcinoma. Benign vascular tumors (juvenile nasopharyngeal angiofibroma) also cause nasal stuffiness and obstruction.

Pharyngeal symptoms most commonly center around irritation and pain. Laryngitis is characterized by hoarseness, throat pain, and dysphonia. Examination of the larynx shows edematous swelling of the both true and false vocal cords along with erythema. Laryngitis may be caused by vocal cord trauma (eg, yelling, loud forced singing), allergy, or infection with either virus or bacteria. Neoplastic disease of the vocal structures is similar to that seen in the oral cavity. Laryngeal papillomatosis is encountered primarily in children and teenagers. On laryngoscopy polypoid masses are seen on the true and false cords. These HPV-induced lesions are difficult to eradicate; recurrence after excision or laser ablation may occur.

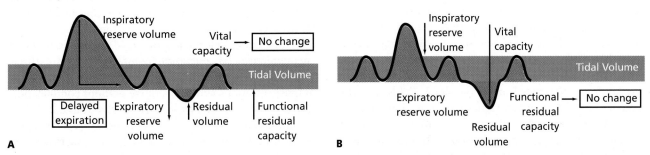

Figure 5–6 Spirometer patterns in obstructed and restricted lung. *A,* In COPD from emphysema, there is an increase in residual volume, a reduction in expiratory reserve volume, and a delay in expiration after maximal inhalation, owing to air trapped in dilatated alveoli. *B,* In restrictive lung disease attributable to pneumoconiosis, the inspiratory reserve volume and vital capacity are decreased because of loss of airway space. COPD = chronic obstructive pulmonary disease.

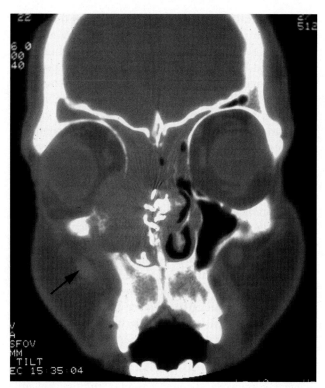

Figure 5–7 Computed tomography scan showing a maxillary sinus malignancy in a patient who complained of nasal obstruction and periodic epistaxis. The lesion perforated the buccal plate, presenting as a maxillary vestibular mass (arrow).

Carcinoma of the laryngeal mucosa is typically associated with smoking. These tumors are squamous cell carcinomas. The signs are hoarseness and dysphonia; symptoms include a scratchy feeling and pain. Occasionally, blood-tinged saliva is found from tumor bleeding. Clinically, early lesions are white, red, or mixed red and white lesions with focal ulcerations. Tumefaction is seen, and when the tumor invades the adjacent cartilages, auscultation discloses a loss of normal crepitus, since the cartilagenous structures become invaded and fixed. Invasion of contiguous structures may also cause true cord paralysis.

The primary clinical manifestations of pulmonary disease include dyspnea, cough (productive or nonproductive), hemoptysis, and respiratory distress. The accumulation of viscous mucin within bronchioles and bronchi, as well as constriction of the airway because of smooth muscle contraction act as impediments to air flow. These obstructive changes may be detectable with the stethoscope placed over the lung fields on the patient's back. A constricted airway causes wheezing on both inspiration and expiration. Mucus accumulation produces crackling and gurgling sounds termed rales and rhonchi. Orthopnea, shortness of breath while supine, is another sign of pulmonary disease. The signs and symptoms may be associated with a variety of pulmonary diseases, and alone are not diagnostic of any one disorder.

The most common infectious diseases to affect the lungs are the common cold and respiratory flu, both of which are viral in origin. These common infections are characterized by productive cough, fever, and malaise, with a 7- to 10-day course. Serious infections of the lungs are the pneumonias. Pneumonia is a widely disseminated lung disease that may be caused by either viruses or bacteria. The more common organisms to cause pneumonia are the bacteria *Streptococcus pneumoniae*, staphylococci, *Haemophilus influenzae*, *Pseudomonas aeruginosa*, and coliform rods. When the infection is widely disseminated within the parenchyma as multiple foci, the disease is termed bronchopneumonia. When the infection diffusely involves an entire lobe it is referred to as lobar pneumonia. In response to infection, the air passages secrete excessive mucins and the fibrovascular septae show vessel engorgement and congestion with exudative fluid accumulation in the airway. This leads to dyspnea along with deep cough that is productive in the beginning, yet as the infection consolidates, a dry cough follows. The patient is febrile. Percussion and auscultation of the chest disclose evidence of fluid accumulation, and radiographs show patchy opacification in bronchopneumonia and diffuse opacification in lobar pneumonia. Patients with pneumonia require hospitalization and selection of appropriate antibiotics when bacteria are causative. In debilitated patients, death is a common outcome. Pneumonia and flu are leading causes of death in the United States. Disseminated malignant neoplasms and immunodeficiencies of various types are often complicated by pneumonia.

Infections of the lung parenchyma may extend to the pleural lining where inflammatory foci develop and fibrin may be deposited, a lesion known as pleuritis. As the lungs expand and contract, these inflammatory foci may scrape across adjacent regions of the parietal pleura lining the internal chest wall. These movements can be painful and upon chest auscultation the scraping sounds often are detectable as a friction rub.

Influenza virus, respiratory syncytial virus, and adenovirus among others cause interstitial pneumonia. *Mycoplasma pneumoniae*, a bacterium, also causes infection, with inflammatory lesions involving the interstitial fibrovascular tissues that constitute the lung septae. Patients complain of headache, extremity muscle pain, fever, and cough. Elevated serum cold agglutinin titers are encountered in *M. pneumoniae* infection, yet are absent in most other viral forms of interstitial pneumonia. Most of these infections run their course without complication; however, fatal outbreaks have been encountered.

Pulmonary infections are commonly seen in cystic fibrosis along with other exocrine lesions, such as bowel obstruction, malabsorption, and xerostomia. Only homozygotes are affected. Children develop bronchiectasis with dyspnea and chronic cough due to a lack of airway wetting. The mucins are thick and ropey (mucoviscidosis) and obstruct the airway. These problems lead to pneumonia or cor pulmonale and eventuate in death for many of the affected children.

Chronic granulomatous infections of the lungs, TB being the most prevalent, begin with coughing in the absence of fever, or there may be a low-grade elevation in temperature. Weight loss and fatigue are frequently associated. As more and more lung parenchyma becomes involved and as granulomas enlarge, they may cavitate in the zones of caseous necrosis. A productive cough ensues and hemoptysis is commonly encountered. These individuals are infectious and can transmit TB organisms. Sputum specimens can be cultured or smeared to identify tubercle baccilus organisms. Recall that deep invasive fungi, such as histoplasmosis, blastomycosis, and coccidioidomycosis, can cause similar granulomatous infections. Chest auscultation and percussion are abnormal in late disease. Radiographs disclose the presence of granulomas and hilar lymph node enlargement. Long-term antibiotic treatment is required for active tuberculosis, and most patients are hospitalized until the infection is controlled. In contrast to the global epidemic, TB in the United States is under control. The main TB problem in industrialized countries resides in poverty areas of large cities, in immunocompromised patients, and with antibiotic-resistant mycobacteria.

Dyspnea is a common sign in congestive heart failure (see Chapter 3). Recall that left-sided failure results in passive congestion of the lungs with accumulation of edema fluid and inflammation in the alveolar spaces. Physical examination, cardiac auscultation, electrocardiography, echocardiography, and radiographic studies identify the nature of the cardiopathy.

Patients suffering from the various forms of COPD manifest dyspnea as the chief complaint. In emphysema and bronchitis, the signs and symptoms begin in midlife and become severe in the elderly. Cigarette smoking is the primary causative factor for both of these conditions. Bronchitis is characterized by chronic productive cough as tobacco irritants stimulate inflammation and mucus secretion in the bronchi and bronchioles (bronchiolitis). Emphysema is characterized by dyspnea. As the terminal airway loses septal surface area for gaseous exchange, expirations must be forced. Affected patients are slender and barrel chested. In most cases, bronchitis, bronchiolitis, and emphysema occur together. Spirometer readings disclose normal tidal volume and

inspiration reserve volume with a significantly decreased expiratory reserve and an increased residual volume (see Figure 5–6). After forced inhalation, there is a delay in the duration of exhalation as air is forced by contraction of the intercostal muscles. Chronic obstructive pulmonary disease in this setting is irreversible. Cessation of smoking is essential to prevent the complications and death that may ultimately occur.

Two common appellations applied to COPD patients define their clinical appearance. The euphoniously so-called *Red Puffer* suffers from emphysema. The facial skin is flushed from over-inspiration and oxygenation, and the lips are puckered as the affected person forces air from the lungs on expiration. These patients have normal blood gas values. The second descriptive term is applied to the patient with chronic severe bronchitis: the *Blue Bloater* is cyanotic with facial palor and a bluish cast to the skin as a result of poor oxygenation with hypercapnia. The neck is full from being distended as a consequence of constant coughing.

Asthma is a complex disease that is divided into two major subtypes: extrinsic and intrinsic (Table 5–1). In both forms, the condition usually evolves in early childhood. Extrinsic asthma secondary to airway-introduced allergens is frequently worsened during episodes of stress and anxiety. As the airway becomes constricted and accumulates mucous plugs, the chief clinical sign is wheezing and coughing, without fever. When the asthmatic attack is severe and prolonged over many days, bronchospasm may occur and can be fatal, a condition referred to as status asthmaticus. Asthmatics are treated with orally administered bronchodilator drugs, corticosteroids, and inhalation bronchodilators. In some forms of childhood allergic asthma, the condition improves with ensuing age. Occupational asthma has similar signs and symptoms and represents and idiosyncratic reaction among select individuals upon exposure to certain chemicals found in the workplace. Epoxy resins, formaldehyde, toluene, cotton fibers, and wood dust are common precipitating elements that can initiate an IgG or IgE response. Intrinsic asthma is caused by hyper-reactivity of the airway to infectious agents, aspirin, or vigorous physical activity.

The restrictive lung diseases are uncommon. As the interstitium becomes scarified, the total lung volume is decreased. The spirometer patterns show decreased inspiratory reserve and vital capacity volumes (see Figure

Table 5–1 Classification of Asthmatic Disease

Extrinsic	Intrinsic
Allergen-induced (IgE response)	Nonreaginic respiratory infections
Occupational chemical exposure (IgE and IgG response)	Sports asthma (high physical activity)
Aspergillosis allergy	Aspirin sensitivity

5–6). Patients may also have a chronic cough secondary to bronchiolitis from toxic irritants. Dyspnea is also a major sign. Pneumoconiosis is a group of lung diseases caused by inhalation of irritant chemicals. Anthracosis (coal minor's black lung disease) results in severe interstitial fibrosis with marked restriction in airway volume. Asbestosis is usually only seen in asbestos miners who have been breathing asbestos dust for many years. As mentioned earlier, these individuals are at increased risk for development of bronchogenic carcinoma and mesothelioma. Other forms of restrictive lung disease include the following: sarcoidosis, a granulomatous inflammatory disease of unknown etiology (see Chapter 24); hypersensitivity to allergens that find their way into the terminal bronchioles; hemorrhagic lung syndromes such as Goodpasture syndrome (a condition that also affects the kidneys; Wegener granulomatosis (see Chapter 24); and lupus erythematosus (see Chapter 21).

Bronchogenic carcinoma is a leading cancer among males and is increasing in females. Morbidity and mortality are high. Most cases are associated with smoking cigarettes. Chronic cough is a sign of pulmonary irritation from inhaled smoke, with COPD developing after many years of use. When these signs are accompanied by hemoptysis, carcinoma should be suspected, and chest films must be secured. If a cough is productive, sputum cytology may show malignant cells. In fact, lung cancer can be a silent killer and is often discovered after routine chest radiographs disclose a mass. In some cases after metastasis has occurred at another site, a biopsy indicates malignant cells primary in the lung. Small-cell cancer of the lung is not smoking-related. Some of these small "oat" cell carcinomas secrete hormones, and the first manifestation of disease is clinical endocrinopathy, with hyperparathyroidism being common, owing to secretion of a parathormone-like peptide by the malignant cells (see Chapter 10).

Oral manifestations

Patients with sinonasal diseases often show oral signs and symptoms. Halitosis can be a common sign of chronic allergic sinusitis and rhinitis whereby postnasal secretions fall upon the base of the tongue and may cause malodor (see Chapter 27 on special senses). Cases of antral cancer are seen in which the tumor erodes the palatal bone and presents as an ulceration or fistula (see Figure 5–7; Figure 5–8). Invasive fungal infections of the sinonasal region can also erode into the palate as can nasal midline necrotizing diseases such as Wegener granulomatosis (Figure 5–9) and malignant reticulosis, a form of angiocentric T-cell lymphoma (Figure 5–10). Infraorbital paresthesia is a sign of antral carcinoma, and when present, appropriate imaging studies must be

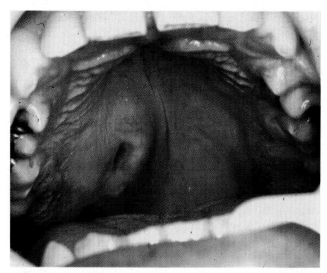

Figure 5–8 Antral carcinoma perforating the palate and presenting as an ulcerated mass.

ordered. Cranial base malignancies may cause neurologic deficits of the cranial nerves including paresthesias and motor deficits of cranial nerves III, IV, V, and VI.

Oral signs are rare in pulmonary diseases. Patients with lung cancer often develop metastases to bone, and the mandible may become a focus of distant spread. Typically, the patient complains of an insidious onset of paresthesia of the lower lip on the affected side as tumor cells invade the inferior alveolar nerve. A dental radiograph discloses a poorly marginated radiolucency, which usually is confined to the posterior body and ramus of the mandible yet may also occur as a soft-tissue mass (Figure 5–11). Biopsy discloses the presence of metastatic malignant cells with morphology consistent with lung carcinoma. As mentioned previously, uncovering a metastatic focus may be the first indication that the patient has a primary cancer in the lung; but it also indicates advanced disease with essentially no chance for cure.

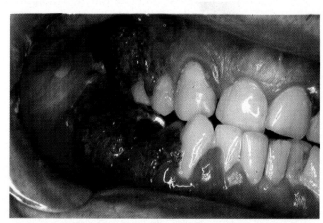

Figure 5–9 Gingival masses in Wegener granulomatosis. Lung involvement is often seen as well.

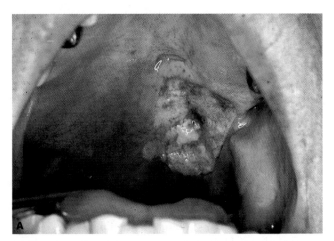
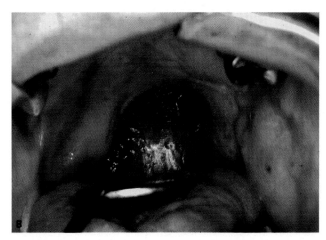

Figure 5–10 Midline destructive lymphoma sometimes referred to as midline lethal granulomas: *A*, prior to therapy; *B*, after radiation therapy.

Tuberculosis and invasive fungi may also spread to the oral cavity from the primary infection in the lung. The organisms gain access to the oral regions by hematogenous spread, and when they adhere to oral tissues, a site of granulomatous inflammation develops. These granulomas may be red and granular or ulcerated with rolled margins, thus resembling a primary carcinoma (Figure 5–12). Tuberculous lymphadenitis occurs in individuals who have ingested nonpasturized milk contaminated with mycobacteria. The nodes are firm to palpation, movable, and often bilateral (Figure 5–13). Tuberculosis and histoplasmosis are the more common granulomatous infections seen in the oral mucosa. Biopsy is required to make the diagnosis, and the pathologist usually needs to apply special stains to identify the microorganisms. Acid-fast Ziehl-Neelsen staining is used to identify mycobacteria; periodic acid-Schiff (PAS) or gram methenamine silver identifies histoplasma and other fungal organisms, all of which have distinct morphologic features. Histoplasmosis in the oral cavity can be an opportunistic infection

among human immunodeficiency virus (HIV)-infected subjects and may or may not be associated with pulmonary disease (see Chapter 14).

In cystic fibrosis, all secretions of exocrine origin are affected, including those of the major and minor salivary glands. Affected children complain of xerostomia and may require artificial saliva preparations to keep the mucosa moist and comfortable.

Dental management

Patients with pulmonary diseases usually do not pose a significant problem for dental care unless general anesthesia is to be performed. It must be realized that the common respiratory infections are transmissible in the dental operatory, necessitating adherence to infection control procedures (see Chapter 19). Currently, in most dental practices, patients are placed in a supine position, and in the patient with a compromised airway, orthop-

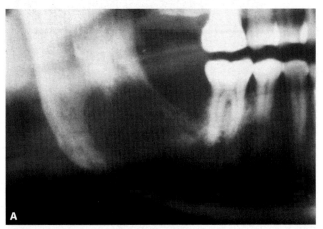
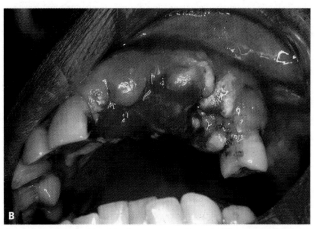

Figure 5–11 *A*, Ill-defined radiolucency of the posterior mandible in a patient with mental nerve paresthesia. Biopsy disclosed metastatic bronchogenic carcinoma. *B*, Soft-tissue metastasis of bronchogenic carcinoma.

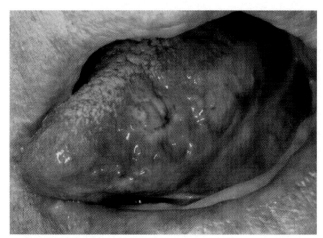

Figure 5–12 Tuberculous ulcer in a patient with concomitant pulmonary tuberculosis.

nea may become a significant problem. When patients have a full stomach and are placed in supine position for prolonged periods, there is always the risk for regurgitation with subsequent aspiration of acidic contents into the lungs. Aspiration of dental instruments, materials, tooth fragments, and prostheses that may be contaminated with oral microorganisms may initiate a lung abscess. The use of the rubber dam helps to eliminate the chance for introduction of such foreign bodies.

Recognition of the patient's pulmonary disease status with regard to severity of dyspnea and orthopnea is an important consideration when long periods of dental therapy are contemplated and the patient is placed in a reclined position. It is advisable to seat the patient upright or to stop all procedures on a regular basis and return them to an upright position periodically. Oxygen should be readily available and equipment should be in place in case assisted breathing is required. It should be noted, however, that forcing air into the lungs of a patient with emphysema, particularly the bullous variant, can burst the pleural lining resulting in pneumothorax, a condition that leads to respiratory arrest, owing to collapse of the lungs.

It is axiomatic that patients with upper respiratory infections with nasal congestion or blockage are unable to receive routine dental care when a rubber dam is to be used, because the oral airway will be blocked. If the nasal mucus can be expelled by blowing the nose, treatment can be implemented; if not, the patient should be rescheduled.

The most severe respiratory emergency is anaphylactic shock. Such an event in the dental office setting is extremely rare, yet can occur if the patient is introduced to a provoking antigen just prior to or during an office visit. Recall that a variety of pharmacologic agents can cause anaphylaxis, particularly penicillins. Most patients are aware of an allergy to penicillin, yet others may be

unaware if they were exposed once before and were never given another prescription after the initial dosing. Food allergens can also induce anaphylactic reactions. At the onset of an anaphylactic event, the patient notices difficulty breathing, and wheezing may be detected. Severe respiratory distress ensues rapidly as histamine and leukotrienes are released in the airway mucosa and submucosa. The blood pressure also drops, and the patient may lose consciousness, owing to hypoperfusion of cerebral vessels. Death may ensue if this medical emergency is not treated. A call to 911 should be undertaken, oxygen should be administered and 1:1000 epinephrine should be injected sublingually, because vascular collapse makes intravenous injection difficult if not impossible. To be effective, diphenhydramine as an intravenous emergency drug can be administered only in the early stages, prior to airway closure and hypotensive shock. Because this antihistamine is a histamine-receptor blocker, its use in late-stage anaphylaxis is of no benefit, since the receptors are already occupied by the IgE-mediated release of histamine; alternatively, epinephrine exerts a direct dilating effect on bronchiolar smooth muscle, opening up the airway within seconds to minutes.

Patients with asthma are at increased risk for an asthmatic attack while undergoing any dental care that may elevate stress levels. Pain and anxiety are common precipitating factors for both allergic and nonallergic

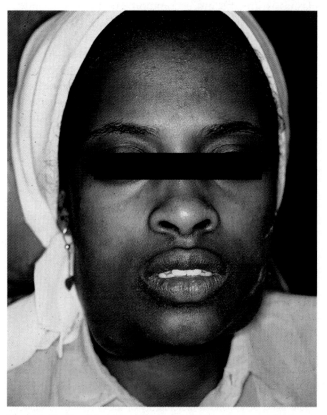

Figure 5–13 Scrofuloderma. Enlarged cervical nodes are evident.

forms of asthma. Sedative drugs with anticholinergic effects are to be avoided. Narcotics and barbiturates are known to trigger an attack. Local anesthetics used in dentistry contain sodium metabisulfite, an antioxidant that prevents oxidation of epinephrine. Twenty percent of asthmatics are allergic to sulfur compounds, and therefore, administration of local anesthetics should be undertaken with caution, always questioning patients as to whether they have experienced any adverse reactions to local anesthetics. The severity and periodicity of asthmatic attacks is highly variable from one affected patient to another. Before engaging in extensive dental procedures, particularly surgical interventions, the history should be explored in detail. If attacks are mild and infrequent, treatment can be initiated with caution. It is always prudent to be certain that patients maintain their bronchodilator daily drug regimen prior to dental treatment and any inhaler devices should be placed within easy reach. Severe asthmatics may also be taking corticosteroids. In these individuals there may be an increased risk for infection. Patients with a history of severe and frequent bronchospasms should be hospitalized for extensive and invasive dental care. Consultation with the physician must be undertaken, and an anesthesiologist should be included on the treatment team.

In rare instances, patients develop asthma after administration of aspirin. Any patient who gives a history of asthma should be questioned about the role of aspirin in the causation of their disease, and obviously, aspirin-containing drugs should be eliminated as analgesic medications. Acetaminophen or propoxyphene should be considered as substitute analgesics for attenuation of dental pain. Oxycodone and hydrocodone should be administered with care since codeine-related drugs and opiates may aggrevate asthmatic attacks. Some asthmatic patients have coincidental complaints of xerostomia. Sialagogues (parasympathomimetics) are contraindicated, because they cause airway congestion.

Children with cystic fibrosis have dry airways, and administration of inhalation sedation can be dangerous when the gases are not humidified. General anesthesia is also problematic because concurrent administration of anticholinergic drugs further aggravates airway dryness. If anesthesia is required for dental care, the patient should be hospitalized and managed by an anesthesiologist.

General anesthetics for adult patients with pulmonary disease must also be used with caution. Mild COPD or restrictive lung disease is generally not problematic. Moderate to severe pulmonary disease can be aggravated and degenerate to severe respiratory distress when inhalation anesthetics are used. This is particularly so in conjunction with intravenous drugs that depress the respiratory center of the central nervous system, and with anticholinergic drugs that may be administered during intubation. When general anesthesia is necessary for patients in this category, they should be hospitalized and managed by an anesthesiologist. In addition, the dentist should consult with the patient's physician prior to rendering treatment.

Suggested reading

Becker DE. Management of respiratory complications in clinical dental practice. Pathophysiological and technical considerations. Anesth Prog 1990;37:169–75.

Hatch CL, Canaan T, Anderson G. Pharmacology of the pulmonary diseases. Dent Clin North Am 1996;40:521–41.

Hoffman MJ, Haug RH, Shepard LS, Indresano AT. Care of the asthmatic and maxillofacial surgery patients. J Oral Maxillofac Surg 1991;49:69–75.

Lapointe HJ, Armstrong JE, Larocque B. A clinical decision making framework for the medically compromised patient: ischemic heart disease and chronic obstructive pulmonary disease. J Can Dent Assoc 1997;63:510–2, 515–6.

Levin JA, Glick M. Dental management of patients with asthma. Compend Cont Educ Dent 1996;17:284, 287–8, 290.

Scannapieco FA. Role of oral bacteria in respiratory infection. J Periodontol 1999;70:793–802.

Zhu JF, Hidalgo HA, Holmgreen WC, et al. Dental management of children with asthma. Pediatr Dent 1996;18:363–70.

Diseases of the Liver and Gastrointestinal Tract

L. Roy Eversole, DDS, MSD, MA

Hepatobiliary diseases

Liver diseases include infections, particularly with viruses, cirrhosis, drug-induced lesions, and neoplasms. Viral hepatitis is discussed in detail in Chapter 16 and is not covered in this chapter. Cirrhosis is the result of progressive degenerative changes in the liver whereby hepatocytes undergo necrosis and are replaced by fibrous scar. The primary causes of cirrhosis include post-viral fibrosis, alcohol abuse, and biliary obstruction. The clinical consequences of cirrhosis are, of course, related to loss of hepatocyte function. Liver cells are the source of many proteins, including albumin, and five factors essential for coagulation; therefore, edema and a hemorrhagic diathesis occur in cirrhotic patients. Estrogen metabolism is impaired and drug clearance is decreased. Scarring in the liver also results in vascular stasis and portal hypertension, which presents clinically with angiectasias of the esophagus, rectum, and periumbilicus.

Biliary disease is usually attributed to bile duct stasis resulting from accumulation of stones (cholelithiasis), although, importantly, obstructive disease can result from tumor compression of the common bile duct (eg, pancreatic carcinoma). Conjugated (direct) bilirubin is typically elevated, as is the liver-specific alkaline phosphatase isoenzyme. In severe prolonged biliary obstruction, cirrhosis develops and results in the same clinical complications of liver failure that occur in alcoholic or post-viral cirrhosis.

Cancer of the liver is more often metastatic than primary. Colon carcinomas metastasize via the portal vein, and cancer cells deposit in the liver via this portal circulation. Hepatocellular carcinoma, or primary liver cancer, is strongly related to infection with hepatitis B, a virus that can trigger oncologic events in hepatocytes. Late-stage liver cancer, either primary or metastatic, culminates in jaundice, bleeding tendency, and eventual emaciation.

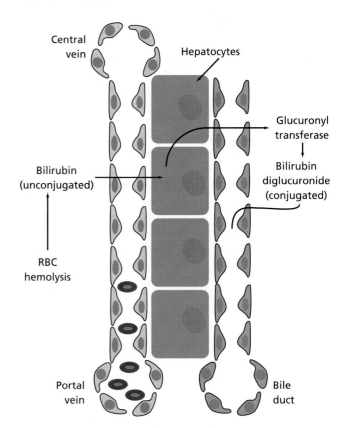

Figure 6–1 Unconjugated bilirubin is derived from red blood cell (RBC) lysis and is transported from the portal vein into the sinusoids where it enters hepatocytes and is glycosylated to become conjugated bilirubin. The conjugated form leaves by way of the bile canaliculi and drains into the bile duct.

Pathophysiology

Erythrocytes are normally lysed after 120-day life spans. The hemoglobin is catabolized to heme, iron, and peptides (Figure 6–1). The heme ring is first converted to biliverdin and bilirubin, which is then transported across the hepatocyte membrane for eventual elimination. Bilirubin enters the hepatocyte from the portal circulation as an unconjugated (indirect) form that is conjugated within the hepatocyte cytoplasm to glucose by an enzymatic process to form bilirubin diglucuronide (direct bilirubin). This conjugated form is transported out of the hepatocyte, into the cholangioles and is then collected in the gall bladder. During the digestive process, bilirubin leaves the bladder along with bile salts to enter the stool where it is converted to stercobilin and then to urobilinogen. Excess amounts of urobilinogen can be reabsorbed into the mesenteric vessels and through the circulation, into the urine.

Jaundice or icterus occurs when bilirubin is retained in the blood stream (Figure 6–2). Elevated serum levels of bilirubin are the consequence of increased hemolysis, hepatocyte damage, and destruction to the outflow of bile through the biliary tree. In hemolytic anemias, excessive hemolysis results in release of high levels of unconjugated bilirubin, more than the liver can assimilate, and the result is a typical unconjugated (indirect) hyperbilirubinemia. Increased amounts of conjugated bilirubin flow into the biliary tract, enter the circulation, and ultimately are lost in the urine, accounting for elevated levels of urine urobilinogen.

When hepatocytes drop out because of infection or toxins, unconjugated bilirubin begins to accumulate. In the remaining functional hepatocytes, bilirubin is conjugated and begins to accumulate in the serum. Thus, in hepatitis and cirrhosis both unconjugated (indirect) and conjugated (direct) hyperbilirubinemia develop. Because bilirubin enters the bile ducts in low quantity, urobilinogen formation is decreased so that urine urobilinogen levels are low. Unlike unconjugated bilirubin, the conjugated form can be filtered through the kidneys with resultant bile in the urine (choluria). Similar findings may be seen in genetic liver diseases, such as rotor, Dubin-Johnson, Crigler-Najjar, and Gilbert syndromes, in which transport and conjugating enzyme proteins are mutated.

Primary biliary cirrhosis is intrahepatic and involves autoimmune mechanisms that lead to inflammatory lesions around bile canaliculi and portal triads. Elevated antimitochondrial antibody titers are observed. Biliary atresia is a congenital defect in which the bile duct system fails to form, thereby leading to severe biliary cirrhosis in children. Secondary or extrahepatic cholestasis is the result of cholangitis, cholelithiasis, and compression from tumors and from strictures of the bile duct. In biliary cirrhosis hepatocytes are capable of bilirubin uptake, conjugation and release such that conjugated bilirubin enters the cholangioles. Owing to stasis resulting from biliary occlusion by stones or tumors, conjugated hyperbilirubinemia occurs with concurrent choluria and absent urinary urobilinogen. Because bile salts are also retained as a consequence of bile obstruction, they cannot reach the small intestine. Intestinal lipids are not emulsified, leading to malabsorption of fat-soluble vitamins and steatorrhea. Avitaminosis K promotes coagulopathy, whereas avitaminosis D can result in osteodystrophy.

Common to all diseases with hepatocyte damage and dropout is coagulopathy, because the liver synthesizes five clotting factors. Prothrombin and partial thromboplastin times are prolonged, and the international normalized ratio (INR) is increased. Certain enzymes are intrinsic to hepatocytes (aminotransferases), and when hepatocytes undergo necrosis, these enzymes become extracellular, and they are absorbed into the liver sinusoids to become elevated in serum. Liver-specific alkaline phosphatase isoenzymes derived from cholangioles become elevated in biliary obstruction.

Primary hepatocellular carcinoma is a malignant tumor of hepatocytes. There is a well-documented marked increased risk for this cancer among persons previously infected with hepatitis B virus. The tumor can remain silent for months or even years. It is not until liver function becomes compromised that symptoms surface. The molecular basis for oncogenesis by the virus is not well-known. Hepatitis B encodes HBx, a

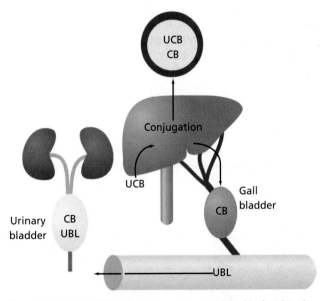

Figure 6–2 In hemolytic anemias, unconjugated bilirubin (UCB) is elevated in the serum and increased levels of conjugated bilirubin (CB) are converted to urobilinogen (UBL), which is reabsorbed from the gut and eliminated in the urine, causing increased levels. In hepatocyte destruction, both UCB and CB are elevated. In biliary obstruction, UCB is elevated in the serum and accumulates in urine (choluria).

protein that transactivates cellular oncogenes and upregulates protein kinase C, an important enzyme involved in signal transduction.

Clinical features

There are signs, symptoms, and complications of liver failure that are common to all forms of hepatonecrosis and cirrhosis, and there are yet other features that are unique to each of the disease processes previously discussed. Common to all forms of liver-cell destruction and failure are jaundice, edema, and a hemorrhagic diathesis. In alcoholic cirrhosis, patients often exhibit vascular dilatations affecting vessels that anastomose with the portal vein. Esophageal, umbilical, and hemorrhoidal veins become distended or varicose as a consequence of portal hypertension. Esophageal varices can be particularly problematic, since they may rupture and lead to uncontrolled internal hemorrhage. The facial skin is prone to show multiple telangiectasias in alcoholic cirrhosis. Hepatocyte damage results in low-level synthesis of albumin, a liver-engendered protein important in the maintenance of osmotic balance. Hypoalbuminemia lowers blood osmotic pressure with resultant exit of fluid from the vascular compartment to the interstitial fluid compartment (edema). Gynecomastia in males is the consequence of diminished catabolism of estrogenic hormones, an enzymatic pathway found in the hepatocyte.

In post-hepatitis cirrhosis, patients may have generalized malaise and low-grade relapsing fevers, depending upon how active or inactive the infection may be. During active infection, hepatomegaly is observed; in cirrhosis, the liver is no longer palpable, owing to scarified shrinkage. In alcoholic cirrhosis, the patient may manifest other signs and symptoms of alcoholism that are readily observable (intoxication behaviors). Patients with biliary cirrhosis may complain of epigastric or infrasternal pain and cramping attributable to gallstones, tumor, or other forms of bile duct stricture. A common symptom in biliary cirrhosis is generalized pruritus. Other findings indicative of biliary obstruction are palmar erythema, particular of the thenar and hypothenar eminences, cutaneous xanthomas secondary to elevated low-density lipoproteins that accompany biliary disease and clubbing of the nails. Children with biliary atresia present with green teeth, owing to the dentinal incorporation of bilirubin pigment.

The diagnosis is made by history, serology for viral antigens and antibodies, laboratory assessment of serum chemistries, and liver needle biopsy. Table 6–1 outlines the salient laboratory findings in the various forms of liver disease.

Patients with end-stage liver disease are candidates for transplantation. Like other organ transplant recipients, patients receiving liver transplants must undergo transplantation antigen testing and tissue cross-matching. Exact tissue matches, except between identical twins, are not feasible, and therefore, recipients are placed on immunosuppressive medications, typically cyclosporine and prednisone.

Dental management

The primary dental management concerns for patients with hepatobiliary disease are infection control for hepatitis viruses, drug metabolism, and importantly, potential coagulopathy. Infection-control issues are of paramount importance, because hepatitis B virus is highly resistant to many disinfectants. Both hepatitis B and C are transmissible from actively infected patients and carriers in the dental office environment. The hepatitides are discussed in detail in Chapter 16, and methods for managing patients with transmissible diseases are discussed in detail in the Chapter 19.

Many drugs are catabolized in the liver by the cytochrome P-450 pathway. In hepatitis and cirrhosis, hepatocyte damage and nonfunction lead to prolonged and cumulative drug activity. This is an important consideration for patients requiring analgesics and sedatives. Pain drugs with codeine, oxycodone, and hydrocodone remain active longer, and either dosage or periodicity of intake should be altered appropriately.

Table 6–1 Blood Chemistries in Jaundice and Liver Disease

Disease Group	Bilirubin	Urobilinogen	Choluria	Hepatitis Serology
Hemolytic anemia	UC	+++	Absent	Negative
Alcoholic cirrhosis	C/UC	+	+	Negative
Postinfectious cirrhosis	C/UC	+	+	Positive
Biliary cirrhosis	C	Absent	+++	Negative
Hepatocellular carcinoma*	Absent	Absent	Absent	Positive

*Carcinoma in the late course may show elevations in bilirubin.

UC = unconjugated or indirect bilirubin; C = conjugated or direct bilirubin.

Antibiotics also are retained longer in circulation; however, this may be a benefit rather than a concern.

Perhaps the most significant aspect of hepatobiliary disease to consider in the dental patient is coagulopathy. In active acute hepatitis, failure to synthesize prothrombin as well as other clotting factors can result in extreme hemorrhage during tooth extraction. In chronic hepatitis and all forms of cirrhosis, prolonged bleeding after periodontal surgery and oral and maxillofacial surgery is commensurate with the degree of hepatocyte destruction and can be assessed by ordering a prothombin time (PT) and INR or partial thromboplastin time (PTT). Recall that any patient with less than 50% of normal coagulability is not a candidate for surgical procedures unless special measures are followed. An INR over 3.0 in a cirrhotic patient is also a cause for modification of dental treatments in which hemorrhage will occur.

In patients needing immediate care owing to an acute oral infection for which periodontal surgery or extraction is necessary, the patient's physician should be consulted, and the patient may have to be hospitalized with intravenous infusion of coagulation-factor replacements. Among patients with only slightly elevated INR or PTs exceeding 50% of normal, added precautions for prolonged bleeding must still be taken. Compression with gauze over wounds should be administered for longer than usual. For postoperative pain, drugs that inhibit platelet adhesion, such as aspirin and other nonsteroidal anti-inflammatory drugs (NSAIDs) only compound the bleeding tendency and should be avoided. Prescription of acetometaphine compounded with codeine, oxycodone, or hydrocodone can be prescribed for pain with the caveat that hepatic catabolism of these drugs is impaired.

The pre- and post-transplant patient poses a risk, owing to the immunosuppression that is induced during and after the transplant. Dental sepsis should be eliminated in the pretransplant subject, extracting teeth with severe periodontitis and periapical foci of infection. Post-transplant patients taking cyclosporine should be informed about the possibility of developing gingival enlargement. When hyperplasia does evolve, gingivectomy can be undertaken. Oral candidiasis may be a complication of transplantation with immunosuppression and can be treated by prescribing the appropriate antifungal medication (see Chapter 18).

Medical management of the patient in liver failure is aimed at preventing life-threatening bleeds, control of edema, and therapy for portal hypertension. Whole-blood transfusions may be administered, and intravenous vasopressor drugs, such as vasopressin, are administered to induce splanchnic constriction. Propranolol has been employed to lessen the degree of esophageal bleeding from varices. In some patients, vascular shunts may be used to lower portal hypertension. Ascites is managed by lowering salt intake and induc-

tion of controlled diuresis with aldosterone blockade. Spironolactone, hydrochlorothiazide, and furosemide may be used to diurese the patient. Weight loss from edema fluids is maintained below 0.5 kg per day, to prevent hypovolemia. In patients with severe hypoproteinemia, infusion of low-salt albumin can be administered to raise the blood osmotic pressure.

In patients with extrahepatic biliary disease, cholecystectomy is the treatment of choice when the disease is chronic and imaging studies reveal the presence of large stones. Smaller stones have been treated with chenodeoxycholic acid or its analogue ursodeoxycholic acid; however, cholesterol stones are resistant to dissolution with these drugs. Small stones may also be lysed with lithotripsy, an ultrasonic device that breaks down the mineralized deposits in situ.

Gastrointestinal diseases

Gastric and duodenal ulcer, atrophic gastritis, gluten enteropathy, chronic inflammatory bowel disease, and intestinal polyposis all have dental implications. Upper gastrointestinal (GI) tract ulcers are considered to be a psychosomatic illness, owing to their association with emotional stress. Hematemesis is a sign of severe gastric ulcer disease. When intestinal ulcers remain untreated, they may progress to perforation with resultant peritonitis. Atrophic gastritis is associated with pernicious anemia, a disease that shows characteristic dorsal tongue changes. Patients with atrophic gastritis are at risk for stomach cancer.

Gluten enteropathy and the two major forms of chronic inflammatory bowel disease (ulcerative colitis and regional enteritis) all have oral manifestations. Indeed, it is the detection of the oral lesions that may herald the presence of gastrointestinal disease. Polyps are common proliferative lesions of the bowel. Some are hereditary, others are not. Certain polyps are prone to malignant transformation. Both hamartomatous polyps and premalignant adenomatous polyps may be associated with oral and jaw lesions. Colorectal cancer can erode the serosal lining of the gut and lead to internal hemorrhaging that may predispose to anemia, leukopenia, and thrombocytopenia.

For the most part, bowel diseases do not directly impact dental treatment. Their significance is primarily linked to the oral and jaw manifestations that are an accompaniment.

Pathophysiology

The stomach is lined by a specialized mucous membrane that secretes hydrochloric acid (HCI) while maintaining a protective mucinous coating that prevents dissolution of its self. The hormone gastrin that is expressed and secreted during active digestion, mediates the secretion of HCl by gastric epithelium. Autoantibodies and autoreactive T cells can exert immunopathologic damage to the mucosal lining, leading to epithelial atrophy. The atrophic lining is no longer capable of acid secretion (achlorhydria), and elaboration of the intrinsic factor required for vitamin B_{12} absorption is significantly diminished. Vitamin B_{12} is a coenzyme required for erythroblastic differentiation and maturation. When vitamin B_{12} is not absorbed, the maturing erythroblasts are enlarged, hence the term megaloblastic anemia. Mature erythrocytes are also enlarged and engorged with excessive amounts of hemoglobin (macrocytic, hyperchromic), yet the total number of erythrocytes is significantly decreased. Oxygen-carrying capacity is low, with patients showing pallor and exhibiting lethargy.

Gastric ulcers occur anywhere in the stomach, although certain regions are more prone. The ulcer is characterized by loss of gastric epithelium. The submucosa is inflamed, and in more severe cases, the inflammatory lesion erodes through the muscularis into the serosa and, in some cases, goes on to ulcerate. Hyperacidity is considered to play a role, yet the presence of *Helicobacter pylori* is also a major factor in the pathogenesis of this disease.

Inflammatory diseases of the small and large intestines are common disorders that appear to involve immunopathologic mechanisms without any known microbial pathogen being isolated from lesional tissue. Gluten enteropathy, also known as celiac disease or nontropical sprue, involves the small bowel and is the result of a hypersensitivity reaction to the wheat gluten allergen, gliadin. IgA antigliadin and antiendomysial antibodies are generally present. Antigen-antibody complexes adhere to the epithelial lining of the gut inducing inflammation with secondary malabsorption of fats (steatorrhea). There is also a defective absorption of fat-soluble vitamins, yet rarely is there significant clinical evidence of osteodystrophy (low vitamin D) or hypoprothrombinemia (low vitamin K). Affected patients suffer from diarrhea and intestinal cramping.

Chronic inflammatory bowel disease consists of two common afflictions: ulcerative colitis and regional enteritis or Crohn's disease. Ulcerative colitis is characterized by irritable bowel symptoms consisting of watery diarrhea with intervening episodes of constipation. Abdominal cramping is also a feature. The etiology is unknown although emotional stress and tension are predisposing factors. Autoantibodies to colonic mucins and a cytotoxic T-cell response to colonic epithelium have been documented and may play a role in the pathogenesis. There are broad areas throughout the colon that develop linear serpentine ulcerative streaks. The colonic epithelium is lost, and the lining is replaced by granulation tissue and microabscesses that form in the epithelial crypts. Most of the ulcers are located in the descending colon.

Regional enteritis is also characterized by irritable bowel symptoms: constipation alternating with episodes of diarrhea and abdominal discomfort. Inflammatory foci are segmentally distributed within the submucosa and are preferentially localized to the ileum yet may extend into the ascending colon. These inflammatory foci are comprised of nonspecific mononuclear inflammatory cell infiltrates that may occasionally include specific granulomatous inflammation with multinucleated giant cells. The inflammatory segments constrict the bowel and obstruction can become a complication. Lower GI contrast imaging discloses the segmental pattern of disease.

Polyps are common nodular lesions of the colon that may occasionally arise in the small bowel. They may be single or multiple, sporadic, or hereditary. Microscopically, intestinal polyps are subdivided into two major categories: benign hamartomatous polyps and adenomatous polyps. The hamartomatous polyps are typically round or oval with a pedunculated stalk. The Peutz-Jeghers syndrome is a heritable condition in which patients develop multiple intestinal hamartomatous polyposis. Importantly, these types of polyps are not precancerous. Colon cancer has been reported to occur in patients with the Peutz-Jeghers syndrome and such cancers are believed to arise from adenomatous polyps that can sometimes be seen in these patients. Adenomatous polyposis coli (APC) is a heritable disease characterized by multiple colonic adenomatous polyps. These polyps are multiple and tend to arise in the transverse and descending colon. The APC gene that encodes a tumor-suppressor protein is mutated in adenomatous polyposis coli, and when both alleles are affected, the polyps transform into adenocarcinomas.

Clinical features and oral manifestations

In pernicious anemia associated with atrophic gastritis, patients often manifest tongue changes. The filiform papillae are denuded and often even the fungiform papillae are lost, giving the dorsum of the tongue a beefy red, bald appearance (Figure 6–3). These same changes may be observed in erythematous candidiasis, which is included in the differential diagnosis (see Chapter 18). A complete blood count, including erythrocyte count, hemoglobin, and hematocrit, discloses a macrocytic hyperchromic anemia. Blood vitamin B_{12} levels are decreased and gastric analysis discloses achlorhydria.

Oral ulcerations resembling aphthae are encountered in patients with gluten enteropathy. These ulcers are oval and small, being less than 5 mm in diameter, and are

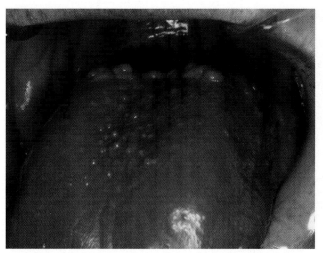

Figure 6–3 Bald, depapillated tongue in pernicious anemia secondary to atrophic gastritis.

multiple (Figure 6–4). Unlike aphthae they are persistant and chronic. Any patient with a history of chronic oral ulcerations and intestinal cramping should be evaluated for gluten enteropathy. Screening for serum IgA anti-endomysial antibodies is recommended. Antigliadin antibodies can be seen in patients who have negative duodenal biopsies and therefore provide no significant diagnostic information. Skin lesions that are red and papular may also occur in gluten enteropathy. Biopsy discloses eosinophilic infiltrates and deposition of IgA in the dermal papillae, diagnostic features for dermatitis herpetiformis. When the patient is started on a gluten-free diet, the signs and symptoms resolve.

Both forms of chronic inflammatory bowel disease show oral manifestations. Some patients with ulcerative colitis develop diffuse serpentine oral erosions that are exudative and erythematous (Figure 6–5). Biopsy dis-

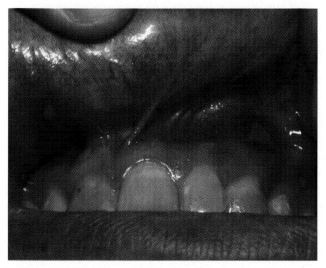

Figure 6–4 Aphthous-like ulcers in celiac disease.

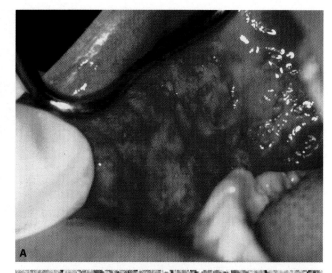

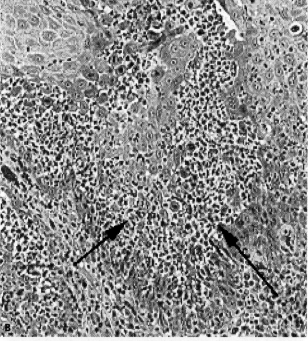

Figure 6–5 Pyostomatitis vegetans. *A*, Clinically, the mucosa shows red and exudative erosions; *B*, microscopically, intraepithelial eosinophilic abscesses are evident; and *C*, immunoreactants (IgG) exhibit a pericellular "fishnet" pattern.

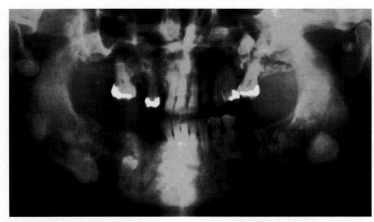

Figure 6–6 Osteomas in the Gardner syndrome.

closes intraepithelial eosinophilic abscesses and immuno-fluorescence staining often shows a pericellular pattern with anti-IgG, -IgM, or -IgA, a pattern identical to that seen in pemphigus vulgaris (see Chapter 21). This condition is termed pyostomatitis vegetans, and lesions with a similar histologic appearance may arise on the skin where they are called pyodermatitis vegetans. In Crohn's disease, patients may have lesions throughout the GI tract, including the small bowel, stomach, and oral cavity. The oral lesions are usually tumefactive and multinodular yet can be erythematous and erosive (see Chapter 24). Histologically, the oral lesions of Crohn's disease are similar to those in the bowel, being represented by noncaseating granulomatous inflammation (see Chaper 24).

Perioral macular pigmentations are encountered in the Peutz-Jeghers syndrome. The lesions are brown to black and appear as numerous freckles (see Chapter 22). Similar melanotic spots may be observed on the hands and fingers. These patients usually indicate that they have had long-term bowel symptoms that include cramping and diarrhea.

The oral and jaw manifestations of the Gardner syndrome are important entities to recognize because they herald the presence of adenomatous polyps. These polyps transform to carcinomas in all patients affected with the syndrome, and once they are detected, colon resection is performed. The jaw manifestations include multiple supernumerary teeth and multifocal radiopaque masses that have been termed osteomas. These bony lesions are readily visualized on dental radiographs where they may be seen overlying the periostium of the jaws or facial bones and within the sinuses (Figure 6–6). They can often be seen clinically and are indurated.

As mentioned previously, patients with GI diseases do not present a problem for routine dental care. Recognition of the oral manifestations is important, since these manifestations may be the first indication that GI disease is extant.

Suggested reading

Douglas LR, Douglass JB, Sieck JO, Smith PJ. Oral management of the patient with end-stage liver disease and the liver transplant patient. Oral Surg Oral Med Oral Pathol Oral Radiol Endod 1998;86:55–64.

Jokinen J, Peters U, Maki M, et al. Celiac sprue in patients with chronic oral mucosal symptoms. J Clin Gastroenterol 1998;26:23–6.

Seow WK, Shepherd RW, Ong TH. Oral changes associated with end-stage liver disease and liver transplantation: implications for dental management. ASDC J Dent Child 1991;58:474–80.

Takeuchi T, Takenoshita Y, Kubo K, Iida M. Natural course of jaw lesions in patients with familial adenomatosis coli (Gardner's syndrome). Int J Oral Maxillofac Surg 1993;22:226–30.

Thomson PJ, Langton SG. Persistent haemorrhage following dental extractions in patients with liver disease: two cautionary tales. Br Dent J 1996;180:141–4.

Thornhill MH, Zakrzewska JM, Gilkes JJ. Pyostomatitis vegetans: report of three cases and review of the literature. J Oral Pathol Med 1992;21:128–33.

Wakefield CW, Throndson RR, Brock T. Liver transplantation: dentistry is an essential part of the team. J Tenn Dent Assoc 1995;75:9–16.

7 Bleeding Disorders

L. Roy Eversole, DDS, MSD, MA

A hemorrhagic diathesis can be a serious life-threatening event to patients undergoing an oral or periodontal surgical procedure. In general, bleeding tendencies occur when there are pathologic conditions that affect (1) platelet adhesion to damaged vascular walls and aggregation of platelets to one another, (2) the coagulation factor cascade and its fibrinolytic counterpart pathways, and (3) fragility of small vessel walls. The latter is rare and is not discussed here.

The clinical findings that herald an underlying bleeding disorder include purpura; spontaneous gingival, nasal, or genital tract bleeds; and hemarthrosis. When a disorder of hemostasis is present, these signs typically occur in the absence of any provocative traumatic event. Two major types of purpura are encountered: petechiae, which are punctate 1- to 2-mm red spots of skin or mucosa and are more common in platelet disorders (Figure 7–1); and ecchymoses, which appear as diffuse macular blue, red, or brown bruises and are more often encountered among patients with clotting factor deficiencies (Figure 7–2).

Pathophysiology

Damage to the endothelium exposes underlying connective tissues, extracellular matrix (ECM) proteins, and glycosaminoglycans of the vascular wall, to the circulation. A serum protein, von Willebrand factor VIII complex, adheres to ECM and then serves as a link for platelets, which have a binding receptor for this adhesion molecule (Figure 7–3). In the von Willebrand group of diseases, this factor is inherited in a mutated hypofunctional form or may not be synthesized in physiologically functional amounts. Platelet adhesion is delayed or does not occur. Assuming an intact von Willebrand factor, the next phase of hemostasis involves aggregation of platelets to those that are adherent to the damaged vascular wall. This is mediated by a group of platelet membrane adhesion molecules that bind to a receptor on the adherent thrombocytes bound to von Willebrand factor. Fibrinogen, a serum clotting factor, is an important platelet–platelet link. The cyclooxygenase pathway is involved in

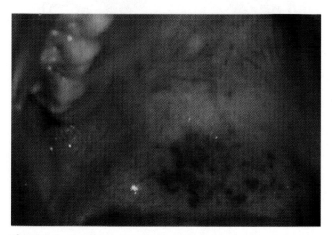

Figure 7–1 Petechial hemorrhages in the palate.

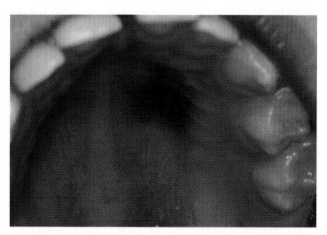

Figure 7–2 Diffuse mucosal hemorrhage or ecchymosis of the palate.

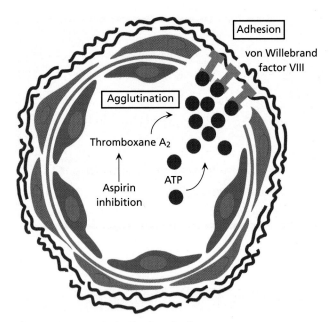

Figure 7–3   Hemostasis. Platelet adhesion.

platelet aggregation by synthesis of thromboxane A₂ from arachidonic acid within the platelet. Acetylsalicylic acid is an inhibitor of this metabolic pathway, and administration of aspirin inhibits aggregation for the entire 160-day life span of the platelet. Clinically relevant bleeding problems are not usually encountered until a patient ingests more than eight 325-mg tablets per day. Many other nonsteroidal anti-inflammatory drugs (NSAIDs) also affect this pathway adversely.

In addition to thromboxane and fibrinogen, there are other platelet adhesion molecules necessary for platelet aggregation. There are rare disorders in which these molecules are inherited in mutated hypofunctional form.

Thrombocytopenia is a condition comprising a wide variety of etiologies. Table 7–1, although not comprehensive, lists the more common diseases that can culminate in thrombocytopenia. The idiopathic forms frequently manifest antibodies that bind to autologous antigens on platelet membranes, resulting in IgG complement-mediated clearance by phagocytes. This form

Table 7–1   Platelet Disorders

Adhesion defect
    von Willebrand factor group of diseases
Aggregation defects
    Aspirin, various NSAIDS
    Inherited platelet adhesion molecule diseases
Thrombocytopenia
    Idiopathic or autoimmune
    Drug-induced
    Leukemia-associated
    Total body irradiation

may be encountered in untreated human immunodeficiency virus (HIV)-infected subjects. The thrombocytopenia seen in leukemia is a consequence of bone marrow depletion of megakaryocyte precursors by malignant leukocyte proliferation and infiltration. Chemotherapeutic agents used to treat cancer, inhibit dividing cells and induce thrombocytopenia, anemia, and leukopenia.

Coagulopathies are the consequence of either inherited or acquired defects in the proteins that constitute the coagulation cascade, a complex stepwise sequence of enzymatic reactions that leads to the formation of a fibrin clot (Figure 7–4) (Table 7–2). Fibrin is formed by activation of an enzyme known as thromboplastin. This enzyme acts upon a precursor protein, prothrombin, which is cleaved to the enzyme thrombin. In turn, thrombin cleaves fibrinogen to form the sticky thread-like protein fibrin. Fibrin intercalates between aggregated platelets to form a stabilized clot within a damaged vessel. In damaged tissues, fibrin forms a diffuse gel-like matrix that serves as a scaffold for organization by granulation tissue in the process of wound healing. These enzymatic steps are collectively referred to as the common pathway.

Clots forming outside of vessels, as in wounds, are initiated by factors of the extrinsic pathway. Tissue thromboplastin is released by fibroblasts during injury and is activated by serum factor VII (Figure 7–5). This activated thromboplastin then propagates through the common pathway. Factor VII deficiency is extremely rare.

Clots that form inside vessels are initiated by factors released from adherent, aggregated platelets that then act upon serum proteins, collectively known as clotting

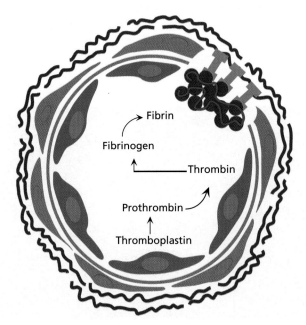

Figure 7–4   Hemostatis. Clotting mechanism.

Table 7–2 Coagulopathies

Heritable extrinsic pathway
  Factor VII deficiency
Heritable intrinsic pathway
  Factor VIII (hemophilia A)
  Factor IX (Christmas disease)
Heritable common pathway
  Factor I afibrinogenemia
Acquired common pathway
  Chronic and acute liver disease
  Malabsorption of lipids and fat-soluble vitamin K
    Drug-induced (Coumadin)
    Consumptive coagulopathy
    Heparinized patients

factors. The factors, derived from aggregated platelets, activate serum factor XII (Hageman factor), which in the presence of calcium, activates a stepwise series of reactions that includes factor IX, factor XI, and factor VIII, to yield the plasma form of thromboplastin (factor X). This constitutes the intrinsic pathway. Subse-

quently, the common pathway is entered, progressing to form a fibrin network that wraps around and through aggregated platelets, thereby forming a stable thrombus over the vessel wound. Endothelial cells can then resurface the wound. The hemophilias are hereditary diseases: in hemophilia A defective factor VIII is derived the material allele, being an X-linked recessive disorder. In Christmas disease or hemophilia B, factor IX is mutated and defective. In von Willebrand disease, there is a defect in the von Willebrand factor VIII adhesion molecule, with impaired platelet adhesion coupled with a mild intrinsic pathway coagulopathy. There are three major subtypes of von Willebrand disease, the more common of which is mild. A less frequent form presents with severe bleeding.

Since the liver synthesizes many clotting factors of the intrinsic and common pathways, it is axiomatic that hepatocyte destruction will result in coagulopathy that is reflected by prolonged intrinsic and extrinsic pathway clotting (see Chapter 6). Fat malabsorption, such as seen in nontropical sprue, is characterized by steatorrhea that also contributes to coagulopathy through the common

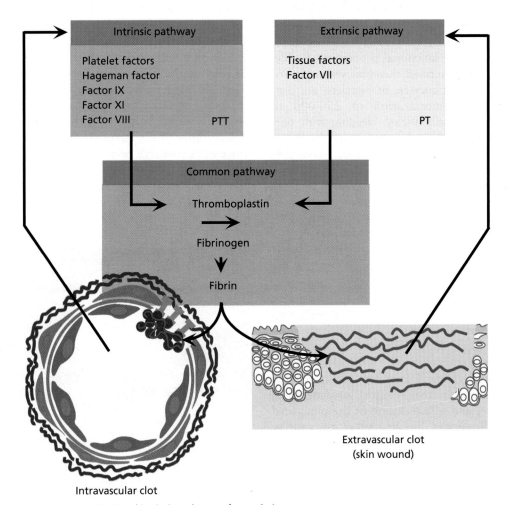

Figure 7–5 Extrinsic and intrinsic pathways of coagulation.

pathway. When the fat-soluble vitamin K, a coenzyme required for prothrombin synthesis, cannot be absorbed because of bowel disease, coagulation is delayed. Similarly, in biliary obstruction, bile salts fail to reach the gut, chylomicrons are not cleared, and vitamin K is not absorbed in adequate quantities. Hypoprothrombinemia then contributes to a bleeding tendency. Coumadin is a vitamin K antagonist and is, therefore, used for control of thromboembolic vascular disease. Patients treated with Coumadin may show prolonged clotting and manifest significant bleeding during oral surgery.

The antithesis to hemostasis is clot dissolution. This is accomplished by the plasminogen-fibrinolysin enzyme pathways that initiate clot lysis. These pathways can be inhibited by pharmacologic agents.

Both platelets and clotting factors can be consumed when disseminated intravascular coagulation occurs as a consequence of serum factors that favor clot formation. Disseminated intravascular coagulation (DIC) is a complication of certain widespread metastatic cancers.

Clinical features and diagnosis

Platelet disease encompasses two major defects. A decrease in absolute numbers is termed thrombocytopenia. A deficiency in the functional properties of adhesion or aggregation is termed thrombocytopathia (or thrombasthenia). Thrombocytes, or platelets, are normally found in a concentration of 250,000 to 500,000/cm^3 of blood. Significant bleeding with purpura is seen when the thrombocyte count falls below 50,000. Defects in adhesion are detected by assessing in vitro aggregation from venipuncture samples. Certain specific adhesion molecules that normally mediate adhesion and aggregation can be measured in special reference clinical laboratories that specialize in analysis of hematologic diseases.

The chief clinical test for assessment of thrombocyte disease is the bleeding time. This simple test can be ordered from the laboratory or can be performed in the office. A blood pressure cuff is placed on the upper arm and is then inflated to 40 mm Hg. A blood lancet is used to make a small puncture through the skin of the forearm. The oozing blood is then blotted with filter paper (a coffee filter will suffice) every 15 seconds until no blood appears on the filter (Figure 7–6). This normally takes 4 to 6 minutes, the time required for platelets to adhere, aggregate, and affect closure of the punctured vascular walls. Prolonged bleeding times are seen in both thrombocytopenia and thombocytopathia.

Defects in clotting factors lead to ecchymosis, spontaneous bleeding and intra-articular bleeding after even minor trauma to a joint. Clotting factors are activated when platelets plug a severance in the endothelium and

their activation culminates in the formation of a fibrin clot. Intravascular hemostasis uses clotting factors of the intrinsic pathway, and blood samples can be subjected to a test that assesses the integrity of this pathway, the partial thromboplastin time (PTT). In a normal patient, the PTT is about 25 to 30 seconds and is an in vitro measure of the actual time required for the intrinsic pathway factors to form a fibrin clot (see Figure 7–5).

The PTT is performed in an instrument that electronically detects the presence of a fibrin thread. The PTT is performed on a blood sample that has been placed in a tube containing anticoagulant. A portion of plasma is obtained, and to this sample, an activator of the intrinsic pathway is added, alleviating the anticoagulant effect and stimulating the Hageman factor activation. This leads to generation of plasma thromboplastin, hence the term partial thromboplastin time, which then progresses through the common pathway to form a fibrin clot, a multistep process that normally occurs in 30 seconds.

The extrinsic pathway is responsible for extravascular coagulation (ie, forming clots in wounded tissues, such as tooth extraction sites). Some of the clotting factors of the extrinsic pathway differ from those of the intrinsic cascade. The test for the extrinsic pathway is the prothrombin time (PT), which is typically 11 to 13 seconds. The PT also uses anticoagulated plasma, to which an activator of the extrinsic pathway is added, thereby stimulating prothrombin (prothrombin time). The PTT and PT are delayed when one or more proteins in their respective pathways are absent or nonfunctional. Both pathways are prolonged when there is a defect in one of the factors from the common pathway, since both converge here.

The most reliable assessment of coagulation status is the international normalized ratio (INR). The INR is based upon the prothrombin time and is controlled over

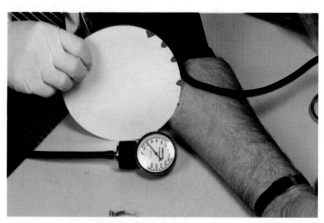

Figure 7–6 The bleeding time is assessed with a cuff inflated to 40 mm Hg. A lancet initiates bleeding on the forearm, and after 4 minutes have transpired, a filter paper is dabbed over the bleeding spot every 15 seconds until bleeding has ceased.

many laboratories, whereby a ratio is generated to indicate coagulation status. An INR of 1.0 is normal, and any ratio from 1.0 to 2.0 is considered to be only mildly decreased, approaching normal coagulability. When the INR is 2.0, this would correspond to a PT of 24, if the control sample across laboratories was 12 seconds, thereby indicating that coagulation is one-half the efficiency of the norm. An INR of 2.0 to 3.0 indicates a moderate-level bleeder, whereas 3.0 to 5.0 is considered to be at high risk for uncontrolled bleeding.

The clinical test for coagulation disorders is the clotting time. To conduct this test, a blood lancet is used to puncture the finger pad. Immediately, eight capillary microhematocrit tubes are placed over the puncture site, one at a time, filling them by capillary action. After waiting 4 minutes, a tube is fractured in the center and gently pulled apart. This procedure is repeated every 15 seconds until a thin threadlike band connects the fractured ends of the tube (Figure 7–7). This thread represents the formation of fibrin, which was activated once blood contacted the glass surface of the tube. Normally, the fibrin thread forms within 4 to 5 minutes. Prolongation of the clotting time equates to a defect of the intrinsic or common pathways of coagulation. The vast majority of coagulopathies can be screened using the clotting time test.

indicative of a bleeding disorder warrants the procurement of appropriate blood tests, such as platelet count, platelet aggregation, PT, and PTT. If leukemia is suspected, a complete blood count should be ordered as well.

If a surgical procedure is undertaken and bleeding becomes problematic, 911 should be called and the patient should be admitted to the emergency department. Thrombin packs with direct pressure should be placed over the wound until the patient can be admitted.

For patients with thrombocyte deficiency who need tooth extraction or other oral surgical interventions, the patient should be treated in the hospital or surgical center with hematologic consultation. A platelet transfusion can then be administered prior to oral surgery. Aspirin or indomethacin toxicity may be encountered in patients with arthritis or chronic headache. The drug should be withdrawn, using a substitute analgesic without aspirin (acetometaphine with codeine or hydrocodone), and surgery postponed for 5 to 7 days.

Patients with factor deficiencies should be hospitalized in consultation with a hematologist. Missing factor can be administered intravenously just prior to dental surgery. Cryoprecipitate and recombinant factors should be obtained in advance. For patients on Coumadin requiring immediate surgery for severe odontalgia, vitamin K can be given intravenously under

Clinical considerations for dental care

Uncontrolled bleeding from tooth extraction, periodontal surgery, or other oral and maxillofacial surgery procedures can occur in patients with either platelet disorders or coagulopathies. As alluded to earlier, the oral manifestations include petechia, ecchymosis, and spontaneous oronasal bleeds that occur in the absence of any significant trauma. Purpura found in conjunction with gingival enlargement and malaise may underlie leukemia. If facial spider telangiectasias are evident and the skin or conjunctivae are jaundiced, cirrhosis of the liver must be considered. Purpura can occur in patients with HIV infection, indicating thrombocytopenic purpura. Ecchymosis of the mucosa or skin in a patient with a history of vascular occlusive disease may be indicative of Coumadin therapy. The medical history should be thoroughly reviewed to explore whether there are any past or present episodes indicative of a hemorrhagic diathesis.

Two dilemmas can occur in dental patients: (1) unknowingly performing a surgical procedure on a hemorrhagic subject, and (2) performing necessary extractions or surgeries in a patient with a known coagulation disorder. The first scenario can often be avoided by taking a thorough medical history, asking the appropriate questions regarding bruisability, spontaneous or poorly controlled bleeding, and drug history (Table 7–3). Any sign

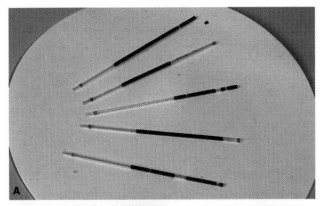

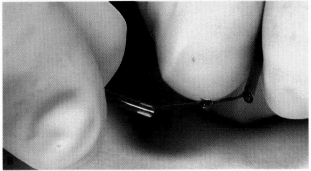

Figures 7–7 The clotting time. Microcapillary tubes (*A*) are filled with blood taken from a finger lancet puncture (*B*) and after 3.5 minutes one is broken every 15 seconds until a fibrin thread is observed across the broken ends.

Table 7–3 Commonly Prescribed Drugs That Can Produce a Hemorrhagic Diathesis

Vitamin K antagonist
Coumadin
Platelet aggregation inhibition
Acetylsalicylic acid
Indomethacin
Ibuprofen
Ketorolac
Persantine*
Acetaminophen*
Corticosteroids*
Heparin sulfate
Platelet synthesis inhibition
Cytotoxic antineoplastic agents
Cyclophosphamide
5-fluorouracil
Methotrexate
Mitomysin
Bleomycin
Doxorubicin
Vinblastine or vincristine
Antihypertensive myelosuppression
ACE inhibitors
Beta blockers

*Mild effect.
ACE = angiotensin-converting enzyme.

direction of the patient's physician, and coagulation status can be monitored by obtaining a prothrombin time. For elective surgery, the dentist should consult with the physician about withdrawing the Coumadin for 3 to 4 days prior to surgery. It should be noted that most physicians managing patients with thromboembolic diseases are reluctant to have them discontinue their anticoagulant for any extended period.

In general, anyone with a platelet count below 50,000 should not have dental or periodontal surgery in the general office setting. Similarly, if platelet aggregation is less than 50% of normal control values, the same holds true. With regard to coagulation disorders or patients receiving anticoagulant therapy, the PT or PTT should be above 50% of normal or prolonged no more than double normal values for in-office procedures, or the INR should be under 3.0. Recent studies have shown that teeth can be safely extracted without altering Coumadin levels, even with ratios up to 5.0, provided extraction sites are sutured and occluded with fibrin sealant. Antifibrinolytic preparations, such as tranexamic acid, may also be used in patients with coagulopathic disorders.

Patients who are heparinized while undergoing hemodialysis for end-stage renal disease should be treated the day prior or 1 day subsequent to dialysis. Heparin is rapidly metabolized, and its anticoagulant effects last only 4 to 6 hours.

Capillary fragility is generally not a problem in dental practice. Although hereditary hemorrhagic telangiectasia involves the oral mucosa, fragile vessels are not present in the periodontal tissues. A case of ascorbic acid deficiency would be so rare as to be a candidate for a grand rounds session!

Suggested reading

Basi DL, Schmiechen NJ. Bleeding and coagulation problems in the dental patient. Hereditary disease and medication-induced risks. Dent Clin North Am 1999;43:457–70.

Bodner L, Weinstein JM, Baumgarten AK. Efficacy of fibrin sealant in patients on various levels of oral anticoagulant undergoing oral surgery. Oral Surg Oral Med Oral Pathol Oral Radiol Endod 1998;86:421–4.

Garfunkel AA, Galili D, Findler M, et al. Bleeding tendency: a practical approach in dentistry. Compend Cont Educ Dent 1999;20:836–8, 840–2, 844. (Passim)

Troulis MJ, Head TW, Leclerc JR. Dental extractions in patients on an oral anticoagulant: a survey of practices in North America. J Oral Maxillofac Surg 1998;56:914–7.

8 Blood Dyscrasias

Douglas E. Peterson, DMD, PhD, Mark M. Schubert, DDS, MSD,
Sol Silverman, Jr, MA, DDS, and L. Roy Eversole, DDS, MSD, MA

The anemias

Anemia is a disease of oxygen transport. Tissues supplied by the circulation receive a deficient quantity of oxygen. This deficient oxygenation can be attributed to a decrease in erythrocyte numbers, decreased amounts of hemoglobin, or defective hemoglobin molecules. Therefore, there are numerous forms of anemia that differ depending upon where the defect lies. The most common form of anemia is attributed to iron deficiency and is, therefore, easily treated by increasing intake of dietary iron or iron-salt tablets. The other forms of anemia are less frequently encountered, particularly those that are heritable and involve defective hemoglobins, which predispose erythrocytes to lysis (hemolytic anemias). In general, anemias do not pose a serious risk for patients seeking dental care, unless general anesthetics are to be administered. Some forms of anemia are associated with oral mucosa lesions and radiographically evident changes in the jawbones.

Molecular and pathologic correlates of disease

Erythroblasts are generated in the bone marrow from hematopoietic stem cells. Their differentiation into mature erythrocytes requires the action of erythropoietin, a growth factor that is secreted into the blood stream by renal tubular epithelium. Other hematopoietic growth factors secreted by connective tissue cells also play a role in red blood cell maturation. Erythrocytes are basically anuclear bags of hemoglobin, the molecule responsible for oxygen transport. Hemoglobin is synthesized in nucleated erythroblasts and requires folic acid and cyanocobalamine (vitamin B_{12}) for full maturation. The molecule is comprised of a heme (porphyrin) ring with ferric ions chelated in the center of the ring; globular protein components are attached to the heme ring to complete the structure of this complex protein. These globin chains are subdivided into alpha and beta subunits. In utero, a special type of hemoglobin is synthesized (fetal Hgb [Hgb F]). After parturition, chemically distinct adult hemoglobin is produced (Hgb A), and subsequently, the cell loses its nucleus. The average life span of an erythrocyte is 120 days, afterwhich it is lysed and phagocytized by macrophages in the liver. The heme ring is transformed to bilirubin and metabolized through the liver, the globin chains are degraded reconstituting the amino acid pool, and the iron is recycled back into newly generated erythrocytes.

Anemia attributable to iron deficiency and blood loss is characterized by a decrease in circulating erythrocytes (Figure 8–1). The cells are small and hemoglobin-deficient (microcytic, hypochromic anemia). Megaloblastic anemias, because of the erythoblasts, faced with a deficiency in the factors that are required for hemoglobin synthesis, tend to enlarge and pack as much hemoglobin into the cell as possible. There is a decrease in erythrocyte numbers, whereas the individual cells are large and contain concentrated hemoglobin (macrocytic, hyperchromic anemia). By comparing the red cell count, hemoglobin concentration per 100 mL of blood, and the packed cell volume, also termed the hematocrit, one can determine cell size and hemoglobin content. Ratios are obtained and are referred to as the red cell indices. Mean corpuscular volume (MCV) is derived by a calculation that compares the red cell numbers with the hematocrit. If cell number is normal (ie, 5×10^6) yet the hematocrit is low (far less than 45%), the MCV will be a lower value, indicating that the cells are microcytic. Conversely, if the red cell count is low (eg, 3×10^6) yet the hematocrit is normal (45%), the cells are macrocytic. The mean

corpuscular hemoglobin concentration (MCHC), is a measure of the amount of hemoglobin within the cell. This ratio is derived by calculating the hemoglobin concentration in reference to the cell size. A low MCHC is seen in hypochromic anemias, whereas a high MCHC is indicative of hyperchromic anemia.

The hemolytic anemias are inherited defects of hemoglobin or red cell structure, sickle cell and thalassemia being the more common forms. In sickle cell anemia, one amino acid is substituted as a single base-point mutation, such that valine is substituted for glutamic acid at the sixth position of the beta chain. The protein conformation is changed by this mutation, and the cells assume a sickled shape and become lysed. Hemoglobin electrophoresis reveals the presence of both Hgb A and Hgb S in heterozygotic carriers, with only Hgb S being detected in homozygous subjects with full-blown sickle cell anemia. There are numerous variants of thalassemia, all of which involve mutations in specific loci of either the alpha or beta globin chains. As in sickle cell, the Mediterranean anemias result in altered erythrocyte morphology and predispose to lysis. There is considerable variability with regard to severity of disease in the different subtypes of thalassemia. Hereditary spherocytosis is a disease of red cell morphology and is probably attributable to a derangement in the erythrocyte cytoskeletal molecule spectrin. The consequence is a change in shape of the erythrocyte, whereby it looses its discoid structure and becomes spherical. The spherocytes are readily lysed in the spleen. In glucose-6-phosphate dehydrogenase deficiency, the red cell is easily damaged and becomes lysed. This occurs because enzyme dysfunction leads to low levels of reduced glutathione, a molecule that when present in normal concentration, protects erythrocytes from oxidants.

In Fanconi anemia, there is a mutation in the DNA repair gene family, a defect that leads not only to ane-

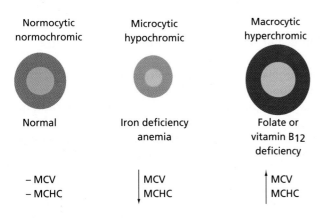

Normocytic normochromic	Microcytic hypochromic	Macrocytic hyperchromic
Normal	Iron deficiency anemia	Folate or vitamin B₁₂ deficiency
– MCV	↓ MCV	↑ MCV
– MCHC	↓ MCHC	↑ MCHC

Normal mean values	Males	Females
Normal RBC count	5,000,000	4,500,000
Hemoglobin concentration	15 mg/dL	13 mg/dL
Hematocrit	45%	36%

Figure 8–1 *Top,* Red cell sizes and hemoglobin content in various anemias. *Bottom,* Normal hemogram. MCV = mean corpuscular volume; MCHC = mean corpuscular hemoglobin concentration; RBC = red blood cell count.

Table 8–1 The Anemias

Maturation defects and deficiency anemias
Iron deficiency anemia
Plummer-Vinson syndrome
Internal hemorrhage
Anemia of end-stage renal disease
Folic acid deficiency
Vitamin B₁₂ deficiency (pernicious anemia)
Aplastic anemia
Fanconi anemia
Hemolytic anemias
Sickle cell anemia
Thalassemia (Mediterranean anemia) syndromes
Glucose-6-phosphate dehydrogenase deficiency
Hereditary spherocytosis

mia but to a predisposition for squamous cancers, many of which affect the facial skin and oral mucosa.

Clinical features

Table 8–1 lists the more common forms of anemia. Iron deficiency is most common and is characterized by palor and lethargy. The hemogram shows low red cell count, hemoglobin, and hematocrit, with hypochromatic microcytic erythrocytes. Females are affected far more frequently than males. The anemia can be reversed by adding adequate levels of iron to the diet. Iron deficiency among women of Scandinavian descent that is associated with atrophic changes in the upper aerodigestive tract mucosa is termed the Plummer-Vinson syndrome, and the atrophic mucosa is prone to malignant transformation to squamous cell carcinomas.

Internal hemorrhaging occurs in a variety of clinical situations, including visceral trauma, esophageal varices accompanying alcoholic cirrhosis, bleeding gastric and pyloric ulcers, and bleeds into the gut from ulcerated colonic cancer. Another systemic disease associated with anemia is end-stage kidney disease. Recall that erythropoietin is synthesized by the kidney tubule, and in tubulointerstitial renal diseases as well as late-stage glomerulonephritis and pyelonephritis, tubular epithelial necrosis occurs with a resultant decrease in erythropoietin levels.

Dietary folic acid deficiency and vitamin B_{12} deficiency secondary to atrophic gastritis and loss of intrinsic factor lead to megaloblastic anemia, with decreased red cell numbers showing macrocytic hyperchromic changes. In fact, one may produce adequate numbers of these cells and still be anemic because the overall oxygen-carrying capacity is diminished. Anemias that occur as a result of dietary or absorption deficiency of folate or vitamin B_{12} are referred to as megaloblastic anemias. Patients are constantly run down and tired, with skin palor. Folic acid deficiency can be corrected by dietary supplementation. Vitamin B_{12} deficiency requires injection administration of vitamin B_{12}, because the atrophic gastric mucosa that is an accompaniment is unable to synthesize adequate levels of intrinsic factor, a protein involved in B_{12} absorption and transport.

Aplastic anemia is a hematologic disease that affects not only erythrocytes but white cells and platelets as well. There is widespread bone marrow arrest in aplastic anemia that is clinically characterized by palor, susceptibility to infections and hemorrhagic diathesis. Bone marrow aplasia is also seen in Fanconi anemia. Patients with Fanconi manifest congenital anomalies, including digital defects of the thumb and radii, and develop facial skin or oral squamous cell carcinomas at a young age.

The hemolytic anemias are encountered in children, since they represent mutations in the hemoglobin molecule. Sickle cell anemia involves a gene that is segregated in individuals of native African descent. Heterozygous carriers generally show no ill effects. Homozygotes who have inherited both defective genes manifest severe anemia. Erythrocyte membranes are unstable, and the cells tend to collapse, sickle, and lyse. During severe episodes (sickle cell crisis), the sickled erythrocytes may occlude small vessels. Weakness, palor, and abdominal pain are features. In thalassemia, defects in either the alpha or beta chains occur, and akin to sickle cell disease, homozygotes are more severely affected.

Oral manifestations

In all forms of anemia, the oral mucosal tissues often show palor. In Plummer-Vinson syndrome and the Fanconi syndrome, pharyngeal and oral squamous cell carcinomas occur, appearing as masses, ulcerations, or erythroplakic lesions (Figure 8–2). Facial skin cancers are also seen in Fanconi anemia.

The classic oral finding in megaloblastic anemia is atrophic glossitis or bald tongue. All the papillae are

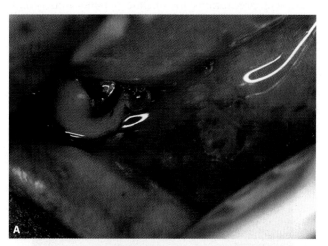

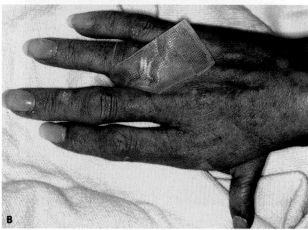

Figure 8–2 Fanconi anemia: *A*, erythroplakia of oral mucosa represents carcinoma; *B*, thumb anomaly. (Courtesy of Dr. C. Choi.)

lost, leaving a smooth, reddened dorsal surface (Figure 8–3). Patients presenting with tongue changes of this nature may also have erythematous candidiasis, but a hematologic workup is required to uncover anemia. Folate and B_{12} serum levels should be ordered along with a hemogram, to disclose macrocytic hyperchromic anemia. Iron deficiency anemia can also be manifested by a depapillated tongue that may also be associated with discomfort.

In sickle cell anemia, stepladder trabeculation may be seen on dental bitewing radiographs, a finding that is common yet may be seen in patients without sickle cell disease. Increased hematopoiesis leads to radiographically defined changes in the calavarium whereby vertical projections of osteophytes are seen, yielding a "hair on end" effect. Similar changes may be encountered in thalassemia syndromes, and additionally, the jaws may exhibit multilocular radiolucencies (Figure 8–4).

Dental management

In general, there are no increased risks that require treatment precautions for anemic patients undergoing dental procedures. If the anemia is severe, patients have a tendency for syncope and should be closely monitored. In aplastic anemia, it must be recalled that a potential bleeding disorder is inherent and, therefore, a

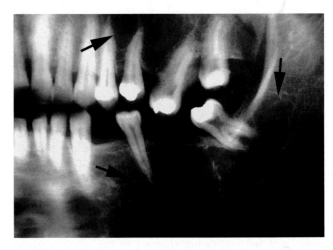

Figure 8–4 Radiolucencies of the jaws in beta thalassemia.

platelet count should be ordered prior to undertaking any surgical procedures. Sepsis is also of concern in aplastic patients with significant neutropenia. If the neutrophil count is less than $2500/mm^3$ and dental, periapical, or periodontal acute infection is evident, antibiotic coverage is recommended after any periodontal, endodontic, or oral surgical procedures. For patients being placed under inhalation anesthesia for dental procedures, oxygenation is crucial. The anesthesiologist should address these issues.

Children with sickle cell anemia should be assessed dentally on a regular basis to ensure that dental and periodontal infections are eliminated, since a severe dental infection may precipitate a crisis attack. If nitrous oxide analgesia is to be administered, high oxygen levels must be maintained with a high flow rate.

Leukemias and lymphomas

Leukemias and lymphomas account for approximately 8% of all malignancies and presently represent almost 95,000 new cases diagnosed each year in the United States. In 2000, it was estimated that 62,300 were lymphomas (54,000 non-Hodgkin type) and 30,800 were leukemias. These malignancies afflict slightly more males than females. More than half of those afflicted will die from their disease. In children ages 1 to 14 years, malignancies are the leading disease-cause of death; leukemia is the most common malignancy within this cohort. Acute myelogenous leukemia (AML) occurs in all decades of life, but is primarily found in patients over the age of 40 years. Chronic myelogenous leukemia (CML) generally occurs in individuals older than 20 years, with frequency increasing with each succeeding decade. Lymphomas collectively represent several types of neoplasias of the lymphoreticular system

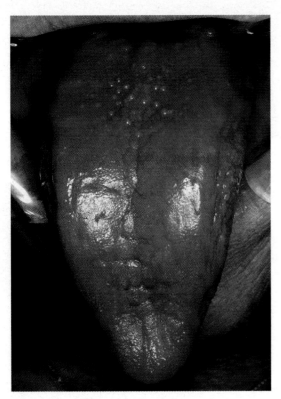

Figure 8–3 Atrophic glossitis in pernicious anemia.

Table 8–2 Oral Complications of Cancer Chemotherapy and Marrow Transplantation

Course of Toxicity	Oral Manifestation	
	Direct Toxicity	*Indirect Toxicity*
Acute	Oral mucosal damage	Myelosuppression
	Mucositis (mucosal atrophy, ulceration)	Neutropenia
	Salivary gland dysfunction	Immunosuppression
	Xerostomia	Anemia
	Neurotoxicity	Thrombocytopenia
	Taste dysfunction	Infection
	Dentinal hypersensitivity	Viral (HSV, VZV, CMV, EBV, other)
	Neuralgias	Fungal (*Candida, Aspergillus*, other)
	Temporomandibular dysfunction	Bacterial
		Gastrointestinal mucositis
		Nausea and vomiting
		Acute graft-versus-host disease
Chronic	Xerostomia–xerostomia decay	Chronic graft-versus-host disease
	Dental and skeletal growth and development (pediatric patients)	Late infections (HSV, VZV, HPV)
	Second primary tumors	Recurrent primary disease (relapse)

HSV = herpes simplex virus; VZV = varicella-zoster virus; CMV = cytomegalovirus; EBV = Epstein-Barr virus; HPV = hepatitis virus.

that share clinical characteristics. Distribution in humans varies. For example, incidence of Hodgkin disease exhibits two peaks: early adulthood and beyond the fifth decade. Multiple myeloma, which is diagnosed in almost 14,000 Americans each year, primarily affects patients older than 40 years.

Leukemia and lymphoma collectively represent a varied pattern of white blood cell abnormalities, a wide spectrum of signs and symptoms, and a spectrum of management approaches. A wide range of oral lesions can arise in patients with these diseases (Table 8–2). Presenting symptoms and signs as well as cancer treatment strategies are relevant to the dental practitioner regarding diagnosis and dental treatment. In many instances, oral lesions may be the first indication of the underlying leukemia or lymphoma. Furthermore, these patients can develop a high risk for systemic infection of oral origin secondary to their underlying disease or cancer therapies, which produce profound, prolonged immunosuppression.

Molecular and pathologic correlates of disease

Leukemias are neoplasms of the white blood cells. The disease occurs in all races and may develop at any age. In the United States, approximately 30,800 new cases of leukemia occurred in 2000. Approximately 50% of leukemia cases observed in Western countries are acute leukemias, about 30% being chronic lymphocytic leukemia (CLL) and about 20% being CML. Leukemias exhibit a slight predilection for males.

Leukemia can be caused by exposure to chemical carcinogens or high-dose ionizing radiation. Chemicals and drugs associated with development of leukemia include benzene, phenylbutazone, arsenic, and chloramphenicol. Genetic susceptibility also appears to increase risk of disease. Although animal models have established a role for oncogenic viruses in causing the disease, viral causation of human leukemia is not fully substantiated. Human T-lymphotrophic virus (HTLV-1) is linked to human adult T-cell leukemia/lymphoma. Despite widespread distribution of this virus worldwide, it accounts for a remarkably low percentage of leukemia in humans. Fulminant infection and hemorrhage are primary causes of death.

The classification of leukemia as acute or chronic principally depends on degree of white cell maturation (Figure 8–5) as well as cell-type of origin (eg, lymphocyte, granulocyte). Immunohistochemistry further aids in classifications that have direct implications for disease course, type, response to therapy, and long-term patient survival.

Clonal expansion of tumor cells can compromise normal hematopoiesis. This impairment results from the relentless mitosis of the leukemic cells, with resultant physical crowding of marrow spaces. In addition, leukemic cells appear to exert a chemically mediated inhibitory effect on normal hematopoiesis. Over time and as tumor burden increases, a functional neutropenia as well as thrombocytopenia and anemia may emerge. Increasing presence of leukemic blast cells in the peripheral blood occurs as disease progresses. Blast cells are incapable of normal physiologic and protective functions. Gene deletions and translocations on various chromosomes have been identified. These findings add to a better understanding of these malignancies regarding causation, patient risks, therapy, and prognosis.

Lymphomas represent malignant disorders of lymphocytes, histiocytes, and their precursors or progeny. The term malignant lymphomas refers to several neoplastic diseases of the lymphoreticular system that include Hodgkin lymphoma, non-Hodgkin lymphoma, Burkitt lymphoma, multiple myeloma, and mycosis fungoides.

An important distinction exists between Hodgkin lymphoma and non-Hodgkin lymphoma. Hodgkin lymphoma is characterized by morphologically distinct neoplastic giant cells (Reed-Sternberg cells), distinctive clinical features, including fever, and an uncertain target cell associated with the neoplastic transformation (Figure 8–6). The disease displays a bimodal age-and-incidence curve; one peak is associated with early adult life (under 30 yr of age), and the second peak with patients older than 45 years. There is no racial predisposition.

By comparison, non-Hodgkin lymphoma represents a wide range of disorders with associated important varia-tions in patient age at onset, primary cell of origin, and therapeutic response. The diseases collectively range from relatively indolent to rapidly fatal malignancies. Etiology of these lymphomas remains unknown, although radiation, viral infections, and immune deficiencies have been implicated. Approximately 55,400 new cases of non-Hodgkin lymphoma were diagnosed in the United States in 2000; a significant proportion occurs in immunosuppressed patients. The 30 to 40% 5-year survival rate associated with the disease is less favorable than that for Hodgkin disease. Non-Hodgkin lymphoma is the most rapidly escalating neoplasm in terms of frequency in human immunodeficiency virus (HIV)-infected patients, and is virtually fatal in this cohort (see Chapter 14).

Less common lymphomas include Burkitt lymphoma, mycosis fungoides, and lymphomas secondary to midline "nonhealing" granuloma. Collectively, these conditions affect all ages of patients. The African form of Burkitt lymphoma has a distinct association with Epstein-Barr virus, whereas the American form shows little association with the virus. The African form

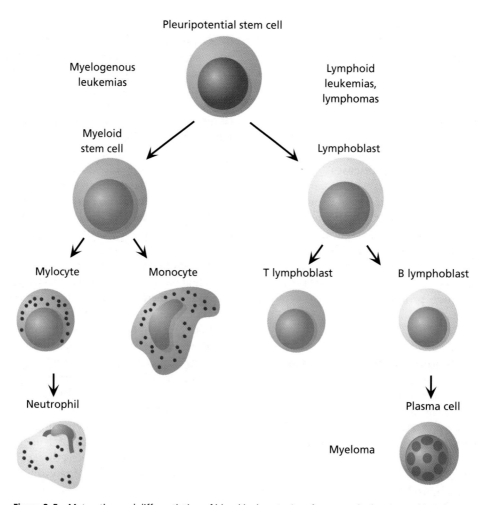

Figure 8–5 Maturation and differentiation of blood leukocytes in reference to leukemias and lymphomas.

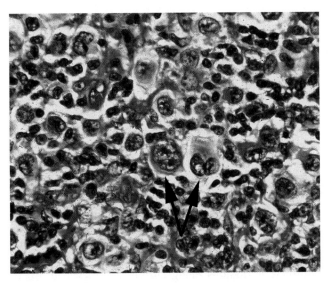

Figure 8–6 Reed-Sternberg cell in Hodgkin lymphoma.

exhibits a predilection for the mandible, whereas the American version typically initially involves lymph nodes and bone marrow. The neoplasms are treated with chemotherapy or radiation. They are not discussed further in this chapter because of their relatively low frequency of occurrence worldwide.

The non-Hodgkin lymphomas are subdivided into numerous variants, based on cellular phenotype, cell size, and formation or lack of formation of follicular structures (Figure 8–7). A combined American and European histopathologic classification system is used to standardize the morphologic diagnosis, which in turn is related to prognosis and response to radiation and specific chemotherapeutic agents. The lymphoid cells may be of B or T origin; immunohistochemical or flow cytometric analysis can be used to phenotype the tumor. All tumor cells in the mass are monoclonal, being derived from a single stem cell that has undergone neoplastic transformation. Clonality can be assessed by gene rearrangement studies that sample fresh tissue and determine if the B-cell immunoglobulin receptor or, in the case of T-cell lymphomas, the T-cell receptor is chemically identical for all tumor cells, thereby confirming monoclonality. As with leukemias, lymphoma cells harbor specific translocations of chromosomes and express increased levels of specific oncogenes and transcription factors, cell cycle regulatory molecules, and mutated tumor-suppressor genes.

Clinical features, diagnosis, and treatment

Leukemia

Acute leukemia can affect any component of the myeloid series (Figure 8–8); classically, the disease can be categorized into acute lymphocytic or acute myelogenous leukemia. The disease is typically aggressive and can lead to death within 6 months unless intensive cancer therapy is promptly initiated. Signs and symptoms of acute leukemia are associated with progressive marrow involvement secondary to expanding tumor burden and loss of normal hematopoietic cells. Patients with leukemia typically complain of fatigue, malaise, and occasional fever; they may also be aware of neck swelling or unexplained gingival bleeding. This constellation of symptoms may prompt them to seek dental evaluation. Infection, lymphadenopathy, night sweats, and weight loss may also be present.

The resulting neutropenia, anemia, and thrombocytopenia can lead to viral, bacterial, or fungal infection as well as fatigue, dypsnea on exertion, pallor, palpitations, and spontaneous hemorrhage. In addition, leukemic infiltrates can involve organ systems, including the oral cavity, especially gingiva. The diagnosis is suspected by history and clinical findings and is confirmed and staged by hematology and bone marrow assessment.

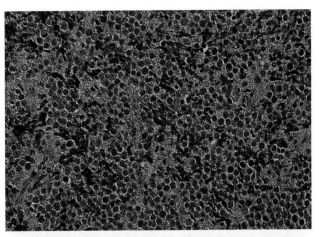

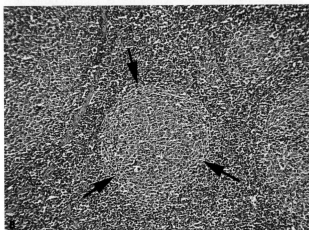

Figure 8–7 Non-Hodgkin lymphomas: *A,* diffuse pattern of lymphoid cells; *B,* nodular (follicular) pattern of lymphoid cells.

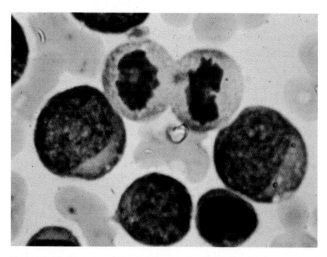

Figure 8–8 Acute myelogenous leukemia. The cells are characterized by prominent nuclei, consistent with the high mitotic rate. Tumor cell-population doubling times can be as frequent as every 18 to 24 hours in an untreated patient.

Treatment of acute lymphocytic leukemia can be divided into three phases. First, high-dose chemotherapy (remission induction) is administered, with a goal of eradicating microscopically detectable disease. Second, central nervous system (CNS) prophylaxis is instituted via intrathecal chemotherapy or carinal radiation, to eliminate tumor burden in the CNS. Third, maintenance chemotherapy is administered over the several years following completion of high-dose chemotherapy, to maximize length of disease-free status. This collective approach is associated with 50 to 80% of patients achieving a 3-year disease-free survival, with 75% of these patients cured of disease and requiring no further chemotherapy. In relapsed patients, allogeneic hematopoietic cell transplantation of bone marrow or peripheral blood origin is associated with approximately 50% long-term remission.

Acute myelogenous leukemia is considerably less sensitive to chemotherapy than is acute lymphocytic leukemia. Thus, AML is typically treated with more intensive therapy, including high-dose chemotherapy (induction phase) followed by moderately intense chemotherapy (maintenance phase). Induction therapy can produce short-term remission in 50 to 70% of patients, but long-term survival is generally only 1 to 2 years. Relapsed disease tends to exhibit increased resistance to subsequent high-dose chemotherapy. However, use of hematopoietic stem cell transplantation in recent years has improved long-term survivor data from less than 20% without transplant to 40 to 50% long-term remission with transplant.

Chronic leukemia can present insidiously, with diagnosis occasionally established during medical evaluations for other purposes. The disease typically progresses in indolent fashion; survival times in general are considerably longer with chronic leukemia than with acute leukemia. Chronic myelogenous leukemia is characterized by a profound leukocytosis characterized by multiple stages: (1) an initial chronic phase, in which an indolent elevation of white blood cells persists for several years; (2) an accelerated phase, in which white blood cell counts continue to increase despite the use of previously effective chemotherapy; and (3) ultimately, blast crisis, in which the disease clinically progresses in ways similar to acute leukemia, including resistance to chemotherapy. Currently, CML is principally managed via combined high-dose chemotherapy. However, expected life span is less than 1 year when the patient enters the blast crisis phase. Supralethal chemotherapy followed by stem cell transplant is emerging as an efficacious modality, with complete remissions being currently achieved in 40 to 50% of patients.

In contrast, CLL generally occurs in older adults; patients less than 35 years of age are rarely affected. The disease in the older age group is only slowly progressive, with patient survival often consistent with otherwise healthy peers. However, younger patients experience a more rapid disease progression, with expected life span of approximately 5 to 7 years.

Lymphomas

Hodgkin lymphoma

Initial clinical disease expression is generally associated with regional lymph nodes above the diaphragm. Head and neck nodes are involved in 60 to 80% of presenting cases. Clinical progression over time is varied and related to stage of disease at diagnosis. Diagnosis and staging involve microscopic lymph node confirmation and assessment of the extent of lymph node involvement. Localized cervical disease conveys an optimal prognosis and is generally responsive to localized radiation. However, in advanced cases, combinations of radiation and chemotherapy are used. The clinical course is typically one of cycles of remission followed by acute flares of the disease. Hematopoietic cell transplantation is being used with increasing frequency and success.

Non-Hodgkin lymphoma

The most prominent presenting feature in non-Hodgkin lymphoma is painless firm lymphadenopathy, with a predisposition to supraclavicular or cervical regions. Tumor masses can be extranodal (Figure 8–9). Patients also typically present with findings that include fever, unexplained weight loss, fatigue, diaphoresis, and pruritus. The diagnosis and staging, in addition to history and physical examination, involve microscopic confirmation (lymph node or extranodal

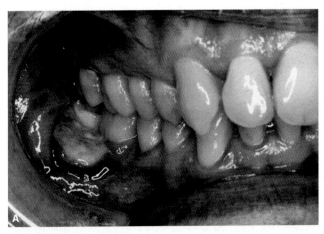 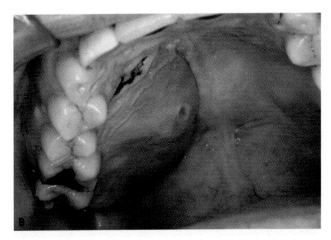

Figure 8–9 Non-Hodgkin lymphoma (NHL): *A*, gingival NHL in an HIV-positive patient who was severely immunocompromised; *B*, palatal NHL manifested as a slow-growing mass.

biopsy), hematologic and bone marrow evaluations, and magnetic resonance imaging (MRI). Treatment involves combinations of high-dose chemotherapy and radiation.

Multiple myeloma

Multiple myeloma represents a neoplasm of plasma cells in which tumor expansion produces a monoclonal gammopathy. Significant marrow compromise develops over time, with attendant leukopenia, anemia, and bleeding diatheses. In addition, multifocal lesions of bone, including the mandible and maxilla, can lead to pathologic fractures and pain. Prognosis is poor, with survivorship usually being less than 2 years following diagnosis.

Oral manifestations and their treatment

Head and neck symptoms and signs, including painless cervical lymphadenopathy or spontaneous gingival hemorrhage, can cause the patient to present for assessment by the dentist. Painless extraoral swelling, acute oral infections, and gingival enlargement or bleeding that cannot be exclusively attributed to local factors should prompt the dentist to consider systemic disease that includes these neoplasms.

Lymphadenopathy

Many of the lymphomas display cervical lymphadenopathy early in the clinical course. Approximately 23% of non-Hodgkin lymphomas occur within Waldeyer ring in the nasopharynx. Characteristics include firm, immobile painless masses with ill-defined borders. Unilateral distribution is a classic hallmark, although bilateral distribution does not rule out neoplasia. Biopsy is required to produce a definitive diagnosis.

Acute oral infections

Infections can be classified in two domains: lesions occurring in the undiagnosed patient and those occurring secondary to cancer therapy.

Infections occurring in the undiagnosed patient

The patient may present with mucosal, periodontal, or periapical infections that are disproportionately severe in relation to local etiologic factors. In addition, diagnosis of oral lesions not responding appropriately to routine therapy should be reconsidered, including a possible systemic basis. These infections should be evaluated in the context of a thorough health history with specific attention to systemic symptoms described previously in this chapter. Although oral infection management, including culturing, antibiotics, and surgical intervention where indicated, is important, referral to a

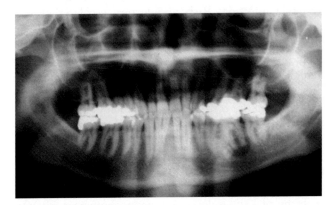

Figure 8–10 Panoramic radiograph delineating periapical pathosis associated with the mandibular left first molar. The patient was newly diagnosed with acute leukemia in blast crisis and had developed left mandibular space infection secondary to functional neutropenia and periapical disease. Despite aggressive oral and systemic therapy, the patient expired several days after presenting with the condition.

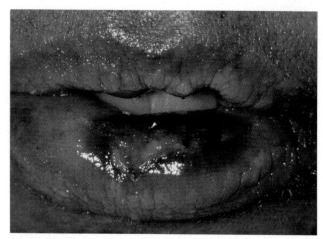

Figure 8–11 Herpes virus infection of mandibular labial mucosa in a neutropenic acute myelogenous leukemia patient.

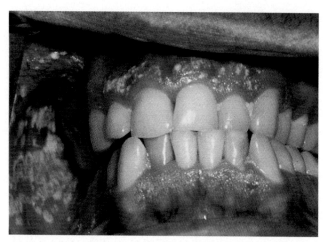

Figure 8–12 Pseudomembranous candidiasis in a xerostomic patient approximately 3 months following allogeneic hematopoietic cell transplantation. The functional compromise in salivary function secondary to graft-versus-host disease provided a setting for opportunistic fungal infection.

physician for additional evaluation of possible systemic cause is warranted.

Upon confirmation that leukemia or lymphoma has been diagnosed, the dental team plays a pivotal role in preparing the patient for cancer treatment, which both directly and indirectly involves oral tissues. Supportive care, including infection prevention, remains a hallmark of treatment of oral lesions prior to cancer therapy. Aspirin and other nonsteroidal anti-inflammatory drugs (NSAIDs) should be avoided, owing to deleterious effects on platelet adhesiveness. Invasive procedures, including periodontal scaling or dental extractions, should be performed in the context of consultation with the oncologist. Hematologic status and need for antibiotic prophylaxis if an in-dwelling catheter is present must be considered.

Infections occurring secondary to cancer therapy
The oral cavity represents a frequent portal of entry for systemic infection. Risk of infection escalates as the degree and duration of myelosuppression increases. In the patient with severe myeloablation, infections, including those of oral origin, can be fatal. Infections can develop at oral sites exhibiting chronic infection pre-chemotherapy (eg, chronic periodontal disease) or can occur in the context of nosocomial organisms.
Bacterial infections. Oral bacterial infections observed in myelosuppressed cancer patients are often those associated with periodontal and endodontic disease, although mucosal infection can emerge as well (Figures 8–10 and 8–11). Organisms typically classified as being of low virulence in immunocompetent patients can produce both local and systemic infection in these patients. Examples include gram-positive organisms including viridans streptococci and *Streptococcus mutans.* Furthermore, pathogens, including *Pseudomonas aeruginosa, Staphylococcus aureus,* and *Escherichia coli* can

emerge and cause infection of oral origin. These latter organisms are highly pathogenic and can result in death or substantial morbidity. Infection management should target these organisms in preventive or therapeutic regimens. Microbiologic documentation of causative organisms is essential in view of the nonspecific presentation of bacterial infections. It is important to recognize that secondary bacterial infection can occur with a wide range of oral lesions that may develop during myelosuppression.

Although not frequent in cancer patients with neutropenia cancer, acute exacerbation of preexistent periodontal disease can develop, with resultant systemic sequelae, including bacteremia. Clinical presentation can be subtle, since erythema and other inflammatory signs are typically suppressed during periods of profound myeloablation. Dental plaque can substantially increase risk of periodontal and associated systemic infection. Broad-spectrum antibiotic therapy should be considered while culture results are pending. In addition to systemic antimicrobials, oral interventions can include irrigation with effervescent (peroxide) agents, which are toxic to anaerobic bacteria colonizing the periodontal pocket, as well as gentle mechanical plaque removal, including dental brushing and flossing.
Fungal infections. Candidal infections are the most frequent oral fungal infections in the myelosuppressed or xerostomic cancer patient (Figure 8–12). The combination of myelosuppression, xerostomia, antibiotic-mediated floral shifts, and mucosal disruption and immune dysregulation contributes to clinical disease. The pseudomembranous variant occurs most often, although erythematous, hyperplastic, or invasive infection may also emerge. During periods of profound immunosuppression, invasive fungal infections caused

by organisms including aspergillus, histoplasmosis and mucormycosis may develop.

Relative to establishing a diagnosis, culturing is indicated for clinically-suspected pseudomembranous candidiasis. However, culturing may produce false-negative results involving other types of fungal infection. Gram stain or potassium hydroxide stain of scrapings is often helpful in identifying the presence of fungus. Biopsy may also be useful; but interventions including antibiotics or platelet support may be indicated depending on the hematologic status of the patient.

Treatment requires the use of antifungal drugs (see Chapter 18). Systemic fluconazole prophylaxis is often effective in preventing fungal infections during myeloablation. Topical medications include clotrimazole troches, nystatin oral suspension, pastilles, and amphotericin oral suspension. Compliance with drug dosing coupled with optimal oral hygiene should be reinforced. Hydrogen peroxide-saline mouthrinses (equal parts 3% hydrogen peroxide and normal saline) and 0.12% chlorhexidine can be effective against mild cases, although the products can be irritating when mucositis is present. Ultimate resolution of infection may not occur until marrow recovery is well established.

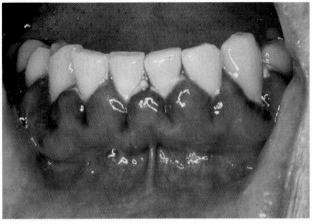

Figure 8–14 Gingival leukemic infiltrate in a patient newly diagnosed with acute myelogenous leukemia.

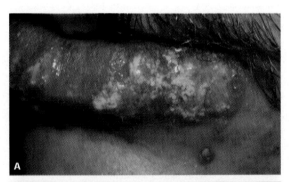

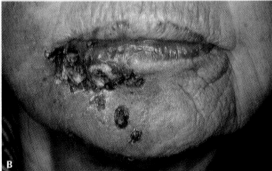

Figure 8–13 *A,* Severe herpes virus infection of mandibular labial mucosa in a myelosuppressed hematopoietic cell transplant patient. This lesion has several clinical features consistent with chemotherapy-induced oral mucositis. Differential diagnosis should thus include both herpes virus and chemotherapy-associated mucositis during the first 3 weeks post-transplantation. *B,* Reactivation of the varicella virus causing herpes zoster (shingles) in an immunosuppressed patient undergoing chemotherapy.

Viral infections. Viral infections represent important and frequent clinical complications in the myelosuppressed cancer patient (Figure 8–13). Many, but not all of the infections represent reactivation of latent virus, including herpes simplex virus (HSV), varicella zoster virus (VZV), or cytomegalovirus (CMV). Resulting ulcerations can be painful and persistent. Oral lesions caused by CMV, VZV, adenovirus, and coxsackie virus are occasionally observed in these patients, although HSV represents the most common viral infection with oral manifestations. Diagnosis is established best by culture techniques.

Treatment requires the use of antiviral drugs (see Chapter 13). Oral or parenteral acyclovir is the drug of choice for HSV prophylaxis and therapy. The drug is highly effective in both settings, with viral resistance being a rare occurrence. Patients who are seropositive prior to myeloablation should receive prophylactic drug during the period of marrow suppression. Oral dosing is often appropriate unless the patient has oral mucositis sufficiently severe to preclude enteral administration. Valacyclovir recently has been shown to provide enhanced plasma levels. Acyclovir or famciclovir are used for VZV infections; CMV is treated with ganciclovir.

Gingival enlargement or bleeding

Gingival infiltrates are classically associated with myelogenous leukemia but can occasionally occur with lymphocytic leukemia or lymphoma (Figure 8–14). Infiltrates are characterized by edematous, engorged, and painful periodontium that can bleed easily. The gingival changes are disproportionately severe in relation to local etiologic factors. Maintenance of optimal oral hygiene is essential to minimizing complications. Supportive care, including topical and systemic antibiotics or hemostatic measures may

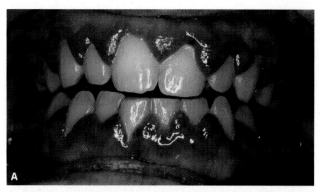 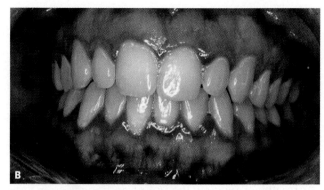

Figure 8–15 Patient with acute myelogenous leukemia. *A,* Sudden onset of painful, bleeding gingiva with associated fever and malaise. *B,* After chemo-induction therapy to control the acute signs and symptoms, a marrow transplant from the patient's histocompatible sister led to a remission.

be necessary prior to performing dental scaling and prophylaxis. However, primary management consists of induction-remission chemotherapy, whereby tumor burden can be substantially reduced or eliminated. Low-dose (eg, 900 cGy) radiation may be indicated in instances of gingival lesions that persist following chemotherapy.

Management of the oral cavity during myelosuppression

As previously noted, the myelosuppressed cancer patient is at high risk for acute local and systemic infection of oral origin. In addition, high-dose chemotherapy with or without stem cell rescue, or high-dose

Table 8–3 Stages of Stem Cell Transplantation

Stage Management Protocol	Reactions or Risks	Oral Implications
Stage I. Pretransplant patient assessment and identification of donor (prior to day –10) Comprehensive medical evaluation Decision on donor (autologous, allogeneic, matched or unmatched)		Elimination of oral foci of infection and trauma
Stage II. Conditioning to early engraftment (days –10 to +21) High-dose chemotherapy, to ablate patient's immune responsiveness and reduce tumor burden	Nausea and vomiting Fevers of unknown origin Veno-occlusive disease Acute GVHD	Institution of neutropenic mouth-care practices Xerostomia management secondary to anticholinergic medications for nausea Supportive care for ulcerative mucositis, xerostomia, pain, nausea Continued surveillance of neutropenic mouth-care practices GVHD management as needed
Stage III. Early engraftment to recovery of circulating counts (Days +22 to +100) Gradual reduction in risk from neutropenia, anemia, and thrombocytopenia	Risk for chronic GVHD	Ongoing supportive care per Stage II Introduction of conventional mouth-care protocols GVHD management as needed
Stage IV. Recovery of circulating counts to immune reconstitution (days +101 to +365) Anticipated immune recovery by 1 year post-transplant		Comprehensive oral care initiated when immune recovery permits Maintenance of optimal oral health over life span of patient
Stage V. Long-term survivorship (>1 yr post-transplant) Monitor for evidence of relapse or secondary malignancies Monitor for growth and development sequelae (pediatric cohorts)		Maintenance of optimal oral health over life span of patient Monitor for evidence of relapse or secondary malignancies Management of craniofacial development abnormalities as needed

GVHD = graft-versus-host disease.

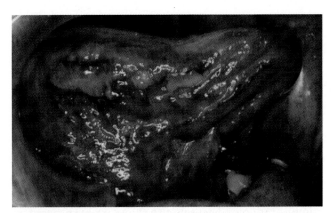

Figure 8–16 Severe pseudomembranous ulcerative oral mucositis in a neutropenic cancer patient. High-dose chemotherapy had been administered for 6 days. This lesion developed approximately 1 week after discontinuation of the chemotherapy. Oral mucositis can contribute to elevated risk of systemic infection, severe oral pain, and nutritional compromise unless comprehensively managed.

upper mantle head and neck radiation, can cause additional oral toxicities.

High-dose chemotherapy with or without stem cell rescue

Patients receiving these therapies typically experience ulcerative oral mucositis, dysgeusia, and xerostomia and are at risk for oral hemorrhage. In addition, allogeneic hematopoietic cell transplant patients may develop treatment-specific complications, including graft-versus-host-disease (GVHD).

Hematopoietic stem cell transplantation is generally used to treat acute myelogenous leukemia following remission induction or to treat other malignancies that have either failed to completely respond to conventional chemotherapy or that directly involve marrow (Figure 8–15). The transplant model can be discussed in the context of five stages (Table 8–3).

Oral mucositis

Severe ulcerative oral mucositis can result from high-dose chemotherapy or radiation to oropharyngeal tissues (Figure 8–16) (see Chapter 20). Etiology of the lesion is multidimensional and appears to include the following:

- direct injury to replicating basal epithelial cells by cytotoxic cancer therapy
- disturbances in mucosal immunity
- exacerbation of injury secondary to factors including metabolites produced by oral microflora
- wound-healing compromise secondary to infection and anemia

Mucositis causes significant pain, interferes with oral intake and other oral functions, and may be a por-tal for systemic infection in the myelosuppressed cancer patient. In addition, it can be a dose-limiting toxicity for selected chemotherapy regimens. Principal management interventions are directed to pain relief and oral hygiene (Table 8–4).

Protocols to topically manage mucositis should address appropriate dosing, efficacy, and patient compliance. A stepped approach in which topical agents are initially used, followed by intermittent or continuously administered systemic agents, can be implemented.

Bland oral rinses (0.9% saline, with or without 1–2 tablespoons/quart sodium bicarbonate) can moisturize, lubricate, and provide temporary relief for patients with mild to moderate mucositis. Patients may use the solution at room or chilled temperatures, depending on preference. A patient can then rinse gently with about 12-oz volumes and expectorate. This dosing scheme can be repeated as often as necessary to maintain oral comfort. It also facilitates production of saliva, thereby enhancing mucosal protection. Antacids and artificial salivas can also be considered, to promote patient comfort. For local areas of ulceration, hydroxypropylcellulose film-forming agents (eg, Zilactin®) can be applied to provide 2 to 6 hours of protection and pain relief.

Topical anesthetics can be introduced as mucositis pain increases. Viscous lidocaine, dyclonine, and diphenhydramine can be sprayed and rinsed, held for 1 to 2 minutes, and expectorated, as frequently as needed. Where possible, focal application is preferred versus

Table 8–4 Management of Oral Mucositis

Degree of Mucositis	Initial Therapy
Mild	Bland rinses
	0.9% normal saline
	Sodium bicarbonate solution
	Mucosal coating agents
	Antacid solutions
	Kaolin solution
	Water soluble lubricating agents, including artificial salivas
Mild to moderate	Topical anesthetics
	Viscous lidocaine
	Dyclonine rinse or spray
	Benzocaine sprays or gels
	Diphenhydramine solutions
	Hydroxypropyl cellulose film-forming agents (eg, Zilactin®)
Moderate to severe	Opiate analgesics
	Morphine: oral time-release, IV (bolus), patient-controlled analgesia
	Fentanyl: patches
	Meperidine

more broad dosing of mucosal surfaces. Rinsing with topical anesthetics carries the risk of reducing the gag reflex, which can potentially result in aspiration pneumonia; this risk is elevated when the rinse is gargled. Risk associated with systemic absorption of anesthetics does not appear to be increased in the setting of ulcerated oral mucosa; however, swallowing anesthetics can result in systemic toxicity. Care should be taken when patients anesthetize their mouths prior to eating, for reasons including increased likelihood of accidental mucosal trauma that can in turn increase the probability of additional trauma and infection.

Topically administered agents have a relatively short duration of effect; therefore, it is important to introduce systemic analgesics as soon as pain management with the above agents is deemed insufficient. Opiates formulated for timed release via tablets, skin patches, or by computerized patient-controlled analgesia (PCA) methods are interventions of choice. Studies have clearly shown that PCA results in superior pain control with significantly fewer drug doses and side effects.

Research is currently delineating interventions designed to prevent or reduce oral mucositis caused by chemotherapy or radiation. Nonsteroidal anti-inflammatory drugs and members of the prostanoid family have shown beneficial effects in initial clinical trials. Of note, benzydamine hydrochloride, a topical anti-inflammatory agent that has also shown analgesic properties, has undergone extensive testing in the United States and is likely to be approved for use for mucositis management. Preventive or therapeutic efficacy of oral sucralfate suspension, which is intended to form a protective coat, is not clear, based on several conflicting studies. New strategies directed at enhancing mucosal immune function or promoting wound healing are currently being tested. Approaches currently under study include low-energy helium-neon laser, cytokines (eg, epidermal growth factor, transforming growth factor-3, α-interferon, keratinocyte growth factor), and misoprostol (a prostaglandin analogue). Modification of oral microflora via administration of defensins also shows promise, based on early clinical trials. Moderation of oral mucositis by the administration of antioxidants has yet to be documented.

Oral hemorrhage

There are multiple reasons for oral hemorrhage in patients receiving cancer therapy, including thrombocytopenia, disseminated intravascular coagulation, hepatic disease, oral infection and mucosal trauma (Figures 8–17 and 8–18). Spontaneous mucosal petechiae and gingival bleeding typically occur at platelet levels of less than 20,000 to 30,000/mm³. Oral bleeding can be of concern to patients and care givers; pooling with whole saliva can give the appearance of more severe bleeding than actually exists.

Topical therapy should address formation of a stable clot and protection of the wound until initial

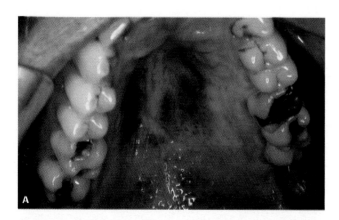

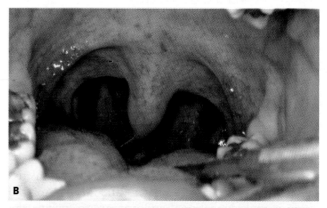

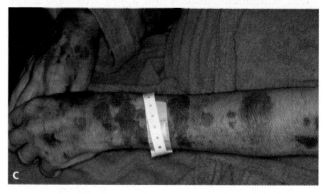

Figure 8–17 *A*, Submucosal bleeding of the palate in a thrombocytopenic cancer patient. Platelet count was approximately 35,000/mm³. *B*, Submucosal bleeding causing purpuric lesions of the posterior pharyngeal wall, in a patient with chemotherapy-induced thrombocytopenia (blood platelets <20,000). *C*, Multiple areas of subepidermal bleeding causing widespread ecchymoses of the skin in a patient with acute myelogenous leukemia and low platelet count.

epithelialization has been established. Gauze soaked in topical thrombin can be applied directly to the bleeding site. Application of ice can enhance vasoconstriction; alternatively, drugs, such as topical cocaine solution or epinephrine, can be used. Agents designed to enhance clot formation (eg, microfibrillar collagen) may contribute to organization and stabilization of clots. Topical or systemic aminocaproic acid may also be of value. Platelet transfusions may be necessary, depending on severity of bleeding diathesis or tissue invasiveness of a procedure.

Salivary gland dysfunction

Intact salivary function is an important component of oral host defenses against infections. Patients with salivary gland dysfunction are thus at risk for infections of the mucosa, dentition, and periodontium. Head and neck radiation can affect salivary gland function (see Chapter 20). Degree of injury is directly proportional to exposure of salivary tissue to ionizing radiation. Glandular doses in excess of 2500 cGy typically produce limitations in saliva production, which at higher dosages may be irreversible. Thus, salivary changes are commonly observed in patients receiving head and neck radiation for squamous cell carcinoma, Hodgkin lymphoma or non-Hodgkin lymphoma. By comparison, degree of salivary gland dysfunction in patients receiving chemotherapy varies. Recovery of gland function generally occurs within several weeks following discontinuation of chemotherapy.

Patients receiving radiation or chemotherapy typically receive a variety of drugs in addition to chemotherapy, including antiemetics or antihistamines. Many of these medications exert anticholinergic effects, resulting in xerostomia. Mouth breathing or oxygen masks can lead to further dessication of oral tissues.

Management of salivary gland dysfunction is important for several reasons, including reduction of mucosal trauma and infection, and improved quality of life (see Chapter 26). Frequent oral rinses with normal (0.9%) saline can stimulate salivary gland function and promote mucosal hydration and oral hygiene. Commercially available artificial saliva may provide temporary symptomatic relief. Salivary gland function can be stimulated via sugarless gum or candies, or by medications that function as secretagogues. For example, pilocarpine hydrochloride directly stimulates salivary gland function and has been shown to be useful for managing xerostomia. Dietary interventions, including use of moist foods (eg, flavored gelatins) and sauces and gravies, can increase the comfort of eating. The type and texture of nutrients that are effective in enhancing food intake varies among patients. Taste bud viability also may play a role regarding appetite and interest in eating. Dry or cracked lips should be kept lubricated

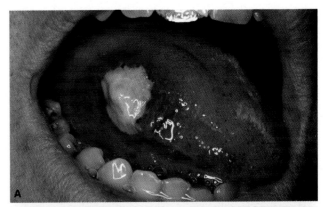

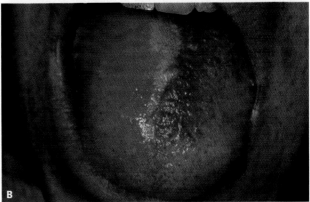

Figure 8–18 Leukemic patient undergoing chemotherapy (platelet count = 4000/mm³; white blood cell count = 700/mm³). *A,* Painful bleeding ulceration of the tongue that biopsy showed to be a leukemic infiltrate not responding to the treatment regimen. *B,* Control of the tongue infiltrate with low-dose radiation therapy.

with agents such as lanolin-based creams and nonmedicated skin moisturizers.

Rapidly progressive dental caries can be a particularly significant oral complication in patients who develop chronic xerostomia following radiation therapy or who have developed chronic GVHD following stem cell transplantation. The carious lesions result from a combination of a loss of remineralizing elements provided by saliva, loss of antimicrobial proteins and substances found in saliva, and an ecologic shift to increasingly cariogenic bacterial flora. Patient compliance with comprehensive management is critical to minimizing risks associated with these changes. This includes effective dental plaque removal via brushing and flossing, diet modifications to reduce sucrose intake, daily application of stannous or neutral sodium fluorides, and topical oral antimicrobial rinses (eg, chlorhexidine or povidone iodine).

Neurotoxicity

Selected chemotherapeutic agents, notably the vinca alkaloids vincristine and vinblastine, can directly cause neurotoxicity. Symptoms include severe, throbbing pain that can mimic pain secondary to dental disease, including irreversible pulpitis. Diagnosis is usually made by exclusion of more overt causes of dental, periodontal, or muscular origin. Opioid-containing analgesics are often effective for pain relief. The lesion generally dissipates over several weeks following discontinuation of the causative chemotherapeutic agent.

Chemotherapy patients may also develop a transient, mild to moderate dental hypersensitivity within weeks following initiation of chemotherapy. Although the etiology is not well understood, symptoms generally are responsive to topical application of fluorides or desensitizing toothpaste. The condition generally resolves several weeks after discontinuation of chemotherapy.

Patients receiving chemotherapy or head and neck radiation may also develop dysgeusia. The lesion apparently develops in the setting of disrupted regeneration of taste buds coupled with xerostomia that reduces delivery of taste stimulants to the taste bud receptors themselves. Olfactory disturbances can exacerbate dysgeusia. Also, cancer chemotherapy can occasionally diffuse into the oral cavity, thereby producing an offensive taste; this process is termed venous taste phenomenon.

Bruxism or clenching may develop in cancer patients owing to stress, sleep dysfunction, or selected medications that cause CNS toxicity. Temporomandibular dysfunction (TMD) can ensue; facial pain or headache are predominant symptoms. Management directed to underlying causative factors may include anxiolytics or muscle relaxants. Physical therapy, including moist heat applications, massage, and gentle stretching may also be effective. Patients with nocturnal bruxism may benefit from wearing customized occlusal splints while sleeping.

Alterations in craniofacial growth and development
High-dose chemotherapy can damage developing dental and skeletal structures in children and adolescents. Addition of radiation to treatment protocols (eg, cranial radiation for leukemia or total body irradiation for

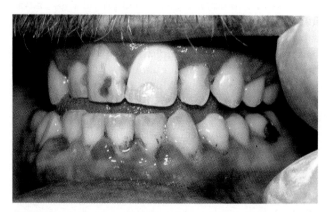

Figure 8–19 Lymphoma involving the gingiva in a patient with cancer previously treated with Cytoxan. Malignancies are a risk of long-term immunosuppression.

marrow transplants) significantly increases propensity for damage to developing teeth. Most severe effects are observed in patients treated for malignancy at ages younger than 5 years. Dental abnormalities include hypoplastic dentin and enamel, tooth crown discoloration, blunted or conical root formation, taurodontism, and diminutive teeth. Complete agenesis of teeth can occur in severe cases. Dental eruption can be compromised secondary to altered tooth development as well as disturbances in alveolar, mandibular, and maxillary osseous growth. These changes often produce the need for orthodontic or cosmetic management.

Second primary neoplasms
Second primary cancers are well recognized as potential complications for long-term survivors of high-dose chemotherapy and radiation therapy for cancer (Figure 8–19). Incidence rate for marrow transplant recipients ranges between 1% and 2%. In a study by the Seattle transplant group, the majority (63%) of the second malignancies associated with marrow transplant were hematologic malignancies (eg, non-Hodgkin lymphoma following treatment for leukemia) whereas 37% represented a wide variety of solid tumors. Skin and mucosal carcinomas are the most commonly diagnosed secondary solid tumors, including oral squamous cell carcinomas.

Graft-versus-host disease
Graft-versus-host disease most commonly occurs in allogeneic transplant recipients, although a clinically similar lesion mimicking acute GVHD can also develop in autologous transplant patients. Specific target tissues include skin, liver, lacrimal glands, and oral mucosa and salivary glands (Figure 8–20). Reasons for this distribution are not well-defined. The process is principally mediated via cytotoxic T cells present in the graft that react against host tissue. The basis for autoreactivity in autologous GVHD is less well understood than for allogeneic GVHD. Matching of patient and donor for major histocompatibility loci (eg, human leukocyte antigen) is a primary means of reducing risk for development of GVHD. Disparities at minor histocompatibility loci partially govern clinical expression as well.

Acute GVHD occurs between days 14 and 100 posttransplantation and is usually more limited in severity than chronic GVHD. Chronic GVHD classically occurs between days 100 and 500 post-transplantation and involves multiple organs. A given patient may develop either acute or chronic GVHD, or progress from acute into chronic forms. Graft-versus-host disease can be fatal, infection being a principal cause of death.

Immunosuppressive drugs are used prophylactically in allogeneic patients to reduce development of acute GVHD. Cyclosporine, methotrexate, prednisone, or FK-506 alone or in combination are drugs of choice for

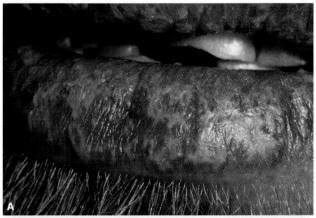

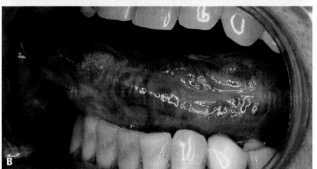

Figure 8–20   *A,* Chronic graft-versus-host disease (GVHD) day +103 following allogeneic hematopoietic cell transplantation. Note the white striae of the lip. This lichenoid presentation is commonly observed in patients with oral GVHD. *B,* Painful tongue ulceration and lichenoid lesion in a transplant patient manifesting GVHD.

administration from approximately day 7 to day 100 after transplantation. Notably, methotrexate given during the first 3 weeks following transplantation can exacerbate severity of oral mucositis. Oral complications secondary to cyclosporine prophylaxis do not usually develop, especially when blood levels are routinely monitored.

In most instances, oral GVHD occurs as a component of multisystem involvement. However, numerous instances of patients with oral GVHD as the only manifestation of disease have been observed. The most common clinical presentations are mucosal erythema and atrophy. Lichenoid changes associated with hyperkeratotic striae, papules, and plaques are also clinically distinctive. Severe disease can result in pseudomembranous ulcerations. The oral lesions are often painful and interfere with oral function. Xerostomia can be prominent, secondary to major and minor salivary gland compromise, and can lead to increased mucosal injury, pain, and infection.

Both systemic and topical therapy are generally indicated, since oral GVHD typically occurs concurrent with lesions at other sites. Systemic treatment includes high-dose immunosuppressive therapy with combination high-dose prednisone and cyclosporine. Steroid rinses, creams, ointment-pastes, or gels applied directly to the oral mucosal ulcerative lesions may promote healing by reducing inflammation. Ongoing maintenance of optimal oral hygiene is important in context of reducing risk for oral infection in the setting of dysregulated mucosal immune systems. Topical administration of cyclosporine or psoralen-ultra violet A (PUVA) intraoral therapy may also be of benefit, although further research is needed. Therapy continues until the GVHD subsides and graft tolerance occurs.

Both GVHD and its prophylaxis and treatment are immunosuppressive and significantly increase risk for infection. Active periodontal disease and dental infections should be eliminated. Patients should perform comprehensive oral hygiene practices, especially when receiving high-dose immunosuppressive therapy. Atypical presentations of recurrent herpes simplex and other viral infections as well as candidiasis can occur. Appropriate antimicrobial agents are frequently required as adjunctive treatment. Clinical vigilance is essential for prompt diagnosis so that treatment can be immediately instituted.

Suggested reading

Cherny NI. The management of cancer pain. CA Cancer J Clin 2000;50:70–116.

Dahllöf G. Craniofacial growth in children treated for malignant diseases. Acta Odontol Scand 1998;56:378–82.

Lucas VS, Roberts GJ, Beighton D. Oral health of children undergoing allogeneic bone marrow transplantation. Bone Marrow Transplant 1998;22:801–8.

Plevoá P. Prevention and treatment of chemotherapy- and radiotherapy-induced oral mucositis: a review. Oral Oncol 1999;35:453–70.

Schubert MM, Epstein JB, Peterson DE. Oral complications of cancer therapy. In: Yagelia JA, Neidle EA, Dowd FJ, eds. Pharmacology and therapeutics in dentistry. St. Louis: Mosby Year Book, 1998:644–55.

Schubert MM, Peterson DE, Lloid M. Oral complications. In: Thomas E, Blume KG, Forman SJ, eds. Hematopoietic cell transplantation. 2nd Ed. Oxford: Blackwell Science, 1999: 751–63.

Silverman S Jr, Kramer AM. Drugs for neoplastic disorders. In: Ciancio S, ed. ADA guide to dental therapeutics. 2nd Ed. Chicago: ADA Publishing, 2000.

Sonis ST. Mucositis as a biological process: a new hypothesis for the development of chemotherapy-induced stomatotoxicity. Oral Oncol 1998;34:39–43.

9 Endocrine Diseases

Carol M. Stewart, DDS, MS

Diabetes mellitus

Diabetes mellitus is a chronic metabolic disorder characterized by a relative or absolute lack of insulin that results in elevated blood glucose levels and produces disturbances in lipid and protein metabolism as well. Being the most common metabolic disorder, it affects 15 to 20 million Americans, roughly 2 to 4% of the population; many are yet undiagnosed. Diabetes mellitus produces multiple systemic complications, including nephropathy, retinopathy, accelerated atherosclerosis, neuropathy, delayed wound healing, and increased susceptibility to infections. It is clearly recognized for adverse effects on longevity and quality of life. With increasing disease prevalence and energized medical research initiatives, it is critical that the dental team maintain contemporary awareness.

The responsibility falls to the dental practitioner to (1) recognize signs and symptoms of diabetes, to facilitate early diagnosis and management; (2) appropriately manage oral conditions, to maximize oral function, comfort, and esthetics for the life of the patient; and (3) work in conjunction with the patient, the patient's physician, and diabetes management team, to facilitate long-term disease control.

The two most common forms of diabetes mellitus are characterized as type 1, autoimmune, which comprises about 5% of the cases, and type 2, non-autoimmune, which accounts for roughly 85% of cases. The term type 1 diabetes mellitus is often used synonymously for insulin-dependent diabetes mellitus (IDDM), and the term type 2 is used to characterize non–insulin-dependent diabetes mellitus (NIDDM). This classification can be confusing in that patients with NIDDM may need insulin to control their disease; however, they do not develop ketoacidosis if their insulin is withdrawn. Hence they are termed non–insulin-dependent. In contrast, patients with IDDM develop ketoacidosis in the absence of insulin (ketoacidosis-sensitive) and are therefore termed insulin-dependent.

Insulin-dependent diabetes mellitus is generally found in individuals under 40 years of age. Because disease onset often occurs during adolescence, it is descriptively called "juvenile onset." However, IDDM may occur at any age. Type 2 diabetes mellitus generally occurs in individuals over 40 years of age, and has been referred to as "adult onset." Secondary diabetes mellitus, which applies to the development of a diabetic state that originated secondary to another disease or condition, has also been characterized. Examples include pancreatic disease from chronic alcohol intake, hormonal diseases, such as hyperthyroidism, or the administration of drugs, such as exogenous corticosteroids. All three types of diabetes may be characterized by hyperglycemia and microangiopathy. This chapter focuses on type 1, IDDM, and type 2, NIDDM.

Molecular and pathologic correlates of disease

Both IDDM and NIDDM have a genetic component involved in their etiology. Studies have shown that the concordance rate between identical twins and type 1 diabetes is 50%, as compared to 80% in identical twins with type 2 diabetes. It is believed that susceptibility to IDDM is linked to specific alleles of the class II major histocompatibility complex. However, an environmental event, such as exposure to a virus, is believed necessary to trigger the development of diabetes. Following exposure to an environmental event, an inflammatory response called "insulitis" develops in the pancreas. The cells that infiltrate the islets are activated T lymphocytes. It is not clear at this time that insulitis is central to the destructive sequence in autoimmune diabetes. Next, the surface of the beta cell is transformed such that it is no longer recognized as "self," but is perceived by the immune system as a foreign cell. This stimulates the development of an immune response in which cytotoxic antibodies develop and act with cell-mediated immune mechanisms to destroy the beta cells. The precise mechanism behind the autoimmune destruction is unknown. When most of the beta cells are destroyed, diabetes mellitus type 1 manifests.

Type 1 diabetics have minimal or no endogenous insulin production as a result of autoimmune destruction of insulin-producing pancreatic beta cells (Figure 9–1). These individuals require exogenous insulin for control of glycemia and, without insulin, develop serious metabolic complications leading to ketoacidosis and coma. More specifically, when ingested food is converted into glucose, insulin secretion is normally stimulated. Insulin is essential for transfer of glucose from blood into muscle, fat, and liver tissues and for preventing the liver from converting glycogen stores into glucose. If insulin is not available, glucose levels increase in the blood and tissue fluids. Blood glucose rises from underuse of blood glucose as well as overproduction owing to glycogenolysis and fat metabolism. When hyperglycemia exceeds the renal threshold (roughly 200 mg/dL) glycosuria ensues. The excessive glycosuria induces an osmotic diuresis with polyuria (passage of large volumes of urine) which results in the loss of water and electrolytes. Increased urinary output coupled with vascular hyperosmolarity tends to deplete fluid reserves. Osmoreceptors in the thirst center of the brain sense the fluid loss and polydipsia (excessive thirst) results. The lack of glucose use by insulin-dependent cells, leads to glucose-starved cells. The patient often increases the intake of food (polyphagia) but, in many cases, still loses weight. Cortisol secretion may be increased in the type 1 diabetic, in response to the stress, which leads to protein breakdown and loss of nitrogen in the urine. As the process continues, the

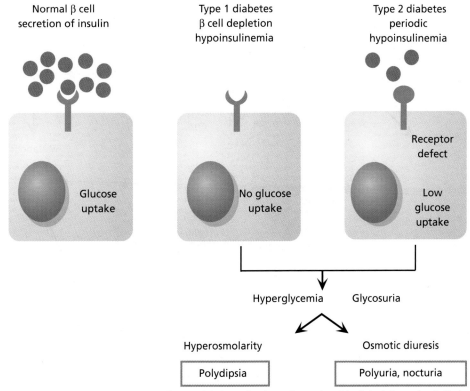

Figure 9–1 Hyperglycemia in both forms of diabetes leads to glycosuria with clinical signs of polydipsia, polyuria, and nocturia.

body metabolizes fat for energy, releasing free fatty acids, which are converted to harmful ketones (acetone and beta-hydroxybutyric acid) that are excreted in the urine. As this progresses, the individual develops metabolic acidosis, which can lead to coma and death if not quickly treated (Figure 9–2). Ketonic acid-buffering by sodium bicarbonate leads to generation of excess carbonic acid with increased respiratory rate (hypernea), a compensatory mechanism that attempts to raise blood pH by elimination of water and carbon dioxide.

Type 2 diabetes mellitus is the most common type of diabetes; but less is known about its etiology and onset. It is believed that genetic factors are more significant for type 2 than for type 1; but type 2 diabetes is not linked to any human leukocyte antigen (HLA) genes, being polygenic. Two metabolic defects may characterize type 2 disease: abnormal insulin secretion and inability of peripheral tissues to respond to insulin, perhaps related to a cell-surface insulin receptor defect. In early phases, glucose levels remain normal, owing to increased insulin release that balances the defective receptor-mediated insulin resistance. As insulin resistance increases, hyperglycemia develops. In the third phase, insulin resistance does not change, but insulin secretion declines, resulting in overt diabetes. It is likely that insulin secretory defects and insulin resistance are both required for diabetes to be expressed. Obesity increases an individual's susceptibility to NIDDM. Many obese type 2 diabetics can reverse impaired glucose tolerance simply by losing weight, especially if weight is lost early in the course of their disease. Obesity may play a critical role in the development of insulin resistance, but one must remember that insulin resistance is also encountered in nonobese patients with type 2 diabetes. As the longevity of the population increases, the prevalence of NIDDM will also increase. Table 9–1 and Table 9–2 summarize the general characteristics and symptoms associated with type 1, IDDM, and type 2, NIDDM.

Clinical features

Reports have indicated that diabetic patients are susceptible to complications that cause morbidity and premature mortality. A given patient may experience several complications simultaneously, or a single problem may dominate the clinical picture. Complications include

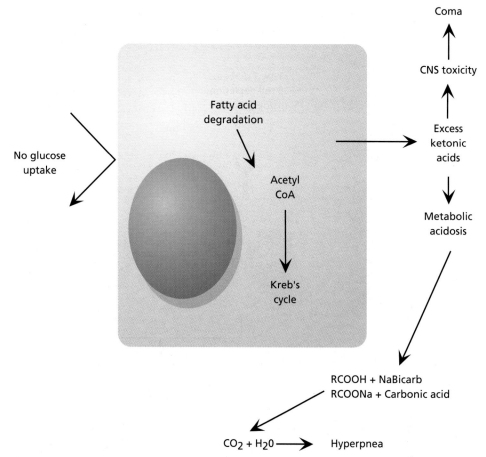

Figure 9–2 Ketosis occurs when fatty acids are required for generation of adenosine triphosphate (ATP) in the absence of intracellular glucose.

Table 9–1 General Characteristics of Type 1 and Type 2 Diabetes

Characteristic	Type 1 (IDDM)	Type 2 (NIDDM)
Frequency	5%	85–90%
Clinical	Onset abrupt	Onset gradual
Age	Onset < 20 yr of age	Onset > 40 yr of age
Weight	Normal	Obese (80%)
Endogenous insulin	Inadequate or absent	Low, normal, or high levels
Islet cell antibodies	Present	Absent
Ketoacidosis	Common	Uncommon
Genetics	HLA-D linked	No HLA association
Concordance in identical twins	50%	90–100%
Pathogenesis	Autoimmunity to pancreatic beta cells	Insulin resistance

IDDM = insulin-dependent diabetes mellitus; NIDDM = non–insulin-dependent diabetes mellitus; HLA = human leukocyte antigen.

retinopathy, nephropathy, neuropathy, macrovascular disease, and impaired wound healing (Figure 9–3). Medical complications are related to the level of hyperglycemia and pathologic changes within the vascular system and the peripheral nervous system. Hyperglycemia appears to play a major role in development of atherosclerotic plaques, which enhance development of hypertension, stroke, and myocardial infarction. Atherosclerosis develops earlier and is more prevalent and more advanced in diabetic than in nondiabetic individuals. Uncontrolled diabetics have higher levels of low-density lipoprotein (LDL) cholesterol and lower levels of high-density lipoprotein (HDL) cholesterol. Myocardial infarction is a leading cause of death in patients with NIDDM. Atherosclerotic lesions also produce intermittent claudication, poor wound healing, and gangrene.

Small-vessel changes, including thickening of the intima and lipid deposition, are especially significant in the retina of the eye and small vessels of the kidney. Diabetic retinopathy is one of the leading causes of blindness. Diabetic nephropathy progresses to end-stage renal disease in 30 to 40% of individuals with IDDM. Nearly one-fourth of individuals using renal dialysis are diabetic.

Diabetic neuropathy may affect every system, with the possible exception of the brain. It is a major cause of morbidity. Peripheral neuropathy is generally bilateral and symptoms include numbness, paresthesias, hyperesthesias, and pain.

The relation between control of glucose levels and progression of diabetic complications is becoming more clear as research continues. Microvascular-related complications can be diminished by good control of glycemia. Improved control of glycemia has also been associated with a reduction in macrovascular complications. Since hyperglycemia also plays a major role in diabetic neuropathy, improved control seems appropriate. Efforts should be made to control hyperglycemia, but such therapy should not introduce a high incidence of dangerous hypoglycemic reactions.

Table 9–2 Symptoms of Diabetes

Type 1 (IDDM)	Type 2 (NIDDM)
Polydipsia	Paresthesias
Polyuria	Nocturnal urination
Polyphagia	Visual changes
Weight loss	Weight loss or weight gain
Visual changes	Loss of sensation
Recurrence of bed wetting	Postural hypotension
Thirst or dry mouth	
Headache	
Irritability	

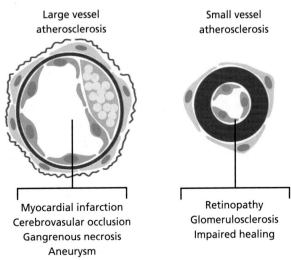

Figure 9–3 Both large- and small-vessel disease are complications of diabetes.

It is uncertain if strict control of glycemia in patients with NIDDM would significantly reduce long-term complications, but improved control has been recommended by the American Diabetes Association. Management of NIDDM may require oral hypoglycemic agents as well as dietary and exercise therapy. Insulin injections may be added to the regimen.

Screening tests are available for individuals who show signs and symptoms and those in risk groups, such as individuals who are over 40 years of age, obese, have diabetic relatives, or females with gestational diabetes. A normal fasting blood glucose level ranges from 60 mg/dL to 100 mg/dL. The National Diabetes Data Groups of the National Institutes of Health, in 1979, provided revised criteria for the diagnosis of diabetes. A fasting blood glucose greater than 140 mg/dL on two occasions is generally considered diagnostic for diabetes mellitus. A 2-hour postprandial glucose assay requires the patient to ingest 75 to 100 g of glucose after a night of fasting. Blood glucose levels taken 2 hours after glucose ingestion that are greater than 200 mg/dL on two occasions are diagnostic of diabetes mellitus. These measures provide the blood glucose level at the time the blood was drawn and reflect intake from the previous 2 to 10 hours. With the availability of home monitoring equipment, many patients, especially those taking insulin, monitor their blood levels at home and are keeping a log to share with their physicians. Patients are taking a more active role in their disease management.

After the diagnosis and implementation of initial therapy, the overall goal of medical management is the prevention of diabetic complications through adequate control of glycemia. The primary assay used for assessing long-term control is the glycosylated or glycated hemoglobin assay, termed the HbA$_{1c}$ or HbA$_1$ assay. This test indicates the blood glucose concentrations during the previous 6 to 8 weeks. The clinical interpretation for this assay is listed in Table 9–3. This assay is not to be used as a screening or diagnostic assay for diabetes.

Although diet and exercise therapy are important in the management of diabetes, all IDDM and some NIDDM patients require insulin therapy to maintain disease control. A variety of insulin preparations are available for use in the treatment of diabetes mellitus. The goal is for the physician to provide the patient a steady supply of insulin through the day and higher concentrations at mealtimes. Insulins vary in time of onset and duration. Most patients require a combination of preparations that include rapid-acting insulins and more slowly absorbed insulin suspensions. Insulin pumps use regular or Lispro insulin to match the peak activity of the injected insulin with the peak absorption of glucose. Table 9–4 provides a list of commonly used insulin products.

Table 9–3   Evaluation of Diabetes: Control of Glycemia

Glycohemoglobin Level (HbA$_{1c}$)	Clinical Interpretation
4–6%	Normal
Less than 7.5%	Good diabetes control
7.6–8.9%	Moderate diabetes control
>9%	Poor diabetes control

The most serious consequence of insulin overdose is hypoglycemia. Drowsiness, irritability, and confusion might signal mild hypoglycemia. Coma, spasms, or seizures could develop if severe hypoglycemia develops. Of special note is the use of beta-adrenergic blockers by diabetic patients. Tachycardia often serves as a warning to patients of impending hypoglycemia. Beta-adrenergic blockers mask the tachycardia and allow hypoglycemia to progress. Long-term use of insulin can also lead to the development of insulin antibodies, requiring larger doses to compensate for antibody-mediated elimination.

Patients with NIDDM often use oral hypoglycemic or anti-hyperglycemic agents to aid control of glycemia (Table 9–5). Oral sulfonylureas represent a commonly used class in this group of medications. The first generation agents include chlorpropamide, tolbutamide, tolazamide, and acetohexamide. Second generation agents include glyburide and glipizide. These agents are commonly given to diabetics whose fasting glucose level is lower than 250 mg/dL.

Sulfonylurea agents activate beta cells to increase insulin output in patients. The second generation drugs appear to be more potent and require a lower daily dosage. In addition, they produce less displace-

Table 9–4   Insulin Preparations

Type	Time of Onset (hr)	Duration (hr)
Fast-acting insulins		
Lispro	15 min	< 5 hr
Insulin injection (regular)	30–60 min	6–8
Prompt insulin zinc suspension (Semilente)	1–2	12–16
Intermediate-acting insulins		
Isophane insulin suspension (NPH)	1–2	18–28
Insulin zinc suspension (Lente)	1–3	18–28
Long-acting insulins		
Protamine zinc insulin suspension	4–8	36
Extended insulin zinc suspension (Ultralente)	4–8	20–36

NPH = neutral protamine hagedorn.

Table 9–5 Oral Agents for Diabetes Mellitus

Agent	Generic Name	Brand Name
Sulfonylureas:		
oral hypoglycemic		
First generation	Chlorpropamide	Diabinese
	Tolbutamide	Orinase
	Tolazamide	Tolinase
	Acetohexamide	Dymelor
Second generation	Glyburide	DiaBeta, Micronase
	Glipizide	Glucotrol
	Glimepiride	Amaryl
Biguanides: oral antihyperglycemic	Metformin	Glucophage
Thiazolidinediones: oral antihyperglycemic	Rosiglitazone	Avandia
	Pioglitazone	Actos
Alpha-glucosidase inhibitors	Acarbose	Precose
Meglitinide: insulin enhancers	Repaglinide	Prandin
	Nateglinide	Starlix

ment from protein binding sites and hence have less frequent interactions with other agents such as salicylates and warfarin. At high dosages, acetohexamide has been associated with additional side effects such as gastrointestinal upset and hypersensitivity to sunlight. All sulfonylurea agents are capable of producing severe hypoglycemia, and patient selection and usage in conjunction with other medications must be carefully evaluated.

Biguanides are used in the treatment of NIDDM, alone or in combination with oral sulfonylurea agents. Biguanides are not chemically or pharmacologically related to oral sulfonylureas. Unlike sulfonylureas, the biguanides do not increase secretion of insulin. They reduce hyperglycemia by improving insulin sensitivity, and enhance the glucose uptake in cells. They also inhibit gluconeogenesis and appear to reduce glucose absorption from the gut. Metformin (Glucophage) does not produce hypoglycemia and does not change insulin secretion. Metformin is contraindicated in patients with renal dysfunction and has been associated with a very low incidence of fatal lactic acidosis.

The class of drugs, thiazolidinediones, appears to heighten cellular responsiveness to insulin in muscle and adipose tissue. One of the first medications in this class, troglitazone (Rezulin) was removed from the market in 2000 because of liver toxicity and associated patient mortality. Two second generation "glitazones," as the class is informally called, were approved in 1999. Rosiglitazone is a highly selective and potent agonist for the peroxisome proliferator-activated receptor gamma (PPAR-γ) found in tissues such as adipose, skeletal, muscle, and liver. The mechanism is thought to involve

binding to nuclear receptors that regulate the transcription of a number of insulin-responsive genes critical for the control of glucose and lipid metabolism. It does not stimulate insulin release, nor does it function in the absence of circulating insulin. Rosiglitazone (Avandia) has been approved for monotherapy use or in combination with metformin in patients with Type 2 diabetes who are not able to be controlled with diet and exercise alone. Pioglitazone (Actos) also functions to decrease insulin resistance and was approved for use as monotherapy or in combination with insulin or a sulfonylurea drug such as glyburide or glipizide. These medications should be used with caution in patients with heart failure, edema, or liver disease, and they may affect ovulation. The second generation thiazolidinedione drugs appear to have less risk of liver toxicity than troglitazone, however, monitoring of liver function is recommended.

Acarbose (Precose) is an alpha-glucosidase inhibitor for use in the management of NIDDM. It slows the digestion and uptake of carbohydrates from the gastrointestinal system, lowering the post-prandial peaks in blood glucose. It does not cause hypoglycemia, but when taken with sulfonylureas or insulin, the delay of glucose into the blood stream could lead to relative insulin excess and hypoglycemia. Acarbose is contraindicated in patients with inflammatory bowel disease and marked disorders of digestion.

The insulin enhancers are very short acting agents that stimulate the release of insulin from beta cells. Repaglinide (Prandin) and nateglinide (Starlix) are designed to be taken with each meal and skipped if a meal is omitted. These medications should be used cautiously in patients with impaired renal function or impaired liver function. The hypoglycemic action may be potentiated by nonsteroidal anti-inflammatory agents, salicylates, and several other medications that are highly protein bound.

For proper management, a thorough medication history with special attention directed at potential drug interactions is critical. New medications and contraindications with existing agents are constantly being recognized. Reference to a current pharmacology text or a recognized drug-interaction program is recommended prior to initiating therapy.

Oral manifestations

Diabetes is associated with several oral manifestations, primarily those related to infections, inflammations, and poor wound healing. Hyperglycemia, ketoacidosis, and vascular-wall disease contribute to the increased susceptibility of uncontrolled diabetics to infection and the decreased ability to manage infections. Hyperglycemia has been shown to reduce the phagocytic function of leukocytes. Associated vascular-wall changes inhibit blood flow and the transport of granulocytes to the area of injury. Xerostomia and effects associated with reduced salivary flow rates are also problematic. These conditions have significant implications for dental care.

Several studies have reported an increased incidence and severity of gingival inflammation, periodontal abscess, and chronic periodontal disease in diabetic patients (Figure 9–4). Microvascular disease in the periodontium adversely affects blood flow and leukocyte migration and predisposes to premature periodontal disease, abscess, and delayed wound healing.

Research strongly supports cessation of cigarette smoking to aid maintenance of periodontal health, especially in patients with diabetes. Data also support the concept that in diabetes-associated periodontitis, the altered host inflammatory response plays a critical role. An unexpected high level of gingival crevicular fluid mediators was found among subjects with IDDM, even in the patients with gingivitis and mild periodontitis. Diabetics had significantly higher gingival cervical fluid levels of both prostaglandin E_2 (PGE_2) and interleukin (IL)-l beta when compared to nondiabetic controls with similar periodontal status. These findings suggest that IDDM is a significant risk factor for more severe periodontal disease, because as compared to nondiabetics, diabetic subjects react with an abnormally high degree of inflammation to an equivalent bacterial burden. Other findings suggest that both hyper- and hypoglycemia might directly impair the biologic functions of periodontal connective tissues through cell–matrix interactions.

Well-controlled diabetic patients, as measured by blood glycated hemoglobin levels, have less severe periodontal disease than poorly controlled diabetics. Recent findings indicate that effective control of periodontal infection in patients with diabetes (IDDM and NIDDM) reduces the level of advanced glycosylation end-products in the serum. If this is confirmed via additional studies, periodontal infection control must be considered as an integral part of medical management of diabetic control.

Oral candidiasis occurs more frequently in diabetics than in nonaffected populations, because of altered response to infections and xerostomia and an altered oral flora (Figure 9–5). After confirmation of diagnosis, topical or systemic antifungal agents can be prescribed as appropriate (see Chapter 18).

Antral mucormycosis is a rare but serious complication associated with immunocompromised status that accompanies uncontrolled or chronic IDDM. Signs and symptoms include nasal obstruction, bloody nasal discharge, facial pain, swelling, and visual dis-

turbances. Progression of disease leads to blindness, seizures, and death (Figure 9–6). The patient should be referred to an infectious disease specialist for appropriate management.

Burning tongue may be associated with fungal infections, such as candidiasis, or peripheral neuropathies associated with diabetes. A cytologic smear can confirm the diagnosis of oral candidiasis and proper treatment can be initiated. The diagnosis of peripheral neuropathy

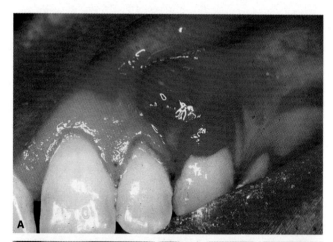
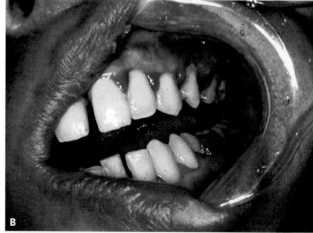
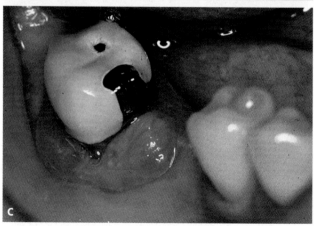

Figure 9–4 Periodontitis and periodontal abscesses in diabetes.

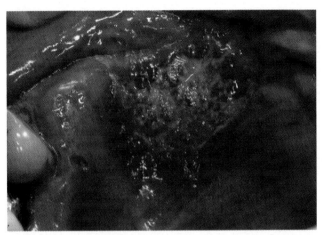

Figure 9–5 Candidiasis in a patient with insulin-dependent diabetes (brittle diabetes).

should be concluded after other probable causes have been ruled out by consultation with the patient's physician and an oral medicine specialist.

Xerostomia may result from hyperglycemia and subsequent polyuria that depletes the extracellular fluids. The overall effect is reduction in secretion of saliva. Adequate salivary flow is recognized to be an essential component for normal mastication, taste, and swallowing functions. Saliva plays a critical role in the lubrication and protection of the oral mucosa, neutralizing harmful acid that can lead to dental caries and destroying microorganisms. Diminished flow can increase susceptibility to oral ulcers, bacterial, viral or fungal infections, and dental caries.

Dental management

Dental management of the diabetic patient should include four primary areas:

1. Screening and diagnosis of previously undiagnosed patients (based upon a health history review and oral examination),
2. Proper dental management of oral manifestations,
3. Prevention of complications during procedures related to hypoglycemic shock, hyperglycemic shock, and acute cardiovascular episodes, and
4. Proper management of medical emergencies.

Screening and referral for diagnosis should be based upon a thorough review of the patient's health history and oral examination. Chairside glucose screening might provide helpful information. Patients suspected of having diabetes should be referred to a physician for definitive diagnosis and long-term management.

An assessment of the impact of diabetes mellitus on oral health should be included in the overall patient

management. All patients diagnosed with diabetes should be identified by history, type of diabetes, treatment regimen, and presence of medical complications. It is extremely beneficial to determine the severity of the disease and degree of control of glycemia. A few screening questions might assist in that process.

- When were you diagnosed?
- When did you last visit your physician and how often do you go?
- What are your current medications?
- When was your last blood glucose measurement and what was the value?
- Do you home-monitor yourself?
- When was the last time you had an insulin reaction?
- When was the last time you went to the local hospital emergency room with complications related to your diabetes?

The diabetic patient who is receiving good medical management and is well controlled without serious complications, such as renal disease, hypertension, or coronary artery disease, can safely receive any indicated dental treatment. A diabetic patient whose disease is well controlled and who is free of infection does not require prophylactic antibiotics for dental treatment. However, some consideration should be given to helping prevent unanticipated events during dental care.

For patients with IDDM, the following special management considerations should be reviewed:

1. Patients should be scheduled when their glucose is high and insulin activity is low—usually morning appointments.
2. Patients should be instructed to take their usual insulin dosage and to eat their normal breakfast before the dental appointment.
3. Nutritional intake and insulin levels should be reviewed with the patient prior to dental procedures.
4. Vital signs should be monitored.

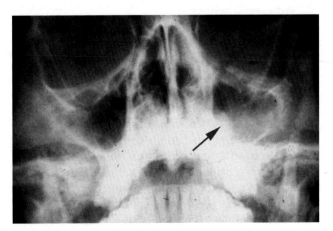

Figure 9–6 Sinus radiograph showing erosion of lateral wall.

5. Patients should be instructed to inform the dentist if they feel the onset of an insulin reaction.
6. The dentist should observe for signs of hypoglycemia and treat as appropriate.
   - Signs of hypoglycemia vary among individuals. The dentist should observe the patient for any of the following signs or symptoms and initiate treatment:
     a. Hunger, weakness, fast heartbeat, tingling, or altered sensations,
     b. Confusion or mood alteration,
     c. Sweating or pallor, and
     d. Disorientation
   - Treatment
     If conscious, administer glucose via beverage (cola or juice) containing glucose.
     If initial signs of hypoglycemia are not apparent, hypotension and a fast weak pulse may develop and the patient may become unconscious.
   - Treatment
     If unconscious, administer 50% dextrose, 30 to 50 mL, intravenously, or 1 mg glucagon, intramuscularly.
     Any patient who has experienced unconsciousness should be taken to a hospital for further evaluation and treatment.
7. The dentist should consider factors that will contribute to development of hypoglycemia.
   - Hypoglycemia can develop if patients received their insulin injections, but failed to eat.
   - Hypoglycemia can result if patients received too much insulin or oral hypoglycemic agent.
   - Hypoglycemia can result through adverse drug interactions.
     a. Sulfonylureas and aspirin enhance the hypoglycemic effect of oral hypoglycemic agents.
     b. Sulfonylureas and fluconazole enhance the hypoglycemic effect of oral hypoglycemic agents.
8. The dentist should treat oral infections promptly and aggressively.
   - Medical consultation regarding glycemic status and insulin therapy is indicated.
   - If purulence is associated with the oral infection, culture should be obtained if possible. Penicillin or amoxicillin could be initiated until culture and sensitivity results are obtained.
   - Close follow-up should be maintained until the patient is stable and the condition has resolved.
9. The dentist should review the following considerations when planning for surgical procedures:
   - If the return to regular food intake is anticipated immediately following the procedure, no alteration in diet or insulin is necessary.
   - If the anticipated procedure will not allow the patient to return to regular food intake, consultation with physician prior to the procedure may be appropriate.
     a. For the insulin-controlled patient, the normal dose of insulin is often decreased the morning of the surgical procedure. Slight hyperglycemia during a procedure is certainly preferable to hypoglycemic shock.
   - In all cases, patients should be advised that the recommended nutritional intake is important to attain anticipated postoperative recovery.
   - Prophylactic antibiotics may be recommended to prevent infection in patients with poorly controlled diabetes and those with a history of recurrent infection.

Diabetes insipidus

Diabetes insipidus is a condition caused by a neurohypophyseal lesion, either inflammatory or neoplastic in nature, in which renal conservation of water is impaired owing to deficient antidiuretic hormone (ADH) release. Vasopressin, also called antidiuretic hormone, affects the control of water conservation and its release in coordination with the activity of the thirst center that regulates fluid intake. Via actions on receptors in the distal tubules of the kidney, ADH conserves water and concentrates the urine. This action assists in maintaining constancy of the osmolarity and volume of body fluids.

Molecular and pathologic correlates of disease

There are five primary causes for the development of diabetes insipidis, all of which result in damage, necrosis, or loss of function of the CNS cells that secrete ADH: (1) infiltrative lesions of the hypothalamus or pituitary as a result of neoplasms, leukemia, sarcoidosis, or histiocytosis (Langerhans cell histiocytosis); (2) pituitary or hypothalamic surgery; (3) severe head injuries; (4) vascular lesions; (5) idiopathic cause.

Clinical features

Polyuria, frequent urination and polydipsia, excessive thirst, are almost invariably present. Characteristically, these symptoms are sudden in onset. Urine may be pale in color and volume immense—up to 16 to 24 L per day accompanied by frequent urination, every hour, day and night. More frequently, urine volume is only moderately increased 2 to 6 L per day or even less. Diagnosis is determined by plasma or urinary ADH levels or by measuring urinary osmolality after dehydration and again after vasopressin administration.

Oral manifestations and dental management

Infiltrative lesions of the neurohypophysis as a result of Langerhans cell histiocytosis have implications for dental treatment. Histiocytes may infiltrate the posterior pituitary, resulting in decreased output of ADH, with resultant polyuria. Retro-orbital infiltrates of histiocytes may lead to exophthalmos, and osseous infiltrates are typically found in the skull and jaws. In addition, osseous infiltrates can be identified via conventional dental radiography. In addition to jaw lesions, one might observe loosening of the teeth or teeth "floating in space" (Figure 9–7). Langerhans cell histiocytosis can be treated successfully with *Vinca* alkaloid chemotherapy. Radiation therapy is sometimes needed. Jaw lesions are usually treated by local curettage. Extraction of involved teeth is often required.

Dental fluorosis has been reported as a complication of hereditary diabetes insipidus. Such patients demonstrate polydipsia and polyuria from early infancy. Drinking large amounts of water, even with lower than accepted fluoride content, can produce fluorosis of the teeth. In one study, six affected members from two families with hereditary diabetes insipidus were reviewed. Two children who drank water fluoridated at optimum levels developed moderate to severe fluorosis. Four affected patients who did not consume fluoridated water showed normal dentitions. In a second study, a mother and her four children presented different degrees of fluorosis directly related to the stage at which hormonal therapy was introduced.

Addison disease

Both hyperfunction and hypofunction of the adrenal glands can have profound effects on dental management of affected individuals. The following sections address primary and secondary adrenal insufficiency and hyperfunctioning of the adrenal cortex.

Molecular and pathologic correlates of disease

The adrenal glands are located on the superior aspect of each kidney and consist of two defined portions that provide several special functions. The outer portion of the gland, the adrenal cortex, produces three groups of steroid hormones: glucocorticoids, mineralocorticoids, and androgens. They are derived from cholesterol and share a common core structure. The adrenal cortex has three zones (Figure 9–8). The outermost zona glomerulosa produces mineralocorticoids, primarily aldosterone, which are critical for sodium and potassium balance and extracellular fluid volume. The zona fasciculata and the innermost zona reticularis secrete the glucocorticoid, cortisol, and androgens. Cortisol is essential for metabolism, anti-inflammatory properties, and maintenance of homeostasis during periods of physical or emotional stress. The inner portion of the gland, adrenal medulla, produces catecholamines, epinephrine (adrenalin), and norepinephrine (noradrenalin).

Cortisol secretion is regulated by the hypothalamic-pituitary-adrenal axis. The circadian rhythm, mediated by the CNS, and responses to stress stimulate the hypothalamus to release corticotropin-releasing hormone (CRH), which stimulates the production and secretion of adrenocorticotropic hormone (ACTH) by the anterior pituitary. The adrenal cortex is stimulated by ACTH to produce and secrete cortisol. Circulating plasma cortisol levels are elevated within minutes after stimulation in a normally functioning gland. The increased levels of cortisol act to inhibit the production of CRH and ACTH, and thereby decrease the output of cortisol This process constitutes the negative feedback loop of cortisol

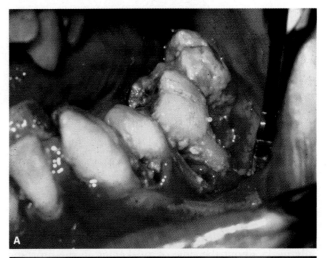

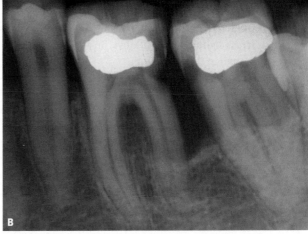

Figure 9–7 *A,* Gingival erosion is seen in Langerhans cell histiocytosis in a child who presented with a chief complaint of polyuria; *B,* radiograph showing alveolar bone resorption from infiltrating histiocytes.

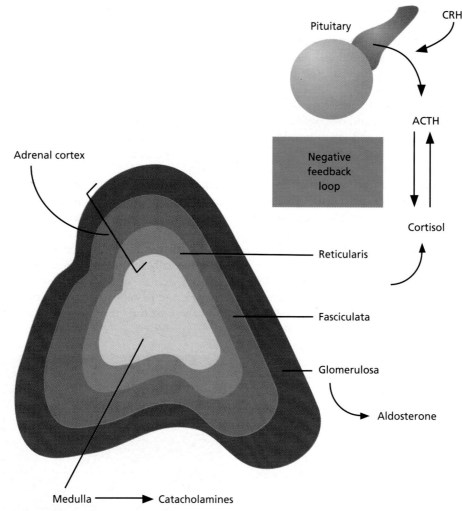

Figure 9–8 Adrenal cortex-pituitary axis. ACTH = adrenocorticotropic hormone; CRH = corticotropin-releasing hormone.

regulation. The normal pattern of cortisol secretion usually peaks about the time of awakening in the morning and is lowest in the afternoon and evening. During a 24-hour period, approximately 20 mg of cortisol are secreted. Stress from trauma, illness, and emotional concerns can enhance this secretion.

Aldosterone secretion is regulated by the renin-angiotensin system, ACTH, sodium, and potassium levels (see Chapter 4). When renal blood pressure decreases, renin is released, which stimulates release of angiotensin and activates the secretion of aldosterone via a negative feedback loop.

Clinical features

Primary adrenocortical insufficiency, known as Addison disease, is an uncommon endocrine condition attributable to a progressive destruction of the adrenal cortex. The gland destruction may be the result of an auto-

immune process, an infectious disease, such as tuberculosis, or a malignancy. Autoimmune disease has surpassed tuberculosis as the primary cause of Addison disease, but tuberculosis still accounts for a significant proportion of cases. As cortisol and aldosterone are primary hormones produced by the adrenal cortex, Addison disease may manifest by a variety of nonspecific symptoms, such as malaise, anorexia, and nausea, related to inadequate levels of these hormones.

The clinical manifestations of Addison disease do not begin to appear until at least 90% of the glandular tissue has been destroyed. The clinical picture is a reflection of the deficiency of cortisol and aldosterone. A lack of cortisol produces altered glucose, fat, and protein metabolism, resulting in weakness, fatigue, weight loss, inability to tolerate stress, and hypotension. This may develop over a period of months. The individual may complain of anorexia, nausea, diarrhea, weight loss, and sometimes a craving for salt. Aldosterone deficiency leads to sodium imbalance, hypovolemia, hyperkalemia, and acidosis. A generalized hyperpigmentation of the skin occurs, classically described as "bronzing," which may be more pronounced on sun-exposed skin. It is caused by increased levels of ACTH, which stimulate melanocytes to increase melanin production.

Secondary adrenocortical insufficiency results from the administration of exogenous corticosteroids. As the plasma cortisol level increases, from exogenous sources, the production of ACTH decreases via the negative feedback system. Inhibition of ACTH production results in suppression of the production of cortisol, but the production of aldosterone is not significantly affected. In general, patients with secondary adrenal insufficiency do not present with symptoms unless the patient is severely stressed. However, they may not have adequate circulating cortisol to manage a stressful event.

The diagnosis of Addison disease may be confirmed by rapid ACTH stimulation test measurement of plasma ACTH levels. A 24-hour urine collection to evaluate the level of 17-hydroxycorticosteroids, and other stimulation and suppression tests may be employed.

Oral manifestations and dental management

The oral manifestations include diffuse patchy brown macular pigmentation of the oral mucosa. Oral mucosal changes may be the first manifestations of the disease, with skin hyperpigmentation following. Patients demonstrating diffuse oral pigmentation should be questioned regarding onset.

Medical management of a patient with Addison disease includes glucocorticoid replacement, usually with daily cortisone or prednisone. The need for glucocorticoid augmentation during times of stress remains for a lifetime. If a patient with Addison disease is suddenly stressed, for example by dental infection or surgery, an adrenal crisis can be precipitated. Although this can occur even in the presence of supplementation, the probability is reduced. Acute adrenal insufficiency can be associated with high morbidity and mortality if allowed to progress unrecognized. The symptoms include extreme weakness, headache, and dehydration. The index of suspicion should be particularly high if the patient also has a history of an autoimmune disease (hypothyroidism, diabetes) or recent prior use of exogenous steroids. Hypotension, fever, and decreasing mental status, should initiate aggressive treatment. Immediate therapy would include injection of glucocorticoid and fluid replacement.

The ongoing concern regarding dental management for secondary adrenal cortical insufficiency is focused on when and to what degree to supplement patients who are on routine steroid regimens. Judgments based on duration and dosage are not always dependable. Studies have demonstrated a lack of correlation between suppression level and clinical reaction to a stressful event. Based on clinical evidence and reports, it appears that patients with secondary adrenal insufficiency undergoing routine dental care (including dental extractions) with local anesthesia do not require supplementation. This recommendation assumes adequate postoperative pain management and blood pressure monitoring. In some situations, however, patients exhibiting extreme dental anxiety may benefit from special anxiety management or supplementation.

When extensive procedures are planned for these patients, especially when the patient exhibits anxiety, doubling the normal amount on the day of the dental procedure is recommended. If postoperative pain is anticipated, a prudent recommendation would be to double the dose on the first postoperative day. Some literature states that the adrenal suppression from exogenous glucocorticosteroids lasts for 12 months. However, the stress response will return in 2 to 4 weeks. Therefore, if less than 30 days have passed since the last dose and extensive procedures are planned, the maintenance dose should be doubled on the day of the procedure.

Patients with adrenal insufficiency for whom dental procedures require general anesthesia should be treated in a hospital setting. Steroid augmentation may include 100 mg of hydrocortisone the morning of the procedure, 100 mg 1 hour before and/or after the procedure and doubled maintenance dose the first postoperative day. Appropriate management of pain and infection should be applied.

Patients with adrenal insufficiency should be monitored for possible hypotension and observed for signs of hypoglycemia. A medical consultation regarding steroid supplementation may be helpful.

Cushing disease

Cushing syndrome is a condition that results from a sustained increase in glucocorticoid levels. In most cases, the increase is attributable to exogenous corticosteroid therapy prescribed for treatment of medical disorders, such as autoimmune conditions and organ transplants. When the excess glucocorticoid is from an endogenous source, such as a functional adrenal cortical tumor or an ACTH-secreting pituitary tumor, the condition is known as Cushing disease. This condition is rare and generally affects young adult females.

Clinical features

Excessive corticosteroid therapy can produce signs and symptoms of hyperadrenalism or Cushing syndrome. The onset is generally slow, with weight gain in the central body area being the most obvious clinical manifestation. A "buffalo hump" may result from the accumulation of fat in the dorsal cervical spine area. Fat deposition in the face results in the rounded facial appearance or moon-shaped facies. In addition, a patient may develop hypertension, osteoporosis, diabetes mellitus, delayed wound healing, and depression. Females may demonstrate hirsutism.

Dental management

Owing to exogenous steroid therapy, the patient with Cushing syndrome is susceptible to an adrenal crisis during stressful events, as previously discussed. The clinician must be aware of the possible complications and plan the patient's dental care appropriately.

Hyperthyroidism

Obtaining an understanding of thyroid dysfunction is of significant importance to the dentist for two reasons. First, the dentist may be the first to suspect a serious thyroid disorder and aid in early diagnosis. The second reason is to avoid possible dental complications resulting from treating patients with poorly controlled hyperthyroid conditions. Although a rare occurrence, a thyrotoxic crisis—a true medical emergency—can occur associated with hyperthyroidism and dental procedures. The patient with hypothyroidism presents risks less critical in nature, but a few precautions are noteworthy. This section reviews hyperthyroidism and pertinent dental management considerations.

Hyperthyroidism is a condition caused by excess levels of circulating triiodothyronine (T3) and thyroxine (T4). The increased levels of these hormones may be a result of Graves disease, multinodular goiter, a functional thyroid adenoma, ectopic thyroid tissue, or disease involving the anterior portion of the pituitary gland. The most common cause of hyperthyroidism is Graves disease, which is the focus of this discussion. Graves disease is thought to be triggered by autoantibodies directed against thyroid-stimulating hormone (TSH) receptors on the surface of the thyroid cells. When the autoantibodies attach to these surface receptors, they stimulate the thyroid cells to release excessive thyroid hormone. The onset is unclear but may be associated with severe emotional trauma or infection.

Molecular and pathologic correlates of disease

The thyroid gland is a butterfly-shaped gland located in the anterior portion the neck just below the thyroid cartilage, and consists of two lateral lobes connected by an isthmus (Figure 9–9). Manual palpation of the thyroid gland should be a routine part of all new patient examinations and annual health updates. The normal thyroid tissue is soft and smooth. The thyroid should move upward during swallowing. The dentist may discover diffuse enlargement, indicative of thyroid hyperfunctioning, or a solitary nodule, suggesting a neoplasm.

To gain an understanding of the manifestations of thyroid hyperfunctioning (thyrotoxicosis) or hypofunctioning (myxedema or cretinism), a review of the hormones produced by the thyroid is appropriate. The thyroid gland secretes three hormones: thyroxine and triiodothyronine, which regulate growth and metabolism, and calcitonin, which regulates serum calcium levels, in conjunction with parathyroid hormone and vitamin D (see Chapter 10).

Circulating levels of T4 and T3 are controlled through a negative feedback mechanism mediated by the hypothalamic-pituitary-thyroid axis. Under steady-state conditions, thyrotropin-releasing hormone (TRH) is released by the hypothalamus in response to external stimuli, such as stress, illness, metabolic demand, and low levels of T3 and T4. Thyrotropin-releasing hormone stimulates the pituitary to release TSH, which causes the thyroid gland to secrete T4 and T3. In addition, high circulating levels of T4 and T3 diminish the release of TSH, and low levels of T4 and T3 increase the release of TSH from the pituitary.

Clinical features

Common manifestations of thyrotoxicosis include nervousness, emotional instability, inability to sleep, tremors, and excessive sweating. Weight loss is usual despite an adequate diet. In older patients, cardiovascular manifestations may predominate, such as exacerbation of angina pectoris.

The primary manifestations of Graves disease include hyperthyroidism with diffuse goiter, ophthalmopathy, and dermopathy (Figure 9–10). All components may manifest, or they may do so independently. Graves disease is 5 to 10 times more common in females than in males and affects nearly 2% of women. It is generally diagnosed during the third and fourth decades of life but may develop at puberty, pregnancy, or menopause. Most patients with Graves disease present with diffuse thyroid enlargement and have complaints associated with excessive thyroid hormones. Weight loss and increased appetite are commonly found owing to increased metabolic rate. Palmar erythema and a rosy complexion may be found. Hair may become fine, and the nails may soften. Skin manifestations are characterized by thickening of the dermis, which is infiltrated with lymphocytes and mucopolysaccharides. The skin change

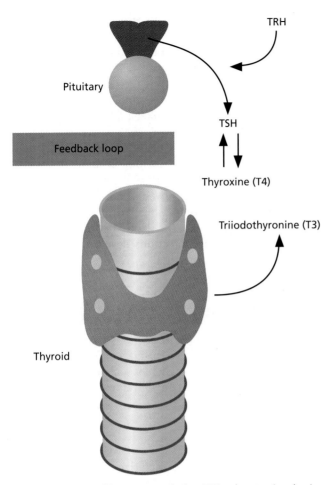

Figure 9–9 Thyroid hormone regulation. TRH = thyrotropin-releasing hormone; TSH = thyroid-stimulating hormone.

Hyperthyroidism during development and eruption of primary teeth can lead to early exfoliation of primary teeth and early eruption of permanent teeth. One may observe a tremor of the tongue.

A small number of patients may exhibit a raised, reddish asymptomatic mass in the dorsal posterior tongue area, near the foramen cecum. This is called lingual thyroid and represents a mass of normal thyroid tissue left along the path of the thyroglossal duct. This appears in females more commonly than in males. Before removal or biopsy of this mass, it should be confirmed that the thyroid gland is present and functional. In many cases, the lingual thyroid is the only functional thyroid tissue present.

The major treatments are focused on limiting the quantity of thyroid hormones produced by the gland. One major approach is to limit hormone production by surgical removal of a portion of the gland or by the use of radioactive iodine. Radioactive iodine is one of the

is often found on the dorsum of the legs and may be pruritic and hyperpigmented with a raised "orange peel" appearance. Hyperpigmentation of the oral mucosa has not been reported. Some patients complain of anxiety, nervousness, heart palpitations, heat intolerance, emotional instability, and muscle weakness. Profuse sweating is common. Patients may demonstrate widened pulse pressure, with an elevated systolic pressure. Another prominent feature is ocular manifestations. In early stages of hyperthyroidism, patients demonstrate a wide stare with eyelid retraction and lid lag. Sometimes jerky movements of the lids are present. If the exophthalmos, protrusion of the eyes, begins unilaterally, it usually progresses to be bilateral. The globe protrusion is attributable to the accumulation of glycosaminoglycans in connective tissues behind the eyes. Corneal ulceration and ocular muscle weakness may develop.

Diagnosis of hyperthyroidism from Graves disease includes characteristic clinical manifestations and laboratory findings. Laboratory examinations include elevated levels for T3, T4, and thyroid-binding globulin (TBG) levels with minimal or undetectable TSH levels.

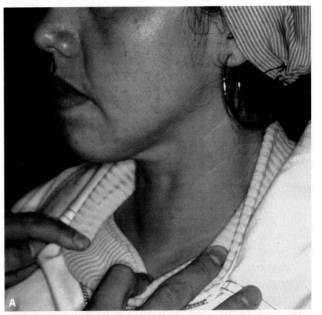

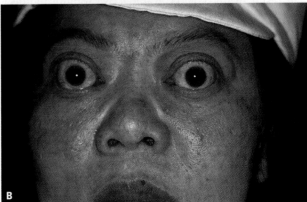

Figure 9–10 *A*, Thyroid enlargement in hyperthyroidism; *B*, exophthalmos.

most effective therapeutic strategies for patients with Graves disease. The radioactive iodine is taken up by the gland, destroying the hyperactive thyroid tissue. Thyroid hormone levels should return to normal. Patients may also be treated via partial or total thyroidectomy. These therapies may lead to hypothyroidism, which can generally be managed with hormone-replacement therapy.

Antithyroid agents, propylthiouracil and methimazole chemically block hormone synthesis by blocking iodine uptake. These agents may cause mild leukopenia. Beta-adrenergic blocking agents, such as propranolol, may alleviate sweating, tremor, and tachycardia.

Medications most useful for treatment of hyperthyroidism include thionamides, iodine, and radioactive isotopes of iodine. The thionamides (propylthiouracil and methimazole [Tapazole]), inhibit oxidation of iodide and coupling reactions to inhibit thyroid hormone formation. Non-radioactive iodides are used to temporarily suppress the gland prior to surgery. Iodides may also produce altered taste sensations, excessive salivation, and enlargement of the parotid and submandibular glands.

Thionamides may be used to control hyperthyroidism before surgery or while the therapeutic effects of radioactive iodide are realized. Thionamides may cause bone marrow suppression, resulting in greater susceptibility to infection, gingival bleeding, or delayed healing. Oral manifestations of agranulocytosis have been reported to have developed in a hyperthyroid patient 2 months after administration of methimazole. These manifestations included fever, sore throat, profound leukopenia, gingival necrosis and mucosal ulceration. When taken during pregnancy, thionamides can cross the placenta and cause fetal hypothyroidism. Thionamides may also cause rash, nausea, and headache. Hepatic toxicity and allergic hepatitis are occasionally associated with thionamides.

Radioactive sodium iodide is used in diagnosis and treatment of hyperthyroidism, and at higher concentrations, the isotope destroys thyroid cells. This treatment can result in myxedema. Radioactive sodium iodide is contraindicated during pregnancy.

Dental management

Patients with uncontrolled hyperthyroidism require special dental management. They are sensitive to epinephrine and pressor amines in local anesthetics and gingival retraction cords. These agents should not be administered until hyperthyroidism is controlled.

Patients with undiagnosed or poorly controlled thyrotoxicosis may develop thyrotoxic crisis, a serious complication with an abrupt onset. Most patients who develop thyrotoxic crisis have a goiter, wide pulse pressure, eye signs, and a long history of thyrotoxicosis. Pre-cipitating factors are infections, trauma, surgical emergencies, and surgery. Symptoms are extreme restlessness, nausea, vomiting, and abdominal pain. Coma and severe hypotension may develop. Immediate treatment consists of anti-hyperthyroid therapies to include propylthiouracil, potassium iodide, propranolol, hydrocortisone, and ice packs or cooling blankets; CPR may be needed until medical help arrives.

Long-term follow-up is necessary for patients with Graves disease and should include an annual physical examination and measurement of serum concentrations of thyrotropin and free thyroxine. These should be maintained in the normal range. After the thyrotoxic patient is well controlled, the dental treatment plan will be unaffected. If acute infections develop, the patient's physician should be consulted.

Hypothyroidism

Acute hypothyroidism (myxedema) is more common in females and occurs between the ages of 30 and 60 years. Childhood hypothyroidism is termed cretinism. Hypothyroidism may be congenital or acquired.

Clinical features

Neonatal cretinism is characterized by dwarfism, a broad flat nose, thick lips, large protruding tongue, poor muscle tone, pale skin, retarded bone age, delayed eruption of teeth, and malocclusions. The long-term effects of severe hypothyroidism on craniofacial growth and dental development have also included impaction of the mandibular second molars, owing to failure of normal resorption of the internal aspect of the ramus. Hypothyroidism in older children and adults is characterized by a dull expression; puffy eyelids, face, and hands; rough skin and brittle, coarse hair; enlarged tongue; slurred speech; and increased sensitivity to cold. Juvenile hypothyroidism has been reported to include evidence of delays in shedding of deciduous teeth, root development, and eruption of permanent teeth as well as retarded skeletal growth. Two years of treatment with L-thyroxine results in dental and skeletal changes.

Hypothyroidism may occur from Hashimoto thyroiditis. This disorder is a chronic inflammatory disease of the thyroid in which autoimmune factors play a prominent role. It occurs in females during middle age and is the most common cause of sporadic goiter in children. Autoantibodies are indicative of disease but cytotoxic T cells probably destroy parenchyma. The most prominent feature is a diffuse goiter, which may be symmetrical or asymmetrical. The gland may feel rubbery to palpation. Hashimoto thyroiditis may coexist with other diseases that are autoimmune in nature, such as pernicious anemia, Sjögren syndrome, systemic lupus erythematosus, diabetes mellitus, and Graves disease. Thyroid failure is manifested first by a rise in TSH concentration. As the condition progresses, serum T4 level declines, then T3 also declines, resulting in hypothyroidism. Autoimmune thyroiditis accounts for a significant percentage of adult hypothyroidism.

Dental management

Detection of hypothyroidism requires medical referral of the patient prior to dental treatment. Patients with hypothyroidism are usually treated with synthetic hormone replacement containing levothyroxine sodium (Levothroid, Levoxine, Synthroid) until normal functional levels are achieved. Unless the hypothyroid condition is transient, patients generally maintain replacement therapy for a lifetime. Levothyroxine should be used with caution in patients with cardiovascular disorders. Hypothyroid patients who are receiving warfarin or other oral anticoagulants along with levothyroxine may have prolonged prothrombin times and could be at risk for hemorrhage. Stressful situations, such as cold, surgery, or trauma, may precipitate a hypothyroid (myxedema) coma in the undiagnosed severely hypothyroid patient. This condition is treated by parenteral T3, steroids, and artificial respiration.

In general, patients with mild symptoms of untreated hypothyroidism are not in danger when receiving dental therapy. However, depressants, sedatives, or narcotic analgesics may produce an exaggerated response in patients with mild to severe hypothyroidism. These medications should be avoided in patients with severe hypothyroidism and minimized for those with mild disease. When the hypothyroid patient is under effective medical care, regular dental care can be provided.

Suggested reading

Clark CM, Lee DA. Prevention of complications of diabetes mellitus. N Engl J Med 1995;332:1210–7.

Davenport J, Kellerman C, Reiss D, Harrison L. Addison's disease. Am Fam Physician 1991;43:1338–42.

Diabetes Control and Complications Trial Research Group. Effect of intensive diabetes management on macrovascular and microvascular events and risk factors in the diabetes control and complications trial. Am J Cardiol 1995;75:894–903.

Diabetes Control and Complications Trial Research Group. The effect of intensive treatment of diabetes on the development and progression of long-term complications in insulin-dependent diabetes mellitus. N Engl J Med 1993;329:977–86.

Glick M. Glucocorticosteroid replacement therapy: a literature review and suggested replacement therapy. Oral Surg Oral Med Oral Pathol 1989;67:7614–20.

Grossi SG, Genco RJ. Periodontal disease and diabetes mellitus: a two-way relationship. Ann Periodontol 1998;3:51–61.

Klein H. Dental fluorosis associated with hereditary diabetes insipidus. Oral Surg Oral Med Oral Pathol 1975;40:736–41.

McDonald JS, Miller Rl, Bernstein ML, Olson JW. Histiocytosis X: a clinical presentation. J Oral Pathol 1980;9:342–9.

Moore PA, Weyant RJ, Mongelluzzo MB, et al. Type 1 diabetes mellitus and oral health: assessment of periodontal disease. J Periodontol 1999;70:409–17.

Nathan DM, Singer DE, Hurxthal K, Goodson JD. The clinical information value of glycosylated hemoglobin assay. N Engl J Med 1984;310:341–6.

Ng'ang'a PM, Chindia ML. Dental and skeletal changes in juvenile hypothyroidism following treatment: case report. Odontostomatol Trop 1990;13:25–7.

Perusse R, Goulet JP, Turcotte JY. Contraindications to vasoconstrictors in dentistry. Part II. Hyperthyroidism, diabetes, sulfite sensitivity, cortico-dependent asthma, and pheochromocytoma. Oral Surg Oral Med Oral Pathol 1992;74:687–91.

Seow WE, Thomsett MJ. Dental fluorosis as a complication of hereditary diabetes insipidus: studies of six affected patients. Pediatr Dent 1994;16:128–32.

Slavkin HC. Diabetes, clinical dentistry, and changing paradigms. J Am Dent Assoc 1997;128:638–44.

Soskolne WA. Epidemiological and clinical aspects of periodontal diseases in diabetics. Ann Periodontol 1998;3:3–12.

Taylor GW, Burt BA, Becker MP, et al. Severe periodontitis and risk for poor glycemic control in patients with non–insulin-dependent diabetes mellitus. J Periodontol 1996;67:1085–93.

Tuomilehto J, Lindstrom J, Eriksson JG, et al. Prevention of type 2 diabetes mellitus by changes in lifestyle among subjects with impaired glucose tolerance. N Engl J Med 2001;344:1343–50.

Werbel SS, Ober KP. Acute adrenal insufficiency. Endocrinol Metab Clin North Am 1993;22:303–28.

Young ER. The thyroid gland and the dental practitioner. J Can Dent Assoc 1989;55:903–7.

10 Parathyroid Disease and Calcium Metabolism

Sol Silverman, Jr, MA, DDS

The parathyroid glands are significant in oral health because of their control of calcium metabolism, which in turn critically influences tooth development and the maintenance of healthy bone. Of concern to the dental professional are a rational basis for an adequate calcium intake, the complex endocrine mechanisms for metabolic control of calcium, and the differential diagnosis of nonendocrine oral diseases or conditions with clinical features that may reflect abnormalities in calcium metabolism and endocrine dysfunction and, thus, confuse diagnoses and management approaches.

Molecular and pathologic correlates of disease

Calcium metabolism depends upon a complex interplay among dietary calcium, absorption, and excretion; hormonal interactions of parathormone, vitamin D, and calcitonin; immobilization or exercise status; and other diseases and medications.

An average daily intake of calcium varies with the type of diet and the amount ingested. For example, consumers of large amounts of dairy products have a high calcium intake. Also, consumption of calcium-containing antacids or mineral supplements containing calcium and vitamin D intake influence calcium levels. The recommended daily allowance for healthy individuals is 1 g. This is increased under various conditions (eg, osteoporosis and pregnancy).

Calcium is poorly absorbed from the small intestine; the average varies from 10 to 30%, with the residual being eliminated in the feces. Vitamin D directly increases serum calcium by increasing protein synthesis in the intestinal wall, which in turn enhances intestinal calcium transport and absorption. Vitamin D also increases renal tubular reabsorption of calcium as well as phosphorus. Vitamin D actually posseses hormonal activity, since, through corresponding blood levels, there is a homeostatic interplay mechanism between serum calcium and parathyroid hormone production. Parathormone, produced in the parathyroid glands, controls calcium levels by influencing bone breakdown or resorption. This hormone is regulated in feedback fashion by the level of serum calcium. Parathormone also influences the hydroxylation of vitamin D as well as the kidney reabsorption of phosphate and calcium.

Calciferol (vitamin D_2) is the most inert form of vitamin D and is obtained from plant sources. This is the active ingrediant in most proprietary vitamin D preparations. Cholecalciferol (vitamin D_3) is obtained through the diet from animal sources or conversion from fat stores in the skin by ultraviolet light. The most active form of vitamin D is the 1,25-dihydroxycholecalciferol. The hydroxylation takes place first in the liver (the 25-position) and then sequentially in the kidney (the 1-position). This process takes place in the mitochondria. Obviously then, liver disease decreases the amount of the active form of vitamin D. Therefore, such conditions as cirrhosis or the ingestion of drugs, such as phenytoin and phenobarital, influence the levels of vitamin D activity.

Circulating parathyroid hormone also influences the 1-hydroxylation in the kidney by feedback control. Thus, if there is excess parathyroid hormone and an increase in serum calcium levels, the 1-hydroxylation kidney activity is depressed. This in turn reduces vitamin D activity and lowers intestinal calcium absorption.

Serum calcium levels have ranges of normal that vary from laboratory to laboratory. However, the limits are rigid, and values slightly above or below normal usually reflect a significant abnormality. Fifty percent of serum calcium is usually protein-bound. Up to 200 mg of calcium may be excreted through the urine daily; but the average amount approximates 125 mg. Tubular reabsorption of calcium is efficient, approximating 97%. This process of reabsorption is influenced by serum levels of calcium, vitamin D, and parathormone. When calcium levels exceed normal, the risk for kidney damage increases. The exchange pool between serum calcium and bone usually approximates 350 mg per day, with accretion equaling resorption, under normal conditions (Table 10–1).

Calcitonin is a hormone that tends to preserve the skeleton by controlling calcium and phosphate levels, probably by reducing bone resorption by inhibiting the action of osteoclasts. Its production is primarily from the ultimobranchial cells distributed in thyroid, parathyroid, and thymus glands.

Clinical features

There are innumerable causes of hypercalcemia. Fortunately, the body's homeostatic mechanisms are capable of maintaining serum calcium within normal limits under most circumstances. Following are some of the common causes of hypercalcemia.

1. Cancer that invades bone. Tumors can elaborate parathyroid hormone-like substances leading to release of calcium; this is seen often in advanced head and neck cancers.
2. Milk-alkali syndrome caused by the ingestion of antacids that contain soluble calcium salts.
3. Hyperparathyroidism.
4. Excess vitamin D ingestion.
5. Diuretic therapy using thiazides.
6. Sarcoidosis.
7. Immobilization.

The clinical picture of excessive circulating calcium depends upon the level and duration of hypercalcemia. Table 10–2 list the variable multisystem manifestations that may complicate this condition.

Primary hyperparathyroidism is caused by the development of benign tumors (adenomas) or hyperplasia of one or more of the parathyroid glands. Early detection and adequate surgical treatment are extremely important, since delay may lead to irreversible kidney damage, hypertension, and death. Tests include the measurement of parathormone as well as biochemical assessment for abnormal calcium, phosphorus, and alkaline phosphatase levels. Secondary hyperparathyroidism is usually a reflection of renal disease, with sequelae of calcium loss and compensatory parathyroid hyperactivity to maintain adequate serum calcium levels. The dental findings between primary and secondary disease are indistinguishable.

The dental findings of hyperparathyroid disease are usually found as abnormalities on dental radiographs

Table 10–1 Hormonal Control of Bone Resorption

Stimulated	Inhibited
Parathyroid	Calcitonin
Thyroid	Estrogen
Cortisone*	Androgen

*Short-term: turns off osteoblastic activity, reducing serum calcium; long-term: stimulates parathormone, increasing serum calcium.

(Figure 10–1). The changes include one or more of the following: (1) complete or partial loss of lamina dura; (2) alveolar bone demineralization (ground-glass appearance); and (3) fibrous giant-cell bone lesions (brown tumor, osteitis fibrosa cystica), which must be confirmed by biopsy. Bone changes almost always reflect late-stage disease.

Hypoparathyroidism is relatively rare and may be attributable to a genetic disorder (congenital), or induced by parathyroid or thyroid surgery, or radiation to that area. These events can lead to a low serum calcium level (hypocalcemia), which can lead to muscular spasms and tetany. The dental manifestations only occur in the congenital form, which affects the teeth at the developmental stage, causing mottling (hypoplastia) and discoloration (Figure 10–2). There are no dental findings in acquired hypoparathyroidism.

Vitamin D-resistant rickets is a congenital genetic condition that lowers serum calcium. In one form of the disease, for unknown reasons, spontaneous pulpal death and abscess formation occurs in one or more teeth.

Diagnosis

From the dental point-of-view, the diagnosis of disturbed calcium metabolism is based upon the abnormal radiographic findings of altered lamina dura, demineralized bone, or radiographic cysts (see Figure 10–1). When biopsy specimens from bone show giant cells in the

Table 10–2 Clinical Features of Hypercalcemia

Site or System	Manifestation
Oral	Jaw bone demineralization, loss of lamina dura, osteitis fibrosa cystica
Gastrointestinal	Anorexia, constipation, nausea, pain
Genitourinary	Polydipsia or polyuria, calculi, nephroinsufficiency
Neurologic	Fatigue, muscle weakness, disorientation or stupor, coma or death
Psychiatric	Apathy, depression, psychotic behavior
Ocular, kidney, vascular, periarticular	Calcifications (no association with salivary stones)

fibrous stroma, hyperparathyroidism must be ruled out. Biochemically, the diagnosis is established by parathyroid hormone levels and, indirectly, by serum levels of high calcium, low phosphate, and high alkaline phosphatase.

Confusion in determining the differential diagnosis often arises because of many nonendocrine conditions that may mimic characteristics found in hypercalcemic states (Table 10–3).

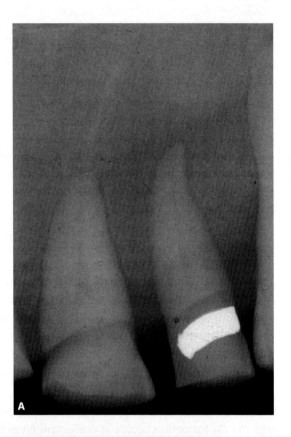

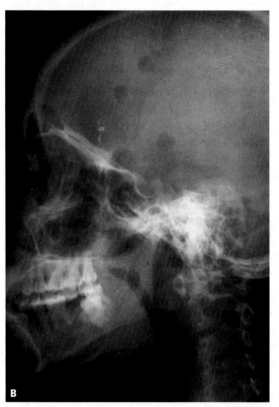

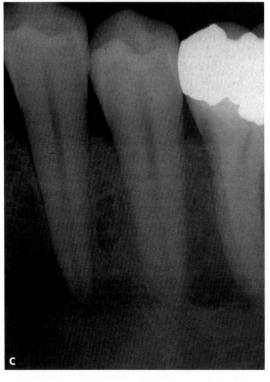

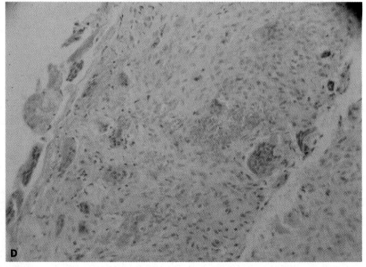

Figure 10–1 Hyperparathyroidism. *A*, Demineralized maxillary bone with ground-glass appearance and loss of lamina dura. *B*, Osteitis fibrosa cystica of skull (multiple radiolucent giant-cell lesions). *C*, Osteitis fibrosa cystica of mandibular bone, which can resemble other types of nonendocrine bone pathology. *D*, Giant-cell lesion (brown tumor) of osteitis fibrosa cystica.

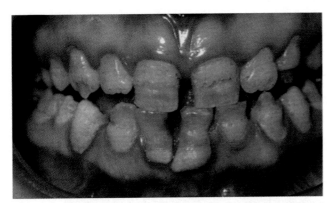

Figure 10–2 Congenital hypoparathyroidism showing mottled enamel from decreased serum calcium during tooth calcification.

Management

Treatment for calcium disorders requires surgery for gland tumors and medications to adjust calcium and phosphorus levels. Abnormalities in bone revert to normal after calcium metabolism is stabilized (Figure 10–3). Therefore, specific local treatment to the dental structures, other than routine care, is contraindicated. It must be remembered that similar radiographic bone alterations may represent several different diseases. Correlations between clinical, radiographic, and microscopic findings are critical to arriving at a definitive diagnosis. For example, giant-cell lesions of bone can be the manifestation of an inflammatory process, neoplasia, or a parathyroid adenoma.

Fibrous dysplasia is a benign, idiopathic demineralization of one bone or a part of a bone (monostotic) or numerous bones (polyostotic). The clinical appearance may show expansion of the mandible or maxilla with confirmation by a ground-glass or demineralized appearance (Figure 10–4). It is usually painless, has limited growth, and requires no treatment. Surgical trimming is sometimes done for esthetics or interference with prostheses. Polyostotic fibrous dysplasia is rare. The bone expansion is differentiated from an osteoma, which has continued growth and usually a radiographic presentation of radiopacity (Figure 10–5).

Paget's disease of bone usually occurs in people over 40 years of age. It is a condition in which osteoclastic activity and compensatory disorganized bone overgrowth occur side by side (Figure 10–6). Mandibular overgrowth and malocclusion are oral manifestations, and sometimes are the first sign of this idiopathic disease. Long bones may bow, and there is often associated pain. Diagnosis can be confirmed by biopsy, radiographs, and chemistry (normal calcium, high alkaline phosphatase). There might be some clinical confusion with acromegaly, since both conditions may present with the Class III malocclusion. But acromegaly is a reflection of anterior pituitary adenoma with an increase in growth hormone that stimulates condylar cartilagenous reactivation and mandibular growth. Other endocrinopathies, such as diabetes mellitus, occur simultaneously.

Osteomalacia is a disease of insufficient bone matrix calcification as a result of intestinal malabsorption of minerals or renal disorders. Osteomalacia commonly follows sprue, a disease of disturbed small intestine function characterized by impaired nutrient absorption. Fractures and bone pain are major findings.

Osteoporosis is an extremely common condition of aging, particularly in postmenopausal women. Osteoporosis is not a primary disorder of calcium metabolism. It may result from inadequate stimulation of osteoblasts (postmenopause, disuse) or excess catabolic agents (adrenal cortex overactivity). Pain and fractures are common findings. Control is usually on the basis of steroid hormone replacement, nutrient replacement (diet, supplements), and exercise. It has been shown that osteoporosis affects jaw bones; however, the clinical implications are not clear.

Table 10–3 Differential Diagnosis: Serum, Radiographic, and Microscopic Findings

Disease or Condition	Parathormone	Serum Calcium	APL	Loss of Lamina Dura	Ground-glass Appearance*	Bone Cyst†	Giant Cells
Hyperparathyroidism	Increase	Increase	Increase	+	+	+	+
Renal rickets and hyperparathyroidism	Increase	Increase	Increase	+	+	+	+
Fibrous dysplasia	0	0	0	+	+	0	0
Paget's disease	0	0	Increase	+	+	0	0
Osteomalacia	0	Decrease	Increase	+	+	0	0
Giant-cell granuloma	0	0	0	0	0	+	+
Hemorrhagic cyst	0	0	0	0	0	+	0
Osteoporosis	0	0	0	0	+	0	0

*Radiolucency.
†Demineralization.
APL = alkaline phosphatase; + = present; 0 = normal or absent.

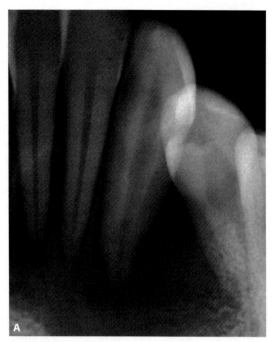 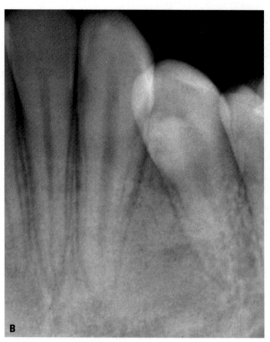

Figure 10–3 Osteitis fibrosa cystica in a patient with hyperparathyroidism. *A*, Asymptomatic mandibular lesion before removal of a parathyroid adenoma. *B*, Six months after parathyroid surgery. There were no interim dental procedures performed.

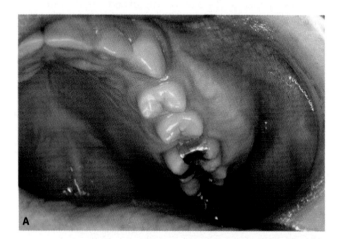 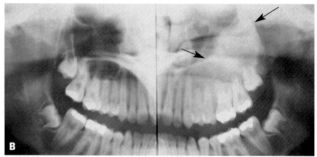

Figure 10–4 Fibrous dysplasia (benign fibroosseus disease). *A*, Non-expanding asymptomatic boney mass in the left maxilla that had been noticed for over 2 years. *B*, Panorex film demonstrating a ground-glass appearance of the left posterior maxilla.

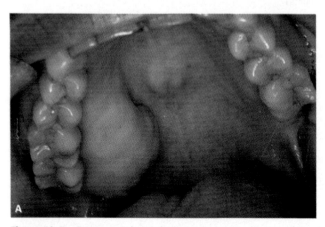 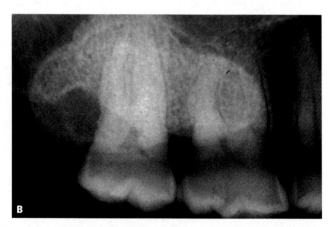

Figure 10–5 Osteoma: *A*, increasing asymptomatic expansion of the right posterior maxilla; *B*, radiograph showing an associated radiopacity.

Hemorrhagic pseudocysts are asymptomatic bone cavities occurring more commonly in the mandible (Figure 10–7). Although they are often called traumatic cysts, their cause is unknown. These areas will usually

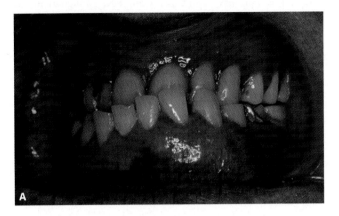

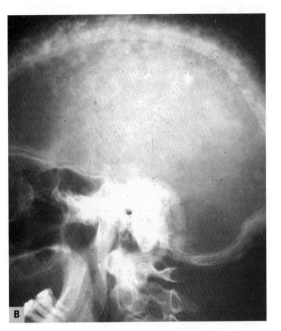

Figure 10–6 Paget's disease: *A*, appositional bone growth of the mandible promoting a Class III malocclusion; *B*, radiograph of the skull showing typical appositional bone growth of the cortex.

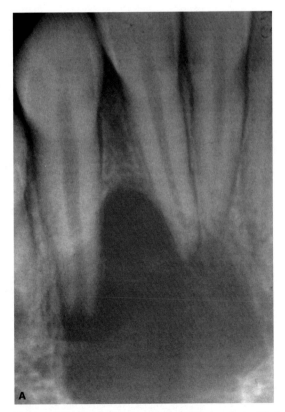

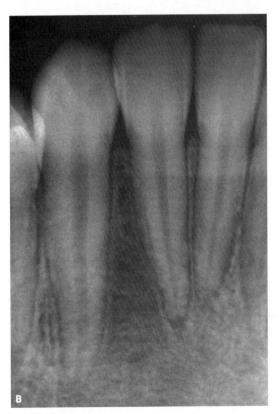

Figure 10–7 Hemorrhagic pseudocyst ("traumatic cyst"). *A*, This radiolucency was found on a routine radiographic survey in an asymptomatic patient. There was no clinically detected bone expansion and no associated history of trauma. Serum calcium was normal, and an attempted biopsy revealed an empty bone cavity. *B*, Follow-up radiograph at 6 months was within normal limits (spontaneous remineralization).

remineralize spontaneously. They can resemble the bone lesions of hyperparathyroid disease.

Suggested reading

Delmas PD, Meunier PJ. The management of Paget's disease of bone. N Engl J Med 1997;336:558–66.

Eastell R. Treatment of postmenopausal osteoporosis. N Engl J Med 1998;338:736–46.

Holick MF, Schnoes THK, DeLuca HF, et al. Isolation and identification of 1,25-dihydroxycholecalciferol. A metabolite of vitamin D active in intestine. J NIH Res 1992;4:88–95.

Jeffcoat MK, Chestnut CH. Systemic osteoporosis and oral bone loss: evidence shows increased risk factors. J Am Dent Assoc 1993;124:49–56.

Reichel H, Klieffler HP, Norman AW. The role of the vitamin D endocrine system in health and disease. N Engl J Med 1989;320:980–91.

Ruggieri P, Sim FH, Bond JR, Unni KK. Malignancies in fibrous dysplasia. Cancer 1994;73:1411–24.

Silverberg SJ, Shane E, Jacobs TP, et al. A 10-year prospective study of primary hyperparathyroidism with or without parathyroid surgery. N Engl J Med 1999;341:1249–54.

Slavkin HC. Building a better mousetrap: toward an understanding of osteoporosis. J Am Dent Assoc 1999;130:1632–6.

White SC, Rudolph DJ. Alterations of the trabecular pattern of the jaws in patients with osteoporosis. Oral Surg Oral Med Oral Pathol Oral Radiol Endod 1999;88:628–35.

11 Adverse Drug Reactions

Peter L. Jacobsen, PhD, DDS

Adverse drug reaction is a broad term comprising many problems associated with drug use. It includes side effects, toxicity, drug–drug interactions, drug–physiology interactions, drug–laboratory test interactions, allergic reactions, and idiosyncratic reactions (Table 11–1). This chapter focuses on two aspects of adverse drug reactions, significant drug–physiology interactions (side effects) and drug–drug interactions. These two areas comprise what is commonly termed, in dentistry, drug interactions. Fortunately, severe problems from drug interactions are rare in dentistry. Avoiding the most common dental interactions is relatively simple and is outlined in this chapter.

Though an awareness of the "at-risk drugs" is important, understanding of the "at-risk patient" is even more valuable. There is a greater risk of having an adverse drug reaction in certain patients than in others. In certain high-risk patients, avoiding the use of erythromycin, ketoconazole, and metronidazole will, essentially, eliminate the risk of drug–drug interactions.

The primary drugs used in dentistry fall into five different groups: local anesthetics, analgesics, antimicrobials (antibiotics, antifungals, antivirals), sedatives, and drugs that affect the autonomic nervous system (anti-histamines, sympathomimetics, and less commonly, anticholinergics). Several other drug groups are uncommonly used in general dental practice. Antidepressants, owing to their serotoninergic action are useful in chronic pain management, and corticosteroids are used to treat oral autoimmune diseases, such as lichen planus, pemphigoid, erythema multiforme, and pemphigus. Since the primary dental drugs are used for a short duration at only moderate dosage, in relatively healthy individuals, the risks of untoward reactions are minimal. At the same time, an understanding of mechanisms of adverse drug reactions assists in avoiding problems.

Mechanisms of adverse drug reactions

Drug–physiology interactions

Drugs have specific effects on body functions and are selected for these effects. For example, aspirin has an antiprostaglandin effect, which leads to the dentally useful effect of decreasing inflammation and pain. At the same time, a drug may have effects on other physiologic systems and, thus, may not be useful to the den-

Table 11–1 Definitions of Terms, All Considered To Be Adverse Drug Reactions

Term	Definition
Toxicity	Overdose of a drug that injures a physiologic system
Side effect	Expected or predictable undesirable effect of a drug that occurs at therapeutic doses
Drug–drug interaction	The presence of one drug effects the pharmacodynamics (absorption, distribution, metabolism, excretion) of another drug
Drug–physiology interaction	The presence of a drug alters the bodies physiology, leading to a harmful condition (may overlap with the concept of side effect)
Drug–laboratory test interaction	Drug will alter laboratory test results without impacting the physiologic system being measured—essentially a false-positive or false-negative laboratory test result
Allergic reaction	Drug triggers an immunologic response
Idiosyncratic reaction	Drug creates a physiologic or psychological response that is unpredictable and is unique to the individual

Table 11–2 Significant Drug–Physiology Interactions

Drug	Desired Dental Response	Undesired Physiologic Response (In Dental Settings)
Aspirin	Analgesic	Bleeding
Barbiturates	Sedative	Respiratory depression
Narcotics	Analgesic	Respiratory depression
Vasoconstrictors	Localize anesthetic solution	Increase cardiac excitability

tist. For example, the antiprostaglandin effect of aspirin also prevents platelets from adhering. Therefore, a side effect or drug–physiology interaction may be excessive bleeding. Such drug–physiology interactions are relatively common, but significant ones, those that are life-threatening, occur only with a few drugs used in dentistry (Table 11–2).

The second drug–physiology interaction is toxicity. This adverse drug reaction is associated with the dose of the drug and may be an extension of its therapeutic effect or may be an effect on another system. Toxic effects of drugs should not happen, since most drugs used in dentistry have a wide margin of safety between the therapeutic dose and the toxic dose. The most common reason for drug overdose is a failure to take into account the size of the patient; overdose toxicity is more common in children and the frail elderly. The second most common reason for overdose is failure to adjust dosing to take into account the patient's inability to metabolize or eliminate the drug. Therefore, if the dentist is aware of the proper dose and alert to the patient's size as well as their liver and kidney function, chances of overdosing are minimized. The practitioner must also keep in mind that the patient may be taking other medication, especially over-the-counter medication, which may have additive toxicity to the medication used in dentistry.

Drug–drug interactions

The classic drug–drug interactions comprise four different aspects of drug pharmacodynamics: absorption, distribution, metabolism, and excretion. Absorption is not a crucial aspect when discussing adverse drug reactions in dentistry. It is possible that food in the stomach may lower the absorption rate, but neither final blood level nor therapeutic effect is substantially altered. All drugs given for dental purposes, at the appropriate dosage, should eventually be adequately absorbed to obtain therapeutic blood levels. Certainly, if the patient regurgitates the bulk of the drug, then therapeutic blood levels cannot be obtained, and it may be necessary for the patient either to retake the drug or to receive it parenterally. In patients with malabsorption, extensive col-

itis, or other gastrointestinal problems, the dentist should consult with the patient's physician to establish ways of ensuring that necessary medications are given in such a way that therapeutic blood levels are achieved.

Drug distribution in the body has the potential to initiate adverse reactions. Some drugs are bound to plasma proteins; once at the site of action, the therapeutic effect is created by the free drug. A drug administered by the dentist may have a higher affinity for the plasma protein, and will therefore displace the drug already bound. This will cause higher concentrations of the original drug in the plasma and a possible toxicity reaction. This primarily occurs with highly protein-bound medical drugs that have narrow therapeutic margins of safety, such as the anticoagulant, dicumarol.

For drugs used in dentistry, problems associated with excretion are important only for those patients with significant kidney problems. When the kidney is not functioning properly, any drug excreted by the kidney is excreted more slowly. This decrease in excretion rate may allow blood levels to rise to potentially toxic levels. Some dental drugs can have a toxic effect on specific organs, including the kidney and liver. For patients with liver and kidney problems, dental drugs should be chosen so as to have minimum impact on the diseased organ (Table 11–3).

The most important area of drug–drug interactions is drug metabolism. Most drugs given in dentistry and most drugs given for medical purposes are metabolized by enzymes in the liver. The primary group of metabolizing enzymes is called the cytochrome P-450 system. These are areas in liver cells that act as latticed processing stations. These surfaces are coated with various enzymes. The cytochrome P-450 enzyme system is subdivided into isoenzyme groups. The enzymes metabolize a wide range of compounds. Some drugs induce the synthesis of these enzymes, thereby accelerating their own metabolism and the metabolism of other drugs. Some drugs inhibit these metabolizing enzymes, thereby slowing their own metabolization or slowing the metabolization of other drugs. The most serious drug–drug interactions are related to either inducing or inhibiting isoenzyme groups within the cytochrome P-450 system. In dentistry, four drugs, the antibiotics, erythromycin, clarithromycin, metronidazole, and the antifungal drug, ketoconazole, are known inhibitors of cytochrome P-450 enzymes (Table 11–4). When using any of these

Table 11–3 Dental Drugs with Toxic Effects on Specific Organs

Drug	Use	Affected Organ
Acetaminophen	Analgesia	Liver
Corticosteroids	Anti-inflammatory	Immune system
Ketoconazole	Antifungal	Liver

four drugs, the dentist should be alert to whether the patient is taking any other medication and be prepared to evaluate a possible interaction. It might be appropriate to choose a different drug to treat the oral problem.

Drug allergies

In dentistry, drug allergies are the most common adverse drug reaction encountered. Patients frequently claim to have allergies to penicillin, aspirin, or codeine. A true allergic reaction is an immune system-mediated response to an allergen. Almost any drug or compound can be an allergen. (Actually most drugs are too small to be antigenic by themselves and must combine with a carrier protein, or hapten, to create an allergic response.) Most severe allergic reactions are immediate type, humoral (B cell) antibody-mediated reactions. The allergen (drug) exposure precipates an antibody response, and the resultant cascade of events includes histamine release that causes swelling, redness, and itching (urticaria). Most commonly, this manifests as a rash on the body, but infrequently it manifests as perioral swelling (angioneurotic edema) or swelling in the throat adequate to restrict or prevent breathing (anaphylaxis). Delayed allergic reactions are mediated through the cellular (T cell) branch of the immune system, and these usually manifest as skin rashes, blisters, and at times, oral ulcerations.

Dental management

The primary approach to allergic reactions is to avoid them by obtaining a thorough patient health history with respect to allergic reactions. The dentist should interview the patient about allergies, especially allergies to medications commonly used in dentistry, including antibiotics, pain medications, or local anesthetics. True allergic reactions to local anesthetic are extremely rare, and, even then, it is usually a reaction to the preservative; nevertheless, this information is necessary to avoid an adverse response to dental treatment.

Table 11–4 Drugs Used in Dentistry that Alter Cytochrome P-450 Enzymes

Drug	Use	Effect on Cytochrome P-450 Enzymes
Erythromycin	Antibiotic	Inhibit
Ketoconazole	Antiflangal	Inhibit
Clarithromycin	Antibiotic	Inhibit
Metronidazole	Antibiotic	Inhibit
Barbiturates	Sedative	Stimulate
Dexamethasone	Steroidal anti-inflammatory	Stimulate

When a patient claims to have had an allergic reaction, further questioning is necessary. If the patient has experienced a true immune system-mediated allergic reaction, such as redness, swelling, rash, or itching, the drug should be avoided. If the "allergic reaction" was actually an adverse physiologic response to the drug or the dental experience, such as stomach upset, dizziness, or nausea, which do not constitute an immune system-mediated reaction, it is not a true allergy. Still, the drug should be avoided, if possible, because the patient's next exposure may precipitate a true allergic response, or it may precipitate the same adverse physiologic response the patient reported. In any event, the patient will be upset at having been exposed to a drug to which he or she reported having an "allergy."

Allergic responses are treated by withdrawal of the drug and possibly antihistamines or corticosteroids. Depending on the severity of the reaction, as in the case of laryngeal swelling (anaphylaxis), it may be necessary to give an injection of epinephrine to physiologically reverse the allergic response.

The management of patients in a dental setting, to minimize the risk of other adverse drug reactions, has two aspects. The first is to avoid adverse drug reactions by identifying the patient who is at high risk. The second is to understand which specific drugs have the greatest probability of causing adverse drug reactions. The practitioner should be aware that some patients are at much higher risk of adverse drug reactions than others. Identifying these patients and treating them accordingly is the most effective way to minimize risk. Patients at greatest risk are those taking multiple medications, those who are medically compromised, and those who are taking specific medications that are closely titrated and have a narrow therapeutic index. The therapeutic dose of highly titrated drugs is just slightly less than the dose that causes adverse reactions. These drug groups are the following:

1. Anticoagulants
2. Anticonvulsants
3. Hypoglycemics
4. Cardiac glycosides
5. Lithium

It is estimated that medically complex patients, depending on the definition used, comprise from 15% to 25% of the average dental practice. The higher estimate includes in the definition of medically complex patients, cigarette smokers and patients over 55 years of age. More traditionally, the definition applies to those patients on multiple medications, those who have multiple medical problems, and patients under the age of 14 years and those older than 65 years. Certainly the decision as to whether a person is medically complex should be taken on a case-by-case basis, and varies with the medical problem as well as the dental procedure being undertaken. Relative to adverse drug interactions, special consideration should be given to those patients who are taking highly titrated drugs. Patients taking Synthroid to normalize their thyroid levels and even those taking blood pressure medications that render them normotensive, though they would be considered medically compromised, are at low risk for adverse drug reactions in a dental setting.

The other way of avoiding adverse drug reactions is to understand the drugs used in dentistry, their metabolism, effects, side effects, and toxicities. Few drugs are used in dentistry; the prescriber should know their uses and the safe maximum dose. It is not the dentist's responsibility to understand the effects, side effects, toxicity, and metabolism of all the medical drugs the patient may be using, but to understand how dental procedures and dental drugs impact the patient and the medication he or she is taking. This may be done in consultation with the patient's physician, though the dentist should not expect the physician to understand dental procedures nor the drugs used in dentistry. It is the dentist's responsibility to be aware of any medical drugs known to interact with drugs used in dentistry.

Many drug interactions are theoretically possible, but few are probable, and of the drug interactions that are probable, even fewer are serious. The adverse drug reactions noted here are considered probable; that is, they occur in more than 3% of patients. With awareness of these adverse drug reactions, familiarity with patients' health status, and use of proper drug dosage, the dentist can essentially eliminate the risk of adverse drug reactions, especially drug–drug and drug–physiology interactions.

Resources

This chapter is designed as a partial overview of adverse drug reactions. It provides precautions and information that should be adequate for the average practitioner to avoid 95% of the potential adverse drug reactions that could occur in dentistry. The resources listed in Table 11–5 provide additional specific information on certain topics, including tables on adverse drug reactions that are considered probable (ie, interactions have been reported in the scientific literature). Adverse drug reactions considered possible (ie, theoretically could occur but are not documented) also can be found in the *Journal of the American Dental Association* series on adverse drug reactions (see Table 11–5). As information available on the Internet evolves, there is no doubt that the most current information and the most accurate data available on adverse drug reactions will be accessible through a variety of Web sites. (Table 11–6 lists some

Table 11–5 Resources Regarding Adverse Drug Reaction

Specific series on dental drug interactions

Moore PA, Gage TW, Hersh EV, et al. Adverse drug interactions in dental practice: professional and educational implications. J Am Dent Assoc 1999;130:47–54.

Hersh EV. Adverse drug interactions in dental practice: interactions involving antibiotics. J Am Dent Assoc 1999;130:236–51.

Haas DA. Adverse drug interactions in dental practice: interactions associated with analgesics. J Am Dent Assoc 1999;130:397–407.

Moore PA. Adverse drug interactions in dental practice: interactions associated with local anesthetics, sedatives, and anxiolytics. J Am Dent Assoc 1999;130:541–54.

Yagiela JA. Adverse drug interactions in dental practice: interactions associated with vasoconstrictors. J Am Dent Assoc 1999;130:701–9.

Useful books

Wynn RL, Meiller TF, Cossley HL. Drug information handbook for dentistry. 5th Ed. Hudson, Ohio: Lexi-Comp, 1999–2000.

Web sites that are available for on-line inquiries about adverse drug reactions.) The dentist should select one or two sites, list them in "favorites," and learn to work effectively within them to gather necessary information. Two of the sites listed have search features that can be used to find information about specific drugs. This is especially important for new drugs that are just being released. These resources often provide a superabundance of information; it is the professional responsibility of each practitioner to identify the information that is relevant to the circumstances of each patient.

Table 11–6 Internet Web Site Resources for Drugs and Drug Interaction Information

www.medscape.com. This is a searchable site or an extensive medical-based home page that can be customized for personal interest. It will send topics, such as pharmacology, updates to your computer, to allow you to keep current on areas of interest.

www.fda.gov/opacom/hpchoice.html. This site within FDA provides information on adverse reactions.

www.nlm.nih.gov. This site has a powerful search feature that looks at a large range of databases and searches out complete articles on specific topics.

www.ada.org. The American Dental Association Web site contains resources and connects to a variety of medically related sites. Members can look through a long, well-researched list of useful Web sites related to drugs and health.

www.healthgate.com. This site provides access to medicine searches as well as health news.

www.dentalgate.com. This site has two different search features, one for the World Wide Web and another for medicine, especially designed for dentistry.

Mechanisms of Infection and Host Defense

L. Roy Eversole, DDS, MSD, MA

Microbial strategies

Microbial agents that cause disease in humans are said to be pathogenic, and those that cause disease only when the host defenses are compromised in some fashion are termed opportunists. The war that is waged between the infectious agent and the infected host constitutes a balance between microbial virulence factors and host defense mechanisms. Highly virulent organisms may propagate rapidly in host tissues and cause death before the immune system has time to respond. Conversely, many infectious agents are controlled by the host's immune response, and after a period of illness, the organisms are killed and eliminated. The host tissues may be fully reconstituted, or in some instances, permanent damage may occur. There are some infectious organisms that may chronically infect the host for years or months without causing death; a subset of these agents may reside within the host tissues as a quiescent reservoir, a process known as latency.

The majority of infections germane to the practice of oral medicine are viruses, fungi, and bacteria. The latter are common and affect the teeth and gums. Odontogenic endodontic infections are usually caused by gram-positive streptococcal organisms, with a minority of cases attributed to anaerobic rods. Periodontal infections are attributed to a heterogeneous group of spirochetes, rods, and pleomorphic bacteria, many of which are gram-negative. These infections constitute the "bread and butter" of dental practice. They are not discussed here, except in the context of focus of infection (see Chapter 17). In the practice of oral medicine, viruses and fungi are responsible for most microbial infections.

Virulence factors for bacteria, viruses, and fungi are presented in Tables 12–1 and 12–2. Bacteria are pathogenic because they synthesize proteins that are toxic to their infected host. Both bacteria and fungi possess cell-wall proteins and glycoproteins that allow for attachment to host-cell membranes. These molecules are referred to as adhesins. The fibrilla of gram-positive cocci bind to a variety of host-cell proteins, and lipoteichoic acid in the cell wall adheres to all eukaryotic cells, leukocytes, and oral epithelium in particular. Gram-negative bacteria have pili on their surfaces, and on the outer projecting surface of these pili are unique amino acid sequences that are specific for each bacterial species. By virtue of the variability in pili, certain bacteria bind only certain human cell types and not others, a factor that determines, in some part, cell tropism.

Molecular mimicry is another mechanism by which bacteria and fungi adhere to cells and tissues. Microorganisms possess surface proteins that bear a close similarity to host-cell proteins and, therefore, are capable of adhering to specific tissue receptors. In this context, both

Table 12–1 Virulence Factors in Pathogenic Bacteria and Fungi

Surface adhesion molecules (adhesins)
  Fibrilla (M proteins, gram-positive cocci)
  Lipoteichoic acid (gram-positive cocci)
  Pili (gram-negative bacteria, heterogenous cell specificity)
  Molecular mimicry (molecules that resemble host binding
    proteins)
    Integrin binding
    Complement receptors on leukocytes
    Extracellular matrix proteins
Intracellular virulence factors
  Hemolysins
  Lysosomal fusion inhibitory factors
  Protein synthesis inhibitory factors
  Cell-wall glycoproteins that resist lysosomal digestion
Endotoxin (lipopolysaccharide [LPS])
Exotoxins
  Diphtheria toxin protein A, arrest of protein synthesis
  Miscellaneous toxins that inhibit host-cell functioning
Bacterial antigen shedding
Leukotoxins
Proteases that degrade immunoglobulins
Proteases that degrade extracellular matrix
K antigens, complement inactivation
Staphylococcal protein A, binding of Fc region of immunoglobulin

Table 12–2 Viral Virulence Factors

Envelope/capsid adhesion molecules
    Specificity for binding to host-cell membrane proteins
    Molecular mimicry
    Cell membrane modification factors
Intracellular molecular alterations
    Specific tropism for selected cell types
    Enzyme and substrate piracy
    Inactivation of host-cell protein synthesis
    Inactivation of host-cell DNA and RNA synthesis
    Propagation-induced lysis
    MHC-I cell-surface presentation
    MHC-I sequestration
    Latency-inducing viral proteins
    Early proteins, cell cycle activation

MHC = major histocompatibility class.

bacteria and fungi have molecular motifs that bind to complement receptors on leukocytes, integrins, or extracellular matrix molecules. The mimicry then allows organisms to bind to host tissues and propagate in that milieu.

Once organisms have penetrated cells or have been phagocytized as intracellular parasites, they exert a variety of escape mechanisms that prevent them from being lysed. Some secrete hemolysins that destroy lysosomal membranes; others synthesize proteins that prevent fusion with lysosomes. Certain specific bacteria, such as mycobacteria, possess cell-wall glycoproteins that are resistant to lysosomal digestion.

Endotoxin is present on the cell membrane of many bacteria. This molecule is a lipopolysaccharide (LPS) that has a wide range of inflammatory effects that include stimulation of proinflammatory cytokines from leukocytes. Such effects contribute to a robust leukocytic response that can result in tissue destruction. Exotoxins are secreted by bacteria and are highly specific. For example, the diphtheria toxin is a bimolecular complex. The protein A subunit interferes with host-cell metabolism by arresting protein synthesis. Many other organisms secrete exotoxins that interfere with host-cell metabolic processes. For example, intestinal pathogens secrete toxins that interfere with G protein signal transduction in host cells, leading to massive accumulation of fluids in the gut.

The shedding of bacterial antigens serves to bind antibodies and complement, allowing the infectious agent itself a form of sequestration and escape. Another group of virulence factors derived from bacteria are enzymes that can be tissue-destructive. Included in this group are the collagenases and glycosidases that lyse collagen and glycosaminoglycan extracellular matrix polymers, laminases, lectinases, and other proteases that degrade integrins. Complement inactivation by K antigens and binding of Fc regions on immunoglobu-lin molecules by staphylococcal protein A are yet other virulence factors found in specific bacteria.

Viral virulence factors include envelope and capsid proteins that act as adhesion molecules and mediate viral entry into cells that express receptors for these adhesins. This molecular interaction is, in part, what governs cellular tropism by viruses. Viral proteins can alter host membranes making them porous or allowing cells to fuse with one another. As with bacteria, some viral proteins mimic normal cell chemistry and find ways of eluding the immune response. Early viral proteins interact with host-cell DNA and promote host-cell proliferation, viral nucleic acid integration (integrase enzymes) and viral replication by synthesis of DNA polymerase in the case of DNA viruses and reverse transcriptase in the case of RNA retroviruses. Once internalized into the host cell, viral parasites usurp normal cell constituents for their own propagation and also result in lysis and necrosis of host cells. Viral proteins are integrated into major histocompatibility complex (MHC) class II molecules in antigen-presenting cells for immunorecognition and into MHC-I molecules which then become targets for cytotoxic T lymphocytes, which can then further destroy host cells that harbor virus. This aids in viral elimination, yet also results in widespread host-cell destruction. Herpes group viruses are able to prevent MHC-I assembly and can hide inside cells without expressing antigen on the cell surface. Most herpesviruses elaborate proteins that enable them to remain latent intracellular parasites. At a later point in time, other viral gene products are elaborated, awakening the virus from latency and promoting a recurrent lytic infection of host cells.

Host defenses

The flip side of virulence is host resistance. Following is a brief overview of host response to challenge by foreign proteins and glycoproteins that are present on microbial cell walls, envelopes, and capsids. The host defends against infectious diseases by mounting an immune response. The primary barrier to infection is the stratified squamous epithelium of the skin and mucous membranes. For many years, this barrier has been considered in the context of a physical barricade that prevents penetration of pathogenic microorganisms, thereby mitigating their access to the connective tissues and vital organs. It is now well documented that the skin and mucosae are biochemical and immunologic organs. Furthermore, it is axiomatic that some infectious agents, particularly viral and fungal pathogens, actually use the epithelium for colonization and propagation.

All microbial agents possess surface proteins and glycoproteins that are recognized as "non-self" or "foreign" to the human host. The foreign molecules are referred to as *antigens*. This foreignness is the sine qua non of the host mechanism of defense. When a viral, bacterial, or fungal pathogen comes in contact with host tissues, it does so with a plan. This plan is to use the host as a substrate for self-propagation. As has been discussed, self-propagation takes place at the expense of host-cell integrity, thereby resulting in disease. When host tissues are violated by microbial pathogens, a group of cells become activated and alert the host that a battle must be engaged. These cells are referred to as *antigen presenting cells* and are comprised of intraepithelial Langerhans cells and migratory as well as fixed tissue macrophages. These ubiquitous cells are able to phagocytize, indiscriminately, foreign antigens and digest their molecular components by an enzymatic organelle known as the proteasome. The digested antigens are then attached to an MHC-II molecule and exteriorized on the cell surface (Figure 12–1). These phagocytes are then activated to motility and migrate via lymphatics to regional lymph nodes where they encounter lymphocytes that bear a specific receptor that recognizes the antigen in the context of the MHC-II molecule (class II restricted lymphocytes). These lymphocytes are destined to help or induce the host immune response and are, therefore, termed helper-inducer lymphocytes. These lymphocytes bear a cell-surface molecule that is their trademark, *CD4*.

The CD4 lymphocytes, so stimulated, peruse one of two specific pathways: Th1 and Th2. The pathway taken is governed by the nature of the pathogen antigens. Some organisms are eliminated more efficiently by Th1 stimulation; others are more effectively eliminated by Th2 pathway stimulation. These pathways are stimulated by certain chemical moieties, known as *cytokines*, synthesized by the antigen-presenting cell. The Th1 pathway stimulates another subset of lymphocytes that bear the surface-marker protein CD8. These lymphocytes are cytotoxic, able to directly destroy cells that are infected with virus or destroy cells that bear the foreign antigen on the membranes. The Th2 pathway involves the stimulation of a subset of lymphocytes that bear surface immunoglobulins, glycoprotein antibodies that bind to foreign antigens. These are known as B-lymphocytes, cells that can migrate into tissues and transform into plasma cells.

Once B lymphocytes are activated, they secrete specific immunoglobulins that specifically bind to foreign antigens (Figure 12–2). There are five classes of

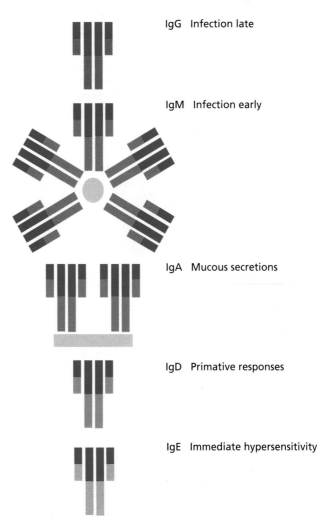

Figure 12–2 Immunoglobulin classes and functions.

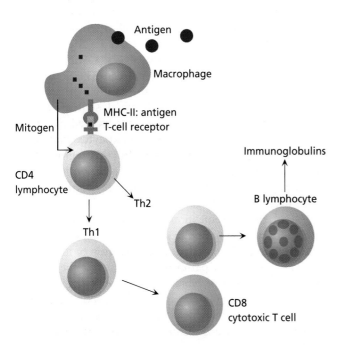

Figure 12–1 Immune response overview. Antigen-presenting cells interact with CD4 lymphocytes that diverge into Th1 and Th2 pathways to activate CD8 lymphocytes and B lymphocytes, respectively. MHC-II = major histocompatibility complex class II.

immunoglobulins (Ig): IgG, IgM, IgA, IgD, and IgE. IgM is the first antibody to be stimulated by an infection and is quickly replaced by B cells that secrete IgG. IgA is a unique antibody that is generated by lymphocytes in the intestines and is found in mucosal secretions, including breast milk, oral, nasal, pharyngeal, pulmonary, intestinal, and urogenital mucous membrane secretions. IgD is an early immunoglobulin that becomes replaced by others during maturation of the immune response to an antigen. IgE is protective against certain parasites and is the key antibody in allergic reactions that occur within minutes of exposure to antigen (immediate hypersensitivity). Antigens that are noninfectious, yet mediate an IgE response are termed *allergens.*

When antigens that trigger the Th2 cytokine profile select a Th2 pathway, B lymphocytes are selected for immunoglobulin synthesis. B cells carry receptors on their surface that recognize specific amino acid sequences on antigens. The receptors are immunoglobulins, and the antigenic sequences are known as epitopes. Once specific B lymphocytes are bound to antigen, they transform into plasma cells that become immunoglobulin secretors (Figure 12–3). When viral, fungal, or bacterial antigens are the stimuli, the B cells secrete IgM and IgG into the serum with resultant hypergammaglobulinemia. If soluble antigens are present in the serum, Ig:Ag complexes, also known as *immune complexes,* form and may filter out into the tissues to cause a pathologic response. This response is

typically seen around vessel walls, forming an immune complex vasculitis. If the stimulatory antigen is an allergen, IgE-bearing B cells respond. The IgE antibody, referred to as reagin, has a binding site on mast cells and when allergenic epitopes are bound, mast cells degranulate, releasing histamine and other vasoactive mediators that culminate in vasodilation, permeability, and edema.

In the context of immunity against infectious agents, the role of immunoglobulin is limited; the function of the antibody molecule is to bind the antigen and precipitate it. To achieve microbial death, lysis, and elimination, immunoglobulins require another group of active proteins. These proteins are collectively known as *complement* (Figure 12–4). The C1qrs trimolecular complex binds to an antigen that is already bound to its complementary IgG or IgM antibody. (There is an alternative pathway that does not require IgM or IgG.) Fractions 2, 4, and 3 are then activated, and it is the binding of C3 that initiates the inflammatory cascade by releasing C3-derived peptides known as cleavage products. These peptides are biologically active, stimulating other complement fractions to form complexes (C5, 6, and 7 chemoattractants), causing mast cells to degranulate (C3a, C5a anaphylatoxins), and coating microbial-cell walls with peptide fragments (opsonins) that facilitate phagocytosis. The final complement components, C8 and C9, form the membrane attack complex, a reaction that eventuates in lysis of the infectious agent cell membrane. Thus, it is Ig with complement activation that results in the inflammatory response with edema, chemotaxis of leukocytes, phagocytosis, and lysis.

Another mechanism for microbial elimination is *antibody-dependent cellular cytotoxicity.* In this scenario, antibody binds to infectious agents or to infected host cells that express microbial antigens (Figure 12–5). The immunoglobulin molecule, on the pole opposite its antigen-binding domain has chemical sequences that bind leukocytes. These sequences are located in the Fc region of immunoglobulin, and leukocytes that have adhesion molecules (Fc receptors) for this region of Ig. Once bound, phagocytosis may proceed or leukocyte enzymes and oxygen free-radical species may then inactivate microbial propagation.

All of the aforementioned pathways involve B-cell activation, immunoglobulin synthesis, secretion and circulation within the blood, and propagation of inflammation via complement pathways. Taken altogether, this is the *humoral-mediated immune response* (Th2). The *cell-mediated immune (CMI) response* is engendered, not by immunoglobulin, but by cytotoxic CD8 lymphocytes. Cell-mediated immune response does not use circulating cell products (ie, Igs); rather the detrimental effects on microbial agents and infected host cells is mediated by the CD8 lymphocyte directly (Th1). In such reactions, these cytotoxic cells must be transported through blood to the

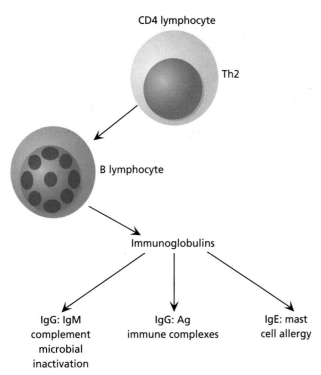

Figure 12–3 The Th2 pathway involves activation of immunoglobulin-secreting B lymphocytes and plasma cells.

site of the infection; such responses usually require up to 48 hours and are, therefore, termed *delayed immune responses*. Once CD8 lymphocytes contact cellular antigens, they bind to them by virtue of specific T-cell receptors (Figure 12–6). These T-cell receptors have the same intricate specificity for antigenic epitopes as do the B-cell immunoglobulin receptors. The antigen is engaged in the context of the cell-surface molecule MHC-I, and therefore, cytotoxic T cells are MHC-I restricted. Once the lymphocyte binds to the infected cell, a class of cytokines termed perforins is released, and these proteins mediate cell lysis of the target cell that harbors the MHC-I:Ag complex. Microscopically, CD8 reactions are characterized by chronic inflammatory cell infiltration.

At the outset it was mentioned that the epithelium of the skin and mucous membranes serves as a physical, immunologic, and biochemical barrier to infection. It is

now well documented that keratinocytes are a vital component of the immune system. These cells elaborated inflammatory cytokines, leukocyte mitogenic factors, adhesion molecules for leukocytes, and chemoattractants. All of these functions are stimulated when a pathogen passes into the epithelial layers.

Immunoglobulins and complement more efficiently eliminate bacterial infections whereas the cellular limb of the immune response is more efficacious for viral and fungal infections. In most infectious diseases, both limbs of the immune response are active, yet one appears to take precedence over the other, depending upon the nature of the offending organism. Recall that both humoral and cellular immunity require induction by antigen-presenting cells and CD4 lymphocytes. It is the CD4 lymphocyte that is the target for the human immunodeficiency virus (see Chapter 14). As CD4 cells

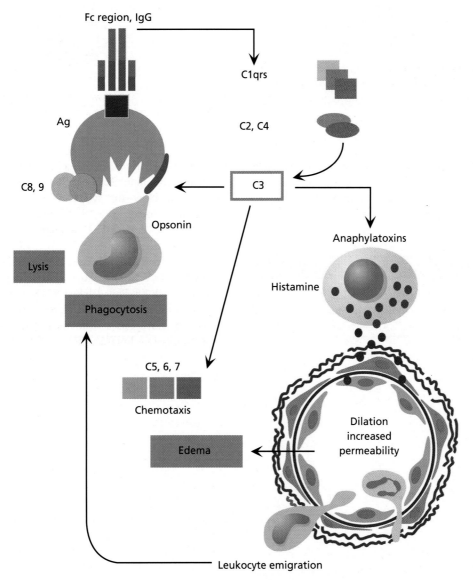

Figure 12–4   The role of complement in the elimination of pathogens and pathogen-infected host cells.

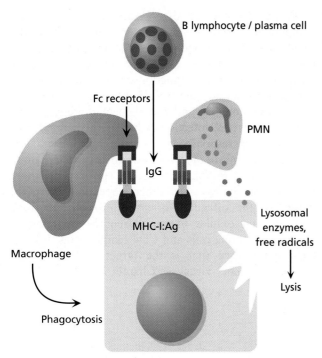

Figure 12–5 Antibody-dependent cellular cytotoxicity: phagocytes bind to Fc regions of Igs that are, in turn, bound to antigen. PMN = polymorphonuclear neutrophil leukocytes; MHC-I = major histocompatibility complex class I.

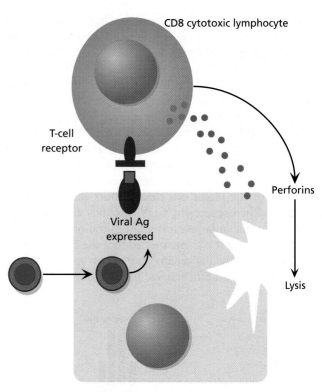

Figure 12–6 The Th1 pathway involves binding of CD8 lymphocytes to target antigens culminating in release of cytolytic perforins.

are progressively eliminated by viral-induced and CD8 cell-induced lysis, the ability to mount an immune response to new antigens becomes impaired, leading to the emergence of opportunistic infections.

Suggested reading

Eversole LR. Defense. In: Eversole L, Leider A, Merrell P, Carpenter W, eds. General pathology and medicine in dental practice. 3rd Ed. Stockton, CA: University of the Pacific Press, 2000:1–60.

Lamont AG, Adorini L. IL-12: a key cytokine in immune regulation. Immunol Today 1996;17:214–7.

Murray JS. How the MHC selects Th1/Th2 immunity. Immunol Today 1998;19:157–63.

Romagnani S. The Th1/Th2 paradigm. Immunol Today 1997; 18:263–6.

Samuelson J, von Lichtenberg F. Infectious diseases. In: Cotran RS, Kumar V, Robbins SL, eds. Robbins pathologic basis of disease. 5th Ed. Philadelphia: WB Saunders, 1994:305–19.

Strober W, Kelsall B, Fuss I, et al. Reciprocal IFN-gamma and TGF-beta responses regulate the occurrence of mucosal inflammation. Immunol Today 1997;18:61–4.

Herpesviruses and Enteroviruses

Sol Silverman, Jr, MA, DDS, and L. Roy Eversole, DDS, MSD, MA

The human herpesviruses (HHV, numbered 1 through 8) represent a large group of DNA viruses that share some common biologic features that account for a great deal of oral pathology. Human herpesvirus infections often lead to acute oral signs and symptoms, are a challenge to diagnosis, and are frequently difficult to treat. This family of viruses includes the herpes simplex viruses (HSV) (HHV-1 and -2), the varicella-zoster virus (VZV) (HHV-3), Epstein-Barr virus (EBV) (HHV-4), cytomegalovirus (CMV) (HHV-5), and the relatively more recently identified viruses, HHV-6, HHV-7, and HHV-8. Because of their different expressions of disease, each of the herpes family viruses is discussed separately.

Although the occurrences of HHV in both health and disease are worldwide, their exact prevalence is uncertain. Because their modes of clinical expressions differ, HHV infections pose frequent and common global problems for both patients and clinicians. The worldwide problem of immunosuppression has an effect on the frequencies and control of HHV oral disease. The details of frequency, severity, diagnosis, and treatment of HHV and immunosuppression are covered in detail in Chapter 14.

Human herpesviruses have a large spectrum of associated pathologic effects on cells and tissues. They are associated with both acute and chronic infections as well as neoplasia. Whereas the history and clinical features sometimes allow an accurate diagnosis, at other times,

sophisticated laboratory testing is required to identify and classify the specific HHV member. Following identification, the management regarding initial treatment, recurrences, and prevention often becomes a challenge.

Molecular and pathologic correlates of disease

The human herpesviruses are comprised of a DNA genome surrounded by an icosahedron protein capsule that is enclosed within an envelope. The average dimension is about 200 nm. These viruses are subclassified into alpha, beta, and gamma subtypes according to their virulence in tissue culture. Human herpesviruses 1, 2 (simplex types), and 3 (varicella-zoster virus) belong to the alpha group, Epstein-Barr virus (HHV-4) to the gamma group, and cytomegalovirus (HHV-5) is a member of the beta group. Human herpesviruses 1 and 2 possess envelope proteins that bind to plasma membrane receptors on keratinocytes and neurons. Upon binding, the virions enter the cytoplasm by endocytosis, and the receptors can then recycle back to the cell membrane (Figure 13–1). Virions under genetic control uncoat, and the DNA enters the nucleus.

Replication ensues within the nuclear envelope, and transcription of proteins takes place in the cytoplasm

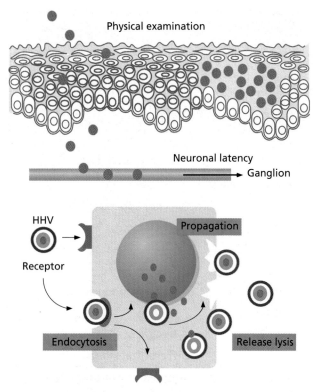

Figure 13–1 *Top*, Diagram of the lytic (keratinocytes) and latent (neuronal) phases of HHV-1 infection. *Bottom*, Viral adhesion to cell-surface receptor, intranuclear propagation, assembly, release, and cell lysis in a keratinocyte.

where new capsids are formed. During replication, thousands of viral copies are generated and the nucleus swells, creating a histologically distinct cytopathic effect termed nuclear ballooning degeneration. The nascent DNA is then packaged into the empty capsids that are exported to the nuclear membrane. There they acquire an envelope consisting of host lipoprotein, viral-specific glycoprotein spikes, and a glue-like material that is interposed between the capsid and envelope, known as the tegument. The mature virions pass into the cytosol and are released through the plasma membrane into the extracellular space. During the process of replication, various HHV gene products cause major alterations in keratinocyte metabolism, the chief effects being membrane leakage and a shutdown of macromolecular synthesis. In the process, the cell becomes lysed and undergoes necrosis. Thus, keratinocyte infections are classified as lytic.

The next phase of HHV infection is the process of latency. When virions bind to receptors on neurons, they are mobilized up axis cylinders by retrograde transport and enter the cell body of the nerve cell. The virus then enters a state of dormancy, residing in the cytosol as an episome. This sleepy phase is termed latency and is accompanied by expression of latency associated transcripts (LATS). Various sensory stimuli may then

reactivate the virus, awaking it from dormancy and allowing transport down to the axonal terminus where the virus passes across the connective tissues to bind and reinfect keratinocytes of the lips or oral mucosa. In the process, patients often perceive paresthetic changes in the skin or mucosa that ultimately manifest a vesicle.

The HHV genome is comprised of multiple inverted repeats that flank a long (L) segment and a short (S) segment of viral-specific DNA sequences. The entire genome is large, with a molecular weight of 96×10^6. The HHV-1, -2, and -5 genes are divided into alpha, beta, and gamma groups, with expression of alpha genes being required for activation of the others. Over 80 viral-specific proteins are transcribed from the genome. There are various alpha gene products that are required for replication. The thymidine kinase gene is one of them and is an important mediator of adenosine phosphorylation. This enzyme is HHV specific and phosphorylates acyclovir, a drug that, once converted to a triphosphate, depresses further replication of herpesvirus DNA. Human herpesvirus type-3 (VZV) and HHV-4 (EBV) have a somewhat different genetic orientation. Epstein-Barr virus genes are usually grouped into immediate, early, and late components, with the immediate and early gene products being responsible for viral propagation and host cell changes, whereas late gene products are involved in capsid assembly. In Burkitt and human immunodeficiency virus (HIV)-associated lymphomas, EBV genomes can be identified and are accompanied by host-cell chromosomal translocations that are thought to be of etiologic importance.

Also included in this chapter are the epitheliotropic enteroviruses, which are comprised of 67 genotype or serotype species, the most important of which are the coxsackieviruses (CSV). These viruses bind to epithelial cell membranes of the oral mucosal, skin, and intestinal epithelia. This group of viruses is elemental, being only 7300 base pairs in length, with an RNA genome. Unlike HHV, they do not induce a latent form of infection. RNA is transcribed into a single protein that is then enzymatically cleaved, to yield functional and structural proteins. The virions are encapsulated, yet not enveloped. The RNA sequences and, hence, protein products are closely related yet vary to some degree, accounting for the classification into four major subgroups: coxsackievirus types A and B, echoviruses, and miscellaneous enteroviruses. Each major subtype is further divided numerically into various serotypes (Table 13–1). More than one serotype can cause a specific form of coxsackie infection.

Herpes simplex viruses

By far, the most common oral HHV infections and problems involve HSV-1. Individuals are usually

Table 13–1 The Enteroviruses

Viral Subgroup	Serotypes	Exanthem or Enanthem
Poliovirus	1–3	Poliomyelitis (1–3)
Coxsackie A	1–22, 24	Lymphonodular pharyngititis (A10)
		Herpangina (A1, 3–10, 16)
		Nonspecific stomatitis (A3, 5, 9, 16)
		Hand, foot, and mouth disease (A4, 5, 7, 9, 16)
Coxsackie B	1–6	Herpangina (B1–5)
		Nonspecific stomatitis (B2, 3, 5)
Echovirus	1–7, 9, 11–27, 29–32*	Herpangina (3, 6, 9, 16, 17, 30)
		Nonspecific stomatitis (6, 9, 16)
Other enteroviruses	68–71	Hand, foot, and mouth disease (71)

*Various echoviruses eliminated from sequential numbering because they have been reclassified as other viral types.

exposed to HSV-1 before puberty. Once infected, the virus remains in a latent form in regional ganglia indefinitely. Asymptomatic shedding and reactivation are common, varying up to 50% in some population studies. Although HSV-2 primarily occurs in the genital area, recurrent lip and oral mucosal lesions are occasionally associated with this type. However, the diagnosis and treatment of these types do not differ.

Clinical features

Upon initial infection early in life (before adolescence), many individuals have signs and symptoms. Some have slight clinical manifestations of malaise and possibly fever, whereas others become quite ill with a primary herpetic gingivostomatitis. The latter can be expressed by skin, lip, and oral mucosal ulcerations, fever, lymphadenopathy, and considerable malaise. It is referred to as a gingivostomatitis, because almost always there is an associated gingival erythema, edema, and erosive lesions (Figures 13–2 to 13–5).

The main therapeutic control is derived from patients developing appropriate antibodies; and almost like clockwork, patient illness increases during the first week of infection and continually improves during the second week. By the third week, all signs and symptoms of primary herpetic gingivostomatitis have disappeared, and the patient has developed lifetime immunity against this acute form of infection. About 10% of the population by the time they reach adolescence either have never been exposed sufficiently to HSV-1 or have not developed antibodies, and they may acquire adult-onset primary herpetic gingivostomatitis upon HSV exposure.

Although the course of infection in adults may be about the same 2 to 3 weeks, the signs and symptoms are often more severe.

When unprotected fingers that have skin breaks come in contact with HSV by oral contact, particularly around the nail bed (cuticle), a herpetic whitlow may develop. These lesions of the fingers are painful and difficult to treat (Figure 13–6). Some patients with HSV infections can inoculate their eyes with HSV by rubbing their eyes with HSV-infected oral secretions (Figure 13–7). These lesions can be painful and even impair vision.

Diagnosis

Primary herpetic gingivostomatitis
Primary herpetic gingivostomatitis is an infection that can often be diagnosed by history (no previous episodes), the short and acute onset, and signs and symptoms. Cultures for HSV and scrapings may be helpful in confirming a viral etiology. The scrapings can

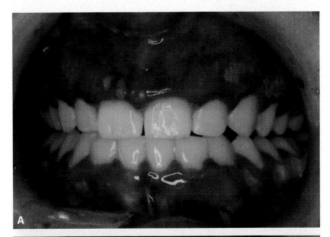

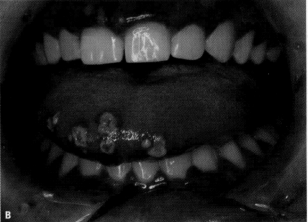

Figure 13–2 Primary herpetic gingivostomatitis in a child. Painful gingival (*A*) and tongue (*B*) lesions had been present for 4 days with associated fever and malaise. This was a first-time attack. In 10 days with only supportive care, the patient was asymptomatic and well.

be processed for immunofluorescent confirmation, or stained for cytologic evidence of pathognomonic pseudogiant cells (Figure 13–8). Blood draws that show a fourfold or more rise in HSV antibodies are also confirmatory, but after the fact. In the differential diagnosis in youngsters, erythema multiforme must be considered (see Chapter 21); in adults, along with erythema multiforme, pemphigus vulgaris is included in the differential diagnosis. If vesicular lesions have lasted more than 3 weeks, primary HSV is not a consideration.

Recurrent herpes labialis

Recurrent herpes labialis manifests as vesicles caused by HHV-1 or, infrequently, by HHV-2 that occur on the lips as "cold sores." Most typically these common lesions appear suddenly, after an episode of lip tingling, and remain intact for about 4 days, after which they enter a crust period for about 4 to 6 days (Figure 13–9). They heal without scarring. Although cold sores are

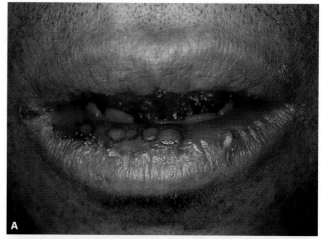

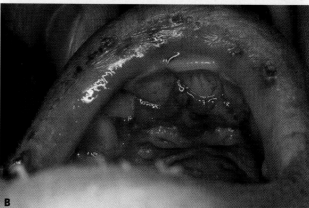

Figure 13–4 *A* and *B*, Adult onset primary herpetic gingivostomatitis in a 32-year-old male with spontaneous severe oral ulcers and gingivitis. There was acute pain and fever with no other findings. Following supportive care only, he was well in 2 weeks, and since then, has had no further similar attacks.

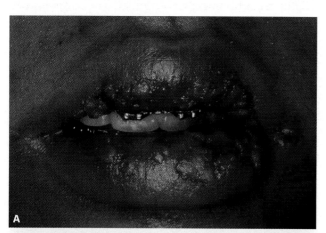

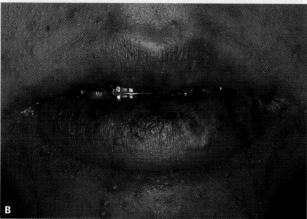

Figure 13–3 Primary herpetic gingivostomatitis in an adolescent. *A,* Intraoral and labial ulcers of 5 days duration associated with sudden onset, fever, pain, and lymphadenopathy. There were no other medical findings or associated causative factors. *B,* One week later, the patient was essentially without signs or symptoms; and at the end of 2 weeks from the onset, she was completely healed. Treatment included acyclovir for 5 days, fluids, and anti-inflammatory-antipyretic analgesics.

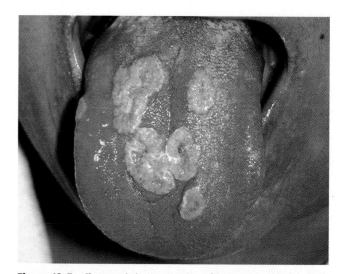

Figure 13–5 Characteristic presentation of tongue ulcerations of primary herpetic gingivostomatitis in an immunosuppressed kidney transplant patient. There was complete healing in a week following acyclovir intravenous medication.

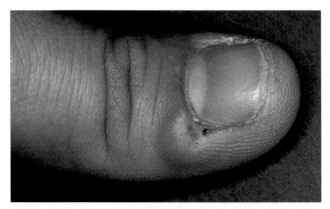

Figure 13–6 Characteristic herpetic whitlow contracted by contact between this patient's finger cuticle and herpes simplex virus type 1-infected saliva.

usually single, they may be multiple, which in turn usually increases the discomfort and can even confuse the diagnosis with erythema multiforme (see Chapter 21). The number and severity of attacks vary from patient to patient, often without a clear explanation; however, many times patients recall stress, fever (often called "fever blisters"), trauma (eg, a dental visit), or climate exposure (sun exposure or cold). Herpes labialis is a consequence of recrudescence from latent ganglionic HHV-1 infection.

Intraoral recurrent herpes

Intraoral recurrent herpes is an infection that almost exclusively occurs in keratinized epithelium, which helps in the differential diagnosis from aphthous-type ulcers, which almost always occur on unkeratinized epithelial mucosa. They usually occur as shallow, irregularly shaped clusters of surface erosions that can

coelesce (Figure 13–10). They may even appear similar to some type of local trauma response (eg, hard or hot foods) or physical irritation. Therefore, the diagnosis is often missed. Importantly, the vesicles cluster in small groups, with the premolar or molar region of the palatal

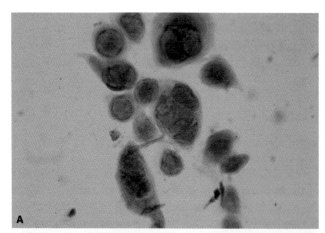

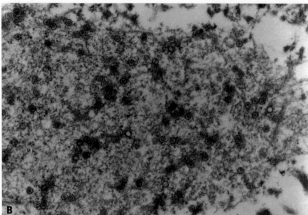

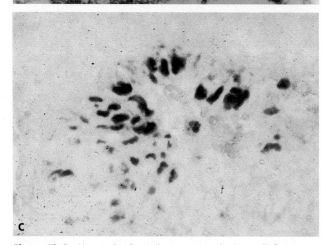

Figure 13–8 Herpes simplex 1 viruses. *A,* Pseudogiant cells from a surface scraping of an oral ulcer in a patient with primary herpetic gingivostomatitis. *B,* Electron microscopic photomicrograph of a nucleus from a herpes simplex virus type 1-infected epithelial cell. Note the numerous viruses with their central core and capsule. *C,* In situ DNA hybridization for herpes virus.

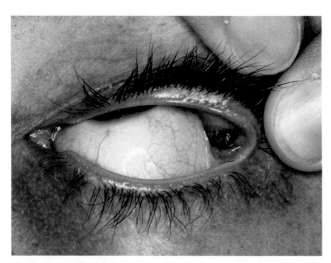

Figure 13–7 Ocular herpes simplex virus type 1 infection from rubbing the eye with a saliva-contaminated finger in a patient with primary herpetic stomatitis.

gingiva being the most commonly involved site. The virions exit the endings of the greater palatine nerve. Occasionally, latent virus travels down the mental or long buccal nerve to culminate in vesicular lesions of the anterior mandibular facial gingiva or posterior mandibular buccal gingiva, respectively. The main significance is that HHV ulcers shed virus for about 3 to 4 days and, hence, may put partners at risk during that time. In the immunocompromised patient, HSV lesions can occur on any mucosal surface with often uncharacteristic appearances, which sometimes complicate identification (see Chapter 14).

Treatment

Treatment for the primary infection with HSV is directed toward control of signs and symptoms, since the cure is based upon production and site migration (chemotaxis) of the appropriate antibodies in the infected host. When indicated in the early stages, antiviral agents are helpful (Table 13–2). The patient may need supportive care with antipyretic analgesics, and must be kept hydrated. Reassurance of the benign nature and the need for some caloric intake and rest is important.

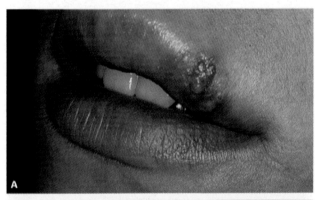
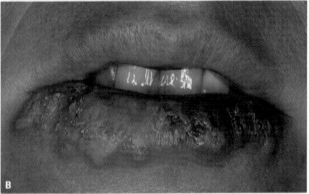

Figure 13–9 Recurrent herpes labialis (cold sores). *A,* Single lesion at day 7 in a 12-year-old boy; *B,* multiple lesions in an adult female at day 10. The lesions spontaneously healed in another 10 days, with only application of lubricant. The sores recurred periodically and would shed virus for about 4 days.

In most individuals, recurrent HSV resolves rapidly from local antibody protection. When infection is identified early (within 3 days), antiviral medication, either systemically or topically may help. After 4 to 5 days, viral shedding is difficult to identify, then the lesions are primarily inflammatory and antiviral medications are not effective. If clinical or physical conditions can be identified with the onset of attacks, obviously, these situations should be minimized or avoided. Prophylaxis with antiviral medications can be tried on a trial-and-error basis.

In the dermatologic literature, there has been reported evidence of an association between HSV serving as an antigen and subsequent attacks of erythema multiforme. Oral manifestations of erythema multiforme and the presence of HSV has only been reported in a few cases. Therefore, it might be assumed that HSV may serve as a causative factor in an oral erythema multiforme reaction (see Chapter 21).

Other human herpesviruses

Epstein-Barr virus

Epstein-Barr virus (HHV-4) is associated with infectious mononucleosis, lymphomas, and nasopharyngeal carcinoma. Although each can have oral manifestations, these are almost always primarily a medical problem. The EBV has been associated with a condition called hairy leukoplakia, primarily seen in HIV-infected patients (see Chapter 14).

Varicella-zoster virus

Varicella-zoster virus (HHV-3) causes chicken pox, then becomes latent. Occasionally, chicken pox is associated with oral eruptions (vesicles and ulcerations). These

Table 13–2 Antiviral Drugs for Herpes Simplex Virus

Classification Generic Name (Brand Name)	Suggested Dosage × Duration (d)
Systemic	
Acyclovir (Zovirax)	400 mg tid × 7
Famciclovir (Famvir)	125 mg bid × 5
Valacyclovir (Valtrex)	500 mg bid × 5
Topical	
Penciclovir (Denavir) cream (1%)	Every 2 hours during the day
Acyclovir (Zovirax) ointment (5%)	Every 3 hours during the day
Docosanol cream (10%)	Every 3 hours during the day
Viroxyn solution	Single application

*Variations in dosage and time are adjusted for clinical severity and response.

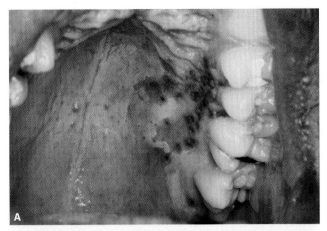

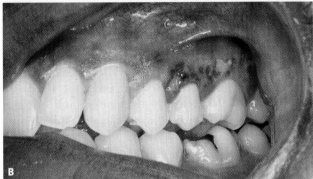

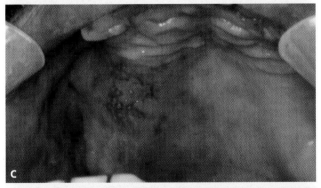

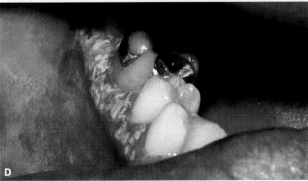

resolve as antibodies are developed in controlling the virus. Somewhat uncommonly, HHV-3 becomes reactivated (usually only once, if at all) and causes the signs and symptoms of herpes zoster or shingles. The virus involves the host with a unilateral, nerve pathway-associated vesicular eruption; usually, a single, unilateral dermatome is involved. This can occur in the mouth and lips as the only manifestation (Figures 13–11 and 13–12). The most frequently involved sites are the face and trunk. It more commonly occurs in elderly or immunocompromised and medically complex patients. Post-zoster neuropathy can become a prolonged post-infection complication of pain that can significantly alter the quality of life.

Antiviral treatment to be most effective must be started within 72 hours. There is no reproducibly effective treatment for post-herpetic neuropathy; antianxiety- or antidepression-type drugs seem to offer some relief.

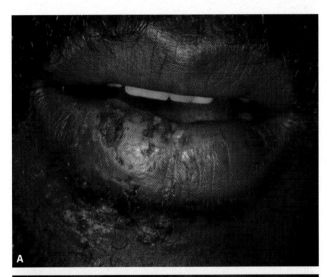

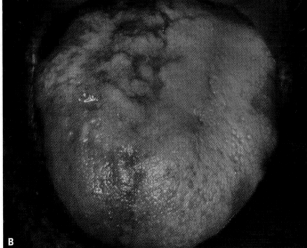

Figure 13–10 Recurrent intraoral herpes infections. *A,* Typical palatal herpes that would occur periodically, last less than 10 days, and were not associated with any specific event. *B,* Classic gingival herpes. These are often mistaken for a response to trauma. *C,* This patient would have occasional outbreaks under a denture. Note how the small herpetic ulcers tend to coelesce. Healing usually occurs within 2 weeks without any treatment. *D,* Long buccal distribution of human herpes virus type 1.

Figure 13–11 *A* and *B,* Herpes zoster (shingles) due to reactivation of the varicella (chicken pox) virus. Note the unilateral distribution of lesions.

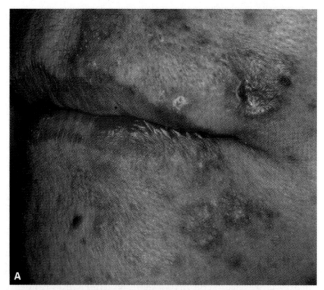

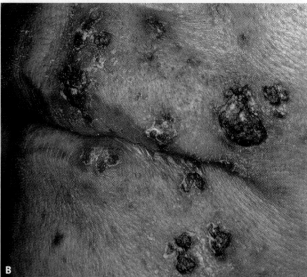

Figure 13-12 Shingles in an elderly and stressed patient. *A,* Painful unilateral ulcers present for 1 week. *B,* At day 11 the ulcers reverted from pain to mainly itching. Note the presence of scabs and healing process. Clinical healing was complete by day 20; but then vague neuropathy in that area began to bother the patient.

Cytomegalovirus

Human CMV (HHV-5) occurs worldwide, and evidence of exposure is found in large segments of the population in both developed and underdeveloped countries. However, CMV clinical oral infections are infrequent, even though antibodies to CMV can be found commonly in blood and urine. Most CMV-infected persons, therefore, have had subclinical infections. Cytomegalovirus can infect major salivary glands and cause xerostomia, or can be identified in some oral ulcerations in the immunocompromised patient (Figure 13-13) (see Chapters 14 and 26).

Lymphotropic viruses

Human herpes viruses type 6 and 7 have been recently identified and tend to produce latent infections in humans. They may become reactivated in a lytic phase, induce various cytokines, as well as proliferation factors, and result in malignant transformation in the susceptible host. Variants of HHV-6 have been found in the peripheral blood of immunocompromised hosts, namely transplant and HIV-positive patients. Adult seroprevalence may exceed 80%, and HHV-6 may be transmitted by saliva. Although HHV-7 has properties similar to those of HHV-6, it has not been definitively associated with human disease; however, its antibodies are found widespread in human peripheral blood. Major and minor salivary glands may harbor and shed this virus in saliva.

Human herpesvirus type 8 has been strongly associated with Kaposi sarcoma (KS) in HIV-infected patients. The appearance of KS, depending upon the stage, can be confused with trauma, hemangiomas, and bacillary angiomatosis and with some amalgam and melanin mucosal depositions (see Chapter 14).

Enteroviruses

Like the herpesviruses, enteroviruses cause oral vesiculo-ulcerative lesions, although a rare syndrome is characterized by nonvesicular papular eruptions. The diseases caused by some enteroviruses crossover, meaning that members of one serotype group can cause the same clinical presentation of infection as those of another serotype. Because these viruses lack the ability to induce latent infections, there are no episodic recurrences. Alternatively, because there are so many serotypes, any given individual may become reinfected and manifest the same disease at a later time. For many subjects,

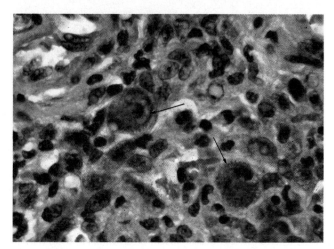

Figure 13-13 Cytomegalovirus inclusions in connective tissue cells.

cross-reactive antibodies may protect against future infections with specific serotypes.

Clinical features

These infections are self-limited, persisting for only 10 to 14 days, and are classically accompanied by constitutional signs of infectious disease, which include malaise, regional lymphadenopathy, and fever. Certain members of this group cause serious myocarditis; the ones under consideration here cause upper respiratory and oral vesiculoulcerative lesions. Coxsackieviruses (CSV) belong to the ECHO group of enteroviruses, and infections with these viruses also induce diarrhea.

Diagnosis

Throat and stool cultures are used for definitive serotyping; however, from a clinical point of view, the diagnosis is made based upon the salient clinical findings and distribution of lesions. A given syndrome may be caused by a variety of enterovirus serotypes. As stated previously, each disease is distinguished by the anatomic distribution of lesions and their character. Some manifest as vesicles, others as papules.

Hand, foot, and mouth disease

Hand, foot, and mouth disease may be caused by various members of the CSV group. The lesional distribution is classic (Figure 13–14, *A* to *C*). Vesicles that breakdown to small ulcers can occur anywhere in the oral cavity, but importantly, do not show a predilection for involvement of the palate or gingiva (keratinized epithelium). The cutaneous lesions are localized to the elbows down and the knees down, with most vesicles appearing on the hands and feet. These lesions are painful and pruritic, resolving in 10 to 12 days. As with other CSV infections, there is no latent phase, and the virus is neutralized by antibody, without recrudescence. Treatment, as with herpangina, is palliative.

Herpangina

So-named because the lesions resemble those of herpes infections and the affected mucosa is painful and burning, herpangina manifests a unique distribution pattern. All of the vesicles are localized posterior to the hard–soft palate junction (Figure 13–14, *D*). The soft palate, uvula, and faucel pillars are the favored sites of involvement. The lesions do not cluster; rather, they are randomly distributed and begin as vesicles that soon rupture to leave open microulcers. There may also be a diffuse erythema of the oropharynx. The combination of pharyngitis and ulceration causes clinical confusion with streptococcal disease (strep throat). Patients are febrile and manifest lymphadenopathy of cervical nodes. The disease runs its course in 10 days, and during the initial 5 to 6 days, it is transmissible as aerosol. Palliative oral rinses, such as antihistamines mixed with kaopectate, offer symptomatic relief. In small children, it is important to maintain fluid and nutritional intake, adhering to a liquid diet, since solids may aggravate the pain symptoms. Analgesics are also helpful.

Enterovirus enanthematous stomatitis

There are many atypical infections of the oral mucosa that do not conform to the classic distribution patterns of the herpes simplex and CSV. These lesions are often confused with herpetiform aphthae (multiple minute aphthae, see Chapter 21) and allergic stomatitis. Importantly, the ulcers can be diffusely distributed throughout the mouth, yet are accompanied by fever. The lesions do not tend to involve the gingiva and, therefore, do not resemble primary herpetic gingivostomatitis. As with CSV infections, various serotypes may be causative, and the lesions resolve within 2 weeks. Treatment is palliative, using anesthetic rinses and analgesic or antipyretic drugs to lower fever.

Lymphonodular pharyngitis

Lymphonodular pharyngitis is a unique CSV infection in that the lesions are not vesiculoulcerative; rather, they appear as yellow-orange papules localized primarily, yet not exclusively, to the soft palate (Figure 13–14, *E*). These papules are multifocal without any tendency to cluster. On biopsy, the small nodules or papules show lymphoid aggregates, hence the term lymphonodular. The chief complaint is throat pain. Similar to other CSV infections, the patient is febrile with cervical lymphadenopathy, and the disease resolves of its own accord in 10 to 12 days.

Treatment

All enterovirus oral enanthems resolve of their own accord in 10 to 12 days. Treatment for oral pain is accomplished by administration of palliative oral rinses containing an anesthetic or antihistamine. Fluid and nutritional intake must be monitored, particularly in infants and young children, and antipyretics minimize fever.

Differential diagnosis

Many of the lesions caused by the herpes and enteroviruses show similar or overlapping features. Differentiating between them is based on anatomic distribution of vesicular eruptions and cutaneous pattern of involvement. Table 13–3 summarizes these features.

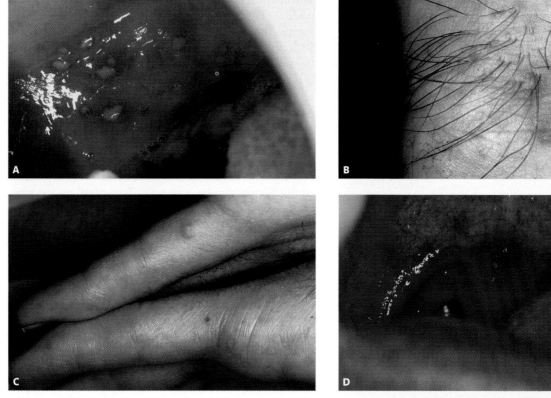

Figure 13–14 Enterovirus stomatitides. *A* to *C,* Clinical presentation of hand, foot, and mouth disease, an infection that is usually associated with coxsackie A16. *A,* Oral; *B,* toe; *C,* fingers. *D,* Soft palate erythema with vesicular eruption in herpangina. *E,* Soft palate papular enanthem in lymphonodular pharyngitis.

Table 13–3 Vesiculoulcerative Viral Lesions of the Oral Mucosa

Lesion	Fever	Distribution	Age
HSV primary herpetic gingivostomatitis	Yes	Gingiva, movable mucosa	Childhood
HSV herpes labialis	No	Lips	Young adults
HSV intraoral herpes	No	Hard palate	Young adults
Primary VZV	Yes	Skin, oral mucosa	Childhood
Secondary VZV, shingles	Mild	Skin, oral mucosa, V1, V2, or V3, unilateral	Adults
Enterovirus herpangina	Yes	Soft palate	Childhood
Enterovirus hand, foot, and mouth	Yes	Oral mucosa, skin of hands and feet	Childhood
Enterovirus lymphonodular pharyngitis	Yes	Soft palate papules	Childhood
Enterovirus nonspecific stomatitis	Yes	Movable mucosa	Childhood

HSV = herpes simplex virus (HHV-1 and -2); VZV = varicella-zoster virus (HHV-3); V1, V2, V3 = divisions 1, 2, and 3 of trigeminal nerve.

Suggested reading

Balfour HH Jr. Antiviral drugs. N Engl J Med 1999;16: 1255–68.

Eisen D. The clinical characteristics of intraoral herpes simplex virus infection in 52 immunocompetent patients. Oral Surg Oral Med Oral Pathol Oral Radiol Endod 1998;86:432–37.

Horwitz E, Pisanty S, Czerninski R, Helser M, et al. A clinical evaluation of a novel liposomal carrier for acyclovir in the topical treatment of recurrent herpes labialis. Oral Surg Oral Med Oral Pathol Oral Radiol Endod 1999;87: 700–5.

Jaffe HW, Pellett PE. Human herpes virus 8 and Kaposi's sarcoma: some answers, more questions. N Engl J Med 1999; 340:1912–13.

Kost RG, Straus SE. Post-herpetic neuralgia: pathogenesis, treatment, and prevention. N Engl J Med 1999;335:32–42.

Logan HL, Lutgendorf S, Hartwig A, Lilly J, Berberich SL. Immune, stress, and mood markers related to recurrent oral herpes outbreaks. Oral Surg Oral Med Oral Pathol Oral Radiol Endod 1998;86:48–54.

Raborn GW, Martel AY, Grace MGA, Eng P, McGaw WT. Oral acyclovir in prevention of herpes labialis. A randomized, double-blind, multi-centered trial. Oral Surg Oral Med Oral Pathol Oral Radiol Endod 1998;85:55–9.

14 Human Immunodeficiency Virus Disease

Michael Glick, DMD, and Sol Silverman, Jr, MA, DDS

Two reports from the Centers for Disease Control and Prevention (CDC) in 1981, describing a cohort of men suffering from opportunistic infections previously only seen in severely immunosuppressed individuals, was the first indication of a brewing global epidemic that would devastate millions of people. Two years later, it became apparent that these, and other similarly afflicted individuals, were infected with a virus that was causing a progressive destruction of their immune systems. The causative agent, the human immunodeficiency virus (HIV) was soon identified, and tests were developed that could identify infected individuals. By the 1990s, every country in the world had reported cases of HIV infection, with sub-Saharan Africa being the most severely affected area. It was estimated that by the year 2001 more than 36 million people worldwide had been infected with HIV, with 11 new infections and 6 deaths occurring every minute. Although numerous medications are available to slow the progression of HIV disease, at the present time there is no cure.

Almost one million HIV-infected people are living in North America. One-third are aware of their HIV infection but are mostly asymptomatic. One-third are already diagnosed with the acquired immunodeficiency syndrome (AIDS), the end-stage of HIV disease, whereas the remaining one-third may not yet be aware of their infection.

As with all viruses, HIV needs to infect a target cell, incorporate its genetic material into the genome of the host cell, and use the host cell's ability to produce proteins for viral replication. Although HIV has been shown to infect several different cell types, the virus has a predilection for cells expressing a CD4 receptor. These cells are mainly T-helper lymphocytes and macrophages. The hallmark of HIV disease, and the measure of immune suppression, is the continuous depletion of CD4+ T lymphocytes. When the reduction of these CD4+ cells reaches a critical number, major opportunistic infections and neoplasms start to develop. These opportunistic infections and neoplasms are the cause of death among HIV-infected individuals.

An understanding of the epidemiology, pathogenesis, and treatment of infected individuals is essential for oral health care providers treating HIV-positive individuals. This chapter addresses these topics and how they relate to the provision of oral health care.

HIV epidemiology

Criteria have been established by the CDC that determine when individuals have reached the clinical stage of HIV disease classified as AIDS. As of January 1, 1993, 25 different clinical diseases and illnesses, as well as a depressed immune system measured by a CD4 cell count below 200 cells/mm^3, define AIDS (Table 14–1).

Since the institution in the middle 1990s of a new class of anti-HIV drugs called protease inhibitors, the incidence of the number of new AIDS cases, as well as the mortality rate of HIV disease, has declined dramatically in the United States. The AIDS incidence decreased 18% between 1996 and 1997, but slowed down to an 11% decrease the following year. The death rate decreased by 25% between 1995 and 1996, 42%

between 1996 and 1997, and 20% between 1997 and 1998. At the same time, the number of persons living with AIDS increased by 10% from the end of 1997 to the end of 1998. By January 2000, approximately 300,000 people were estimated to be living with AIDS in the United States. As only 34 states report cases of HIV-infected persons, no accurate figures are available of the number of people living with HIV. However, it is estimated that in the United States by the beginning of 2000 there were between 500,000 and 600,000 people living

Table 14–1   Definition of Acquired Immunodeficiency Syndrome*

CD4+ T lymphocyte categories

The lowest accurate CD4+ T lymphocyte count should be used for classification purposes, even though more recent and possibly different counts may be available.

Clinical categories
Clinical Category A

  Conditions
    Asymptomatic HIV infection
    Persistent generalized lymphadenopathy (PGL)
    Acute HIV infection with accompanying illness or history of
      acute HIV infection.
  Conditions listed in *Category B* or *Category C* must not have
    occurred.

Clinical Category B

  Symptomatic conditions in HIV-infected adolescents or adults
    that are not included in *Clinical Category C* and meet at least
    one of the following criteria:
    a. The conditions are attributed to HIV infection or are
      indicative of a defect in cell-mediated immunity.
    b. The conditions are considered by physicians to have a clinical
      course or to require management that is complicated by HIV
      infection.
  Examples are the following conditions (not exclusive):
    Bacillary angiomatosis
    Candidiasis, oropharyngeal (thrush)
    Candidiasis, vulvovaginal; persistent, frequent, or poorly
      responsive to therapy
    Cervical dysplasia (moderate or severe) or cervical carcinoma
      in situ
    Constitutional symptoms (eg, fever [38.5°C] or diarrhea lasting
      >1 mo)
    Herpes zoster (shingles), involving at least two distinct episodes
      or more than one dermatome
    Idiopathic thrombocytopenia purpura
    Listeriosis

Oral hairy leukoplakia
Pelvic inflammatory disease, particular if complicated by
  tubo-ovarian abscess
Peripheral neuropathy

Clinical Category C

  Conditions
    Candidiasis of bronchi, trachea, or lung
    Candidiasis, esophageal
    Cervical cancer, invasive
    Coccidiomycosis, disseminated or extrapulmonary
    Cryptococcosis, extrapulmonary
    Cryptosporidiosis, chronic intestinal (persisting >1 mo)
    Cytomegalovirus disease (other than liver, spleen, or nodes)
    Cytomegalovirus retinitis (with loss of vision)
    Encephalopathy, HIV-related
    Herpes simplex: chronic ulcer(s) (persisting >1 mo); or
      bronchitis, pneumonitis, or esophagitis
    Histoplasmosis, disseminated or extrapulmonary
    Isosporiasis, chronic intestinal (persisting >1 mo)
    Kaposi sarcoma
    Lymphoma, Burkitt (or equivalent term)
    Lymphoma, immunoblastic (or equivalent term)
    Lymphoma, primary, of brain
    Mycobacterium avium complex or *Mycobacterium kansaii*,
      disseminated or extrapulmonary
    Mycobacterium tuberculosis, any site (pulmonary or
      extrapulmonary)
    Mycobacterium, other species, or unidentified species,
      disseminated or extrapulmonary
    Pneumocystis carinii pneumonia
    Pneumonia, recurrent
    Progressive multifocal leukoencephalopathy
    Salmonella septicemia, recurrent
    Toxoplasmosis
    Wasting syndrome due to HIV

		Clinical Categories		
Clinical Category	CD4+ (T cells/mm³) (Percentage)	(A) Asymptomatic Acute HIV or PGL	(B) Symptomatic not (A) or (C) Conditions	(C) AIDS-Indicator Conditions
1	≥ 500 (≥ 29%)	A1	B1	C1†
2	200–499 (14–28%)	A2	B2	C2†
3	< 200 (14%)	A3†	B3†	C3†

*Adapted from Centers for Disease Control and Prevention. 1993 revised classification system for HIV infection and expanded surveillance case definition for AIDS among adolescents and adults. MMWR 1992;41(No. RR-17):1–19.
†Expanded AIDS surveillance case definition.

with HIV disease without an AIDS diagnosis. The CDC has recommended that all states need to report cases with HIV and not only AIDS, which will enable a much better surveillance of the HIV epidemic in the United States. By mid-2000, close to a half million Americans with AIDS had reportedly died from their disease.

Although the mode of transmission of HIV is known, new infections occur daily. An additional 47,083 new cases of AIDS were reported from July 1998 through June 1999. This is a decrease in the number of new AIDS cases compared to the two preceding 12-month periods, in which 54,140 and 64,597 cases, respectively, were reported. Since the beginning of the AIDS epidemic, over 725,000 cases of AIDS have been reported in the United States. The states and the cities with the most reported cases have not changed significantly since the beginning of this epidemic (Table 14–2).

An additional problem appears to be occurring: as HIV-infected individuals develop a resistance to current antiretroviral drugs, adverse side effects and costs increase, and compliance remains questionable, plus there is an increasing number of people living with HIV infection serving as a reservoir for transmission, the downturn of newly reported cases and deaths is probably at an end.

A disproportionate number of minorities have been infected with HIV. Whereas African-Americans constitute only 12% of the population in the United States, 33% of all reported male AIDS cases and 57% of all reported female AIDS cases belong to this ethnic group. Hispanics total 11.5% of the population in the United States, but 18% of all reported male AIDS cases and 20% of all reported female AIDS cases are from Hispanic descent. In the reporting period between July 1998 through June 1999 women accounted for 23% of all adult cases, and 80% of these women were African-Americans or Hispanics. During the same time period, 61% of all reported male cases were African-Americans or Hispanics.

The global trend of the HIV epidemic is not encouraging. A total of 5.6 million new HIV infections and 2.6 million deaths from HIV disease were reported in 1999 alone. By the beginning of 2001, it was estimated that more than 36 million people worldwide would be living with HIV/AIDS, 1.2 million of these being children under the age of 15 years. Sub-Saharan Africa is hardest hit with this epidemic, harboring more than 25 million people living with HIV/AIDS. This translates into approximately an 8% adult prevalence rate. However, the areas with the fastest rising rates in 2000 were Eastern Europe and Central Asia (700,000), East Asia and the Pacific (640,000), and South and Southeast Asia (5,800,000). New infections in these regions contributed 26%, 23%, and 22% to the total number of people in these geographic areas already living with HIV/AIDS.

Transmission of HIV may occur during sexual intercourse, by exchange of infected blood and blood products, and from infected mothers to their offspring during pregnancy or delivery, and post partum through breast-feeding. Although other modes of transmission have been proposed, such as exposure to aerosol, aerosol from dental rotary instruments, tears, urine, sweat, hepatitis B vaccination, insect bites, or causal contacts, none has ever been documented. Because of rigid testing standards, blood-bank products are more than 99% safe.

Since the beginning of this epidemic the largest number of people infected in the United States have been homosexual and bisexual men, totaling 48% of all cases through June 2000. Although the infection rate among this transmission category has decreased, new infections among homosexual and bisexual men are still prevalent.

Most new infections occur among injection drug users. Twenty-two percent of all men and 42% of all women have reported injection drug use as their primary mode of transmission. Sharing of needles, as well as sexual practices, contribute to the increased transmission rate in this risk category. Although there are no age limits to HIV infection, the diagnosis of AIDS is most frequently made in individuals between the ages of 30 and 39 years. Because of prolonged incubation periods and

Table 14–2 Number of Aids Cases and Rate per 100,000 Population: July 1998–June 1999

Residence	Number of Cases	Rate
Area		
District of Columbia	750	143.4
New York State	7655	42.1
Florida	5683	38.1
Puerto Rico	1448	37.5
Maryland	1634	31.8
Virgin Islands, US	33	27.9
South Carolina	984	25.7
New Jersey	2061	25.4
Delaware	177	23.8
Georgia	1635	21.4
Louisiana	904	20.7
Massachusetts	1250	20.3
City		
New York, NY	6513	74.9
Miami, FL	1561	72.5
Fort Lauderdale, FL	989	65.8
San Francisco, CA	904	53.7
Newark, NJ	963	49.3
San Juan, PR	971	48.4
Columbia, SC	242	47.2
Baltimore, MD	1171	47.1
West Palm Beach, FL	546	45.3
Jersey City, NJ	245	44.0
Houston, TX	1339	34.1
New Orleans, LA	442	33.8

delayed occurrence of signs and symptoms, it can only be inferred that infection has occurred many years prior to recognition and diagnosis. This is confirmed in states where HIV is reported; in those areas, the highest age range for initial reporting is 25 to 34 years.

In heterosexuals, who are HIV positive, male-to-female contact is the most common route of transmission. Whereas 4% of all male AIDS cases can be attributed to this mode of transmission, 40% of all female AIDS cases have been infected via heterosexual contacts. Drug abuse is a significant associated factor in this group.

Transmission of HIV in health care settings is rare. Through June 2000, 56 health care workers reported documented occupational transmission of HIV. None of these health care workers were dentists, hygienists, or dental assistants. Two cases have been reported in which health care workers have been identified as the possible source of infection to patients. The first case was a dentist with AIDS in Florida, who was implicated in transmitting HIV to six of his patients. Although the mode of transmission was never identified, all patients had almost identical viral genetic makeup to that of the dentist. An additional case, in France, reported an orthopedic surgeon transmitting HIV to one of his patients. Again, the mode of transmission was never clearly elucidated. Relative to transmission, the evidence supports a conclusion that the dental office setting is a safe environment for both health care workers and patients (see Chapter 19).

Molecular and pathologic correlates of disease

Human immunodeficiency virus is a double-stranded RNA virus belonging to the lentivirus family. The viral RNA is surrounded by a core that also contains reverse transcriptase, an enzyme necessary to transcribe the viral RNA into viral DNA. The core is surrounded by a lipid membrane with a transmembrane protein, gp41, and an outer envelope protein, gp120. This gp41-gp120 complex is intimately involved with attaching the virus to a target cell (Figure 14–1). This fusion of the viral and cellular membranes enables the viral RNA to be transferred from the viral core into the cytoplasm of the host cell. After successful transfer of the viral RNA, it is transcribed by the reverse transcriptase to viral DNA, which gets incorporated into the host cell's genome. The "viral template" remains intact indefinitely. When the host cell gets stimulated, cellular and viral proteins are produced. The viral proteins are cleaved into appropriate building blocks with the help of proteases, and new viruses are formed that bud out of the host cell to infect other susceptible cells. Stimulating factors or agents and the rate of producing new viruses vary among patients. It is also

in this step that most viral mutations occur, which in turn influence morbidity, disease progression, and response to treatment.

The gp120 protein recognizes and attaches to the CD4 receptor on the target cell, whereas gp41 enhances the fusion between the viral membrane and the cellular membrane by using a cellular chemokine receptor. It is of interest to note that some individuals have specific mutations of their chemokine receptors that protect them against HIV infection.

The initial HIV infection may be accompanied by nonspecific viral signs and symptoms, including a sore throat, high fever, lymphadenopathy, photophobia, macular rashes, and oral ulcerations. This acute seroconversion syndrome appears 10 to 14 days after the initial infection and lasts for approximately 5 to 7 days. During this time, the virus is disseminated to various anatomic sites; this includes seeding of the virus into lymphoid tissues, where it can remain latent for varying periods and also escape detection. The body mounts a partially effective immune response, which results in downregulation of viral replication but not viral elimination.

The second stage of HIV infection is associated with persistent viral replication despite the immune response, and the virus eventually enters into the mantle regions of lymph nodes. At this time, chronic activation of T lymphocytes and secretion of different cytokines initiate a chronic immune system activation. During the last stages of HIV infection there is an accelerated viral replication that is associated with increased viral diversity and more cytopathic isolates. Viral replication in lymphocytes eventually results in escape of virus to peripheral blood cells and advanced HIV disease.

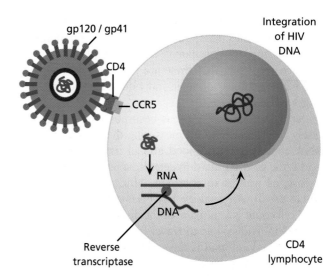

Figure 14–1 HIV uses gp120 to adhere to the CD4 receptor and gp41 to adhere to the chemokine CCR5 receptor. Once inside the CD4 lymphocyte, the viral RNA is released, linearizes, and is reverse transcribed to DNA. Proviral DNA is then integrated into the host genome.

Table 14-3 CD4 Cell Count, Viral Load, and HIV Disease Progression*

CD4 Cell Count (Cells/mm³)	Viral Load (Copies/mL)	Percentage of Patients with AIDS-Defined Complications		
		3 Years	6 Years	9 Years
≤ 350	< 3000	–	–	–
	3001–14,000	0	18.8	30.6
	14,001–41,000	8.0	42.2	65.6
	41,001–110,000	40.1	72.9	86.2
	> 110,000	72.9	92.7	95.6
351–500	< 3000	–	–	–
	3001–14,000	4.4	22.1	46.9
	14,001–41,000	5.9	39.8	60.7
	41,001–110,000	15.1	57.2	78.6
	> 110,000	47.9	77.7	94.4
>500	< 3000	1.0	5.0	10.7
	3001–14,000	2.3	14.9	33.2
	14,001–41,000	7.2	25.9	50.3
	41,001–110,000	14.6	47.7	70.6
	> 110,000	32.6	66.8	76.3

*Adapted from Mellors JW, Munoz A, Giorgi JV, et al. Plasma viral load and CD4+ lymphocytes as prognostic markers of HIV-1 infection. Ann Intern Med 1997;126:946–54.

Destruction of the immune system is reflected in the continuous decrease in CD4+ lymphocytes in the blood. The absolute number and percentage of CD4+ T lymphocytes is used to assess an infected individual's ability to defend against opportunistic infections. Accordingly, at specific CD4 cell levels, prophylactic medications are instituted. A normal CD4 cell count is above 700 cells/mm³; initial immune suppression is characterized by a CD4 cell count below 500 cells/mm³; and severe immune suppression is defined as a CD4 cell count below 200 cells/mm³. Because T lymphocytes are the body's primary defense against viral infections, fungal infections, and parasitic infections and, to some extent, control neoplastic growth, it is not surprising that these are the types of infections and manifestations found in individuals during the later stages of HIV disease.

Since the late 1990s it has been possible to routinely assess viral replication by measuring the number of viral RNA copies found in blood and in tissue. Plasma viral load is the gold standard to determine progression of HIV disease, as well as to determine efficacy of medications (Table 14–3). An analogy has been made in which the CD4 cell count is a measure of the distance of the route an infected individual has to travel from infection to death, whereas the viral load is the speed by which this process takes place along this route. Thus, when the viral load is very low, or even undetectable, the disease progression is slowed or even halted. Thus, if the viral load can be kept low for an extended period, the body can sometimes reconstitute its immune system. Routine viral load deter-

minations can measure a minimum of 20 to 400 RNA equivalent/mm³. Below this value an infected individual is considered to have an undetectable viral load.

An astounding number of viruses are replicating every day. It has been estimated that an infected individual can produce more than 10×10^9 virions per day. Unfortunately, the mutation rate of HIV is also extremely high. One mutation in every three base pairs of the HIV genome of 10^4 bases occurs every time the virus replicates. This explains some of the difficulties encountered during the search for effective medications and vaccines.

Treatment for HIV disease

Elimination of HIV from infected individuals is the goal of HIV therapy, but this has yet to be achieved. Current antiretroviral medications reduce viral replication, which enables the immune system to remain functional or, in more advanced cases, to reconstitute. Successful cases of HIV treatment have resulted in a dramatic and sustained increase in CD4 cell count for several years. Although the primary treatment for HIV disease is focused on reducing viral replication, treatment and prophylactic interventions for opportunistic infections are also common.

Several different types of antiretroviral medications are employed (Table 14–4). The oldest and most commonly used class of anti-HIV drugs is nucleoside reverse transcriptase inhibitors. These medications reduce viral replication by competitively inhibiting the reverse transcriptase enzyme, which reduces the number of viral RNA being transcribed into viral DNA. Similar classes of medications that also inhibit viral RNA being transcribed into viral DNA are non-nucleoside reverse transcriptase inhibitors and nucleotide reverse transcriptase inhibitors. The difference between these classes of drugs is the method of terminating the effect of the reverse transcriptase enzyme. Protease inhibitors are another type of commonly used anti-HIV medications. Medications belonging to this class of drugs prevent the breakdown of viral proteins into the necessary building blocks for new virus production. Other classes of anti-HIV drugs are also used but are less common.

Infected individuals take a combination of at least two, preferably three different types of antiretroviral medications, usually two reverse transcriptase inhibitors together with one protease inhibitor. This type of therapy is called highly active antiretroviral therapy (HAART). The protease inhibitors need to be taken according to very strict regimens; failure to do so may induce rapid resistance to these drugs. New combinations are continually tried when viral loads increase or CD4 counts precipitously drop. Compliance is an additional problem, since so many drugs and schedules are involved.

Table 14–4 Common Antiretroviral Medications

Generic Name	Trade Name	Toxicity Relevant to Dentistry	Interaction with Medications Used in Dentistry
Nucleoside reverse transcriptase inhibitors (NRTIs)			
Abacavir (ABC)	Ziagen	Xerostomia	
Didanosine (ddI)	Videx	Peripheral neuropathy, xerostomia	
Lamivudine (3TC)	Epivir		
Stavudine (d4T)	Zerit	Peripheral neuropathy	
Zalcitabine (ddC)	HIVID	Peripheral neuropathy, oral ulcerations	
Zidovudine (AZT, ZDV)	Retrovir	Anemia, neutropenia	
Zidovudine + lamivudine	Combivir		
Non-nucleoside reverse transcriptase inhibitors (NNRTIs)			
Delavirdine	Rescriptor		Inhibits cytochrome P-450 enzymes
			Contraindications: midazolam
			Delavirdine levels decreased by phenobarbitol
			Delavirdine increases levels of clarithromycin, dapsone
			Avoid buffered medications ≥ 1 hr
Efavirenz	Sustiva		Inhibits and induces P-450 enzymes
			Contraindications: midazolam, triazolam
			Interacts with clarithromycin, phenobarbitol
Nevirapine	Viramune		Induces cytochrome P-450 enzymes
Protease inhibitors			
Amprenavir	Agenerase	Perioral paresthesias	
Indinavir	Crixivan	Thrombocytopenia	Inhibits cytochrome P-450 enzymes
			Avoid concurrent use: midazolam
			Indinavir levels increased by ketaconazole
Nelfinavir	Viracept		Inhibits cytochrome P-450 enzymes
			Avoid concurrent use with midazolam
Ritonavir	Norvir	Dysgeusia	Inhibits cytochrome P-450 enzymes (potent)
			Contraindication for concurrent use with diazepam, meperidine, midazolam, piroxicam, and propoxyphene
			Ritonavir decreases levels of clarithromycin
Saquinavir	Invirase		Inhibits cytochrome P-450 enzymes
			Saquinavir levels reduced by dexamethasone
Ribonucleotide reductase inhibitor			
Hydroxyurea	Hydrea	Bone marrow suppression, oral ulcerations	
Nucleotide reverse transcriptase inhibitor			
Adefovir	Preveon	Anemia	

All antiretroviral medications are associated with side effects. The most common complaint from patients on HAART is reduced salivary flow. This may be so severe that their speech and masticatory functions are impaired. Individuals taking protease inhibitors may experience several side effects with systemic implications that may necessitate additional treatments. Some of the most prevalent side effects are hyperglycemia, increased levels of triglycerides, redistribution of body fat, hepatitis, increased demand for methadone, hair loss, and loss of the effect of birth control pills. Furthermore, these medications are associated with drug interactions that limit the usefulness of many concomitantly administered medications.

Treatment and prophylaxis for opportunistic infections are instituted based on the presence of an infection, or patient susceptibility to develop an infection, according to an individual's immune status. Treatment options are constantly changing as are the criteria for prophylaxis against opportunistic infections. Usually medications are instituted as prophylaxis after an individual's CD4 cell count drops below 200 cells/mm³. Such individuals start to receive prophylactic medications against *Pneumocystis carinii* pneumonia (PCP). At even lower CD4 cell counts, prophylactic medications against opportunistic fungal infections, such as cryptococcosis or esophageal candidiasis, or opportunistic viral infections, such as cytomegalovirus, may be instituted.

Oral health care for HIV-positive patients

Oral health care workers need to provide dental care for HIV-infected patients and recognize as well as understand the significance of oral manifestations associated with HIV infection. Dental care for patients infected with HIV does not differ from that provided to noninfected individuals. Several studies have reported that the complication rates among HIV-positive patients after extractions, endodontic procedures, periodontal procedures, biopsies, or routine operative or prosthodontic procedures are the same as for HIV-negative patients. Even procedures such as dental implants have not revealed impaired osseous integration or impaired healing.

One important key to successful treatment of all patients is an appropriate and relevant medical assessment. Although the medical status of patients with HIV infection may change rapidly during the later stages of the

disease, the evaluation of the patient is not different than for other patients. Concerns regarding impaired hemostasis, susceptibility to infections, drug actions, and drug interactions, as well as the ability to withstand the stress of dental care are the same concerns as with all patients.

Impaired or altered hemostasis is not a common finding in patients with HIV infection. However, a small percentage of patients may present with idiopathic thrombocytopenia purpura (ITP), secondary to a dysfunctional immune system or as a side effect to medications. Routine dental care, including simple extractions, can safely be performed in patients with platelet counts down to 50,000 to 60,000 cells/mm³, if all other hemostatic values are within normal limits. There are HIV-infected dental patients with hepatic disease, which predispose them to increased bleeding due to impaired coagulation. In such patients, prothrombin time (PT) and partial thromboplastin time (PTT) indicate the level of hepatic function and bleeding tendency. Obviously HIV-infected patients with hemophilia also have impaired coagulation functions.

Neutropenia is not an uncommon finding in HIV-infected patients. However, the degree of neutropenia determines whether antibiotic prophylaxis is necessary prior to dental procedures. As a rule, an absolute neutrophil count below 1000 cells/mm³ usually requires antibiotic prophylaxis. The regimen may require 5 to 7 days of antibiotic coverage. Other reasons for antibiotic premedication are uncontrolled hyperglycemia, as

Table 14–5   Medical Questionnaire for Patients with HIV Disease

Specific Data	Pertinence
Date	Updated information is needed, since patients' conditions may change rapidly.
Personal and demographic information	As with all other patients
Chief complaint or history of chief complaint	As with all other patients
Medical history	HIV-infected patients may also suffer from other non-HIV-related illnesses and conditions.
HIV test results	(a) Date of first HIV test, (b) date of last negative HIV test, (c) date of first positive HIV test, and (d) reason for being tested provide information regarding the patient's HIV awareness, possible time of infection, and possible risk behavior or risk category.
Risk behavior or risk category	May indicate need for dental modification, such as anticipated bleeding tendencies in hemophiliac patients, or increased incidence of cardiac disease among injection drug users, or modification of prescription of narcotics for present and former drug users.
HIV-associated illnesses	May indicate type of medications patients are using or immune status or diseases that may be associated with different oral conditions.
CD4 level	Indicates immune status or specific medications patients are using or indicate specific immune-related oral manifestations.
Viral load	Plasma viral load indicates rate of progression of HIV disease.
CBC with differential	May indicate need for antibiotic prophylaxis or impaired hemostasis.
Current medications	Indicate patients past and present HIV-associated conditions and illnesses, immune status, and potential for drug reactions and drug interactions. Be aware of rapidly changing types and regimens.
Allergies and drug sensitivity	As with all other patients
Tobacco, alcohol, and recreational drug use	As with all other patients

determined by glycosylated hemoglobin (hemoglobin A1C [Hgb$_{A1C}$]), or conditions were the American Heart Association's prophylactic regimens need to be implemented (see Chapter 9 and Chapter 17).

Patients with HIV infection usually take numerous medications. Some of these medications may have significant side effects and may interact with medications commonly used in dentistry. Oral health care providers should familiarize themselves with the more common medications used in HIV disease and be aware of patients' rapidly changing drug regimens (see Table 14–4). Furthermore, patients with hepatic and renal disease may require alterations to the type and dosage of medications that dental care providers may use.

Although patients with HIV disease tolerate dental procedures well, providers need to be aware of possible concomitant cardiac, adrenal, or gastrointestinal conditions that require modification of dental procedures. Assessment of HIV patients follow the same rationale and guidelines used with non-HIV-infected patients. However, some questions regarding immune status, disease progression, and HIV-associated conditions may be specific for HIV-positive patients (Table 14–5).

Oral manifestations

Since the first reports of the AIDS epidemic, oral lesions have been recognized as important clinical markers. Although none of the lesions found in patients with HIV are absolutely unique to HIV disease, they may be more prevalent, more severe, or manifest slightly differently than what is reported among other cohorts. Oral health care providers need to screen for, diagnose, and treat these lesions, as well as recognize the significance of the lesions as markers for immune suppression and HIV disease progression.

Oral manifestations observed in HIV-infected patients are associated with opportunistic pathogens, with immune suppression, with side effects from medications or are idiopathic in nature. The prevalence and incidence of lesions vary depending upon environmental and geographic differences, habits and behavioral characteristics, or general treatment protocols used for HIV disease and non-oral-related infections. Because oral lesions among immunodeficient patients may present with atypical appearances, laboratory confirmation should accompany clinical impressions, to allow selection of the most effective treatment.

Xerostomia

Reduced salivary flow is a common finding in patients with HIV disease. This condition can be secondary to

medications or attributable to infections of salivary glands. There may be other associated factors. Several antiretroviral medications have been associated with impaired salivary flow, including zidovudine, didanosine (ddI), and numerous protease inhibitors; salivary glands may get infected with viruses, such as cytomegalovirus, with associated oral dryness; lymphocytes may infiltrate the parotid glands, which may also cause unilateral or bilateral enlargement; and radiation therapy that includes salivary glands in the field may also be a factor. Common complications associated with xerostomia include increased incidence of caries, increased incidence and severity of periodontal disease, overgrowth of *Candida* species, and impaired ability to chew and swallow.

Symptomatic relief from oral dryness can be achieved by continuously sipping water, sucking on crushed ice, or administration of saliva substitutes. Stimulation of saliva flow can sometimes be accomplished by chewing sugarless gum or sucking on sugarless candies. Cholinergic agonists can also be used. Bethanechol and pilocarpine are the most commonly used compounds (see Chapter 26). Discontinuation of xerostomia-inducing medications should also be attempted, but always in consultation with patients' physicians.

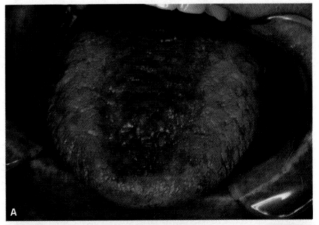

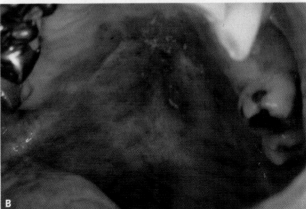

Figure 14–2 Erythematous candidiasis of the tongue (*A*) and palate (*B*). Both fungal infections were the first signs and symptoms of HIV infection.

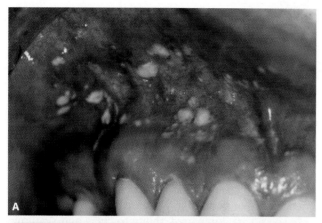

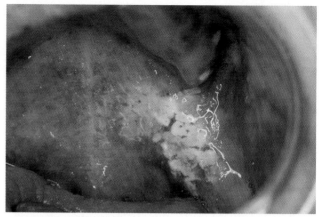

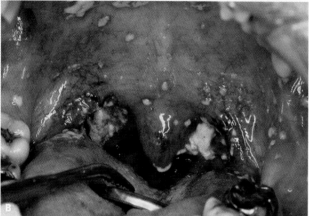

Figure 14–4 Chronic hyperplastic candidiasis. A biopsy revealed candidal hyphae in the surface epithelium. The lesion was reversed with systemic antifungal medication.

Figure 14–3 *A* and *B*, Pseudomembranous candidiasis (thrush) in HIV-positive patients.

Fungal infections

A localized fungal infection is the most common opportunistic oral manifestation found in patients with HIV disease. Different species as well as different clinical manifestations may determine type of treatment intervention as well as suggest level of immune suppression. *Candida albicans* is the predominant fungal species in the oral cavity. However, during the progression of HIV disease and owing to specific medications, other candidal species (yeasts) may become more dominant.

Four different clinical presentations of oral candidiasis have been described. Erythematous or atrophic candidiasis presents as red areas on any mucosal surface, and more commonly on the hard and soft palate, tongue, or gingiva (Figure 14–2). When the tongue is affected, atrophic areas are noted on the dorsal surface. This type of candidiasis may be present all through the course of HIV disease but is usually the first to appear during mild immune suppression. Although it is often asymptomatic, longstanding infections may cause painful inflammation and even ulcerations.

Pseudomembranous candidiasis, or thrush, presents as white or yellowish plaques that can easily be wiped off the oral mucosa (Figure 14–3). All oral mucosal surfaces may be affected, but the palate and the mucobuccal folds are the most common sites. Pseudomembranous candidiasis usually appears during the early stages of immune suppression. This type of candidiasis may be accompanied by symptoms such as a burning sensation, pain, and difficulties chewing and swallowing. Patients often refer to a sensation of having pieces of cotton in their mouth. Altered taste and halitosis also may occur.

Hypertrophic (hyperplastic) candidiasis is usually chronic and is a more severe form of pseudomembranous candidiasis (Figure 14–4). It is characterized by the accumulation of plaques that cannot be wiped off, and may coalesce into larger areas that have typical white or yellow appearances. This form of candidiasis is associated with severe immune suppression and is usually accompanied by xerostomia. Patients complain of pain, great difficulties with chewing and swallowing, and a persistent bad taste in the mouth.

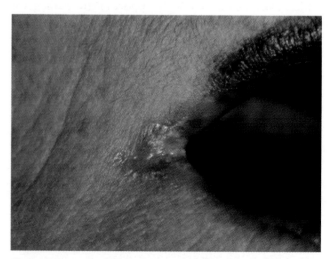

Figure 14–5 Angular cheilitis secondary to candidiasis.

Angular cheilitis or perlèche is a form of candidal infection affecting oral and perioral tissue (Figure 14–5). A pseudomembrane overlying red fissures at the corners of the mouth that may extend beyond this area onto the surrounding skin, is the typical appearance. Although usually painless, longstanding infections may be associated with discomfort when the tissue is distended during wide mouth openings.

Diagnosis of candidiasis is mainly clinical but can be confirmed with laboratory methods through staining of oral mucosal surface scrapings with either potassium hydroxide (KOH), periodic acid-Schiff stain (PAS), or Gram stain.

Treatment of oral candidiasis is based on the severity of the manifestation and the status of the patient's immune system (see Chapter 18). Atrophic candidiasis can be successfully treated with clotrimazole troches, or itraconazole and amphotericin suspensions. Nystatin suspension is also used, but it is not as effective as other topical formulations. Furthermore, the high concentration of sucrose in nystatin suspensions may contribute to increased incidence of caries in long-term users.

Topical antifungal therapy is also effective for treatment of pseudomembranous candidiasis in patients with CD4 cell counts above 150 to 200 cells/mm³. Systemic therapy should be instituted for patients with more severe immune suppression. The most commonly used systemic antifungal medication is fluconazole. Side effects in long-term users with severe immune suppression include resistance to the drug. Itraconazole has shown to be a good alternative for patients with side effects to fluconazole, especially those patients exhibiting drug resistance. Ketoconazole is another effective systemic antifungal medication. This medication is potentially hepatotoxic, and patients taking this drug need to have frequent liver-function evaluations. All of the systemic antifungal medications can also be used for patients with hyperplastic candidiasis. However, intravenous administration of amphotericin B is the most effective treatment for this type of candidal infection. Treatment often must be prolonged, involve high dosage regimens, and demands alertness to resistant species. Xerostomia can complicate control. Prophylactic antifungal use is common.

Angular cheilitis as well as atrophic candidal infections found underneath dentures can be treated with nystatin ointment or ketoconazole cream. Addition of triamcinolone to nystatin has shown to be highly effective for angular cheilitis. In some cases, topical antibiotic creams or ointments need to be added to treat bacterial superinfections.

Deep-seated fungal infections have also been described in the oral cavity among patients with HIV disease. They are rare, are usually associated with severe immune suppression, and are signs of systemic involvement.

Other fungal infections include histoplasmosis, aspergillosis, geotrichosis, and cryptococcosis. They most commonly present as oral ulcerations, but may appear as pseudomembranous lesions. Diagnosis depends upon biopsy and culture. Medical care is required.

Viral infections

Herpes viruses

Oral manifestations of herpes simplex virus (HSV)-1 and -2 are found in both immunocompetent and immunodeficient individuals. However, the typical lesions found among immunosuppressed patients usually become more severe, last longer, and require different interventions in patients whose immune system cannot limit the infection (Figure 14–6). These include recurrent intraoral herpes as well as herpes labialis (cold sores). Lesions attributable to HSV-1 or -2 in patients with HIV disease may present as large confluent ulcers that are present for more than 2 to 3 weeks. These ulcers can be found on any mucosal surface and may be surrounded by a raised white margin. The diagnosis may be difficult, because of the atypical appearance. Cultures and biopsy may be necessary. Treatment consists of antiviral drugs until resolution of the ulcers has been achieved (see Chapter 13).

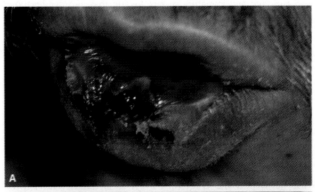
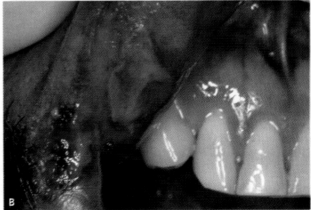

Figure 14–6 *A* and *B*, Herpes simplex-1 infections in HIV-positive patients. These painful ulcerations required antiviral drugs for control.

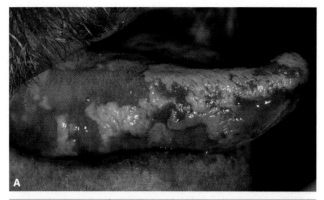

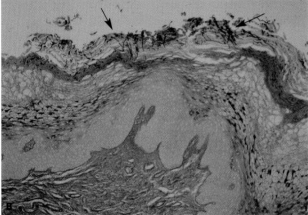

Figure 14–7 HIV-associated oral hairy leukoplakia. *A*, Asymptomatic tongue lesion; *B*, histopathology showed typical epithelial hyperplasia, vacuolization, and immature surface keratin that also demonstrated coincidental candidal colonization (PAS stain).

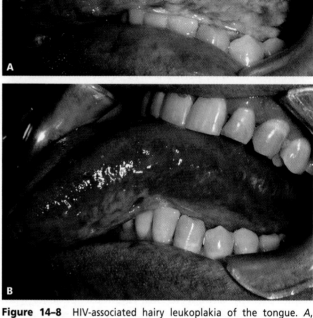

Figure 14–8 HIV-associated hairy leukoplakia of the tongue. *A*, Patient complained of mild roughness and irritation. *B*, One week after one topical application of 25% podophyllin. The control lasted for 3 months.

Epstein-Barr virus (EBV) has been implicated in the appearance of oral hairy leukoplakia (OHL). This lesion was first described in HIV-infected patients, but has since also been reported to occur among other immune suppressed and immune competent individuals. Oral hairy leukoplakia typically appears on the lateral borders of the tongue as corrugated, white lesions that cannot be wiped off (Figure 14–7). It is usually asymptomatic, but can get superinfected with bacteria that may cause a burning sensation. More than 50% of OHL may also be infected with candidiasis. This lesion is more frequent among homosexual or bisexual men and in patients with CD4 cell count below 200 cells/mm^3.

Diagnosis is based upon clinical characteristics and biopsy. The biopsy rules out other conditions, such as dysplasia, as well as displaying diagnostic features of epithelial hyperplasia, epithelial cell vacuolization, and immature surface keratin. Inflammation is not a consistent feature. Treatment for OHL is instituted only upon request of the patient. Several treatment options are available, but a 10- to 14-day course of high-dose acyclovir (2 g daily) is effective. Topical applications of 25% podophyllin or 0.05% Retin-A solution have

been reported to be helpful (Figure 14–8). Recurrences are common.

Cytomegalovirus (CMV) infection has presented as ulcerations in the oral cavity. These ulcers are non-

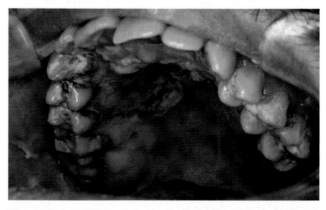

Figure 14–9 Painful and progressive palatal ulceration of 1 month duration in a patient with AIDS. The patient had lost 20 pounds of weight from inability to eat. A biopsy revealed a combination of cytomegalovirus and herpesvirus. The infection responded to antiviral agents within 10 days.

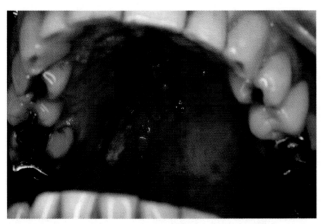

Figure 14–10 Herpes zoster (shingles) in an HIV immunocompromised patient. He had unilateral oral and facial skin lesions, which responded to high-dose acyclovir.

specific, and a biopsy is required for a definitive diagnosis. The lesion may appear on any mucosal surface as a shallow or a deep ulcer, sometimes with an eroded base with or without raised borders (Figure 14–9). Cytomegalovirus-associated ulcers are associated with severe immune suppression with CD4 cell counts below 100 cells/mm³, and usually are a sign of a disseminated CMV infection. Diagnosis is established by biopsy. Treatment for these lesions includes ganciclovir, but glucocorticosteroids have also been used to achieve healing of the ulcers. Patients with CMV-associated ulcers need to be referred to an ophthalmologist for evaluation of CMV retinitis, which is a common cause of impaired vision in HIV-infected patients.

Varicella-zoster infection of multiple dermatomes is a sign of immune suppression among HIV-infected patients. Both intraoral ulcerations and facial manifestations of zoster have been reported in patients with HIV disease. The lesions are unilateral, painful, and require high-dose antiviral therapy. No consistent associations have been documented between the appearance of these lesions and HIV disease progression. The diagnosis is usually established by clinical features of sudden onset, pain, fever, and the unilateral distribution of skin or mucosal lesions (Figure 14–10). Treatment involves high-dose antiviral medications. Post zoster neuropathy may be a chronic and troubling complication.

Kaposi sarcoma (KS) is the most common tumor in HIV-infected persons and is the AIDS-defining condition in 10 to 15% of all reported AIDS cases in the United States. It is more frequent in homosexual men. Recent reports have implicated HHV-8 as an etiologic agent for the development of KS. It is not clear if this virus causes progression of KS or if the presence of HHV-8 may only have a supporting and sustaining effect.

Intraoral KS initially presents as asymptomatic flat, vascular-like discolorations. Since KS is a progressive

reactive neoplasm, the lesions soon become nodular growths associated with pain, bleeding, and oral dysfunction. Although KS can occur on any mucosal surface, the palate and gingiva are the most frequent sites (Figure 14–11 and 14–12). Although KS is traditionally regarded as a cutaneous lesion, studies have suggested that intraoral KS may be the first sign of the lesion in over 20% of cases. Kaposi syndrome worsens during the course of immune deterioration seen in HIV disease. Most lesions are found in patients with CD4 cell counts below 200 cells/mm³. The diagnosis is established by biopsy, displaying both angiogenesis and cellular proliferation.

Treatment for KS is instituted to reduce the number and the size of lesions. Low-dose radiation therapy, as well as chemotherapy, is effective. Intralesional injections with vinblastine and sclerosing solutions have been used successfully for localized intraoral lesions. Kaposi syndrome is rarely the primary cause of death.

Human papillomaviruses

Since the institution of more effective antiretroviral therapy, the overall incidence of oral lesions has diminished. However, the incidence of intra- and perioral papilloma-

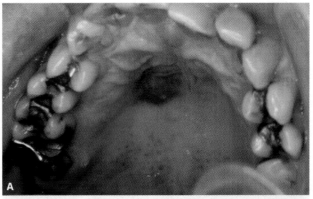

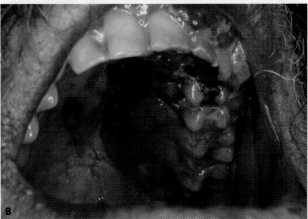

Figure 14–11 Kaposi sarcoma (KS), which usually occurs when the CD4 lymphocyte counts are below 200, is an AIDS-defining disease in the HIV-positive patient. A, Early, flat, asymptomatic palatal lesion; B, painful, advanced nodular lesion, which was treated with low-dose radiation.

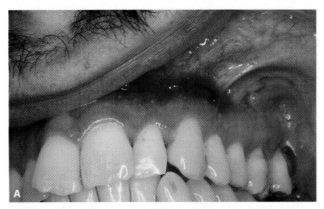
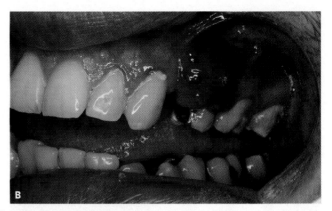

Figure 14–12 Kaposi sarcoma of the gingiva. *A*, Flat, early, asymptomatic lesion; *B*, painful, nodular, advanced lesion, which was controlled with an intralesional sclerosing agent.

virus infections has shown a slight increase. The manifestations present as wart-like lesions (condyloma acuminatum), often referred to as venereal warts. Most commonly the lesions are multiple, covering large areas of the gingiva, palate, buccal mucosa, the inside of the lips, and the skin surrounding the lips (Figure 14–13). Sometimes they appear as clusters of small "fibromas."

The diagnosis is made by history, clinical appearance, and biopsy. Treatment for papilloma lesions consists of relatively aggressive surgical removal together with adjunct chemotherapeutic interventions. Topical

application of 25% podophyllum resin as well as intralesional interferon-α injections have also been helpful. Recurrences are common.

Bacterial infections

Significant atypical periodontal conditions have been described in individuals with HIV disease. Although these conditions have not been associated with a different bacterial flora from that found in conventional

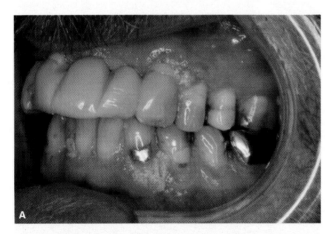
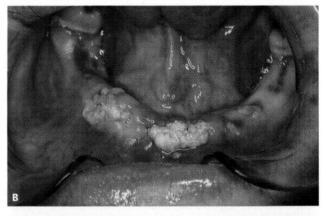
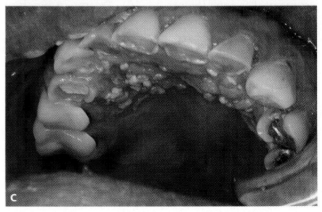

Figure 14–13 Condyloma acuminatum (venereal warts) in HIV patients. These are related to transmissible human papillomaviruses. *A*, Irritating gingival lesions; *B*, alveolar mucosa warts causing irritation under the lower denture; *C*, uncomfortable palatal condylomata.

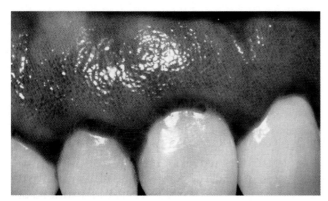

Figure 14–14 Linear gingival erythema associated with HIV infection.

periodontitis, aggressive soft and hard tissue destruction has been documented.

Linear gingival erythema (LGE) has been described as a 2- to 3-mm red band-like lesion of the marginal gingiva. Numerous studies have indicated a variable prevalence. Diagnosis is made from history and clinical features (Figure 14–14). Laboratory tests have not been helpful. Treatment with conventional therapies, including scaling, root planing, and curettage, generally is not effective. However, mechanical debridement together with antibiotics and antifungal medications may result in improvement or even resolution of the lesion. The significance of this asymptomatic lesion is not clear.

Necrotizing ulcerative gingivitis (NUG) presents as an ulcerative lesion affecting the marginal gingiva, but without concomitant alveolar bone destruction (Figure 14–15). This lesion may be associated with pain and complaints of a bad taste in the mouth. Diagnosis is established by clinical characteristics. Successful treatment of this lesion with mechanical debridement in combination with antibiotics has been achieved. Necrotizing ulcerative gingivitis usually only appears in patients with severe immune deterioration.

Necrotizing ulcerative periodontitis (NUP) is an aggressive form of periodontal disease that left untreated may result in rapid destruction of both soft and hard tissues (Figure 14–16). This lesion is usually very painful, with patient complaints of a deep-seated, bony-type pain. Presence of spontaneous gingival bleeding and fetor oris typically also accompany NUP. In severe cases, 1 to 2 mm of bone loss has been documented to occur within 1 to 2 weeks. Treatment with mechanical debridement, antiseptic mouthrinses (chlorhexidine), and antibiotics usually results in fast improvement and arrest of the periodontal destruction. Several studies have indicated that NUP is associated with severe immune deterioration with CD4 cell counts below 100 cells/mm^3 and poor overall survival.

Neoplasms

Non-Hodgkin lymphoma (NHL) is the fastest increasing malignancy in HIV-infected individuals. In some patients, it may be the first sign of HIV infection. Non-Hodgkin lymphoma occurs in a younger age group of HIV-infected patients compared with NHL in non-HIV-infected individuals. The prevalence of oral NHL is low, but the severity of a diagnosis of NHL is evident by the usual low survival rate of only 4 to 16 weeks after diagnosis. Less than 20% survive 2 years. The lesion may appear as an ulceration or as a mass with varying symptoms (Figure 14–17). The diagnosis is established by biopsy. Treatment involves aggressive chemotherapy and radiation.

Nonspecific etiology

Necrotizing stomatitis
Necrotizing stomatitis (NS) is a rapidly progressive, painful ulceration that may affect adjacent bony struc-

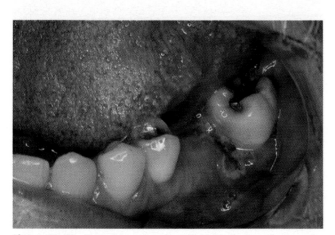

Figure 14–15 Necrotizing ulcerative gingivitis that requires aggressive curettage, antiseptic mouthrinses, and antimicrobial support.

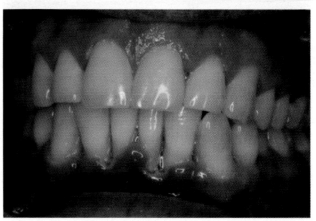

Figure 14–16 Painful necrotizing ulcerative periodontitis of sudden onset and rapid progression, with associated alveolar bone loss.

tures (Figure 14–18). Long-standing lesions may impair chewing and swallowing. Although the etiology is not clear, NS is associated with CD4 cell counts below 100 cells/mm³. The lesions usually respond to topical and systemic glucocorticosteroid therapy in combination with systemic antibiotics. A biopsy is often required in new cases to rule out other causes, such as granulomatous diseases and neoplasia.

Aphthous ulcers

Both minor and major recurrent ulcerations occur in HIV-infected patients (Figure 14–19). These ulcers are not more common but may be more aggressive and last longer than in non-HIV-infected individuals. Minor aphthous ulcers can be treated symptomatically with analgesic mouthrinses and, in more severe cases, with topical glucocorticosteroids. Major aphthous ulcers usually persist for more than 3 weeks and often heal with a scar. These lesions are associated with severe immune suppression with CD4 cell counts below 100 cells/mm³.

When the clinical diagnosis is uncertain, a biopsy might be indicated to rule out a more serious lesion. The usual treatment consists of high doses of systemic glucocorticosteroids for 10 to 14 days. However, sometimes major aphthae persist and require high-dose corticosteroids for longer periods (see Chapter 21). Recurrences are a certainty.

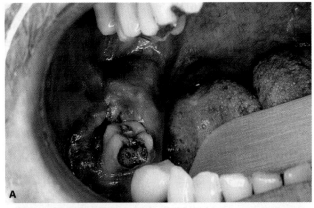

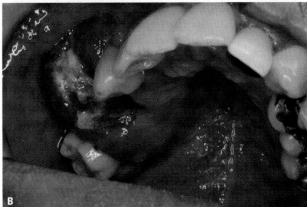

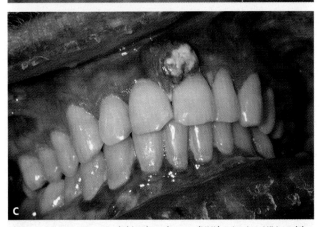

Figure 14–17 Non-Hodgkin lymphoma (NHL). *A,* An HIV-positive patient reported to the emergency department for a mandibular dental abscess. There was no response to antibiotics. A biopsy showed NHL. *B,* Extraction of the involved tooth and biopsy of this maxillary growth that was noticed for several weeks revealed NHL. This was the first clinical manifestation of HIV or lymphoma in this patient. *C,* This squamous cell carcinoma of the maxillary gingiva in this HIV-infected patient was at first thought to represent an infection. It also mimicked a lymphoma.

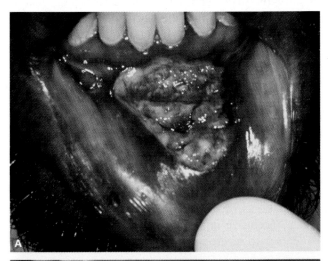

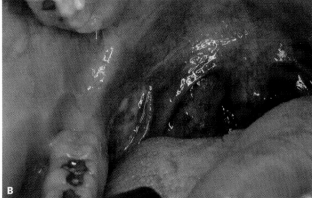

Figure 14–18 Idiopathic necrotizing stomatitis in immunocompromised HIV patients. *A,* Progressive, painful labial-mandibular gingiva-alveolar bone ulceration; *B,* chronic, extremely painful ulceration of the right soft palate in an patient with AIDS with a rapidly failing immune system.

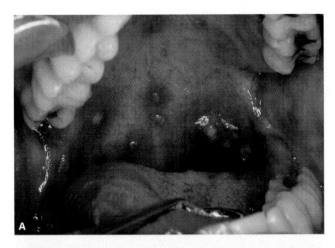

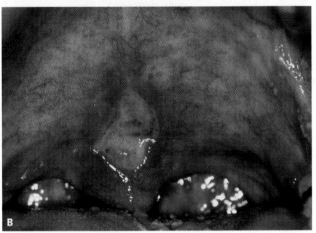

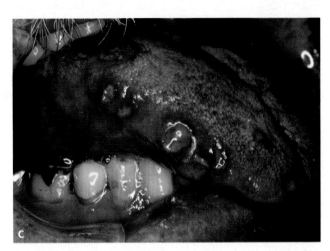

Figure 14–19 Aphthous ulcers in HIV-positive patients. *A*, Multiple minor aphthae of the soft palate; *B*, major aphthous ulcer of palate; *C*, multiple major and minor aphthae of the tongue, which required high-dose daily prednisone for 8 days for control of signs and symptoms. The lesions had been present for almost 2 weeks and caused an acute weight loss of about 10 pounds from inability to eat.

Suggested reading

Abel SN, Croser D, Fishman SL, et al. Principles of dental management for the HIV/AIDS patient. New York: Dental Alliance for AIDS/HIV Care (DAAC), 1999.

Bartlett JG. Medical management of HIV infection. Baltimore, MD: Johns Hopkins University Press, 1999.

Glick M, Muzyka BC, Lurie D, Salkin LM. Oral manifestations associated with HIV-related disease as markers for immunosuppression and AIDS. Oral Surg Oral Med Oral Pathol 1994;77:344–9.

Glick M. Dental management of patients with HIV. Carol Stream, IL: Quintessence, 1994.

Palelle FJ, Delaney KM, Moorman AC, et al. Declining morbidity and mortality among patients with advanced human immunodeficiency infection. N Engl J Med 1998; 338:853–60.

Patton LL, McKaig R, Strauss R, et al. Changing prevalence of oral manifestations of human immunodeficiency virus in the era of protease inhibitor therapy. Oral Surg Oral Med Oral Pathol Oral Radiol Endod 2000;89:299–304.

Silverman S Jr. Color atlas of the oral manifestations of AIDS. 2nd Ed. St. Louis, MD: CV Mosby, 1996.

15 Human Papillomaviruses and Papillary Oral Lesions

L. Roy Eversole, DDS, MSD, MA

Papillary lesions are those that are tumefactive with a cauliflower surface. Some are pedunculated others are sessile. Some are single, others are multiple or diffusely involve broad areas of the oral mucosa. The vast majority of papillomas are associated with or indeed caused by members of the human papillomavirus (HPV) family, yet there are a few papillary growths that have not been associated with HPV. One lesion in particular, molluscum contagiosum, is caused by a member of the poxvirus group. When the papillomas show minimal surface keratinization histologically, they appear pink, with the same coloration as normal mucosa. When surface hyperkeratosis is extant, the papillary lesions show a white surface. When the clinical appearance is that of multiple projections or stalks, much like a sea anemone, they are usually said to be papillary; conversely, when the lesions are white and keratotic with a roughened surface, they are said to be verrucous.

Because most papillary and verrucous lesions are of viral origin, they are transmissible. In general, oral mucosal papillomas are only mildly contagious and transmission requires direct mucosal contact. Viral transfer or inoculation to another individual probably requires an erosion or laceration of the recipient's mucosal epithelium for virus to gain access to the basal cells of the stratified epithelium.

Molecular and pathologic correlates of disease

There are over 100 genotypes of HPV, all of which are closely related, with DNA sequences showing some homology between genotypes (conserved sequences). In turn, there are unique sequences that separate one genotype from another. The HPVs are classified by number, and these numbers have no bearing on the pathogenesis of each specific genotype. They are numbered in sequential order of their discovery. Computerized gene banks have recorded complete DNA sequences for each type.

The virus is epitheliotropic, and those that tend to infect mucous membranes more readily than skin are termed mucosatropic. The virus is about 7200 bases long and is encased within an icosahedron capsid, lacking an out envelope. The circularized genome is organized into various reading frames within early (E) and late (L) region DNA sequences. The late region genes encode proteins that engender viral assembly and formation of the capsid. The early region genes encode proteins that are important in viral replication and also transactivate regions of the human genome. Specifically E6 and E7 genes within the early region of HPV induce transformation of basal keratinocytes, activating the cell cycle. Most HPVs induce benign hyperplasias or neoplasias of the epithelium. The genotypes that induce malignant transformation of keratinocytes with genesis of squamous cell carcinomas are referred to as mucosatropic oncogenic HPVs. Whereas oncogenesis may be the consequence of oncogene activation by transactivation, it has been demonstrated that E6 binds to the p53 tumor-suppressor protein and activates its degradation by the ubiquitin pathways. E7 binds the Rb tumor suppressor, releasing E2F, a transcription factor that activates cell cycling. Figure 15–1 summarizes these biologic activities of HPV and Table 15–1 presents a brief list of the genotypes associated with oral lesions.

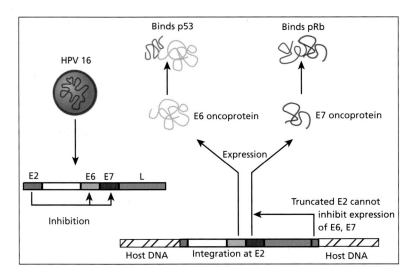

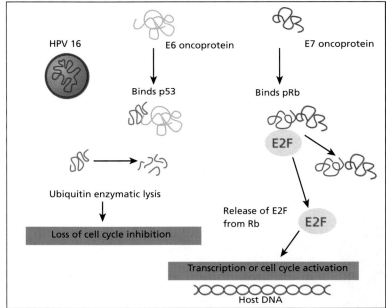

Figure 15–1 Schematic diagram showing human papillomavirus (HPV) infection of keratinocytes leading to either benign or malignant neoplasias.

Molecular methods can be used in lesional tissue to demonstrate the presence of virus. Viral presence does not prove causation. Since normal mucosa is often found to harbor viral DNA, it is conceivable that the virus is merely a passenger. Basic cell biology studies have shown, however, that E6 and E7 sequences transfected into human keratinocytes induces transformation into papillomas (HPV 6, 11) or carcinomas (HPV 16, 18). The footprints of the virus are detected by the sensitive method of polymerase chain reaction (PCR), and RNA transcripts can be detected by reverse transcriptase PCR. Only rarely do immunohistochemical markers for HPV capsid antigens stain positive in papillomas that have been shown to contain DNA or RNA. In any case, it is now well documented which genotypes are associated with specific histopathologically defined papillomas. HPV 2, 4, 6, and 11 are associated with and

cause the benign warts of oral mucosa and vermilion epithelia; the role of HPV 16, 18 and other oncogenic

Table 15–1 Human Papillomavirus and Oral Papillary or Verrucous Lesions

Lesion	Associated HPV Genotypes
Verruca vulgaris	2, 4
Squamous papilloma	6, 11
Condyloma acuminatum	6, 11
Focal epithelial hyperplasia	13, 32
Squamous cell carcinoma	16, 18, 31, 33, 35
Proliferative verrucous leukoplakia	6, 11, 16
Verrucous carcinoma	2, 6, 11, 16
Verruciform xanthoma	None
Molluscum contagiosum	None, poxvirus
Denture papillary hyperplasia	None
Keratoacanthoma	None

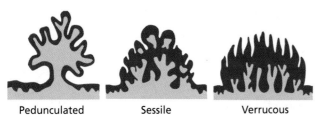

Pedunculated   Sessile   Verrucous

Figure 15-2 Histologic configurations in papillary and verrucous lesions.

genotypes in the pathogenesis of oral carcinoma is equivocal. The association for upper aerodigestive tract epithelium is not as convincing as for genital tract mucosa, in which HPV oncogenic viruses are identifiable in over 95% of lesional tissues. Since HPV DNA, RNA, or protein has been identified in some oral squamous cell carcinomas, specific HPV genotypes may be a causal cofactor in some patients, particularly in those individuals who have no evident risk factors.

Microscopically the benign verrucae and papillomas show exophytic, finger-like projections of stratified squamous epithelium, showing wide variations in the thickness of the keratin layer, which is usually parakeratinized (Figure 15-2). Verrucous lesions tend to have acute "churchspire" projections, whereas papillary lesions tend to have rounded surface projections. The cells of the spinous layer show normal cytology, yet in the upper layers, the nuclei are swollen, a cytopathic effect of HPV termed koilocytosis. The histology of proliferative verrucous leukoplakia and carcinomas is discussed in the chapter on precancerous and cancerous lesions (see Chapter 20).

Clinical features

The specific types of solitary papillary lesions that occur in the oral cavity include the common squamous papilloma, verruca vulgaris, condyloma acuminatum, verruciform xanthoma, molluscum contagiosum, and keratoacanthoma. Condylomas may also occur in crops of multiple papillomas, either clustered or widely separated. Denture papillomatosis, proliferative verrucous leukoplakia, verrucous carcinoma, and papillary exophytic squamous cell carcinoma are diffuse sessile lesions.

Squamous papilloma

The squamous papilloma is the most common benign epithelial neoplasm of oral epithelium. It may occur anywhere in the mouth with a predilection for the ventral tongue and frenum area, palate, and mucosal surface of the lips. Nonkeratinized lesions appear coral pink; if keratinized, they are white (Figure 15-3). Some have a cauliflower surface whereas others have discrete

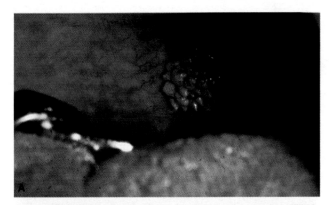

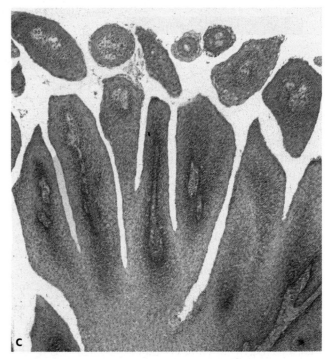

Figure 15-3 Squamous papilloma. *A*, Clinical appearance; *B*, gross specimen showing finger-like projections; *C*, microscopic appearance of papilloma.

finger-like projections. They may be pedunculated or sessile in configuration. Papillomas are typically single, yet occasionally, more than one may occur. They occur at any age and are frequently seen in children and adolescents. There is no clearly defined mode of transmission, most occurring spontaneously. The solitary simple squamous papilloma has not been considered to be a sexually transmitted lesion, and when these lesions occur in children, sexual abuse is not to be suspected.

Verruca vulgaris

The common skin wart may be seen on the vermilion border, or less often, in the oral cavity. This type of oral wart is the least common and may occur at any age, being more frequent in children and adolescents. In the mouth, verruca vulgaris has a tendency to arise most frequently on the keratinized surfaces of the gingiva and palate. Verrucae are sessile, oval, and white, owing to the thickened keratin layer on the surface (Figure 15–4). In children with warts on their fingers, autoinoculation may occur to the lips in those with a thumb-sucking habit. Rarely, there may be more than one lesion present.

Condyloma acuminatum

Sexually transmitted warts tend to occur in multiples yet may be single lesions. They are usually broad-based and sessile. They occur in both sexes but are more common in homosexual males. Although oral condylomas can occur on any mucosal surface, they are more commonly found on the lips, commissure region, and gingiva. When multiple, they tend to arrange themselves into regional clusters, although some cases are widely distributed throughout the oral mucosa, particularly in human

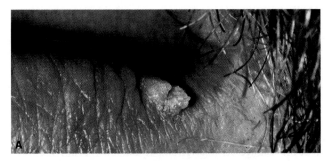
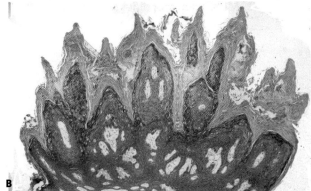
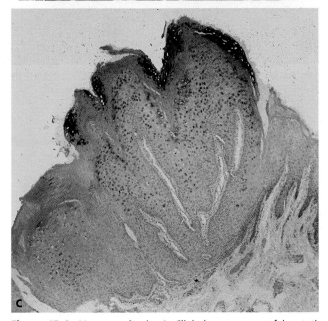

Figure 15–4 Verruca vulgaris. *A,* Clinical appearance of keratotic lesion on the lip; *B,* microscopic appearance; *C,* DNA in situ hybridization showing HPV-2 positivity in most keratinocyte nuclei.

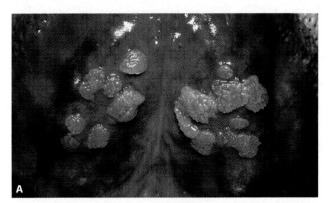
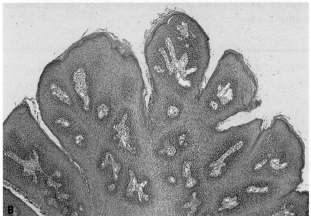

Figure 15–5 Condylomas. *A,* Clinical appearance of multiple confluent and clustered condylomas; *B,* microscopic appearance showing papillary projections.

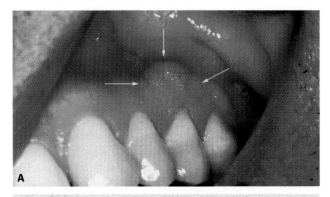

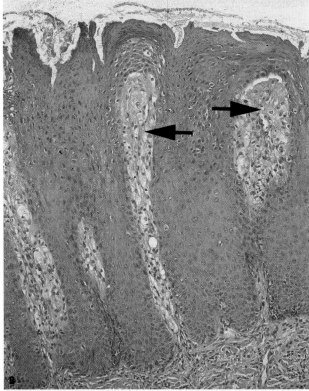

Figure 15–6 Verruciform xanthoma. A, Sessile lesion of the gingiva in a bone marrow transplant patient; B, Photomicrograph showing bubbly foam or xanthoma cells in the connective tissue papillae between epithelial cells.

immunodeficiency virus (HIV)-infected patients (see Chapter 14). Most are coral pink in color, have a warty appearance, but are slightly keratinized (Figure 15–5). These lesions of the oral mucosa are often transmitted by oral, genital, and anal sex. Multiple papillary lesions in a child should arouse suspicion of sexual abuse, warranting investigation of persons in contact with that child.

Verruciform xanthoma

An association between verruciform xanthoma and HPV has not been substantiated. These lesions clinically resemble the other papillomas that frequent the oral

cavity; however, they are relatively rare (Figure 15–6). They have a unique histology in which the papillary projections of the epithelium overlie connective tissue fronds that are populated by foam-cell histiocytes. Unlike cutaneous xanthomas, there has not been a correlation with hyperlipoproteinemia. Verruciform xanthoma occurs anywhere in the oral mucosa, being more common on the gingiva and buccal mucosa, where it is usually of normal mucosal coloration.

Molluscum contagiosum

Caused by a large virus of the poxvirus group, molluscum contagiosum (MC) is an uncommon lesion of the oral mucosa since the tropism of the virus is primarily cutaneous. In the head and neck area, the lesions are usually seen on the facial skin and around the lips. The classic wart of molluscum is a crateriform papule, a small normal colored skin nodule with a depressed central pit (Figure 15–7). When present, MC lesions tend to be multiple. Molluscum contagiosum is most often seen

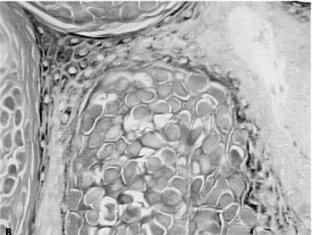

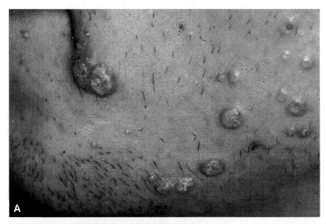

Figure 15–7 Molluscum contagiosum. A, Multiple facial skin lesions in an HIV-positive subject; B, molluscum bodies representing huge viral inclusions in keratinocytes.

on the trunk, and when they are located on the face, it is usually an indication that the patient is immunocompromised, particularly as a consequence of HIV infection and subsequent immunosuppression. The virus is only mildly contagious, requiring prolonged skin-to-skin contact for transmission.

Keratoacanthoma

Keratoacanthoma (KA) is usually encountered on the facial skin and lips yet can also arise, albeit rarely, in the mouth. An association with HPV is not well established. Clinically they are characterized by a tumefaction with round, mounded borders that surround a central core of hard keratinized material that may appear pale yellow or brown. The brown appearance is caused by extrinsic pigments that become incorporated with the excessive keratin. Intraoral KAs are generally nonpigmented. The peripheral mounded borders show an abrupt transition into normal skin or mucosa, both clinically and histologically (Figure 15–8). Since these warts can be large, they may cause the clinician to suspect carcinoma. Although the clinical appearance can be confusing, the symmetrical nature, oval or round configuration, and keratotic core are indicative of KA. If left untreated, most KAs spontaneously regress.

Denture papillomatosis

Underlying maxillary dentures one may encounter diffuse papillary projections. These proliferations are found even more commonly with dentures that afford negative pressures or are ill-fitting. Clinically, the entire hard palatal vault has the appearance of a mushroom garden with coalescing small polyps (Figure 15–9). The individual polyps are easily separated with a dental explorer. They are not hyperkeratotic, and for this reason their coloration is that of normal mucosa. If there is a complicat-

ing *Candida* infection, the papillary surface may be white or red (pseudomembranous and erythematous forms of candidiasis). This condition is known as denture papillomatosis or papillary inflammatory hyperplasia and represents a hyperplastic reaction. The papillary pavement may extend from the vibrating line posteriorly to the incisive papilla anteroposteriorly and laterally across the palatal vault without extention onto the edentulous alveolar ridges. This is an important clinical feature, since the differential diagnosis for diffuse papillary lesions includes proliferative verrucous leukoplakia, verrucous carcinoma, and papillary exophytic squamous cell carcinoma, all of which tend to occur in the vestibule, yet frequently extend onto edentulous alveolar ridges.

Precancerous diffuse papillary lesions

Proliferative verrucous leukoplakia, verrucous carcinoma, and the papillary, exophytic variant of squamous

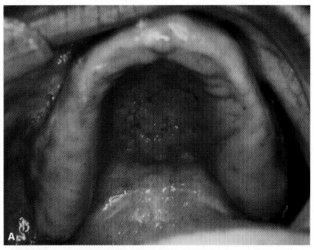

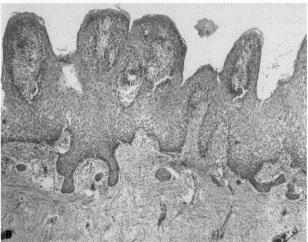

Figure 15–9 Denture inflammatory papillary hyperplasia (papillomatosis). *A*, Clinical appearance of palatal lesions found under an old denture; *B*, microscopic appearance of diffuse papillary projections.

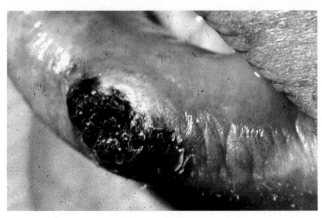

Figure 15–8 Keratoacanthoma of the lip.

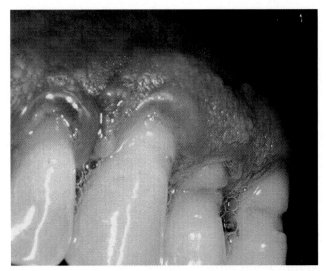

Figure 15–10   Diffuse papillary lesions of the gingiva in the Cowden syndrome.

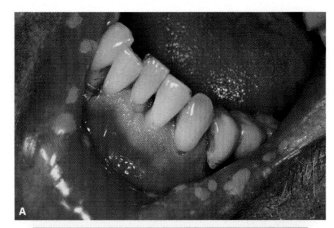

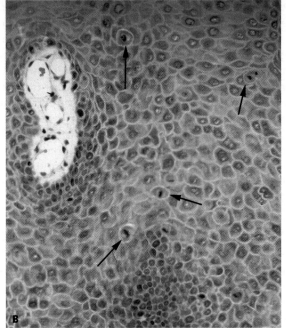

Figure 15–11   Focal epithelial hyperplasia. *A*, Multiple lip nodules; *B*, mitosoid bodies in spinous cells.

cell carcinoma are diffuse verrucous and papillary lesions of the oral mucous membranes. These entities are HPV-associated and are discussed in detail in Chapter 20.

Cowden syndrome

Multiple hamartomas are encountered in this syndrome, which is a multisystem disease. The importance in recognizing the oral manifestations of Cowden syndrome is to explore for the other manifestations, since some of the hamartomatous lesions can progress to cancer. The disease is inherited as an autosomal dominant trait. Cutaneous papules are seen around the nose and lips and also on the palmar surfaces, most represent hair follicle hamartomas (trichilemmomas). The patients develop goiters, thyroid adenomas, and fibrocystic disease of the breast, and some manifest hamartomatous intestinal polyps. As mentioned previously, carcinomas can develop in the breast and thyroid. The oral lesions are diffuse sessile papillomas that have the appearance of a cobblestone street (Figure 15–10). Histologically they are benign papillary and papular proliferations of epithlium, supported by fibrous cores. No viral association has been discovered.

Focal epithelial hyperplasia (Heck disease)

Caused by HPV 13 and 32, focal epithelial hyperplasia is an infection confined to oral mucosa (ie, there are no genital or cutaneous foci of involvement). The lesions occur in children and young adults and are more common in central and south America than in other areas, yet the disease has a worldwide distribution. Similar infections can occur in HIV-infected subjects. The lesions appear on the mucosal surfaces of the upper and

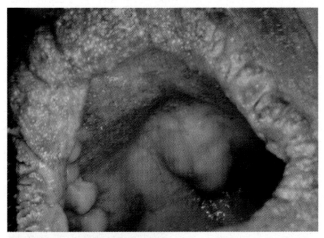

Figure 15–12   Diffuse papillary lesions in acanthosis nigricans showing an absence of pigmentation.

lower lips, commissures, and buccal mucosa. They are multiple, measure from 3 mm to 10 mm, and are smooth dome-shaped papules that lack a pebbly surface (Figure 15–11). The lesions persist for many months then spontaneously resolve with no treatment.

Acanthosis nigricans

There are two forms of acanthosis nigricans, a benign form and a malignant form. The malignant form is associated with an internal malignancy, usually in the gastrointestinal tract, whereas the benign form fails to show any such association. Acanthosis nigricans occurs on the skin and may also affect the lips and oral mucosa. The papillary lesions are diffuse and sessile with a cobblestone or pebbly appearance (Figure 15–12). They are pigmented pale gray, a clinical finding attributable to basilar melanosis in the papillary epithelium. Once the diagnosis has been made, a workup for internal malignancy is indicated.

Treatment and management

Single papillomas, verruca, and condylomas are treated by local excision or laser ablation. Their focal appearance is classic; however, microscopic examination is recommended since some forms of early squamous cancer may present as papillomas. If laser ablation is to be performed, it is recommended that the exophytic lesion be laser excised and submitted for biopsy, followed by direct ablation of the lateral and deep margins. Since these lesions are superficial and exophytic, deep excision is not necessary. However, if squamous cell carcinoma is strongly considered in the differential diagnosis, an incisional biopsy should be performed prior to treatment.

The colonization of oral mucosa, particularly in immunocompromised patients, by condylomas is a management dilemma. Multiple widespread excisions are painful during the healing phase and even after excision, multiple recurrences are common. Human immunodeficiency virus-infected patients placed on antiretrovirals and proteinase inhibitors and other multiple drug regimens have been shown to undergo regression of their oral warts in some cases. If the patient does not show a favorable response to anti-HIV drug interventions, laser ablation should be considered.

Proliferative verrucous leukoplakia, verrucous carcinoma, and the papillary variant of squamous cell carcinoma have been discussed in more detail in Chapter 20. These three premalignant and malignant papillary growths are treated by surgical excision with wide mar-

gins. Even though complete excision is accomplished with microscopically confirmed clear margins, all of these HPV-associated tumors have a tendency to recur, and some become more histologically advanced with each recurrence. Sometimes, radiation therapy is combined with surgical removal. Chemotherapy has not been found to be effective.

Suggested reading

Carlos R, Sedano HO. Multifocal papilloma virus epithelial hyperplasia. Oral Surg Oral Med Oral Pathol 1994;77:631–5.

Eversole LR, Laipis PJ. Oral squamous papillomas: detection of HPV DNA by in situ hybridization. Oral Surg Oral Med Oral Pathol 1988;65:545–50.

Eversole LR, Laipis PJ, Merrell P, Choi E. Demonstration of human papillomavirus DNA in oral condyloma acuminatum. J Oral Pathol 1987;16:266–72.

Flaitz CM, Hicks MJ. Molecular piracy: the viral link to carcinogenesis. Oral Oncol 1998;34:448–53.

Garlick JA, Taichman LB. Human papillomavirus infection of the oral mucosa. Am J Dermatopathol 1991;13:386–95.

Green TL, Eversole LR, Leider AS. Oral and labial verruca vulgaris: clinical, histologic, and immunohistochemical evaluation. Oral Surg Oral Med Oral Pathol 1986;62:410–6

Koch WM, Lango M, Sewell D, et al. Head and neck cancer in nonsmokers: a distinct clinical and molecular entity. Laryngoscope 1999;109:1544–51.

Mignogna MD, Lo Muzio L, Ruocco V, Bucci E. Early diagnosis of multiple hamartoma and neoplasia syndrome (Cowden disease). The role of the dentist. Oral Surg Oral Med Oral Pathol Oral Radiol Endod 1995;79:295–9.

Miller CS, White DK. Human papillomavirus expression in oral mucosa, premalignant conditions, and squamous cell carcinoma: a retrospective review of the literature. Oral Surg Oral Med Oral Pathol Oral Radiol Endod 1996;82:57–68.

Mostafa KA, Takata T, Ogawa I, et al. Verruciform xanthoma of the oral mucosa: a clinicopathological study with immunohistochemical findings relating to pathogenesis. Virchows Arch A Pathol Anat Histopathol 1993;423:243–8.

Nelen M, Padberg GW, Peeters EA, et al. Localization of the gene for Cowden disease to chromosome 10q22-23. Nat Genet 1996;13:114–6.

Porter S, Cawson R, Scully C, Eveson J. Multiple hamartoma syndrome presenting with oral lesions. Oral Surg Oral Med Oral Pathol Oral Radiol Endod 1996;82:295–301.

Praetorius F. HPV-associated diseases of oral mucosa. Clin Dermatol 1997;15:399–413.

Ramirez-Amador V, Esquivel-Pedraza L, Caballero-Mendoza E, et al. Oral manifestations as a hallmark of malignant acanthosis nigricans. J Oral Pathol Med 1999;28:278–81.

Viraben R, Aquilina C, Brousset P, Bazex J. Focal epithelial hyperplasia (Heck disease) associated with AIDS. Dermatology 1996;193:261–2.

16 Hepatitis B and Hepatitis C Virus Infections

Craig S. Miller, DMD, MS

There are many infectious agents that can cause hepatitis or inflammation of the liver. Of the infectious agents, six hepatitis viruses (ie, hepatitis A virus [HAV], hepatitis B virus [HBV], hepatitis C virus [HCV], hepatitis D virus [HDV or delta], hepatitis E virus [HEV], and hepatitis G virus [HGV or GB virus]) that target the liver for replication and disease have been identified. Features of each virus are listed in Table 16–1. Hepatitis B and C viruses are the focus of this chapter because they are endemic throughout the world, the majority of the public remains unvaccinated and at risk of infection, and both viruses can cause acute and chronic infections that impact on human health and the ability to withstand dental procedures. During the acute phase of viral hepatitis, the patient's liver is inflamed and damaged. A damaged liver has diminished capacity to effectively excrete bile; metabolize drugs and cholesterol; perform gluconeogenesis; synthesize glycogen, coagulation factors and albumin; and mount an effective immune response. The dentist should realize that a significant percentage of patients with HBV and HCV infections progress to chronic infection. These patients can shed and transmit virus, have oral manifestations, and suffer from persistent virus replication that damages hepatocytes and increases the risk of development of hepatocellular carcinoma.

Molecular and pathologic correlates of disease

Acute viral hepatitis is characterized by virus replication in hepatocytes, inflammation, degeneration, and necrosis of liver cells. The injured hepatocytes undergo ballooning degeneration, and spread of the infection throughout the liver lobule results in infiltrates of lymphocytes and mononuclear phagocytes. As a result, the damaged liver inefficiency conjugates bilirubin with glucuronic acid; bilirubin accumulates in the blood and is deposited in the tissues and excreted in the urine. The skin and sclerae turn yellow and the urine darkens. Failure to excrete bile results in stools that are tan in color. More severe disease diminishes the liver's ability to produce coagulation factors (I, II, V, VII, VIII, IX, X, XI, XIII, and fibrinogen), resulting in persistent elevations in the prothrombin time and abnormal hemostasis.

Recovery from infection is determined by the level of virus replication, the host response, and the appearance of antibodies. Greater morbidity and mortality is associated with very young and older patients. Although most patients recover from viral hepatitis, sequelae include persistent infection (or carrier state), dual infection (HDV [a defective virus] with HBV), chronic active hepatitis, fulminant hepatitis (characterized by massive hepatocellular destruction), cirrhosis, hepatocellular carcinoma, and death. Dual infections increase the risk for fulminant hepatitis, the latter having a mortality rate of about 80%.

Chronic hepatitis results when (1) HBV or HCV escape the host's immune surveillance, (2) virus persists within the liver, and (3) virus or viral antigens can be detected in the serum for longer than 6 months.

Hepatitis B virus

Hepatitis B virus is a 42 nm DNA virus of the Hepadnaviridae family (Figure 16–1). The DNA genome is

Table 16–1 Comparison of Hepatitis Viruses

	HAV	HBV	HCV	HDV	HEV	HGV
Virion	28nm RNA	42nm DNA	40–55 nm RNA	35 nm RNA	32nm RNA	
Transmission	Fecal-oral	Parenteral, sexual	Parenteral, sexual?	Parenteral, sexual?	Fecal-oral	?
Incubation (d)	15–60	45–180	14–180		15–64	?
Dx markers	Anti-HAV	Anti-HBs, Anti-HBc, Anti-Hbe	Anti-HCV		Anti-HEV	Anti-HGV
		HBsAg	HCV RNA			
Chronic carrier state	No	Yes	Yes	Yes	No	?
Vaccine	Yes	Yes	No	No	No	No

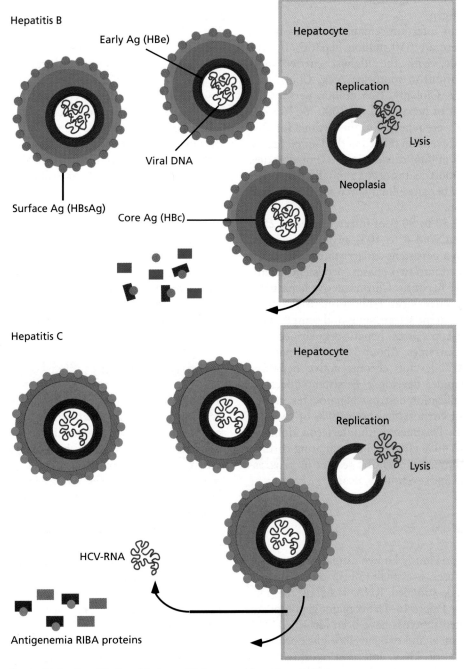

Figure 16–1 Hepatitis B and C viruses. RIBA = recombinant immunoblot assay.

circular and comprised of two strands, with one strand being partially incomplete (~80% full length). It is a highly infectious virus that produces three distinct particles during replication: (1) the Dane particle or complete virus (HBV), composed of an outer shell and an inner core, (2) 22-nm noninfectious spherical particles, and (3) noninfectious filamentous units. The outer shell of the Dane particle carries the hepatitis B surface antigen (HBsAg), which is anchored in a lipid bilayer derived from the host cell. Internally is the inner core that is composed of a protein known as the hepatitis B core antigen (HBcAg), and the hepatitis B early antigen (HBeAg), an antigenic component derived from cleavage of the core antigen.

Hepatitis B virus infection remains a serious health care problem. There are 350 million hepatitis B virus carriers worldwide, with the highest carrier rates (8–20% of population) in southeast Asia, China, and sub-Saharan Africa. Globally, 1.25 million persons die per year as a result of hepatitis B. In 2000, 6646 cases of type B hepatitis were reported to the Centers for Disease Control and Prevention (CDC) in the United States. There are over 1.5 million carriers in the United States, and an estimated 6000 deaths occur annually due to cirrhosis and primary hepatocellular carcinoma associated with HBV infection.

Approximately 50 to 90% of infected infants, 25% of infected children, and 6 to 10% of adults infected with HBV develop a persistent carrier state. The carrier state may be divided into two phases: persistent hepatitis or chronic active hepatitis. Chronic active hepatitis is characterized by active virus replication in the liver, HBsAg and HBeAg in the serum, signs and symptoms of chronic liver disease, persistent hepatic cellular necrosis, and elevated liver enzymes. About 3 to 5% of patients infected with HBV develop chronic active hepatitis, whereas the remainder develop a persistent infection. Persistent virus replication destroys hepatocytes, resulting in fibrosis and cirrhosis in about 20% of cases of chronic hepatitis B. Treatment with interferon alpha-2b (IFN-α 2b) is 30 to 40% effective in eliminating chronic HBV infection. Untreated cirrhosis results in progression of the disease and, eventually, death.

Hepatitis C virus

Hepatitis C virus, previously known as one of the non-A non-B hepatitis viruses, is a small (38–55 nm diameter), positive-sense, single-stranded RNA virus of the Flaviviridae family (see Figure 16–1). Six major genotypes of HCV and 40 related subtypes have been identified. The virus has a core protein and two envelope glycoproteins.

The prevalence of HCV infection worldwide is between 0.3% and 1.5%, with an estimated 300 million carriers worldwide. In the United States, 30,000 acute new infections occur annually; approximately 25% of these are diagnosed, and 1.8% of the population 6 years old or older (or approximately 4 million) have antibodies against HCV. About 2.7 million Americans are chronically infected with HCV. Hepatitis C is responsible for an estimated 10,000 deaths annually and is the leading cause of liver transplantation in the United States.

The genetic diversity of HCV, and its ability to mutate, allows the virus to avoid neutralization and establish a chronic infection in about 85 to 90% of infected persons. The majority of HCV-infected patients develop chronic active hepatitis that is characterized by persistent and intermittent viremia, fluctuating elevations of serum alanine aminotransferase (ALT) levels and slow but progressive liver damage. The first decade is usually marked by inflammatory cell infiltration of the portal tracts and focal liver cell necrosis. Mild fibrosis ensues that is followed by more severe fibrosis, bridging between portal tracts and bridging between portal tracts and hepatic veins. By the second decade after infection, fibrosis progresses to cirrhosis in at least 20% of patients with chronic HCV infection. Progression is more likely if patients consume excessive amounts of alcohol. Untreated cirrhosis is accompanied by liver failure, portal hypertension, ascites, jaundice, esophageal varices, and encephalopathy (end-stage liver disease). Portal hypertension contributes to splenic abnormalities that enhance platelet destruction, whereas esophageal varices can rupture, resulting in life-threatening hemorrhage. The 5-year survival is 50 to 90%, depending on whether the hepatitis C patient develops compensated or decompensated cirrhosis.

Clinical features

Hepatitis B and C viruses are present in the blood, serum, plasma, saliva, menstrual and vaginal discharge, seminal fluid, and occasionally, urine of infected persons. Hepatitis B virus is highly infectious in blood. Both viruses are transmitted to susceptible individuals by horizontal routes (ie, parenteral, hetero- or homosexual, and injecting drug use) and vertical routes (mother to fetus). Blood transfusion, dialysis, percutaneous inoculation (tattooing, body piercing), absorption of infective serum or plasma through mucosal surfaces, and organ and tissue transplantation are other modes of transmission. Transmission of HBV and HCV via a human bite has been reported, and transmission from inanimate objects (eg, blood-tinged gauze) is possible. In the United States, HBV and HCV are transmitted primarily by horizontal routes, yet 30% and 40% of HBV- and HCV-infected patients, respectively, have no identifiable risk factor for infection. Hepatitis C virus was the major etiologic agent of post-transfusion hepatitis until the introduction of sensitive blood testing for HCV in the 1990s. Since then, the risk of transfusion-related hepatitis has been reduced to approximately 1 in 100,000 units transfused.

Hepatitis B and C virus infections can occur at any age, but are more common after puberty. The incubation period for HBV is 45 to 180 days (average, 75 d); for HCV it is 14 to 180 days (average, 50 d). Hepatitis B and C viruses produce symptoms in 10% and 25 to 30% of patients, respectively. Symptoms initially are flu-like and include fatigue, fever, loss of appetite, diarrhea, headache, malaise, myalgia, nausea, vomiting, and weakness. During acute HBV infection, about 50% of symptomatic persons become icteric within about 10 days of the onset of symptoms. A minority become icteric with HCV infection. Icterus is the stage of infection in which patients demonstrate jaundice (yellow bile deposits) in the skin, conjunctiva of the eye, oral mucosa, and urine as a result of serum bilirubin levels rising three- to fourfold above normal levels (0.2–1.2 mg/dL). About 10% of patients infected with HBV also demonstrate serum sickness-like manifestations, including angioedema, arthralgia, and a rash. As the disease progresses, abdominal pain increases and hepatomegaly and splenomegaly develop. Two to 8 weeks are required for recovery from symptoms, with hepatomegaly and abnormal liver function persisting for weeks to months. The course of the disease varies with alcohol use and the viral strain and load. The acute infection rarely requires medical treatment other than rest and the avoidance of hepatotoxic drugs. Patients who fail to produce an adequate immune response can develop fulminant hepatitis or a chronic infection.

Diagnosis

The diagnosis of acute HBV infection is made by recognition of the clinical features, specific serologic tests for viral antigens and antibodies, and elevated liver enzymes. The hepatitis B surface antigen (HBsAg) is the first detectable specific marker (Figure 16–2). Hepatitis B surface antigen appears in the blood usually by the fourth week of infection and is followed within a week by the hepatitis B early antigen (HBeAg). Two to 4 weeks after the appearance of surface antigen, antibodies against the core antigen (anti-HBcAg) appear. Subsequently, antibodies against the hepatitis B early antigen (anti-HBeAg) appear by about the sixteenth week, and finally the appearance of antibodies against the surface antigen (anti-HBsAg) appear by about week 28. Clearance of the virus is marked by the disappearance of HBeAg, appearance of anti-HBeAg and the eventual dis-

appearance of HBsAg. Failure to produce anti-HBsAg results in a chronic carrier state. Carriers persistently display HBsAg in their serum for more than 6 months. The presence of the HBeAg in a carrier's serum indicates virus replication in the liver and an infectious state.

Antibody against HCV (anti-HCV) can be detected in 50 to 70% of patients at the onset of symptoms and in 90% within 3 months after onset of infection. Anti-HCV is commonly detected using an enzyme immunoassay (EIA) that contains HCV antigens from the core and nonstructural genes. A supplemental recombinant immunoblot assay (RIBA) and the qualitative reverse transcriptase polymerase chain reaction (RT-PCR) for HCV RNA can be performed for confirmation. The RIBA is often positive after the third week of infection, whereas HCV RNA can be detected in blood as soon as 1 week after initial exposure.

Since a delay of several weeks occurs before antibodies can be detected in the serum of a patient with acute hepatitis, other laboratory abnormalities are helpful in the diagnosis. Early features include a relative leukocytosis with a shift to the left and a mild proteinuria in the urine. More specific for acute hepatitis are elevations in the serum transaminase levels (aspartate aminotransferase/serum glutamate oxaloacetate transaminase [AST/SGOT], alanine aminotransferase/serum glutamate pyruvate transaminase [ALT/SGPT], and gamma-glutamyltransferase [GGT]). They become elevated (often more than 10 times normal) during the late prodromal phase. Subsequently, a rise in the serum bilirubin occurs, the serum alkaline phosphatase level

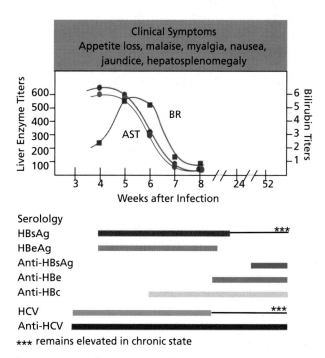

Figure 16–2 Serologic changes in hepatitis B and C virus infections.

elevates mildly and the prothrombin time (PT) may become prolonged. Elevation of the serum bilirubin often corresponds with the peak of the icteric phase. During recovery, the transaminase level begins to fall, however, elevations in the bilirubin level regress more slowly. Failure of the PT to return to normal is a significant prognostic sign of extensive hepatic cellular destruction, indicative of a fulminant clinical course or a chronic rather than an acute infection.

Extrahepatic and oral manifestations

Patients with chronic hepatitis C occasionally present with extrahepatic manifestations considered to be of autoimmune origin, including antinuclear and anti-smooth muscle antibodies, autoimmune thyroiditis, rheumatoid arthritis, essential mixed cryoglobulinemia, glomerulonephritis, (Gougerot)-Sjögren-like syndrome, keratoconjunctivitis sicca, lichen planus, porphyria cutanea tarda, vasculitis, and thrombocytopenic purpura. The patients affected with Sjögren-like syndrome often have features of secondary Sjögren syndrome (ie, keratoconjunctivitis sicca, hypergammaglobulinemia, and anti-DNA antibodies), but rarely have the typical primary autoimmune disorders of secondary Sjögren syndrome (ie, rheumatoid factor, anti–SS-A and anti–SS-B antibodies); the clinical abnormalities of oral dryness and abnormal sialography are variable. The lichen planus associated with chronic HCV can be intraoral or extraoral and appears in about 5 to 10% of patients with chronic HCV, with higher prevalence in Italy and Japan. The dermal eruptions of lichen planus associated with chronic liver disease can also result from adverse drug effects of IFN-α 2b administration.

The oral cavity manifests several features of hepatitis. Hepatitis B and C viruses are present in whole saliva of infected humans. During the icterus, jaundice can be seen in the oral mucosa. Jaundice becomes clinically evident as the serum bilirubin level approaches 2.5 mg/100 mL. Levels of bilirubin are highest during peak icterus and gradually subside during convalescence. Jaundice is best visualized in the posterior palate, the floor of the mouth along the lingual frenum, and the buccal mucosa. Although children under 2 years of age are often asymptomatic, hepatitis that results in jaundice can result in yellow-green bile deposition of the dentin of developing teeth. Viral-induced liver disease can cause intraoral bleeding, petechiae, and ecchymoses.

Neoplasia

Chronic HBV and HCV can deregulate RNA transcription and the replication machinery of the hepatocyte, leading to hepatocellular carcinoma. Hepatitis B virus induces neoplasia by integrating its DNA into the hepatocyte genome and facilitating the activity of oncogenes, such as *ras*. The mechanism by which HCV induces malignant transformation may involve inactivation of the tumor suppressor gene p53. Hepatocellular carcinoma (HCC) develops in 1 to 5% of patients with chronic HCV hepatitis after 20 years and is associated with chronic HBV and HCV infection in 20 to 50% of cases. Once cirrhosis is established, the rate of HCC development is 1 to 4% per year. The risk of liver cancer is 30- to 100-fold higher for chronic hepatitis virus carriers compared with uninfected persons.

Diagnostic tests for HCC include an elevated α-fetoprotein (AFP) and the liver biopsy. Metastases of HCC to the orofacial complex are rare. Generally they appear as rapidly expanding, hypervascular, and hemorrhagic masses located posterior to the premolar region and extending into the mandibular ramus.

Chronic hepatitis C infection has been associated with lymphoproliferation, lymphoid cancer (B-cell non-Hodgkin lymphoma), and gammopathies.

Therapy and prevention

Chronic hepatitis is managed with antiviral agents when HCV RNA levels and ALT levels remain elevated and the liver biopsy shows portal or bridging fibrosis and moderate inflammation and necrosis. Interferon-α 2b is the drug of choice for patients with chronic viral hepatitis. It regulates cytokine activity, increases activity of natural killer cells and macrophages, augments lymphocytic T-cell cytotoxicity via enhanced maturation, and modulates immunoglobulin production. Approximately a third of patients chronically infected with HBV and 20% of patients with HCV have a sustained response to therapy when 3 million units of IFN-α 2b are administered twice weekly subcutaneously for 12 months. Recent studies of chronically infected HCV patients have shown that combination therapy of interferon with ribarivin or lamuvidine improves the sustained virologic response to above 30%. Patients who fail to respond to therapy require liver transplantation to survive. Currently, HBV and HCV infections are the leading cause of chronic liver disease and liver transplantation in the United States.

Vaccination is the most effective means of preventing HBV infection. An effective vaccine against HBV has been available since 1982. Currently, the vaccine is available as a recombinant synthetic formulation as Recombivax and Engerix. Three injections are required, with the injections at 0, 1, and 6 months after the initial dose. The injections should be provided in the deltoid muscle to obtain the highest antibody titers. Both vaccines provide over 96% efficacy in preventing HBV infection. Currently, the HBV vaccine is recommended for all infants and health care workers in the United States. No booster dose is currently recommended and protective antibodies persist for at least 9 years in most vaccinated persons. There is no vaccine available against HCV at this time.

Dental management

The dentist should perform a thorough medical history on all patients, to identify those with active or chronic hepatitis. Questions should be asked that specifically determine the diagnosis of hepatitis and risk for hepatitis. Positive responses regarding blood transfusions, recipient of blood products, hemodialysis, injecting and illicit drug use, multiple sexual partners, and close contacts with infectious patients indicate risk and the need to inquire specifically of hepatitis. Serum liver function tests and hepatitis antigen and antibody tests are required to confirm the type of hepatitis present.

Patients with a known history of HBV and HCV should be evaluated to determine carrier status, activity of disease, and liver function. Consultation with the physician is recommended if moderate-to-severe liver disease is present and significant dental procedures are planned. Elevations of serum transaminases indicate risk for altered drug metabolism. Drugs that are metabolized primarily in the liver are listed in Table 16–2. These drugs encompass a large percentage of commonly used dental drugs. Thus, their avoidance may be impossible, to effectively perform dental treatment. However, upon consultation with the patient's physician usually the drugs are used in reduced amounts administered at increased intervals.

There is always concern for proper hemostasis in a patient with liver disease. The presurgical evaluation should include a platelet count and bleeding time as well as a prothrombin time (PT), which measures the extrinsic pathway, and the activated partial thromboplastin time (aPTT), which measures the intrinsic pathway. Platelet counts above 50,000/mm^3 are generally considered safe when conservative surgical technique is employed and other measures of hemostasis are within the normal reference range.

The prothrombin time is reported as a value normalized to a standard factor (ie, the international normalized ratio [INR]) (see Chapter 7). When INR values are between 1.0 and 3.5, it is usually considered safe to perform surgical procedures as long as the other measures of hemostasis are normal and local hemostatic measures (gel foam, topical thrombin, pressure dressings, and soft diet) are employed. Hemorrhagic procedures on a patient with an INR above 3.5 require a hospital-

like environment and potentially vitamin K supplementation or fresh frozen plasma prior to the surgical procedure. After an extraction or surgery, patients should be advised to minimize aspirin intake if gastrointestinal bleeding is a concern. Likewise, acetaminophen intake should be reduced and avoidance of alcoholic beverages is advised, as both are hepatotoxic. Severe liver disease (ie, cirrhosis) increases the risk for infection, and perioperative antibiotics may be indicated for extractions and surgical procedures.

Patients with chronic hepatitis may experience adverse drug effects from medical therapy. Interferon-α 2b induces a flu-like illness, muscle aches, fatigue, and arthritis. In addition, it causes various autoimmune disorders, such as interstitial pneumonia, systemic lupus erythematosus, autoimmune hemolytic anemia, hypothyroidism, immune thrombocytopenia, and recurrent sarcoidosis with or without bilateral swelling of parotid glands. Anemia, anorexia, nausea, diarrhea, depression, irritability, pharyngitis, and alopecia are potential adverse effects of IFN-α 2b when used in combination with ribavirin. A complete blood count and differential is recommended prior to surgical and sedation procedures for patients taking IFN-α 2b and ribavirin.

Post-exposure protocol

In situations of known exposure, the CDC recommendation for post-exposure prophylaxis is dependent on the type of virus suspected or known, and whether the exposure is from a person with acute or chronic disease. If a dental health care worker (DHCW) is exposed (eg, percutaneous exposure by a sharp or needlestick) to the blood or bodily fluid of an HBsAg-positive person with

Table 16–2 Dental Drugs Metabolized in the Liver

Classification	Drug
Analgesics	Aspirin
	Acetaminophen
	Ibuprofen
	Codeine
	Meperidine
Antibiotics	Ampicillin
	Macrolide antibiotics (azithromycin, clarithromycin, erythromycin)
	Tetracyclines (doxycycline, minocycline)
Amide local anesthetics	Lidocaine
	Mepivacaine
	Prilocaine
	Bupivicaine
Anxiolytics or sedatives	Benzodiazepines (diazepam, triazolam)
	Barbiturates (pentobarbital, thiopental sodium, methohexital sodium)

acute disease, then hepatitis B immune globulin (HBIG) is to be given (within 24 hr) along with the vaccine within 14 days if the DHCW is previously unvaccinated. If a DHCW is exposed to a person with chronic disease, then HBV vaccine is recommended within 14 days, to be given if the DHCW is previously unvaccinated. The CDC does not currently recommend post-exposure prophylaxis for HCV. However, higher rates of resolved infection have been documented when IFN-α 2b treatment was initiated early in persons acutely infected with HCV. The CDC current guidelines recommend as a minimum that (1) the source person be baseline tested, (2) the person exposed be baseline and follow-up (6 mo) tested for antibodies against the virus and liver enzyme activity, (3) the antibody results be confirmed by repeating the test or use of an alternate test, and (4) health care workers be educated about risk and prevention of blood-borne infections.

Suggested reading

Gumber SC, Chopra S. Hepatitis C: a multifacted disease. Review of extrahepatic manifestations. Ann Intern Med 1995;123:615–20.

Iwarson S, Norkrans G, Wejstal R. Hepatitis C: natural history of a unique infection. Clin Infect Dis 1995;20:1361–70.

Komiyama K, Moro I, Mastuda Y, et al. HCV in saliva of chronic hepatitis patients having dental treatment. Lancet 1991;338:572–3.

Lauer GM, Walker BC. Hepatitis C virus infection. N Engl J Med 2001;345:41–52.

Ray RB, Steele R, Meyer K, Ray R. Transcriptional repression of p53 promoter by hepatitis C virus core protein. J Biol Chem 1997;272:10983–6.

Wisnom CJ, Kelly M. Medical/dental management of a chronic hepatitis C patient: a case report. Oral Surg Oral Med Oral Pathol 1993;75:787–90.

17 Bacterial Infections

Jed J. Jacobson, DDS, MS, MPH, and Sol Silverman, Jr, MA, DDS

In this chapter, oral focal infections caused by bacteria are discussed with primary emphasis on the occurrence of bacteremias of oral cavity origin that result in endocarditis and infection in the vicinity of prosthetic joints. Subsequently, bacterial infections of the oral mucosa are reviewed, emphasizing sexually transmitted disease and cat scratch fever.

Oral focal infection and prophylaxis

The oral focal infection theory, a concept generally neglected for several decades, is controversial yet has gained renewed interest with progress in classification and identification of oral microorganisms. Additionally, recent evidence associating dental infections with atherosclerosis and other chronic diseases has also helped resurrect the focal infection theory. The detrimental effect of focal infection on general health has been known for decades. Prophylactic antibiotics are routinely prescribed before some dental procedures to immunosuppressed and other at-risk patients, to combat the spread of oral bacteria into the blood stream. But which bacteremias, in what patients, and which intervention is appropriate after what dental procedures has been the source of controversy since early in the twentieth century in Britain, where the focal infection theory arose. In spite of the lack of scientific foundation, the dental profession readily accepted the notion that bad teeth were one of the major sources of infection and the cause of many diseases. In general, the theory relates a number of general conditions to septic foci from which toxic products spread to different parts of the body. The specification of "spreading to different parts of the body," separates the metastatic dissemination of infection through the blood stream from local invasive spread of infection (Figure 17–1). The three pathways that may link oral bacteria to secondary disease distant from the oral nidus are (1) metastatic infection attributable to transient bacteria in the blood; (2) metastatic immunologic injury; and (3) metastatic toxic injury. The scientific evidence, weak as it is, best supports the first pathway of transient bacteremias of oral origin and is the focus of this chapter. As the science evolves, it may reveal that all three pathways are operant, and they may not be independent mechanisms, but interrelated. Nonetheless,

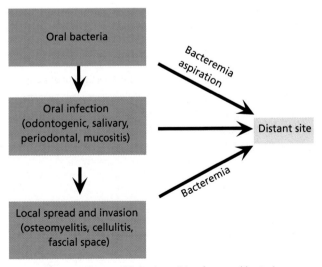

Figure 17–1 Pathways of infection arising from oral bacteria.

this chapter focuses on the hematogenous dissemination of oral bacteria to cause bacterial endocarditis, infections of prosthetic devices, and a group of diseases for which immunosuppressed patients are at risk.

In a healthy person the daily transient bacteremias following tooth brushing, flossing, or activities of daily living are usually controlled by host defenses. Some bacteremias, however, can overwhelm defense mechanisms and lead to infections at distant sites. Bacteremias related to a variety of dental conditions or procedures have been documented and have been associated with infections at distant sites. In immunocompromised patients, bacteremias of oral origin can involve many organisms, including rare pathologic microorganisms, such as *Capnocytophaga* or *Leptotrichia* species.

Overlooking the oral cavity as a possible origin for bacteremias can complicate and delay the necessary removal of the etiologic source. Fever of unknown origin in the hospital setting can often result from bacteremia of oral origin.

Bacterial endocarditis

A major group of infections that dental health care workers must acquire current knowledge about are those that begin with hematogenous dissemination of an oral organism to endocardium. The most commonly studied of these infections is bacterial endocarditis, often attributable to alpha-hemolytic streptococci, or viridans streptococci. Bacterial endocarditis is a severe infection of the cardiac valves and supporting endocardial structures by blood-borne bacteria that gain entry to the blood stream from the mouth, gastrointestinal tract, skin, and genitourinary tract following procedures and activities that initiate bleeding. Bacterial endocarditis may present as acute, subacute, or chronic disease. Acute endocarditis is usually caused by virulent organisms and an intact endocardium not damaged by previous disease, such as rheumatic fever. Cases of endocarditis of oral origin are almost always caused by bacteria of low virulence that slowly (subacutely) attack a previously damaged endocardium, resulting in a subacute bacterial endocarditis. Acute and subacute endocarditis can lead to a chronic disease state.

Acute endocarditis is frequently caused by *Staphylococcus aureus,* and metastatic foci of infection are common. If untreated, the infection carries a high risk of mortality within days to weeks. Subacute endocarditis infection takes 6 or more weeks or even years to become fatal.

Pathophysiology

Almost any species of bacteria is capable of producing infective endocarditis. However, streptococci and staphylococci account for the vast majority of cases (Table 17–1). Enterococci and group A beta-hemolytic streptococcus can attack normal or previously damaged heart valves and may cause rapid destruction.

Bacterial endocarditis results from bacterial proliferation on cardiac (endothelial) surfaces. It appears that a number of factors interacting in sequence and, at times, simultaneously, are needed to result in this serious infection. The initiation of endocarditis first requires the presence of microorganisms in the blood stream (see Figure 17–1). These microorganisms stick or attach themselves to sterile, preformed platelet thrombi vegetations found on the endocardium, particularly damaged surfaces. Recent evidence suggests that bacteria such as streptococci have special adherence properties, which make them likely to stick and form vegetations on endocardium (Figure 17–2). The damaged endothelium may result from trauma to the endothelial cells or a subendothelial inflammatory reaction, as in rheumatic fever. Nevertheless, once the characteristic vegetation of infective endocarditis is formed, the continued deposition of platelets and fibrin over the proliferating bacteria protects the vegetation from phagocytic cells. Additionally, bacteria are continuously released from these vegetations and disseminate to other parts of the heart.

The sites of involvement suggest an important role for hydrodynamic forces. Endocarditis occurs down-

Table 17–1 Microbial Organisms Involved in Infective Endocarditis

Organism	Involvement (%)
Alpha-hemolytic streptococcus	50
S. viridans	
S. sanguis	
S. mitior	
S. pneumoniae	
Staphylococci	20
S. aureus; S. epidermidis	
Enterococcus (*E. coli* and *S. faecalis*)	15
Fungi or gram-negative bacteria	10
Neisseria gonorrhoeae	< 5

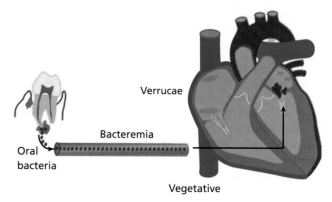

Figure 17–2 Bacterial endocarditis.

Table 17–2 Cardiac Conditions Associated with Endocarditis

Endocarditis Prophylaxis Recommended	Endocarditis Prophylaxis Not Recommended
High-risk category	Negligible-risk category (no greater risk than the general population)
Prosthetic heart valves	Isolated secundum atrial septal defect
Previous bacterial endocarditis	Surgical repair of atrial septal defect
Complex cyanotic congenital heart disease (eg, transposition	Previous coronary artery bypass graft surgery
of the great arteries, tetralogy of Fallot)	Mitral valve prolapse without valvular regurgitation
Surgically constructed systemic pulmonary shunts	Physiologic, functional, or innocent heart murmurs
Moderate-risk category	Previous Kawasaki syndrome or rheumatic fever without valvular
Most other congenital cardiac malformations	dysfunction
Acquired valvular dysfunction (eg, rheumatic heart disease)	Cardiac pacemakers and implanted defibrillators
Hypertrophic cardiomyopathy	
Mitral valve prolapse with valvular regurgitation	

stream from where blood flows through a narrow orifice at a high velocity. It is speculated that disturbed flow across these high-pressure gradients may result in eddies downstream, allowing the bacteria to linger in a specific area. The increased risk of bacterial endocarditis in heart conditions listed in Table 17–2 underscores the implicated link to altered hydrodynamic forces.

The pathogenesis of endocarditis is a result of the vegetations themselves and an immune reaction to the infection. The vegetations can lead to destruction of valvular tissue, resulting in valvular insufficiency. Even upon healing, scar formation may lead to valvular insufficiency, resulting in congestive heart failure. Further, the infection may extend into the myocardium, forming burrowing abscesses.

Portions of the vegetation can break off, embolizing to the brain, kidneys, spleen, lungs, extremities, and other parts of the heart itself. These emboli and continuous release of bacteria trigger an immune response, resulting in immune complexes. Immune complex deposition is responsible for the vasculitis of endocarditis

that causes many of the cutaneous and glomerular manifestations (Table 17–3).

Clinical features
Endocarditis is a life-threatening disease that is relatively uncommon, particularly among children, with the mean age of occurrence in the mid to late 40s. Despite improvements in outcomes, owing to advances in diagnosis and antimicrobial therapy, significant morbidity and mortality result from this infection. The rise in the mean age of occurrence is probably attributable to the decline in incidence of rheumatic heart disease in the younger population and the increased incidence of degenerative heart disease, cardiovascular surgery, and endocarditis among drug abusers. Additionally, the aged constitute a larger proportion of individuals who develop endocarditis in that the elderly are retaining their teeth, and those that are edentulous are having prostheses fabricated to replace their missing teeth. Teeth and their prosthetic replacements provide an ecologic niche for streptococcal

Table 17–3 Manifestations of Infective Endocarditis

Category	Manifestation
General	Weakness, malaise, fever, weight loss
Cardiopulmonary	Valvular damage, marked changing heart murmurs, pulmonary emboli, hemoptysis, congestive heart failure, coronary embolism, myocarditis
Gastrointestinal	Splenomegaly, abnormal pain, splenic infarcts, abnormal liver function tests, mesenteric vascular occlusion
Central nervous system	Emboli, brain abscess, meningitis, cerebrovascular accidents, paresis, encephalitis, subarachroid hemorrhage, coma
Genitourinary	Embolic glomerulonephritis, hematuria, flank pain, albuminuria, uremia
Dermatologic	Splinter hemorrhages: small, red, linear, splinter-like spots under the proximal two-thirds of the nails
	Osler nodes: tender, pink-to-red, painful lumps in the finger and toe pads
	Janeway lesions: asymptomatic, irregular hemorrhagic macules of the palms and soles
	Petechial hemorrhages: pinpoint bleeding of skin and mucosa
Ocular	Roth spots: pale retinal hemorrhages
Extremities	Myalgia, arthralgia, clubbing, arthritis, osteomyelitis
Hematologic	Leukocytosis, anemia, elevated sedimentation rate

organisms likely to become the etiologic bacteria arising from the oral cavity.

The most common underlying heart condition that predisposes patients to bacterial endocarditis is rheumatic heart disease (25–40%). Congenital heart disease is the underlying risk in 5 to 20% of the patients with endocarditis. The incidence of endocarditis in individuals with no underlying heart disease is increasing (20–40%), as it is in newly recognized lesions, such as hypertrophic myocardiopathies, Marfan syndrome, and degenerative heart disease.

Since most cases of endocarditis arising from dental procedures are subacute, only the clinical manifestations of subacute bacterial endocarditis are discussed. Common early symptoms of subacute bacterial endocarditis include unexplained low-grade fever, malaise, anemia, lethargy, weight loss, and joint pains. These symptoms generally start within 2 or 3 weeks of the dental procedure if the cause of endocarditis is a bacteremia of dental or oral origin. A history of a dental procedure can be elicited in only 15 to 20% of the patients with endocarditis caused by streptococci of the viridans group. The onset of symptoms is usually gradual, with mild fever and malaise. These symptoms persist for weeks eventually leading to orthopnea and dyspnea, as deterioration of cardiac function progresses. Concurrently, a significant and changing heart murmur is evident, and embolic phenomena and multiple manifestations of disseminated immune-medicated vasculitis can occur. Table 17–3 lists the clinical manifestations of bacterial endocarditis.

The diagnosis of subacute bacterial endocarditis is frequently made by the elimination of other conditions that may produce mild febrile symptoms, weakness, and loss of weight. The final diagnosis is made by blood culture and echocardiography to detect the valvular vegetations. An elevated erythrocyte sedimentation rate (ESR), mild anemia, slight leukocytosis, and circulating immune complexes are evident in a majority of patients.

Patients with streptococcal endocarditis are hospitalized and provided high-dose antibiotic therapy to minimize cardiac damage. Streptococci usually respond to high doses of penicillin combined with streptomycin, gentamicin, or tobramycin. Formerly, this disease was frequently fatal, because of overwhelming infection. Currently, fatalities are reduced and attributable to congestive heart failure secondary to valve damage and cerebral vascular accidents. The mortality rate in treated streptococcal endocarditis is about 10%.

Dental management
The most important responsibility of the dentist is to protect against bacterial endocarditis in high-risk patients. Although it is not possible to know the likelihood that a patient will develop endocarditis subsequent to dental therapy, it is estimated that 6 to 15% of endocarditis cases arise following dental treatment, and the extremely serious nature of this disease warrants use of prophylactic measures to preclude bacteremia in patients at risk for endocarditis. Antimicrobial protection is the best method of prevention for patients susceptible to infective endocarditis. Although there is no direct evidence that antibiotic prophylaxis prevents endocarditis, there is adequate evidence that it decreases the incidence of bacteremia. To prevent bacterial endocarditis, dentists are strongly encouraged to follow the most current American Heart Association Guidelines (1997): (1) identify the susceptible patient, (2) identify dental procedures likely to cause a bacteremia requiring antibiotic prophylaxis, (3) select the appropriate antimicrobiologic regimen, and (4) eliminate all sources of infection.

How is the susceptible patient identified? As mentioned previously, patients with cardiac conditions associated with alteration in hemodynamic forces are predisposed to development of endocarditis. Antibiotic prophylaxis is recommended in individuals who have a higher risk for developing endocarditis than the general population. Table 17–2 stratifies these conditions into high- and moderate-risk categories. Consequently, a dental patient should be questioned regarding a history of those cardiac conditions prior to initiation of dental pro-

Table 17–4 Dental Procedures and Endocarditis Prophylaxis

Endocarditis Prophylaxis Recommended	Endocarditis Prophylaxis Not Recommended
Dental extractions	Restorative dentistry (operative and prosthodontic) with or without retraction cord. Clinical judgment may indicate antibiotic use in selected circumstances that may create significant bleeding.
Periodontal procedures including surgery, scaling and root planing, probing, and recall maintenance	Local anesthetic injections (nonintraligamentary)
Dental implant placement and reimplantation of avulsed teeth	Intracanal endodontic treatment; post placement and buildup
Endodontic instrumentation or surgery only beyond the apex	Placement of rubber dams
Subgingival placements of antibiotic fibers or strips	Postoperative suture removal
Intraligamentary local anesthetic injections	Placement of removable prosthodontic or orthodontic appliances
Prophylactic cleaning of teeth or implants where bleeding is anticipated	Taking of oral impressions
	Taking of oral radiographs

cedures likely to result in a transient bacteremia. If a dentist is unable to determine the need for antibiotic prophylaxis based upon a thorough history, a recommendation from the patient's physician or cardiologist should be obtained. Although bacterial endocarditis can occur in patients without previously documented cardiac lesions, antibiotic prophylaxis is only indicated for patients with known underlying abnormalities. Frequently the dentist is confronted with a patient giving a history of a heart murmur of unknown origin and an implication by the patient that the murmur is of little consequence and does not affect the activities of daily living. A heart murmur is created by turbulence in blood flow and is usually detected with the aid of a stethoscope. Occasionally, the heart murmur may be labeled as functional or innocent. Functional murmurs do not reflect cardiac abnormalities and do not require antibiotic prophylaxis. However, clinically significant murmurs usually result from valvular or other cardiac abnormalities and may require antibiotic prophylaxis. Only careful cardiac examination reveals which murmurs place a patient at high risk for endocarditis.

Dental procedures that are likely to cause bacteremias and, thus, require antibiotic prophylaxis must be identified. As stated previously, bacteremias occur daily through such activities as tooth brushing, flossing, and chewing. Only those bacteremias of organisms commonly associated with endocarditis and attributable to identifiable procedures are significant. Those procedures known to produce such bacteremias that require antibiotic prophylaxis are specified by the American Heart Association (Table 17–4). Further, the risk of orally introduced bacteremias appears to be dependent upon the degree of oral inflammation and infection as well as the amount of soft-tissue trauma induced by the dental procedure. Consequently, individuals at risk for developing bacterial endocarditis should establish and maintain optimum oral health. Lastly, unanticipated bleeding may occur or recognition of a high-risk patient may become evident after manipulation of tissue that results in bleeding. In such an event, antimicrobial prophylaxis administered up to 2 hours following the procedure has been shown to be effective in animal models.

The choice of antibiotics for prophylaxis is largely an empirical decision. The drugs chosen should be bactericidal, directed at the organisms commonly found in the oral cavity etiologically associated with endocarditis, and administered in doses sufficient to ensure adequate antibiotic concentrations in the serum during and after the procedure. To reduce the likelihood of microbial resistance, it is important that antibiotics be initiated shortly before the procedures and not continued for extended periods. If a series of dental procedures is required, it may be prudent to observe an interval of time between procedures (9–14 d) to allow repopulation of the mouth with antibiotic-susceptible flora. Based upon the above considerations, clinical experience, experimental models, and reviews of MEDLINE database searches, the American Heart Association currently recommends the regimens listed in Table 17–5.

Elimination of all sources of infection that could serve as a nidus for a bacteremia should be undertaken. Poor oral hygiene or oral infections (ie, pulpal or periodontal) may induce a bacteremia even in the absence of dental procedures. The dentist needs to eliminate these infections and provide oral hygiene instruction. This instruction includes proper use of manual and powered toothbrushes, dental floss, and other plaque-removal devices. Antiseptic mouthrinses applied immediately prior to dental procedures may reduce the incidence and magnitude of a bacteremia. However, sustained use is not indicated, as this may lead to selection of resistant microorganisms.

Antibiotic prophylaxis in high-risk dental patients does not guarantee prevention, but only reduces the probability of endocarditis. Therefore, the dentist should be mindful of the vague symptoms of malaise, unexplained mild fever, and joint pain in patients having received invasive dental procedures and make a timely referral to a physician for further diagnostic evaluation.

Late prosthetic joint infection

The ability to replace diseased organs and tissues with prosthetic devices is a major accomplishment of bio-

Table 17–5 Prophylactic Regimen for Dental and Oral Procedures

Category	Prophylaxis
Standard general prophylaxis	Amoxicillin 2.0 g 1 hour before procedure
Unable to take oral medications	Amoxicillin 2.0 g IM or IV within 30 min before procedure
Allergic to penicillins	Clindamycin 600 g 1 hr before procedure *or* cephalexin or cefadroxil* 2.0 g 1 hr before procedure *or* azithromycin or clarithromycin 500 mg 1 hr before procedure
Allergic to penicillins and unable to take oral medications	Clindamycin 600 mg IV within 30 min before procedure *or* cefazolin* 1.0 g IM or IV within 30 min before procedure

*Cephalosporins should not be used in individuals with immediate-type hypersensitivity reaction (urticaria, angioedema, or anaphylaxis) to penicillins.

logic science. Many prostheses are implanted permanently, some are used for short periods of time, and still others are used to bridge the period from failure of the natural organ to transplantation of a donor organ. Individuals with painful or debilitating joint disease are often recipients of prosthetic joints. Approximately 450,000 total-joint arthroplasties are performed annually in the United States. Deep infections of these prostheses usually result in failure, removal with high morbidity, and costly hospitalizations.

A late prosthetic joint infection is a deep infection in and around a prosthetic joint, which occurs 6 months after placement and is caused by hematogenous dissemination of bacteria from a distant source. The 6-month symptom-free time interval from initial placement is essential to distinguish late prosthetic joint infections from early or perioperative infections, which are caused by bacteria implanted at the time of placement of the prosthetic joint. As in bacterial endocarditis, bloodborne bacteria can gain entry to the blood stream from the oral cavity, skin, respiratory, gastrointestinal, and genitourinary tract following procedures that initiate bleeding. Once bacteria, particularly those with the ability to adhere to foreign surfaces, enter the blood stream and attach to the surface of the prosthesis, they can persist and propagate. These bacteria may then invade the surrounding tissues. Although infrequent, infection at a prosthesis is a serious complication and occasionally results in death.

Pathophysiology

Dental patients with prostheses, both hip and knee, are at increased risk of infection, because bacteria can persist on avascular surfaces, sequestered from circulating immune factors and circulating antibiotics. Once established, these infections are difficult to manage. As in bacterial endocarditis, almost any species of bacteria is capable of producing a late prosthetic joint infection. In contrast to bacterial endocarditis arising from an oral source, the predominant etiologic bacteria are staphylococci (48%). Streptococci are still associated in a significant percentage of infections (38%), but are not the predominant organisms (Table 17–6).

Prosthetic devices and the compounds used in their formulation and insertion may directly alter the host's susceptibility to infection. These devices may promote infection by providing a physical refuge from circulating leukocytes. Adherence of bacteria directly to the surface of prosthetic devices is also important in the pathogenesis of infection. Mechanisms of attachment and protection may involve bacterial glycocalyx or extracellular slime substance. Viridans streptococci, *S. aureus*, and *Pseudomonas aeruginosa* have been shown to produce a glycocalyx. This complex carbohydrate mucoid layer blocks penetration of antibiotics, complement, and phagocyte cells. Consequently, this protective layer can lead to the persistence and propagation of bacteria, promoting infection.

The surgical procedure and the cementation of the prosthetic joint into bone with methyl methacrylate may also impact the host's defense mechanisms. Scar-tissue formation around the prosthetic device is inherent in the surgical placement. Owing to the relatively avascular nature of scar tissue, the host's immune response is reduced. Further, animal studies suggest that infection is attributable to the thermal and chemical effects of methyl methacrylate. Excess monomer and heat from the curing process depress the host's ability to react to bacteria attached to the prosthesis, and the most critical period for risk of deep infection appears to be up to 2 years after joint placement.

Given the low estimated incidence of hematogenous late prosthetic joint infection in the United States, less than 1%, it seems unlikely that all patients with prosthetic joints who experience a bacteremia are at high risk. More likely, chronic bacteremias and associated disease processes, such as rheumatoid arthritis, diabetes mellitus, and immunosuppressive states, increase the risk of late prosthetic joint infection. Retrospective

Table 17–6 Microbial Organisms Associated with Hematogenous Late Prosthetic Joint Infections

Organism	Incidence (%)	Incidence following Dental Treatment (%)
Staphylococci	60	48
S. epidermidis	40	10
S. aureus	20	38
Streptococci	20	38
Alpha-hemolytic	5	19
Beta-hemolytic	5	14
Gamma-hemolytic	10	5
Anaerobes	10	9
Gram-negative bacilli	10	5

Table 17–7 Patients at Potential Increased Risk of Hematogenous Total-Joint Infection

Patient Group	Risk Factor
Immunocompromised/ immunosuppressed	Inflammatory arthropathies: rheumatoid arthritis, systemic lupus erythematosus
	Disease-, drug-, or radiation-induced immunosuppression
Others	Type 1 diabetes
	First 2 years following joint placement
	Previous prosthetic joint infections
	Malnourishment
	Hemophilia

analyses have also revealed that patient groups with previous prosthetic joint infections, hemophilia, malnourishment, and placement of the prosthesis within 2 years may be at increased risk (Table 17–7).

Although staphylococci do not account for a large percentage of the cultivable organisms of the oral cavity, there are reports that *S. aureus* may be more prevalent in the mouths of elderly subjects with rheumatoid arthritis. It is not clear whether this increased prevalence of *S. aureus* is attributable to immunosuppression caused by long-term steroid therapy, associated xerostomia, changes in salivary immunoglobulins, poor oral hygiene, or decreased chemotaxis of polymorphonuclear leukocytes in individuals with rheumatoid arthritis.

Clinical features

Dental health care workers should maintain a high index of suspicion for any unusual signs and symptoms in patients with total-joint prostheses. Commonly, the patient complains of pain in the infected joint, especially in a weight-bearing joint. The patient may also complain of swelling and have a fever. The infected joint may also be warm to the touch. Early definitive treatment is essential. The goal of management is to eliminate the infection, to retain the prosthetic joint and the limb, and to enable the patient to independently participate in activities of daily living. Therapeutic modalities include antibiotic therapy, incision and drainage, surgical removal of the prosthetic joint (57%), and occasionally, amputation of the limb (10%). Death either directly from the infection or from complication during treatment is between 1% to 10%.

Dental management

Prevention of a late prosthetic joint infection is a major responsibility of the dentist. Patients with total-joint arthroplasty should perform effective daily oral hygiene procedures to remove plaque. The risk of bacteremia is far more substantial in a mouth with inflammation than in one that is healthy. Bacteremias can cause hematogenous seeding of prosthetic joints, and it appears that a critical period is up to 2 years following placement. Also, it is likely that bacteremias associated with acute infection in the oral cavity can cause late prosthetic joint infection. Any patient with a prosthetic joint with acute orofacial infection should be treated vigorously to eliminate the source of the infection. Owing to the high morbidity and mortality associated with late prosthetic joint infection, use of prophylactic measures in high-risk patients may be warranted. The most current American Dental Association/American Academy of Orthopedic Surgeons Advisory Statement is recommended as an effective guide for care of patients susceptible to late prosthetic joint infections: (1) identify the susceptible patient, (2) identify dental procedures likely to cause a bacteremia requiring antibiotic prophylaxis, (3) select the appropriate antibiotic regimen, and (4) eliminate all sources of infection. Figure 17–3 provides an explicit algorithm for management of dental patients with total joint prostheses.

The susceptible patient must be identified. Table 17–7 lists conditions at potential increased risk of hematogenous total-joint infection. Antibiotic prophylaxis is not indicated for dental patients with pins, plates, or screws nor is it routinely indicated for most dental patients with total-joint replacements. However, there is some limited evidence that a patient who reports a condition listed in Table 17–7 may be at higher risk for hematogenously disseminated infection. Therefore, a

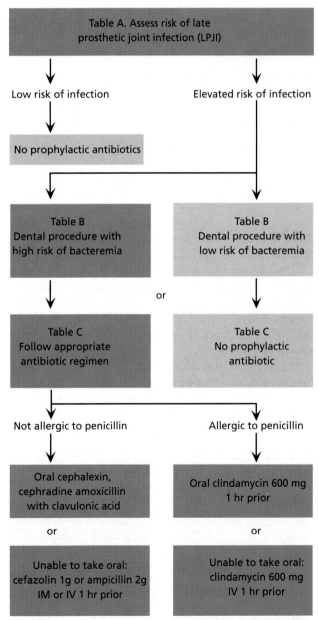

Figure 17–3 Pre-procedural action plan for dental patients with prosthetic joints.

Table 17–8 Incidence Stratification of Bactermic Dental Procedures

Incidence	Dental Procedure
Higher	Dental extractions
	Periodontal procedures: surgery, subgingival placement of antibiotic fibers or strips, scaling and root planing, probing, recall maintenance
	Dental implant placement and reimplantation of avulsed teeth
	Endodontic (root canal) instrumentation or surgery only beyond the apex
	Initial placement of orthodontic bands but not brackets
	Intraligamentary local anesthetic injections
	Prophylactic cleaning of teeth or implants where bleeding is anticipated
Lower	Restorative dentistry (operative and prosthodontic) with or without retraction cord
	Local anesthetic injections (non-intraligamentary)
	Intracanal endodontic treatment (postplacement and buildup)
	Placement of rubber dam
	Postoperative suture removal
	Placement of removable prosthodontic or orthodontic appliances
	Taking of oral impressions
	Fluoride treatments
	Taking of oral radiographs
	Orthodontic appliance adjustment

dental patient should be questioned regarding a history of these conditions prior to invasive dental procedures.

Dental procedures likely to cause a bacteremia that requires antibiotic prophylaxis should be identified. Table 17–8 provides a stratification of incidence of bacteremic dental procedures. Antibiotic prophylaxis for the higher-incidence procedures in higher-risk patients should be considered.

As in bacterial endocarditis the choice of antibiotics for prophylaxis is an empirical regimen, and should be (1) bactericidal, (2) directed at the oral organisms most likely to be associated with late prosthetic joint infection,

Table 17–9 Suggested Antibiotic Prophylaxis Regimens Prior to Dental Procedures for Patients with Total-Joint Replacements

Patient Group	Prophylaxis
Not allergic to penicillin	Cephalexin, cephradine, or amoxicillin 2 g orally 1 hr prior
Allergic to penicillin	Clindamycin 600 mg orally 1 hr prior
Not allergic to penicillin and unable to take oral medicine	Cefazolin 1 g or ampicillin 2 g IM or IV 1 hr prior
Allergic to penicillin and unable to take oral medicine	Clindamycin 600 mg IV 1 hr prior

and (3) administered in doses sufficient for adequate serum concentrations during and after the procedure. Unlike the regimen for bacterial endocarditis, there is a subtle difference of including cephalosporins, to diminish the likelihood of staphylococcus in a bacteremia of oral origin. Based upon the available evidence, the Advisory Statement regimens are listed in Table 17–9.

On occasion a dentist may be faced with recommendations from a patient's physician that are not consistent with the Advisory Statement. This may be owing to a lack of familiarity with the Advisory Statement or because of special circumstances about the patient's medical condition that are not known to the dentist. On those occasions the dentist is encouraged to consult with the physician to determine if there are special circumstances, or the dentist may wish to share a copy of the Advisory Statement with the physician, if appropriate. The dentist is ultimately responsible for making dental treatment recommendations based on professional judgment. The potential benefit of antibiotic prophylaxis must be weighed against known risks of allergy, toxicity, and development of microbial resistance.

Oral mucosal bacterial infections

Syphilis

Syphilis is a complex infectious disease caused by the spirochete *Treponema pallidum*. Transmission is mainly by sexual contact. There are three stages following infection, primary, secondary, and tertiary, all of which may involve oral and paraoral structures, manifested by a variety of signs and symptoms.

This global disease still remains in epidemic proportions in the United States, although the number of reported cases to the Centers for Disease Control and Prevention (CDC) decreases each year. In 2000, there were 113 new cases reported every week of the year; but underreporting is likely.

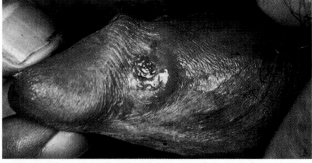

Figure 17–4 Primary syphilis of the penis. Similar appearing chancres may also be seen on the lips and tongue.

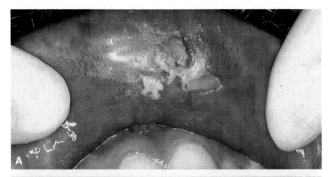

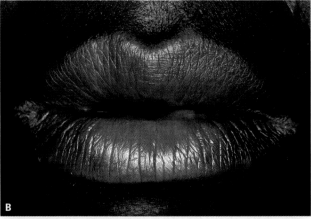

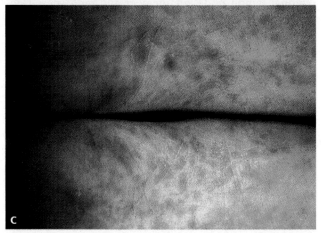

Figure 17–5 Seconday syphilis. *A*, Mucous patches on the lips; *B* split papules in the commissures; *C* maculopapular rash on the soles of the feet.

If not treated in the early stages, there can be varying periods of latency. In the later stages of syphilis, almost every organ system can be involved, leading to considerable morbidity.

Oral features of syphilis are identifiable in four settings.

1. Primary (3–12 wk after contact): a painless ulcer with rolled borders that occurs on the genitalia, yet may occasionally be seen on the tongue or lip (chancre), and possibly, cervical lymphadenopathy (Figure 17–4).

2. Secondary (2–10 wk following the primary stage with widespread spirochetal infection): mucosal ulcers covered by pseudomembranes and associated erythema (mucous patches) and, sometimes, angular cheilitis (Figure 17–5).
3. Tertiary (years later following a latency period): ulceration with a raised, firm border, frequently on the tongue or palate (gumma) (Figure 17–6); tongue depapillation and fissuring (syphilitic glossitis); neural and cardiovascular changes; and nasal bone involvement, causing a "saddle nose" appearance.
4. Congenital syphilis: dental malformations (Mulberry molars and notched, abnormally shaped incisors).

The diagnosis is established by laboratory tests. In the early stages, *T. pallidum* can be smeared or cultured from lesions or infected lymph nodes. Antibodies can be identified by complement fixation tests. Biopsy in the late stages reveals vasculitis and necrosis. The two most common tests are the non-treponemal Venereal Disease Research Laboratory (VDRL) test and rapid plasma reagin (RPR) test (flocculation tests). The VDRL (the most widely used) becomes positive 4 to 6 weeks after infection, and is invariably positive in the secondary stage. The fluorescent treponemal antibody absorption test (FTA-ABS) is slightly more accurate.

Treatment is the use of antibiotics; penicillin remains the drug of choice. When primary syphilis is adequately treated, the secondary and tertiary stages are prevented.

Gonorrhea

Gonorrhea is caused by *Neisseria gonorrhoeae*, a gram-negative diplococcus. It is a common infection worldwide. In the United States in 2000, there were over 6000 new cases reported each week to the CDC. The greatest prevalence is in the 15 to 30 years age group. After contact, the incubation period varies between 2 and 8 days.

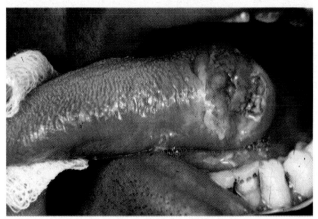

Figure 17–6 Tertiary syphilis. Gumma of the tongue.

Although oral manifestations are rare, there have been infrequent associations with oropharyngeal ulcers, pharyngitis, and temporomandibular joint (TMJ) pathology. However, the main problem is that gonorrheal infection usually reflects unprotected sexual activity, thus increasing the risks for other sexually transmitted diseases (acquired immunodeficiency syndrome [AIDS] virus, hepatitis viruses, herpesviruses, and human papillomaviruses).

The diagnosis is established by smears, staining for gram-negative diplococci in neutrophils, or by using culture techniques. Treatment incorporates the use of antibiotics. Because of the many gonococcal strains resistant to penicillin, one of the fluoroquinolones (eg, ciprofloxacin) or trimethoprim-sulfamethoxazole are effective. Reinfection is common.

Chlamydia

Chlamydia are a large group of obligate intracellular parasites that are closely related to gram-negative bacteria. These common worldwide infectious organisms primarily affect the genitourinary tract, followed by lung and eye involvement. The three species are identified as *C. trachomatis* (genitourinary, lung, eye), *C. pneumoniae* (repiratory), and *C. psittaci* (psittacosis, mainly from bird contact). In the United States, it is the most commonly reported infection, with more than 12,000 new cases identified to the CDC each week.

Regarding the oral cavity, no definitive lesions have been documented, even among clinics for sexually transmitted disease. However, some poorly established reports have emerged possibly linking *Chlamydia* to TMJ dysfunction.

The differential diagnosis is difficult, since the signs and symptoms (pain, suppuration, lymphadenopathy, ulcerations) must be differentiated from neoplasia, and other infections, including gonococcal. The diagnosis is primarily established by culture techniques, but can also include specific immunofluorescence for IgM, complement fixation, enzyme-linked immunoassays, and DNA probes.

Treatment with antibiotics (tetracyclines, doxycycline, erythromycin, and trimethoprim-sulfamethoxazole) is effective.

Cat-scratch disease

Cat-scratch disease is an acute infection of children and young adults. It is caused by *Bartonella henselae* (previously classified as *Rochalimaea* species). It is a relatively uncommon infection and is not contagious between humans; rather, cats harbor the organism under their claws and may then transmit the organism to humans by inducing a scratch that breaks the skin barrier.

The clinical features include a papule or ulcer at the site of injury or scratch within a few days, followed by regional lymph node enlargement and tenderness (Figure 17–7, *A*). Frequently, there is associated fever and malaise. Mucosal ulcers can occur.

The lymph nodes may become suppurative, but special cultures are necessary to identify the organism. The diagnosis is usually deduced by history, clinical features, and ruling out neoplasia and other infections. Cat-scratch disease is self-limiting and rarely requires excision of the involved lymph nodes. When an affected node is subjected to biopsy, it shows necrotizing granulomas characterized by a zone of caseous necrosis

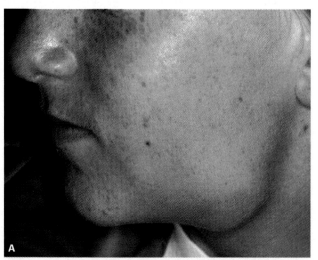
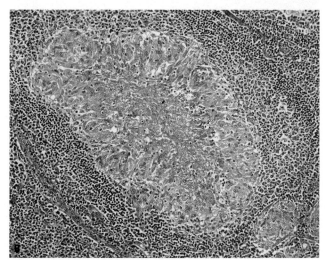

Figure 17–7 Cat-scratch disease. *A*, Lymph node enlargement at the angle of the mandible. *B*, Necrotizing lymphadenitis showing a central focus of necrosis surrounded by palisaded histiocytes.

enveloped by palisading histiocytes (see Figure 17–7, *B*). Therefore, treatment incorporates ruling out other diseases, and supportive care.

Suggested reading

American Dental Association and American Academy of Orthopaedic Surgeons. Advisory statement. Antibiotic prophylaxis for dental patients with total joint replacements. J Am Dent Assoc 1997;128:1004–8.

Beck J, Garcia R, Heiss G, et al. Periodontal disease and cardiovascular disease. J Periodontal 1996; 67(Suppl 10):1123–37.

Ship J, Mohammad A, eds. Clinician's guide to oral health in geriatric patients. New York: The American Academy of Oral Medicine, 1999:45–7.

Tyler M, Lozada-Nur F, eds. Clinician's guide to treatment of medically compromised dental patients. New York: The American Academy of Oral Medicine, 1995:13–16.

Dajani AS, Taubert KA, Wilson W, et al. Prevention of bacterial endocarditis: recommendations by the American Heart Association. J Am Dent Assoc 1997;128:1142–51.

Dussault G, Sheiham A. Medical theories and professional development. The theory of focal sepsis and dentistry in early twentieth century Britain. Soc Sci Med 1982;16:1405–12.

Jacobson JJ, Millard HD, Plezia R, Blankenship JR. Dental treatment and late prosthetic joint infections. Oral Surg Oral Med Oral Pathol 1986;61:413–7.

Jacobson JJ, Patel B, Asher G, et al. Oral staphylococcus in older subjects with rheumatoid arthritis. J Am Geriatr Soc 1997;45:590–3.

Mattila KJ, Valtonen VV, Nieminen MS, Asikainen S. Role of infection as a risk factor for atherosclerosis, myocardial infarction, and stroke. Clin Infect Dis 1998;26:719–34.

Meurman JH. Dental infections and general health. Quintessence Int 1997;28:807–11.

18 Oral Fungal Infections

Joel B. Epstein, DMD, MSD, FRCD(C), Sol Silverman, Jr, MA, DDS, and Jacob Fleischmann, MD

Oropharyngeal candidiasis

Candida is a yeast-like fungus. *Candida* species are common in the normal oral flora and have been reported to be present in from 40% to 60% of the population. *Candida albicans* is the most common species, although other species (eg, *Candida tropicalis*, *Candida glabrata*, *Candida krusei*) are less commonly identified and may cause infection, particularly in immunosuppressed and neutropenic patients. Overgrowth of *Candida*, plus other biologic factors, such as adhesion to epithelial cells, leads to clinical candidiasis (infection) with concomitant signs and symptoms.

Table 18–1 Risk Factors for Development of Oropharyngeal Candidiasis

Local factors
  Xerostomia (hyposalivation attributable to medications, radiotherapy)
  Topical corticosteroids (epithelial cell glycogen → glucose)
  Leukoplakia, epithelial dysplasia, oral cancer
  Dentures (eg, poor fit, trauma, uncleanliness)
  Cigarette use
Systemic factors
  Neonate and advanced age (developing and declining immune systems)
  Systemic and topical antibiotics
  Corticosteroids (liver, muscle glycogen → increase salivary glucose)
  Diabetes, pregnancy (hormonal changes)
  Anemia, nutritional deficiencies (iron, folate, or vitamin B_{12} deficiency)
  Cytotoxic cancer therapies (leukopenia, neutropenia)
  Immunosuppression (AIDS, transplantation)
  Sjögren syndrome

An increasing frequency of oropharyngeal infection by *Candida* species has occurred, owing to the presence of both local and systemic risk factors that increase the possibility of infection (Table 18–1). Also, the mucosa of the dorsum of the tongue (filiform papillae) may represent a site of residual colonization and reservoir of organisms. Topical and systemic steroids increase the risk of candidiasis by facilitating the conversion of glycogen to glucose, thus increasing substrate for candidal growth. Millions of denture wearers are at increased risk of candidiasis, owing to increased adherence of *Candida* species to acrylic, reduced salivary flow under tissue–fitting surfaces, and poor oral hygiene. Denture reline materials may become permeated with *Candida* species, providing an additional site for a reservoir of organisms.

Additionally, changes in salivary flow impact upon antimicrobial proteins and enzymes in the saliva, potentially increasing the risk of colonization and secondary infection. Salivary gland hypofunction may be caused by immune disorders, cancer therapy (radiation and some chemotherapeutic agents), and many systemic medications (eg, antidepressants, antihistaminics, diuretics), all of which may cause a dry mouth (xerostomia) from decreased amounts of saliva (hyposalivation). Oropharyngeal candidiasis is common in patients with leukemia, secondary to therapy, mainly stemming from depressed white cell counts and function, and in patients receiving chemotherapy or marrow transplantation, in whom granulocytopenia occurs (see Chapter 8). Increasing prevalence of oral *Candida* and candidiasis in patients receiving head and neck radiation therapy is expected and creates considerable morbidity. Oral candidiasis is extremely common with human immunodeficiency virus (HIV) and acquired immunodeficiency syndrome (AIDS) infection as immunosuppression progresses (see Chapter 14).

Molecular and pathologic correlates of disease

The pathogenesis of *C. albicans* infection is closely linked to two microbial phenomena: (1) genetic control of the process of mycelial or hyphal transformation from yeast and (2) the ability of the organism to adhere to mucosal keratinocyte membranes.

The molecular analysis of *C. albicans,* the most common species causing candidiasis, has accelerated in the past decade. *Candida albicans* has no known sexual phase, which has significantly delayed analysis of this fungus. Interestingly, homologues of mating loci of *Saccharomyces cerevisiae* have been identified in *C. albicans,* but their role remains unknown. *Candida* is diploid, and as complete sequencing of its genome is nearing completion, it appears that these fungi contain over 3000 genes. Electrophoretic karyotypic analysis indicates that candidal organisms have chromosomes numbered 1 through 7, decreasing in size, and one variable sized fragment designated as chromosome R.

A number of virulence factors have been postulated for this organism. Among these is this yeast's capacity to transform into hyphae and pseudohyphae. A number of genes, with apparent divergent functions have been found to play a role in this process. Data suggest that this organism uses more than one signaling pathway for hyphal transformation. *CPH*1, is a transcription factor involved in the mitogen-activated protein (MAP) kinase cascade. When both alleles are inactivated, hyphal transformation is suppressed on solid media, but remains intact when stimulated by serum. When one allele of the *EFG*1 gene is inactivated, true hypha formation is suppressed, but pseudohypha form in serum. Overexpression of this gene stimulates pseudohypha. A double mutant, involving both alleles of *CPH*1 and *EFG*1, abrogates germination even in serum, and when injected into mice this mutant is avirulent, suggesting that hyphal transformation is a virulence factor. However, this remains debatable as *C. glabrata,* a yeast that has never germinated, causes infections similar to those cause by *C. albicans* and with increasing frequency. Disruption of *RBF*1, coding for a DNA binding protein and *TUP*1, a transcriptional repressor, results in organisms growing in filamentous form only.

These data would imply that the default state of the organism is filamentous and that genes need to be activated to transform to yeast. In *C. albicans,* disruption of *INT*1 results in suppression of hyphal growth and in the capacity to adhere to epithelial cells, indicating a dual role for this gene.

The capacity to adhere to tissue is clearly a virulence factor. A number of adhesion molecules have been identified and their genes have been cloned. One of the most interesting among these is a hyphae-specific, proline-rich protein that is coded for by the *HWP*1 gene. It appears to be a target for mammalian transglutaminases in human buccal epithelial cells, leading to a covalent bond between cells and the fungus. When the gene is disrupted, stable adherence to buccal epithelial cells is lost, and its capacity to cause systemic candidiasis in a murine model is diminished.

A number of other properties of this organism are thought to be virulence factors. Several secreted enzymes, such as proteases and phospholipases, have been identified, and their genes cloned. Studies employing disruption of some of these genes or their insertion into surrogate nonpathogens, such as *S. cerevisiae,* clearly indicate a pathogenic role for them. *Candida albicans* is capable of switching between phenotypic states, but the significance of such switching in disease is unknown. Candidal hyphae are capable of moving along cell surfaces, which has been referred to as thigmotropism. The molecular basis for this behavior is unknown, and any role in pathogenesis remains unproven.

Clinical features

The presentation of *Candida* may include symptoms of burning, sensitivity, altered taste, and altered smell. If it involves the pharynx or esophagus, dysphagia may be present. Regarding signs, patients may be aware of cracking and sensitivity at the corners of the mouth (angular cheilitis). Clinical intraoral signs may vary from a red form (erythematous) to a pseudomembranous form (white, thrush), with or without angular cheilitis (Figures 18–1 to 18–4; Table 18–2). Simultaneous red and white changes are common. Infrequently, a hyperplastic form occurs that can be mistaken for leukoplakia. In this form, white keratin patches that cannot be scraped off appear on oral mucosal surfaces, because of a proliferative keratin-formation response of epithelial cells to the presence of *Candida.* Although rare, oral candidal infections may be associated with involvement of other sites, such as skin and nails (mucocutaneous) and may be genetic rather than acquired. This has been associated with an absence of myeloperoxidase. The erythematous form may present with involvement of the dorsal surface of the tongue, leading to a partial blunting or absence of the filiform papillae, which resembles median rhomboid glossitis (see Chapter 25).

Oral candidal overgrowth is almost always superficial, and rarely penetrates deeper than surface epithelial cells. Characteristic of the pseudomembranous form, the colonies of organisms that attach to the surface can be removed with rubbing, frequently leaving red or bleeding sites. The least common presentation, an ulcerative form that may be seen in severely immune and hematologically compromised patients, is rare. In this form, invasion by *Candida* species occurs deep into the stratified squamous epithelium, leading to ulceration. Candidemia from any form of oral and oropharyngeal candidiasis is extremely rare. In the past, oral presentations were described as acute or chronic forms. However, this terminology

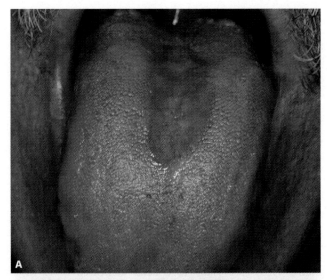

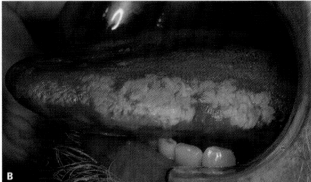

Figure 18–2 Candidiasis. *A*, Painful, depapillation of the tongue dorsum. A fungal culture was positive The area repopulated with filiform papillae following antifungal medication and became asymptomatic. *B*, Painful hyperplastic *Candida* of the lateral tongue mistaken for leukoplakia. It completely disappeared following antifungal medication.

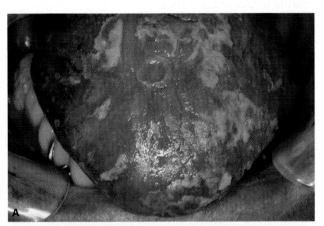

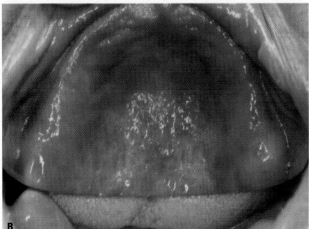

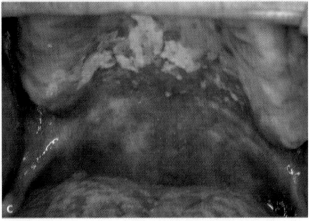

Figure 18–1 Forms of candidiasis: *A*, pseudomembranous form; *B*, erythematous form; *C*, pseudomembranous-erythematous form.

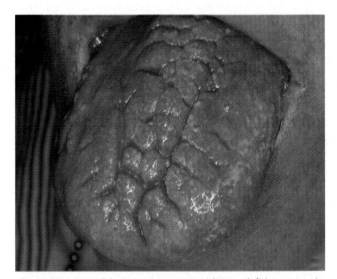

Figure 18–3 Candidiasis in a teenager with iron deficiency anemia. Note the angular cheilitis and yeast involvement of the tongue. Topical antifungal medication and iron supplements controlled the candidiasis.

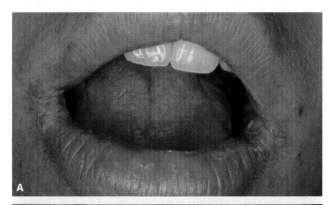
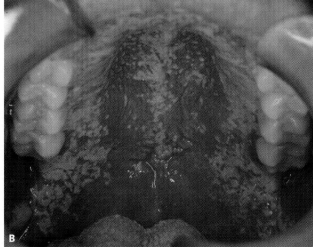

Figure 18–4 Genetic mucocutaneous candidiasis in a 15-year-old girl who, although otherwise healthy, had a myeloperoxidase deficiency: *A*, candidal-induced angular cheilitis; *B*, pseudomembranous candidiasis. This was controlled by the chronic use of combinations of systemic and topical antifungal medications.

Table 18–2 Forms of Oropharyngeal Candidiasis

Pseudomembranous (thrush)
Erythematous; denture stomatitis (atrophic)
Angular cheilitis
Hyperplastic candidiasis (leukoplakic-type hyperkeratosis)
Mucocutaneous (genetic, missing myeloperoxidase)
Ulcerative (erosions associated with white or red changes)

can be performed by candidal counts and speciation. Quantitation is done by plating *Candida* brom cresol green (BCG) agar, incubating, and counting colony-forming units. Qualitation is accomplished by using germ tube growth (for albicans) and carbohydrate assimilations (for other species). Biopsy specimens can be stained with the periodic acid-Schiff (PAS) stain, which effectively reveals pseudomycelia and hyphae when present.

Angular cheilitis, with or without oral signs and symptoms, should always raise the possibility or probability of candidiasis. In establishing the diagnosis, etiologic factors must be taken into consideration (see Table 18–1). Additionally, bacterial and viral infections (see Chapters 13 and 17) as well as immunopathologic diseases (see Chapter 21) must also be considered, particularly if there is no response to antifungal treatment. Epithelial dysplasia often manifests as white, red, and white-red lesions (see Chapter 20) and must be ruled out.

Treatment

Therapeutic approaches can use either topical or systemic antifungal medications (Table 18–3). The choice depends upon the probability of compliance, degree of oral pain, ability to use a topical agent, and patient preference (Figures 18–6 to 18–9).

Topical antifungals are available in rinses, suspensions, creams, tablets, and lozenges. The form of the medication chosen should reflect the conditions in the oral cavity. Factors such as taste, texture, and sucrose sweetening of the medication should be considered in selecting the drug to be used. In patients with dry mouth, tablets given to dissolve in the mouth may be poorly soluble and may become irritating during dissolution. Therefore, oral rinses may be a better choice in these patients. Topical creams may be easily applied on the tissue contacting surfaces of dentures, and to the corners of the mouth.

Systemic medications may provide convenience of therapy, although cost and medical and toxic considerations related to systemic use are factors. The duration of use of such medications should be considered as well as the underlying risk factors that caused the candidiasis. Therefore, prophylaxis versus intermittent therapy must be determined. Also, prophylaxis of high-risk

should be avoided, because any of these forms may present in a persisting and chronic fashion with periodic flares, particularly in the medically compromised patient. Angular cheilitis associated with *Candida* species is sometimes co-infected with a staphylococcus, which may have implications in clinical management.

Diagnosis

The diagnosis of *Candida* overgrowth (candidiasis, candidosis) is often made on the basis of clinical suspicion of the somewhat typical white, red, and white-red mucosal changes. Associated angular cheilitis substantially enhances the probability of candidiasis. These findings are almost always associated with some degree of discomfort or pain.

The diagnosis can be confirmed by scrapings that are processed by potassium hydroxide or Gram-stained before microscopic examination or by cultures (Figure 18–5). With the cultures, quantitation and qualitation

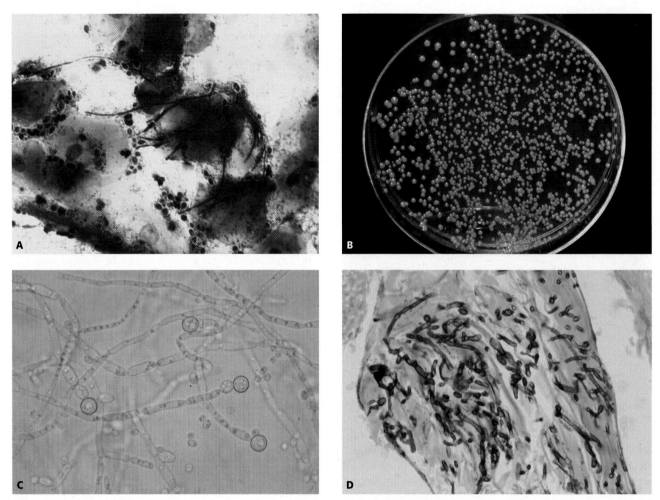

Figure 18–5   *Candida* diagnosis. *A*, Gram stain of a surface scraping from a patient with pseudomembranous candidiasis showing yeast spores and mycelia among epithelial cells. *B*, Corn meal agar culture from a patient with suspected candidiasis, demonstrating overwhelming growth of yeast (speciation showed *C. albicans*). *C*, Photomicrograph of *C. albicans* smeared from the culture in Figure 5, *B*, revealing the yeast morphology of mycelia and spores. *D*, PAS-stained buccal biopsy from a patient with candidiasis, demonstrating candidal hyphae and pseudomycelia in surface stratified squamous epithelium.

Table 18–3   Antifungal Drugs

Generic Drug	Brand Name	Dosage	Considerations
Systemic			
Ketoconazole	Nizoral (tablets)	200–400 mg/d	Metabolized in liver; taken with food for optimal absorption
Fluconazole	Diflucan (tablets)	100–200 mg/d	Metabolized in kidney; food elective; resistance can occur
Topical (dissolve, swish, swallow)			
Clotrimazole	Mycelex		
	10-mg oral troches	5/d	
	100–200-mg vaginal troches	1–2/d	
Amphotericin B	Fungizone solution	1 mL qid (400 mg)	
Nystatin	Mycostatin		
	500,000-U/tsp suspension	3 times/d	
	100,000-U vaginal troches	3–5 times/d	
Itraconazole	Sporanox solution	10 mL bid (400 mg)	

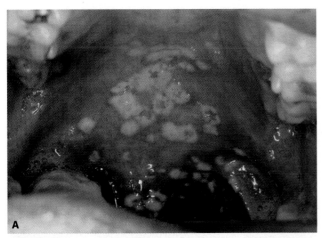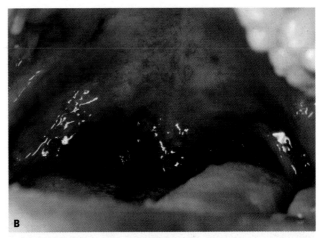

Figure 18–6 *A*, Acutely painful pseudomembranous candidiasis of the palate. *B*, Signs and symptoms were controlled after 200 mg ketoconazole daily for 3 days.

patients, such as those being treated for leukemia and with bone marrow transplantation, must be considered (see Chapter 8). Systemic prophylaxis for fungal infections is the standard of care in most oncology centers when immunosuppression (leukopenia) is anticipated.

Topical therapies

Nystatin can be used as initial treatment for patients with oropharyngeal candidiasis. The suspension (500,000 U/5 mL) is highly sucrose-sweetened and should be used for short periods of time only, with particular caution in patients who are dentate and who are xerostomic. Swallowing is not mandatory, since nystatin is not absorbed in the gut. Nystatin may induce nausea, which may result in limited compliance in patients undergoing systemic chemotherapy and who may already be at risk of nausea. Nystatin in the form of a vaginal troche (100,000 units dissolved orally up to 5 times daily) is appropriate and often is effective in controlling the candidal overgrowth. Nystatin powder

(100 mg/g in spray containers) is useful for applying to the tissue-bearing surfaces of dentures. A cream form also may be applied to denture surfaces and the corners of the mouth. Nystatin pastilles (200,000 U) may provide increased contact time when dissolved in the mouth, but clinically have not proved effective.

Amphotericin B is available as a topical suspension (100 mg/mL). This swish-and-swallow form (1 mL up to 4 times daily) provides an additional topical alternative agent. Patient compliance, dosage, and efficacy have not been fully determined. Nystatin and amphotericin B are polyene antimicrobials, and have shown to be rarely associated with the development of resistance.

Azole antifungals are fungistatic and are available as topical therapy. Clotrimazole oral and vaginal troches are available. The oral troche (Mycelex) is sweetened with sugar for taste. They are dispensed in 10-mg strength to be dissolved orally up to 5 times daily. The vaginal troches when dissolved in the mouth (100 mg, 1 or 2/d) are useful because of the higher dosage and less frequent

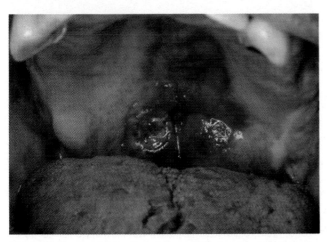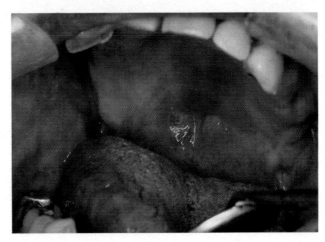

Figure 18–7 *A* and *B*, Erythematous candidiasis controlled after a 1-week course of fluconazole (100 mg/d).

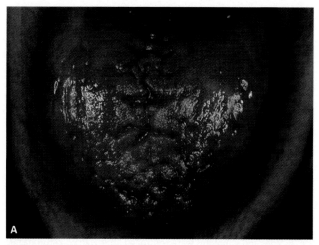

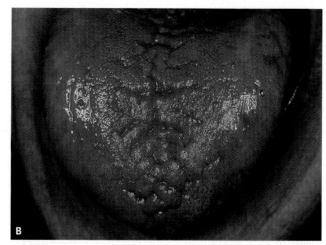

Figure 18–8 *A*, Painful candidiasis of the tongue present for 3 weeks in a patient with polycythemia vera. *B*, Clotrimazole (100 mg troches) dissolved orally twice daily for 1 week controlled the signs and symptoms.

usage. Both forms provide prolonged contact with the yeast and have proved to be efficacious. Itraconazole has limited usefulness in the control of oral candidiasis.

Miconazole cream represents a useful topical therapy for angular cheilitis or the tissue-bearing surfaces of dentures. This is based upon its antifungal effect as well as the effect on staphylococcus that may be present. The need for frequent and prolonged contact between topical antifungal agents and oral microorganisms is always a challenge for patient compliance.

Antiseptic mouthrinses may be helpful in the initial treatment of candidiasis, or as a prophylactic measure to help control recurrent infections. Chlorhexidine (Peridex, Periogard) has an antifungal spectrum and may suppress colonization. Nystatin is incompatible with the use of chlorhexidine, and the products should not be used concurrently. Also, Listerine mouthrinse, comprised of essen-

tial oils, possesses antifungal properties along with antibacterial activity that may be helpful.

Systemic therapies

Amphotericin B is an important and effective broad-spectrum, systemic antifungal. The agent is, however, associated with risk of kidney toxicity. This medication is primarily used intravenously. However, it is also provided as a swish-and-swallow solution (see Table 18–3).

The azoles, which include ketoconazole and fluconazole (see Table 18–3), have been widely used for systemic control of oral fungal infections. Ketoconazole (200–400 mg once daily) is an effective anticandidal agent. It must be taken with food, since it is absorbed in an acid (low pH) environment. It is metabolized in the liver, so its use is limited in patients with hepatitis. Also, its absorption is diminished in the presence of antacids.

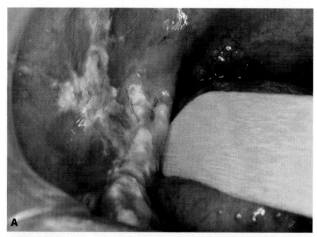

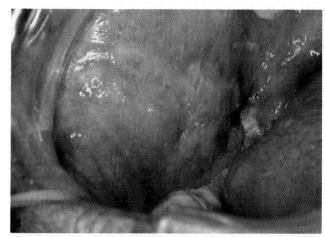

Figure 18–9 Hyperplastic candidiasis, that was mistaken for leukoplakia, was completely reversed with 400 mg ketoconazole daily for 1 week in a patient with xerostomia caused by head and neck radiation therapy. Because of constant recurrences, the patient was maintained and controlled using nystatin troches (100,000 U) dissolved orally up to 3 times a day. *A*, Before treatment; *B*, after 3 days of treatment.

Fluconazole is the most readily tolerated of the azoles, but carries a risk of inducing fungal resistance. The infrequent dosing may facilitate compliance. It is also useful in prophylaxis and in individuals who require treatment over extended periods of time, for example, medically compromised patients. Fluconazole in therapeutic dosing (200 mg stat and 100 mg daily thereafter) has been an effective oral antifungal medication. It is metabolized in the kidney, and can be taken with or without food.

The question of resistance is often raised. Many times a lack of response is a reflection of inadequate dosage rather than a drug-resistant yeast, but because of the possibility of developing resistant organisms, extended periods of treatment are usually discouraged, to diminish this transformation risk. With patients at risk for frequent recurrences, combinations of systemic and topical therapies can be effectively prescribed. It must also be remembered in treatment that salivary hypofunction and xerostomia promote yeast overgrowth. Therefore, adequate amounts of saliva are fundamental to effective control. Sugarless gums or candies are helpful; if necessary, systemic salivary gland stimulation may be required as follows: pilocarpine (Salagen 5-mg tablets, 1 or 2 tablets tid); bethanechol (Urecholine 25 mg, 1 or 2 tablets 3 or 4 times daily); or cevimeline (Evoxac 30-mg capsules tid).

Invasive fungi

Whereas *Candida* species are superficial fungal pathogens, they can invade tissues when patients are immunocompromised, such as seen in patients with genetic T-cell deficiencies, leukemia and malignant lymphoma, and other severe immunodeficiency diseases. There are other fungi that are tissue-invasive, even among immunocompetent persons, although immunodeficient patients harbor a heightened susceptibility to these mycoses. The infections that are most often encountered in the oral cavity, and maxillary antrum are histoplasmosis, blastomycosis, cryptococcosis, and phycomycosis (mucormycosis). Only the latter is typically found in tissue in its mycelial form, the others invade tissues as budding yeast forms. Bipolaris fungi are not truly invasive; however, they cause accentuated host immune responsiveness that leads to antral destructive lesions.

Histoplasmosis

Granulomatous inflammation is caused by *Histoplasma capsulatum*, and the lesions may become disseminated throughout the body. Histoplasmosis is a chronic pulmonary infection, similar to tuberculosis, in which granulomas form in the lungs. It is endemic to the Ohio and Mississippi river valleys. The organisms are phagocytized

by histiocytes and are readily visualized by periodic acid-Schiff staining in tissue sections. As the fungus propagates, more and more granulation tissue evolves, thereby compromising the airway and leading to chronic cough. In advanced stages, organisms enter vessels and become disseminated to various tissues and organs. This "metastatic" spread can seed organisms into the oral mucosal tissues in a manner similar to that seen in miliary tuberculosis. Immunocompromised patients can contract

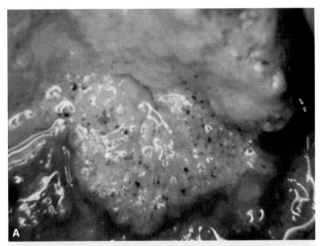

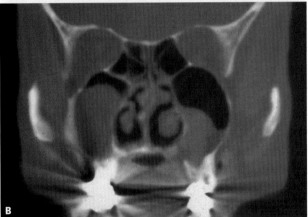

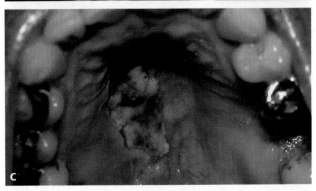

Figure 18–10 Invasive fungal disease. *A*, Diffuse pebbly granuloma of oral mucosa in blastomycosis; *B*, antral and nasal lesions with palatal perforation appear as soft-tissue opacifications on CT in an HIV-infected patient with histoplasmosis; *C*, palatal view.

histoplasmosis directly, bypassing the pulmonary locus. Particularly in HIV-infected subjects (see Chapter 14), oral granulomas may develop or infection may involve the sinonasal tissues and perforate into the oral mucosa. The oral lesions of histoplasmosis are similar in clinical appearance to those of blastomycosis and cryptococcosis. The mucosa is raised, pebbly, erythematous, and may show foci of ulceration (Figure 18–10). Intravenously administered antifungals, such as griseofulvin and amphotericin B are the favored therapeutic agents.

Mucormycosis

Phycomycetes are large fungi with nonseptate branching hyphae. The disease mucormycosis commonly affects the maxillary sinus and is rarely seen among healthy patients. The organism gains entry to tissue among immunocompromised patients and patients with brittle diabetes mellitus. Mucor has a propensity for vascular invasion, a pathologic event that eventuates in thrombosis, vascular occlusion, and widespread necrosis. In the maxillary antrum, the sinus fills with microbial colonies and necrotic tissue, with rapidly evolving destruction of the osseous antral walls (Figure 18–11). Large foci of necrosis can evolve in the palate with osseous destructive oral–antral communication and bony sequestration. Teeth loosen and spontaneously exfoliate. Treatment consists of systemic antifungals and surgical débridement of the infected and necrotic tissues.

Allergic fungal sinusitis

Certain soil fungi may become aspirated into the airway and become deposited in the mucous membranes of the

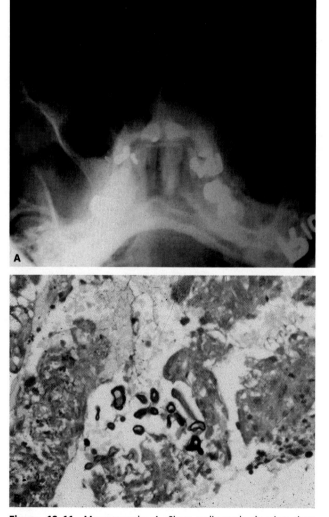

Figure 18–11 Mucormycosis. *A*, Sinus radiograph showing sinus clouding and osseous destruction; *B*, periodic acid-Schiff staining reveals the large hyphae in an area of necrotic tissue from the sinus.

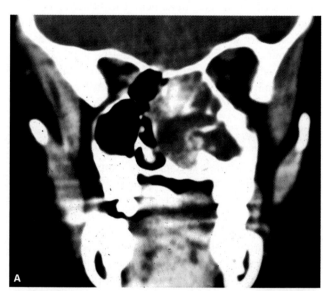

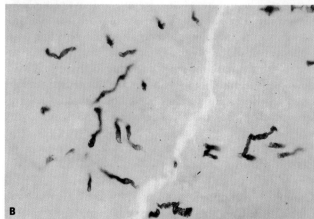

Figure 18–12 Allergic fungal sinusitis. *A*, Computed tomogram showing deformation of sinus walls with antral opacification and osseous remodeling. *B*, *Bipolaris* fungi engender an intense allergic response in the sinus with compacted eosinophils and Charcot-Leyden crystals.

nose and maxillary sinus. These organisms, collectively known as *Bipolaris* fungi, are not pathogenic; however, they stimulate a robust immune response with massive infiltration of eosinophils. The sinus becomes impacted with exudates and fungal organisms, leading to nasal speech and congestion. Progressive allergic reaction can lead to maxillary enlargement and osseous resorption with remodeling of the antral walls. Most affected individuals are young adults. The sinuses show osteolytic changes and clouding on sinus radiographs and CT scans (Figure 18–12). At surgery, they are filled with a smudgy brown material that resembles peanut butter. Diagnosis is made by biopsy of the sinus contents with identification of laminated aggregates of esosinophils, Charcot-Leyden crystals, and large pleomorphic fungal hyphae. Treatment is débridement and systemic prednisone.

Suggested reading

Cannon RD, Holmes AR, Mason AB, Monk BC. Oral *Candida*: Clearance, colonization, or candidiasis? J Dent Res 1995;74:1152–61.

Epstein JB, Ransier A, Lunn R, et al. Prophylaxis of candidiasis in patients with leukemia and bone marrow transplants. Oral Surg Oral Med Oral Pathol Oral Radiol Endod 1996;81:291–6.

Hull CM, Johnson AD. Identification of a mating type-like locus in the asexual pathogenic yeast *Candida albicans*. Science 1999;285:1271–5.

Navazesh M, Wood GJ, Brightman V. Relationship between salivary flow rates and *Candida albicans* counts. Oral Surg Oral Med Oral Pathol Oral Radiol Endod 1995;80:284–8.

Ramirez-Amador V, Silverman S Jr, Mayer P, et al. Candidal colonization and oral candidiasis in patients undergoing oral and pharyngeal radiation therapy. Oral Surg Oral Med Oral Pathol Oral Radiol Endod 1997;84:149–53.

Silverman S Jr, Gallo JW, McKnight ML, et al. Clinical characterisics and management responses in 85 HIV-infected patients with oral candidiasis. Oral Surg Oral Med Oral Pathol Oral Radiol Endod 1996;82:402–7.

19 Infection Control

Eve Cuny, MS, and William M. Carpenter, DDS, MS

The Centers for Disease Control and Prevention (CDC) is a division of the United States Public Health Service and is the primary source of infection control recommendations. Over the years, a number of recommendations for the prevention of disease transmission have been issued by the CDC, with updates and revisions as knowledge and science advance. Several common terms for various protective measures for the dental health care worker (DHCW) are used in health care today.

Precautions

Universal precautions

First introduced in 1985, universal precautions instruct DHCW to follow the same infection-control precautions for all patients regardless of infectious status. Many individuals may be infected with the human immunodeficiency virus (HIV), hepatitis B virus (HBV), or other blood-borne disease and are not identified through the medical history. Certain precautions are known to prevent the transmission of these viruses and should be applied during the care of all patients. These precautions should protect both the health care worker and the patient from disease transmission. More recent guidelines address infections that are not necessarily blood-borne.

Standard precautions

In 1996, a new set of precautions, called standard precautions was introduced to the medical community. These precautions are a synthesis of the major features of universal precautions and body substance isolation precautions. They apply to blood; other bodily fluids, secretions, and excretions except sweat (BBF), regardless of whether they contain visible blood; nonintact skin; and mucous membranes. Therefore, standard precautions apply to blood and all moist body substances. These guidelines are "first tier" in the prevention of nosocomial infections in hospitals and other medical patient-care settings. Although these guidelines have replaced universal precautions in hospital settings, they do not apply to most dental offices and clinics. Isolation precautions had been developed to address the need to tailor infection control precautions to the various epidemiologic features of individual diseases. These precautions were updated and improved over time, as more became known about disease transmission and hospital personnel became more sophisticated in their knowledge of precautions for specific diseases.

Transmission-based precautions

Transmission-based precautions are designed for patients documented or suspected to be infected or colonized with highly transmissible or epidemiologically important pathogens. These are used when standard precautions may not be adequate to interrupt transmission in hospitals. As with standard precautions, these were developed for the treatment of patients in a hospital setting and are not applicable to dentistry.

Several aspects of disease transmission are addressed (Figure 19–1).

Medical history

Certainly, the medical history is a necessary part of comprehensive dental care. However, prior to the CDC recommendations of various precautions to be followed, the importance of detecting patients with infectious diseases was considered paramount. This was especially crucial in patients with the highly transmissible HBV. Once dentistry followed strict infection control guidelines and adopted the concept of universal precautions, as regulated by the Occupational Safety and Health Administration (OSHA), this goal carried far less importance in disease transmission. Since all patients are now regarded as potentially infectious, the approach has been simplified.

The two major exceptions to universal precautions in dentistry are the patient with untreated, active tuberculosis (TB) and the immunocompromised patient. The patient with active TB should not be treated for elective procedures, and emergency procedures should be undertaken following special precautions (ie, laminar air flow, ultraviolet light, and HEPA filter masks). Immunocompromised patients may require special treatment to protect them from infection, such as the use of sterile irrigation and prophylactic antibiotics. For protection of the DHCW, vaccinations should be considered for other highly transmissible infectious diseases.

Vaccination

Vaccination (immunization) is an important tool in preventing the transmission of diseases. Since health care workers are often at an increased risk for acquiring diseases because of occupational exposure, maintaining immunity to vaccine-preventable diseases is an important part of any infection control program.

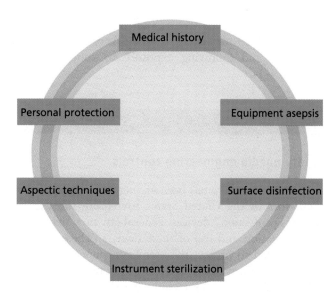

Figure 19–1 Elements of infection control.

Public Health Service guidelines regarding the need for health care worker immunizations should be considered, in addition to recommendations by the individual's primary care physician. Health care workers in specific geographic locations or with underlying medical conditions may need additional immunizations that are not routinely recommended for health care workers. Immunizing agents strongly recommended for health care workers in the United States include hepatitis B, influenza, measles, mumps, rubella, and varicella vaccines. If the health care worker is already naturally immune to these infections, immunization is not necessary. All adults should be protected against diphtheria and tetanus (usually administered in childhood as the diphtheria, pertussis, and tetanus (DPT) vaccine). Pneumococcal vaccine is recommended for all adults, age 65 years of age and older.

Table 19–1 Work Restrictions for Infected Health Care Workers, as Recommended by the Public Health Service

Infection	Restriction
Diphtheria	Exclude from duty
Mumps	Exclude from duty during active and postexposure period
Hepatitis A virus	Restrict patient contact, food handling
Hepatitis B virus	Seek counsel of expert review panel until HBeAg-negative
Upper respiratory infection	Avoid contact with high-risk patients
Measles	Exclude from duty during active and postexposure period
Herpes zoster (shingles)	Cover lesions

Work restrictions are recommended by the Public Health Service for health care workers with certain infections and following exposure to some diseases (Table 19–1).

Personal protection

Safety needle engineering controls

In recent years there has been an increased emphasis by regulators in the United States to require the use of "sharps protection" devices. Federal law now mandates the evaluation and use of these devices. These devices are intended to protect the user from puncture with a sharp instrument or device that is contaminated with patient BBF. Examples include self-sheathing needles, needleless intravenous systems, disposable scalpels that do not require removal of the blade from the handle, and plastic materials in place of glass, in situations where contaminated glass is at risk of breakage.

Work practice controls

Work practice controls alter the manner in which a person performs a given task, reducing the risk of contact with a patient's BBF. Examples of work practice controls include one-handed needle recapping and safe instrument transfer techniques.

Eye protection

In the course of many dental procedures, body fluids of the patient may be present in the splash or spray from dental devices. Additionally, blood or saliva may be present in particles generated and released during the procedure. The DHCW performing, assisting, or closely observing procedures where it is reasonable to suspect that droplet, aerosol, or particles may be produced, must wear protective eyewear. Eyewear should provide a lens large enough to protect the eye and should have solid side shields to prevent foreign objects from entering the eye through the side of the glasses. A face shield that meets these criteria is also acceptable, as is a shield attached to a surgical or procedure mask. Eye protection that is reusable should be washed with soap and water or surface disinfected between patients, to avoid cross-contamination during handling.

Masks

Masks should be worn under the same conditions as those that require eye protection. A variety of types are available for use. Surgical and procedure masks are adequate during most dental procedures to protect the nose, mouth, and airway from contact with body fluids generated during dental procedures.

An important aspect of mask use is that the DHCW wear the mask in the manner intended. Masks should be placed in a manner that allows the mask to contact the wearer's face around the periphery of the mask. If possible, direct contact of the mask with the wearer's nose and mouth should be avoided, to reduce the moisture absorbed by the mask.

A new mask should be used for each patient. Additionally, a mask should be replaced during long procedures, especially when the mask becomes moistened. Moisture affects the barrier properties of the mask and may allow contamination to reach the DHCW.

Special masks are required when lasers are used. Personnel conducting or assisting in laser procedures should wear masks that are labeled and approved for use with lasers.

Protective clothing

Attire that prevents the contact of BBF with work clothes, street clothes, skin, and undergarments must be worn, when it is reasonable to anticipate contact. For most dental procedures, a gown or lab coat with long sleeves and collar sufficient to cover exposed clothing and skin will suffice. Surgical procedures may require the use of attire made from material with fluid resistant properties. The dentist-employer should determine if BBF is penetrating the protective attire and make any changes necessary to ensure adequate protection is provided.

Protective attire should be changed daily, or between patients if it has become visibly soiled. OSHA requires that the employer arrange for the laundering of protective attire. This may be done either in the office, if there is space available for a washing machine and dryer, or at a commercial laundry.

Disposable gowns are also acceptable, as long as they meet the criteria for barrier protection. If disposable gowns are used, they should be discarded at the end of each day or between patients if necessary. Disposable gowns may be disposed with the regular trash, unless they meet the guidelines for medical waste disposal. These guidelines vary from state to state, so the local agency should be consulted regarding specific rules.

Gloves

Medical examination gloves are considered adequate for most dental procedures. The gloves should be selected on the basis of quality, comfort, and fit. A plethora of glove brands exists on the dental market today, and selection can be a difficult process, particularly if any DHCW or patient in the practice is latex-sensitive. Examination gloves are nonsterile, single-use, and usually manufactured using latex, although there is an increasing number of brands using alternative materials. Sterile gloves should be worn when undertaking surgical procedures.

Hand washing

Hands should be thoroughly washed with soap and water, before placing and after removing gloves to reduce the number of transient organisms. Rings should be removed from workers' fingers and fingernails kept short to allow thorough cleaning of all areas of the hands. Antimicrobial handwashing agents should be used when undertaking surgical procedures.

Hand care and latex allergy

The greatly increased use of gloves for infection control has come with attendant negative aspects. The incidence of latex hypersensitivity and nonspecific dermatitis directly linked to use of latex products in health care has increased significantly in recent years. Numerous articles in the scientific literature explore the issue of latex allergy. Irritant dermatitis and delayed or immediate hypersensitivity can result from contact with latex gloves.

Steps can be taken to minimize the occurrence of problems related to glove use. Failing to wear gloves or not hand washing are not reasonable options. Being aware of potential irritants and protecting the hands from unnecessary exposure should be of concern to every health care worker, whether or not they have ever experienced a skin problem. Chemicals that are used in the manufacturing process for latex gloves that may cause delayed hypersensitivity include accelerators and antioxidants. Avoiding powdered gloves is also useful in minimizing the transfer of latex chemicals into the environment and minimizing irritation. A true allergy to latex is relatively uncommon. A physician should be consulted to evaluate any case of hand irritation so that an accurate diagnosis and proper treatment can be rendered.

Exposure incidents

In spite of the use of protective attire, the risk of accidental exposure to BBF continues to exist in the dental setting. Punctures and scrapes with contaminated instruments and splashes to DHCW mucous membranes with BBF may carry the risk of infectious disease transmission. OSHA requires employers of health care workers to have a plan in place to respond to exposure incidents. At a minimum, the employee should be provided with immediate first aid, followed by referral to a qualified health care provider for exposure follow-up. The source patient must be asked to submit to testing for hepatitis B, HIV, and hepatitis C. The CDC provides complete guidelines for postexposure management. The guidelines are updated regularly as more information is available regarding the treatment and prevention of disease transmission from patient to health care worker.

Equipment sterilization

Sterilization of instruments between uses is a fundamental aspect of good infection control practices. Numerous guidelines exist that aid the DHCW in determining the appropriate method for a given type or classification of instrument.

Instrument classification

Dental instruments are classified according to their intended use. These classifications assist the practitioner in determining the appropriate method of reprocessing instruments between uses. Sterilization methods that can be verified through the use of biologic indicators are preferable to chemical methods, that cannot be verified. Verifiable methods include steam autoclave, chemical vapor (Chemiclave®, Getinge/Castle Inc., Rochester, NY), dry heat, and ethylene oxide (ETO).

Critical instruments are those instruments intended to penetrate soft tissue or bone. These instruments should be sterilized between use or must be disposable.
Semicritical instruments are not intended to penetrate tissue, but do contact oral tissues. These instruments also require sterilization between uses. If heat sterilization is not feasible, immersion in a high-level sterilant/disinfectant is accepted.
Noncritical instruments contact only intact skin. These items may be processed using an appropriate intermediate or low-level disinfection.

Sterilization procedures

Instruments should be thoroughly cleaned as a first step in reprocessing. Throughout the cleaning process and until instruments have been sterilized, personnel should wear heavy-duty gloves to provide additional protection against puncture injury. Mechanical means of cleaning, such as an ultrasonic or washer-disinfector are preferable to hand scrubbing. Instruments should be inspected following mechanical cleaning for residual debris, which can then be removed by hand.

Once instruments are free of debris, they should be placed in pouches or wraps that are intended for the type of sterilization process in use. It is important to note that most heat sterilizers are programmed to provide a sterilization cycle that will accomplish sterilization if items are under single layers of wrap. Placing multiple packs together or inside one another must be avoided. If multiple layers of wrap are used, such as for surgical trays, sterilizer cycle times must be adjusted accordingly. Refer to the manufacturer's handbook for specific directions.

Heat sterilization methods

There are three types of heat sterilizers commonly used in dental offices in the United States. They are steam under pressure (autoclave), dry heat, and chemical vapor (Chemiclave®). The characteristics and many of the advantages and disadvantages of the three types are outlined in Table 19–2.

Chemical sterilization and disinfection

There are three levels of disinfectants available for use. Intermediate and low-level disinfectants are registered by the Environmental Protection Agency (EPA). The Food and Drug Administration (FDA) registers high-level disinfectants. Only products that have been appropriately registered should be used in the dental office.

Low level. Low-level disinfectants are not capable of killing the tubercle bacillus (TB) but are registered by the EPA as hospital-level disinfectants. These germicides are not considered effective against TB, a highly resistant organism selected to identify the bactericidal activity of disinfectants. Low-level disinfectants are most commonly used for housekeeping purposes in health care settings. Many quaternary ammonium compounds fit into this category.

Intermediate level. Intermediate disinfectants are registered by the EPA as hospital-level and are effective against most organisms, including TB, when used according to the manufacturer's instructions. These chemical germicides should be used for the management of environmental surfaces in the dental operatory after each patient. These products are not intended for the management of contaminated critical and semicritical instruments. Examples of product classifications that fit this category include combination synthetic phenolics, chlorine compounds, iodophor, sodium bromide, chlorine, and some alcohol-phenolic combination products.

High level. High-level disinfectants are capable of killing all microorganisms, including spores, when specific conditions are met. These germicides are intended for use on instruments and devices and should be used for immersion only.

Glutaraldehyde is a high-level disinfectant used to disinfect and sterilize dental instruments. When used undiluted to immerse instruments for 6 to 10 hours, glutaraldehyde may be used for the sterilization of heat sensitive items. This method should be used only when heat sterilization of critical and semicritical items is not possible because of the nature of the instrument or device. Glutaraldehyde is an intermediate-level disinfectant when used either in dilute solution or undiluted for immersion of instruments for approximately 20 minutes. Glutaraldehyde is a volatile solution and may be irritating or sensitizing to tissues. Solutions should be kept covered when not in use, and workers should wear gloves, a mask, and eye protection when mixing, discarding, or decanting this disinfectant and when placing and removing instruments.

More recently, peroxide formulations have become available to the dental market for chemical sterilization. This liquid germicide can provide sterilization or high-level disinfection, if the manufacturer's instructions are followed.

Surface disinfection

Disinfection is the destruction of most, but not all microorganisms. Equipment and surfaces that may have become contaminated during patient treatment and are not capable of being sterilized by a heat method must be managed by disinfecting after each use, or by the use of impervious barriers. Contamination may occur by touching with contaminated gloves or from spray or

Table 19–2 Sterilization Methods

Method	Temperature	Time	Advantages	Disadvantages
Steam autoclave	121°C (250°F)	15–20 min	Short cycle, good penetration, material compatibility	Carbon steel corrosion, dulling of cutting edges, wet packaging
Dry heat	160°C (320°F) or 170°C (340°F)	2 hr 1 hr	No dulling, no rust/corrosion, effective and safe	Long cycle, poor penetration, not for handpieces
Chemiclave	131°C (270°F)	20–40 min	Short cycle, no rust or corrosion, no dulling, suitable for stainless	Instruments must be dry, chemical product needed, requires ventilation, may produce hazardous waste

splashing through the use of dental devices, such as handpieces and air or water syringes.

Chemical disinfectants are intended for use on clean, nonporous surfaces. Efficacy of the disinfectant may be affected by material remaining on the surfaces, incorrectly mixed product, expired shelf-life, and several other factors. The best method for accomplishing both cleaning and disinfection is to purchase a product that serves a dual purpose. Many intermediate-level disinfectants contain surfactants that allow the user to clean surfaces before disinfecting them, using a single product. The procedure for surface disinfection should be conducted to allow cleaning of all affected surfaces and to provide sufficient contact time for disinfection to occur. The contact time for disinfectants may vary depending upon the brand and type of product used. Some germicides require a contact time of only 2 minutes, although the majority require a contact time of 10 minutes.

Important features to consider when selecting a chemical disinfectant are equipment compatibility, odor and staining properties, ease of use, ability to remain wet on surfaces for the required contact time without evaporating, shelf-life, tuberculocidal activity, and cost.

Barriers

Barriers can offer an effective and time-efficient alternative to surface disinfection. Barriers are plastic or other impervious materials placed over equipment or surfaces to protect them against contamination with BBF from the patient during dental treatment. If barriers are used, they must be changed after each patient.

Aseptic techniques: (avoiding cross-contamination)

Cross-contamination may occur both during and after dental procedures. Items and areas that are touched with contaminated gloves during dental procedures may act as a transfer surface for organism transmission from person to person. Inappropriate or inadequate disinfection and sterilization procedures may also result in cross-contamination. Clean examination or surgical gloves should be placed on the worker's hands just prior to initiating dental treatment. After placing gloves, the DHCW should not touch charts, pens, x-rays, telephones, or other objects or areas with the gloves, to prevent inadvertent transfer of oral fluids from patients to objects that do not routinely receive decontamination and that may be touched subsequent to the procedure. Likewise, areas and objects, such as doors, counters, walls, and dental materials that are not aseptic, must be handled in a manner to avoid the transfer of contamination to gloves that will later enter the patient's mouth or contaminate equipment. Organisms may survive for periods of time ranging from hours to weeks, allowing the opportunity for exposure if contaminated areas are not sterilized or disinfected properly.

Summary

Time has shown that the dental office is not a common source of disease transmission. Epidemiologic studies are being closely followed, especially in regard to DHCW. The most significant disease transmission has been with the HBV, and the incidence in the DHCW has dropped precipitously. Since the late 1980s, no cluster of dentistogenic transmission to patients has been identified. Both strict adherence to these infection control regulations and the hepatitis B vaccine have been efficacious in this regard.

Suggested reading

Black SS, editor. Disinfection, sterilization, and preservation. Philadelphia: Lippincott Williams & Wilkins, 2001.

CDC guidelines for preventing the transmission of *Mycobacterium tuberculosis* in health-care facilities. 1994. MMWR Morb Mortal Wkly Rep 1994;43(RR-13):1–132.

CDC immunization of health-care workers: recommendations of the Advisory Committee on Immunization Practices (ACIP) and the Hospital Infection Control Practices Advisory Committee (HICPAC). MMWR Morb Mortal Wkly Rep 1997;46(RR-18):1–42.

CDC Public Health Service guidelines for the management of health-care worker exposures to HIV and recommendations for postexposure prophylaxis. MMWR Morb Mortal Wkly Rep 1998;47(RR-7):1–33.

CDC recommendations for prevention and control of hepatitis C virus (HCV) infection and HCV-related chronic disease. MMWR Morb Mortal Wkly Rep 1998;47(RR-19):1–39.

CDC recommendations for preventing transmission of human immunodeficiency virus and hepatitis B virus to patients during exposure-prone invasive procedures. Bull Am Coll Surg 1991;76:29–37.

Cottone JA, Terezhalmy GT, Molinari JA. Practical infection control in dentistry. Philadelphia: Lea & Febiger, 1991.

Crawford JJ. Clinical asepsis in dentistry. United States: RA Kolstad, 1986.

Garner JS. Guidelines for isolation precautions in hospitals. Hospital Infection Control Advisory Committee. Infect Control Hosp Epidemiol 1996;17:53–80.

Martin MV. Infection control in the dental environment. London: Kavo, 1991.

Runnells RR. Dental infection control update '88. Utah: IC Publications, 1988.

20

Oral Premalignancies and Squamous Cell Carcinoma

Sol Silverman, Jr, MA, DDS, and L. Roy Eversole, DDS, MSD, MA

Worldwide, oral cancer is a prevalent malignancy, mainly associated with a variety of tobacco-related habits and forms (eg, unrefined tobacco in bidi cigarets, and areca "betel" nut chewing), as well as poor diets with low intake of vegetables and fruits. It is the cause for significant morbidity, suffering, and death.

However, cancer is primarily a disease of aging and associated cell dysregulation; more than 90% of all oral cancers in developed countries occur in individuals over the age of 45 years, with the mean age of onset being the sixth decade of life. But there are now some indications from worldwide tumor registry data that the age of onset of oral cancer is decreasing. In fact, it is becoming more and more common to have reports of persons under 40 years of age with no evident risk factors that have developed a cancer of the oral or oropharyngeal area. Studies indicate probable genetic chromasomal alterations as potent risk factors, although familial clustering has not been documented.

In the United States, the oral cancer rate is highest in African-Americans compared with other ethnic groups; they also have the greatest mortality rate (Table 20–1). This prevalence may be a reflection of access to the health care system, level of education, and late diagnosis. The most common intraoral site is the tongue. This is followed by the lip and floor of the

mouth. If cancer of the lip is excluded (highly predominant in males), the gender ratio of males to females is now less than 2 to 1.

Oral cancer is associated with significant morbidity, pain, and death. Five-year survival rates for oral squamous cell carcinoma are poor (Table 20–2). Even in developed countries with the advances made in surgery, radiation therapy, and chemotherapy, the overall survival for oral cancer only approximates 50%. As a result, therapy is usually aggressive in attempts to improve survival; but in turn, when this is accomplished, morbidity is increased, which tends to significantly lower the quality of life.

This bleak picture is primarily attributable to delays in diagnosis and, subsequently, a large number of advanced-staged tumors. This compromises surgical tumor margins, increases regional metastases, and

Table 20–1 Oral Cancer Rates in the United States

Population	Incidence (%)	Mortality (%)
Blacks	12.3	4.8
Whites	10.0	2.5
Asian	6.0	2.3
Hispanics	5.7	1.7

Table 20–2 Five-Year Relative Survival Rates for Oral Cancer of Three Leading Sites

	Tongue		Lip		Floor of Mouth	
	n	5-yr RS	n	5-yr RS	n	5-yr RS
White males						
1973–84	2637	0.41	3653	0.94	1740	0.52
1985–96	2966	0.47	2538	0.95	1465	0.52
Black males						
1973–84	335	0.25	15	0.84	229	0.38
1985–96	433	0.27	8	0.44	241	0.33
White females						
1973–84	1367	0.48	423	0.87	805	0.64
1985–96	1591	0.58	465	0.95	669	0.63
Black females						
1973–84	131	0.40	5	1.00	68	0.41
1985–96	140	0.32	10	0.81	77	0.59

5-yr RS = 5-year relative survival.
Reproduced from SEER data, National Cancer Institute, 1973–1996.

Table 20–3 Localized Oral Cancers 1973–96: Comparing 11-Year Intervals

Site	1973–1984		1985–1996	
	Cases	L (%)	Cases	L (%)
Tongue	4794	44	5993	45
Lip	4014	86	3402	94
Floor of mouth	3042	43	2804	44
Other	4135	41	4701	43

L = localized cancers (stages 1 and 2).
Reproduced from SEER data, National Cancer Institute, 1973–1996.

reduces the effectiveness of radiation, owing to biologic factors related to tumor size.

Therefore, because of delays in diagnosis, prevention becomes a priority. Prevention, if possible, involves controlling the known risk factors of tobacco and alcohol consumption. Another important factor in reducing the occurrences of oral cancers is the recognition and management of established precancerous lesions. Currently, it seems that no matter what is attempted to prevent cancer, some oral carcinomas still develop. Therefore, early detection is critical in decreasing morbidity and mortality. Unfortunately, the trend in diagnosing early, localized oral squamous cell carcinomas has not been successful (Tables 20–3 and 20–4).

Oral premalignancies

Oral premalignancies can be best characterized as lesions in which there is a risk for uncontrolled cellular growth and transformation into cancer, followed by the disruption of normally functioning tissues. This pathologic process of oral premalignancies primarily affects the stratified squamous epithelium that lines the entire oral cavity and oropharynx. The most frequent clinical manifestations are the leukoplakias that are attributable to the biochemical process of hyperkeratosis. A sound scientific explanation of the association between excess keratin formation and malignant transformation is unknown; the relation is based upon epidemiologic findings of an excess occurrence of carcinomas in these individuals compared with what would be found in that general population (Tables 20–5 and 20–6).

Hyperkeratosis leads to a white patch or plaque that cannot be scraped from the mucosal surface. Another high-risk lesion is the red-appearing patch (erythroplakia or erythroplasia). Often there is a combined white and red appearance (erythroleukoplakia). These lesions are more likely to progress to dysplasia or carcinoma compared with the homogeneous white patch.

In most cases, prediction of the transformation to malignancy is inaccurate. Therefore, cellular markers are being developed and tested to improve the accuracy of discerning those lesions that are most likely to become cancerous. Molecular genetics will also contribute eventually to this assessment. Currently, however, practitioners are limited to the recognition of clinical risk factors and microscopic morphology to help formulate clinical assessments and management.

Pathologic and molecular correlates of disease

Premalignancy and dysplasia

The microscopic changes that occur in leukoplakias range from simple hyperkeratosis to early squamous cell carcinoma. Although a mixed red and white lesion may have a greater chance of exhibiting dysplastic changes, the clinical appearance of a leukoplakia is not predictive of its microscopic appearance. The benign keratoses include hyperparakeratosis, hyperorthokeratosis, acanthosis, and

Table 20–4 Oral and Pharyngeal Cancer in the United States: Staging and 5-Year Survival

	Spread	Whites (%)	Blacks (%)
Stage	Localized	49	26
Survival	Localized	82	48
	Regional	44	31
	Distant	20	10

Table 20–5 Malignant Transformation in Oral Leukoplakia

Investigator (Country)	Year	Number of Patients	Malignant Transformation (%)	Years Observed Number (Average)
Silverman (India)	1976	4762	0.13	2
Gupta (India, Bhavnagar)	1980	360	0.30	1–10 (7.0)
Gupta (India, Ernakulam)	1980	410	2.20	1–10 (7.0)
Roed-Petersen (Denmark)	1971	331	3.60	>1
Einhorn (Sweden)	1967	782	4.00	1–20
Pindborg (Denmark)	1968	248	4.40	1–9
Kramer (England)	1969	187	4.80	1–16
Banoczy (Hungary)	1977	670	5.90	1–30 (9.8)
Silverman (USA)	1968	117	6.00	1–11 (3.5)
Schepman (The Netherlands)	1998	166	12.00	0.5–17 (2.7)
Silverman (USA)	1984	257	17.50	1–39 (7.2)

combinations of these changes. Parakeratosis with acanthosis is a common finding in smokeless tobacco-induced lesions (Figure 20–1). When cells begin to undergo malignant changes, they do so in the basal and parabasal layers. The cells show classic cytologic atypical changes indicative of rapid cell cycling that include pleomorphism, hyperchromatism, and increased nuclear size. The rete pegs become bulbous or teardrop in shape and fuse with one another (Figure 20–2). Changes of this nature, confined to the lower strata of the stratified squamous epithelium are collectively termed mild dysplasia. It is important for the clinician to understand that a diagnosis of mild dysplasia does not presage the evolvement of a cancerous lesion. Irritation and inflammatory changes in the mucosa may cause these changes. Alternatively, these same changes can be seen in cases that progress into cancer.

Atypical cytologic changes that are encountered in the basal, parabasal, and low to mid spinous layer, are referred to as moderate dysplasia; when most of the layers of the epithelium are affected, the term severe dysplasia applies. When cytologic atypia extends from the basal layer to the outer surface of keratinocytes, the appelation is carcinoma-in-situ (Figure 20–3). Importantly, moderate and severe dysplasia as well as carcinoma-in-situ are considered unequivocal precancerous lesions and have the highest propensity to progress to squamous cancer. However, some of these dysplastic lesions, if left untreated, may persist without progressive changes for many months or even years; and some may regress or spontaneously resolve. Unfortunately, it is not possible to predict accurately which course all dysplasias will take based only on the histopathologic diagnosis alone.

Malignancy and carcinoma

The term carcinoma is applied only after cytologically atypical keratinocytes have lost their continuity with the

Table 20–6 Reports of Progression of Dysplasia to Carcinoma in Patients with Oral Leukoplakia

Author (Country)	Year	Number of Dysplasias	Cancers Number (%)	Follow-up (yr)
Mincer (USA)	1972	45*	5 (11)	1–8
Banoczy (Hungary)	1976	68†	9 (13)	1–20
Pindborg (India)	1977	21	3 (14)	7
Silverman (USA)	1984	22‡	8 (36)	1–39
Lumerman (USA)	1995	44	7 (16)	1–7
Sudbo (Norway)	2001	150	36 (24)	1–14

*22 persisted; 3 disappeared; 20 were excised (7 recurred).

†45 of 68 were excised; 8 of the cancers in untreated lesions.

‡20 of 22 lesions presented as erythroleukoplakia.

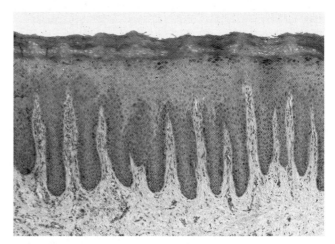

Figure 20–1 Benign keratoses; hyperparakeratosis with acanthosis. No cytologic atypia can be seen. (H&E. Original magnification, ×50)

Figure 20–2 Moderate epithelial dysplasia. Atypical cytologic features including pleomophism and hyperchromatism are evident. (H&E. Original magnification, ×100)

overlying stratified squamous epithelium and islands of tumor cells have invaded the submucosa. This early event in carcinogenesis is termed superficially invasive squamous cell carcinoma. Although this change usually evolves from a dysplastic lesion that has progressed to carcinoma-in-situ, it can also occur when only lower strata cells are dysplastic. Not all early cancers need to progress from carcinoma-in-situ to begin invasion of the submucosa. This invasive event is often said to reflect penetration of the basement membrane; however, even the invasive tumor nests in the submucosa often are enveloped by a basement membrane structure. It is evident that the sequence of events in invasion is modulated by an array of cell proteins.

Once the submucosa is invaded by carcinoma cells, penetration of lymphatic vascular walls may ensue, and the intralymphatic tumor cells can then be passively transported to regional lymph nodes as nodal metastases, which significantly worsens the prognosis. The main route of metastases is by the lymphatic system,

with hematologic spread being less frequent. Blood vascular metastases is the principal route for the rare spread to other organ systems.

As the primary tumor grows and invades deeper into the underlying connective tissues, it often initiates a chronic inflammatory response. The cells from different tumors grow at different rates, and the cell cycle turnover rate is inversely related to differentiation of the tumor. Cells that make mature-appearing keratinocytes, squamous eddies, and keratin pearls are well differentiated, whereas those without keratin differentiation resemble basaloid cells and are poorly differentiated. In general, the latter have a higher turnover rate, are more aggressive, and are more sensitive to radiation therapy. In general, tumors in the anterior part of the mouth are more differentiated, whereas those in the posterior (tonsillar, tongue base) are less differentiated.

Cell cycling

Oral cancer and oral precancerous lesions evolve as a consequence of uncontrolled cell cycling. The etiologic factors that have been alluded to earlier are responsible for genetic events in the keratinocyte that favor continual movement through the cell cycle. This increase in cycling is usually the consequence of multiple mutations, perhaps four to eight mutations in various genes that regulate the process of cell division. Oral keratinocytes have surface membrane receptors that bind cytokine ligands and many of these cytokines are growth factors. Epidermal growth factor, platelet-derived growth factor, and even fibroblast growth factors all have keratinocyte receptors, and once these ligands bind to them, they trigger conformational protein changes with phosphorylation of the receptor's intracytoplasmic domains (kinase activity). This in turn triggers a series of biochemical activations that involve secondary messengers, such as mitosis-associated protein (MAP) kinases, within the cytoplasm that culminate in the DNA transcription of proteins. These proteins transactivate other DNA-binding proteins through structures known as ring fingers.

The so-called transcription factors, such as C-*myc*, *fos*, and *jun*, may then activate the regulatory molecules of the cell cycle (Figure 20–4). Many of the genes that encode growth factors, their receptors, internal signaling molecules, and transcription factors are collectively termed proto-oncogenes. If they are activated or upregulated, the cell may progress to rapid mitotic turnover. Damage or mutations in molecules that downregulate the expression of proto-oncogenes then allows for amplified or sustained expression and drives the cell to increased mitotic cycling.

The cell cycle operates under the influence of molecular engines known as gatekeepers that serve as check-

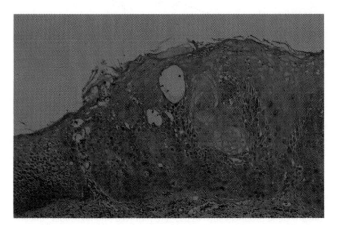

Figure 20–3 Carcinoma-in-situ. Atypical cytologic features are seen to involve all strata of the epithelium. (H&E. Original magnification, ×100).

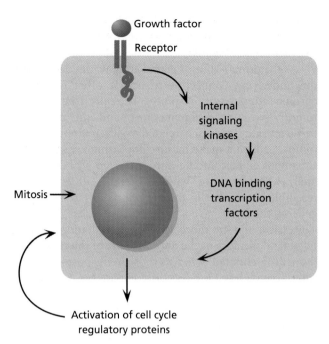

Figure 20-4   Growth factors, their receptors, internal signaling pathways, and activation of transcription factors that can activate regulatory proteins of the cell cycle.

points for each phase. The G1 phase is a gap of minimal activity just prior to initiation of the S phase in which DNA is unwound and polymerases then duplicate the strands. This is followed by another rest or gap termed G2. The next phase is recruitment of the cytoskeletal molecules that assemble the mitotic spindle, and metaphase is initiated. The gatekeepers are the cyclins and the cell cycle-dependent kinases (CDK). When specific cyclins bind to their corresponding kinases, the cell machinery responsible for progression of mitosis is initiated. Proliferating cell nuclear antigen (PCNA) is a cofactor that interacts with cyclins and CDK and is expressed before and during the S phase.

Tumor suppressor genes

There is a group of genes that encode proteins with negative affects on cell division. These are known as tumor suppressor genes (TSG). Importantly, these gene products inhibit the cell cycle when DNA damage occurs. This damage may develop as a consequence of exposure to carcinogens or infection with oncogenic viruses. If damage is severe and nonreparable, the TSG proteins may push the cell into programmed cell death or apoptosis. One of the major gene products that operates in this fashion is the protein p53. This protein is activated when DNA is damaged. P53 is a transcription factor that activates the transcription of another protein, p21, which in turn inhibits the interaction of the cell cycle

regulatory proteins CDK and cyclin. This inhibition prevents the cell from progressing into S phase (Figures 20–5 and 20–6). Importantly, if p53 is mutated in both alleles, or one allele is mutated and the other is not expressed, there are no brakes on the cell cycle and mitosis progresses unchecked. Most oral carcinomas have p53 mutations (mutant p53).

In addition to proto-oncogenes, tumor suppressor genes, and gatekeeper molecules, there is a group of DNA repair genes that may also be mutated in oral carcinomas. The products of these genes repair single- and double-strand breaks and DNA nucleotide mismatches. Since the repair-gene products correct errors that may occur during replication, they are collectively known as caretaker molecules. It is axiomatic that if these genes are mutated, DNA damage occurs unchecked, and such damage, if it occurs in the appropriate site, may have a profound effect

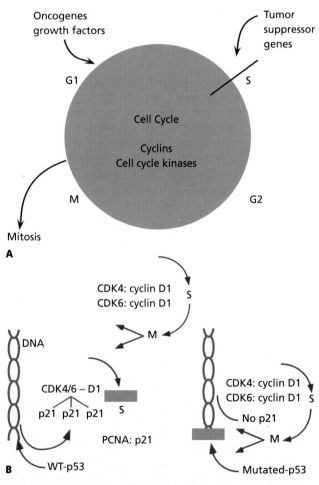

Figure 20-5   Genes involved in cancer. *A,* The cell cycle is regulated by cyclins and cell cycle-dependent kinases, which are influenced by oncoproteins, which activate the cycle, and tumor suppressor gene products, which arrest the cycle. *B,* The cell cycle is activated when tumor suppressor gene products, such as p53, are mutated and no longer function to arrest mitotic division. CDK = cycle-dependent kinase, PCNA = proliferating cell nuclear antigen.

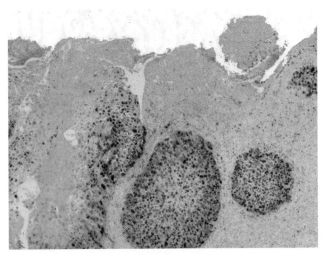

Figure 20–6 Immunohistochemical staining for p53 shows nuclear labeling in dysplasia with early squamous cell carcinoma in which both basal and spinous cells label, indicating the presence of a mutated p53 tumor suppressor protein (3-amino-9-ethylcarbazole [AEC] immunostain. Original magnification, ×50).

on the dysregulation of the mitotic clock. Table 20–7 represents a partial list of molecular lesions identified in oral precancerous and cancerous lesions.

The cause of these genetic alterations is not always identifiable; however, an association with the mucosatropic oncogenic human papillomaviruses (HPV) has been implicated. Human papillomaviruses types 16 and 18 are found in truncated form in over 98% of uterine cervix squamous cell cancers. These types have also been identified in anorectal and oral squamous cell carcinomas. The role of HPV in the pathogenesis of oral cancer is not as clear as it is for cervical cancer; yet, many investigators have identified HPV DNA, mRNA, and viral proteins in oral carcinomas and carcinoma cell lines. Interestingly, HPV 16 encodes an early protein (E6) that transactivates the host cell genome to synthesize a protein that is capable of binding to p53. This binding event promotes the enzymatic degradation of p53 via a ubiquitin-proteasome pathway, thereby eliminating the p53-p21 mitotic arrest regulatory mechanism. If this is coupled with a mutation on one allele, cell cycling proceeds without the appropriate braking mechanism.

Adhesion molecules

Aside from cell cycle activation, oral malignancy is characterized by the ability of cancer cells to migrate, adhere to vascular endothelia and enter vessels, which transport tumor cells to distant sites. The invasive and metastatic potential of carcinoma cells is not a case of cells gone terrorist. Rather, it is a biologically contrived event that allows the stealthy cancer cell to pass through the extra-

cellular matrix (ECM) by virtue of cell:matrix adhesion molecule expression (or loss of certain attachment proteins) with internal signaling that promotes cytoskeletal alterations in the cells that promulgate motility. Oral carcinomas have been shown to downregulate a variety of integrins that are necessary for attachment to cells and to ECM proteins and proteoglycans. Loss of alpha-2, 3, 4, 5, 6, and beta 1 as well as the 64 dimer is seen in carcinomas, and the loss of these adhesins probably serves to mitigate immobilization. The integrin ligand laminin 5 in the basement membrane is also lost or weakly expressed. Conversely, v6 integrin is upregulated as is the internal signaling enzyme focal adhesion kinase, both of which are involved in activation of cell motility. Other adhesion molecules that are underexpressed and presumed to be correlated with invasiveness and metastasis are E-cadherin, the catenins, and the hyaluronate binding molecule CD44.

Host responses

Host defenses against transformed oral keratinocytes can be seen histologically as an intense mononuclear leukocytic infiltrate that surrounds the invasive cancer cells. Indeed, precancerous lesions may also stimulate a submucosal inflammatory response. Tumor cells express a variety of antigens that are found on fetal, yet not on adult cells, and are known as cancer-fetal antigens. In

Table 20–7 Molecular Lesions in Oral Precancerous and Cancerous Lesions

Oncogene overexpression	Epidermal growth factor
	Epidermal growth factor receptor
	MAP kinases
	ras
	myc
	jun
	fos
Tumor suppressor gene mutation	p53
	p21
	pRB
	MDM2
	Sonic hedgehog/patched
	APC
Gatekeeper molecules	Cyclins
	CDKs
	p21
DNA repair gene mutation	Microsatellites
	hMSH 2
	hMLH 1
	MMR genes

MAP = mitosis-associated protein; APC = adenomatous polyposis coli; CDK = cell cycle-dependent kinase.

addition, some cancer cells express unique cancer-specific antigens. These antigens are targets for cytotoxic T cells whose T-cell receptor complex recognizes antigens if they are displayed in the context of major histocompatibility complex class I (MHC-I) molecules on the cancer cell membrane (Figure 20–7). Therapeutic strategies are being developed to target these antigens with immunospecific antibodies and cytotoxic lymphocytes.

Clinical spectrum of oral premalignant and cancerous lesions

As illustrated earlier, oral premalignant lesions may appear white, red, or mixed red and white (Figures 20–8 and 20–9). Additionally, the keratotic (leukoplakic) lesions may show variation in their appearances. Those that are white and smooth and lack textural irregularities are termed homogeneous leukoplakias. Yet others show a fissured or a rough corrugated surface and are referred to as verrucous leukoplakias (Figure 20–10). When these verrucous white lesions are diffuse or multifocal, they conform to the criteria for a specific type of keratosis termed proliferative verrucous

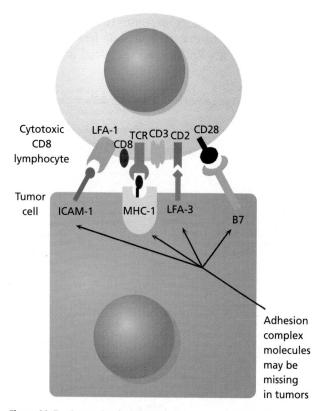

Figure 20–7 Cytotoxic T lymphocytes can recognize cell-surface tumor-specific antigens on cancer cell membranes, bind to these targets, and release cytoxic cytokines. ICAM = intracellular adhesion molecule; LFA = leukocyte function-associated antigen; MHC = major histocompatibility complex; TCR = T-cell antigen receptor; TSA = tumor-specific antigen.

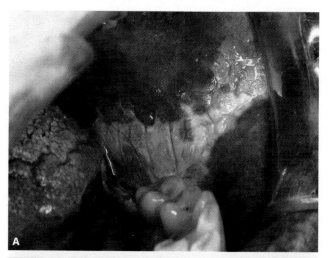

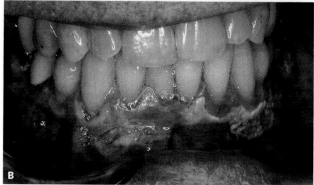

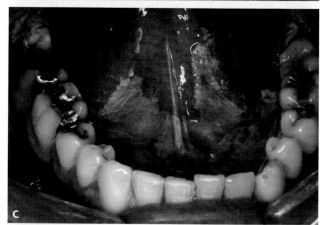

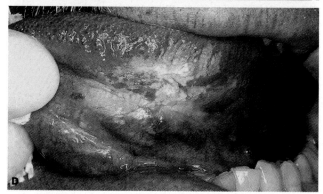

Figure 20–8 Leukoplakia: *A*, buccal mucosa; *B*, gingiva; *C*, ventral tongue and floor of mouth; *D*, tongue, associated with mild dysplasia.

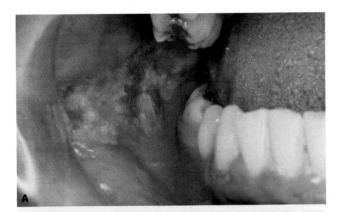

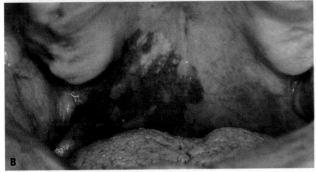

Figure 20–9 *A,* Erythroleukoplakia of the buccal mucosa that later was associated with moderate dysplasia. *B,* Erythroplakia of the soft palate and oropharynx with a minimal keratotic component. This later transformed into squamous cell carcinoma.

leukoplakia. This form of leukoplakia is commonly found in elderly females, smoking habits are often absent, and there is a high risk for malignant transformation (Figure 20–11).

Leukoplakias of the lip are associated with ultraviolet radiation (the counterpart of skin actinic keratoses) and are appropriately termed actinic cheilitis. The lesions are usually smooth, covering all or part of

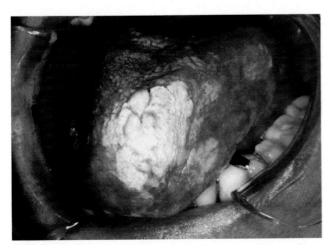

Figure 20–10 Verrucous leukoplakia. After 14 years, squamous cell carcinoma developed in this area.

the vermilion lip border. Occasionally, they are markedly crusted or thickened. When a zone of ulceration or induration appears in an actinic lip, suspicion of dysplasia and early carcinomatous transformation should be high (Figure 20–12).

Erythroplakia is typically a homogeneous velvety red diffuse macule. Erythoplakias may also be intimately associated with white plaque lesions (erythroleukoplakias) (Figure 20–13). Erythroplakias with multiple small white spots are often referred to as speckled leukoplakias (Figure 20–14). Whereas other benign diseases of the oral mucous membranes also may appear white, red, or mixed, this clinical presentation may suggest dysplasia or carcinoma and warrants a biopsy to secure a definitive diagnosis.

Oral squamous cell carcinomas may arise in the site of preexisting leukoplakias and erythroplakias or may arise de novo. Clinically, the lesions have the appearance of the aforementioned precancerous lesions in the early stages of carcinogenesis (Figure 20–15). Once there is substantial invasion of the submucosa, squamous cell carcinomas appear as indurated, nonhealing ulcerations with raised borders (Figure 20–16).

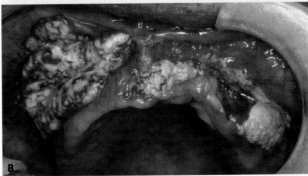

Figure 20–11 Proliferative verrucous leukoplakia: *A,* involving the oropharynx, buccal mucosa, and gingiva that eventually was associated with moderate to severe dysplasia; *B,* of the maxillary gingiva and labial mucosa that, after many years, became symptomatic, started proliferating rather rapidly, and transformed into squamous cell carcinoma. Previous biopsies over the years showed only benign epithelial hyperkeratosis and hyperplasia.

Verrucous carcinoma and the papillary variant of oral squamous carcinoma are exophytic, diffuse, white papillary-type lesions that can at first be limited in size, but can eventually involve large surface areas in late-stage disease (Figure 20–17). Although these variant forms of carcinoma may be locally aggressive, they rarely metastasize.

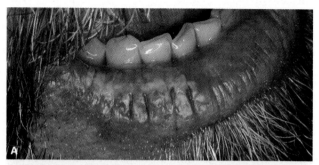
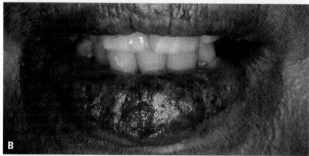
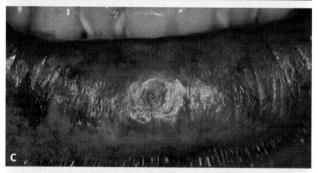
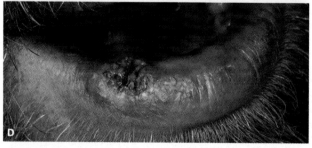

Figure 20–12 *A*, Chronic cheilitis associated with leukoplakia; *B*, chronic actinic cheilitis that eventually transformed into a squamous cell carcinoma involving the entire lower vermilion border; *C*, squamous cell carcinoma of the lower lip, at first thought to be a "cold sore," occurring in a patient with long-standing cheilitis and incidental melanosis; *D*, squamous cell carcinoma of the lip noticed for 2 months in a patient with chronically "chapped" lips.

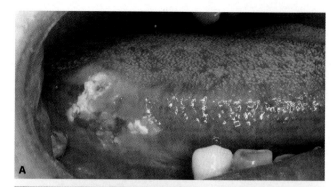
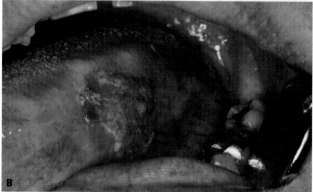

Figure 20–13 *A* and *B*, Erythroleukoplakia of the tongue. Each lesion proved to be a squamous cell carcinoma.

Like cancers elsewhere, oral carcinomas are staged clinically to set the basis for treatment planning. The staging system used in most centers is the tumor-node-metastasis (TNM) classification, where T designates the primary tumor size (T1 is small; T4 is massive), N signifies the presence or absence of metastatic lesions in lymph nodes, and M refers to the presence or absence of distant metastases in some other organ or site, the most common being the lungs. The complete scheme for oral TMN staging is given in Table 20–8.

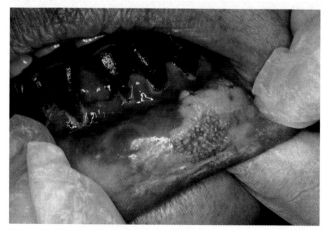

Figure 20–14 Speckled leukoplakia of the lip in a chronic snuff user. A biopsy showed severe epithelial dysplasia.

Risk factors for premalignancies

Probably the most accurate prediction of transformation is based upon microscopic epithelial dysplasia (Figure 20–18). Although frequently there is some disagreement with respect to the degree of dysplasia, as well as carcinoma-in-situ, transformation rates following microscopic recognition of dysplasia have been significantly high (see Table 20–6). Because of that risk, excision is usually indicated. Whereas regression of dysplasia can occur, it is unusual.

A red-appearing lesion may also be a manifestation of epithelial dysplasia, or even carcinoma. Therefore, a mucosal change of this nature must either disappear or be microscopically evaluated. As already cited, a red component to a clinically white lesion increases the possibility of dysplasia and carcinoma. Therefore, this appearance increases the risk of transformation and must be investigated. Since leukoplakias are usually not associated with discomfort, symptomatic lesions may indicate a transformation and should be recognized as a risk factor.

The clinical appearance and behavior of a leukoplakic lesion may, at times, signal an increased risk. Proliferative verrucous leukoplakia has demonstrated a high risk for malignant transformation (see Figure 20–11). Thus, a more aggressive treatment approach is indicated. There may be an association with a type of human papillomavirus (type 16) that may account for this behavior.

Candida species are often associated with leukoplakia, since candidal hyphae are often seen in microscopic sections from oral leukoplakia. Their role is uncertain. However, *Candida* are capable of producing

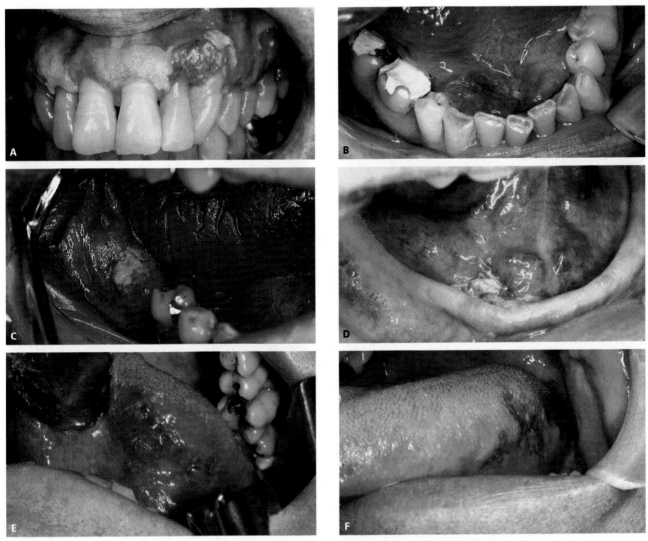

Figure 20–15 Early squamous cell carcinoma: *A*, developing in an area of gingival leukoplakia, *B*, developing in an area of erythroplakia; *C*, at first mistaken for a benign traumatic lesion from the saddle of the lower partial denture; *D*, of the floor of the mouth, at first mistaken for a benign traumatic keratosis induced by an overextended lingual denture flange; *E*, of the tongue, at first mistaken for a benign inflammatory lesion or infection; *F*, of the tongue, at first mistaken for a vesiculo-erosive disease lesion.

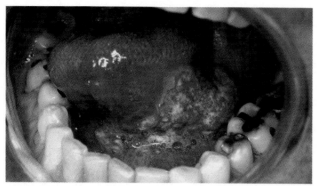

Figure 20–16 Advanced squamous cell carcinoma of the tongue and floor of mouth with metastases to regional lymph nodes.

carcinogenic nitrosoamines through biochemical tissue reactions. Although the association with carcinogenesis is not clear, the presence of *Candida* must be considered to be a potential risk factor (Figure 20–19).

Smoking has been associated with hyperkeratosis and leukoplakia. This may be because of physical or chemical irritants. However, a paradox also exists: in

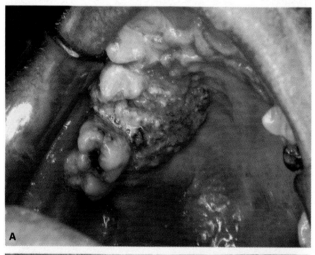

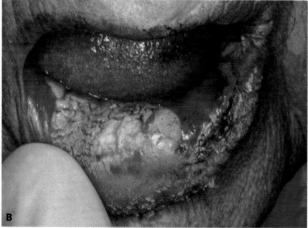

Figure 20–17 Verrucous carcinoma; *A*, palatal gingiva, *B*, labial mucosa.

those patients with oral leukoplakia who do not smoke, malignant transformation risks appear to be higher. It must be that a more lethal factor is present in those individuals. Whereas smokeless tobacco is associated with an increased risk for developing carcinoma, the primary factor is the long-time usage. Cessation of the habit usually leads to disappearance of an associated epithelial change. Alcohol consumption alone or in conjunction with tobacco usage increases the risk for cell dysregulation and carcinogenesis.

The most common association with oral cancer is aging, which is also true for the leukoplakias. This makes biologic sense, since the sensitive homeostatic mechanism controlling epithelial growth is influenced by the behavior of oncogenes that, in turn, appear to be responsive to time-related exposures to viruses and

Table 20–8 Tumor-Node-Metastasis (TNM) Staging System for Oral Carcinoma

Primary tumor (T)

TX	Primary tumor cannot be assessed
T0	No evidence of primary tumor
Tis	Carcinoma-in-situ
T1	Tumor 2 cm or less in greatest dimension
T2	Tumor more than 2 cm but not more than 4 cm in greatest dimension
T3	Tumor more than 4 cm in greatest dimension. Lip: tumor invades adjacent structures (eg, through cortical bone, into deep [extrinsic] muscle of tongue, maxillary sinus, skin)
T4	Oral cavity: tumor invades adjacent structure (eg, through cortical bone, into deep [extrinsic] muscle of tongue, maxillary sinus, skin)

Regional lymph nodes (N)

NX	Regional lymph nodes cannot be assessed
N0	No regional lymph node metastasis
N1	Metastasis in a single ipsilateral lymph node, 3 cm or less in greatest dimension
N2	Metastasis in a single ipsilateral lymph node, more than 3 cm but not more than 6 cm in greatest dimension; in multiple ipsilateral lymph nodes, none more than 6 cm in greatest dimension; in bilateral or contralateral lymph nodes, none more than 6 cm in greatest dimension
N2a	Metastasis in single ipsilateral lymph node more than 3 cm but not more than 6 cm in greatest dimension
N2b	Metastasis in multiple ipsilateral lymph nodes, none more than 6 cm in greatest dimension
N2c	Metastasis in bilateral or contralateral lymph nodes, none more than 6 cm in greatest dimension
N3	Metastasis in a lymph node more than 6 cm in greatest dimension

Distant metastasis (M)

MX	Presence of distant metastasis cannot be assessed
M0	No distant metastasis
M1	Distant metastasis

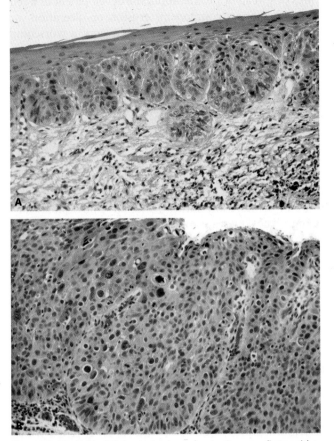

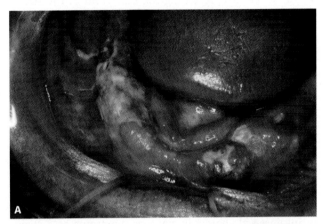

Extremely useful, because of accuracy, low cost, quickness, simplicity, and noninvasive nature, is the application of toluidine blue dye (Figure 20–20). This involves applying a 1% aqueous solution of toluidine blue to the lesion, rinsing with water, applying a 1% solution of acetic acid, rinsing with water, and observing any binding. The accuracy has been found to exceed 90%. The probable mechanism is the affinity or binding of toluidine blue with DNA and sulfated mucopolysaccharides, both of which are selectively high in dysplastic and malignant

Figure 20–18 Epithelial dysplasia: *A*, moderate; *B*, severe (intraepithelial carcinoma).

chemical or physical agents. It must be remembered, even if a patient with leukoplakia does not demonstrate any of the above risk factors, transformation to malignancy may occur. Therefore, long-term follow-up of all leukoplakic lesions is mandatory.

Diagnosis

The diagnosis of premalignant lesions depends upon clinical suspicion and microscopic assessment following biopsy. Obviously, disappearance of a lesion helps rule out malignancy and premalignancy at that time. Many times, biopsy is delayed because of patient or clinician choice, or the institution of other treatment to rule out infection or local irritation. However, these reasons should not delay a definitive diagnosis for more than 3 to 4 weeks.

Sometimes, the extensiveness of a lesion complicates the most appropriate area to biopsy to rule out dysplasia or carcinoma. Therefore, other adjuncts to clinical judgment (not substitutes) are helpful in both accelerating biopsy and selecting the most appropriate area to sample.

Figure 20–19 *A*, Gingival leukoplakia associated with *Candida albicans* that eventually transformed into squamous cell carcinoma of the anterior gingiva. *B*, Note microscopic hyperkeratosis and candidal hyphae in surface cells.

oral epithelium compared with normal epithelium and benign lesions. Additionally, toluidine blue dye binds to cytoplasmic negatively charged mitochondrial membranes, which are stronger in dysplastic and malignant epithelial cells compared with normal tissue.

Exfoliative cytology has been helpful as well as accurate in determining a diagnosis (Figure 20–21). However, the difficulty of cell collection and the increased time and cost have limited its usefulness. The brush biopsy technique, using a specially designed brush, has extended the usefulness of cytology by improving collection of cells representing the full width of the stratified squamous epithelium (Figure 20–22). The accuracy has exceeded 95%. The procedure is essentially painless, and therefore, anesthesia is not necessary. Microscopic evaluation involves a rapid and effective computer-assisted analysis.

The question often arises as to when rebiopsy is in order once a precancerous lesion has been initially evaluated. First, if there is evidence of dysplasia, removal and follow-up is recommended. If there is no dysplasia or it is only classified as mild and a lesion is not removed, then at least periodic follow-up is essential. This involves a thorough clinical examination as well as toluidine blue application or cytologic analysis. If there is any interval change in signs or symptoms or a suspicious stain or cytology, then rebiopsy is indicated. Any change in dye uptake, abnormal cytology, clinical fea-

tures of spread or proliferation, the development of a red or erythematous component, erosion or ulceration, or discomfort or pain may indicate dysplasia, a worsening of existing dysplasia, or transformation to carcinoma.

Management

As indicated, a thorough initial evaluation of signs and symptoms is essential, which includes a biopsy and subsequent follow-up. An alternative to the incisional biopsy with a scalpel, is the use of a 5-mm punch biopsy (Figure 20–23). The punch technique is quick, usually does not require any sutures, and may allow more sampling. The question of incisional versus excisional biopsy usually arises when a lesion is small. If dysplasia or carcinoma is suspected in the differential diagnosis, then incisional biopsy is rcommended. This allows for better planning regarding mode of therapy and margins and gives the therapist an opportunity to actually visualize and palpate the lesion.

If a biopsy shows the lesion to be squamous cell carcinoma (invasion of dysplastic cells into the underlying connective tissue), then the patient should be referred to a cancer therapist or a tumor board to discuss and plan treatment approaches. At present, the only potentially curative therapy involves surgery or radiation. Chemotherapy is used sometimes as an adjunct, which

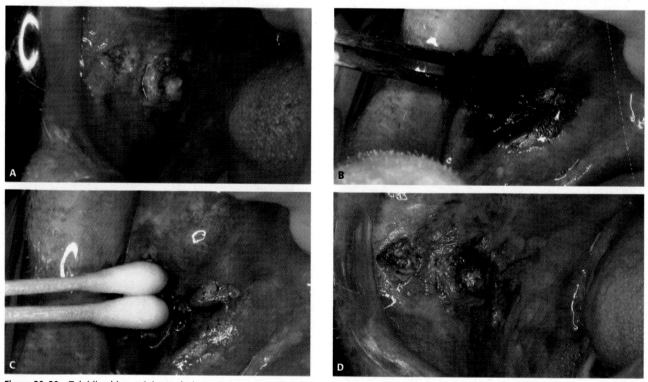

Figure 20–20 Toluidine blue staining technique: *A,* squamous cell carcinoma and leukoplakia, buccal mucosa; *B,* applying 1% aqueous toluidine blue stain; *C,* after water rinse, decolorize with 1% acetic acid; and *D,* dye retention in area of carcinoma and surrounding dysplasia.

may slightly improve response rates in some tumors. The aggressiveness of therapy depends upon the stage of the cancer: early (small and localized) or late (large and spread). The clinical evaluation is significantly aided by advanced radiation imaging techniques, magnetic resonance (MR) and computed tomography (CT). A newer technique, positron emission tomography (PET), also can be helpful in determining lymph node involvement. These techniques aid therapists in determining margins and aggressiveness of treatment, as well as prognosis for survival and function.

Relevant to precancerous lesions, periodic follow-up is indicated even if what appears to be a precancerous

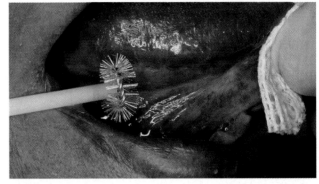

Figure 20–22 Brush biopsy can be used to obtain cells that represent the full thickness of the epithelium. The evaluation is a cytologic assessment.

lesion disappears. Treatment of persistent suspicious lesions requires surgical removal. Margins often create a problem and explain recurrences, since epithelial cells that both clinically and microscopically appear normal may have subcellular proteins that can reestablish the pathologic process. Biologic markers may help diminish this problem.

Laser techniques have helped improve surgical approaches and ultimate control of leukoplakia (Figure 20–24). Chemoprevention using vitamin A analogues (retinoids) and other antioxidant vitamins and nutrients (ie, beta carotene, vitamins C and E) have not been effective in well-designed, prospective studies. The theory is that antioxidants help stabilize cellular free radicals (mainly unstable oxygen) that can serve as promotors of chromosomal mutagenesis and carcinogenesis. Problems in chemoprevention involve toxicities during administration and recurrences when the agent is discontinued. Eventual effectiveness will follow when we learn more about and are able to coordinate dosages, regimens, and patient profiles. In the meantime, a helpful nutritional approach would be the daily intake of a diet rich in fruits and vegetables. These foods contain antioxidants and cell-suppressor proteins that are helpful in diminishing mutagenesis and carcinogenesis activity. This has been supported by dietary and epidemiologic studies.

In summary, recognition and control of premalignant lesions is an effective approach to reducing the occurrence and, thus, the morbidity and mortality from oral cancer.

Oral cancer: complications of therapy

Smaller and localized tumors have a far lower mortality rate and less morbidity than advanced lesions. Staging of oral cancers is critically important, since the more advanced tumors require more aggressive therapy. As would be expected, the more intensive therapeutic approaches used to improve survival also increase the

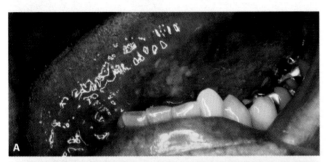

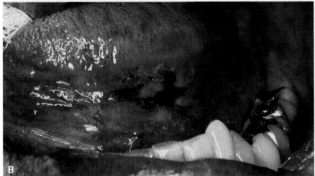

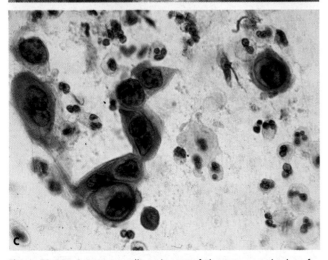

Figure 20–21 Squamous cell carcinoma of the tongue, mistaken for trauma or infection, that had been present for over a month. *A,* Clinical lesion; *B,* toluidine blue positive; *C,* cytology specimen showing malignant cells.

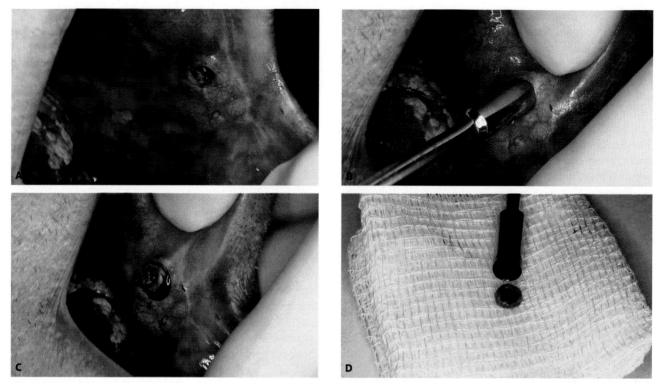

Figure 20–23   Punch biopsy technique in a patient being seen on a routine recall for widespread oral leukoplakia: *A*, routine toluidine blue application revealed dye binding in the commissure; *B*, incision with a 5-mm punch instrument; *C*, specimen to be removed by scissors or scalpel; *D*, specimen and punch instrument. The biopsy showed early squamous cell carcinoma.

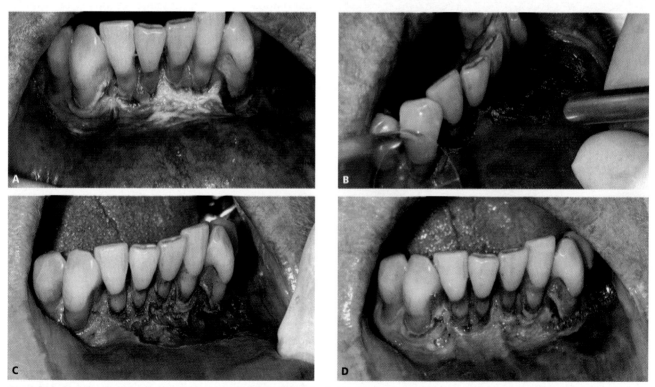

Figure 20–24   Carbon dioxide laser management of gingival leukoplakia: *A*, a biopsy showed associated moderate epithelial dysplasia; *B*, laser vaporization under local anesthesia; *C*, immediately following laser removal; *D*, complete healing by 4 weeks. The patient was asymptomatic and without recurrence after 3 years.

complications. Therefore, preventing or minimizing these complications is vital to quality-of-life and successful rehabilitation.

Radiation effects

Ionizing radiation delivered in doses that kill cancer cells induces unavoidable changes in the surrounding normal tissues, causing compromises in function and host defenses and severe complications.

Mucocutaneous changes

Unless intraoral or interstitial treatment is used, most patients develop some erythema and moderate tanning of the skin in the treatment portal. Hair follicles are radiosensitive; therefore, if hair is in the treatment beam, it will cease to grow and will fall out. This is often transient and related to dosage.

The acute oral mucosal reaction (mucositis) is secondary to radiation-induced mitotic death of the basal cells in the oral mucosa (Figure 20–25). If the radiation is delivered at a rate equivalent to the ability of the oral mucosa to regenerate, only mild mucositis will be seen. Oral microorganisms probably play a role in aggravating the impaired epithelium. Smoking is also a negative factor. Clinically observed late or radiation-induced atrophy and telangiectasis of the mucosa often increase the risk for pain or necrosis.

Management of acute mucositis may sometimes require a 1-week interruption of therapy. Topical anesthetics (viscous xylocaine) may be of some value, but the pain usually requires systemic analgesic drugs. Opioid medication is often required for pain control. Since infections may be associated, appropriate diagnosis and antimicrobial agents must be considered for either fungal or bacterial organisms. Viral infections are rarely a complication of radiation-induced mucositis. A short course of systemic prednisone (40–80 mg/d for not more than 1 week) has been helpful in reducing inflammation and discomfort.

Loss of taste

Taste buds, which occur primarily in the circumvallate and fungiform papillae, are sensitive to radiation. Because of their location in the tongue, they are included in the beam of radiation for most oral cancers. Therefore, patients develop a partial (hypogeusia) or most usually, complete (ageusia) loss of taste during treatment. The cells comprising taste buds usually regenerate within 4 months after treatment. However,

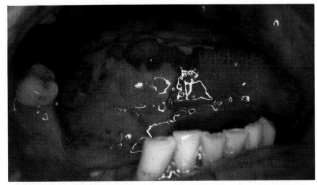

Figure 20–25 Radiation-induced mucositis at fifth week of therapy (4500 cGy).

the degree of long-term impairment of taste varies from patient to patient.

Dietary consultations regarding recipes with pleasing texture and perceptible and pleasing tastes are essential to improve intake of food. However, there are tremendous patient-to-patient differences that preclude standard recommendations. Failure in taste perception, in addition to pain, dysphagia, hyposalivation, and depression, is associated with the loss of pleasure in eating and, thus, a loss of appetite. Weight loss, weakness, malaise, and dehydration often follow. This is further complicated when prior surgery has caused problems in mastication and swallowing. Trials with zinc supplements (as $ZnSO_4$) exceeding the usual recommended daily intake (RDI) appear to be helpful (50–100 mg elemental zinc daily have been prescribed with success in some patients). Whereas zinc serves as a critical enzyme in many biochemical reactions, its role in taste and saliva remains unknown. Saliva probably has a modulating effect on the acuity of some tastes (sour, bitter, salt, sweet) through biochemical interactions, as well as providing an ionic environment in signal transduction for taste cells.

Salivary function

Exposure of the major salivary glands to the field of ionizing radiation induces fibrosis, fatty degeneration, acinar atrophy, and cellular necrosis within glands. A critical dose level has not been identified. The serous acini appear to be more sensitive than the mucinous. During irradiation, the glandular secretions are usually diminished, thick, sticky, and bothersome to the patient. Some patients are unable to produce more than 1 mL of pooled saliva in 10 minutes. The duration of this depressed salivary function varies from patient to patient. Some regeneration can occur several months after treatment, and the undesirable signs and symptoms of xerostomia (discomfort, difficulty in speech and swallowing) may be modified. However, recovery of adequate saliva for oral comfort and function may take up to 12 months; in others, the saliva remains inadequate indefinitely and is the source of major post-treatment complaints. When both of the parotid glands are exposed to the treatment beam, saliva diminution is most marked, and the prognosis for recovery is the worst. Obviously, the higher the dosage of irradiation, the worse the prognosis for xerostomia.

Frequent sips of water and water rinses are essential for partial control of radiation-induced xerostomia. Sugarless chewing gum and tart candy may be helpful. In some patients, pilocarpine hydrochloride solution or tablets (Salagen®, MGI Pharma, Minneapolis, Minnesota) have been effective in stimulating saliva production (5 mg, 3–4 times daily). Another effective sialogogue is cevimeline HCl (Evoxac®, Daiichi Pharmaceutical, Montrale, New Jersey), taken as a 30-mg capsule three times daily. Side effects can include sweating and stomach discomfort. Bethanechol (Urecholine®, Odyssey Pharmaceuticals, East Hanover, New Jersey), a salivary gland stimulant, administered as tablets in divided doses varying from 75 to 200 mg daily, has been helpful in many patients with xerostomia. However, it is not FDA-approved for this effect.

Synthetic saliva solutions and saliva substitute lubricants have been of limited help in the majority of patients with dry mouth, although some favorable reports have been published. Oral Balance, an over-the-counter lubricating gel, has been useful in many patients. In some patients in whom the salivary complaint is related to the "thickness" (excess mucous-type secretions), guaifenesin (Organidin® NR, Wallace, Cranbury, New Jersey) may help as a mucolytic agent (200–400 mg, 3–4 times daily).

Nutrition

Because of the painful mucositis, loss of taste, and partial xerostomia, the lack of desire or frank inability to eat is a common and almost universal complaint in patients receiving external irradiation to the oral cavity. A resultant weight loss tends to weakness, inactivity, discouragement, further anorexia, and susceptibility to infection. Therefore, close attention is given to food intake and weight maintenance during treatment and follow-up. Anemia, bleeding, or immune deficiencies have not been complications of head and neck radiation.

Dental caries

Patients who have not shown any degree of caries activity for years may develop dental decay and varying

degrees of tooth disintegration after irradiation. The cervical areas are most typically affected. This condition appears to be attributable to the lack of saliva as well as to changes in its chemical composition.

Radiation-induced dental effects primarily depend upon salivary changes, but direct irradiation of teeth also may alter the organic or inorganic components in some manner, making them more susceptible to decalcification. Remineralization of enamel by a salivary substitute has been reported. There do not appear to be any clinical or histologic pulpal differences in noncarious human adult teeth, whether they have been in or out of the primary field of radiation.

To prevent or at least minimize radiation caries, oral hygiene must be maximal, including intensive home care and frequent office visits for examination and prophylaxis. Mouthrinsing is essential. Antiseptic mouthrinses, for example, chlorhexidine (Peridex®, Proctor and Gamble, Mason, Ohio; PerioGard®, Colgate Canton, Massachusetts), if tolerated, are helpful in eliminating debris and controlling microbial flora. Daily topical fluoride applications, as a solution for mouthrinsing, a gel delivered by means of a tray, or brushed on as a paste or gel, are effective. Attempts should be made to increase salivary flow either by local or systemic means. Foods and beverages containing sucrose should be avoided as much as possible. If carious lesions develop, removal and restoration should take place immediately. Appropriate use of dental radiographic imaging is in order when indicated to monitor caries activity.

Candidiasis

Infections of the mouth by *Candida albicans* are commonly seen in patients receiving irradiation, and are related to the alterations in saliva (Figure 20–26). Clinically, the signs may be confused with radiation mucositis or other sources of infection. Candidiasis is usually painful. Management is primarily with the use of antifungal drugs (see Chapter 18). Systemic administration (200 mg ketoconazole daily with food, or fluconazole 100 mg daily) is usually more effective for both response and compliance. Duration of treatment depends upon control of signs and recurrences, since complete elimination of *Candida* from the oral flora usually does not occur. Topical administration entails the use of nystatin or clotrimazole tablets dissolved orally. Because of pain from mucositis and dryness, patients may experience difficulty in dissolving tablets topically. Suspensions are an alternative form of treatment, but often are not as effective because of limited contact time between drug and fungi. Antiseptic mouthrinses similar to those used for caries control may be helpful, if tolerated. In addition, topical (viscous xylocaine) or systemic analgesics may be

Figure 20–26   Pseudomembranous candidiasis associated with xerostomia at the fourth week of radiation therapy for oropharyngeal carcinoma.

required. Keeping the mouth moist is essential. There is always the possibility of developing fungal resistance, or the need of higher dosages, when these agents are used for prolonged periods of time. Candidal overgrowth remains a problem even after radiation is completed in patients with persistent xerostomia and those wearing dental prostheses.

Osteoradionecrosis

Osteonecrosis is one of the more serious complications of head and neck irradiation for cancer (Figure 20–27). Bone cells and vascularity may be irreversibly injured. Fortunately, in many cases, devitalized bone fragments sequestrate and lesions spontaneously heal. However, when radiation osteonecrosis is progressive, it can lead to intolerable pain or fracture and may necessitate jaw resection.

The risk for developing spontaneous osteoradionecrosis is somewhat unpredictable, but it is related to the dose of radiation delivered and bone volume (usually more than 6000 cGy). The mandible is at higher risk than the maxilla. The risk is increased in dentulous patients, even more if teeth within the treatment field are removed after therapy. Spontaneous bone exposure is usually delayed and on average occurs more than 1 year after radiation is completed. The risk for osteonecrosis continues indefinitely following radiation therapy (Table 20–9).

If osteonecrosis does not progress clinically or radiographically, the usual management involves periodic observation. If flares (swelling, suppuration, pain) occur only occasionally, antibiotics are usually effective. Clindamycin (Cleocin, 600–1200 mg daily) and amoxicillin-clavulanic acid (Augmentin, 1500–2000 mg daily) have

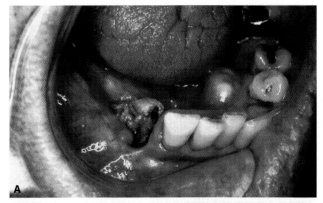

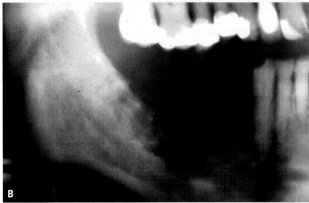

Figure 20–27   Osteonecrosis 2 years after the completion of radiation therapy (6800 cGy). *A,* Painful exposed bone following an uncomplicated bicuspid extraction. *B,* Panorex film showing irregular and extensive mandibular decalcification.

been useful antibiotics in managing osteoradionecrosis. If pain or flares occur too frequently or present other difficulties for the patient, surgery must be considered. Hyperbaric oxygen treatments along with surgery and antibiotics may be helpful in healing, based upon angiogenesis induced by increased oxygen. However, reproducible benefits remain uncertain.

Soft-tissue necrosis

Soft-tissue necrosis may be defined as the occurrence of a mucosal ulcer in irradiated tissue that has no residual

Table 20–9   Occurrence of Osteonecrosis after Irradiation for Oral Cancer

Tooth Extraction	Dosage (cGy) Range (mean)	Osteonecrosis Incidence 19/78 (24%)	Time after Diagnosis (mo)
None	6940–9280 (7871)	5/41 (12)	29
Before	7580–9610 (8500)	3/19 (16)	41
After	6700–8100 (7346)	11/18 (61)	20

cancer. The incidence of soft-tissue necrosis is related to dose, time, and volume irradiated. The risk is far greater with interstitial implantation and intraoral techniques because of the higher irradiation doses used.

Soft-tissue necrosis is usually painful. Optimal hygiene is required and analgesics are usually helpful, but antibiotics are generally of little help in relieving pain and promoting healing. Since these ulcerations are often at the site of the primary tumor, periodic assessment for recurrence is essential until the necrosis heals.

Dental treatment planning

In view of the risk that accompanies high-dose irradiation, special attention to preradiation dental planning appears critical. Factors important in the dental management of these patients include (1) anticipated bone dose; (2) pretreatment dental status, dental hygiene, and retention of teeth that will be exposed to high-dose irradiation; (3) extraction techniques; (4) allowance of adequate healing time for teeth extracted before radiotherapy; and (5) patient motivation and capability of compliance to preventive measures.

Since many infections occur months or years after treatment, it is evident that the tissue changes induced by radiation persist for long periods and may be irreversible. Therefore, extreme care must be taken in evaluating the status of the teeth and periodontium before, during, and after treatment. Optimal oral and periodontal hygiene must be maintained because of the lowered biologic potential for healing in response to physical irritation, chemical agents, and microbial organisms. Such attention is critical because of the potentially progressive nature of radiation osteonecrosis, which may involve large segments of bone and present a major therapeutic problem, possibly requiring extensive resection.

It is impossible to establish precise formulas for managing preradiation and postradiation dental problems. Extractions are considered primarily for teeth with a poor prognosis owing to such conditions as advanced periodontal disease, extensive caries activity, and periapical lesions. Other considerations are sources of chronic soft-tissue irritation (trauma), and the degree of patient cooperation in preventive home care and dental office programs. The decision is modified further for each patient on the basis of the prognosis, age, desires, economic aspects, and radiation delivery.

Reported studies and personal experience do not substantiate the advisability of extracting all teeth before treatment as a good preventive measure. When teeth are extracted before or after radiation, the alveolar bone must be evenly trimmed and carefully smoothed so that primary tissue closure is possible. This is necessary because suppression of bone cell viability

diminishes remodeling, and if a suitable alveolectomy is not performed, the resulting alveolar ridge will be irregular and may increase the risk of subsequent bone exposure and discomfort. A minimum of 1 week to 10 days is arbitrarily allowed for initial healing before radiation is instituted. However, if the situation permits, more time is preferable, up to 14 or even 21 days. Since dosages are fractionated, healing can usually continue before damaging levels of radiation are delivered to a surgical area. Obviously, teeth completely out of the treatment field are not affected similarly.

The use of antibiotics during the healing period is important to minimize infection. Whenever possible, an attempt is made to retain teeth to support tooth-borne appliances for the tentatively planned rehabilitation of these patients.

The periodontium is maintained in optimal condition by periodic routine periodontal procedures. When areas exposed to radiation are treated, extreme care is exercised and antibiotics may be selectively administered. Fluoride applications (daily, in the form of mouthrinses or gels) appear to aid in minimizing tooth decalcification and caries in these patients. There are no unusual contraindications for endodontic procedures.

In conclusion, review of the literature and experience indicate that carefully controlled studies are necessary before more definitive guidelines can be formulated for managing dental structures that have been or are to be radiated. This is particularly true because of newer fractionation and dose regimens of radiation, as well as combinations with chemotherapy, to attain better responses and survival rates. Each case must be managed individually, based on the needs of the patient, the status of the tumor, and the risks known to exist for dental health in irradiated tissues, and a one-formula approach for all patients is contraindicated.

The time for construction or use of dentures is individually determined and based upon the needs of the patient, appearance of tissues, and the ability of the patient to tolerate wearing appliances. Obviously, any irritation should be minimized and the dentures kept immaculately clean. Many edentulous patients never stop wearing their dentures, even during therapy. This has not produced any unusual morbidity or pathology.

Surgery

Surgical approaches to cancer control include removal of malignant and adjacent normal tissue (margins) in an attempt to remove all cancerous cells. This surgery results in defects that cause problems with appearance and function, which in turn can cause severe emotional disturbances. If the margins are inadequate, recurrences follow. Rehabilitation is usually planned at the time of initial treatment and frequently involves maxillofacial prosthodontics for oral and facial appliances. Intraoral prostheses may require obturators and implants.

Chemotherapy

Chemotherapy alone is not an effective treatment for oral cancers, although some regimens can enhance radiation and surgery. The toxic effects of chemotherapy are usually acute and may add to the morbidity of treatment. Therefore, treatment must often balance between the adverse side effects of chemotherapy and the benefits of trying to increase response and survival.

When using cytotoxic chemotherapeutic drugs, it is extremely important to keep patients free from the oral foci of infection and pain, to minimize local infection and bacteremia and to enable them to maintain a nutritious diet. The chemotherapeutic agents used to eradicate tumor production also adversely affect normal cells, particularly those that have relatively high turnover rates, such as oral epithelial tissues. The depressant effect of therapy on oral epithelial mitoses can result in thinning and ulceration of the tissues as well as salivary gland and taste dysfunctions. The oral ulcerations may be caused by direct cellular cytotoxicity from the chemotherapeutic agents; increased susceptibility to microorganisms, owing to neutropenia (bone marrow suppression); trauma; or a combination of these factors. Therefore, mucositis becomes a major adverse side effect of chemotherapy. Fortunately, it is usually transient. Herpes reactivation can complicate the mucositis. Dental work must be correlated with the medical oncologist, because of the induced neutropenia (susceptibility to infection) and thrombocytopenia (bleeding risk from low platelets).

Suggested reading

Abbey LM, Kaugars GE, Gunsolley JC, et al. Intraexaminer and interexaminer reliability in the diagnosis of oral epithelial dysplasia. Oral Surg Oral Med Oral Pathol Oral Radiol Endod 1995;80:188–91.

Bagutti C, Speight PM, Watt FM. Comparison of integrin, cadherin, and catenin expression in squamous cell carcinomas of the oral cavity. J Pathol 1998;186:8–16.

Epstein JB, Chin EA, Jacobson JJ, et al. The relationships among fluoride, cariogenic oral flora, and salivary flow rate during radiation therapy. Oral Surg Oral Med Oral Pathol Oral Radiol Endod 1998;86:286–92.

Krebs-Smith SM. Progress in improving diet to reduce cancer risk. Cancer 1998;83:1425–32.

Lilly JP, Cox D, Arcuri M, Krell KV. An evaluation of root canal treatment in patients who have received irradiation to the mandible and maxilla. Oral Surg Oral Med Oral Pathol Oral Radiol Endod 1998;86:224–6.

Lumerman H, Freedman P, Kerpel S. Oral epithelial dysplasia and the development of invasive squamous carcinoma. Oral Surg Oral Med Oral Pathol Oral Radiol Endod 1995;79:321–29.

Niedermeier W, Matthaeus C, Meyer C, et al. Radiation-induced hyposalivation and its treatment with oral pilocarpine. Oral Surg Oral Med Oral Pathol Oral Radiol Endod 1998;86:541–9.

Partridge M, Emilion G, Pateromichelakis S, et al. Allelic imbalance at chromosomal loci implicated in the pathogenesis of oral precancer: cumulative loss and its relationship with progression to cancer. Oral Oncol 1998;34:77–83.

Ramirez-Amador V, Silverman S Jr, Mayer P, et al. Candidal colonization and oral candidiasis in patients undergoing oral and pharyngeal radiation therapy. Oral Surg Oral Med Oral Pathol Oral Radiol Endod 1997;84:149–53.

Ripamonti C, Zecca E, Brunelli C, et al. A randomized, controlled clinical trial to evaluate the effects of zinc sulfate on cancer patients with taste alterations caused by head and neck irradiation. Cancer 1998;82:1938–45.

Schoelch ML, Secandari N, Regezi JA, Silverman S Jr. Laser management of oral leukoplakias: a follow-up study of 70 patients. Laryngoscope 1999;109:149–53.

Shiboski CH, Shiboski SC, Silverman S Jr. Trends in oral cancer rates in the United States, 1973–1996. Community Dent Oral Epidemiol 2000;28:249–56.

Silverman S Jr, Gorsky M. Proliferative verrucous leukoplakia: a follow-up study of 54 cases. Oral Surg Oral Med Oral Pathol Oral Radiol Endod 1997;84:154–7.

Sugerman PB, Shillitoe EJ. The high-risk human papillomaviruses and oral cancer: evidence for and against a causal relationship. Oral Diseases 1997;3:130–47.

Takes RP, Baatenburg de Jong RJ, Schuuring E, et al. Diffences in expression of oncogenes and tumor suppressor genes in different sites of head and neck squamous cell. Anticancer Res 1998;18:4793–800.

van Merkesteyn JPR, Baker DJ, Borgmeijer-Hoelen AMMJ. Hyperbaric oxygen treatment of osteoradionecrosis of the mandible. Oral Surg Oral Med Oral Pathol Oral Radiol Endod 1995;80:12–6.

21 Immunopathologic Mucosal Lesions

Sol Silverman, Jr, MA, DDS, and L. Roy Eversole, DDS, MSD, MA

The immunopathologic mucosal diseases (vesiculobullous, vesiculoerosive) as a group present as somewhat commonly occurring inflammatory mucocutaneous lesions. In the mouth they can appear as erythematous mucosal changes with associated keratoses, ulcerations (erosive areas), desquamation, and occasionally, bullae. Frequently there is accompanying pain, varying from mild discomfort to severe symptoms that can alter significantly the ability to function. Although external irritants aggravate existing lesions, the etiology is on an idiopathic autoimmune basis.

The exact occurrence has not been established because of an absence of well-designed population-based studies, the often cyclical nature, and asymptomatic patients whose lesions are never diagnosed or recognized.

Lupus erythematosus and recurrent aphthous stomatitis are considered here, because both are immunopathologic conditions, and sometimes they are a confusing factor in the differential diagnosis.

Pathologic and molecular correlates of disease

Lichen planus

Lichen planus (LP) is a fairly common immunopathologic mucocutaneous disorder that is mediated by a T-

Diagnosis

The diagnosis is based upon a combination of clinical characteristics and biopsy. At times, immunofluorescent preparations of biopsied specimens aid in establishing the classification. These diseases can occur as either chronic or cyclical flares, and can appear independently or in combination in the mouth, lips, and skin. Other mucosal surfaces are occasionally involved, also.

The most common of these lesions is lichen planus, followed by pemphigoid, erythema multiforme, and pemphigus. Each condition has its own characteristics both clinically and microscopically. However, there can be an overlap of uncertain, confusing clinical changes, as well as a microscopically observed inflammation that is nonspecific and termed interface mucositis.

Figure 21–1 Histology of lichen planus. A band of lymphocytes, all of which immunolabel as T cells (both CD4 and CD8), infiltrates the epithelial–connective tissue interface.

lymphocyte reaction to antigenic stimuli residing in the epithelial layer (Figure 21–1). Immunomarker studies have disclosed that the lymphocyte population is exclusively T-cell in nature with a mixture of CD4 and CD8 lymphocytes that express integrin molecules of the α_1 Class (Figure 21–2). These integrin ligands bind to other adhesion molecules that are upregulated on endothelial cells (vascular cell adhesion molecule [VCAM]) and epithelial cells (intracellular adhesion molecules [ICAM]). Lower strata keratinocytes, which also express major histocompatibility complex class II (MHC-II) molecules (human leukocyte antigen-D/DR [HLA D/DR]) in lichen planus, are able to present antigens to cells bearing the CD4-associated T-cell receptor. CD8 lymphocytes are able to bind to antigen-complexed MHC-I molecules on keratinoctyes.

The basement membrane is altered in LP, and in this region, excessive amounts of fibrinogen are deposited, a feature with diagnostic value when direct immunfluorescence is applied (Figure 21–3, *A*). Other basement membrane molecules, such as fibronectin, laminin, and types IV and VII collagens are upregulated. Angiogenesis and vasodilation are considerably increased in lesional submucosa. In the inflamed epithelium, lower strata keratinocytes express and secrete chemokines that are chemotactic to lymphocytes. Thus, following antigenic challenge, lymphocytes adhere to vascular endothelia,

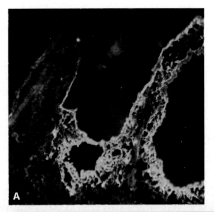

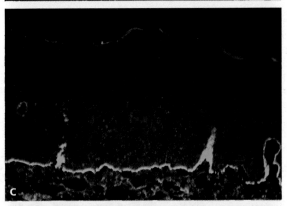

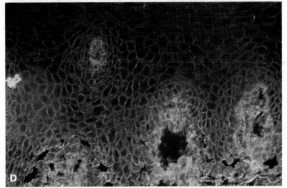

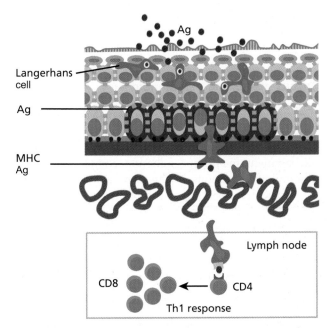

Figure 21–2 The afferent limb of immunoreactivity in lichen planus. Antigenic challenge comes from the external environment or may be the result of keratinocyte autoantigen expression. Dendritic Langerhans cells and antigen-bearing class II molecules on keratinocytes relay molecular information to reactive CD4 cells in the regional lymph nodes, which engender an effector T helper cell (Th1) pathway response. MHC = major histocompatibility complex; Ag = antigen.

Figure 21–3 Immunoflourescent patterns in bullous or desquamative oral lesions: *A*, sub-basement membrane deposition of fibrinogen in lichen planus; *B*, perivascular complement fraction 3 localization in erythema multiforme; *C*, basement membrane IgG deposition in mucous membrane pemphigoid; and *D*, pericellular, desmosomal localization of IgG in pemphigus vulgaris.

emigrate into the submucosa, and migrate under the influence of the epithelial secreted chemoattractant molecules. Lymphocytes are then able to adhere to extracellular matrix (ECM) molecules that are overproduced along the basement membrane. Upon crossing the epithelial–mesenchymal interface, ECM molecules are able to bind, via integrins, to cell-surface adhesion molecules pathologically expressed on keratinocytes (Figure 21–4).

Therefore, LP is a T-cell mediated immunologic mucosal and cutaneous disease and, as such, it responds to T-cell immunosuppressive drugs. As previously alluded to, the antigenic agent responsible for this reaction has remained elusive in most cases. This has prompted some investigators to propose an autoimmune pathogenesis.

Lichenoid is a term used to describe lesions that clinically and histologically can resemble LP. As an example, and although rare, some instances of LP-like lesions are found adjacent to corroding dental amalgams, and such lesions are referred to as contact lichenoid lesions. When such an association occurs, these lichenoid lesions resolve after removal of the adjacent amalgam. Both clinical and laboratory studies have shown delayed-type hypersensitivity to dental metals, particularly mercury. Another lichenoid process with a known allergenic challenging agent is the reaction to cinnamon. Clinically, the lesions are lichenoid, as they are histologically, manifesting a unique and characteristic perivascular lymphoid infiltrate in the submucosa. Lastly, with regard to pathogenesis, topically and systemically administered medications may cause a lichenoid drug reaction of skin and mucosa.

Erythema multiforme

Erythema multiforme (EM), a mucocutaneous inflammatory reaction, arises as a consequence of immune complex mechanisms. Although some cases are of unknown origin, the majority are sequelae to drug administration, usually sulfa drugs (both antibiotic sulfas and hypoglycemic sulfonylureas), or in some cases even represent postherpetic immune complex phenomena. In oral mucosal EM, herpes simplex virus (HSV) allergenicity is an uncommon associated factor. Furthermore, causative agents (antigens) are rarely identified in oral EM. However, in both cases, antigenic peptides form complexes with IgG complement-fixing immunoglobulins, and these complexes filter out into vessel walls, where they bind complement and initiate a leukocytic infiltrate, consisting of neutrophils and macrophages (Figure 21–3, B). These leukocytes release oxygen free radical species and lytic enzymes that culminate in necrosis of the epithelium, which results in bulla and diffuse desquamation (Figure 21–5). Some investigators have identified viral antigens and even viral DNA in EM lesions, yet no active infectious organisms are extant.

Mucous membrane pemphigoid

The mucous membrane pemphigoid (MMP) phenotype is the consequence of autoimmune humoral disease. The antigenic targets that become immunogens reside within the basement membrane adhesion complex (BMAC). Immunologic reactions in this region dissociate adhesion molecules, resulting in sub-basilar cells. The basal cells attach to this membrane via extracellular integrins and collagens, which bind ligands in the lamina lucida. These ligands include laminins 1, 5, and 6, which in turn extend into the lamina densa where they bind type IV collagen. The lamina densa is bound to the connective tissue collagens (types I and II) by anchoring fibrils comprised of type VII collagen (Figure 21–6). In bullous pemphigoid (BP) of skin, both BP antigen BP230 and collagen XII are the antigenic targets, which are bound by autoreactive complement-fixing IgG or IgM. Complement-binding to the BMAC stimulates leukocyte infiltration of the submucosa whereby neutrophils and macrophages may directly damage and dissociate the adhesion molecules.

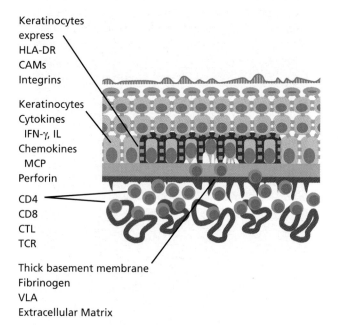

Keratinocytes
express
HLA-DR
CAMs
Integrins

Keratinocytes
Cytokines
  IFN-γ, IL
Chemokines
  MCP
Perforin

CD4
CD8
CTL
TCR

Thick basement membrane
Fibrinogen
VLA
Extracellular Matrix

Figure 21–4 The efferent limb of immunoreactivity in lichen planus. Reactive T cells leave submucosal vessels and enter the connective tissues. Chemokines from keratinocytes direct lymphocyte traffic along extracellular matrix using cell–matrix adhesion molecules. Cytotoxic T cells release perforin and other enzymes, which lyse basal cells, particularly in the erosive form of the disease. CAMS = cell adhesion molecules; CD4 = helper inducer T cells; CD8 = cytotoxic T cells; CTL = cytotoxic T lymphocyte; HLA-DR = human leukocyte antigen class II antigen presentation molecules; IFN-γ = interferon gamma; IL = interleukin; MCP = monocyte chemoattractant protein; TCR = T-cell antigen receptor; VLA = very late activation.

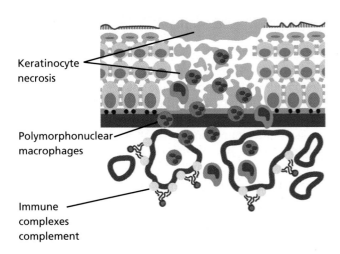

Keratinocyte
necrosis

Polymorphonuclear
macrophages

Immune
complexes
complement

Figure 21–5 Pathogenesis of immune complex vasculitis in erythema multifome. Immune complexes settle in vessel walls where complement fixation occurs and promulgates an inflammatory reaction with leukocyte trafficking into the submucosa and epithelium. Vasculitis may also contribute to ischemic necrosis of the overlying epithelium.

There are other antigenic targets in variants of MMP. Therefore, pemphigoid is a specific phenotype with sub-basilar cell separation and deposition of BMAC immunoreactants (Figure 21–3, C), characterized by a heterogeneous group of antigenic targets unique to the basement membrane. In linear IgA disease, a specific antigenic target resides in the lamina lucida. In antiepiligrin cicatricial pemphigoid, the target antigen is laminin-5 (epiligrin). It is noteworthy that these same adhesion molecules can be mutated in the inherited collective group of bullous diseases known as epidermolysis bullosa (EB). Oral lesions do in fact occur in the genetic forms of EB, and in one genotypic form, ameloblasts are damaged, with resultant enamel pitting and hypoplasia (see Clinical characteristics).

Pemphigus vulgaris

Pemphigus vulgaris (PV) is a disease that involves IgG and sometimes IgA and IgM autoantibodies directed to the intercellular desmosomal adhesion molecule desmoglein III. This molecule mediates cell–cell adhesion between contiguous keratinocytes, and when antibodies bind, they sterically interfere with the ability of the desmogleins to adhere to one another. The result is a suprabasilar clefting with acantholysis and a pericellular or desmosomal distribution of immunoreactants (Figure 21–3, D; Figure 21–7). There are some drugs, such as captopril and penicillamine, that possess sulfhydryl groups that can induce the formation of PV antibodies to desmoglein, a process that is reversible once the drug is withdrawn.

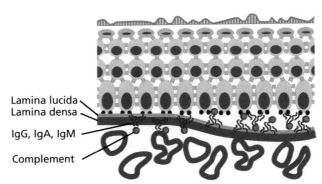

Lamina lucida
Lamina densa

IgG, IgA, IgM

Complement

Figure 21–6 The hemidesmosome basement membrane adhesion complex: basement membrane antigens and the pemphigoid phenotype. Numerous chemical species are involved in the adhesion of basal cells to the basement membrane. These adhesion molecules may become antigenic targets for IgG, and IgM complement-fixing antibodies as well as IgA.

Paraneoplastic pemphigus is a disease characterized by mucocutaneous bullae and ulcerations with a predilection for the lips and conjuntiva. These patients harbor an underlying neoplasm, usually lymphoma. Both suprabasilar clefting and lichenoid histologic presentations are seen. These patients have autoantibodies that target the desmoplakins, plaque proteins of the desmosome that are independent from desmoglein. A positive pericellular distribution of immunoreactants can be seen with indirect immunofluorescence using patient serum and urinary bladder epithelium as a substrate.

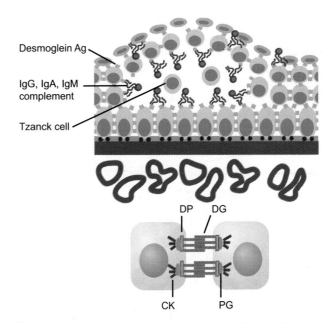

Desmoglein Ag

IgG, IgA, IgM
complement

Tzanck cell

DP   DG

CK   PG

Figure 21–7 Desmoglein is the antigenic target in pemphigus vulgaris. Antidesmoglein antibodies sterically interfere with the interaction of adhesion proteins with similar molecules on neighboring cell desmosomes. CK = cytokeratin; DG = desmoglein; DP = desmoplakin; PG = plakoglobin.

Lupus erythematosus

Lupus erythematosus (LE) is an autoimmune disease that is characterized by the presence of serum circulating antibodies directed against cell nucleus components. Antinuclear antibodies (ANA) are of major diagnostic importance in LE and include anti-DNA, antihistone, antiribonuclear, and antinucleolar antibodies. In addition, antibody directed toward basement membranes is demonstrable using direct immunofluorescent staining, generating the so-called lupus band test, which shows IgG and IgM localization along the skin and oral mucosal basement membranes. Immunoreactants are also localized to glomerular basement membranes in systemic lupus. Many other antibodies are found in lupus, which is now considered to be a dysregulation of immune tolerance to self antigens. These various autoantibodies form immune complexes, which are pathogenic and responsible for vascular and renal lesions seen in the disease.

Recurrent aphthous stomatitis

The earliest lesion of recurrent aphthous stomatitis is a preulcerative inflammatory focus within the oral epithelium that is characterized by an influx of T lymphocytes. Cytotoxic T cells appear to be directed to some antigenic determinant located on or within keratinocytes (Figure 21–8). The release of various immunoreactive cytokines and chemokines induces a cell-mediated response that is believed to result in keratinocyte lysis. Many studies have demonstrated both antibody and T cell-mediated immunologic reactions with oral keratinocytes; however, the antigen remains unidentified and could be a hapten, a virus, or an allergen. The antigenic stimulus, whatever it may be, is short-lived and focal, since the lesions are separated by unaffected mucosa and last only 10 to 14 days.

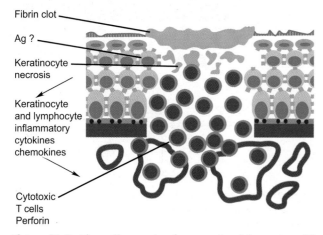

Fibrin clot

Ag ?

Keratinocyte necrosis

Keratinocyte and lymphocyte inflammatory cytokines chemokines

Cytotoxic T cells Perforin

Figure 21–8 The pathogenesis of recurrent aphthous stomatitis involves T cell infiltration to antigenic targets in the surface epithelium.

Lichen planus (LP) has a reticular form (reticular surface keratoses), an atrophic form (erythematous mucosa alternating with keratoses), and the erosive form (combination of ulcerations, erythematous mucosa, and keratosis) (Figure 21–9). The reticular form is characterized by lacey interconnecting stria of Wickham that occur typically on the buccal mucosa with extention into the mandibular vestibule, and such lesions are usually without symptoms. Gingival involvement is common, particularly in the erosive form, where it may present as desquamative gingivitis (a descriptive clinical term) with interspersed foci of keratosis. Over time, patients may exhibit all three forms of the disease and, therefore, show longitudinal variation in the manifestation of symptoms, since usually, only the atrophic and erosive forms are painful. Oral LP usually appears in midlife and is more common among females; it rarely occurs in children or even adolescents. Unusual presentations include a papular variant of the keratotic reticular form and a pigmented form in which white and red lesions can be associated with brown or black diffuse melanosis. The primary microscopic feature is hyperkeratosis combined with subepithelial white cell (mainly lymphocytic) infiltrate. Often there is deterioration of the basement membrane and irregular epithelial hyperplasia.

Pemphigoid can occur in a cicatricial or bullous form. The former is most common, and it most often occurs on mucosal surfaces. Clinically, it may present as an erythematous mucosal surface, and frequently, there are associated areas of pseudomembrane-covered erosive lesions stemming from ruptured vesicles (Figure 21–10). The most common site is the gingiva, where the lesions may present as a desquamative gingivitis. Other oral mucosal sites may be involved with or without gingival manifestations. Occasionally there is eye involvement, with scar tissue forming between the lower eye lid and the conjunctiva (symblepharon). There is a marked female predilection, and the lesions usually appear in mid- to late life.

Erythema multiforme is a hypersensitivity reaction that can occur as a mild to severe reaction. In mucosal erythema multiforme, an offending antigen cannot always be identified. The lesions may occur independently or in combination in the mouth, lips, and skin. They appear as nonspecific erythematous lesions and often as ulcerations that are irregular in appearance (Figure 21–11). Whereas any mucosal tissues can be involved, crusting ulcerations of the lips are often present. Multiple mucosal sites can be involved, and onset, whether for a chronic or cyclical form, is usually acute. When a triggering event can be identified, it is usually a sulfa drug (antibiotic and hypoglycemic). Erythema multiforme can be seen in either gender and at any age.

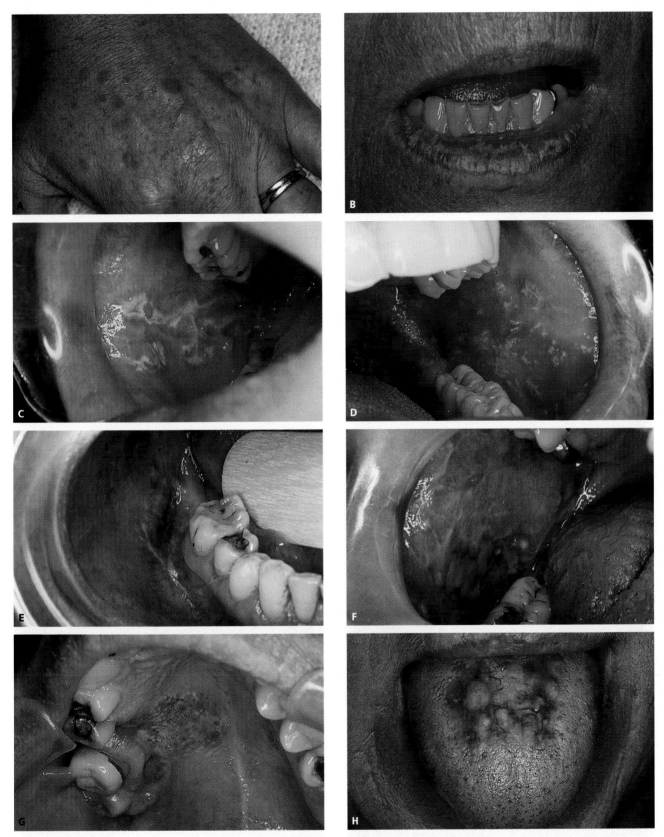

Figure 21–9 Lichen planus (LP) forms. *A*, Classic appearance of skin-involved LP. About 20% of patients with oral LP have a history or active skin lesions. *B*, Reticular LP occurring on the vermilion border of the lip. *C*, Classic reticular LP. *D*, Punctate LP that could be confused with leukoplakia, frictional keratosis, or candidiasis. *E*, A common site of atrophic LP in the posterior mandibular buccogingival reflex. It is usually bilateral. *F*, Erosive LP of the buccal mucosa. *G*, Erosive LP of the palate. *H*, Erosive LP of the tongue dorsum.

Pemphigus in the mouth is fairly uncommon but may occur prior to skin involvement; rarely, only oral lesions are present. The ulcerations of pemphigus are usually somewhat characteristic because of their irregular and cavernous appearance (Figure 21–12). There is often considerable associated pain. These ulcerations can occur anywhere in the mouth, with a common location being the pillar of fauces–soft palate region. The patients are usually adults, with both genders being equally affected.

Lesions of lupus erythematosus (LE), whether discoid or systemic, are rarely found in the mouth. When present, they can appear as nonspecific, chronic, red-white, erosive lesions (Figure 21–13). The diagnosis is based upon clinical suspicion, confirmation of LE involving skin or other organ systems, and suggestive microscopic findings.

Recurrent aphthous stomatitis (RAS) most typically presents as characteristic shallow single or multiple ulcerations with surrounding inflammatory halos (Figure 21–14). It recurs at varying intervals based upon patient differences and a variety of initiating physical and chemical factors. Almost always, RAS occurs on nonkeratinizing oral epithelium (buccal and labial mucosae, lateral and ventral tongue, floor of the mouth,

and soft palate). The diagnosis is usually supported by a history of recurrence, pain, and spontaneous healing. Whereas certain foods and local trauma can initiate these ulcers, the prime etiology appears to be based on lymphocytes that are chemotactically attracted to these various sites, which in turn pathologically react with epithelium. Before an ulcer becomes apparent, patients can often sense an aura of discomfort. Duration of RAS usually does not exceed 1 to 2 weeks.

Usually, RAS lesions do not exceed 5 mm, but they can be multiple. Sometimes, the clustering and irregularity in size almost suggests a hypersensitivity reaction (EM). When RAS ulcers exceed 6 mm, they are designated as major aphthae. This indicates a deeper inflammatory infiltrate, a longer duration, and increased pain. In immunocompromised patients, major aphthae can be confused with granulomatous or malignant lesions. If the diagnosis is indefinite or an ulcer persists, a biopsy is indicated. When RAS lesions are associated with genital or eye lesions, arthritis, or dermatologic pathoses (ie, erythema nodosum), the condition is termed Behçet's syndrome.

Epidermolysis bullosa is an incurable symptom complex, with the main oral finding being mucosal

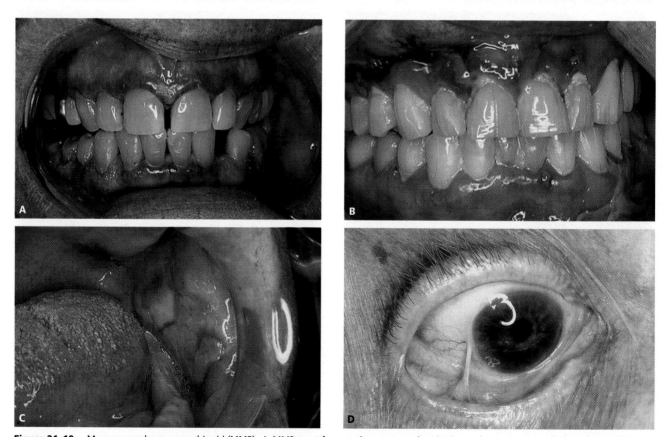

Figure 21–10 Mucous membrane pemphigoid (MMP). *A*, MMP most frequently occurs on the gingiva and appears as marked erythema. This presentation is often referred to as desquamative gingivitis. *B*, Ulcerative MMP of the gingiva. Note pseudomembrane-covered erosive areas from collapsed vesicles. *C*, Buccal involvement of MMP. *D*, A symblepharon occurring in a patient with oral lesions of MMP.

ulcerations that can vary from epithelial friability causing moderate dysfunction to life-threatening bullae.

With all these lesions, the differential diagnosis is of utmost importance. First, since these are chronic or recurring incurable immunologic diseases, patients and their primary care physicians desire an exact classification. In turn, this is necessary to justify the regimens of toxic drugs often required to control the symptoms and signs. It should always be kept in mind that dysplastic, or even malignant lesions, can resemble some of the clinical presentations, and this must be ruled out in the initial diagnosis as well as in follow-up.

Treatment

Since these diseases are chronic and incurable, management is focused upon the severity of symptoms and the patient's general health. The approach is to neutralize offending lymphocytes that do not recognize some host cells, releasing cytokines that initiate the inflammatory response and the signs and symptoms. Assurance that these are not infectious (contagious) diseases, and ruling out malignancy are both important components of management and patient care.

Systemically, the most useful drug to control the damaging lymphocyte response is prednisone. Usually 40 to 80 mg daily reduces signs and symptoms; if it is taken for

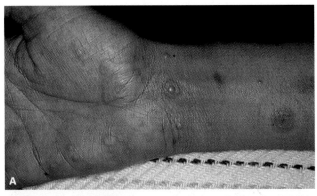

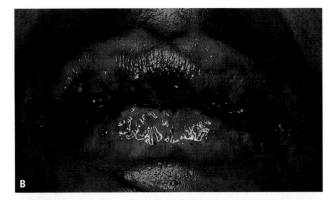

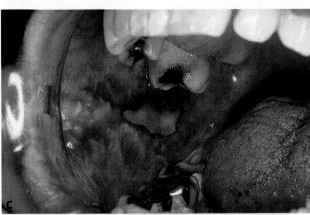

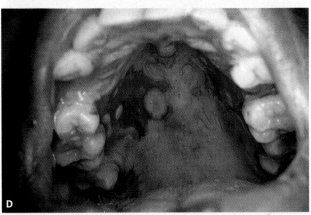

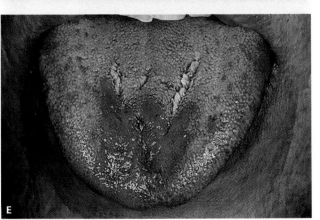

Figure 21–11 Erythema multiforme (EM). *A*, Classic "bull's-eye" lesion of EM involving skin. *B*, Acute EM of the lips present for 1 week. No antigen could be identified. The lesion responded to a combination of prednisone and azathioprine. *C*, EM involving the buccal mucosa. *D*, EM involving the palate. *E*, EM of the anterior tongue manifested by erythema, loss of filiform papillae, and burning pain. The spontaneous signs and symptoms, present for 2 weeks, disappeared after a 3-day course of systemic prednisone.

less than 2 weeks tapering is unnecessary. The philosophy of treatment is "high dose, short course." This minimizes the adverse side effects of longer-term therapy that might be necessary with a lower dose. If an increased dosage or time is required, then tapering is in order (Figures 21–15 to 21–17). The most common side effects from short-term administration of prednisone are insomnia, mood alterations, and fluid retention (bloating).

Care also must be taken in patients with certain systemic diseases. Prednisone converts liver and muscle glycogen to glucose, thereby putting diabetic patients at risk from hyperglycemia. Because of fluid retention from decreased sodium elimination, hypertension may create a problem. Potassium diuresis is a small problem, but can be accentuated in patients taking diuretics. This

can interfere with muscle function. Caution must also be taken in patients with a history of gastrointestinal ulcers, to avoid the possibility of promoting ulcer bleeding. Because of possible changes in ocular pressure, patients with glaucoma should be cleared before usage. Long-term administration of prednisone can complicate osteoporosis, because of calcium loss from bone and lack of replacement.

Sometimes, combining the cytotoxic (antimetabolite) drug azathioprine (Imuran) with prednisone synergistically enhances the anti-inflammatory effect. The usual effective daily supplemental dose when needed varies between 50 and 100 mg daily. At times, when a patient is intolerant to the prednisone dosage necessary to control signs and symptoms, a lower dose of pred-

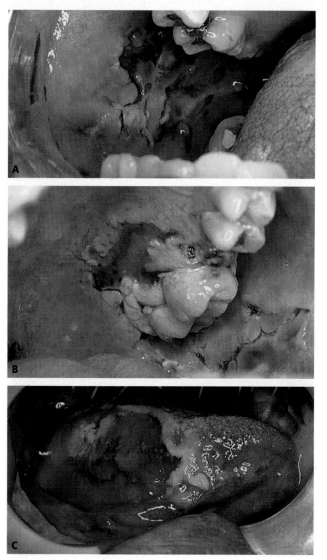

Figure 21–12 Pemphigus vulgaris (PV). *A,* PV of the buccal mucosa. The patient also had skin lesions. *B,* PV of the palate. The buccal mucosa were also involved. *C,* PV of the tongue in a patient who had skin involement that occurred after the oral lesions appeared.

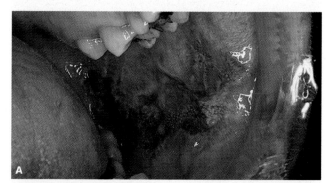

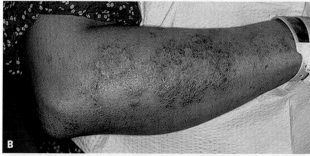

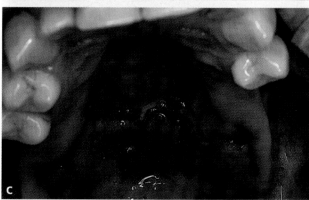

Figure 21–13 Lupus erythematosus (LE). *A,* Typical oral manifestation of LE on the buccal mucosa in a patient with the discoid form. (LE lesions can sometimes be confused with lichen planus.) *B,* Skin lesions of LE, seen in the same patient. *C,* An advanced palatal lesion of LE in a patient with systemic LE.

nisone can be made effective by adding azathioprine. The combination is also considered in patients with acutely severe inflammatory signs and symptoms.

Topical agents are used when there are medical reasons not to use systemic medication or if the patient has personal objections. In addition, topicals may be preferable for patients with mild disease. When used, the corticosteroids must be those with high potency, otherwise they are not effective. The corticosteroids that currently have shown topical efficacy are fluorinated (which increases the half-life and potency) and include fluocinonide (Lidex), clobetasol (Temovate), and halobetasol (Ultravate). They are all 0.05% and can be used as a gel, or the ointment form can be mixed with equal parts orabase as a paste. They can be applied up to three times daily, with long-term studies showing no adverse side effects (Figures 21–18 and 21–19). Mouthrinses

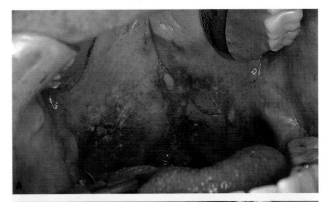

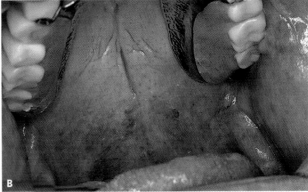

Figure 21–15 *A*, Painful mucous membrane pemphigoid present for more than 1 year. *B*, One week after daily oral intake of 80 mg of prednisone and 100 mg of azathioprine the signs and symptoms dramatically regressed. There were no adverse side effects, and the drugs were slowly tapered.

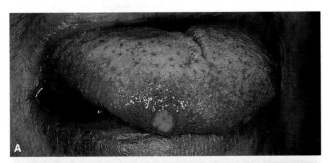

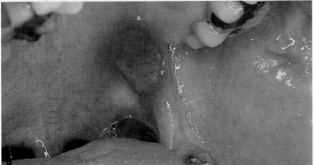

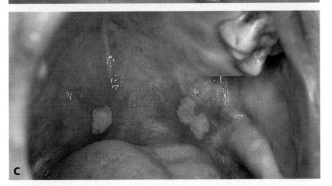

Figure 21–14 Recurrent aphthous stomatitis (RAS). *A*, Typical minor RAS in unkeratinized mucosa of the tongue. *B*, Major RAS of the soft palate. The patient would have about four attacks a year, without any evident initiating factor. *C*, Multiple RAS of unknown etiology. The attacks were almost constant, with only 2 to 3 weeks between flares.

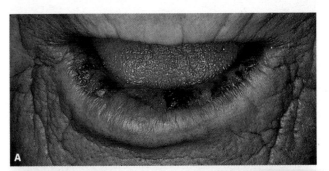

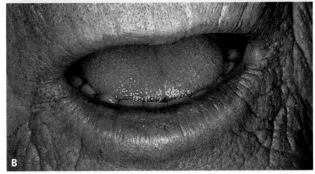

Figure 21–16 *A*, Erythema multiforme of unknown etiology present for 4 months. *B*, 60 mg of prednisone daily for 1 week led to remission. The patient would have occasional recurrences managed in the same manner.

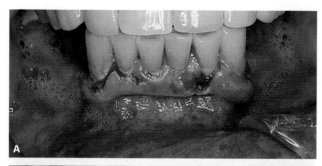

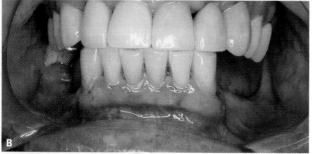

Figure 21–17 Pemphigus vulgaris present on the gingiva for 7 months, without any skin involvement. One week after 80 mg prednisone daily there was complete control. The patient was then maintained on topical corticosteroids.

also may be helpful. The one with which we have experience is elixir of dexamethasone, 0.5 mg/5mL (1 teaspoonful held in the mouth for up to 3 minutes, then spit out) used up to four times daily. No rinsing or eating for half an hour afterward is advised to have maximum tissue and lesion contact.

Sometimes the use of either systemic or topical corticosteroids causes a flare of candidal overgrowth (candidiasis). This is based upon the ability of these drugs to convert glycogen to glucose, leading to increased substrate upon which these yeasts (fungi) can feed, replicate, and infect. Topical or systemic antifungal medication can control this somewhat infrequent complication (see Chapter 18). Studies with the use of dapsone, thalidomide, cyclosporine, and levamisole to reduce the causative immunologic activity have been inconclusive. These treatments also incur risks of side effects and considerable expense.

In conclusion, a differential diagnosis of mucosal lesions must be established, the patient must be oriented to the chronic and benign nature of these diseases, and treatment must be symptom-specific. The patient's medical provider must be involved, so that there is a team approach to disease management. It is important to follow these patients periodically to reinforce the perception of chronicity, to manage flares, and to examine for

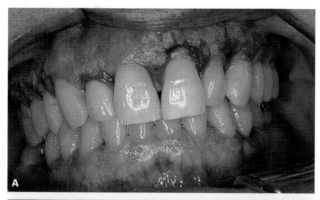

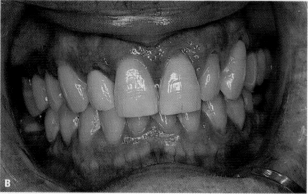

Figure 21–18 *A*, Painful erosive lichen planus of the gingiva present for 3 years. The patient preferred not to use systemic medication, if possible. *B*, After 2 weeks of fluocinonide ointment mixed with equal parts orabase applied three to five times daily, there was marked regression. The patient is now maintained with lower daily applications.

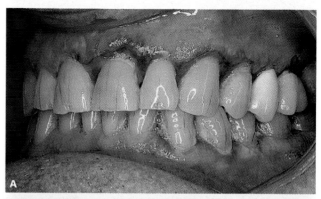

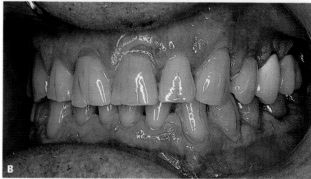

Figure 21–19 Painful mucous membrane pemphigoid present for 1 year. After 3 weeks of daily applications of fluocinonide paste (0.05% Lidex ointment mixed with equal parts orabase), there was control of the signs and symptoms.

the possibility of additional tissue changes. Follow-up is especially significant in oral LP, since there is a risk that a small number of LP patients (approximately 2%) may develop an oral squamous cell carcinoma over time.

Suggested reading

Anhault GJ, Kim S, Stanley JR. Paraneoplastic pemphigus: an autoimmune mucocutaneous disease associated with neoplasia. N Engl J Med 1990;323:1729–35.

Chainani-Wu N, Silverman S Jr, Lozada-Nur F, et al. Oral lichen planus: patient profile, disease progression and treatment responses. J Am Dent Assoc 2001;132:901–9.

Dabelsteen E. Molecular biological aspects of acquired bullous diseases. Crit Rev Oral Biol Med 1998;9:162–78.

De Rossi SS, Glick M. Lupus erythematosus: considerations for dentistry. J Am Dent Assoc 1998;129:330–39.

Eversole LR. Oral mucosal diseases. In: Millar HD, Mason DK, eds. 2nd World Workshop on Oral Medicine. Ann Arbor: University of Michigan, 1993.

Eversole LR. Immunopathology of oral mucosal ulcerative, desquamative, and bullous diseases. Selective review of the literature. Oral Surg Oral Med Oral Pathol 1994;77: 555–71.

Eversole LR. Immunopathogenesis of oral lichen planus and recurrent aphthous stomatitis. Semin Cutan Med Surg 1997;16:284–94.

Flier JS, Underhill LH. The hypothalamic-pituitary-adrenal axis and immune-mediated inflammation. N Engl J Med 1995;332:1351–60.

Jonsson R, Mountz J, Koopman W. Elucidating the pathogenesis of autoimmune disease: recent advances at the molecular level and relevance to oral mucosal disease. J Oral Pathol Med 1990;19:341–50.

Lamey PJ, Rees TD, Binnie WH, Rankin KV. Mucous membrane pemphigoid. Treatment experience at two institutions. Oral Surg Oral Med Oral Pathol 1992;74:50–3.

Lozada-Nur F, Miranda C, Maliski R. Double-blind clinical trial of 0.05% clobetasol propionate ointment in orabase and 0.05% fluocinonide ointment in orabase in the treatment of patients with oral vesiculoerosive diseases. Oral Surg Oral Med Oral Pathol 1994;77:598–604.

Lozada-Nur F, Miranda C. Oral lichen planus: topical and systemic therapy. Semin Cutan Med Surg 1997;16:295–300.

Lozada-Nur F, Shillitoe EJ. Erythema multiforme and herpes simplex virus. J Dent Res 1985;64:930–31.

Mobini N, Nagarwalla N, Ahmed R. Oral pemphigoid. Subset of cicatricial pemphigoid? Oral Surg Oral Med Oral Pathol Oral Radiol Endod 1998;85:37–43.

Porter SR, Kirby A, Olsen I, Barrett W. Immunologic aspects of dermal and oral lichen planus: a review. Oral Surg Oral Med Oral Pathol Oral Radiol Endod 1997;83:358–66.

Rojo-Morena JL, Bagan JV, Rojo-Moreno J, et al. Psychologic factors and oral lichen planus. Oral Surg Oral Med Oral Pathol Oral Radiol Endod 1998;86:687–91.

Scully C, Carrozzo M, Gandolfo S, et al. Update on mucous membrane pemphigoid. A heterogeneous immune-mediated subepithelial blistering entity. Oral Surg Oral Med Oral Pathol Oral Radiol Endod 1999;88:56–68.

Ship JA. Recurrent aphthous stomatitis: an update. Oral Surg Oral Med Oral Pathol Oral Radiol Endod 1996;81:141–7.

Silverman S Jr, Bahl S. Oral lichen planus update: clinical characteristics, treatment responses, and malignant transformation in 95 patients. Am J Dent 1997;10:259–63.

Silverman S Jr, Gorsky M, Lozada-Nur F, Giannotti K. A prospective study of findings and management in 214 patients with oral lichen planus. Oral Surg Oral Med Oral Pathol Oral Radiol Endod 1991;72:665–70.

Silverman S Jr, Lozada-Nur F, Migliorati C. Clinical efficacy of prednisone in the treatment of patients with oral inflammatory ulcerative diseases: a study of 55 patients. Oral Surg 1985;59:360–5.

Snow JL, Gibson LE. A pharmacogenetic basis for the safe and effective use of azathioprine and other thiopurine drugs in dermatologic patients. J Am Acad Dermatol 1995;32:114–16.

Vincent SD, Lilly GE, Baker KA. Clinical, historic, and therapeutic features of cicatricial pemphigoid. A literature review and open therapeutic trial with corticosteroids. Oral Surg Oral Med Oral Pathol 1993;76:453–9.

Weinberg MA, Insler MS, Campen RB. Mucocutaneous features of autoimmune blistering diseases. Oral Surg Oral Med Oral Pathol Oral Radiol Endod 1997;84:517–34.

Wood AJJ. Management of acquired bullous skin diseases. N Engl J Med 1995;333:1475–84.

22 Pigmentations of the Oral Mucosa and Facial Skin

L. Roy Eversole, DDS, MSD, MA, and Sol Silverman, Jr, MA, DDS

Blue, gray, and black skin and mucosal pigmented lesions are usually attributable to exogenous tattoos or melanin. Brown pigmentations are represented by either melanin or hemosiderin. Yellow discolorations may be the result of bilirubin deposition or the ingestion of large amounts of β-carotene. Blue and purple discolorations are generally the consequence of vascular lakes within the dermis or submucosal connective tissues. Pigmented lesions may be focal and macular or raised, or they may be diffuse or multifocal. In general, diffuse and multifocal pigmentation is attributable to melanosis, and there may be systemic or pharmacologic factors in the etiopathogenesis. The most common causes of oral pigmentations are genetic, related to ethnicity, and those caused by accidental amalgam implantation (Table 22–1).

Table 22–1 Pigmentations of the Facial Skin and Oral Mucosa

Lesion	Macular	Nodular	Papillary
Focal	Amalgam tattoo Graphite tattoo Ephelis, melanotic macule, melanoacanthoma Junctional nevus Blue nevus Ecchymosis, petechia Macular hemangioma, Kaposi sarcoma	Compound and intradermal (mucosal) nevi Seborrheic keratosis (skin) Angiomas, varices, Kaposi sarcoma Melanoma	
Diffuse	Physiologic (ethnic) pigmentation Addison disease, Cushing syndrome McCune-Albright syndrome Neurofibromatosis Peutz-Jeghers syndrome Minocycline HIV-associated oral melanosis Smoker's melanosis Melasma, chloasma	Malignant melanoma Kaposi sarcoma	Acanthosis nigricans Black or brown hairy tongue

Molecular and pathologic correlates of disease

Exogenous pigments in the oral mucosa are iatrogenic or traumatically introduced; amalgam is the most common. Cavity preparation of a tooth with an existing restoration results in the entrapment of fine particles in the fissures of the rotary bur. Laceration of the soft tissue deposits the particles in the submucosa (Figure 22–1). The silver particles in the amalgam slowly leach out and stain reticulum fibers. If there are other materials admixed with amalgam particles, a foreign body giant cell reaction is seen microscopically. There are no untoward effects of amalgam tattoos, the pigment remaining in place for the patient's lifetime. Graphite, from lead pencils, is another source of exogenous pigment. Deposition usually occurs in the palate when some poor unfortunate sole has placed their pencil between the upper and lower teeth with the lead resting against the hard palate. Someone accidently bumps them and the graphite is fractured off the pencil tip and deposited into the palatal tissues.

Blood pigments are deposited in the connective tissues as a consequence of extravasation. Erythrocytes are lysed, releasing hemoglobin. The hemoglobin is converted by enzymes into hemosiderin, which in turn is broken down to bilirubin and biliverdin, which are phagocytized and cleared in the spleen. Blood pigments are usually cleared from the skin or mucosa within 2 weeks. The extravasation is attributable to trauma, capillary fragility, platelet defects, or clotting-factor disorders.

Melanocytic lesions all involve synthesis of melanin pigment granules by melanocytes. When there is no melanocytic proliferation, only increased synthesis of melanin in melanocyte-containing melanosomes, the pigment is released into the basilar keratinocytes, and when their capacity to retain this pigment is exceeded, pigment spills into the underlying connective tissues. These processes are referred to as basilar melanosis and melanin incontinence, respectively (see Figure 22–1). Keratinocytes containing melanin migrate to the surface. During this maturation process, the melanin is broken down by intracellular proteolytic enzymes.

On skin, melanosis occurs in response to excessive sun exposure. In the mouth, melanosis may occur in traumatized areas, and the traumatized epithelia that regenerate may do so with concomitant overproduction of melanin by melanocytes that repopulate the region. Other stimuli for melanin production are certain hormones and drugs. The adrenal cortical–hypothalamic axis is affected by hypofunction of the adrenal cortex. As serum corticosteroid levels decline, adrenocorticotropic hormone (ACTH) production by the posterior pituitary increases, and because ACTH has melanocyte stimulatory function, it can induce melanosis. Minocycline is a

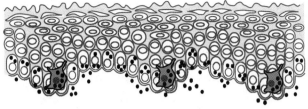

Oral melanotic macule
"increased melanin synthesis"

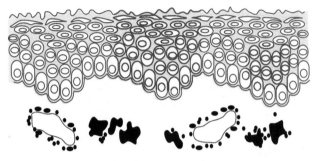

Amalgam and graphite tatoos
"extrinsic pigments"

Figure 22–1   Illustration of basilar melanosis with incontinence into the submucosa (*top*) and pigmentation resulting from traumatic implantation of amalgam or graphite into the connective tissues (*bottom*).

tetracycline derivative that is used to treat acne. It has been shown to stimulate mucosal melanocytes to produce excessive amounts of melanin pigment; the mechanism is unknown.

Melanin pigment is synthesized in melanocytes by a progression of molecular events that take place within small membrane-bound organelles, the premelanosomes. As the biochemical processes progress, the pigment becomes compacted into electron dense melanosomes. Tyrosinase is a key enzyme required for the synthesis of melanin pigment; the corresponding gene is mutated in albinism. Thus, albinos contain normal numbers of melanocytes, but they are unable to produce melanin. On the other hand, vitiligo is a term describing acquired depigmented patches caused by a dimished number of melanocytes.

Proliferation of melanocytes occurs in benign nevi and in melanoma. Melanocytic nevi develop during childhood and rarely arise in adult life. Most nevi originate as basal layer melanocytes that proliferate in the lower strata of the epithelium along the junction with the connective tissue, and are therefore termed junctional nevi (Figure 22–2 and Figure 22–3, A). Later, the nevocytes (melanocytes) drop off into the connective tissue to form theques and islands, a feature that labels them as compound nevi. Their eventual fate is to leave the surface epithelium entirely, whereby all the clusters of nevus cells reside in the dermis or submucosa as

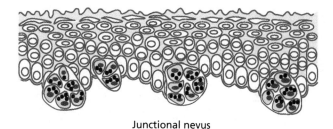

Junctional nevus

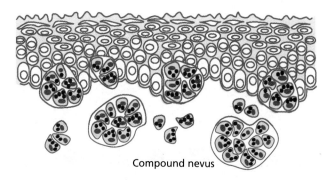

Compound nevus

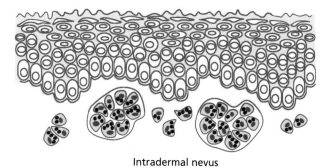

Intradermal nevus

Figure 22–2 Illustration of the progression of nevi from junctional to compound to intramucosal (intradermal).

intradermal or intramucosal nevi (Figure 22–3, *B*). Junctional activity is generally lost by age 18. Blue nevi are unique in that they arise from dermal or mucosal melanocytes that remained in the connective tissues during embryonic neural crest migration and, therefore, did not evolve from junctional nevi. Blue nevi are comprised of spindle-shaped melanocytes that synthesize copious amounts of melanin pigment (Figure 22–3, *C*).

Malignant transformation of melanocytes can often be attributed to genetic alterations that result from solar radiation. The earliest change is junctional. In an adult, junctional proliferation with nuclear atypia is referred to as atypical melanocytic hyperplasia. When cytologic atypia becomes more advanced, the lesions are superficial spreading melanomas (Figure 22–3, *D*). When invasion of the connective tissue ensues, they are invasive or nodular melanomas and metastatic potential has been reached. There are pathologic stages that correlate the depth or level of invasion with survival. The Clark classification

system for skin is commonly used for this purpose (Figure 22–4). Malignant melanocytes confined to the epithelium represents level I, invasion into the superficial papillary dermis is level II, invasion through the papillary dermis down to the reticular dermis is level III, invasion through the reticular dermis is level IV, and deep invasion of the subcutaneous fat is level V. The Breslow system utilizes a micrometer to precisely measure depth of invasion.

Focal pigmentations

Melanotic macule, ephelis

Ephelides, or freckles, are generated or intensified by sun exposure to the skin. They are commonly seen on the faces of redheads and appear as small brown macules. Focal macular pigmentations of the oral mucosa and lower lip are mucosal equivalents to the ephelis and are termed oral melanotic macules. On the lip, there is often a history of trauma. Intraoral melanotic macules are most often seen on the gingiva, palate, and lips, but can be found anywhere in the mouth, including the tongue. They are usually small, brown or black, and have smooth borders (Figure 22–5). Biopsy confirmation is recommended to rule out a melanocytic proliferation. Melanotic macules are focal forms of basilar melanosis, a nonproliferative process. A unique form of melanotic macule is the melanoacanthoma, a lesion usually encountered in persons of native African descent. This form of macule is microscopically characterized by basilar melanosis with concomitant presence of dendritic, pigment-forming melanocytes spread throughout an acanthotic spinous cell layer.

The differential diagnosis on the skin includes senile lentigo or age spots, melanoacanthoma, and superficial spreading melanoma The latter two can arise in oral mucosa.

Melanocytic nevi

As previously discussed, junctional, compound, intramucosal, and blue nevi can arise on the face or in the mouth. Junctional nevi are macular and brown, whereas blue nevi are black or blue, because the melanin pigment is deep within the connective tissue (Figure 22–6). Compound and intramucosal nevi typically present as nodules that are round and symmetric. Most, yet not all, compound and intramucosal nevi are pigmented. On the face, nevi can arise in any location. In the mouth, nevi are more often encountered on fixed mucosa of the palate and gingiva. Biopsy is recommended to confirm the diagnosis, because unlike skin nevi, oral nevi are rare, and it is prudent to obtain histologic confirmation.

Amalgam and graphite tattoo

Tattoos are iatrogenic or factitial and represent the most common focal pigmentation of the oral mucosa.

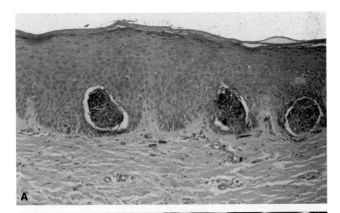

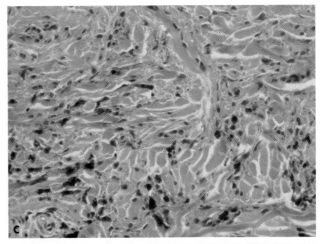

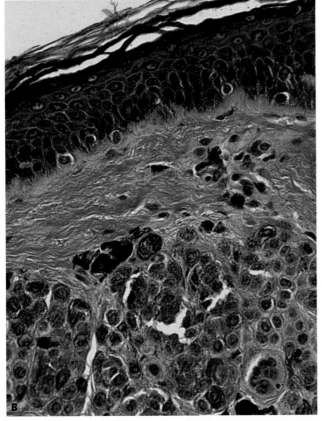

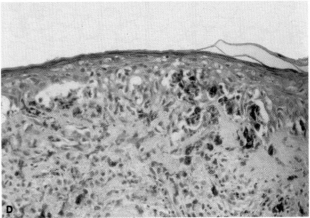

Figure 22–3 Microscopic appearance of, *A*, junctional nevus, *B*, intradermal nevus, *C*, blue nevus, and *D*, malignant melanoma.

Amalgam tattoos are introduced during condensation of amalgam fillings or cavity preparation of an existing alloy-filled tooth, or caused by fragments that may break away during tooth extraction and fall into open extraction sites. Another source is through leaching of a retrofilled endodontically treated tooth in which there is an opening from the cortex to the gingiva or vestibule. The pigment is usually black or gray, unlike the brown pigmentations seen with melanin and blood pigments (Figure 22–7). In general, amalgam tattoos are located adjacent to a restored tooth. A radiograph is recommended to confirm the presence of foreign metallic particles. When there is no evidence of amalgam on the radiograph and there is no adjacent restored tooth, biopsy is recommended to rule out a melanocytic lesion. It should be recalled that failure to detect an opacity from an amalgam tattoo may be encountered when the imbedded particles are below the resolution of dental radiographs.

Graphite tattoos are black or gray and are typically found in the hard palate where a pencil lead was accidentally and traumatically implanted. This usually occurs in individuals who hold pencils between their teeth with the pencil point inside the mouth. Both amalgam and graphite are inert, yet a foreign body reaction is sometimes encountered.

Ecchymosis

Trauma to the soft tissues of the skin and mucosa often lead to venous severage with extravasation of erythrocytes. These bruises or ecchymoses are bright red if the traumatic episode is recent and superficial, or after 2 days they are "black and blue" or, more often, brown, owing to conversion of hemoglobin to hemosiderin (Figure 22–8). If there is no history of trauma, a coagu-

Clark levels

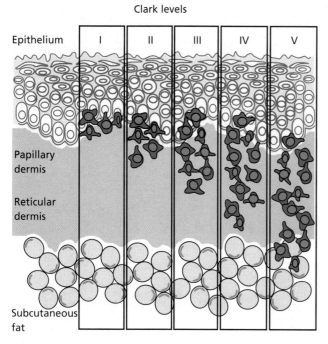

Figure 22–4 Diagram showing Clark classification of levels of invasion in cutaneous malignant melanoma. This classification is not applicable to mucosal melanomas, since the submucosal tissue layers are different.

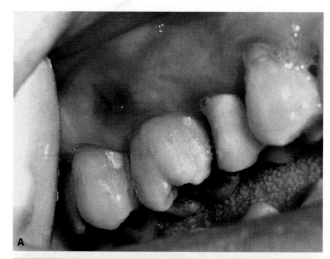

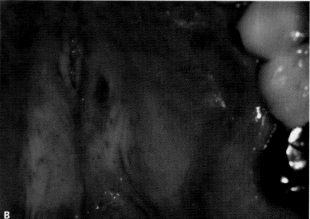

Figure 22–6 *A,* Intramucosal nevus; *B,* intraoral blue nevus.

lopathy or platelet disorder should be suspected, and a hematologic evaluation (prothrombin time, partial thromboplastin time, platelet count, and platelet aggregation assay) should be obtained (see Chapter 7). Because the blood pigments are extravascular, diascopy or point-pressure yields no blanching.

Angiomas

Vascular anomalies are discussed in more detail in Chapter 25. Blood vascular growths (hemangiomas) are usually

raised nodules or multinodular lesions that are red, blue, and purple; however, some are flat and macular. These macular hemangiomas can be red or purple. Trauma to the lower lip often damages venous channels, with forma-

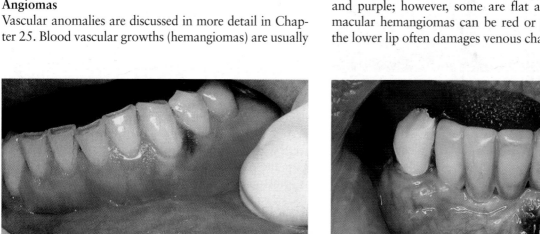

Figure 22–5 Oral melanotic macule.

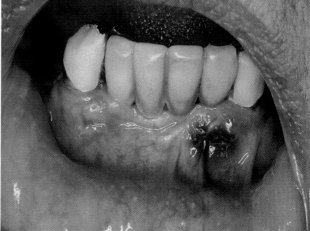

Figure 22–7 Amalgam tattoo.

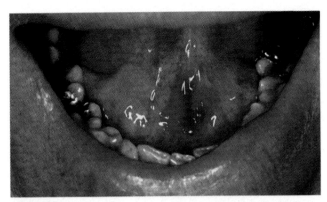

Figure 22–8   Ecchymosis.

tion of a varix (Figure 22–9, A). Diascopy of the lesions usually produces blanching, since the erythrocytes yielding the pigment changes are located within the lumens of vessels. In children, treatment is generally withheld, since most hemangiomas spontaneously regress after puberty. The hemangiomas seen in the Sturge-Weber syndrome, port-wine stains, and the blue rubber bleb nevus syn-

drome do not regress. In persistant small hemangiomas and varices of the oral cavity and face, sclerotherapy with injection Sotradecol® or laser ablation are treatment options. Kaposi sarcoma appears as a red, blue, purple, or brown mucosal lesion that can be macular or tumefactive (Figure 22–9, B). This unique form of human immunodeficiency virus (HIV)-associated angiosarcoma is described in detail in Chapter 14. Lymphangiomas and hemangiomas are discussed in Chapter 25.

Melanoma

Melanomas of the facial skin are commonly found on the forehead and malar skin, areas that are prominent and subject to direct sun exposure. Early lesions are macular, can vary greatly in size, and are characterized by two major clinical findings that distinguish melanoma from nevi. First, they tend to show pigment heterogeneity. The pigment varies from black to brown to gray, and there are foci of depigmentation. Secondly, the borders tend to be irregular. Melanotic freckle of Hutchinson is the term applied to these flat early melanomas that are histologically represented by super-

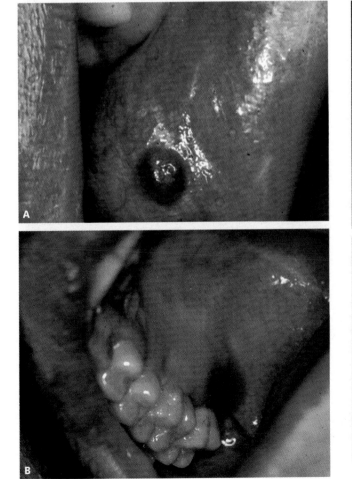

Figure 22–9   A, Varix. B, Kaposi sarcoma.

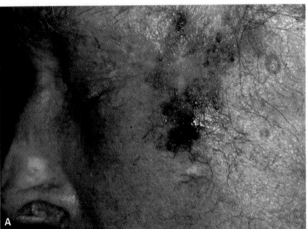

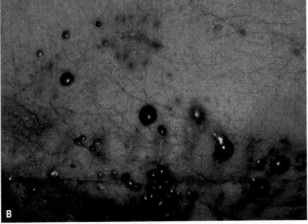

Figure 22–10   A, Superficial spreading melanoma of facial skin. B, Nodular melanoma with satellite lesions.

ficial spreading melanoma (Figure 22–10, *A*). These varigated lesions may ultimately progress to nodular lesions that are also pigmented, tumefactive, and often ulcerated. Nodular melanoma is microscopically invasive, and the prognosis worsens with increasing Clark or Breslow levels of invasion (Figure 22–10, *B*).

Oral melanomas are extremely rare and can present as macular superficial spreading lesions or as invasive nodular tumefactions (Figure 22–11). For unknown reasons, they are more common in certain islands of Japan than in other parts of the world. Oral melanomas have a predilection for the anterior maxillary gingiva and palate. However, they can occur on any mucosal surface. They are black, gray, or brown and, like skin, may harbor foci of depigmentation. Because of the poor prognosis for oral melanomas, treatment requires extensive surgical excision, often followed by radiation therapy. Vaccines remain experimental. Although melanomas are rare in the mouth, suspicious pigmented lesions should be biopsied. There is no concrete evidence that an incisional biopsy encourages metastases.

Diffuse and multiple pigmentations

Diffuse pigmentations are generally forms of basilar melanosis and appear brown or gray. The facial skin and oral mucosa may appear yellow in jaundice (see Chapter 6) and yellow-orange in patients who consume excess carotenoids, primarily beta carotene.

Physiologic pigmentation

Most Caucasians and Asians manifest coral pink oral mucous membranes. Black individuals, many Mediterranean region Caucasians, Asians, and Hispanics who are dark skinned often have pink mucosa with widespread diffuse macular fields of brown, gray, or even black pigmentation. This physiologic melanosis can be found anywhere in the mouth, the facial gingiva being the most common location (Figure 22–12).

Black or brown hairy tongue

Elongation of the filiform papillae is accompanied by superficial pigments in the condition known as hairy tongue. These pigments are derived from foods and endogenous oral bacteria (Figure 22–13). This condition is described in Chapter 25.

Smoker's melanosis

Patchy brown macular pigmentations are sometimes present in the buccal mucosa among heavy cigarette smokers. These macules are 0.5 to 1.0 cm spots that are multiple and bilateral (Figure 22–14). Microscopically they are forms of basilar melanosis without melanocyte proliferation. The mechanism for this association is unknown.

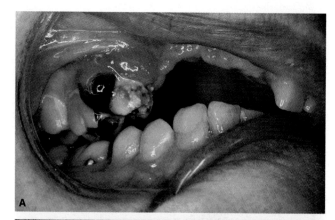
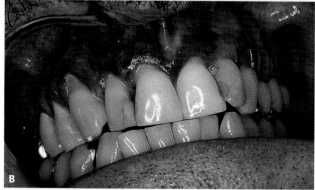

Figure 22–11 Oral mucosal melanoma. *A*, Nodular melanoma of the gingiva. *B*, Gingival melanoma.

Addison disease

Adrenal cortical insufficiency is the consequence of destructive pathologic processes, such as neoplasms and inflammatory lesions. Decreased corticosteroid production leads to increased ACTH, a hormone with melanocyte stimulatory action. As a consequence, the skin darkens or becomes bronzed and multifocal pig-

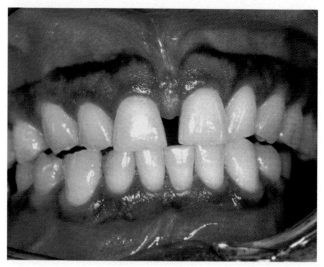

Figure 22–12 Physiologic oral mucosal diffuse pigmentation.

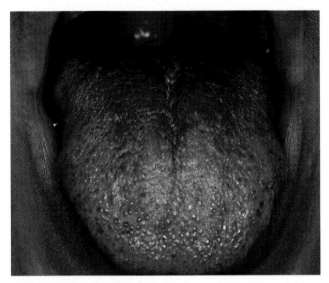

Figure 22–13 Brown hairy tongue.

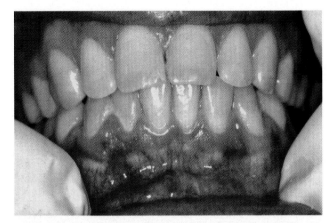

Figure 22–15 Oral melanotic pigmentation in Addison disease.

mentations appear in the mucous membranes of the oral cavity, conjunctiva, and genital regions (Figure 22–15). A tumor of the posterior pituitary or certain small cell carcinomas may also secrete excessive amounts of ACTH with the same pigmentary changes. In ACTH-secreting tumors, the patient manifests features of the Cushing syndrome (see Chapter 9).

Café au lait pigmentation

Bronze and tan diffuse and multifocal macular pigmentations appear on the skin in neurofibromatosis, an autosomal dominantly inherited disease characterized by multiple skin nodules or even pendulous tumors. These pale brown macules may be several centimeters wide (Figure 22–16). They can occur anywhere, including the face and neck, and occasionally, oral mucosal pigmentations arise. Owing to their pale brown color, they are referred to as café au lait spots. Similar pig-

mented lesions occur in the McCune-Albright syndrome, an osseous disease with endocrine accompaniments. Severe fibrous dysplasia is polyostotic in this syndrome and may affect the jaws and facial bones. In addition, patients can develop thyroid goiter, and females may undergo precocious puberty.

Acanthosis nigricans

The diffuse pigmentations seen in acanthosis nigricans are encountered in the context of papillary surface changes. This disease can affect the oral mucosa as well as skin and may be a harbinger of gastrointestinal cancer. It is discussed in more detail in Chapter 15.

Minocycline melanosis

The tetracycline derivative minocycline is used to treat acne and is, therefore, a drug that is consumed over a long period. In some patients undergoing minocyline therapy, oral pigmentations evolve. They are broad brown, gray, or black foci of pigmentation accounted for by the presence of basilar melanosis. Most minocycline melanotic lesions are located in the palate (Figure 22–17).

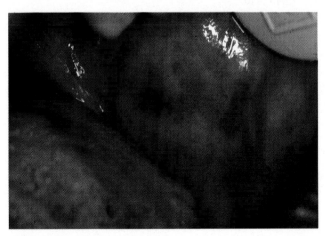

Figure 22–14 Smoker's melanosis.

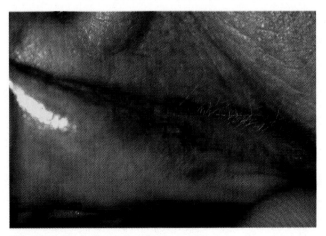

Figure 22–16 Café au lait melanotic patch.

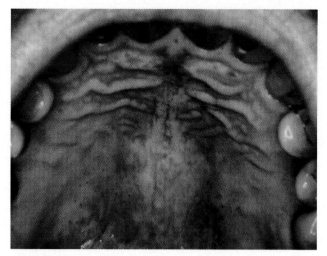

Figure 22–17 Minocycline-induced oral melanosis.

Melasma, chloasma

Melasma, the so-called mask of pregnancy, is a pigmentary lesion of the facial skin that occurs in the third trimester. Chloasma is clinically identical, yet occurs in patients taking birth control pills. These basilar melanoses of the skin may also involve the lips, indeed, perioral and periorbital diffuse brown macular pigmentations are the hallmark of these two conditions (Figure 22–18). Following delivery and upon cessation of birth-control administration, the cutaneous lesions slowly involute. Their genesis is probabably related to hormonal changes that affect melanosome stimulation.

Peutz-Jeghers syndrome

Hereditary intestinal polyposis syndromes are variable, some leading to colorectal carcinoma. The polyps encountered in the Peutz-Jeghers syndrome are hamartomatous and do not have a propensity for malignant transformation, although these patients may also develop adenomatous polyps that may indeed undergo carcinomatous change. There are numerous small peri-

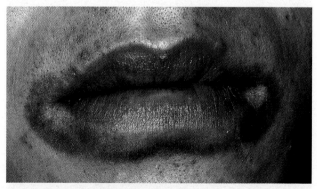

Figure 22–18 Chloasma presenting with perioral pigmentation in a woman who takes the birth control pill.

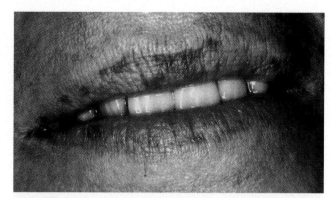

Figure 22–19 Perioral melanotic macules in Peutz-Jeghers syndrome.

oral macular pigmentations that appear around the mouth and on the fingers (Figure 22–19). When these lesions are encountered, the patient should be questioned about any gastrointestinal complaints and a family history of polyps. No treatment is necessary.

Suggested reading

Barrett AW, Bennett JH, Speight PM. A clinicopathological and immunohistochemical analysis of primary oral mucosal melanoma. Eur J Cancer Oral Oncol 1995;31:100–5.

Buchner A, Leider AS, Carpenter WM, Littner MM. Melanocytic nevi of the oral mucosa: a clinicopathologic study of 60 new cases. Refu Hashinayim 1990;8:3–8.

Buchner A, Leider AS, Merrell PW, Carpenter WM. Melanocytic nevi of the oral mucosa: a clinicopathologic study of 130 cases from northern California. J Oral Pathol Med 1990;19:197–201.

Doval DC, Rao CR, Saitha KS, et al. Malignant melanoma of the oral cavity: report of 14 cases from a regional cancer centre. Eur J Surg Oncol 1996;22:245–9.

Eisen D, Hakim MD. Minocycline-induced pigmentation. Incidence, prevention, and management. Drug Saf 1998; 18:431–40.

Eisen D, Voorhees JJ. Oral melanoma and other pigmented lesions of the oral cavity. J Am Acad Dermatol 1991;24: 527–37.

Gorsky M, Epstein JB. Melanoma arising from the mucosal surfaces of the head and neck. Oral Surg Oral Med Oral Pathol Oral Radiol Endod 1998;86:715–9.

Heine BT, Drummond JF, Damm DD, Heine RD 2nd. Bilateral oral melanoacanthoma. Gen Dent 1996;44:451–2.

Kaugars GE, Heise AP, Riley WT, et al. Oral melanotic macules. A review of 353 cases. Oral Surg Oral Med Oral Pathol 1993;76:59–61.

Kitagawa S, Townsend BL, Hebert AA. Peutz-Jeghers syndrome. Dermatol Clin 1995;13:127–33.

Moghadam BK, Gier RE. Melanin pigmentation disorders of the skin and oral mucosa. Compendium 1991;12:14,16–20.

Nandapalan V, Roland NJ, Helliwell TR, et al. Mucosal melanoma of the head and neck. Clin Otolaryngol 1998;23: 107–16.

Ramirez-Amador V, Esquivel-Pedraza L, Caballero-Mendoza E, et al. Oral manifestations as a hallmark of malignant acanthosis nigricans. J Oral Pathol Med 1999;28: 278–81.

Tyler MT, Ficarra G, Silverman S Jr, et al. Malignant acanthosis nigricans with florid papillary oral lesions. Oral Surg Oral Med Oral Pathol Oral Radiol Endod 1996;81: 445–9.

WESTOP Group. Oral mucosal melanomas: The WESTOP Banff Workshop Proceedings. Oral Surg Oral Med Oral Pathol Oral Radiol Endod 1997;83:672–79.

Swellings and Tumors of the Oral Cavity and Face

L. Roy Eversole, DDS, MSD, MA, and Sol Silverman, Jr, MA, DDS

The primary disease processes that give rise to swellings and tumors of the oral cavity include cysts, mucous extravasation and retention in the minor salivary glands, foci of granulation tissue and inflammation, abscesses and connective-tissue proliferations that are well defined or encapsulated, as well as infiltrative sarcomas. Figure 23–1 is a representation of the processes that cause soft-tissue tumefactions in the mouth. Both epithelial and connective-tissue disease processes can present as masses. Benign and malignant surface epithelial tumors are discussed in the Chapters 15 and 20, respectively. From a clinical perspective the three most important defining characteristics of any soft-tissue swelling are location, coloration, and palpable nature.

As for location, certain diseases tend to occur in specific sites to the exclusion of others. Table 23–1 lists the most common lesions according to site. This is not to say that these sites are exclusive, since many lesions can in fact occur anywhere in the mouth; rather, this tabulation catalogues the most likely lesions for that site in terms of overall prevalence. Coloration is dependent upon the tissues present in the mass and the depth of the lesion. Table 23–2 lists the most frequently encountered colorations observed with soft-tissue masses and indicates the lesions that most often present with a given coloration. In general, yellow-appearing lesions are comprised of lymphoid tissue or adipose tissue, red

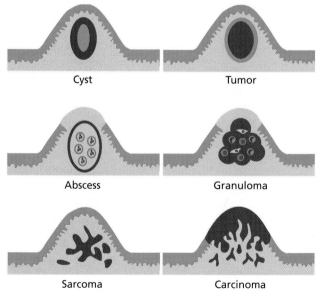

Figure 23–1 Schematic diagram showing the various pathologic processes that can manifest as a submucosal or subcutaneous mass.

Table 23–1 Orofacial Soft-Tissue Swellings according to Site

Site	Type of Lesion
Intraoral	
Lips and buccal mucosa	Fibroma, mucocele, mesenchymal tumor, salivary tumor, squamous cell carcinoma
Gingiva	Parulis, pyogenic granuloma, peripheral fibroma, peripheral giant cell granuloma, peripheral ossifying fibroma, gingival cyst, peripheral odontogenic tumors, squamous cell carcinoma
Palate	Abscess, torus, salivary gland tumor
Dorsolateral tongue	Fibroma, granular cell tumor, pyogenic granuloma, squamous cell carcinoma
Ventral tongue and oral floor	Mucocele, ranula, lymphoid aggregates, lymphoepithelial cyst, osteocartilagenous choristoma, squamous cell carcinoma
Face and neck swellings	
Masseteric region	Cellulitis, space infection, jaw cysts and tumors, masseteric hypertrophy
Parotid region	Sialadenitis, sialolithiasis, salivary neoplasm
Submandibular region	Lymphadenopathy, sialolithiasis, salivary neoplasm
Lateral neck	Lymphadenopathy, mesenchymal neoplasm, branchial cleft cyst, metastatic carcinoma, lymphoma, carotid body tumor
Anterior neck	Goiter, thyroid neoplasm, thyroglossal cyst
Face	Seborrheic keratosis, basal cell carcinoma, adnexal skin tumors, squamous cell carcinoma, melanoma

swellings are vascular, blue swellings are mucinous or venous, and brown swellings contain melanin or blood pigments. Lesions with normal mucosal pink coloration are generally composed of fibrous tissues or some other tissues lying deeper in the connective tissues.

Table 23–3 groups swellings according to their palpation characteristics. Firm movable masses are usually neoplasms or granulomas; soft movable masses are fatty or myxoid tumors; fluctuant masses are cysts, mucoceles or mucous-duct retention cysts and abscesses; and indurated fixed masses are probably malignant and may represent carcinomas, salivary adenocarcinomas, lymphomas, and sarcomas.

In terms of frequency, the majority of oral mucosal masses are reactive proliferations, such as fibrous hyperplasias, pyogenic granulomas, and mucous extravasation reactions. Mesenchymal and salivary neoplasms are uncommon, and lymphomas and sarcomas are rare causes of oral swelling. Indeed, the probability that a mucosal mass is a reactive or hyperplastic process is probably 50-fold compared to a true neoplastic process. In most instances, biopsy is necessary to arrive at a definitive diagnosis. Aspiration or incision and drainage may be performed as a diagnostic procedure when the mass is consistant with an abscess.

Molecular and pathologic correlates of disease

The molecular aspects or oral soft-tissue swellings are poorly understood and have not received much attention in the experimental literature. Conversely, the underlying pathologic processes associated with the various lesions

that produce tumefaction in the oral cavity are well defined in the oral and maxillofacial pathology literature.

As an overview of pathologic mechanisms, basic concepts are briefly presented here. The common masses that represent hyperplasias evolve as a consequence of irritation to the mucosal tissues by a dental appliance or by trauma, often the consquence of biting. The injured tissues respond to chronic and sometimes acute injury by proliferation of cells. The most commonly encountered hyperplasias are those involving fibroblasts. Injury to connective tissue results in fibroblastic proliferation of a benign nature, followed by collagen fibrillogenesis. Many fibrous hyperplasias are comprised of loose collagen and are soft to palpation, such as denture-induced fibrous hyperplasia and the common traumatic fibromas of the tongue and labial and buccal mucosae. In the gingiva, the periodontal tissues may be the targets of injury, particularly from irritants that may become entrapped in the gingival sulcus. Calculus, food particles, and foreign objects may be introduced into the sulcus, where they irritate the

Table 23–2 Masses with Coloration or Pigmentation

Color	Soft-Tissue Mass
Blue–purple	Hemangioma, varix, hematoma, peripheral giant cell granuloma, mucocele, Kaposi sarcoma
Red	Hemangioma, pyogenic granuloma, Kaposi sarcoma
Brown	Nevus, hematoma, seborrheic keratosis, Kaposi sarcoma, melanoma
Black	Melanoma
Yellow–orange	Lymphoid aggregates, lymphoepithelial cyst, lipoma, granular cell tumor

Table 23–3 Masses according to Palpation Characteristic

Palpation Characteristic	Mass
Soft, fluctuant	Mucocele, ranula
	Developmental cysts
	Sialocysts
	Gingival cysts
	Parulis
	Space infections and abscesses
Soft, nonfluctuant	Lipoma
	Fibroma
	Organized mucocele
Firm, movable	Mesenchymal tumors
	Granulomas
	Salivary adenomas
	Adnexal skin tumors
Firm, fixed	Granular cell tumor
	Seborrheic keratosis
	Keratoacanthoma
	Fibromatosis
Indurated, fixed	Basal cell carcinoma
	Salivary adenocarcinomas
	Squamous cell carcinoma
	Melanoma
	Sarcomas
	Lymphomas

fibrovascular connective tissues, periosteum, and periodontal ligament fibrous tissues. Proliferation of the fibrovascular connective tissue, along with inflammation, gives rise to pyogenic granulomas, whereas proliferation of the periosteal tissues, which contain osteoblasts and osteoclasts, gives rise to peripheral giant cell granulomas. When periodontal ligament fibroblasts proliferate, they retain the potential to elaborate bone and cementum, thereby giving rise to peripheral ossifying fibromas.

Minor salivary glands are located everywhere in the oral cavity except on the anterior dorsal tongue and the attached gingiva. They are most easily damaged from accidental biting in the lower lip and sometimes in the buccal mucosa, whereas injuries to the palatal and upper lip glands are rare. Therefore, severence of the minor gland ducts after an acute biting episode frequently leads to mucous extravasation into the connective tissues of the lips and buccal mucosa. In these mucoceles, the extravasated mucus becomes encapsulated, or walled-off, by fibrous and granulation tissues, giving the appearance of a cyst. Less commonly, mucous plugs form in the ducts of minor glands and cause retention of mucus. The ducts undergo cystic dilation and are epithelial lined; such lesions are referred to as mucous retention cysts or sialocysts. Although rare, true salivary stones may arise in minor salivary ducts, and as they grow, they result in an enlargement within the submucosa that is movable and hard.

Acute infections of the soft tissues are uncommon; however, occasionally a foreign body, such as a small fish bone or material from a dental procedure may be implanted into the soft tissues and cause an acute reaction. These submucosal fluctuant abscesses are more often seen on the tongue. Of course the most common location for abscess in the oral cavity is the gingiva and vestibule. In such instances the abscess is a parulis from odontogenic infection or a periodontal abscess arising in a periodontal pocket. Pulp vitality testing of adjacent teeth, periapical radiographs, periodontal probing, and aspiration are all important procedures when attempting to establish a definitive diagnosis. For accurate cultures procured for identifying causative microorganisms, a pure suppurate is essential; this is to avoid contaminants.

Chronic foci of inflammation may also account for submucosal masses. Lymph nodes are located in the buccal mucosa and in health are not palpable. Sometimes they become irritated or drain a local viral or bacterial infection and become enlarged. This enlargement is referred to as reactive lymphoid hyperplasia in which both T cells and germinal-center B cells undergo immune-mediated proliferation. Foreign bodies, in addition to acute infections, may induce granuloma formation. Recall that many foreign bodies can cause a giant cell reaction with accompanying chronically inflamed granulation tissue. Oral mucosal foreign body granulomas are seen with many dental materials, including amalgam and dental cements, handpiece oil (oil granulomas), and vegetable particles (legume or pulse granulomas).

A group of idiopathic diseases, collectively known as orofacial granulomatosis, is histologically characterized by multiple, often confluent foci of granulation tissue with giant cell formation in the absence of foreign material or a specific infectious agent. These are termed noncaseating granulomas, because unlike the granulomas of tuberculosis, there is no focus of caseous necrosis. Included in the orofacial granulomatosis group of lesions are Crohn disease, sarcoidosis, Melkersson-Rosenthal syndrome, and cheilitis granulomatosa (see Chapter 24). Submucosal masses comprised of granulomas also occur in response to infectious agents and are known as specific granulomatous inflammatory lesions. Included here are such specific infections as tuberculosis and deep fungal infections, the most common of which is histoplasmosis. The specific infectious granulomas are typically multinodular with an erythematous granular surface. Wegener granulomatosis is a systemic disease with multiple organ involvement that also manifests as a red granular swelling, usually confined to the fixed gingiva, so-called strawberry gums.

Swellings that diffusely involve the gingiva are the result of pathologic leukocytic infiltrates, such as might be encountered in leukemia, proliferation of granulation tissue in instances of nonspecific hyperplastic gingivitis, and overproduction of collagen in cases of drug-induced gingival hyperplasia (eg, Dilantin, nifedipine, cyclosporine), or the rare hereditary condition, familial fibromatosis gingivae.

As stated previously, true connective-tissue neoplasms are uncommonly seen in the oral cavity as compared with reactive and inflammatory masses. They may derive from any of the submucosal tissues, such as fibroblasts, lipocytes, nerve sheath, smooth muscle, skeletal muscle, vessels, osteoblasts, and chondroblasts. Sarcomas of these tissues are extremely rare. The proliferations contain cellular elements that are histogenically related to the normal tissues from which they arise and are named according to their histologic differentiation. The benign entities derived from mesenchymal or connective-tissues are variably encapsulated or are at least well circumscribed. A specific microscopic diagnosis is essential, since not all connective-tissue tumors behave in the same way. Some are aggressive, such as myofibromatoses, and have a tendency for local recurrence. Others are benign and have no tendency for recurrence after excision.

Minor salivary tumors also present as submucosal masses (see Chapter 26). They are most commonly found in the palate and buccal mucosa, but can arise in any location where minor glands are located. Clinically, benign salivary gland tumors are nonulcerated and show normal surface coloration, whereas the malignant types often exhibit surface telangiectasia, can be ulcerated, and are usually firm to palpation, owing to cellular proliferation. As with connective-tissue tumors, the salivary adenomas and adenocarcinomas are classified according to histologic patterns of differentiation. Recall that normal glands are comprised of ducts, acini, and myoepithelial cells. The various salivary-gland tumors are segregated and classified according to the patterns of these various cell types. The common pleomorphic adenoma is a lesion comprised of benign proliferations of ducts and myoepithelial cells. In the malignant category, adenoid cystic carcinoma and polymorphous low-grade adenocarcinoma are composed of solid-tumor islands with additional foci of ductal formations. Mucoepidermoid carcinoma shows both acinar and ductal cells with squamous (epidermoid) and mucous acinar cell differentiation. Mucoepidermoid carcinomas show variations in cell patterns that allow for assignment into low- or high-grade subgroups that correlate with good and poor prognosis, respectively.

Masses of the facial skin can also, as in the mouth, be represented by inflammatory, infectious, developmental, and neoplastic processes. Diffuse swellings occur in edematous states and in inflammatory conditions, such as dental-space infections, cellulitis, and allergic reactions. Focal masses are often the consequence of either benign or malignant tumors that arise from the surface epithelium, adnexal structures (hair follicles, sweat glands, sebaceous glands), and the dermal connective tissues. The most common focal cancerous swelling of the face is basal cell carcinoma. It has been shown that these tumors, as well as those associated with the basal cell nevus syndrome, harbor mutations in the "patched" gene, a membrane tumor suppressor involved in the sonic hedgehog morphogen pathway. Jaw keratocysts harbor these same mutations.

Clinical features of oral swellings

The clinical features for the more common mucosal swellings vary according to each specific entity. As has already been emphasized, it is crucial that the clinician take note of the location, coloration, surface texture, and palpable nature of the mass before attempting to secure a definitive diagnosis. If the lesion shows the features of an abscess, then diagnostic testing for odontogenic or periodontal origin must be performed by obtaining radiographs, pocket probing, pulp vitality testing, and identifying pyogenic suppuration. If no apparent infectious source is uncovered, then biopsy may be the chief method for procurement of a definitive diagnosis. In the case of diffuse gingival enlargement, interrogation with regard to drug use is imperative. As in all cases of oral lesions, the clinician must obtain a thorough medical history, knowing that some swellings may be associated with systemic diseases. When biopsy is to be undertaken, a decision must be made as to whether the biopsy will be incisional or excisional, a consideration based on both the size of the lesion and the possibility of malignancy. If malignancy has a high priority in the differential diagnosis, then incisional biopsy is indicated (see Chapter 20). The lesional and diagnostic tissue lies deep in the submucosa, and therefore, an incisional biopsy must be taken to a significant depth within the tumefaction. A wedge or pie-shaped incisional biopsy is advisable in these situations, to get an adequate specimen.

Traumatic fibroma

Focal fibrous hyperplasia as a consequence of trauma underlies the pathogenesis of this common benign oral tumor. It is pink in color yet may have a white keratotic surface if it is repeatedly irritated. Most fibromas are round, dome shaped sessile, soft masses (Figure 23–2). They vary greatly in size and are usually asymptomatic. The most common sites are the lips, commissures, buccal mucosa, and tongue. When traumatic fibromas occur on the gingiva they are commonly referred to as peripheral fibromas. Some show unique histologic features and are designated gingival fibromas. Another variant that can occur anywhere in the mouth is the

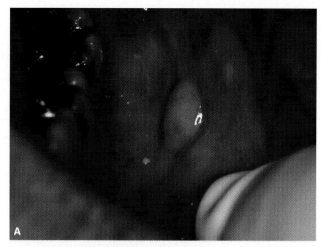

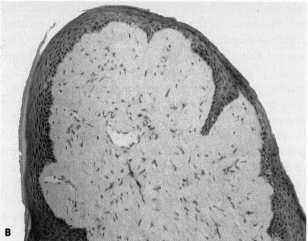

Figure 23–2 *A*, Clinical appearance of traumatic (irritation) fibroma; *B*, microscopic appearance of fibroma.

giant cell fibroma, not to be confused with giant cell granuloma, an aggressive lesion of the gingiva. Fibromas are treated by simple excision as well as trying to identify and remove a possible causative irritant, which is not often apparent.

Inflammatory fibrous (denture) hyperplasia

The irritation from an overextended denture flange can irritate the submucosal connective tissue. This tends to occur under dentures when alveolar ridge resorption has caused the denture to overseat. The irritating flanges induce multinodular flabby masses along the maxillary or mandibular vestibule (Figure 23–3). This so-called epulis fissuratum, an older term for fibrous hyperplasia associated with denture irritation, was used in a descriptive sense because so many of these common lesions are lobulated, with intervening fissural depressions. The most common locations are the anterior maxillary and mandibular vestibules, but they can be located anywhere along the sites of denture compression and irritation. Recall that in the palatal vault denture hyperplasias are diffuse and papillary, a lesion termed inflammatory papillary hyperplasia.

Mucous extravasation phenomenon (mucocele)

Mucoceles are the result of minor salivary gland duct severage with resultant escape of mucus into the submucosal connective tissues. With no conduit for excretion, the mucus collects in the connective tissues, creating a pseudocyst (they lack an epithelial lining) which becomes walled-off with granulation tissue and if not removed, the wall becomes fibrotic. The duct severage is the consequence of biting, usually in the lower lip. Mucoceles rarely involve the upper lip yet may occur at any site where minor salivary glands are located.

The clinical presentation is that of a soft-tissue cyst that is soft and fluctuant (Figure 23–4). When superficial they are faintly blue; if walled-off or fibrosed they may feel more solid and have normal mucosal coloration. Occasionally, the patient pops the lesion (with a pin or by biting) and it resolves; however, it usually recurs. More often, is the tendency to remain or even enlarge. Surgical excision of the cystic tissue should be accompanied by removal of the underlying "feeder" minor glands. Large mucoceles in the floor of the mouth arise from severage of the sublingual or even the major submandibular duct and are referred to as ranulas. Some of these mucous extravasations extend deeply into the intrinsic muscles of the tongue and mylohyoid, so-called plunging ranulas.

Mucous retention cyst

True cysts of the minor salivary ducts are referred to as mucous retention cysts or sialocysts. These lesions mani-

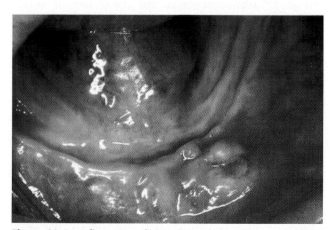

Figure 23–3 Inflammatory fibrous hyperplasia under a mandibular denture.

fest the same clinical characteristics as the mucocele, being soft fluctuant bluish masses. Whereas some are probably true blind cysts lined by salivary ductal epithelium, others are ductal dilatations that develop as a consequence of ductal obstruction or occlusion by mucous plugs. These latter retentive cysts tend to occur in the buccal mucosa of older adults. Treatment is complete excision.

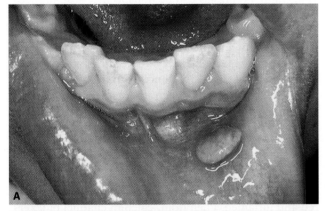

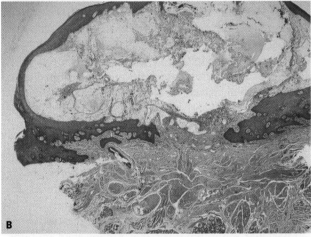

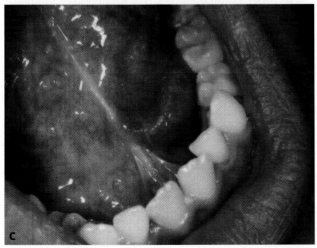

Figure 23–4   *A*, Mucocele of the lower lip; *B*, photomicrograph showing pooling of mucin under the surface epithelium with minor gland lobules in the deeper connective tissue; *C*, ranula in the floor of the mouth.

Reactive gingival tumefactions

Four pathologically related proliferations are encountered on the gingiva, usually arising in the interdental or gingival papilla region. All are reactions to irritation from calculus or particles that become wedged into the gingival sulcus (toothpick fragments, popcorn kernels, etc.). The host reacts to the irritant by hyperplasia of the endogenous tissues in the site, which include fibrovascular connective tissues, periodontal ligament fibroblasts, and periosteal tissues. Proliferation of granulation tissue gives rise to *pyogenic granulomas*, which may fibrose to peripheral *fibroma*; periodontal ligament cells give rise to cells capable of osteogenesis and cementogenesis, causing the *ossifying fibroma*; periosteal progenitor cells, including osteoblasts and osteoclasts, proliferate, producing a lesion termed *peripheral giant cell granuloma* (Figure 23–5). The term peripheral is employed to distinguish these common lesions from their less common counterparts that arise within the jaw bones. Pyogenic granulomas and peripheral ossifying fibromas are common in pregnancy.

Clinically either facial-buccal or lingual gingiva may be involved and there may be a history of rapid growth. The pyogenic granuloma is usually red; fibromas and ossifying fibromas are pale pink; and giant cell granulomas are bluish; and all can become ulcerated with a white pseudomembranous surface (Figure 23–6, 23–7, and 23–8). The peripheral giant cell granuloma is the more aggressive of these lesions, often eroding underlying alveolar bone and even causing root resorption (Figure 23–9).

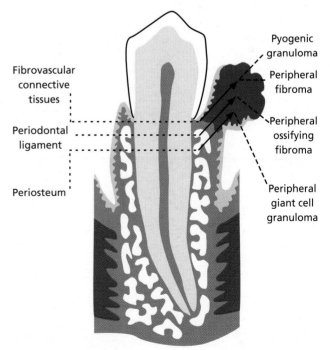

Figure 23–5   Diagram depicting the various reactive lesions of the gingiva.

Wide surgical excision is the treatment. Recurrence occurs in over 20% of the cases, which can be minimized by adequate surgical excision coupled with root planing.

Peripheral odontogenic cysts and tumors

Although odontogenic tumors are encounted central in the jaws, recall that the dental lamina arises from the alveolar mucosa, and odontogenic rests, which can give rise to neoplasms and cysts, are located in the gingiva. The most common entity is the gingival cyst of the adult, a lesion that appears as a nodule on the attached gingiva and may erode the underlying cortex (Figure 23–10). Benign odontogenic tumors also occur here, the periph-

eral odontogenic fibroma being the most common (Figure 23–11). Rare peripheral odontogenic tumors that appear as gingival masses include ameloblastoma, dentinogenic ghost-cell tumor, and calcifying epithelial odontogenic tumor.

Diffuse gingival enlargements

Gingival hyperplasias can be nonspecific, drug-induced, hormonally-related, granulomatous, or even neoplastic. Nonspecific gingival hyperplasias often have the appearance of multifocal pyogenic granulomas, being soft, hemorrhagic, and fiery red. There is a systemic underlying hormonal influence in the pathogenesis of hyperplastic gingivitis when the patient is a female entering puberty or gravid (Figure 23–12). Such instances are often referred to as puberty and pregnancy gingivitis, respectively. The gingival lesions are typically associated with formation of pseudopockets.

Drug-induced gingival hyperplasias are diffuse, and the lesions may be of normal coral pink coloration or red and inflamed. Phenytoin, calcium channel blockers, and cyclosporine used in the treatment of seizure disorders, hypertension and cardiovascular disease, and immunosuppression for organ transplantation, respectively, are all responsible (Figures 23–13 and 23–14). The fibrosis of cyclosporine enlargement is not limited to the gingival tissues; indeed, renal, pulmonary, and retroperitoneal fibrosis are complications of this drug. These lesions do not resolve with drug withdrawal.

Familial fibromatosis gingivae is a rare disorder that is inherited as an autosomal dominant trait. The enlarged gingivae are firmly fibrotic and devoid of significant inflammatory erythema as a rule (Figure 23–15). Periodic gingivectomies are often requested by the patient for esthetic as well as functional reasons.

Wegener granulomatosis is a multisystem immunopathologic disease that affects the lungs, kidneys, skin, and middle ear. The enlarged gingiva is red and granular, often termed strawberry gums (Figure 23–16). A histopathologic diagnosis of Wegener granulomatosis warrants a systemic workup to examine for other sites of involvement. The serologic marker antineutrophil cytoplasmic antibody (ANCA) is of diagnostic importance, being found in over 85% of cases.

Varix

Focal varices are most common in the lower lip and are probably the consequence of trauma, such as lip biting, to the submucosal vessels. Venous channels proliferate and become dilatated. These lesions may be flat or, more often, raised blue or purple masses (Figure 23–17). Some will blanch on diascopy (exerting direct pressure on the

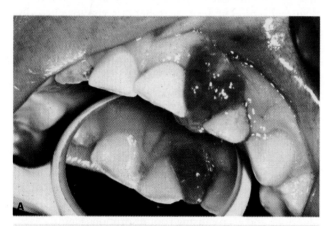
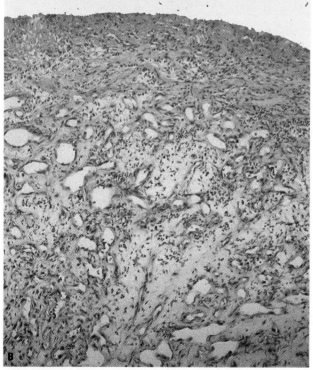

Figure 23–6 *A,* Pyogenic granuloma with red coloration; *B,* photomicrograph of pyogenic granuloma showing fibrovascular tissues.

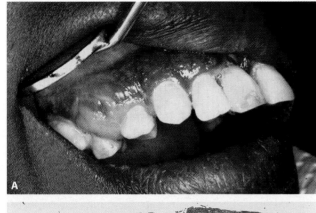

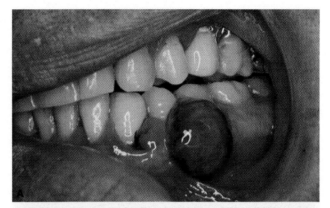

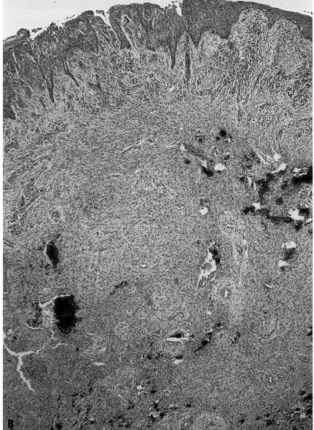

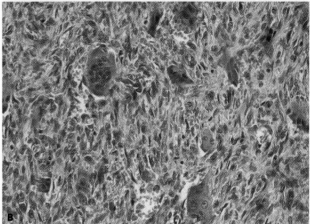

Figure 23–8 *A*, Peripheral giant cell granuloma; *B*, photomicrograph depicted the multifocal nature of giant cell granuloma extending to the base of the cut margin.

Figure 23–7 *A*, Peripheral ossifying fibroma is coral pink in color; *B*, photomicrograph of peripheral ossifying fibroma.

gated mass of the lower lip. The lesion is usually of normal color because the vessel is deep and surrounded by the usual arterial muscularis coat. Sometimes pulsations can be observed visibly; in others palpation is required to detect the pulsatile nature of this vascular anomaly. If the patient elects to have the lesion removed, the

lesion to detect blanching of vascular channels). Those that fail to blanch are often thrombosed. Treatment is elective. Injection with a sclerosing agent, such as Sotradecol™, may be effective. Surgical excision and laser ablation are common treatment options.

Pulsatile labial artery

The labial branch artery may develop a small aneurysmal dilatation that appears as a nodule or linear elon-

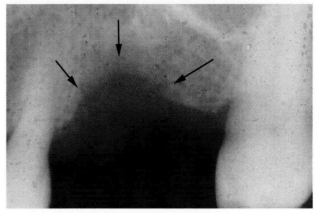

Figure 23–9 Radiograph showing saucerized zone of alveolar ridge resorption from an overlying peripheral giant cell granuloma.

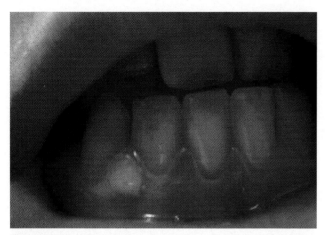

Figure 23–10   Gingival cyst.

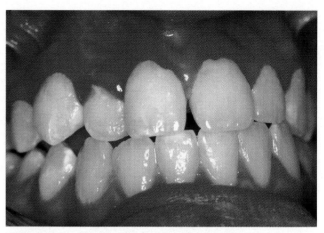

Figure 23–12   Nonspecific puberty-associated hyperplastic gingivitis.

mucosa should be incised and the vessel blunt dissected, followed by ligation and excision.

Parulis

Odontogenic infections that evolve into periapical inflammatory lesions may perforate the cortex, with drainage into the oral soft tissues. Focal drainage of an acute inflammatory process creates a tract that delivers suppurative material into the gingival submucosa. These drainage tracts may occur anywhere from the free gingival margin down to the vestibule (Figure 23–18). This submucosal abscess, or parulis, is associated with an endodontically involved necrotic tooth. Radiographs and pulp vitalometry testing disclose the incriminating tooth. If all teeth in the region of the parulis are vital, then the lesion may represent a focal periodontal abscess, and in such cases, a deep pocket is identifiable and probing causes exudation.

Specific granulomas

Granulomatous inflammation is characterized by granulomas with multinucleated giant cells. This type of histologic reaction is seen in foreign body reactions, orofacial granulomatosis, and such specific infections as tuberculosis and deep fungal infections. Specific granulomas occur most often in the tongue, vestibule, and buccal mucosa, where they appear as submucosal nodules, some being multinodular. Foreign body reactions are commonly found to contain fruit or vegetable material (pulse granulomas), dental materials, or oil from handpieces, thereby representing iatrogenic lesions. Granulomas that represent specific microbial infections are often red with a granular "strawberry" appearance. They are generally firm to palpation. Biopsy with specific microbial stains usually allows the pathologist to identify the genus of the microorganism. Orofacial granulomatosis includes sarcoid, sarcoid-like diseases, and Crohn disease (see Chapter 24).

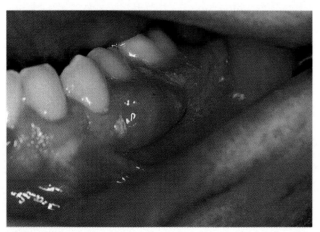

Figure 23–11   Peripheral odontogenic fibroma appearing as a gingival mass.

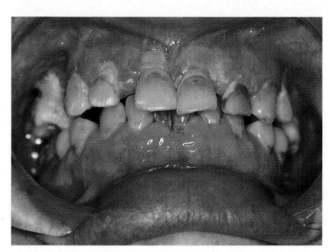

Figure 23–13   Dilantin-induced gingival hyperplasia.

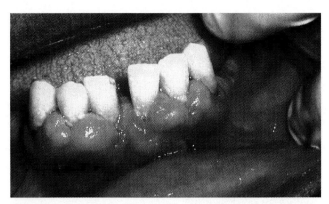

Figure 23–14 Gingival enlargement associated with a calcium channel blocker.

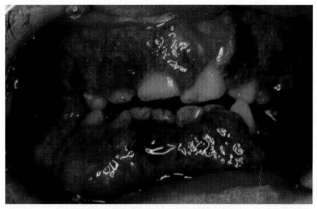

Figure 23–16 The "strawberry gums" of Wegener granulomatosis.

Ectopic lymphoid tissue and benign lymphoepithelial cysts

Ectopic lymphoid tissue is commonly seen in the oral cavity where it appears as a yellow nodular or multinodular mass (Figure 23–19). The common sites are the floor of the mouth and the soft palate. Many of these lymphoid aggregates emulate tonsilar tissue in that epithelial lined crypts extend into the lymphoid tissue and some become impacted with keratin, exhibiting a cystic appearance.

Amyloidosis

Amyloid is a pathologic fibrillar protein that accumulates within the connective tissues and is associated with certain neoplasms. Chemically, there are over 15 separate varieties, yet only three are of clinical significance: amyloid light chain (AL) protein, derived from plasma-cell-generated immunoglobulin light chains; amyloid-associated (AA) protein, which is made in the liver, and

beta-2-microglobulin. Amyloid light chain protein is associated with primary amyloidosis and becomes deposited in tissues in patients with B lymphocyte proliferations, multiple myeloma being the most prevalent. Amyloid-associated protein is deposited in secondary amyloidosis, such as inflammatory lesions and tuberculosis, and beta-2 microglobulin is associated with long-term renal dialysis. In the oral cavity, these deposits are usually encountered on the tongue as multiple or, less

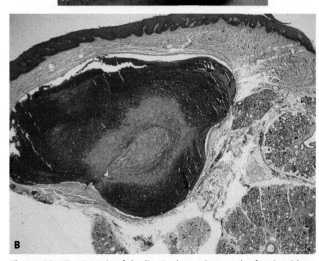

Figure 23–17 *A,* Varix of the lip; *B,* photomicrograph of varix with an organizing thrombus.

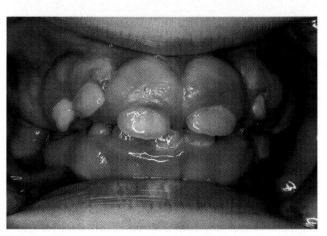

Figure 23–15 Familial gingival hyperplasia.

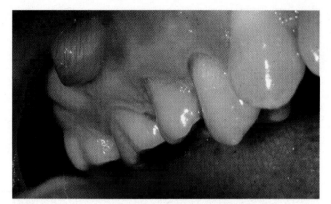

Figure 23–18 Parulis associated with periapical infection.

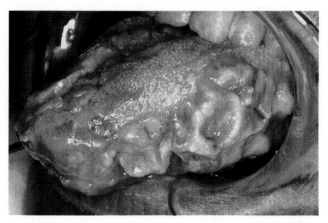

Figure 23–20 Amyloidosis presenting as multiple tongue nodules.

often, single nodules (Figure 23–20). The presence of amyloid in oral biopsies is determined by Congo red staining with subsequent demonstration of green birefringence under polarized light. The fluorochrome thioflavin T also stains amyloid, yet is not specific.

Mesenchymal neoplasms

A variety of neoplasms arise from the submucosal connective tissues, and such tumors appear as nodular swellings. They may show distinct clinical features, such as hemangioma and lymphangioma, or they may be nondescript, simply presenting as pink, smooth-surfaced tumefactions. Hemangiomas and lymphangiomas are considered to be developmental lesions, since these lesions often proliferate in infancy or childhood, and may spontaneously resolve during teenage years (see Chapter 25). Most mesenchymal tumors are found in the tongue or buccal mucosa, but they can occur anywhere in the mouth. The more common are nerve sheath tumors, including neurilemoma (shwannoma) and neurofibroma (Figure 23–21). The granular cell tumor is generally considered to be a nerve sheath tumor as well (Schwann cell origin) and is most com-

monly found in the tongue, where it appears as a yellow, smooth-surfaced, firm plaque or nodule (Figure 23–22).

Lipomas are typically located in the buccal mucosa, appearing as soft, yellow, single or multinodular masses (Figure 22–23). Choristomas are benign growths that aberrantly arise in locations that do not harbor the progenitor cells from which they arise. In the oral cav-

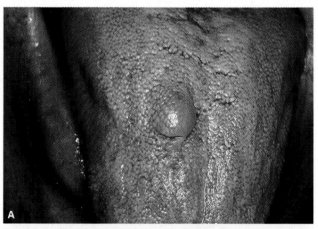

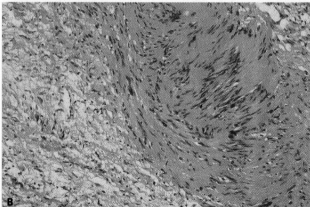

Figure 23–21 *A,* Nerve sheath tumor of the tongue; *B,* photomicrograph of a neurilemoma showing nuclear palisading (Antoni type A tissue).

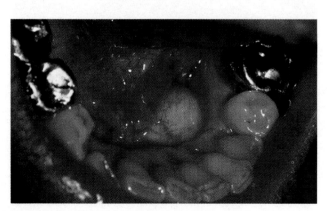

Figure 23–19 Ectopic lymphoid tissue in the oral floor.

ity, chondroid (cartilaginous) choristomas are typically encountered as hard nodules in the submucosa of the tongue. Other benign mesenchymal neoplasms that are occasionally encountered in the oral cavity are rhabdomyoma, leiomyoma, nodular fasciitis, solitary fibrous tumor, and fibrous histiocytoma, to mention but a few (Figures 23–24 and 23–25). These specific entities are all treated by surgical excision, and have variable tendencies for recurrence.

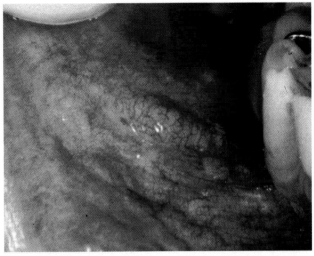

Figure 23–23   Lipoma with yellow coloration of the buccal mucosa.

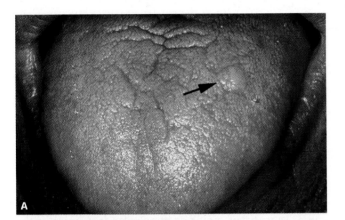

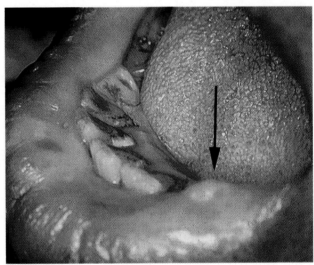

Figure 23–24   Submucosal tumor of the lip.

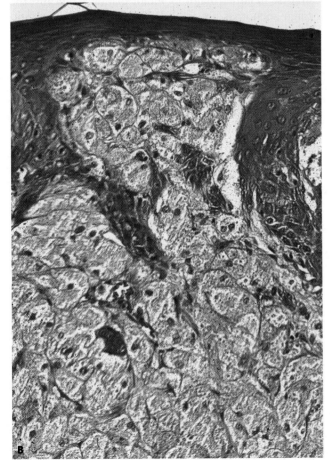

Figure 23–22   *A*, Granular cell tumor of the tongue; *B*, photomicrograph of granular cell tumor with overlying pseudoepitheliomatous hyperplasia.

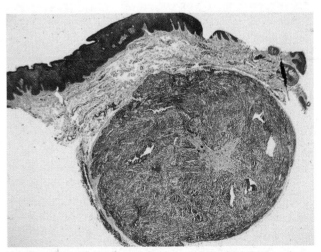

Figure 23–25   Photomicrograph of a well-defined mesenchymal neoplasms, in this case a leiomyoma.

Aggressive proliferations

Certain mesenchymal proliferations are characterized by rapid growth and can reach large proportions; some actually invade adjacent soft and hard tissues despite their inability to metastasize. All are defined by their microscopic appearance. These aggressive mesenchymal tumors often lie deep within the facial tissues, floor of the mouth, tongue, or neck, and are firm to palpation. If there is any invasion of contiguous tissues, they are partially fixed, as assessed by palpation. Included in this group are fibrous histiocytoma, aggressive juvenile fibromatosis, hemangiopericytoma (some of which show malignant behavior), and hemangioendothelioma. Open biopsy or needle aspiration cytology are acceptable diagnostic procedures. Wide excision is generally required.

Squamous cell carcinoma

Chapter 20 discusses oral malignant epithelial neoplasms in detail. Late-stage tumors often present as indurated ulcerated masses, although some are non-ulcerated. Most squamous cell carcinomas are located in the tongue and lips and in the floor of the mouth (Figure 23–26). For oral cancers in general, the more anterior the carcinoma is located in the mouth, the better the prognosis; the more posterior, the worse the prognosis. This may be attributable to delayed diagnosis (advanced stages), intrinsic cell proliferation differences, or greater lymphatic drainage in those areas. Incisional biopsy is recommended for diagnosing these tumefactive indurated lesions. Treatment planning is complex, with the more advanced-stage lesions requiring more aggressive treatment. Overall prognosis is poor, with only about 50% surviving.

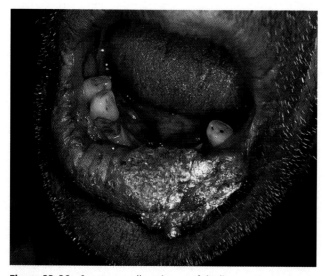

Figure 23–26   Squamous cell carcinoma of the lip.

Salivary gland tumors

Chapter 26 discusses each of the histologic types of salivary gland tumors. Some types that are commonly found in the major glands are rare or may never be found in the minor glands of the mouth, conversely, there are minor salivary gland tumors that rarely arise in the major glands. Intraoral minor gland tumors present as submucosal masses and are as apt to be malignant as they are to be benign. The most common site is the palate, where the mass is off the midline, arising in the posterior aspect of the hard palate or at the hard–soft palate junction (Figure 23–27). The buccal mucosa, upper lip, and ventral tongue are also common sites for these neoplasms. The benign tumors that occur in minor glands include the pleomorphic adenoma, monomorphic adenoma, and canalicular adenoma, the latter arising almost exclusively in the upper lip, where it may be multifocal. Polymorphous low-grade adenocarcinoma is a common malignant minor salivary gland tumor that almost never arises in the major glands. Other adenocarcinomas arising in the oral mucosa are mucoepidermoid carcinoma, adenoid cystic carcinoma, and adenocarcinoma not otherwise specified. There are many other rare histologic types that can arise in either major or minor glands. Clinically, the benign adenomas are typically smooth surfaced, nonul-

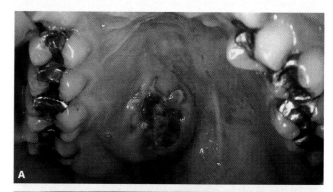

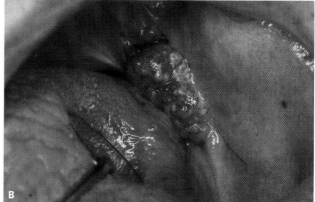

Figure 23–27   *A,* Adenocarinoma of the minor salivary glands of the palate, the most common site for oral salivary gland tumors. *B,* Retromolar adenocarcinoma.

cerated nodules that are movable, unless located in the palate, where the tumor is trapped between the palatal bone and mucosa. Malignant salivary gland tumors are indurated (low-grade mucoepidermoid carcinoma being the exception) and may show surface ulceration and telangiectasia. Incisional biopsy is the diagnositic procedure of choice; fine-needle aspiration is also useful for diagnosis. Primary treatment is surgical removal. Based on the histologic type and surgical margins, postsurgical radiation therapy can be used. Adenomatous hyperplasia is seen in the soft palate and floor of the mouth and represents a benign nonneoplastic growth of normal salivary tissue (Figure 23–28).

Sarcomas and lymphomas

Malignant mesenchymal neoplasms are rarely encountered in the oral soft tissues, being much more prevalent in the neck. Sarcomas can arise anywhere, and cases have been reported in the tongue, buccal mucosa, and oral floor, being extremely rare in other locations (Figure 23–29). Rhabdomyosarcoma, fibrosarcoma, and malignant fibrous histiocytoma have been the more frequent sarcomas reported to arise in the oral cavity (Figure 23–30). These malignancies account for less than 5% of all oral cancers.

Whereas lymphomas are usually seen in the cervical lymph node chain, extranodal non-Hodgkin lymphomas are encountered in the oral cavity. They are far more common in the human immunodeficiency virus (HIV)-infected patient, where they tend to occur on the buccal and palatal gingiva. The masses are firm, rapidly growing, often multinodular, and may show surface ulceration. Microscopically they are usually high-grade lesions populated by monoclonal B lymphoblasts with a diffuse medium or large cell morphology. Patients with acquired immunodeficiency syndrome (AIDS) present-

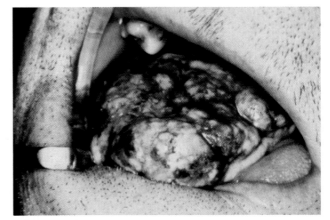

Figure 23–29 Rhabdomyosarcoma of the tongue is a massive, aggressive malignancy that is rare in the oral cavity.

ing with lymphoma generally succumb within 6 months of diagnosis. In the United States, HIV-associated lymphomas account for approximately 25% of all lymphomas reported each year (see Chapters 8 and 14).

Atypical lymphoproliferative lesions represent a lymphoid infiltrative disease of the palate that invades minor salivary tissue while leaving the extralobular ducts relatively well preserved. These lesions appear as unilateral, soft, boggy, diffuse swellings at the hard–soft palate junction. Some are polyclonal B-cell lesions that are probably reactive; others are monoclonal and likely represent low-grade mucosa-associated lymphoid tissue (MALT) lymphomas. These lesions are responsive to low-dose radiation therapy.

Clinical features of facial tumors and swellings

The swellings that are seen on the face can be clinically divided into two major types: those that are diffuse

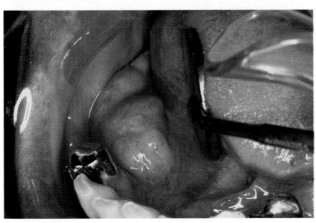

Figure 23–28 Adenomatous hyperplasia of salivary glands in the lateral oral floor.

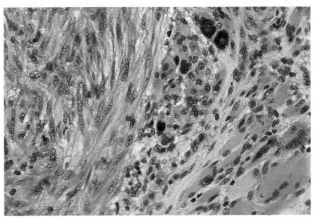

Figure 23–30 Photomicrograph of a sarcoma showing a spindle cell lesion (fibrosarcoma) with marked nuclear pleomorphism.

and those that are focal nodules. As alluded to previously, diffuse swellings are usually inflammatory lesions, such as edema, emphysema, space infection, or cellulites. Facial asymmetry also may be seen when there is an underlying central lesion of the maxillary or mandibular bone and, of course, such lesions are bony hard. Radiographs are necessary diagnostic and evaluative tools.

Focal nodules of the face may be covered by normal skin or they may be verrucous, ulcerated, or pigmented. Most small facial nodules are sebaceous cysts, basal cell carcinomas, nevi, and seborrheic keratoses, the latter two being pigmented. Less common are squamous cancers, melanomas, and mesenchymal neoplasms.

Odontogenic infections

Buccal drainage from a periapical abscess can result in significant facial swelling, which may localize over the mandible or, less frequently, below the zygoma. As the infection progresses through the buccal plate, bacteria and the host response to it result in purulent exudates. If this suppurative process is confined to spaces bordered by muscle and fascia, the diffuse swelling is soft or fluctuant and tender to palpation. Alternatively, if the infectious process infiltrates into muscle and leukocytic infiltrates are interposed within the substance of the muscle itself, then the lesion becomes indurated, a process termed cellulitis. The clinical distinction between cellulitis and space infection is germane to treatment, since the former cannot be incised and drained, whereas the latter is amenable to such intervention. Of course, the incriminated tooth must be treated as well. Depending upon the status of the tooth, endodontic therapy or extraction must be performed, and antibiotic therapy is indicated in these examples of more extensive spread of infection. In some instances, the periosteum reacts to underlying odontogenic infection, giving rise to proliferative periostitis (Figure 23–31).

Soft-tissue emphysema

On rare occasion, air may be forcefully introduced between tissue planes. This may occur during maxillary endodontic, periodontal, and oral surgery procedures in which compressed air is applied and separates the tissue planes. The entrapped air causes a diffuse facial swelling that is crepitant to palpation. A potentially lethal compliction is vascular air embolism, an event that usually occurs shortly after the introduction of compressed air into the tissues. Aspiration of the swollen area may be attempted with caution, making sure not to puncture a major vessel in the process. Eventually, the trapped air is absorbed by the tissues.

Seborrheic keratosis

Sun exposure to the facial skin damages DNA and may induce proliferative responses in the surface epithelium. This exposure may result in the formation of seborrheic keratosis, a benign entity. This common lesion is usually seen on the forehead, temples, or malar regions of the face. The lesions are slightly tumefactive, brown in color, and have an oily texture. They vary considerably in size and are typically symmetrical, with smooth well-delineated borders. The differential diagnosis includes nevus and basal cell carcinoma. Most "seb Ks" can be removed by shave biopsy or laser ablation.

Melanocytic lesions

The common nevi are discussed in more detail in Chapter 22 on pigmentations; not all nevi, however, are pig-

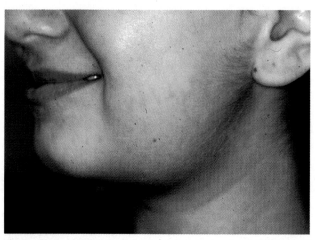

Figure 23–31 Cellulitis of the masseteric region from an abscessed mandibular molar.

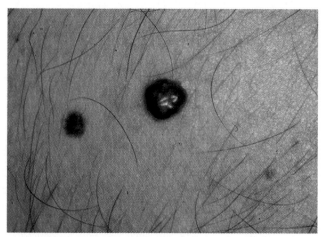

Figure 23–32 Red nodular hemangioma (a nevus is also present as a brown macule).

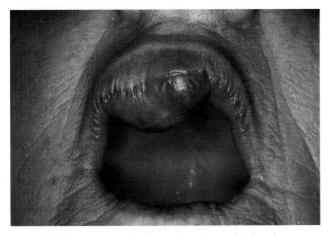

Figure 23–33   Intramuscular hemangioma is not discolored.

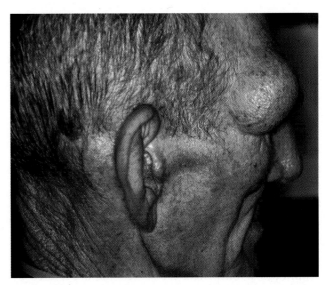

Figure 23–34   Supraorbital subcutaneous lipoma.

mented. They can occur anywhere on the facial skin and are present from early childhood, with no history of any change or increase in size. In adults, they all represent intradermal nevi. The pigmented nevi are symmetrical, round and nodular. The nonpigmented nevi simply appear as nonproliferative nodules of normal skin coloration. Treatment is deferred unless the patient wants them removed for esthetic reasons, or if they are near the hairline and become easily irritated. Should any longstanding nevus begin to increase in size, ulcerate, or deepen in color, biopsy is recommended to rule out dysplastic change in a preexisting nevus. Melanomas are also discussed in Chapter 22.

Mesenchymal neoplasms

A variety of mesenchymal tumors can arise from the subcutaneous tissues of the facial skin. Hemangiomas appear red or purple when superficial (Figure 23–32), or they may not be discolored when they are deep and intramuscular (Figure 23–33). Neurilemomas, neurofibromas, and lipomas are relatively common connective-tissue tumors that appear as subcutanous masses (Figure 23–34).

Basal cell carcinoma

Basal cell carcinomas (BCC) are the most frequently occurring malignancy in the United States, accounting for more than one million new cases each year. Sun exposure is also a factor in the etiology of BCC, which explains why those with fair skin and less melanocytic protection are more prone to the development of these skin cancers. They may appear as pearly nodules with surface telangiectasia, or they may present as nonhealing ulcers (Figure 23–35). The ulcerated basal cell carcinomas usually develop rolled borders. It is common for

these skin cancers to be multifocal. They are more often seen on the upper face, helix of the ear, and scalp than on the lower face and lips. Wide local excision is required for cure, and despite adequate surgery, some recur, presumably owing to a field effect of dysplastic change that many occur in many areas of the facial skin. Radiation therapy is also effective in controlling BCC.

Prognosis is good, since few BCCs metastasize. However, they spread locally and insidiously, so if not diagnosed and treated early, the treatment defect can be disfiguring. Basal cell carcinoma does not arise in the mucosal tissues of the mouth. Some interesting cases have been reported of BCC occurring in skin grafts that have been placed in the mouth for repair or closure purposes.

Variant benign tumors of skin appendages are known as adnexal skin tumors. These lesions present as

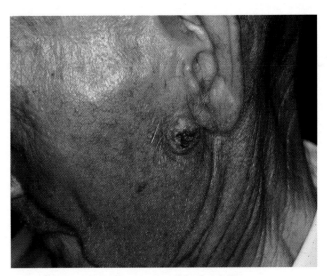

Figure 23–35   Basal cell carcinoma of the facial skin.

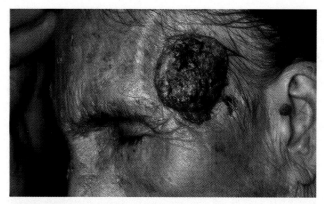

Figure 23–36 Squamous cell carcinoma.

smooth-surfaced nodules, because the cells of origin lie within the dermis. Most are benign and are treated by simple excision.

Squamous cell carcinoma

Arising de novo or from preexisting actinic keratoses, squamous cancers of the facial skin have potential for both regional node and distant metastases. The actinic keratoses are reddish-brown macules with a superficial scaley keratotic crust. They are typically found on the forehead, nose, cheeks, and lower lip. When carcinomatous change arises from these precancerous dysplasias, the lesions become tumefactive, indurated, and ulcerated (Figure 23–36). Ulcerated growths on the eyelids, particular the lower lid, tend to arise from malignant transformation of the dermally situated sebaceous glands (sebaceous carcinoma). Regional nodes become palpably enlarged when metastases evolve. Treatment consists of wide local excision and/or radiation therapy; management of the neck is contingent upon clinical or imaging findings of nodal disease. On the lips, squamous cell carcinoma is common, and BCC is rare (see Chapter 20).

Suggested reading

Desai P, Silver JG. Drug-induced gingival enlargements. J Can Dent Assoc 1998;64:263–8.

Eversole LR, Rovin S. Diagnosis of gingival tumefactions. J Periodontol 1973;44:429–35.

Katz AD, McAlpin C. Face and neck neurogenic neoplasms. Am J Surg 1993;166:421–3.

Manor Y, Merdinger O, Katz J, Taicher S. Unusual peripheral odontogenic tumors in the differential diagnosis of gingival swellings. J Clin Periodontol 1999;26:806–9.

Rees SR, Gibson J. Angioedema and swellings of the orofacial region. Oral Dis 1997;3:39–42.

Rossiter JL, Hendrix RA, Tom LW, Potsic WP. Intramuscular hemangioma of the head and neck. Otolaryngol Head Neck Surg 1993;108:18–26.

Som PM, Norton KI. Lesions that manifest as medial cheek and nasolabial fold masses. Radiology 1991;178:831–5.

Stewart CM, Watson RE, Eversole LR, et al. Oral granular cell tumors: a clinicopathologic and immunocytochemical study. Oral Surg Oral Med Oral Pathol 1988;65:427–35.

Tunkel DE, Baroody FM, Sherman ME. Fine-needle aspiration biopsy of cervicofacial masses in children. Arch Otolaryngol Head Neck Surg 1995;121:533–6.

Van Dis ML. Swellings of the oral cavity. Dermatol Clin 1996;14:355–70.

Orofacial Granulomatosis and Other Inflammatory Lesions

L. Roy Eversole, DDS, MSD, MA

Granulomas are inflammatory lesions that evolve in response to irritation, infectious agents, and foreign bodies (Table 24–1). Those that are represented by localized masses of fibrovascular granulation tissue accompanied by a nonspecific chronic or sometimes subacute inflammatory infiltrate as seen microscopically are simple granulomas; in the oral cavity, lesions of this nature are most frequently encountered intraosseously as endodontically related periapical granulomas. Simple granulomas in the oral cavity are generally localized to the gingiva, yet may actually arise anywhere in the mouth or on the facial skin, where they appear as cherry-red tumefactions, termed pyogenic granulomas (see Chapter 23).

Specific granulomas are those in which the histologic picture is augmented by the presence of multinucleated giant cells. The peripheral giant cell granuloma of the gingiva and alveolar ridge is a reactive lesion without an infectious etiology. Such lesions are not included with the specific granulomas, all of which evolve in response to infection with specific microorganisms. In the oral cavity, specific granulomas are usually associated with mycobacteria or deep invasive fungi, appearing microscopically as caseating and noncaseating granulomas, respectively (see Chapters 17 and 18).

Certain types of foreign materials elicit a granulomatous reaction characterized by chronically inflamed granulation tissue and giant cell formation, although not all foreign agents are capable of inducing a giant cell response. In most cases, the foreign body can be seen microscopically, and polarized light is frequently used to locate crystalline foreign particles. Oil (from dental handpieces), dental materials, foodstuffs (particularly pulses or legumes), are all common exogenous agents that stimulate foreign body granulomas. The giant cells are fused macrophages, and the foreign agent is usually seen as phagocytized material within the cytoplasm.

Noncaseating granulomas with no identifiable infectious agent may occur as single or multifocal nodules or diffuse swellings in the head and neck area. These lesions constitute an enigmatic group of inflammatory disorders that are subsumed under the rubric of orofacial granulomatosis.

Other inflammatory conditions discussed in this chapter include Wegener granulomatosis, angioedema, and subcutaneous (submucosal) angiolymphoid hyperplasia with eosinophilia and a variant form known as Kimura disease.

Molecular and pathologic correlates of disease

A granuloma comprised of chronically inflamed granulation tissue and containing multinucleated giant cells is pathologically referred to as specific granulomatous inflammation. As previously mentioned, this type of inflammation occurs with infectious agents (specific granulomas), foreign body reactions, and orofacial granulomatosis. The granulomas of orofacial granulomatosis are similar and, in some instances, identical to those of sarcoidosis. They are composed of fibrovascular connective tissue with chronic inflammatory cell infiltration, a

Table 24–1 Oral Granulomas

Classification	Type or Infectious Agent
Nonspecific granulomas	Periapical granuloma
	Pyogenic granuloma
	Traumatic granuloma (eosinophilic granuloma of soft tissue)
	Giant cell granuloma (central and peripheral)
Foreign body granulomas	Particulate materials (dental cements, abrasives, other dental materials)
	Foodstuffs (pulse granuloma)
	Oil granuloma (central and peripheral)
Specific granulomas	
Caseating granulomas	*Mycobacterium tuberculosis*
	Tularemia
	Cat-scratch fever
Noncaseating granulomas	*Mycobacterium avium intracellulare*
	Histoplasmosis
	Blastomycosis
	Coccidioidomycosis
	Cryptococcosis
Wegener granulomatosis	Focal or localized noncaseating granuloma
Orofacial granulomatosis	Cheilitis granulomatosa
	Melkersson-Rosenthal syndrome
	Heerfordt syndrome
	Crohn disease
	Sarcoidosis

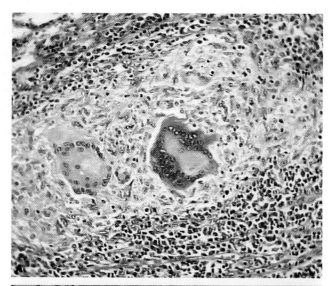

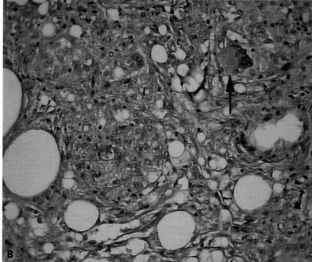

Figure 24–1 *A,* Photomicrograph of noncaseating specific granulomatous inflammation. Note epithelioid histiocytes and multinucleated giant cells. *B,* Oil granuloma showing vacuolated oil spaces, histiocytes, and a multinucleated giant cell (*arrow*).

preponderance of epithelioid macrophages, and multinucleated giant cells with randomly dispersed nuclei (Figure 24–1, *A*). Occasionally the nuclei are arranged in circular (Touton cells) or wreath (Langhans cells) configurations; yet, importantly, special stains fail to identify a specific microorganism or any foreign bodies present within tissue sections. When specific granulomatous inflammation is observed microscopically, the pathologist is obligated to order special stains, to explore for the presence of microorganisms. Acid-fast stains are ordered for mycobacteria and either periodic acid-Schiff (PAS) or Gram methenamine silver is employed to demonstrate invasive fungi. Foreign bodies are often seen on routine hematoxylin-eosin (H&E) sections, whereas some materials, particularly crystalline, are observed using crossed polars that render the foreign particles refractile and thus easily visualized. Many foreign bodies are easily identifiable with routine stains (Figure 24–1, *B*).

The molecular basis for the formation of sarcoid-like granulomas in the oral cavity and face is unknown, as is the etiology. Some of these granulomas are markers of internal disease, others are localized lesions that have no other disease association. There is experimental evidence that mycobacterial antigens and DNA are present in lesional tissue even though intact organisms cannot be identified. Elevated IgG antibody titers directed to a 65 kDa mycobacterial stress protein (mS p65) have been identified in some patients with orofacial granulomatosis. This has led to the speculation that noncaseating granulomatous inflammation is a noninfectious immunologic response to various antigenic stimuli. In addition to microbial antigens, other allergenic substances have been implicated in this response. The classification of orofacial granulomas is given in Table 24–1.

Angioedema is an inflammatory lesion of the face that typically is caused by allergy to an extrinsic chemical substance. The antigen binds to IgE antibodies, which are bound by receptors on mast cells (Figure 24–2). Antigen binding leads to bridging of adjacent IgE antibodies, which evoke internal signaling in the mast

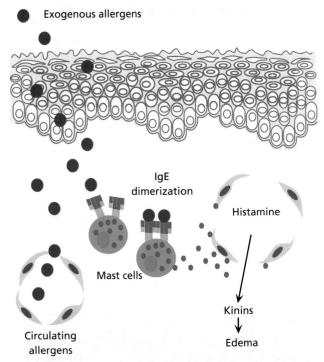

Figure 24–2   Schematic diagram showing the mechanisms of immediate hypersensitivity in angioedema. IgE binds to allergen, and via mast cell signal induction, granules release histamine with resultant vasodilatation and capillary permeability, with release of serum kininogens into the tissues that are converted to bradykinin, another potent vasodilator.

cell to inititiate histamine degranulation. Histamine then acts on vascular smooth muscle and endothelial cell receptors to induce vasodilatation and increased vascular permeability, respectively. As the vessels maintain porosity and leak protein, osmotic forces draw increasing amounts of fluid into the extracellular space with resultant diffuse edema. This process is accentuated by bradykinin, which is released from high-molecular-weight kininogens that leak out of the porous vessels. Angiotensin-converting enzyme (ACE) inhibitors have been found to be common pharmacologic allergens involved in the pathogenesis of angioedema. The main inactivator of bradykinin is kininase II, a mediator with action identical to that of ACE. It may be that bradykinin mediates ACE-inhibitor-dependent angioedema. The hereditary form of angioedema occurs in patients with a genetic deficiency in complement fraction 1 esterase inhibitor (C1 esterase inhibitor).

Clinical features

Focal noncaseating granuloma

Focal granulomas may occur anywhere in the oral mucosa or in the subcutaneous tissues of the skin, where

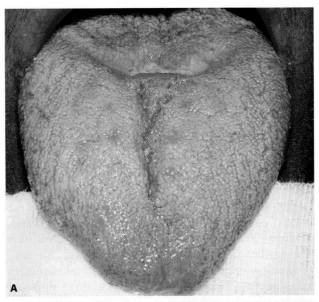

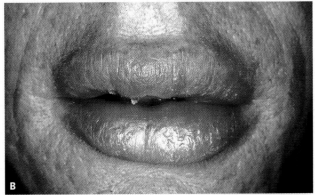

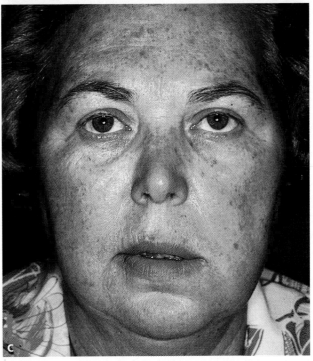

Figure 24–3   Melkersson-Rosenthal syndrome. *A,* Fissured tongue; *B,* granulomatous cheilitis; *C,* facial nerve palsy.

they present as localized firm masses that are occasionally multinodular. Once the diagnosis has been made microscopically, a search should be undertaken to determine whether lesions are present in other organs. When no other lesions can be identified, the diagnosis is secured; however, the etiology and pathogenesis remain unknown.

Melkersson-Rosenthal syndrome

A classic triad of lesions is seen in Melkersson-Rosenthal syndrome, consisting of nodular lip swellings, fissured tongue, and unilateral facial palsy (Figure 24–3). Experience has shown that this classic syndrome triad is rare. Recently, many authors have relaxed the criteria for the diagnosis and include noncaseating granulomas located in oral mucosal sites other than the lips; furthermore, two of the three signs are accepted for the diagnosis of Melkersson-Rosenthal syndrome. Perhaps it is more appropriate to simply designate such cases as orofacial granulomatosis and eliminate the syndrome designation all together. The granulomas of the lips are identical to those seen in cheilitis granulomatosa. Clinically, the lower lip is involved more diffusely than the upper lip, being enlarged with palpable nodularity throughout the submucosa. Microscopically, multiple granulomas are seen to replace or infiltrate the lip minor salivary glands. Nodular tumefactions that are firm to palpation may be encountered in the buccal mucosa, vestibule, and tongue.

Cheilitis granulomatosa

Granulomas located as multiple nodules throughout the lips constitute cheilitis granulomatosa, provided these lesions are the only manifestation of the condition. As previously mentioned, lip granulomas with identical appearance to cheilitis granulomatosa are encountered in the Melkersson-Rosenthal syndrome. The lower, upper, or both lips may be involved (Figure 24–4). Although the swelling may appear to be diffuse, palpation discloses multiple and often confluent nodules within the submucosa. Biopsy shows multiple noncaseating granulomas replacing minor salivary lobules.

Sarcoidosis

Epithelioid noncaseating granulomas are the hallmark of sarcoidosis, a systemic disease with widespread distribution. Geographically, there appears to be a higher incidence among central and northern Europeans. Similar to tuberculosis, sarcoid granulomas are commonly encountered in the lungs, with a penchant for hilar

lymph node involvement. Pulmonary lesions contribute to the elevated levels of serum ACE. Granulomas may be identified in other sites, including internal organs, skin, and mucous membranes. Osseous lesions may be encountered, and hypercalcemia is a common accompaniment in such cases. Other laboratory abnormalities seen in systemic sarcoidosis include anemia, leukopenia, and thrombocytopenia. Accelerated erythrocyte sedimentation rate and elevated serum alkaline phosphatase levels may also be encountered.

In the head and neck, the major salivary glands may be involved; in particular, painless bilateral parotid enlargement may be seen. When parotid and lacrimal gland infiltration by granulomas occurs, the condition is referred to as the *Heerfordt syndrome*. The enlarged parotids are firm and nodular. Mild xerostomia and xerophthalmia may be present. In more widespread sar-

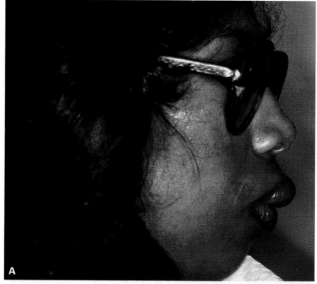

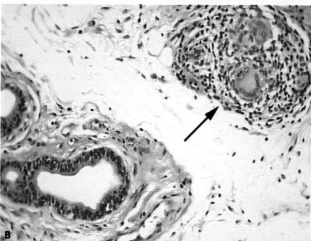

Figure 24–4 Cheilitis granulomatosa. *A,* lip lesions are diffuse; *B,* noncaseating granuloma (*arrow*) replacing the minor salivary glands located in the submusoa.

coidosis, oral and facial skin nodules may be encountered. These nodules are often multifocal or multinodular and are firm to palpation. In the mouth, they are more often encountered in the lips, buccal mucosa, and tongue. Both white and red mucosal lesions may also be seen in sarcoidosis. Sarcoid lymphadenitis of cervical nodes may be a feature as well.

Crohn disease

Regional enteritis is an inflammatory bowel disease characterized by segmental submucosal inflammatory lesions of the small bowel with extention into the ascending colon. The patients complain of lower right quadrant pain, diarrhea, periods of constipation, and episodic obstruction. Extraintestinal manifestations include ankylosing spondylitis, arthritis, and skin lesions. Microscopically, nonspecific chronic inflammation is typically seen, and in older long-standing lesions, noncaseating granulomas are observed.

Granulomatous inflammatory lesions can be seen anywhere along the intestinal tract as well as in the oral mucosa. As many as 60% of patients with Crohn disease present with oral lesions. Males are more commonly affected than females, with most lesions being detected in young adults. The lips, gingiva, vestibule, and buccal mucosa are the predilected intraoral sites for lesions that may be nodular, papular with a cobblestone appearance, or ulcerated (Figure 24–5). The oral lesions may be the first indication of this intestinal disease.

Wegener granulomatosis

Often included as a form of midline lethal granuloma, Wegener granulomatosis represents an inflammatory

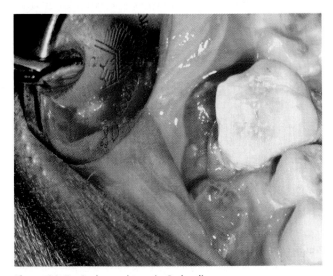

Figure 24–5   Oral granulomas in Crohn disease.

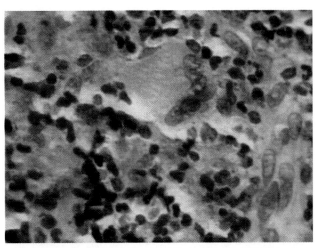

Figure 24–6   Giant cells and eosinophils are seen in oral biopsies from Wegener granulomatosis.

destructive disease that may have widespread systemic involvement. The granulomas of Wegener granulomatosis are usually localized in the lung and kidneys. The middle ear, gingiva, and nasal mucosa are also commonly affected. Microscopically, vasculitis is a dominant finding, along with fibrinoid necrosis. The adjacent granulation tissue is often infiltrated with eosinophils and occasional multinucleated giant cells are seen (Figure 24–6). Antibodies directed to neutrophil cytoplasmic antigens (ANCA) are detected using indirect immunofluorescence with neutrophils as substrate, being positive in over 90% of cases.

Although midfacial destructive lesions may be present, they are not frequently seen. The most common disease to cause both soft- and hard-tissue midline destruction is malignant lymphoma. The term midline lethal granuloma is a clinical term that should be abandoned, since this is not a specific disease. More often, the head and neck manifestations of Wegener granulomatosis are erythematous granular appearing mucosal lesions, and on the gingiva, such lesions have been termed *strawberry gums* (see Chapter 23). Limited forms of Wegener syndrome are often encountered in which lung or kidney involvement is missing.

Traumatic ulcerative granuloma with stromal eosinophilia

Traumatic ulcerative granuloma with stromal eosinophilia (TUGSE) is an ulcerated granuloma that is often mistaken for carcinoma (Figure 24–7). The lesions are usually large (>1 cm in diameter) and often have raised or indurated borders. Although TUGSE may occur at any age, it is more common in middle-aged adults, and a slight female predilection is seen. Most

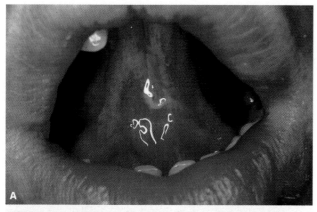

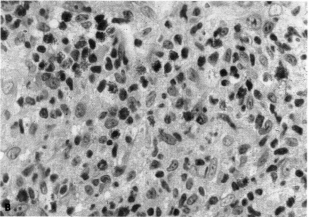

Figure 24–7 Traumatic eosinophilic granuloma. *A*, Tongue ulcer; *B*, microscopic appearance showing histiocytes, other leukocytes, and eosinophils.

instances occur on the dorsum of the tongue and buccal mucosa. Although trauma has been suggested in the etiology, few patients can recall a traumatic episode, and therefore, the cause is unknown. Microscopically, ulceration is seen and a mixed inflammatory infiltrate extends into the connective tissues, where, in the tongue, exten-

sion into muscle is typically seen. The infiltrate is comprised of histiocytes and eosinophils, bearing a resemblance to Langerhan cell histiocytosis. A rare variant of TUGSE is atypical histiocytic granuloma. This variant is often mistaken for malignant lymphoma microscopically because mitotic figures are present and mononuclear histocytoid cells are pleomorphic. Clinically, the lesions are broad-based erosions or ulcerations (Figure 24–8).

Angiolymphoid hyperplasia with eosinophilia

Epithelioid hemangioma, also termed subcutaneous angiolymphoid hyperplasia with eosinophilia (ALHE) is an uncommon lesion of the facial skin and may sometimes occur intraorally. The patients are usually adults, and there is no significant gender predilection. The lesions are diffuse, firm, or even manifested by painless indurated broad subcutaneous plaques of the face. Histologically, the terminology conforms to the findings. Vessels are prominent with large epithelioid-appearing endothelial cells, and dispersed throughout are aggregates of lymphocytes with a diffuse infiltration of eosinophils (Figure 24–9). Peripheral blood eosinophilia may be present as well.

Kimura disease is a variant form of ALHE that is more common among Asians. In Kimura disease, the lesions tend to be more extensive and diffuse than in simple ALHE, and the lymphoid aggregates show germinal center formation. The term epithelioid hemangioma is probably inappropriate, since these benign inflammatory lesions are self-limited and are not truly neoplastic in their natural history.

Angioedema

Angioedema is an allergic reaction that involves IgE antibody-mediated vasodilatation and vascular perme-

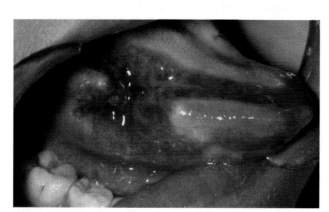

Figure 24–8 Diffuse ulceration of 4 weeks' duration is an atypical histiocytic granuloma that resolved in 2 weeks following an incisional biopsy.

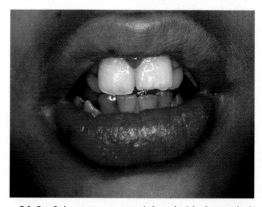

Figure 24–9 Subcutaneous angiolymphoid hyperplasia with eosinophilia of the lower lip is a diffuse indurated submucosal plaque. This case showed microscopic features consistent with Kimura disease.

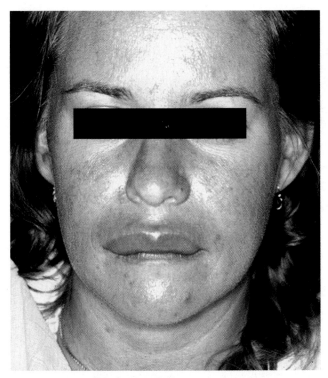

Figure 24–10 Diffuse facial swelling in angioedema.

ability, with resultant diffuse edema. The entire face may become suddenly edematous, or localized regions of edema may develop, such as periorbital or labial swellings (Figure 24–10). Being edematous, these swellings are soft; they are painless, yet may be pruritic. When facial edema is of sudden onset, search for an allergen should be undertaken. Suspected antigenic substances include foods, wine, meats, medications, and dental materials. Angiotensin-converting enzyme inhibitors are common agents responsible for angioedema, and interestingly, the facial edema may not evolve for months, or even after years of use.

The hereditary form of angioedema develops as a consequence of a complement pathway deficiency (C1 esterase inhibitor). Affected individuals typically develop widespread urticarial skin lesions, yet many show facial edema similar to that of the aforementioned allergic reactions. It is noteworthy that ACE-inhibitors may initiate a recrudescence in hereditary angioedema.

Treatment

Orofacial granulomatosis may be treated surgically or medically. Localized granulomas, once excised, usually do not recur. Multifocal lesions, such as cheilitis granulomatosa and subvariants of Melkersson-Rosenthal syndrome can be managed with steroid injection. Local anesthesia is delivered, followed by intralesional cortisone or methylprednisolone (Kenalog 40™, Bristol Myers Squibb), injecting from a tuberculin syringe in 0.1-mL increments. In all instances of orofacial granulomatosis, a workup for regional enteritis and sarcoidosis must be persued. In Crohn disease, systemic steroids or azathioprine are recommended, beginning with moderate doses and tapering down as lesions begin to undergo resolution.

Traumatic ulcerative granulomas and atypical histiocytic granulomas have no known etiology. After biopsy, even incisional biopsy, most lesions resolve within a matter of 2 to 3 weeks

Wegener granulomatosis is treated by combination chemotherapy that includes cyclophosphamide and prednisone.

Angiolymphoid hyperplasia with eosinophila and Kimura disease are self-limited. Smaller lesions can be surgically excised, whereas more diffuse lesions often respond to systemic prednisone.

Angioedema secondary to allergenic hypersensitivity can be treated by oral administration of antihistamines. Diphenhydramine (50 mg twice daily) resolves edema, provided the allergen has been identified and withdrawn. In extensive cases, systemic prednisone (40 to 80 mg) for less than 1 week is generally effective. Angiotensin-converting enzyme inhibitor-induced angioedema may take weeks to resolve after withdrawal of the medication. The edema of hereditary angioedema eventually resolves of its own accord, only to recur at a later date. Antihistamines may be of some use in resolution of the swelling.

Suggested reading

Agostoni A, Cicardi M, Cugno M, et al. Angioedema due to angiotensin-converting enzyme inhibitors. Immunopharmacology 1999;44:21–5.

el-Mofty SK, Swanson PE, Wick MR, Miller AS. Eosinophilic ulcer of the oral mucosa. Report of 38 new cases with immunohistochemical observations. Oral Surg Oral Med Oral Pathol 1993;75:716–22.

Eveson JW. Granulomatous disorders of the oral mucosa. Semin Diagn Pathol 1996;13:118–27.

Ivanyi L, Kirby A, Zakrzewska JM. Antibodies to mycobacterial stress protein in patients with orofacial granulomatosis. J Oral Pathol Med 1993;22:320–2.

Li TJ, Chen XM, Wang SZ, et al. Kimura's disease: a clinicopathologic study of 54 Chinese patients. Oral Surg Oral Med Oral Pathol Oral Radiol Endod 1996;82:549–55.

Plauth M, Jenss H, Meyle J. Oral manifestations of Crohn's disease. An analysis of 79 cases. J Clin Gastroenterol 1991; 13:29–37.

Rees TD. Orofacial granulomatosis and related conditions. Periodontology 2000 1999;21:145–57.

Rogers RS. Melkersson-Rosenthal syndrome and orofacial granulomatosis. Dermatol Clin 1996;14:371–9.

25 Developmental Mucosal Conditions

Sol Silverman, Jr, MA, DDS

Some common oral mucosal defects that often are major patient complaints, and sometimes cause confusion among clinicians, include hairy tongue, geographic tongue (glossitis migrans), stomatitis migrans, fissured tongue, Fordyce granules, median rhomboid glossitis, white sponge nevus, and lymphangiomas and hemangiomas. These conditions may cause some difficulties in establishing a definitive diagnosis and appropriate management. This dilemma not only causes some concern to patients because of thoughts regarding infection, transmission, and malignancy, but it can complicate both the use of clinical or laboratory tests and patient orientation and treatment. Because of patient concern, and sometimes symptoms, it is always important to be able to assure patients that these conditions are neither precancerous nor contagious.

The frequency of these conditions is speculative, since well-designed population epidemiologic studies have not been performed or are inconclusive. Nevertheless, clinical experience allows for gross estimates of disease prevalence.

Since the clinical appearance of these benign conditions varies so greatly, the signs and symptoms, diagnosis, and management are discussed separately as each condition is described.

Pathologic and molecular correlates of disease

The basic explanation of these developmental and acquired conditions is best characterized as manifestations (phenotypic expression) of subtle and unidentified genetic defects, probably at specific chromosomal loci. The variations in penetrance have not been explained by familial tracings or recessiveness. These enigmatic variations include time of onset (first noticed clinically), family history, clinical manifestations, and symptoms. Acquired influences, such as environmental factors, habits, and health, do not seem to play a critical role in explaining the appearance of these conditions. Additionally, cause-and-effect associations have not been established with any systemic diseases. Therefore, an accurate differential diagnosis is critical, to be able to advise patients regarding potential complications or problems, prognosis (natural history), diagnostic confirmation, and management.

White sponge nevus is the only disease or condition in this group that has been investigated by genetic and molecular means. It is an inherited disease in which there is a defect in regulation of mucosal keratinization. Specifically, the keratin family is clustered on chromosome 17. The keratin 13 gene has been found to harbor a missense mutation, and the keratin 4 gene shows a three-base pair deletion in families with white sponge nevus.

Hairy tongue

Hairy tongue (HT) is a clinical manifestation of elongation of the filiform papillae located on the dorsum of the tongue. This condition is often a response to infections, fever, xerostomia, and a variety of substances, such as antibiotics and tobacco. However, often there is no identifiable etiologic agent or factor, thus leading to a working diagnosis of idiopathic HT. It is almost never symptomatic; but it is the appearance that frequently bothers the patient and is the basis for the chief complaint.

Clinical findings

Hairy tongue presents with varying degrees of a "hairy" appearance of the dorsum of the tongue, owing to the elongation of the filiform papillae (Figure 25–1, A and B). Variations can be found in the distribution of the elongated papillae, the length, and the color, but the findings are obvious to both clinician and patient. Usually a slight burst of air will further reveal the elongated keratin hair-like overgrowth.

Diagnosis

The diagnosis can usually be made on the basis of appearance and history. As indicated above, HT can appear grossly discolored, depending upon chromogens from bacteria, foods, drugs, and mouthrinses, and a variety of products with oral mucosal contact, such as combustible and smokeless tobacco, lozenges, and wines. These various substances are absorbed by the thickened keratin covering the elongated papillae causing the transient staining.

A biopsy is elective. Histopathology shows elongated hair-like projections of keratinized surface epithelial cells, some interspersed debris and microbial flora, and a moderate inflammatory infiltrate (Figure 25–1, C). Whereas candidal overgrowth can be found in some cases, it is usually a result, and not the cause of HT.

Treatment

Patient approach involves orientation to the causes, implications, and benign nature, along with reassurance that HT is not contagious or an indicator of a specific systemic disease. Often patient concerns focus on gastrointestinal disease of some sort, or even sexual activities.

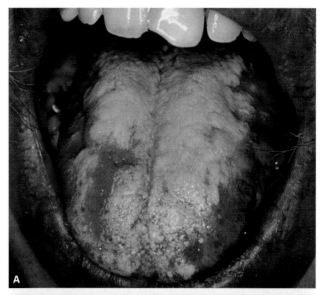

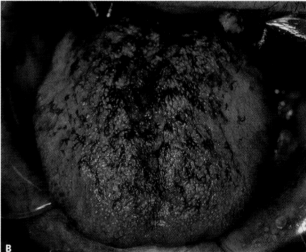

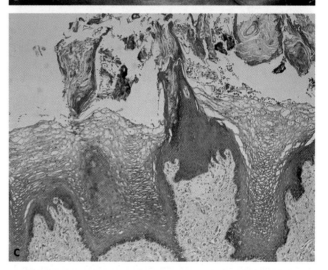

Figure 25–1 Hairy tongue. *A,* Hairy tongue associated with allergies and xerostomia. *B,* Hairy tongue in a patient taking antibiotics and discolored black from bacterial chromogens. *C,* Typical histologic picture of a patient with hairy tongue. Note the surface projections of keratin that forms the "hairs."

Treatment involves orientation to the condition and empirical approaches. The latter include mouthrinse trials, normalizing oral flora if indicated, correcting hyposalivation (see Chapter 26), and tongue brushing or scraping in moderation. Periodic in-office applications of a keratinolytic drug, podophyllin (25% in tincture of benzoin), can sometimes be useful in idiopathic cases (30-second applications followed by rinsing with water). Halitosis may be an associated complaint that persists and requires treatment (see Chapter 27). Again, reassurance of the benign and noninfectious nature of the condition is an extremely important part of management.

Geographic tongue (glossitis migrans)

Geographic tongue (GT) or glossitis migrans is a condition that can be observed at any time in life, even as early as the second year of life. The occurrence of GT appears to be spontaneous and only occasionally associated with a physical, chemical, or environmental exposure. Since the manifestations are often subtle and without symptoms, an exact prevalence remains unknown, but could involve as many as 10% of a pop-

ulation. Some patients, fortunately the minority, are symptomatic and can have idiopathic spontaneous flares, chronic discomfort, or irritation in response to physical or chemical irritants. Once GT occurs, it usually remains in a chronic or cyclic form indefinitely.

Clinical findings

There are classic clinical findings of depapillation of the filiform papillae on the dorsum of the tongue, causing erythematous configurations that can be variable in size, shapes, and number (Figure 25–2, A). These areas are bordered by a slight increase in the surrounding filiform papillae, forming a white-appearing, narrow, peripheral margin. Geographic tongue can be chronic or migratory, or may periodically disappear.

Diagnosis

The diagnosis is based upon clinical appearance and history. When there is clinical confusion because of a rather bizarre manifestation, or deep concern on the part of the patient, a biopsy can be performed. Histo-

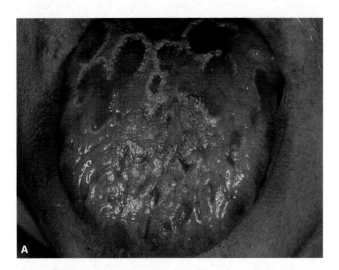

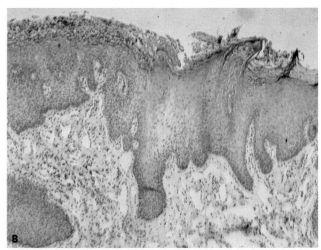

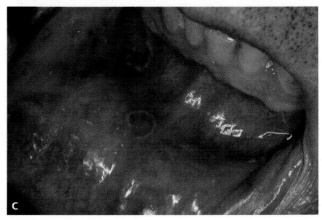

Figure 25–2 Geographic tongue (glossitis migrans). *A*, Classic appearance of depapillated, erythematous areas surrounded by a margin of hyperkeratosis. These lesions were only mildly symptomatic. Although they were chronic, there were week-to-week variations in appearance. The patient was in excellent health and not taking any medications. *B*, Typical microscopic picture of depapillation, adjacent elongation of filiform papillae, connective tissue inflammation, and irregular epithelial hyperplasia. *C*, A patient with geographic tongue, with similar lesions occurring on the labial mucosa, reflex, and buccal mucosa. This variant of geographic tongue is called stomatitis migrans. The lesions would periodically disappear and reappear at different oral mucosal sites.

logically, there is chronic connective tissue inflammation covered by a thin or atrophic epithelium (Figure 25–2, *B*). Elongation of peripheral filiform papillae at the margins can be seen, corresponding to the clinical findings. There is no associated dysplasia.

Treatment

Most important, patients must be reassured that although this is a chronic or cyclic condition, GT does not represent a neoplastic, infectious, or contagious disease. Biopsy is elective. If a patient has generalized complaints or findings, then a physical examination should be suggested to rule out a coincidental systemic problem.

When a patient is asymptomatic, no further treatment is necessary. Since some patients may be uncomfortable or experience considerable pain, identifiable irritants (mainly food types) should be avoided. Symptoms are treated empirically. Trials can include placebos (vitamins), mouthrinses, antianxiety medications, and anti-inflammatory drugs. The latter can include nonsteroidal anti-inflammatory drugs (NSAIDs) and topical or systemic corticosteroids. Analgesic agents are sometimes needed.

Stomatitis (erythema) migrans

This condition is a benign and infrequent variant of GT in which similar-appearing lesions can occur on other mucosal surfaces (Figure 25–2, *C*). The lesions are oval with a red macular center surrounded by a circinate white border. As with geographic tongue, these lesions are typically painless and resolve only to reappear in an adjacent location. Management often involves biopsy and blood tests to rule out dyscrasias. Otherwise, the therapeutic approach is similar to that of GT; that is, empirical approaches for symptomatic patients.

Median rhomboid glossitis

Median rhomboid glossitis (MRG) is thought to be a congenital abnormality related to the persistence of an embryonic midline tongue structure, the tuberculum impar. Its existence is questioned, since this abnormality is not seen in the newborn or infants. Furthermore, many of these observed "lesions" have been associated with candidal organisms, and the clinical changes disappear or are greatly modified following antifungal treatment. However, some uncertainty still remains, since some of these lesions are not controlled by the use of antifungals. Central papillary atrophy is the most currently accepted term to describe these variable-appearing changes.

Diagnosis

Median rhomboid glossitis appears as an atrophic, fissured change on the posterior dorsum of the oral tongue, just anterior to the circumvallate papillae and in the midline (Figure 25–3). The diagnosis is made by the clinical appearance and location as well as a history of

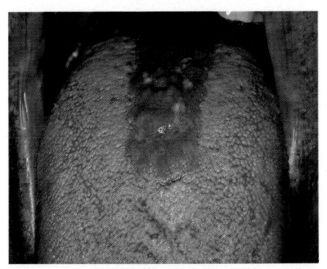

Figure 25–3 This adult patient presented with asymptomatic, chronic depapillated lesion of the tongue. A culture was negative for *Candida*, and there was no clinical response to a course of antifungal medication. On follow-up, there was no change in signs or symptoms. The patient was in good health. This lesion is consistent with median rhomboid glossitis (a developmental anomaly).

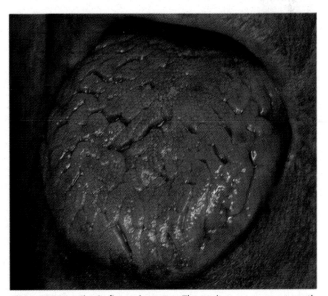

Figure 25–4 Classic fissured tongue. The patient was asymptomatic and in good health. There were no changes in signs or symptoms after long-term follow-up.

no change and no symptoms. If there is any question regarding the possibility of neoplasia, dysplasia, or a granulomatous disease, a biopsy would be appropriate. However, there is no association between MRG and a risk for subsequent pathology. A scraping for fungal hyphae or a fungal culture can be considered.

Treatment

No treatment is indicated for the developmental defect. However, because of the possible uncertainty in diagnosis, a short trial with antifungal medications can be tried, particularly if there are any associated symptoms.

Fissured tongue

The fissured tongue (FT) is a condition, either inherited or acquired, that manifests variable degrees of grooves or fissures on the tongue dorsum. Although these epithelial-lined splits are seen commonly, the frequency is unknown. The etiology is uncertain, because the time when the fissures first appeared cannot be documented with certainty. Whereas there has been some testimonial association with nutritional and vitamin deficiencies, this has not been frequent or well-confirmed.

Clinical findings

There is such a wide range of fissuring appearances that there is no standard classification or adequate description (Figure 25–4). Occasionally, when a patient notices a FT for the first time or feels that the fissures are increasing, there is concern over the significance. In some patients, there are complaints of discomfort, or coincidental tongue symptoms; these are eventually shown to be unrelated to the fissuring (see Chapter 34).

Diagnosis

The diagnosis is made by clinical findings and history. If there are indications of a systemic disease or condition based on signs and symptoms, then the appropriate referral or laboratory tests should be carried out. By simply stretching the tongue with mild pressure, the epithelial-lined fissures become obvious.

Treatment

The prime treatment involves counseling the patient regarding the benign nature, the common occurrence, and the lack of association with infections or other conditions or diseases. Management is empirical, including optimal hygiene and mouthrinses. Rarely, when a fis-

sure is deep and associated with debris and exudate, débridement and closure of the defect is in order.

Fordyce granules

Fordyce granules (FG) are manifestations of ectopic sebaceous glands that can vary clinically from subtle to prominent mucosal irregularities. Fordyce granules are inherited, can be found in most mouths, and are not representative of any disease or pathologic process.

Clinical findings

Fordyce granules appear as submucosal granules or nodules that can vary in size from 1 mm to 2 mm (Figure 25–5). The presentation is yellowish-white, clus-

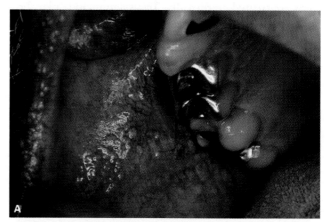

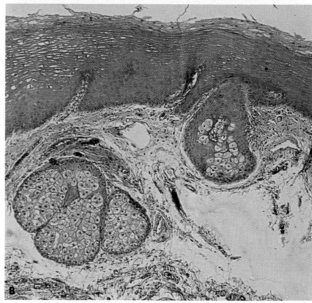

Figure 25–5 Fordyce granules. *A,* Typical appearance of Fordyce granules. These ectopic sebaceous glands are not associated with any pathology. *B,* Microscopic confirmation of ectopic sebaceous glands that are normally found in skin.

tered or dispersed, dense or sparse. They most commonly occur on the buccal and labial mucosa, although they can be found on any mucosal oral site.

Diagnosis

The diagnosis is almost always based on history, lack of symptoms, and clinical appearance. If there is doubt because of an atypical presentation, a biopsy can be performed. Histology shows typical sebaceous glands that are normally found in skin.

Treatment

No treatment is necessary for FG. However, reassurance that these granules are a variation of normal anatomy and not a disease process is important.

White sponge nevus

White sponge nevus (WSN) is a benign genetic condition found in blood-related family members. However, WSN may occur de novo in a family member without any previous family history. Not only is family history, dominance, and recessiveness not clear, but frequently the clinical features (penetrance) are not observed until adolescence or adulthood.

Clinical findings

The characteristics of WSN can be variable, ranging from a mild, irregular epithelial surface keratosis to bothersome, accentuated mucosal surface projections or hairs (Figure 25–6). These irregularities of the mouth lining are often misdiagnosed and blamed on local irritation from foods, biting, or other habits. Occurrence is usually bilateral on the buccal mucosae, which can be accompanied by similar changes on the lateral tongue. Why this is so frequently noticed many years after childhood is not clear.

Diagnosis

White sponge nevus features can often be confused with leukoplakia and a precancerous risk. Therefore, biopsies are often performed to rule out risks for dysplasia or malignancy. Histopathology of WSN shows irregular surface projections of keratin, epithelial hyperplasia, and vacuolation. Staining with toluidine blue accentuates clinically the irregular mucosal surface projections. (Because of the rapid WSN epithelial turnover rate, there is a high concentration of DNA to which the toluidine blue binds.) White sponge nevus is not associated with any other disease or condition and has no premalignant implications.

Treatment

It is important to confirm the diagnosis and reassure a patient of the chronic and benign nature, reemphasizing that WSN is not neoplastic or infectious. Because patients become cognizant of the surface irregularities, they irritate the surface projections by nibbling or sucking on their mucosa. This can be precluded or mitigated by splints or medications, if necessary. In some accentuated cases, smoothing the mucosal surface with laser vaporization has been helpful.

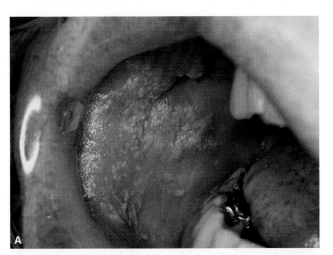 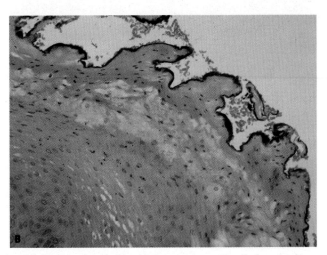

Figure 25–6 White sponge nevus. *A*, Clinical appearance of the hyperplastic epithelium associated with white sponge nevus. Usually there is a long-standing history of a white appearance and complaints of an irregularity of the mucosal surface that prompts biting and involves "sloughing." It is not a precancerous lesion. *B*, The biopsy shows no dysplasia associated with the typical hyperplasia, surface projections, and spongiosis of the epithelium.

Hemangiomas and lymphangiomas

Hemangiomas and lymphangiomas are benign growths, usually self-limiting, which most often occur independently of one another. Occasionally, they occur as a mixed lesion. These proliferations of vessels can be inherited (genetic) or acquired (injury). Their frequency in any population has not been accurately quantified. Depending upon their oral location, they can interfere with esthetics and function. Associated pain is uncommon. However, the lesions may be sub-

jected to acute or chronic irritation (based primarily on size and location) and can lead to clinical complaints of discomfort.

Clinical findings

Hemangiomas can appear as flat, sessile, or lobulated reddish-purple growths that have extreme variations in size (Figure 25–7, *A* and *B*). They are usually soft to palpation and do not blanch to pressure. Lymphangiomas

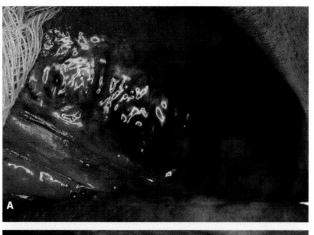

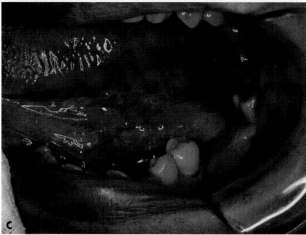

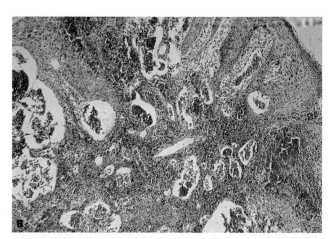

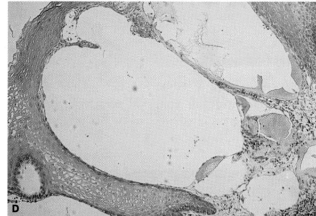

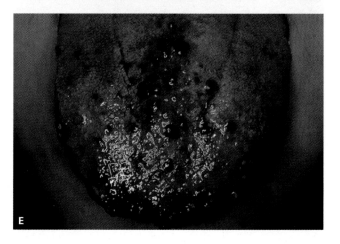

Figure 25–7   Blood and lymph vessel proliferations. *A*, Hemangioma of the tongue present for over a decade. *B*, Microscopic picture of a capillary hemangioma. Note the increase in size and number of capillaries. *C*, Lymphangioma with the usual finding of a soft, sessile, asymptomatic mucosal proliferation. *D*, Microscopic picture of a lymphangioma. Note the grossly enlarged lymph vessels. *E*, Lymphhemangioma in a youngster followed for over 6 years without change. The lesion was asymptomatic.

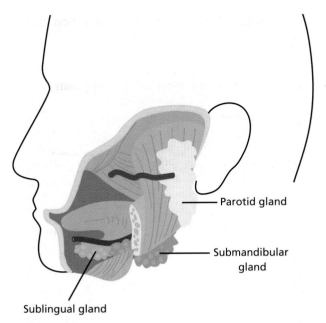

Figure 26–3 Anatomic locations of the three major salivary glands in humans.

Parotid gland

Submandibular gland

Sublingual gland

vary glands connect with the mucosa through short ducts and secrete a mucinous fluid with a high immunoglobulin content.

The secretion of saliva is controlled by the sympathetic and parasympathetic nervous systems. The stimulus for fluid secretion is primarily via muscarinic-cholinergic receptors and, for protein release, through adrenergic receptors. Ligation of these receptors induces a complex signaling and signal transduction pathway within the cells involving numerous membrane transport systems. It is important to consider that loss of acini, as occurs in a number of clinical conditions, limits the ability of the gland to transport fluid and produce saliva; also, muscarinic agonists have the greatest effects in increasing saliva output, as they are primarily responsible for stimulus of fluid secretion. These two points have implications for treatment of salivary gland dysfunction.

Clinical features

Most patients with salivary gland hypofunction have obvious signs of mucosal dryness. The lips are often cracked, peeling, and may be atrophic. The buccal mucosa may be pale and corrugated in appearance. The tongue is often smooth and reddened, with loss of papillation (Figure 26–5). Patients may report that their lips stick to the teeth and one may see shed epithelial cells adhering to the dry enamel. There is often a marked increase in erosion and caries, particularly decay on root surfaces and even cusp-tip involvement. The decay

may be progressive even in the presence of excellent and vigilant oral hygiene. Whereas caries is unquestionably increased, it is unclear if there is an increased prevalence or severity of periodontal pathology associated with salivary gland hypofunction. Candidiasis is frequent, most commonly of the erythematous form. Other oral microbial infections are increased as well. Enlargement of the salivary glands is seen with some frequency. In these cases, one must distinguish between inflammatory, infectious, or neoplastic etiologies (Figure 26–6).

Symptoms in the patient with salivary gland hypofunction are related to decreased fluid in the oral cavity. Patients complain predominantly of dryness of all the mucosal surfaces, including the throat, and also of difficulties chewing, swallowing, and speaking. Many patients report a need to drink fluids while eating to help swallowing, or an inability to swallow dry foods. Most carry fluids at all times for oral comfort and to aid speaking and swallowing. Pain is a common complaint. The mucosa may be sensitive to spicy or coarse foods, which limits enjoyment of meals.

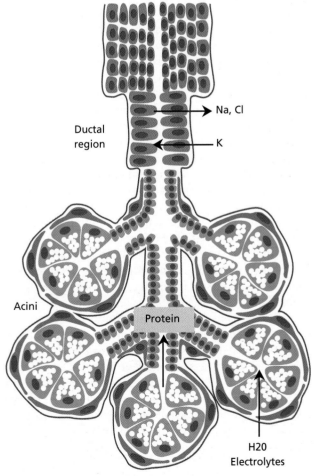

Ductal region

Na, Cl

K

Acini

Protein

H20
Electrolytes

Figure 26–4 Schematic drawing of the basic anatomic structure of the salivary glands showing the branching ductal system and the acinar endpieces.

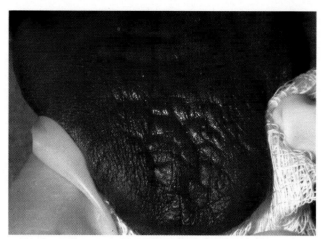

Figure 26–5 The tongue of a patient with Sjögren syndrome and salivary hypofunction. Note the loss of normal papillation and the dry, corrugated appearance.

Diagnosis

The differential diagnosis of xerostomia and salivary gland dysfunction is a lengthy process. The optimal approach to diagnosis is a coherent, sequential plan that should first establish the cause of the complaint, then determine the extent of salivary gland hypofunction that is present, and finally assess the potential for treatment. The goal is to identify patients who require treatment and to recognize associated systemic conditions.

A critical first step is a thorough history. If the past and present medical history reveal medical conditions or medications that are known to be associated with salivary gland dysfunction, the diagnosis may be obvious. Examples would be the patient who has received radiotherapy for a head and neck malignancy or an individual who has recently started a prescription for a tricyclic antidepressant. Often the temporal association of symptom onset with the treatment is a valuable clue. When the history does not suggest an obvious diagnosis, further detailed exploration of the symptomatic complaint should be undertaken. Particular attention should be paid to the specific dryness symptoms. Unfortunately, the general complaint of oral dryness is not well correlated with decreased salivary function; however, specific symptoms may be. For example, whereas complaints of dryness at night or on awakening have not been found to be associated with reduced salivary function, complaints of oral dryness while eating, the need to sip liquids to swallow dry food, or reports of difficulties in swallowing dry food all are highly correlated positively with measured decreases in secretory capacity (Table 26–3). Patient responses to questions that focus on oral activities (eg, swallowing, eating) that rely on stimulated salivary function, when combined with the clinical signs of salivary hypofunction, are

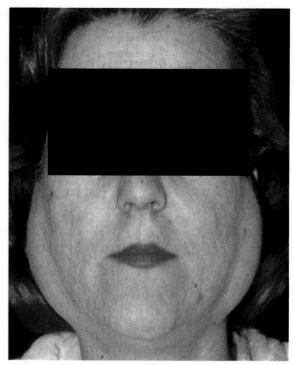

Figure 26–6 A patient with Sjögren syndrome with persistently enlarged major salivary glands. This was found to be a benign condition.

highly predictive of reduced secretory performance and help identify an individual who requires further evaluation and treatment. Therefore, the patient who presents with a complaint of "dry mouth" should be asked specific questions, to help determine whether salivary gland hypofunction exists. Patients should also be questioned concerning dryness at other body sites. It may be a significant indication of a systemic condition, such as Sjögren syndrome, if a patient reports eye, throat, nasal, skin, or vaginal dryness, in addition to xerostomia.

Signs of salivary gland dysfunction should be sought through careful examination. As noted above, dryness of

Table 26–3 Questions Helpful in Evaluating Patients with Complaints of Dry Mouth

1. Do you have difficulty swallowing dry foods?
2. Does your mouth feel dry while eating a meal?
3. Do you sip liquids to aid in swallowing dry food?
4. Does the amount of saliva in your mouth most of the time seem to be too little, too much, or do you not notice it?

Positive responses to questions 1 to 3, or the perception of too little saliva (question 4), are significantly associated with reduced salivary gland function.

Adapted from Fox PC, Busch KA, Baum BJ. Subjective reports of xerostomia and objective measures of salivary gland performance. J Am Dent Assoc 1987;115:581–4.

the mucosal surfaces with erythematous or atrophic changes can be seen. Partial or total papillary atrophy may be present on the tongue. Fissuring of the tongue may also occur. One should look for active caries and judge whether the caries experience and current condition are consistent with the patient's oral hygiene practices. Two additional indications of oral dryness that have been gleaned from clinical experience are the "lipstick" and "tongue blade" signs. In the former, the presence of lipstick on the labial surfaces of the anterior maxillary teeth is indicative of reduced saliva that would normally wet the mucosa and aid in cleansing the teeth. For the latter, the examiner can hold a tongue blade against the buccal mucosa. In a dry mouth, the tissue adheres to the tongue blade as it is lifted away. Both signs suggest that the mucosa is not sufficiently moisturized by the saliva.

The major salivary glands should be palpated to detect masses and also to determine whether saliva can be expressed via the main excretory ducts. Normally, saliva can be expressed from each major gland orifice. The consistency of the secretions should be examined. The expressed saliva should be clear, watery, and copious. Viscous or scant secretions suggest chronically reduced function. A cloudy exudate may be a sign of bacterial infection, although some patients with low salivary function have hazy, flocculated secretions that are sterile. In these cases, there may be mucoid accretions and clumped epithelial cells that lend the saliva a cloudy appearance. Particularly in the case of an enlarged gland, the exudate should be cultured if it does not appear clear. Distinct masses within the body of the gland should not be present and the consistency of the gland should be slightly rubbery, but not hard. Palpation should be painless. Enlarged, painful glands are indicative of infection or acute inflammation.

Salivary output can be measured as well. One can either examine the whole saliva (ie, the combined product of all the salivary glands) or look at individual gland function. The latter is not difficult, but requires specialized collectors and, therefore, is usually done in research settings. Unstimulated saliva is the saliva secreted without exogenous stimulus, often termed the resting flow. Stimulated saliva is secreted in response to a stimulus, usually gustatory, masticatory, or pharmacologic.

Whole saliva can be collected easily by the spitting or drooling methods. Patients are instructed to have nothing by mouth for at least 1 hour prior to collections, to first collect an unstimulated sample. The mouth is rinsed initially with deionized water, and the sample is obtained by having the patient expectorate into a graduated cylinder at regular intervals. Standard collection times are 5 or 15 minutes. Stimulated whole saliva then can be obtained by having the patient chew at a controlled rate on an inert material, such as paraffin wax, unflavored gum base, or a rubber band. During stimulated collection, patients are usually asked to expectorate every minute for 2 to 5 minutes.

Parotid gland collection is performed with Carlson-Crittenden collectors. Individual collectors are placed over Stensen duct orifices on the buccal mucosa and held in place with gentle suction. Submandibular-sublingual individual gland collection uses a suction device. Gauze is placed sublingually to dry and isolate the sublingual region. The gauze and tongue are guided in a posterior direction, away from the duct orifices. Saliva is collected as it is released from the glands into the oral cavity. Stimulation for individual gland collection is obtained by applying 2% citric acid bilaterally to the anterior dorsolateral surface of the tongue with swabs every 30 seconds. Pre-weighed tubes are used for salivary gland collections. Tubes are weighed again following collection to determine flow rate in milliliters per minute per gland, assuming 1 mg = 1 μL saliva.

Although definitive guidelines are not available, primarily because of the wide variability of normal salivary function, there is a consensus among most investigators that unstimulated whole saliva flow rates of less than 1.5 mL per 15 minutes or stimulated whole saliva rates of less than 0.5 mL per minute clearly are abnormally low.

In addition to measuring the volume of saliva produced, one may characterize the constituents. A diagnostic dilemma has been that most causes of salivary gland dysfunction demonstrate similar alterations in the saliva composition. This has limited the diagnostic value of sialochemistries for specific diseases. Recent work in Sjögren syndrome is beginning to identify changes in salivary cytokine and other protein levels that may have diagnostic significance. Saliva may play a greater diagnostic role in monitoring for the presence and concentrations of drugs of abuse and therapeutic agents.

There are numerous salivary gland imaging techniques that may be useful in selected situations. These include salivary scintiscans using ^{99m}Tc pertechnetate, sialograms with opaque contrast materials, computed tomography (CT), magnetic resonance imaging (MRI), and ultrasonography of the major glands.

Technetium scintigraphy uses ^{99m}Tc pertechnetate, a radionuclide with affinity for salivary, thyroid, and gastric glands. Technetium 99m is injected intravenously, and the uptake into the major salivary glands and subsequent secretion into the oral cavity are imaged (Figure 26–7). The Tc scan is a dynamic test of salivary activity. Scintigraphy can serve as a measure of the amount of functional water-transporting acinar tissue remaining in the glands. This is useful in determining the potential benefit from the use of sialagogues in a patient with markedly reduced function. However, this technique does not indicate the cause of gland destruction.

Sialography involves cannulation of the main duct of a major salivary gland and retrograde instillation of radiographic contrast material into the body of the gland, followed by radiographic visualization. The contrast material fills the ductal tree of the gland and shows the main excretory duct and branching into the secondary and terminal ductules (Figure 26–8). Sialography is useful to detect disruption of the gland architecture, either by demonstrating the absence of contrast material within the ducts (as is seen with salivary stones) or the abnormal distribution or displacement of the ducts (as might be seen with a salivary tumor). This technique is also useful for detection of fistulas and duct strictures. The procedure is contraindicated in patients with acute salivary gland inflammation, as the procedure may cause retrograde spread of infection. Since the contrast material contains iodine, this technique should be avoided in patients allergic to this halide.

The boundaries of the salivary glands and the quality of the parenchyma are well delineated by both CT and MRI. The retromandibular vein, the external carotid artery, and intraglandular lymph nodes are well visualized. Volumetric determinations of the major glands also may be obtained.

Computed tomography images transverse planes of tissue. Dental amalgam produces scatter and can obstruct the image. Coronal and axial images are usually viewed. Iodinated contrast can be used to enhance imaging. Computed tomography is most useful in detecting and localizing tumors in the body of the glands.

Magnetic resonance imaging is dependent on the varying water content to distinguish different tissue types. It is predominantly used for imaging soft tissues, and is useful in the salivary glands to distinguish the location, size, and quality of masses and their relation to surrounding structures (Figure 26–9). The differentiation of cystic versus solid masses is particularly accurate. Visualization of the facial nerve within the parotid gland has been reported by MRI. Advantages of MRI as an imaging modality include (1) the patient is not exposed to ionizing radiation, (2) intravenous iodine-containing contrast media is not required, and (3) there is minimal artifact from dental restorations. Magnetic resonance imaging is contraindicated in patients with pacemakers or any metallic implants, such as aneurysmal bone clips.

Ultrasonography of the major salivary glands has been recommended primarily for visualization of cystic masses. Resolution is often low and diagnostic specificity is lacking.

More definitive diagnosis can be obtained with tissue biopsy. A minor salivary gland biopsy is the most accurate sole diagnostic criterion available for diagnosis of the salivary component of Sjögren syndrome. Histologic examination of labial minor glands demonstrates a characteristic focal, periductal, mononuclear cell infiltrate with acinar cell loss (see Figure 26–2). Ductal

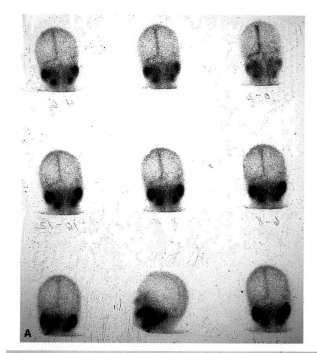

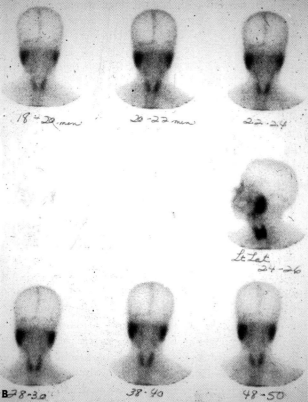

Figure 26–7 Technetium scintiscan of the salivary glands using technetium 99m (^{99m}Tc) pertechnetate. The timed sequence shows the initial uptake of tracer into the parotid glands. *A*, Prompt uptake is seen in both the parotid and submandibular glands in this healthy individual. Appearance of tracer in the oral cavity is seen in the final frame. *B*, The submandibular glands are not seen in this patient, owing to gland dysfunction. The uptake is slowed in this patient with dry mouth, and release of tracer into the oral cavity is not apparent. The thyroid gland can be visualized at the inferior of the frame.

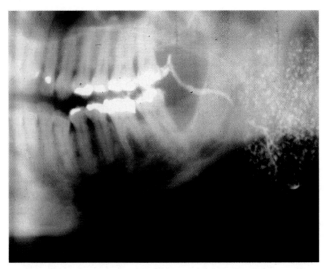

Figure 26–8 A sialogram of the parotid gland using an iodine-containing contrast material. This film shows punctate sialectasis, characteristic of Sjögren syndrome.

structures are relatively well preserved. The extent of mononuclear cell infiltration can be described by the focus score, which quantifies the number of lymphoid aggregates per 4 mm^2 within the glands. A focus score above 1, in the appropriate clinical setting, has been reported to be highly specific for Sjögren syndrome.

Minor salivary glands are easily accessible and biopsy can be obtained with minimal morbidity. Procedures to biopsy the major salivary glands are more invasive, requiring an external incision in the orofacial region, and have higher morbidity. Parotid biopsy carries a risk of damage to the facial nerve and formation of postoperative fistula. Minimally invasive procedures sampling tissue from the parotid tail region are less hazardous and may be performed in an outpatient setting. The choice of biopsy site—major versus minor gland—is determined by the diagnostic requirements in each case.

Parotid gland biopsy is not more accurate than minor gland biopsy for routine diagnostic evaluation of Sjögren syndrome and has given false-negative results. However, major salivary gland biopsy is indicated when tissue must be examined to evaluate an enlarged gland. Patients with Sjögren syndrome often have chronic major salivary gland enlargement. If persistent unilateral enlargement exists or changes in an enlarged region are noted, one should be suspicious of malignant lymphoma and biopsy the affected gland. An open biopsy provides a larger tissue sample than a fine-needle biopsy. It allows one to view a lesion in context of surrounding tissue and indicates if a mass has a distinct margin. However, fine-needle aspiration is useful for repeat biopsies to monitor lesions that have been reported to be benign. In Sjögren syndrome there may be progression of the so-called benign lymphoepithelial lesion to a malignancy. Needle

aspirates are effective in sampling tissue to examine the infiltrate for monoclonality, a sign of lymphoma. An additional advantage to use of fine-needle aspiration is that there is less disruption of the field for subsequent surgery or radiotherapy.

A final diagnostic procedure is examination of peripheral blood. Serologic markers of autoimmunity can be found in patients with Sjögren syndrome and can aid in diagnosis, but a lack of abnormal findings does not exclude the diagnosis of Sjögren syndrome. Antinuclear antibodies (ANA) are present in 80% of patients with Sjögren syndrome. The two most specific autoantibodies in Sjögren syndrome are anti-SS-A/Ro and anti-SS-B/La, found in approximately 60% and 40% of patients, respectively. Rheumatoid factors (RF) are also found in Sjögren syndrome. Other autoantibodies, such as anti-SM, anti-DNA, and anti-RNP (ribonuclear proteins) are rarely found. Patients with Sjögren syndrome often demonstrate elevated total serum protein and marked hypergammaglobulinemia, with one or all (IgG, IgM, IgA) of the immunoglobulin subtypes elevated. The sedimentation rate may be elevated, and the white blood cell count decreased. In cases of salivary gland enlargement or inflammation, the serum amylase is often increased.

At the conclusion of the diagnostic evaluation, one should have a clear indication of the adequacy of salivary function, a possible cause for salivary gland dysfunction (if it exists), and a plan for management based on the diagnosis and the extent of the dysfunction present.

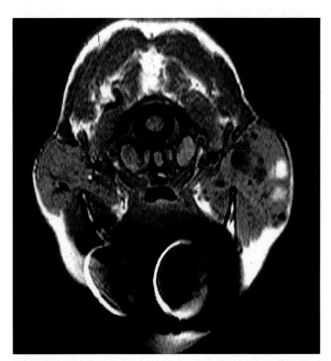

Figure 26–9 MRI of the head showing enlarged parotid glands. This is a T1-weighted image and demonstrates cystic areas and the presence of lymph nodes within the glands.

Treatment

Management of the patient with dry mouth can be characterized as symptomatic, preventive, or curative. Symptomatic treatment is directed at alleviating or minimizing the complaints associated with decreased salivation. These range from simple methods of hydration and lubrication, to use of systemic secretagogues to stimulate salivary function. The goal of preventive treatments is to limit the consequences of salivary gland hypofunction on the oral hard and soft tissues. Curative approaches address the underlying cause of the symptoms.

The use of water cannot be overemphasized for the patient with dry mouth. Patients should be encouraged to carry non-sugar-containing fluids with them and take frequent small sips. This helps hydrate the oral mucosa and also rinses retained debris. The patient must be counseled specifically to avoid fluids that contain sugar, which exacerbate caries problems. Sugar-free soft drinks can be used, but one must be aware of the caffeine-content of these beverages, as caffeine can contribute to the feeling of oral dryness. Patients may benefit from use of humidifiers, particularly placed near the bed at night. Moisturizers and emollients applied to the lips are essential. Although many patients find that petrolatum-based products give relief, more penetrating creams may be preferable. Products containing lanolin and vitamin E seem to be especially well tolerated.

Sensitivity of the mucosal surfaces is a common complaint in patients with dry mouth. Avoiding spicy foods, alcohol, and strong flavorings may limit this symptom. Many dental products have flavorings that can irritate dry tissues. Also, patients should be cautioned to avoid mouthrinses with high alcohol content that can induce mucosal irritation and sensitivity.

Many saliva-replacement products are available. There are a number of oral rinses and gels that may be used to cleanse the mouth and wet the mucosa. Some have gained moderate patient acceptance, but controlled studies have not demonstrated superiority to regular use of sips of water. Often patients prefer sipping water or sucking on ice chips. The taste and mechanical stimulation of salivation from chewing sugarless candy and gum can increase saliva output and provide relief for some patients.

Several systemic sialagogues have been investigated. These agents are only useful for patients who have remaining salivary gland function that can be stimulated. Anethole-trithione has been found to be helpful for mild medication-induced xerostomia in limited clinical studies. It is not available in the United States. Clinical trials have also been conducted with the mucolytic agent bromhexine, but objective evidence of enhanced salivary function is lacking. Pilocarpine hydrochloride is a parasympathomimetic agonist that increases exocrine output. It is the most widely tested secretagogue and has been shown to be effective in relieving symptoms of oral dryness in both radiation and Sjögren syndrome-induced salivary hypofunction. Side effects are common but tolerable. Recommended doses are 5 mg given three or four times daily. Recently (January 2000) a new secretagogue, cevimeline hydrochloride, has been approved for use in the United States for relief of symptoms of dry mouth in patients with Sjögren syndrome. There is limited published information on this compound. It is also a parasympathomimetic agonist and appears to have an activity and adverse event profile similar to that of pilocarpine, based on the prescribing information provided by the manufacturer. The recommended dose is 30 mg three times daily.

Patients with dry mouth have increased susceptibility to dental caries. Oral applications of topical fluorides have been shown to reduce caries and to help preserve the dentition. The fluoride is incorporated into the enamel of the teeth during the demineralization-remineralization process and increases resistance to decay. Fluorides are available as rinses and as higher-concentration gels. The latter can be applied by brush or in custom-made carriers that hold the material against the teeth. The frequency and mode of application must be determined for each patient based on the extent of salivary hypofunction and caries activity. When coupled with increased attention to dental hygiene and frequent professional dental care, supplemental fluoride can protect against the rampant dental decay that can accompany salivary dysfunction. However, sometimes even with daily topical fluoride and meticulous oral hygiene, patients may continue to have increased caries.

There has been research with use of rinse solutions high in calcium and phosphate to help prevent loss of tooth structure in patients with dry mouth. These preparations appear to be helpful, replacing the important function of saliva in promoting remineralization of the teeth. None is presently available commercially in the United States.

If salivary gland hypofunction is related to medication use, it may be possible to stop or change the offending pharmaceutical. The issue should be explored with the prescribing physician. Often patients may have fewer side effects with a different drug of the same class. If possible, a trial with an alternative medication should be done.

If a bacterial infection is identified, appropriate antibiotics should be prescribed. Salivary gland infections often can require prolonged therapy to eradicate an infection completely. Use of sensitivity testing is recommended to select the appropriate medication. Patients should maintain high fluid intake and use a strong secretagogue, such as sour lemon candies, at least three times daily to promote fluid flow. If there is enlargement caused by an inflammatory (and not an infectious) cause, such as in Sjögren syndrome, antibiotics are not indicated. In these cases, short courses of systemically administered corticosteroids, may be beneficial. In general, the nonsteroidal anti-inflammatory drugs have not been useful in this setting.

As noted previously, owing to the loss of the antifungal activity of saliva, candidal and other fungal infections are a common and recurrent problem for patients with dry mouth. Treatment with topical or systemic antifungal agents may be prolonged. A particular concern is that most topical preparations (troches or lozenges) sold for treatment of oral fungal infections contain high concentrations of sugar. Although this improves the taste, it creates a problem for patients with salivary dysfunction who may need to be treated for several weeks to resolve a fungal infection completely. Non-sugar-containing antifungal rinse solutions can be formulated with nystatin powder or a nonflavored vaginal troche can be used orally.

Although secretagogues can provide transient relief of oral dryness, a limitation is that they are directed at the symptoms but fail to address the underlying causes of the gland dysfunction. In conditions such as Sjögren syndrome, patients are left with a gradual decline in function over time, worsening symptoms, and functional deficits.

Since the changes that take place in the salivary glands in Sjögren syndrome are of a chronic, inflammatory nature, the agents that have been tested have been primarily anti-inflammatory drugs used in other connective tissue diseases: nonsteroidal agents, steroids, or members of a large group of more potent drugs known as disease-modifying antirheumatic drugs.

The nonsteroidal anti-inflammatory drug (NSAID) piroxicam was tested in a placebo-controlled, double-masked, randomized clinical trial and was not beneficial in improving either the salivary or the lacrimal component in patients with primary Sjögren syndrome, based on objective and subjective criteria. In the same study, the steroid prednisone was effective in improving the serologic alterations found in Sjögren syndrome and in relieving symptoms of oral and ocular dryness. However, there was not significant improvement in major salivary gland function. More critically, there was no change in the extent of mononuclear cell infiltration of the labial minor salivary glands or of the proportion of individual glandular cellular elements (acini, ducts, other). Therefore, steroids were not helpful in addressing the underlying pathologic tissue changes. Steroids may be used in selected cases of Sjögren syndrome, particularly in managing acute inflammatory swelling of the glands, but cannot be recommended routinely for treatment.

A number of other disease-modifying antirheumatic drugs have been proposed or tested for treatment of Sjögren syndrome. Most have either been ineffective or have had unacceptable risk:benefit ratios. Currently, there is a great deal of interest in hydroxychloroquine. This drug was originally developed as an antimalarial, as an alternative to chloroquine, with fewer adverse effects. It has been used for many years in systemic lupus erythematosus and rheumatoid arthritis, two autoimmune connective tissue diseases with many similarities, histopathologically and serologically, to Sjögren syndrome. There were initial uncontrolled studies suggesting benefit in certain aspects of Sjögren syndrome; however, in later controlled trials the results were not positive. The beneficial effects of hydroxychloroquine on salivary and lacrimal functions in Sjögren syndrome remain unproven.

A series of studies have demonstrated beneficial effects of alpha interferon (IFN-α) on salivary function in Sjögren syndrome. Trials have been conducted with both high-dose injectable formulations and a low-dose oral lozenge form of the drug. In addition to significant increases in salivary output, improvement has been shown in exocrine histopathology. A reduction in inflammatory infiltrating cells and an increase in normal-appearing salivary epithelial tissue have been demonstrated following 6 months of low-dose IFN-α therapy. If confirmed in additional studies, this represents the first disease-modifying therapeutic for Sjögren syndrome.

Infectious, obstructive, and neoplastic salivary diseases

Infections of the salivary gland are not common, with the exception of endemic parotitis, or mumps. Bacterial sialadenitis is usually a complication of obstructive disease and evolves as a consequence of retrograde extention through ducts that no longer transmit salivary secretions. Obstructions can occur from tumors and other inflammatory lesions that encroach upon and compress major salivary gland ducts; however, the most common cause is sialolithiasis (intraductal calcific masses, salivary stones). The submandibular gland is affected more often than the parotid, and occasionally, sialoliths evolve within the ducts of minor salivary glands.

Neoplastic lesions of the salivary glands occur most frequently in the parotid, less frequently in the submandibular gland, and are extremely rare in the sublingual gland. The minor glands of the oral cavity are a common site for salivary tumors, the palate, buccal mucosa, and labial mucosa glands being involved most frequently.

Molecular and pathologic correlates of disease

The histologic compartments of the salivary glands are illustrated in Figure 26–10. The individual components

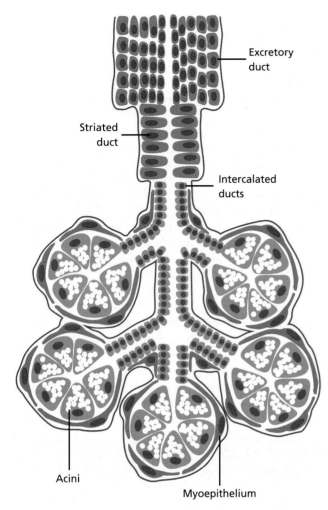

Excretory duct

Striated duct

Intercalated ducts

Acini

Myoepithelium

Figure 26–10 Schematic illustration of the microscopic structure of the salivary glands, depicting ductal system, acinar units, and myoepithelial cells.

include the ductal orifice leading down into the extralobular duct that then branches into smaller extralobular ducts before entering the salivary parenchyma. These ducts are lined by stratified squamous epithelium. Once in the gland proper, the ductal lining becomes high, columnar, and oncocytic, a region referred to as the striated duct zone. These ducts branch further into terminal or intercalated ducts that then enter the acini. Myoepithelial cells encircle these ducts as well as the acini. These contractile cells expel saliva into the lumens, propelling the secretions out through the ductal tree. Recall that acini may be serous, mucous, or seromucous.

The mumps virus, which causes endemic parotitis, is an organism that shows tropism for salivary tissue yet can also infect the testes, pancreas, and central nervous system. The virus is a member of the paramyxovirus family, and its surface is occupied by large glycoproteins with neuraminidase and hemagglutinin activities. The virus is transmitted by aerosol droplets and can propa-

gate in salivary epithelium as well as T lymphocytes. Following infection of the parotid glands, it can be disseminated to other sites via a transient viremia.

Sialolithiasis occurs in the absence of hypercalcemia; rather, the process is a local one whereby detritus accumulates within the ductal lumen. This material forms a mucinous plug that is comprised of viscous glycoproteins, bacteria, and epithelial debris. The ropy and viscous saliva of the submandibular duct appears to be more prone to be associated with stone formation. Upon this organic matrix, calcium salts become precipitated in an accretional, laminated manner such that, microscopically, concentric layering is encountered in decalcified specimens. Small stones may continue to be only partially obstructive, whereas larger sialoliths can cause total blockage (Figure 26–11). Once complete obstruction ensues, the parenchyma continues to function, secreting saliva into a closed space, which then becomes distended with elevated intraluminal pressure that causes atrophy and, ultimately, necrosis of acini. Whereas ductal conduits are preserved, the lobules show mononuclear infiltrates with fibrosis, a process referred to as chronic sclerosing sialadenitis. Other forms of obstruction include mucous plugs, which can be dislodged, and mucous extravasation.

Microscopically, the vast majority of salivary tumors derive from parenchyma and are either adenomas, if benign, or adenocarcinomas, if malignant. In children, some parotid region tumors originate from the fibrovascular supportive tissues of the gland, and in adults, a salivary mass may in actuality represent malignant lymphoma. The nosology of salivary tumors is based exclusively on tumor cell differentiation. Recall that salivary tissue is comprised of three major cellular compartments: acini, ducts, and myoepithelia. The diagnosis is rendered by histopathologic examination. The pathologist bases the diagnosis on two major features: (1) tumor margin characteristics, and (2) resemblance of tumor cells to normal glandular components. With regard to the first feature, encapsulation is perhaps the most important criterion for arriving at a diagnosis of adenoma, whereas invasion of contiguous tissues is the hallmark of adenocarcinomas. The second feature refers to the differentiation of the tumor with respect to ductal, acinar, and myoepithelial components. In most salivary tumors, the differentiation of the cells and their pattern of growth constitute the criteria for establishing a diagnosis.

Clinical features of infectious diseases

Endemic parotitis is a viral infection of the parotid glands that may also infect the submandibular gland. The patient complains of malaise and fever, accompanied by painful bilateral parotid enlargement. The

usually appear as sessile growths or swellings, maintaining the color of adjacent mucosa (Figure 25–7, *C* and *D*). They are soft to palpation and can vary greatly in size. When the mixed type occurs (lymphhemangiomas), the lesion appears as clustered nodules with discolorations varying from purplish-red to yellow-brown (Figure 25–7, *E*).

Diagnosis

Establishing the diagnosis is usually based on the history and clinical appearance. In some cases, a biopsy is necessary, particularly if there is induration or some indication of growth, and the possibility of neoplasia must be evaluated. Aspirating blood from hemangiomas can be helpful in reaching a diagnosis. Fine-needle aspiration biopsy may also serve as an adjunct to the clinical diagnosis (see Chapter 20). Imaging with magnetic resonance can often define the extent and help clarify the diagnosis. Angiograms may be helpful, but are seldom needed.

Treatment

Management depends upon an exact diagnosis as well as signs and symptoms. If lesions appear before puberty, they should be monitored, because often they are self-limiting or even show regression in adoles-cence. After puberty, treatment is elective, depending upon esthetics or interference with function. Treatment is primarily surgical. Laser energy of different wave lengths (ie, argon, carbon dioxide) has been a useful modality. Local injections with sclerosing agents, low-dose radiation, and occluding feeding vessels all may play a role in specific cases. Again, treatment decisions are based upon signs (esthetics, bleeding), symptoms (discomfort, function), the type and extent of the lesion, and progression.

Suggested reading

Banoczy J, Rigo O, Albrecht M. Prevalence study of tongue lesions in a Hungarian population. Community Dent Oral Epidemiol 1993;21:224–6.

Brooks JK, Balciunas BA. Geographic stomatitis: review of the literature and report of five cases. J Am Dent Assoc 1987; 115:421–4.

Jarvinen J, Kullaa-Mikkonen A, Pesonen E. Histoquantitative study of inflamed tongue mucosa. Scand J Dent Res 1991; 99:424–30.

Richard G, De Laurenzi V, Didona B, et al. Keratin 13-point mutation underlies the hereditary mucosal epithelial disorder white sponge nevus. Nat Genet 1995;11:453–5.

van der Waal I, Pindborg JJ. Diseases of the tongue. Chicago: Quintessence, 1986.

26 Diseases of the Salivary Glands

Philip C. Fox, DDS, and L. Roy Eversole, DDS, MSD, MA

Salivary glands are subject to a variety of diseases, including inflammatory, infectious, obstructive, degenerative, and neoplastic processes. Many of these diseases culminate in salivary dysfunction, a problem seen frequently in oral medicine practice. In this chapter, emphasis is placed on xerostomia, followed by a discussion of infectious, obstructive, and neoplastic lesions.

Salivary dysfunction and xerostomia

Saliva plays an essential role in maintaining oral health. Alterations in salivary function lead to compromise of oral tissues and functions and have a large impact on a patient's quality of life. Reductions in salivary flow most commonly manifest as symptoms of oral dryness. This subjective complaint of dry mouth is termed xerostomia, whereas objective alterations in salivary performance, quantitative or qualitative, are referred to as salivary gland dysfunction. This distinction, between symptoms and functional impairment, should be remembered when the evaluation of salivary gland disease is discussed. Although xerostomia is most often indicative of reduced salivary output, it is not invariably associated with objective salivary gland hypofunction. One cannot assume a diagnosis of salivary gland dysfunction based on reports of oral dryness alone. Conversely, the absence of symptoms of dry mouth is not a guarantee of adequate salivary function. Full and systematic evaluation is essential to determine if salivary gland dysfunction is present. This determination is important, as individuals who have true salivary gland hypofunction require aggressive management to prevent or minimize the deleterious effects of reduced salivary function.

Multiple functions of saliva have been recognized. Saliva is important for taste, mastication, deglutition, digestion, maintenance of oral hard and soft tissues, control of oral microbial populations, voice, and speech articulation (Table 26–1).

Saliva plays a role in taste perception by serving as a solute for tastants. Although taste can be maintained in the absence of major salivary gland function, complaints of dysgeusia and hypogeusia are increased in patients with decreased salivary gland function (see Chapter 27). Lubrication of the oral cavity is another important function of saliva. Adequate salivary flow enhances movement of the tongue and lips, which aids in cleansing the oral cavity of food debris and bacteria. This also allows for ease of proper tongue and lip movement necessary for clear articulation. The oral preparatory stage of swallowing requires the formation of a food bolus. Efficient chewing and bolus formation are dependent upon

Table 26–1 Major Functions of Saliva

Hydration
Cleansing
Lubrication
Digestion
Remineralization of dentition
Maintenance of mucosal integrity
Antimicrobial

a moist, lubricated oral mucosa, an intact dentition and periodontium, and fluid to wet the food. Transport during swallowing requires the lubricating and wetting properties of salivary secretions. Saliva plays other roles in digestion beyond aiding in mastication. A variety of digestive enzymes, such as amylase and lipase, are present in saliva and initiate the process of food digestion. Saliva also helps protect the upper gastrointestinal tract by rinsing gastric secretions from the esophageal regions.

Saliva coats the oral mucosal tissues, helping maintain an effective barrier to external insults. Salivary constituents aid in maintaining mucosal integrity by binding to and hydrating the oral tissues. Saliva also contains factors that support tissue growth and differentiation.

Saliva contains numerous antimicrobial agents that help maintain a normal oral flora and control microbial overgrowth. These include both specific and nonspecific factors, such as secretory IgA, mucins, lactoferrin, lysozyme, and lactoperoxidase. The histatins, a family of histidine-rich proteins, have been shown to have potent antifungal properties and the proline-rich proteins influence bacterial colonization by modulating attachment. The combination of saliva's cleansing properties and ability to influence microbial colonization helps prevent the establishment of pathogenic oral flora and decreases the chance of the oral cavity becoming a source of systemic infection.

The dentition is continuously undergoing a process of demineralization and remineralization. Saliva is critical to maintain tooth integrity. Salivary calcium and phosphorus, which are maintained at supersaturated concentrations, owing to specific salivary proteins, are important for remineralization of the teeth. Additionally, the buffering capacity of saliva helps maintain a neutral pH in the oral cavity. Acid production by bacteria at the tooth surface following ingestion of carbohydrates initiates the carious process. Saliva acts to return plaque pH rapidly toward neutrality. Patients who suffer from salivary gland hypofunction are prone to dental decay. Caries is often noted on dental examination, and the incisal and cervical aspects of the teeth are particularly susceptible to decay in these individuals. In spite of meticulous oral hygiene and frequent dental visits, patients with diminished salivary gland function may continue to have a high rate of caries.

As can be appreciated, normal salivary function is central to many aspects of oral health. Additionally, general health can be impacted when salivary function is affected. Altered salivary function has such a major impact on quality of life because saliva plays a critical role in two essential human needs: eating and communicating. Both are compromised when significant salivary gland dysfunction exists.

There are numerous causes of salivary gland dysfunction and xerostomia (Table 26–2). The most com-

mon cause of symptoms of oral dryness is therapeutic drug use. Over 500 agents have been associated with xerostomia symptoms. Interestingly, many of these have not been demonstrated to reduce secretory output quantitatively. Although there is no fully satisfactory explanation for this phenomenon, it may relate to qualitative alterations in saliva composition or to nonsalivary factors. Included among the agents that do directly affect salivary function are antidepressants, anticholinergics, antihypertensives (some), and antihistamines.

Radiotherapy that includes the salivary glands in the treatment fields leads to profound and permanent loss of secretory function at doses above approximately 40 Gy. Salivary function can also be diminished by radioiodine therapy for thyroid carcinoma, particularly if multiple doses are administered. Other cancer treatments may lead to salivary gland hypofunction. These include bone marrow transplantation, which can induce a salivary autoimmune reaction, and head and neck surgery, which can physically disrupt salivary output or secretory neural stimuli.

Many systemic conditions can affect salivary function. Perhaps most prominent is Sjögren syndrome, an autoimmune exocrinopathy. Sjögren syndrome is characterized by symptoms of oral and ocular dryness related to an autoimmune-mediated reduction in salivary and lacrimal function. A distinctive focal mononuclear inflammatory infiltrate can be seen in these glands (Figures 26–1 and 26–2). This condition can also affect other organ systems and, in approximately half of the cases, is associated with another autoimmune connective tissue disorder, such as rheumatoid arthritis or systemic lupus erythematosus. This is then termed secondary Sjögren syndrome. Sjögren syndrome also includes marked serologic autoimmune reactivity, with

Table 26–2 Causes of Salivary Gland Hypofunction

Pharmaceuticals
External beam irradiation to the head and neck and internal radionuclides (eg, ^{131}I)
Systemic diseases
Sjögren syndrome, primary and secondary
Granulomatous diseases (sarcoidosis, tuberculosis)
Graft-versus-host disease
Cystic fibrosis
Bell palsy
Diabetes (uncontrolled)
Amyloidosis
Human immunodeficiency virus infection
Thyroid disease (hypo- and hyperthyroidism)
Late-stage liver disease
Salivary gland disease (tumors)
Psychologic factors (affective disorder)
Malnutrition (anorexia, bulemia, dehydration)
Idiopathic

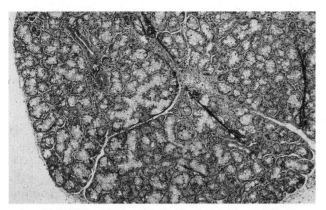

Figure 26–1 Human labial minor salivary gland showing normal histology. The gland is composed primarily of acinar cells. There are a smaller number of ducts and only rare mononuclear cells. (H&E stain)

the majority of patients demonstrating autoantibodies against nuclei (antinuclear antibodies [ANA]) or extractable nuclear antigens (anti-SS-A/Ro and anti-SS-B/La). There is also a 40-fold increased risk for development of malignant lymphoma.

Other systemic conditions with associated salivary gland dysfunction include cystic fibrosis, poorly controlled diabetes, human immunodeficiency virus (HIV) and other viral infections, and thyroid disease (see Table 26–2). Nonsalivary factors that have been associated with xerostomia and salivary gland dysfunction include psychological disorders, malnutrition and eating disorders, and cognitive alterations. Since symptoms of xerostomia usually are not perceived until saliva output is reduced by 50% or more, dry mouth associated with secretory hypofunction is almost always related to involvement of multiple major salivary glands. This implies more generalized systemic involvement. Signs

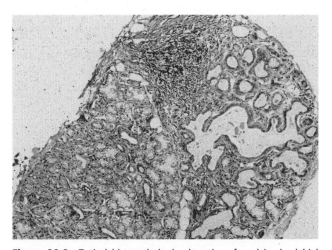

Figure 26–2 Typical histopathologic alterations found in the labial minor salivary glands of a patient with Sjögren syndrome. Note the presence of focal accumulations of mononuclear cells and the loss of acinar elements. (H&E stain)

and symptoms of salivary gland hypofunction should prompt a full oral and medical evaluation to uncover potential underlying systemic disease.

There is continuing debate concerning the role of aging in salivary gland dysfunction. Symptoms of dryness and measurable reductions in salivary function are increased in an older population. However, most investigators believe that this can be explained by the increased incidence of medication use and systemic disease in this group. In healthy, nonmedicated subjects, there is no consistent reduction in salivary gland function with aging. Interestingly, this is true in spite of an approximately 30% decline in total salivary epithelial tissue with aging. For the clinician, the message is that one cannot dismiss symptoms of dryness and salivary gland dysfunction simply as a consequence of aging without a thorough search for other, more probable, causes.

Molecular and pathologic correlates of disease

Saliva is the product of three major salivary glands and the many minor glands dispersed throughout the oral cavity (Figure 26–3). It is a complex mixture of water, organic, and nonorganic components. Most constituents are produced locally within the glands; others are transported from the circulation. The three major salivary glands, the parotid, submandibular, and sublingual, are paired glands that share a basic anatomic structure (Figure 26–4). They are composed of acinar and ductal cells. The acinar cells are the secretory endpiece and are the site of fluid transport into the glands. The acinar cells of the parotid are serous, of the sublingual mucous, and of the submandibular, mixed mucous-serous. The duct cells form a branching system that transports the saliva into the oral cavity. The duct cell morphology changes as it progresses from the acinar junction toward the mouth, and different distinct regions can be identified. The excretory duct of the major glands is named as it enters the oral cavity. Stensen duct is the main duct of the parotid gland and enters the mouth in the buccal mucosa opposite the maxillary molar teeth. Wharton duct is the main duct of the submandibular gland, which runs along the floor of the mouth entering on either side of the lingual frenum. The main duct of the sublingual gland often joins Wharton duct and the secretions cannot be separated from it reliably.

Although fluid secretion occurs only through the acini, proteins are produced and transported into the saliva through both acinar and ductal cells. The primary saliva within the acinar endpiece is isotonic with serum, but undergoes extensive modification within the duct system, with resorption of sodium and chloride and secretion of potassium. The saliva as it enters the oral cavity is a protein-rich hypotonic fluid. The minor sali-

swollen glands typically cause the lobe of the ear to project upward and outward. The glands are extremely tender to palpation and milking them produces a thick white secretion from the parotid ducts. Histologically there is an interstitial infiltrate of mononuclear cells, although neutrophils are often seen within ductal lumens. As acinar cells undergo lysis, the amylase stored in secretory granules is liberated and results in serum elevations of this enzyme. In prepubertal males, the risk of testicular infection is extremely low, yet in postpubertal males, orchitis develops in 20% of cases. Testicular infection follows parotid infection by 1 week and is more often unilateral. Because of the interstitial nature of the inflammatory response in the testes, sterility is rare. There are no effective antiviral agents for mumps.

In rare instances, bacterial sialadenitis develops following extensive or prolonged abdominal surgery. The etiopathogenesis for this complication is unknown, yet may be the consequence of prolonged xerostomia during anesthesia. Patients are febrile and lethargic. The glands swell bilaterally and purulent exudate may be expressed from the duct orifices. This material should be subjected to culture and sensitivity, to allow selection of the appropriate antibiotic. Healing is usually uneventful.

Clinical features of obstructive salivary disease

Obstruction of the salivary ducts is usually attributable to calculus (sialolithiasis). Mucous plugs may congeal within salivary ducts, particularly those of the minor glands and cause intraoral swellings, owing to ductal ectasia. Neoplasms can also compress major ducts and cause the symptoms indicative of obstructive salivary disease; importantly, the gland should be palpated and imaged, to be certain that a neoplastic process is not present, since most instances of obstruction are not related to tumor compression. Magnetic resonance imaging is the preferred modality of imaging in these instances.

The classic clinical findings include episodic glandular enlargement secondary to distention by retained mucus (Figure 26–12, A). This enlargement is accompanied by pain, particularly during eating. The pain is stated to be "drawing" or of a stretching or stinging nature. When these symptoms appear, selected radiographs should be obtained, to explore for the presence of a sialolith. When the symptoms are referable to the submandibular gland, a mandibular occlusal film should be taken (Figure 26–12, B). If no opacity in the vicinity of the course of the submandibular duct can be detected, a panoramic and submental vertex plain film should be taken. Ultrasonography is also a useful imaging technique for discovery of salivary calculi. The more rare occurrence of parotid stones usually requires that a panoramic film be obtained, in which the sialolith can be

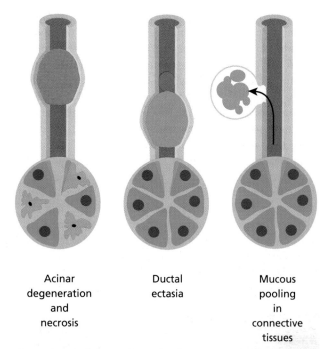

Acinar degeneration and necrosis

Ductal ectasia

Mucous pooling in connective tissues

Figure 26–11 Salivary obstruction from stones, mucous plugs, and mucous extravasation phenomenon.

visualized anterior to the overlying ramus of the mandible. When radiographs fail to reveal any evidence of sialolithiasis, lacrimal probe progressive ductal dilation is indicated, to open any strictures or remove mucinous plugs. Sialography is also a useful diagnostic tool when no reason can be found for obstructive disease.

Mucous extravasation occurs when a salivary duct is severed, usually as a consequence of trauma, and mucus escapes into the connective tissue. The resulting mucocele is soft and fluctuant and is walled-off by a rim of connective tissue yielding a cystic appearance. Most mucoceles are located on the lower lip, yet they may be found anywhere in the mouth where minor salivary glands are located. The buccal mucosa and ventral tongue are other areas where mucoceles are seen. Clinically, they appear as bluish dome-shaped elevations of the mucosa (Figure 26–13).

Clinical features of salivary neoplasms

As mentioned previously, salivary tumors are either benign or malignant with variability in clinical behavior for both groups of neoplasms (Table 26–4). Benign tumors, because of their encapsulation are typically freely movable, except in the hard palate, and are soft or firm, yet not indurated (Figure 26–14). The overlying skin or mucous membrane is unremarkable, ulceration being extremely rare. There are some general principles to be remembered when considering a salivary tumor in the differential diagnosis. In general, all salivary tumors present as visual and palpable masses, with one exception: the deep lobe of the parotid, where the tumor is within the pharyngeal space and small neoplasms may go unnoticed. Parotid gland tumors are more often benign, whereas oral cavity tumors have a 1:1 ratio for benign versus malignant. Unlike other malignancies, malignant parotid tumors are not always indurated and fixed; they may be soft and well defined on palpation, masquerading as a benign tumor. Importantly, malignancy in the parotid often is attended by facial nerve weakness. Oral mucosal malignant salivary tumors often show surface ulceration or overlying telangiectasia.

Adenomas are histopathologically subdivided into monomorphic and pleomorphic subtypes. There are numerous monomorphic adenoma subtypes that vary in their site of occurrence. The monomorphic adenomas

Table 26–4 Classification of Salivary Gland Tumors

Benign tumors with low propensity for recurrence
    Oncocytoma
    Papillary cystadenoma lymphomatosum
    Basal cell adenoma
    Canalicular adenoma
Benign tumors with a propensity for recurrence
    Pleomorphic adenoma (major glands)
Malignant tumors with high-grade behavior
    Adenoid cystic carcinoma
    Salivary duct carcinoma
    Epithelial-myoepithelial carcinoma of intercalated ducts
    High-grade mucoepidermoid carcinoma
    Squamous cell carcinoma of salivary origin
Malignant tumors with low-grade behavior
    Polymorphous low-grade adenocarcinomas
    Low- and intermediate-grade mucoepidermoid carcinoma
    Cystadenocarcinomas

share the common feature of having a single cell type. Most are comprised of ductal cells that resemble either the striated ducts or the intercalated ducts. In the parotid gland, oncocytoma, papillary cystadenoma lymphomatosum (PCL), and basal cell adenoma are the more commonly encountered types. All are encapsulated and relatively soft to palpation. Oncocytoma is a tumor of ductal cells that are enriched with mitochondria, giving the cell a swollen eosinophilic appearance, a feature in common with normally occurring oncocytes within the glands of elderly individuals (Figure 26–15, A). Likewise, oncocytomas are usually encountered in elderly females. Males are more often affected by PCL (Warthin tumor), a lesion that feels like dough on palpation. This characteristic is the result of the histologic pattern of growth. The tumor is well encapsulated and the striated duct-like cells surround cystic spaces into which they project as papillary fronds (Figure 26–15,

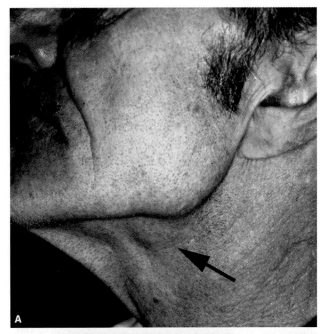

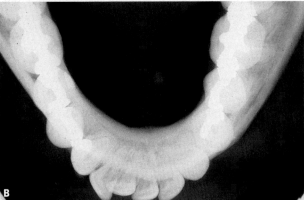

Figure 26–12 *A,* Submandibular enlargement associated with sialolithiasis; *B,* occlusal radiograph showing a sialolith in the floor of the mouth.

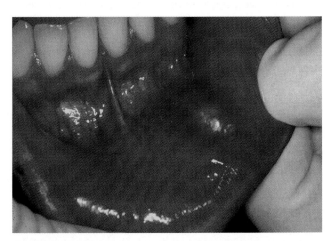

Figure 26–13 Clinical photograph depicting a fluctuant mucocele.

B). Within the cystic zones are mucinous secretions. The intervening stroma, unlike in most tumors, is comprised of lymphoid tissue rather than fibrous tissue. Some cases are bilateral. Basal cell adenomas tend to occur at a younger age and are firmer to palpation. They are comprised of monomorphic islands of basilar-appearing cells and may have only occasional duct-like structures (Figure 26–15, *C*).

In the minor glands of the oral cavity, the monomorphic adenomas are subdivided into basal cell adenoma and a unique variant known as canalicular adenoma. These are movable nodules found in the lip and buccal mucosa. Canalicular adenoma, so-named because of the anastomosing ductal strands that form canal-like structures, is found almost exclusively in the upper lip (Figure 26–15, *D*). Multicentricity is occasionally seen, presenting as multiple small submucosal nodules.

The most common benign salivary neoplasm is pleomorphic adenoma or mixed tumor. The term pleomorphic is applied, not in the sense of cytologic atypia, but rather as a descriptor that defines the diversity of histologic cell types seen in these lesions. There are ductal structures with circumferential myoepithelial cells that fan out into a myxomatous component. Cartilage, fat, and bone may also be seen in the stroma (Figure 26–15, *E*). There is a well-defined capsule that surrounds mixed tumors; however, a feature that accounts for recurrences after enucleation is the extention of satellite tumor nodules beyond the capsule. When these nodules remain behind, particularly in the parotid gland, they tend to recur as multinodular tumor masses. In the oral cavity, the palate is the most common site, followed by the buccal mucosa and lips. Most mixed tumors occur during midlife.

Adenocarcinomas of salivary origin are varied in their histologic appearance and behavior. Some are low-grade with limited potential for metastasis; others are slowly progressive yet metastasize and recur locally after durations of 10 or more years, and yet others are rapidly progressive, with both regional lymph node and distant metastases. The diagnosis is based on microscopic patterns of growth and cell differentiation. The parotid is the most common site for adenocarcinomas, followed by the intraoral minor glands. In the parotid, the lesions are firm to indurated tumefactions, and when the facial nerve is invaded, seventh nerve palsy is commonly observed (Figure 26–16). In the oral cavity, the palate is the most commonly involved site, followed by the buccal mucosa, lips, and tongue base. The tumor mass is often ulcerated or exhibits surface telangiectasia.

Adenoid cystic carcinoma (ACC) is comprised of small dark-staining cells that are arranged in solid nests, cribriform "Swiss cheese" patterns, and trabecular cords (Figure 26–17, *A*). These tumor cells are differentiated along the lines of intercalated ducts with surrounding myoepithelial cells. Clinically, these tumors are solid and usually indurated. In the parotid, they induce seventh nerve weakness when they invade the facial nerve that passes through the substance of the gland. In the oral cavity, ACC is usually located in the palate and may show a normal, telangiectatic, or ulcerated surface. These tumors can invade perineural lymphatics and spread for great distances along nerve trunks. This feature explains the tendency for local recurrences, even when the surgeon is certain that the entire tumor has been excised. The 5-year survival is generally good; however, because of the slow indolent course and tendency for recurrence, the survival rate drops significantly at 10 and 15 years post-treatment. Adenoid cystic carcinoma metastasizes both locally and distantly.

Mucoepidermoid carcinomas (MEC) are a varied group of malignancies with regard to natural history and metastatic potential. They are most commonly located in the parotid and intraoral minor glands. In the mouth, they are found in the palate, buccal mucosa, and tongue base. As the term implies, the tumor is repre-

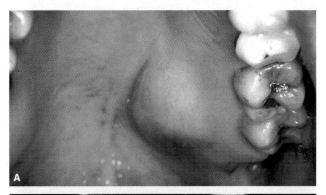

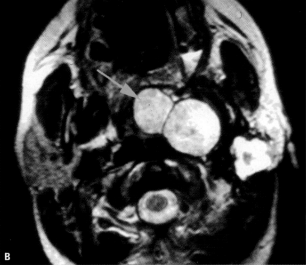

Figure 26–14 *A*, Clinical photograph of a benign adenoma of the palate (pleomorphic adenoma); *B*, MRI of a recurrent parotid pleomorphic adenoma. Note the circumscription of the tumor nodules in this T-2 weighted image. Lesions that recur after inadequate surgery are often multilobular as seen in this case.

sented by cells that differentiate along stratified squamous lines and acinar (mucous cell) lines (Figure 26–17, *B*). Those that are cystic, with a high proportion of mucous cells, are low-grade tumors. They have a limited potential to metastasize; indeed, when located in the mouth, they rarely spread to regional lymph nodes when totally excised. Clinically, a low-grade MEC is soft and often feels encapsulated. Conversely, high-grade MECs are characterized microscopically by a preponderance of epidermoid or squamous cells with small numbers of mucous cells. They tend to be solid rather than cystic. Such tumors have behavior not unlike squa-

mous cell carcinoma with both local and distant metastases. High-grade MECs are indurated and fixed when in the parotid; in the oral cavity they may show surface telangiectasia or ulceration. Tumors with histologic features midway between high and low grade are referred to as intermediate grade MEC, and their prognosis is likewise somewhere between the two extremes.

Acinic cell carcinoma is a tumor that is found almost exclusively in the parotid gland, only rare instances having been reported to arise from intraoral minor glands. This tumor is firm to palpation, yet may sometimes have cystic components. The tumor cells

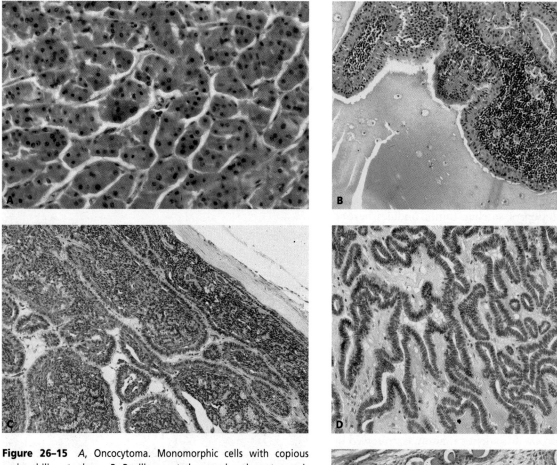

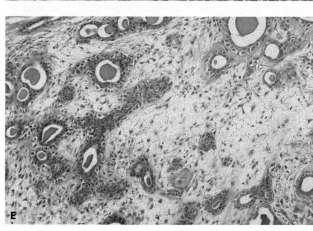

Figure 26–15 *A*, Oncocytoma. Monomorphic cells with copious eosinophilic cytoplasm. *B*, Papillary cystadenoma lymphomatosum is represented by columnar ductal cells, cystic spaces, and a lymphoid component. *C*, Basal cell adenoma is a monomorphic proliferation of basilar darkly stained cells. *D*, Canalicular adenoma of the upper lip shows a maze of anastomosing ductal channels. *E*, Pleomorphic adenoma is characterized by ductal structures, spindled myoepithelial cells, and a diverse myxoid stroma.

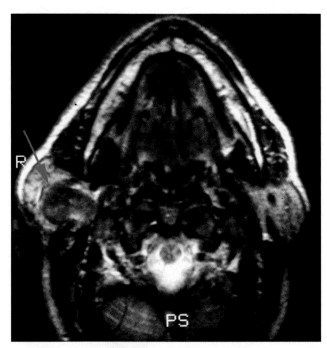

Figure 26–16   MRI shows a parotid adenocarcinoma.

may differentiate as serous or mucous cells, and some are comprised of clear cells (Figure 26–17, C). The tumor cells are arranged in solid sheets, microcystic arrays, or cystic with papillary projections. The 5-year survival after parotidectomy is good, yet declines with ensuing years when local recurrence and metastasis may be encountered.

Polymorphous low-grade adenocarcinoma is a low-grade salivary tumor that is confined to minor glands. For all practical purposes, it does not arise in the major glands. As the term implies, the tumor cells assume a variety of growth patterns (Figure 26–17, D). The cells are arranged in solid sheets, cribriform patterns, ductal structures, and linear cords that bear a resemblance to ACC. These tumors are located in the palate and buccal mucosa as firm, relatively well-delineated submucosal masses. They recur when removed by excision, and their metastatic potential is low.

There are many other histopathologic types of salivary tumors that are rare. Included in this group are primary squamous cell carcinomas of salivary origin, adenocarcinoma arising in a benign mixed tumor (car-

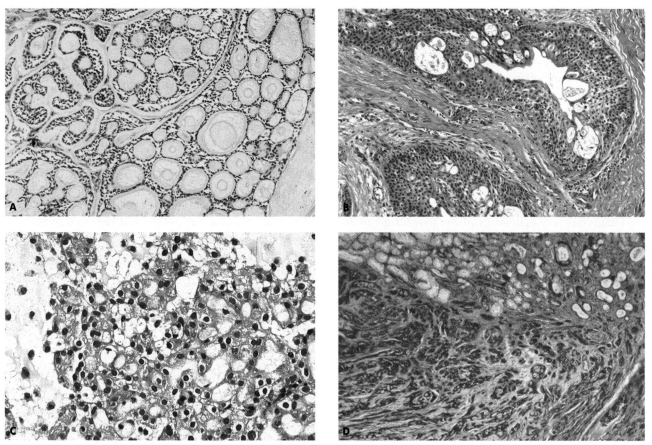

Figure 26–17   *A*, Adenoid cystic carcinoma showing a "Swiss cheese" cribriform pattern; *B*, mucoepidermoid carcinoma comprised of mucous-secreting cells and squamous or epidermal-like cells; *C*, acinic cell carcinoma; *D*, polymorphous low-grade adenocarcinoma of the oral minor glands. Solid and tubular areas are admixed.

cinoma ex pleomorphic adenoma), clear cell adenocarcinoma, basal cell adenocarcinoma (the malignant counterpart to basal cell adenoma), epithelial-myoepithelial carcinoma of intercalated ducts, and the highly malignant salivary duct carcinoma. As mentioned previously, lymphomas can arise from intraparotid lymphoid tissue; some of these lymphomas are derived from mucosa-associated lymphoid tissue (MALT lymphomas), lesions that have a better prognosis than the other non-Hodgkin lymphomas.

Treatment

Sialadenitis is managed according to the causative infectious agent. In mumps, there are no effective antiviral drugs; treatment consists of palliation. Bed rest and NSAID therapy are instituted until the disease runs its course. Bacterial sialadenitis is treated with antibiotics, the selection of which should be based on the results of culture and sensitivity of salivary exudates.

Obstructive disease is, of course, managed by elimination of the obstructive source. In the case of sialolithiasis, the stone must be removed. Small stones located near the duct orifice can often be extruded by manually "walking" the stone through the duct and out the opening. Larger stones require surgical removal. In some instances lithotripty has proved successful in dissolution of large stones. Long-standing sialolithiasis of the submandibular gland may result in diffuse parenchymal sclerosis with an absence of salivary flow from the affected gland. In these instances, sialectomy is recommended, since the nonfunctioning gland is subject to retrograde bacterial infection.

Mucoceles, if enucleated, recur. They need to be excised followed by surgical harvesting of the underlying minor gland lobules. In this way, there are no remaining glands to cause a recurrence.

Benign salivary neoplasms of the parotid gland are treated by local excision or enucleation, if they are monomorphic adenomas. Pleomorphic adenomas should not be treated by enucleation because of the high chance for recurrence, owing to the tendency of these tumors to harbor pericapsular satellites. For this reason, parotid mixed tumors are treated by partial or total parotidectomy. Facial nerve palsy is a potential complication, yet the neurologic deficit can usually be mitigated in benign tumors. Intraoral benign adenomas are treated by local excision, and recurrence, even with pleomorphic adenoma, is unlikely.

Malignant salivary neoplasms of the major glands are treated by total sialectomy, and lymph node dissection is undertaken if there is clinical or imaging evidence of metastasis. Malignant intraoral salivary tumors are treated by wide local excision, with histologic examination of margins for completeness of the surgery. Palatal malignancies require partial or subtotal maxillectomy, since bony invasion is usually present. More radical surgery is performed for adenoid cystic carcinomas, because of their tendency for perineural extension. Lymph node dissection is performed when evidence of metastasis is encountered. Radiation therapy may be used as an adjunct, although most salivary tumors, with rare exceptions, are not radiosensitive.

Suggested reading

Ellis GL, Auclair PL, Gnepp DR. Surgical pathology of the salivary glands. Philadelphia: WB Saunders, 1991.

Epstein JB, Chow AW. Oral complications associated with immunosuppression and cancer therapies. Infect Dis Clin North Am 1999;13:901–23.

Fox PC. Management of dry mouth. Dent Clin North Am 1997;41:863–75.

Fox PC, Brennan M, Pillemer S, et al. Sjögren's syndrome: a model for dental care in the 21st century. J Am Dent Assoc 1998;129:719–28.

Jensen JL, Barkvoll P. Clinical implications of the dry mouth. Oral mucosal diseases. Ann N Y Acad Sci 1998;842: 156–62.

Malamud D. Saliva as a diagnostic fluid. BMJ 1992;305:207–8.

Narhi TO, Meurman JH, Ainamo A. Xerostomia and hyposalivation: causes, consequences, and treatment in the elderly. Drugs Aging 1999;15:103–16.

Sreebny LM, Schwartz SS. A reference guide to drugs and dry mouth: 2nd edition. Gerodontology 1997;14:33–47.

27 Special Senses: Disorders of Taste and Smell

Jonathan A. Ship, DMD, and Elisa M. Chávez, DDS

The chemosensory functions of taste and smell play a vital role in human physiology. They determine the flavor and palatability of foods and beverages, the selection of nutrients essential for life, and the warning of fire, toxic vapors, and spoiled foodstuffs. The hedonic role of chemosensation is experienced daily by everyone. Alterations in these pleasurable sensations have serious implications for the preservation of oral and systemic health, with dramatic effects on quality of life.

Chemosensory disorders can be caused by a variety of oral conditions, upper respiratory tract problems, peripheral or central nervous system (CNS) pathologies, systemic complications, and other factors (aging, circadian variations, menses, and pregnancy). Many patients initially complain to their dentist of altered taste or smell. Unfortunately, it is difficult to diagnose many chemosensory disorders, and occasionally no effective treatment can be found. However, oral health practitioners can assess smell and taste function, identify and treat disorders with orofacial causes, and refer patients to other medical providers when appropriate.

When eating, smell is first perceived through the nasal passages before food is placed into the mouth. Taste is then perceived when food comes in contact with taste receptors located throughout the mouth. A second smell perception occurs retronasally via the nasopharynx as the food bolus is chewed and swallowed. Trigeminal stimulation (pain, tactile, temperature) contributes to flavor perception throughout the eating process.

Smell and taste disorders are common in the general population, although accurate epidemiologic information is lacking. In the 1970s, the consensus was that more than 2 million adults in the United States had a disorder of taste or smell. A large nonrandom survey conducted by the National Geographic Society in 1987 found that 1% of their 1.2 million respondents could not smell three or more of six odorants using a "scratch and sniff" test. A 1994 National Health Interview Survey given to 42,000 randomly selected households reported adjusted national estimates of a prevalence of 2.7 million (1.4%) adults with an olfactory problem and 1.1 million (0.6%) adults with a gustatory problem. When smell or taste problems were combined, 3.2 million (1.65%) adults indicated a chronic chemosensory problem. The prevalence rates increased exponentially with age, with nearly 40% of all problems (1.5 million) existing in adults aged 65 years or older.

Before considering disorders of these special senses in detail, it would be advisable to define the terminology in this field of oral medicine. *Smell* is the perception of odor by the nose, whereas *taste* is the perception of salty, sweet, sour, or bitter by the tongue. *Flavor* is the combination of taste, smell, and trigeminal sensation. *Halitosis* is defined as bad breath, and can contribute to taste and smell changes. Alterations in taste and smell are defined with relative and absolute terms (Table 27–1).

Oral sources of altered taste function are common and can be evaluated by a dentist. Trauma (burns, lacerations, local anesthesia, surgery, reflux), local antiplaque medicaments and drugs excreted into saliva, infections (periodontal, dentoalveolar, soft tissue), vesiculobullous conditions, removable prostheses, metallic dental restorations, and salivary dysfunction can directly or indirectly affect taste function. Oral

Table 27–1 Commonly Used Terms for Gustation and Olfaction

Term	Definition	Example
Gustation		
Normal taste	Normal taste	Healthy adult (any age)
Hypogeusia	Diminished taste	Alzheimer or Parkinson disease
Dysgeusia	Distortion of taste with or without a stimulus present	Poor oral hygiene, medications
Ageusia	Loss or absence of taste	Exposure to toxic chemicals, stroke
Olfaction		
Normosmia	Normal smell	Healthy young adult
Hyposmia	Diminished smell	Older adult
Dysosmia	Distortion of smell	Oral candidiasis, brain tumor, migrane
Phantosmia	Perception of smell without a stimulus present	
Parosmia	Distortion of smell with a stimulus present	
Anosmia	Loss or absence of smell	Upper respiratory infection, stroke

sources of olfactory problems are also common. Halitosis, gingivitis, poor oral hygiene, and periodontal diseases can cause abnormal smell sensations.

Molecular and pathophysiologic correlates of disease

Taste buds mediate taste sensation (Figure 27–1). Three types of lingual papillae contain taste buds: fungiform (anterior two-thirds of the tongue), folate (lateral borders of the tongue in vertical folds), and circumvallate (crateriform nodules on the posterior border of the tongue). Taste buds are also present in the soft palate, pharynx, larynx, epiglottis, uvula, upper third of the esophagus, lips, and cheeks. Taste buds are constantly replaced, approximately every 10 days; if damaged, they can be repaired rapidly.

Taste receptors detect four basic tastes (sweet, salty, bitter, sour) and also perceive a wide range of other tastes that are poorly described by these categories (eg, astringent, metallic, savory, electric). Each taste bud has receptors at the apical portion exposed to the oral cavity and a basolateral area separated by a tight junction. The apical portion of the taste bud begins the chain of events leading to taste sensation (Figure 27–2). Saliva plays a major role in this process since it dissolves and carries tastants to, and rinses them away from the taste buds. Saliva also serves as a protective agent for the taste and epithelial cells by diluting stimulant concentration.

Smell receptors reside in the olfactory epithelium of the nasal septum, superior turbinate, and the roof between the two (Figure 27–3). The bipolar ciliated neurons of olfactory receptors are replaced approximately every 30 to 60 days. They are connected by the olfactory nerve to the olfactory bulb via the cribriform plate. Signal transduction begins at the peripheral neurons when the stimulus is inhaled and transported or dissolved in the mucosal secretions, and processing is completed in the olfactory bulb.

Input received by the taste buds is transmitted by three cranial nerves (CN): VII (chorda tympani and greater petrosal components), IX (glossopharyngeal), and X (vagus) via the nucleus of the solitary tract and the thalamus to the cortex and the hypothalamus. The gustatory innervation system is designed so that contralateral nerves or those with overlapping functions frequently compensate for nerve damage.

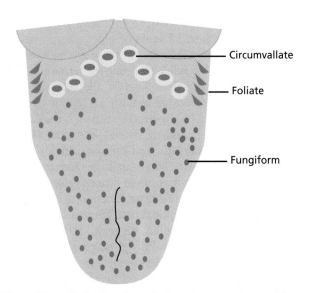

Figure 27–1 Distribution of taste buds on the tongue dorsum. Adapted from Annals of the New York Academy of Sciences.

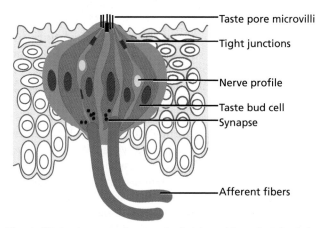

Figure 27–2 Anatomy of a taste bud. Adapted from Annals of the New York Academy of Sciences.

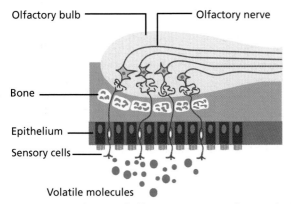

Figure 27–3 Distribution of olfactory receptors and nerves in the nasal cavity.

Several cranial nerves contribute to taste sensation, whereas only one cranial nerve (CN I, olfactory) is responsible for smell. Olfactory neurons aggregate to form glomeruli in the olfactory bulb. Information is sent to and processed in the pyriform lobe, the hippocampal formation, and the hypothalamus. Since the olfactory receptors are themselves nerves with long turnover rates, dysfunction caused by damage to either the peripheral or central components of this system is more common than gustatory dysfunction.

The trigeminal nerve (CN V) also plays a role in olfactory and gustatory sensation by identifying noxious chemicals or irritants. This has been referred to as a "common chemical sense" or as "chemesthesis." Pungent spices and chemicals that cause tearing or sneezing stimulate the trigeminal nerve and its related branches. The ethmoid (branching from the ophthalmic division of CN V) and the nasopalatine (branching from the maxillary division of CN V) both arrive in the nasal cavity and become "free" nerve endings in the nasal mucosa. Some are so close to the surface that chemical stimuli may act directly on the nerve endings.

The maxillary and mandibular branches of the fifth cranial nerve give rise to the lingual, nasopalatine, posterior palatine, and buccal nerves in the oral cavity. The trigeminal nerve (CN V) functions as a nociceptor primarily in the anterior region of the oral cavity, and the glossopharyngeal nerve (CN IX) serves as the main receptor in the posterior regions. Several free nerve endings also reside in the oral mucosa. They occur primarily in the anterior region in the filiform papillae and around the circumvallate papillae, although they can be found in any of the taste papillae.

Disease and the process of aging are often difficult to segregate. Aging, even independent of major medical problems and medications, has significant deleterious influences on olfaction. Detection and recognition thresholds for smell are raised in elderly individuals. The glomeruli of the olfactory bulb deteriorate with age, and

alterations in the olfactory epithelium and the reduction in protein synthesis that occurs with normal aging may contribute to diminished smell perception and identification. Olfaction can be further compromised by medications, chemotherapy, radiotherapy, and systemic diseases. There is little information about possible degenerative changes in the neural pathways attributable to normal aging; however, there is some evidence of losses in trigeminal (CN V) sensitivity with aging.

Losses in gustatory function are not a common sequela of aging, and most changes occur later in life than olfactory dysfunction. Taste-specific (ie, sweet, salty, sour, bitter) changes have been reported, yet it appears that global changes in gustation do not occur as a result of the aging process. Further, there is no evidence that numbers of papillae and taste buds decrease over time. However, numerous older adults are treated for systemic conditions that may affect the gustatory system either directly or indirectly. For example, many medications taken by the elderly directly affect taste perception and inhibit salivary output, impairing gustation. Head and neck cancer treatment (surgery, chemotherapy, radiotherapy) causes short- and long-term damage to the anatomic and nerve pathways responsible for transmitting taste sensation.

Many older adults complain of taste losses, but they are typically attributable to problems with olfaction. Age- and disease-related losses in olfaction play a large role in diminished gustatory function. Any condition that results in a compromised environment for the mediators of chemosensation (eg, tongue, saliva, oral and nasal mucosa, neural pathways, neurotransmitters) results in altered taste and smell perception at any age.

There are three major processes that result in loss of taste and smell function: transport, sensory, and neuronal disorders that involve the oral cavity, head and neck region, and major organs (Table 27–2).

Taste

Many oral and systemic diseases affect the gustatory system (Table 27–3). Antiplaque mouthrinses, toothpastes, and gels are associated with taste alterations. Iatrogenic injury during or subsequent to dental treatments and the use of local anesthetics can cause a taste disorder. Other trauma, such as exposure to excessively hot food or liquids or chemical burns, is common. Metal restorations have been reported to cause a transient metallic taste in some patients. Complete and partial dentures can block access to taste receptor cells. Intraoral infections and inflammatory conditions, such as candidiasis, gingivitis, periodontal disease, dental caries, dental-alveolar infections, herpetic lesions, pulpal necrosis, traumatic lesions, vesiculobullous diseases

Table 27–2   Overview of Mechanistic Causes of Gustatory and Olfactory Disorders

Disorder	Description	Gustatory Examples	Olfactory Examples
Transport problem	Stimulus cannot reach receptor	Salivary dysfunction, oral candidiasis	Blockage of nasal airway, nasal polyp
Sensory problem	Damage to peripheral sensory organs	Radiotherapy, chemotherapy, burn, trauma	Radiotherapy, chemotherapy, upper respiratory tract infection
Neuronal problem	Damage to peripheral nerves or CNS	Tongue surgery, neoplasm, brain tumor	Brain tumor, head trauma, Alzheimer disease

(eg, pemphigus, pemphigoid, lichen planus), and burning mouth syndrome, can all contribute to unpleasant tastes or altered taste function (Figure 27–4).

Defective salivary function can result in altered taste perception or elevation of detection thresholds (Figure 27–5). Numerous medical problems (eg, Sjögren syndrome, diabetes, Alzheimer disease), prescription and nonprescription medications (eg, anticholinergics, antihypertensives, antipsychotics, antihistamines), head and

Table 27–3   Common Causes of Gustatory and Olfactory Disorders

Oral causes
  Trauma (burns, lacerations, chemical damage, anesthetic, surgical)
  Oral mouthrinses, dentifrices, gels
  Gingival and periodontal diseases
  Dentoalveolar infections
  Viral infections
  Soft-tissue lesions
  Candidiasis, denture stomatitis
  Removable prosthodontic appliances
  Burning mouth syndrome
  Salivary dysfunction, drugs in saliva
  Galvanism
Upper respiratory tract problems
  Lesions or tumors of the nose or airway
  Viral and bacterial infections
  Exposure to toxic airborne contaminants, pollutants
  Tobacco use
Peripheral or CNS problems
  Head trauma
  Tumors, lesions
  Neurologic diseases (Alzheimer, Parkinson, Huntington disease; stroke)
Systemic complications
  Systemic diseases (diabetes, thyroid diseases, renal failure)
  Nutritional deficiencies, alcoholism
  Prescription and nonprescription medications
  Chemotherapy and radiotherapy
  Psychiatric disorders
Other
  Aging
  Circadian variation
  Menses and pregnancy
  Idiopathic

neck radiotherapy, and chemotherapy cause salivary dysfunction. The extent to which salivary hypofunction affects gustation is still under debate. Nevertheless, it is hypothesized that in the absence of saliva there is a diminished ability to transport stimuli to taste buds and an increased risk of developing oral-pharyngeal microbial infections that alter taste perception. Saliva may also act as a reservoir for medications or their metabolites, resulting in an unpleasant taste.

Numerous medical problems and their treatment with medications and chemotherapy have been associated with altered taste sensation. Infections (eg, influenza, sinusitis, herpes zoster, human immunodeficiency virus syndrome [HIV]), trauma (eg, motor vehicle accident), and head and neck surgery can result in temporary or permanent damage. Endocrine and metabolic disorders, including diabetes and hypothyroidism, have been associated with altered taste sensation. For example, diabetic neuropathies have been shown to increase taste thresholds. Finally, there is some evidence that genetics may determine the number of taste buds in an individual, which could cause variable gustatory ability and perhaps even predisposition to or increased risk of developing taste disorders.

The effect of medications on the gustatory system may be transient, modifiable, or chronic (Table 27–4). For example, 0.12% chlorhexidine rinse has been reported to produce a reversible impairment of peripheral taste receptors. Whereas some medications cause alterations of specific tastes (sweet, bitter, salty, sour), others increase taste or recognition thresholds. Several drugs have been associated with total loss of taste: local anesthetics (lidocaine), antineoplastics (bleomycin), and antirheumatics (penicillamine). The mechanisms behind these effects are complex and not yet clearly defined, but medication-induced taste dysfunction can occur at any of the transport, sensory, or neuronal levels of the gustatory system.

Finally, little is known regarding pollutants and their effect on the gustatory system. Environmental pollutants range from airborne chemicals, to metallic particles, to dust. Some pollutants, such as insecticides, can actually bind to the tongue, altering taste-bud morphology and, consequently, function.

Smell

Olfaction, entirely dependent upon neural function at peripheral receptor sites and centrally at the first cranial nerve, is especially at risk from any disease or event with neurologic sequelae. The most common cause of smell changes is upper respiratory infection, which also alters gustation. These frequent viral and bacterial infections alter or block peripheral receptor sites. Nonrespiratory bacterial or viral infections, such as acute dentoalveolar infections, HIV, and candidiasis, can adversely affect olfaction.

Head trauma also results in a diminished sense of smell, owing to the location and fragility of the olfactory neurons and the susceptibility to fracture of the cribriform plate. Tumors and surgical procedures that affect olfaction-related structures in the brain or nasal cavity are associated with smell loss. Similarly, neurologic diseases, such as epilepsy, Parkinson disease, Huntington chorea, and Alzheimer disease, impair olfaction. For example, patients with Alzheimer disease develop problems with smell perception because many of the same anatomic and neural structures destroyed by their disease also affect normal olfaction. Further-more, the limbic system is adversely affected in Alzheimer disease, resulting in poor recognition, identification, and recall of odorants.

Other diseases may have indirect effects on the sense of smell because of treatments or medications used to treat the disease. Numerous medications cause olfactory changes, including cardiovascular (nifedipine), antithyroid (methylthiouracil), antibacterial (streptomycin), and analgesic (codeine) drugs (Table 27–5). Radiation, chemotherapy, and hemodialysis regimens can also interfere with olfactory pathways. Environmental pollutants (eg, acrylates, petrochemicals) have been reported to alter neurotransmitters, damage the structures involved in olfaction, or accumulate in the olfactory bulbs. These losses may be transient or chronic.

Halitosis

Halitosis, oral malodor, or bad breath can originate from physiologic or pathologic sources (Table 27–6), and has been estimated to occur chronically in approximately half the population. Odor-producing com-

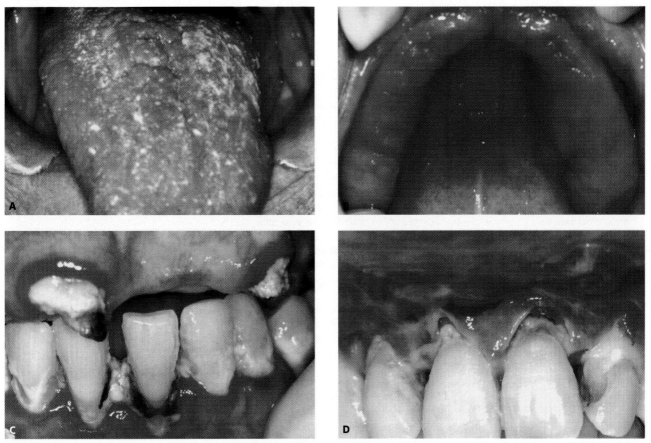

Figure 27–4   Common etiologies of taste, smell, and halitosis problems: *A*, pseudomembraneous candidiasis of the tongue dorsum; *B*, atrophic candidiasis beneath a maxillary denture; *C*, gingivitis, material alba, and impacted food; and *D*, pemphigus vulgaris and desquamative gingivitis.

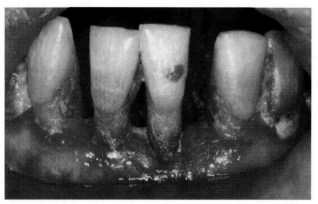

Figure 27–5 Salivary hypofunction and the sequelae of dessicated oral mucosal and dental tissues are common etiologies of taste, smell, and halitosis problems.

pounds are inspired into the lungs and then expired. This occurs when odors (from foods or tobacco) are ingested and inhaled or when pathologically produced odiferous compounds (intraoral or systemic) are introduced into the lungs. Halitosis has been estimated to be from oral sources in 40 to 90% of cases, however, it can also arise from systemic diseases.

Bad breath originating from the mouth is caused by volatile sulfur compounds (VSCs), such as hydrogen

sulfide, methylmercaptan, and dimethyl sulfide. Precursors to these molecules (cysteine, methionine) are found in saliva. The dorsum of the tongue and the gingival sulcus are reservoirs for microbes that can produce VSCs, specifically gram-negative anaerobic bacteria (eg, *Porphyromonas gingivalis, Prevotella intermedia, Fusobacterium nucleatum,* and *Treponema denticola*). Several factors can result in a shift from gram-positive to gram-negative bacteria in the oral cavity: alkaline salivary pH, diminished salivary flow, and inflammatory diseases (ie, gingivitis, periodontitis, major aphthous stomatitis, herpetic gingivostomatitis).

Salivary hypofunction diminishes the self-cleansing action of the oral cavity, and lower levels overnight frequently result in "morning breath." When saliva evaporates, nonsulfur-containing gases (eg, cadaverine, putrescine, butyric, indole) can be released in addition to the VSCs, contributing to halitosis in the patient with salivary hypofunction. Sources of necrosis or hemorrhage in the oral cavity (dentoalveolar infections, periodontal diseases, oral cancers) produce foul odors. Although dental caries does not produce bad breath, it creates food traps as do overhanging, subgingival, and open restorations. Debris remaining in these areas decomposes and produces fetid odors. Similarly, poor maintenance and overnight use of dental prostheses can

Table 27–4 Drugs that Cause Gustatory Disorders

Drug Category	Drug
Amebicide and anthelmintic	Metronidazole, niridazole
Anesthetic (local)	Benzocaine, procaine HCl, lidocaine
Anticholinergic and antispasmodic	Dicyclomine, glycopyrrolate, hyoscyamine
Anticoagulant	Phenindione
Antihistamine	Chlorpheniramine maleate
Antilipidemic	Cholestyramine, clofibrate
Antimicrobial	Amphotericin B, ampicillin, bleomycin, cefamandole, ethambutol HCl, ethionamide, griseofulvin, lincomycin, metronidazole, sulfasalazine, tetracyclines
Antiproliferative and immunosuppressive	Azathioprine, bleomycin, carboplatin, carmustine, cisplatin, doxorubicin, 5-fluorouracil, interferon gamma (INF-γ), methotrexate, vincristine
Antirheumatic, analgesic, antipyretic, anti-inflammatory	Allopurinol, auranofin, colchicine, dexamethasone, flunisolide, gold, hydrocortisone, levamisole, d-penicillamine, phenylbutazone, salicylates
Antithyroid	Carbimazole, iodide, methimazole, methylthiouracil, propylthiouracil, thiouracil
Dental hygiene agent	Sodium lauryl sulfate, chlorhexidine gluconate mouthrinses
Dermatologic agent	Isotretinoin
Diuretic and antihypertensive	Acetazolamide, amiloride and its analogues, captopril, diazoxide, diltiazem, enalapril, ethacrynic acid, hydrochlorothiazide, nifedipine
Hypoglycemic	Glipizide, phenformin and derivatives
Muscle relaxant and drugs for treatment of Parkinson disease	Baclofen, chlormezanone, levodopa
Psychopharmacologic and antiepileptics	Carbamazepine, flurazepam HCl, lithium carbonate, phenytoin, trifluoperazine
Sympathomimetic	Amphetamines, amrinone
Vasodilator	Dipyridamole, nitroglycerin patch, oxyfedrine
Other	EDTA, etidronate, germine monoacetate, idoxuridine, iron dextran complex, vitamin D

EDTA = ethylenediaminetetraacetic acid.

Table 27–5   Drugs that Cause Olfactory Disorders

Drug Category	Drug
Anesthetic (local)	Benzocaine, procaine HCl (Novocain), lidocaine
Antiarrhythmic	Propafenone HCl, tocainide HCl
Anticoagulant	Phenindione
Antihistamine	Chlorpheniramine maleate
Antilipidemic and cholesterol-reducing agents	Cholestyramine, clofibrate, lovastatin
Antimicrobials	Amphotericin B, ampicillin, bleomycin, cefamandole, ciprofloxacin HCl, doxycycline, ethambutol HCl, griseofulvin, lincomycin, lomefloxacin HCl, metronidazole, niridazole, ofloxacin, pentamidine, rifabutin, silver nitrate, sulfasalazine, tetracyclines, terbinafine HCl
Antiproliferative and immunosuppressive	Azathioprine, bleomycin, carmustine, doxorubicin, 5-fluorouracil, methotrexate, vincristine sulfate
Antirheumatic, analgesic, antipyretic, anti-inflammatory	Allopurinol, auranofin, colchicine, dexamethasone, flunisolide, gold, hydrocortisone, levamisole, D-penicillamine, phenylbutazone, salicylates, 5-thiopyridoxine
Antithyroids	Carbimazole, methimazole, methylthiouracil, propylthiouracil, thiouracil
Dental hygiene agents	Sodium lauryl sulfate, chlorhexidine digluconate mouthrinses
Diuretic and antihypertensive	Acetazolamide, amiloride and its analogues, amilodipine besylate, captopril, diazoxide, diltiazem, enalapril, ethacrynic acid, felodipine, lisinopril, losartan potassium, nifedipine, propranolol, spironolactone
Hypoglycemic	Glipizide, phenformin and derivatives
Muscle relaxant and drugs for treatment of Parkinson disease	Baclofen, chlormezanone, levodopa, pergolide mesylate, selegiline HCl
Psychopharmacologic and antiepileptic	Carbamazepine, lithium carbonate, phenytoin, psilocybin, triazolam, trifluoperazine
Sympathomimetic	Amphetamines, amrinone
Vasodilator	Bamifyline HCl, dipyridamole, nitroglycerin patch, oxyfedrine
Other	Etidronate, germine monoacetate, idoxuridine, iron sorbitex, vitamin D

produce malodors as a result of poor hygiene or decreased nighttime salivary flow. *Candida* may arise in similar circumstances, and whereas *Candida albicans* itself does not produce malodors, it can change the oral environment, creating a shift in bacterial flora. A fissured tongue and tonsillar crypts provide reservoirs for food, bacteria, cellular debris, and stagnating saliva, conditions conducive to oral malodor.

Medications, radiotherapy, and chemotherapy can directly affect the oral cavity, resulting in halitosis. The most common medications associated with halitosis are those that inhibit salivary output. Chronic use of inhaled corticosteroids alters the respiratory tract flora and leads to malodors. Cancer treatments (chemotherapy, head and neck radiation) have transient or persistent effects on the salivary system, oropharyngeal tissues, and oral flora, resulting in oral malodors.

Several systemic diseases also produce halitosis. Respiratory diseases are a common source of these odors. Infections involving gram-negative anaerobic bacteria (tuberculosis, pneumonia), obstructions (foreign bodies), tumors (lung cancer), and the production of pus (empyema, bronchiectasis) can all contribute to the emission of foul odors from the nasal cavity, sinuses, nasopharynx, pharynx, and lungs. The postnasal drip associated with upper respiratory viral infections and allergic or infectious sinusitis is a common source of halitosis.

Odiferous by-products may result from drug metabolism, systemic diseases (diabetic ketoacidosis), and diet (alcohol, high fat, garlic). The circulatory system carries these metabolites through the lungs, and they are expired, resulting in halitosis. Individuals with gastrointestinal diseases suffer from halitosis. Hiatal hernias, gastroesophageal reflux, and pyloric stenosis permit the release of gastric odors into the oral cavity. Achalasia is a swallowing disorder in which there is a failure of the contents of the esophagus to empty into the stomach; these patients experience halitosis when food debris and saliva are trapped and decay in the esophagus. Gastric ulceration, infection, carcinoma, and malabsorption can also contribute to oral malodors.

Diabetes is another common systemic cause of halitosis. Diabetic ketoacidosis produces oral malodors, and diabetics are at increased risk of infections and poor wound healing, predisposing them to odor-producing periodontal diseases and other intraoral infections. Dehydration, a major component of diabetes, can result in decreased salivary flow, and a subsequently increased risk of developing halitosis. Hepatic and renal failure, leukemias and other blood dyscrasias, and trimethylaminuria produce malodors as well.

Finally, some persons suffer from a psychogenic halitosis. They do not have detectable malodors, yet they believe it is present (halitophobia). This phenomenon is associated with depression, hypochondriasis, schizophrenia, suicidal ideation, and temporal lobe epilepsy. Importantly, some individuals who have altered taste and smell may perceive their changes as halitosis.

Clinical findings of common taste and smell problems

Most patients who present with a chemosensory problem complain of a taste loss or diminished taste sensitivity. However, the majority of chemosensory deficits are attributable to olfactory losses. True taste loss is relatively rare, and a careful interview can help distinguish between the two problems (Table 27–7). Dysgeusia is a distortion of taste, or a persistent unexplained or unelicited taste sensation. It is particularly difficult to assess, especially when a taste is perceived without a stimulus present (eg, phantom taste).

Objective findings may occur anywhere in the head and neck region. Oral disorders associated with taste changes should be evaluated by the dentist. Examples include pseudomembraneous candidiasis, dentoalveolar abscesses, and salivary dysfunction. Suspected neural injuries to cranial nerves, brain trauma, systemic dis-

Table 27–6 Common Causes of Halitosis

Oral causes
  Gram-negative anaerobic bacteria
  Impacted food
  Gingivitis, periodontitis
  Dentoalveolar infections
  Vesiculobullous and erosive mucosal diseases (eg, aphthous
    stomatitis, herpetic gingivostomatitis)
  Salivary dysfunction
  Candida albicans
  Tongue coating, fissured tongue
  Mouth breathing
  Oral cancers
  Chronic use of alcohol-containing mouthwashes
Pharyngeal and esophageal problems
  Tonsillar crypts
  Cancers
  Achalasia
Respiratory problems
  Bacterial infections
  Nasal congestion, postnasal drip
  Deviated septum
  Allergies
  Tumors
Gastrointestinal disorders
  Reflux
  Hernia, gastric stenosis
  Gastric ulceration, infection
  Carcinomas
Systemic complications
  Medications, chemotherapy, radiotherapy
  Blood dyscrasias
  Diabetes
  Hepatic failure
  Renal failure
  Alcoholism
  Trimethylaminuria (fish odor syndrome)
Other
  Diet (use of herbs, spices, garlic)
  Tobacco use
  Halitophobia

Table 27–7 Steps for the Examination and Diagnosis of Chemosensory and Oral Malodor Disorders

  I. History of chief complaint
    When did the patient first notice the altered taste, smell,
     or halitosis?
    Was there a specific stimulus or coinciding event?
    What relieves and exacerbates the problem?
    Questions specific to taste, smell, and halitosis problems
     (Table 27–8)
 II. Medical, surgical, and family history
    Review of systems
    Dates of medical diagnoses and surgeries
    Current management of medical problems
     Medications (prescription, nonprescription)
     Chemotherapy, radiotherapy, surgery
     Diet, homeopathy
     No treatment
    Unresolved medical issues
    Family history
III. Social history
    Tobacco and alcohol use (past and present)
    Exposure to environmental toxins
    Has anyone else noticed a problem (for smell and halitosis
     problems)?
    Dietary habits (before and after onset of chief complaint)
    Living arrangements (recent changes, reliance on caregivers)
IV. Dental history
    Oral chief complaint
    History of dental and oral surgical treatments
    Use of mouthrinses, gums, candies, mints, sprays, etc.
    Regular and irregular oral hygiene routine
    Presence of head, neck, nasal, and oral discomfort
 V. Oral examination
    Extra- and intraoral lesions, masses, or swellings
    Salivary output from major glands
    Oral hygiene, presence of gingivitis or periodontitis
    Status of tongue, palate, posterior oropharynx
    Status of removable prostheses
    Status of teeth (erupted, erupting, and exfoliating), caries,
     restorations
    Evaluate breath and nasal odor separately (putrid, sweet,
     ketonic, etc.)
    Imaging (intraoral and extraoral radiographs, CT, MRI)
    Laboratory tests (biopsy, culture, serologic tests)
    Specific taste, smell, and halitosis tests (see text and Tables 27–9
     and 27–10)
VI. Interdisciplinary consultation or referral

eases, and medications should be evaluated by medical specialists, with appropriate testing.

As with taste problems, a careful history can help elucidate the problem and distinguish between a smell or taste disorder. For example, smell changes following the use of nitrous oxide analgesia can assist in establishing a diagnosis. Halitosis may be the primary complaint, and is usually attributable to oral-pharyngeal problems that should be evaluated by the dentist. Conduction injuries in the nasal cavity (eg, rhinosinusitis, nasal polyposis) and obstructions in the ear (eg, serous otitis media) should be evaluated by medical specialists and may require computed tomography (CT) and magnetic resonance imaging (MRI) studies to assist with a diagnosis. Patients suspected of having neural injuries to olfactory-related structures (eg, head trauma, neoplasms) or certain medical problems (see Table 27–3), or taking medications (see Table 27–5) should be evaluated by medical specialists with appropriate tests.

Subjective complaints of halitosis and objective findings are often incongruent. Many people think they have bad breath but do not actually have halitosis, and others are unaware that they have a problem. Typically, females are more likely than males to complain of malodor and their self-estimates of bad breath are significantly higher than those made by males. If a patient complains of chronic halitosis that is unrelenting, it is usually a result of chronic oral or systemic disease (eg, periodontitis, diabetes). Alternatively, complaints of intermittent halitosis may be more likely attributable to a gastrointestinal disturbance (eg, gastroesophageal reflux disease).

Volatile sulfur compounds contribute to oral malodor and are produced by gram-negative anaerobic bacteria. Subgingival plaque has the highest levels of these bacteria, and therefore, gingivitis, impacted food material, and periodontal disease are objective markers of oral malodor. Salivary hypofunction, tongue coatings, and tonsillar crypts are additional findings in patients with oral malodor.

Diagnosis and treatment of common taste problems

Diagnosis begins with a careful history of the complaint. The history must include critical questions on the history of the taste problem, a comprehensive dental and medical history, review of medications (prescription, nonprescription, oral-hygiene aids), and social history. Some questions can assist in defining whether the chemosensory loss is related to smell or taste (Table 27–8). For example, the complaint of taste loss following an oral procedure involving injection of a local anesthetic in the vicinity of the chorda tympani helps establish a diagnosis. A frequent complaint is the loss of

taste; however, if upon further questioning, it is revealed that the patient *can* taste the bitterness of coffee, sweetness of ice cream, saltiness of potato chips, and sourness of lemons, then they probably have a smell disorder.

Document the severity by asking the patient to rate their smell/taste/halitosis problem on a scale of 0 to 10. The best score is 0, which should be described to the patient as having "no problem," and 10 is the worst score, or a "severe problem." Recording this subjective ranking helps determine whether the patient perceives his or her problem to be improving, worsening, or not changing over time.

After the most common etiologic agents for a taste disorder have been eliminated from the differential diagnosis (see Table 27–3), specific taste tests are indicated (Table 27–9). The use of topical anesthetics is helpful, particularly when the patient complains of dysgeusia or a phantom taste without any obvious stimulus. If the dysgeusia persists or even gets worse after topical anesthesia has been sequentially applied to the dorsum of the tongue, then a local etiology is unlikely and a central mechanism should be pursued. If the taste

Table 27–8 Questions Useful in the Diagnosis of Chemosensory Disorders

I. General questions
1. Have you experienced a loss in taste, smell, or both?
2. Have you experienced changes in hot, cold, texture, or feeling sensations in your mouth or nose?
3. How long have you had smell or taste loss? Was the loss sudden or gradual, intermittent or continuous, bilateral or unilateral, seasonal (describe the history)?
4. What was the precipitating event for your smell or taste problem?
5. Does eating food mask the smell or taste problem or does the smell or taste distortion mask your enjoyment of eating food?
II. Specific taste questions
1. Can you taste anything? What is it?
2. Can you taste the bitterness of coffee?
3. Can you taste the sweetness of ice cream?
4. Can you taste the sourness of lemons?
5. Can you taste the saltiness of potato chips?
6. Do you have altered tastes without a stimulus, with a stimulus?
7. Describe the altered taste.
III. Specific smell questions
1. Can you smell anything? What is it?
2. Have you lost your taste for steak?
3. Do you have altered smells without a stimulus, with a stimulus?
4. Describe the altered smell.
IV. Specific halitosis questions
1. Do you have a bad taste in your mouth?
2. Have you had any changes in your sense of smell?
3. Has anyone told you that you have bad breath?

problem is eliminated or diminished by topical anesthesia, then an oral etiology must be pursued.

The success of treatment for gustatory problems depends upon the etiology. An orofacial source of a taste problem can usually be treated and followed by dental professionals. Once oral problems have been eliminated from the differential diagnosis, referral to the appropriate medical provider is warranted (eg, neurologist for suspected central or peripheral neurologic problem; internists for underlying metabolic disorder). Unilateral surgical ablation of a damaged chorda tympani nerve has been described for severe dysgeusia. Another cause for a taste problem may be psychologic or behavioral. For example, if dysgeusia is associated with patient-described episodes of stress, advise the patient to see a specialist in stress management. Ultimately, if a cause cannot be established, patients should be referred to a multidisciplinary taste and smell center.

Table 27–9 Clinical Evaluation of Gustatory Function

I. Methylene blue staining of the tongue
  1. Used to test gross innervation of taste buds.
  2. Taste pores remain stained (blue) if they are innervated.
  3. Taste pores do not remain stained if there is an interruption of innervation.
II. Topical anesthesia applied to the tongue
  1. Used to distinguish between oral and nonoral sources of dysgeusia.
  2. Apply 2% unflavored viscous lidocaine or 1% dyclonine hydrochloride to four quadrants of the tongue in a sequential fashion (left anterior 2/3, left posterior 1/3, right anterior 2/3, right posterior 1/3) with a cotton-tipped applicator.
  3. Total-mouth rinse with topical anesthetic to anesthetize taste buds located in the anterior portion of the oropharynx and hard and soft palate.
  4. Caution patients about a reduced gag reflex after application of anesthetics.
  5. Advise patients to avoid eating and drinking until anesthetics have worn off.
  6. If dysgeusia is reduced, cause may be local.
  7. If dysgeusia is greater, cause may be central (eg, phantom taste).
  8. If no changes in dysgeusia, cause is probably not oral.
III. Taste test
  1. Used to test for local and test-specific taste loss.
  2. Four standardized tastants applied to four quadrants of the tongue in a sequential fashion (left anterior 2/3, left posterior 1/3, right anterior 2/3, right posterior 1/3) with cotton-tipped applicators.
  3. Number of correct identifications noted.
  4. Four commonly used tastants easily prepared by a pharmacy:
    a. 1.0 M sodium chloride
    b. 1.0 M sucrose
    c. 0.03 M citric acid
    d. 0.001 M quinine hydrochloride

Taste as well as smell impairments are stressful for patients, particularly if a diagnosis is not established and treatments are not effective. Practitioners should counsel patients with coping strategies and behavioral modification techniques. Moreover, patients need to be advised on nutrition and appetite issues to prevent nutritional deficiencies. The efficacy of zinc supplementation for chemosensory deficiencies is controversial but probably not harmful. High dosages are necessary (ie, 100 mg zinc sulfate daily). Finally, supplementation of foods and beverages with taste (eg, herbs, spices), smell, temperature, and textural stimulants (eg, crunchy, smooth, fizzy) improves palatability and flavor as well as the desirability of eating.

Diagnosis and treatment of common smell problems

The approach to diagnosis and treatment of smell problems is similar to that for taste disorders. A comprehensive subjective assessment of the chief complaint, objective head, neck, oral evaluation, and review of the patient's medical, dental, medication, and social history is necessary. Complaints should be recorded (see Table 27–7), and responses to certain questions can be useful in the establishment of a diagnosis (see Table 27–8). It is important, as with taste complaints, to differentiate between a gustatory and an olfactory disorder. Since there are intimate interactions of taste and smell in the perception of flavor, most chemosensory complaints are related to taste losses, whereas most problems are attributable to smell losses.

A thorough oral, head, neck, and medical examination is required to evaluate the patient for stomatologic, neurologic, endocrinologic, and other systemic diseases that may cause smell losses. Any oral source of malodor should be identified and treated. The nasal cavity and sinuses require examination for any masses, inflammation, or obstructions; this is best accomplished by a specialist in otolaryngology. A complete neurologic examination of cranial nerves, cerebellar function, and sensorimotor function may be required. Head and neck imaging with CT and MRI may be warranted if an intracranial or nasal-sinus abnormality is suspected. If a psychiatric etiology is suspected, referral to qualified specialists is recommended.

Several olfactory tests are available for use in the dental office (Table 27–10). The University of Pennsylvania Smell Identification Test (UPSIT, Sensonics, Inc., Haddonfield, New Jersey) is a commercially available standardized scratch and sniff test consisting of 40 microencapsulated odorants. Scores may be particularly useful in longitudinal serial examinations to determine if a patient's performance is constant or deteriorating over time compared to age- and gender-matched adults. If UPSIT scores diminish more rapidly that those of age- and gender-matched controls, then appropriate referral and treatment is justified, since the evidence suggests that smell losses are greater than attributed to aging alone. When a diagnosis cannot be established or treatment is unsuccessful, patients should be referred to a multidisciplinary research and clinical care taste and smell center, where additional olfactory testing can be administered.

Treatment for olfactory problems is based upon the determination of a diagnosis. Any organ-based etiology (eg, oral candidiasis, nasal polyp, hypothyroidism, use of nifedipine) should be treated by the appropriate specialist. Dentists can treat any orofacial cause. If halitosis is suspected as the etiology, then diagnosis and treatment should be performed. As with gustatory disorders, patients should be referred to appropriate health care providers or smell and taste centers for evaluation and treatment of systemic diseases, medications, environmental toxins, psychobehavioral problems, central or peripheral neurologic disorders that could be responsible for the olfactory dysfunction. Medical and surgical correction of nasal disorders and upper respiratory infections, and the use of topical (nasal) and systemic steroids has some success.

Another aspect of treatment is counseling on four major issues: (1) use of additional smoke detectors in the living environment, (2) avoidance of dwellings with natural gas, (3) use of additional food spoilage precautions, and (4) maximum use of flavor enhancers to improve the flavor of foods. Refrigerated food items must be dated to keep track of potential spoilage. Spices, herbs, and other food additives can be used to stimulate taste, temperature, and textural sensation and to enhance the flavor of foods and the hedonic experience of mealtime. Finally, patients should be reminded that a diminished ability to smell is a sequelae of growing older. Importantly, these losses do not present as sudden disruptions of smell function or dysosmias, but occur gradually and do not become clinically observable until the sixth or seventh decade of life.

Diagnosis and treatment of halitosis

Diagnosis requires a careful review of the chief complaint, dental, medical, medication, and social history (see Table 27–7). A thorough head, neck, and oral examination must be completed to identify a cause of oral malodor (see Table 27–6). On the day of the appointment the patient should be instructed not to wear any perfumes, colognes, or other scented products (eg, cosmetics, hairsprays, powders), and not to eat, drink, smoke, or perform oral hygiene 2 hours before the appointment.

Table 27–10 Clinical Evaluation of Olfactory Function

I. Odor stix
  1. Used to evaluate gross perception of olfaction.
  2. Commercially available odor-producing magic marker-like pen.
  3. Wave approximately 3 to 6 inches in front of patient's nose.
II. Twelve-inch alcohol test
  1. Used to evaluation gross perception of olfaction.
  2. Open an isopropyl alcohol packet and wave it approximately 12 inches in front of patient's nose.
III. Scratch and sniff cards
  1. Used to evaluate gross sensation of olfaction.
  2. Commercially available three-odorant card.
IV. UPSIT (University of Pennsylvania Smell Identification Test)
  1. Used to quantitate olfactory loss (anosmia, hyposmia) and adjusts for age and gender of the patient.
  2. Commercially available test of 40 scratch and sniff odors.
  3. Delivered by forced choice testing.
  4. High test-retest reliability.

There are three types of evaluation for halitosis: organoleptic examination, molecular evaluation of expired air, and bacterial identification tests. Organoleptic measures (odor judge) are qualitative and based upon directly sniffing sources, such as expired air from the nose or mouth, dried saliva, or plaque scrapings from the anterior or posterior of the tongue, teeth, or gingiva. Gas chromatography units, such as sulfide monitors (eg, Halimeter; Interscan Corp., Chatsworth, California), detect volatile sulfur gases in expired air. Gas chromatography combined with mass spectrometry can provide more elaborate analyses of expired air but are costly and impractical. Plaque or saliva samples can be measured for the presence of bacteria capable of producing odor-causing gases (eg, BANA or Perioscan; Oral-B Laboratories, Redwood City, California). Of these techniques, the most subjective (organoleptic) is still the most reliable method of assessment and diagnosis and can be performed by any health care provider. The other methods are useful in monitoring treatment progress. These measures should be used in conjunction with a thorough examination and, if necessary, further diagnostic testing, or referral, to identify the source of the malodor.

Treatment for halitosis begins with improved oral hygiene. Reducing the oral microbes, specifically anaerobes, improves halitosis. Patients should be instructed in proper and daily toothbrushing and flossing techniques, and regular prosthesis hygiene (when applicable). Tongue cleaning, particularly the posterior portion, is essential for the treatment of bad breath, and can be accomplished with tongue cleaners, scrapers, and brushes. Nonprescription mouthwashes may provide some improvement, but only for brief periods, and they can actually exacerbate halitosis, because of the drying effect caused by high alcohol content. Oxidizing agents (dioxide, peroxide), zinc chloride, and triclosan rinses, and prescription antimicrobial rinses (chlorhexidine) are slightly more effective, but all have side effects and lack prospective long-term research confirmation.

If the source of the malodor is suspected to arise from oral disorders, such as defective dental restorations and prostheses, periodontal diseases, or candidiasis, definitive treatment diminishes the number of oral microbes. Salivary hypofunction contributes to halitosis; sugarless candies, mints, or gums, artificial salivas, and pilocarpine (5 mg tid and qhs) can increase salivary output and may improve malodor.

It has been estimated that only 10% of all cases of oral malodor are of systemic origin. However, if an oral source of halitosis has been ruled out and the problem persists, referral to the appropriate health care practitioner is indicated. Ultimately, if an oral and systemic cause cannot be discerned and the patient does not respond to conventional therapy, a psychobehavioral etiology should be considered and a referral made to a trained specialist.

Suggested reading

Ackerman BH, Kasbekar N. Disturbances of taste and smell induced by drugs. Pharmacotherapy 1997;17:482–96.

Ayers KM, Colquhoun AN. Halitosis: causes, diagnosis, and treatment. N Z Dent J 1998;94:156–60.

Cullen MM, Leopold DA. Disorders of smell and taste. Med Clin North Am 1999;83:57–74.

Deems DA, Doty RL, Settle RG, et al. Smell and taste disorders: a study of 750 patients from the University of Pennsylvania smell and taste center. Arch Otolaryngol Head Neck Surg 1991;117:519–28.

Fox PC. Management of dry mouth. Dent Clin North Am 1997;41:863–76.

Getchell TC, Doty RL, Bartoshuk LM, Snow JB Jr. Smell and taste in health and disease. New York: Raven Press, 1991.

Jones N, Rog D. Olfaction: a review. J Laryngol Otol 1998;112:11–24.

McDowell JD, Kassebaum DK. Treatment of oral and nonoral sources of halitosis in elderly patients. Drugs Aging 1995;6:397–408.

Rosenberg M. Clinical assessment of bad breath: current concepts. J Am Dent Assoc 1996;127:475–82.

Schiffman SS. Perception of taste and smell in elderly persons. Crit Rev Food Sci Nutr 1993;33:17–26.

Schiffman SS. Taste and smell losses in normal aging and disease. J Am Med Assoc 1997;278:1357–62.

Ship JA. Gustatory and olfactory considerations in general dental practice. J Am Dent Assoc 1993;124:55–61.

Ship JA. The influence of aging on oral health and consequences for taste and smell. Physiol Behav 1999;66:209–15.

Spielman AI. Interaction of saliva and taste. J Dent Res 1990;69:838–43.

Spielman AI. Chemosensory function and dysfunction. Crit Rev Oral Biol Med 1998;9:267–91.

28 Pain Mechanisms

Edmond L. Truelove, DDS, MSD

The process of pain generation is perhaps the most complex biologic and behavioral process of human behavior, and pain is generally considered to consist of four components: sensory discriminative, cognitive, motivational, and affective. This chapter predominantly addresses the processes of pain recognition that occur through sensory and discriminative neurologic processes. The trigeminal nerve is the focus, since orofacial pain is predominantly initiated and transmitted through trigeminal pathways, but the role of other cranial and cervical nerves is discussed as well as general processes for transmission of neurologic signals. At the outset it is useful to define a few key working definitions of words commonly used in describing pain sensations (Table 28–1).

Neuronal components of pain-signal recognition and transmission

The basic component of all pain-signal recognition and detection is the primary afferent neuron located at the site of the painful (nociceptive) stimulus (Figure 28–1). Detection of the stimulus that is generated by noxious injury that comes from physical, chemical, or other forms of local trauma results in transduction of the stimulus from its initial mode of action to electrical activity within the neuron. Primary afferent neurons are composed of dendrites located at the most peripheral region of the nerve, a nucleus, and an axon that caries the signal centrally. Primary afferent neurons are unipolar and have only one axon but may have multiple dendrites and sensory receptors. Multiple neurons suspended in axoplasm and covered by a nerve sheath make up a nerve fiber. The fiber may be covered with myelin, which acts to insulate the nerve and speed nerve-signal conduction. At the end of the axon are one or more presynaptic terminals and a synaptic cleft that acts as a gap between the primary afferent neuron and the second-order neuron that carries the signal to the central nervous system (CNS).

The signal is detected at the dendritic end of the primary afferent neuron by a sensory receptor that may have specialized functions. Exteroceptors react to the external environment and include tactile receptors in the mucosa and skin such as Merkel and Meissner corpuscles and Ruffini corpuscles that detect changes in pressure and warmth. Krause corpuscles respond to cold, and free nerve endings sense pain and touch. Proprioceptive nerve-end organs have specialized functions, including specialized mechanoreceptors located in muscles, Golgi tendon organs that respond to muscle tension during stretching and contraction, pacinican receptors that also detect pressure, mechanoreceptors in periodontal tissues, and deeper free nerve endings that sense painful and other stimuli. Visceral tissues are innervated by deep primary afferent neurons with sensory receptors called interoceptors including pacinian corpuscles that detect deep pressure, and free nerve endings that detect painful stimuli. Innervation of vascular tissues is some-

Table 28–1 Pain Descriptors

Term	Description
Allodynia	Painful sensation triggered by mechanical non-nociceptive stimuli
Anesthesia	Complete lack of neurologic sensation during nerve stimulation
Anesthesia dolorosa	Persistent pain in a region of anesthesia secondary to denervation or deafferentation of the area
Causalgia	Persistent burning pain thought to be caused by deafferentation of sensory innervation
Dysesthesia	Unpleasant sensation that is also abnormal and may include some level of paresthesia
Heterotopic pain	Pain felt in an area not associated with the true site of stimulation
Hypalgesia	Decreased sensation or sensitivity to a painful stimulus
Hyperesthesia	Increased sensitivity to stimulation of a region
Hyperpathia	Development of exaggerated pain after stimulation that is normally painful
Hypoesthesia	Decreased sensitivity to stimulation of a region
Neuralgia	Pain felt along the distribution of a nerve
Neuropathic pain	Pain that is triggered within the nervous system secondary to neurologic injury or change
Nociception	Neurologic stimulation that normally provokes a painful sensation
Nociceptor	Stimulus that normally provokes a pain
Paresthesia	Altered or diminished sensation in all or part of a region of nerve distribution usually associated with local or central injury
Primary hyperalgesia	Increased sensitivity due to local inflammation
Secondary hyperalgesia	Pain that is heterotopic and provoked by stimulation at the site of pain
Secondary pain	Pain that is evoked by deep somatic pain but felt at a different site

what different than that of cutaneous and musculoskeletal tissues and is provided by a matrix of fibers that are myelinated and respond to sensory stimulation.

Once triggered, the nerve impulse is carried along the neuron via action of calcium, potassium, and sodium channels that depolerize and repolerize as these ions flow out of or into the cell. The signal is transmitted along the neuron past the cell body to the axon, which can be of different thicknesses, which significantly affect the speed of pain or stimulus conduction. Large A fibers (1–20 μm) transmit the signal more rapidly than smaller C fibers (0.5–1.0 μm). There are four size categories of A fibers: alfa fibers are 12 to 20 μm in diameter, beta are 6 to 13 μm in diameter, gamma fibers are 3 to 8 μm in diameter, and delta fibers are 1 to 5 μm in diameter. The speed of signal conduction ranges from over 70 m per minute along the largest fibers (A-alfa) to less than 2 m per second for C fibers, and between 5 to 15 m per second for A-delta fibers. Pain is transmitted via these slower C and A-delta fibers that also transmit touch, itch, cold, and warmth. Tactile and other signals are transmitted over the faster A-alfa, -beta, and -gamma fibers. The transmission of pain is therefore provided through a variety of A-delta and C fiber primary afferents: high threshold mechanoreceptive neurons of the A-delta class that respond to strong mechanical challenge, mechanothermal fibers that are also A-delta and triggered by intense mechanical and thermal challenge, and polymodal C fibers that respond to chemical, thermal, and mechanical stimulation.

The components of the central brain stem trigeminal complex of V include the motor nucleus, the sensory nucleus, and the trigeminal spinal tract (Figure 28–2). Afferents from V entering the motor nucleus trigger reflex motor responses. Most primary afferents from V, however, communicate with second-order neurons located in the trigeminal spinal tract nucleus. After synapsing in the trigeminal spinal tract, second-order neurons cross the midline and migrate through either the reticular formation, where communication with other interneurons occurs, or through the neospinothalamic tract (Figure 28–3). The speed of transmission along these paths depends on the primary afferent type and second-order neuron. Fast pain is often described as bright and is usually well localized, whereas slow pain, which is usually transmitted over C fibers is diffuse and thought to generate deep aching and sensations associated with suffering. Impulses carried along the neospinothalamic tract that are mechanical or thermal pain signals are carried by A-delta fibers and are fast in

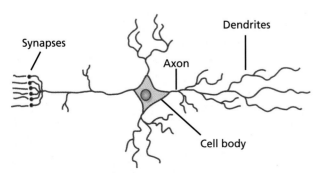

Figure 28–1 Primary afferent neuron.

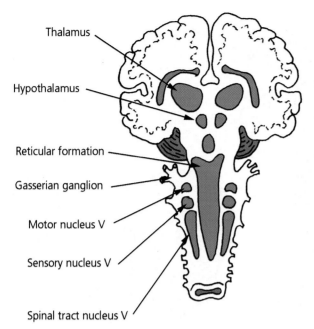

Thalamus

Hypothalamus

Reticular formation

Gasserian ganglion

Motor nucleus V

Sensory nucleus V

Spinal tract nucleus V

Figure 28–2   Nuclear tracts of V. Adapted from Okeson JP. Bell's orofacial pains. 5th ed. Carol Stream (IL): Quintessence Publishing Co., Inc.; 1995.

transmission directly to the thalamus. Those carried by C fibers and transmitted through the reticular formation are slow. Signals passing through the reticular formation move through several interneurons before transmission on to the thalamus. These signals can be modulated by a number of inputs within the reticular formulation, depending upon their location. The bulboreticular facilitatory region speeds transmission and stimulates the entire brain to attention, with acetylcholine acting as an excitatory agent. The other reticular region of importance in pain transmission is the reticular inhibitory area, which inhibits or modulates pain transmission, in part, owing to the action of serotonin, which is concentrated there. Signals generated from the cerebral cortex in response to nociceptive or other stimuli pass downward into the reticular region and are also up- or downregulated by excitatory or inhibitory actions within the reticular formation. Signals moving either directly along the neospinothalamic tract or through the reticular formation are routed to the thalamus, where synapse occurs and the signal is directed onward to the sensory cortex and through thalamic connections to the hypothalamus and limbic system, where emotional or affective aspects of sensation are triggered, including instinctual expressions of anger, rage, escape, and fear. The cortical reactions are modulated by memory and prior associations with pain. Only when the signal is carried to the higher cortical centers of the brain does perception and interpretation of the signal occur, resulting in an integrated pain experience, which can include denial, suffering, pain behaviors, and

alterations in other psychological parameters dependent upon the pain sensation and prior pain experiences. Thus, the pain experience consists of signal transduction, transmission, modulation, and perception.

While sensory signals are being transmitted to the CNS via nerve conduction pathways, other neurologic mechanisms are also operating to alter sensation. The axon transport system operates to transmit signals through the nerve cell using fluid channels in the axon. Neurotransmitters are released either orthodromically (centrally) or antidromically (peripherally). Substance P is one of the agents that is released by the axon transport system and, when released at the peripheral junction of the neuron, triggers sensitization of other neurons and contributes to the process of neurogenic inflammation in peripheral tissues that includes edema, inflammation, vasodilation, and hyperalgesia. This process occurs in both somatic and autonomic nerves, including components of the sympathetic nervous system.

Transmission of pain through the trigeminal system

The orofacial structures receive most of their innervation from the trigeminal nerve (V) with some innervation provided by cervical nerves to the mandible (Figure 28–4). Major transmitters of painful stimuli within the mouth and orofacial complex are the free nerve endings from the trigeminal nerve. Peripheral afferents from the trigeminal are thought to react to specific noxious stimuli and respond to stimulation of different duration, nature, and intensity. The free nerve endings of V transmit via small-diameter, slow-conducting, myelinated A-delta nerves and through slow-conducting C fibers that are unmyelinated. The response of a peripheral free nerve fiber to stimulation provides a specific receptive field that is often less than a millimeter in diameter. The free nerve endings respond to nociceptive stimuli depending on the strength of the stimulation, resulting in a graded response. Other A-delta and C fibers of V respond to stimulation from cooling, temperature change from warmth, and direct tactile irritation. The signals produced are transmitted to trigeminal sensory nucleus or to dorsal horn components of the cervical innervation. Other trigeminal components of the orofacial complex involve A-beta, fast-conducting fibers that transmit tactile and proprioceptive sensations to other areas of the brain.

The trigeminal provides several types of receptors: mechanothermal, polymodal nociceptive C afferents sensitive to chemical and mechanical stimulation, mechanoreceptive fibers that respond to strong mechanical stimuli, and nociceptive afferents excited by mechanothermal stimuli that is intense. Some nociceptive nerve endings are relatively resistant to stimula-

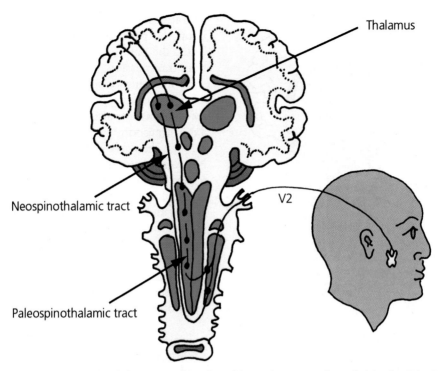

Figure 28–3 Neospinothalamic tract of V. Adapted from Okeson JP. Bell's orofacial pains. 5th ed. Carol Stream (IL): Quintessence Publishing Co., Inc.; 1995.

tion but may become active after injury to tissue, resulting in peripheral sensitization of the injured tissues via peripheral and central mechanisms. After injury, normally silent nerve endings may become activated, resulting in increased pain response from only modest stimulation or even stimulation that is not normally painful (allodynia). A number of physiologic and neurochemical factors are responsible for the sensitization, which is an important clinical phenomenon responsible for much of the discomfort in painful injuries. Agents that increase response to painful stimuli can be released from a variety of sources, including free nerve endings themselves, peripheral tissues, and cellular elements of the hematologic system (neutrophils, basophils, platelets, endothelial cells, etc.). Peripheral tissues, including nerve endings, can release inflammatory mediators, including substance P, which triggers neurogenic inflammation via capillary dilation and extravasation of plasma.

These findings are significant, because they implicate neural reactions in some forms of peripheral inflammation and intensification of pain responses. The innervation of the dental pulp has been extensively studied and found to have many of the same neurologic and neurochemical pain mechanisms as other free nerve endings and nociceptive fibers.

A more recently investigated component of the nervous system is autonomic innervation within the face (Figure 28–5). It appears that sympathetic innervation

can affect nociceptive afferents, causing sensitization to stimuli with a possible role in some forms of chronic neuropathic pain. It is clear that sympathetic innervation of vascular tissues of the face and dental structures

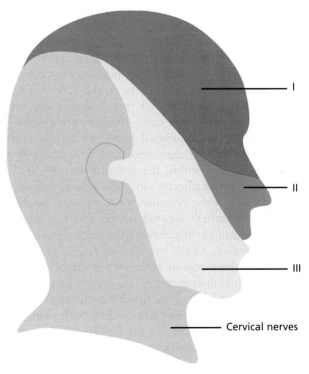

Figure 28–4 Distribution of trigeminal and cervical nerves.

is important and may regulate pain via control of circulatory responses, nociceptive afferents, and by altering local neuropeptides.

Peripheral neurochemical factors in the initiation and transmission of pain at the nerve synapse include substance P, enkephalin, nerve growth factor, norepinephrine, serotonin (5-HT), calcitonin gene-related peptide (CGRP), and other neurokinins and peptides (Figure 28–6) (Table 28–2). Obviously, peripheral inflammatory mediators, including prostaglandins, leukotrienes, and other components of the arachidonic cascade can trigger pain through direct mechanisms of inflammation. Bradykinin is an important component of the inflammatory reaction of tissue to damage and also one of the most potent agents associated with pain sensation. It causes sensitization of nerve receptors and nociceptors. The peripheral mediators of inflammation and injury pain can cause pain by direct stimulation of receptors and by making them hypersensitive to stimulation. Histamine released during tissue damage also provokes painful sensations and triggers release of substance P, which acts to excite nerve receptors and trigger inflammation.

Significant amounts of orofacial pain come from deeper tissues, such as muscles, connective tissue, and components of the temporomandibular junction (TMJ). Nociceptive receptors from those regions are thought to contain high-threshold afferents that respond to stimuli only at ranges close to the maximum level of movement or distortion of that tissue. These high-threshold responders help to explain why only extremes of movement or strain trigger painful responses.

It appears that afferent input from gingival and pulp tissues may project into the brain and communicate such that gingival stimulation of nociceptors can cause painful responses that appear to come from within the pulp or other tissues. Stimulation of pulpal afferents can be projected within the brain to stimulate sensations of pain in nonpulpal tissues of the head, neck, and face. These mechanisms of projection and pain referral can cause great confusion during the clinical assessment of patients with pain that is not readily diagnosed and can lead to inappropriate therapy since the site of felt pain is not the site of nociception in cases of projected or referred pain. It even appears that nociception coming from one tooth

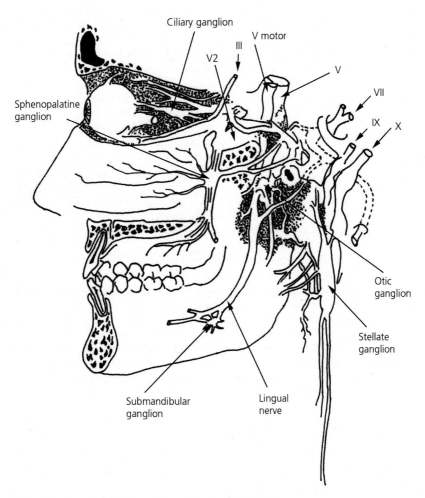

Figure 28–5 Autonomic innervation of the head and neck.

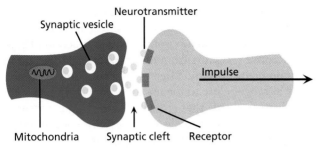

Figure 28–6 Nerve synapse and synaptic cleft.

can be projected via peripheral and central mechanisms to an adjacent tooth or tissues, potentially confusing the diagnosis of the site of pulp pathology.

Interest in headache mechanisms and migraine has stimulated studies of both neurotransmission and neurochemical modulation and stimulation of nociception of cranial structures, including blood vessels, dura, and other connective-tissue sheaths. Some of the same projection and sensitization processes appear to operate from these tissues as occurs with dental and pulp affer-

Table 28–2 Neurochemical Agents Important in Pain Generation and Transmission

Agent	Action
Acetylcholine	Released at site of injury, sensitizes nociceptive nerves, secreted by motor neurons, common neurotransmitter, also secreted by autonomic nerves (sympathetic and parasympathetic), excitatory in function
Arachidonic acid	Released at site of injury, metabolized by cyclooxygenase or lipoxygenase pathway to produce prostaglandins and leukotrienes, which are strong inflammatory mediators, prostaglandin sensitizes nociceptive nerves, increases response of A-delta fibers to mechanostimulation, leukotrienes cause hyperalgesia at site of injury
Aspartate (NMDA)	Excitatory amino acid found at nerve presynaptic terminals in sensory nerves
Adinosine triphosphate (ATP)	Released at site of injury, activates or sensitizes nociceptors
Beta-endorphin	Found in CNS, binds to morphine receptors to block pain, component of placebo analgesia, potentiated by serotonin, blocked by naloxone, contributes to pain tolerance and increases with exercise, has long-term action in pain control, effect may be decreased by the central action of norepinephrine
Bradykinin	Acts peripherally as strong inflammatory agent, released at site of injury; activates nociceptors; requires prostaglandin to act; vasodilator, increases capillary permeability; triggers pain by sensitizing receptors, including high-threshold receptors
Calcitonin gene-related peptide (CGRP)	Released into meningeal vessels of the dura by fibers of the trigeminal nerve; triggers degranulation of mast cells resulting in release of histamine, in response vessels dilate; role in migraine symptoms
Dopamine	Inhibitory in function, secreted in CNS in region of substantia nigra
Enkephalins	Act to decrease or inhibit pain, act rapidly, found in cerebrospinal fluid
Gamma-aminobutyric acid (GABA)	Inhibitory function, produced in spinal cord
Glutamate	Excitatory function, secreted in sensory neurons at presynaptic terminals, also found in spinal dorsal horn region
Glycine	Secreted in spinal cord and trigeminal spinal nucleus, normally inhibits transmission
Histamine	Released at site of injury, sensitizes or activates nociceptor; peripheral functions includes vasodilation, contraction of smooth muscles in respiratory structures, increase of permeability in small vessels, CNS neurotransmission functions
Leukotrienes	Product of metabolism of arachidonic acid via lipoxygenase pathway, cause hyperalgesia in sites of injury
Neurokinin A (NKA)	Neurotransmitter released from afferents, role in vascular responses in migraine
Neuropeptide Y (NYP)	Neurotransmitter released from central sympathetic fibers, active in vascular headaches
Norepinephrine-noradrenaline	Usually excitatory, produced by neurons within brain in pons region
Peptide histidine isoleucine (PHI)	Neurotransmitter released from central parasympathetic fibers, active in vascular headaches
Potassium	Released at site of injury, sensitizes or activates nociceptors
Prostaglandin E_2	Produced at site of injury by metabolism of arachidonic acid by cyclooxygenase, strong inflammatory mediator, sensitizes nociceptive nerves, increases response of A-delta fibers to mechanostimulation
Serotonin (5-HT), 5-HT subtypes	Released at site of injury, sensitizes or activates nociceptors, located centrally in brain stem region and is anti-nociceptive in that area with a function in descending suppression of pain; subtypes are found in the brain in association with the trigeminal vascular system and play a role in vasoconstriction, vasodilation, and pain of migraine
Substance P	Secreted by nociceptive neurons to transport pain signal; functions at central level as excitatory nociceptive agent; also found in spinal cord and released by nociceptive fibers; also present in neurogenic inflammation; causes inflammation in tissues and joints when released; released by peripheral neurons at site of injury to cause pain, inflammation, histamine release, and vasodilation
Vasoactive intestinal peptide (VIP)	Neurotransmitter released from central parasympathetic fibers, active in vascular response in migraine

ents, leading to vasodilation and inflammation of neurogenic origin. The concept that neurologic tissues and nerve endings can produce neuropeptides and other agents that provoke peripheral inflammation has gained increasing importance as a source of possible inflammation within pulpal tissues and the TMJ. Some of these same neurochemical mediators appear to be important in tissue regeneration and repair even within the dental pulp, which was once thought to have no reparative potential. Peripheral control of nociceptive stimulation is gaining recognition as a mechanism for controlling pain, as seen by use of nonsteroidal anti-inflammatory drugs (NSAIDs) for reduction of peripheral inflammatory generators and nociceptive agents within the tissue, and by blocking 5-HT receptor agonists on nociceptors of afferents of cranial blood vessels sensitized during some forms of vascular headaches. Recently, it has been shown that peripheral injection of very small quantities of morphine into an area of inflammation and pain results in significant pain reduction without evidence of the opioid in the blood stream, thus ruling out a central effect.

Trigeminal central pain processes

Painful signals from trigeminal afferents are transmitted to the gasserian ganglion where the nerve cell bodies are located and on to the brain stem (see Figure 28–2). The

afferents entering the brain stem ascend and descend in the trigeminal spinal tract. Second-order neurons in the trigeminal sensory nuclear complex tract carry the signal further. The trigeminal sensory nuclear complex is divided into the principal sensory nucleus and the spinal nucleus with three subnuclei. The subnucleus caudalis, which is the most caudal of the nuclei, is laminated and may receive stimulation from other cranial nerves and upper cervical nerves. Neurochemical agents within the subnucleus caudalis that increase pain responses include substance P and glutamate. A number of other agents are also present that can modulate or suppress pain transmission, including 5-HT, γ-aminobutyric acid (GABA), and enkephalin.

The subnucleus caudalis appears to be the main source of nociceptive transmission from the trigeminal nerve to the brain, whereas it has a less important role in tactile and mechanical signal transmission. Innervation of the subnucleus caudalis is also from nociceptive-specific and wide dynamic-range neurons that are low-threshold mechanoreceptive in nature. These second-order neurons are also stimulated by input of nerves in the TMJ and other deeper structures, in addition to their responsiveness to cutaneous nociceptors in the tissues of the face and mucosa. Of clinical significance is the extensive convergence in the subnucleus caudalis of nontrigeminal innervation from upper cervical and other nerves (Figure 28–7). The innervation of non-

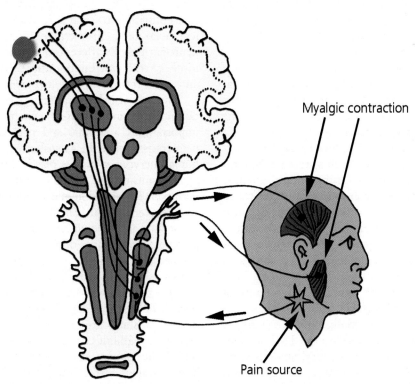

Figure 28–7 Referred pain to trigeminal tract via cervical input. Adapted from Okeson JP. Bell's orofacial pains. 5th ed. Carol Stream (IL): Quintessence Publishing Co., Inc.; 1995.

trigeminal input via convergence of other fibers contributes to pain referral and difficulties in pain localization in some clinical conditions. The other two nuclei of the trigeminal tract, interpolaris and oralis, also have some participation in pain transmission.

Tooth pulp afferents do project to the subnucleus oralis, and it appears that oralis is important in transmission of pain from the pulp into the brain, with subnucleus caudalis apparently participating as an essential modulating agent. These complex processes, coupled with the high degree of convergence of nociceptive input into caudalis, contribute to the poor localization and significant rate of referral and widespread sensitization of tissues to painful stimulation in the oral cavity and orofacial complex, contributing to difficulties in diagnosis of orofacial pain.

Painful signals move from the trigeminal brain stem sensory nucleus (subnucleus caudalis, etc.) primarily to the contralateral thalamus with minor innervation to the ipsilateral aspect of the thalamus. Innervation from the mouth stimulates several regions of the thalamus that have specific response patterns (low-threshold mechanoreceptive, etc.). The thalamus also receives input from the somatosensory cerebral cortex that appears to participate in motivational and affective components of pain perception (see Figure 28–7). Other parts of the thalamus have also been associated with discriminative analytic aspects of pain perception. Convergence of neuronal input from deeper noncutaneous tissues occurs in the thalamus just as in the trigeminal spinal tract. Some fibers from the thalamus project to the somatosensory cortical region and are thought to assist in pain localization and discriminating properties of noxious stimuli. Nociceptive signals originating from trigeminal innervation pass upward through the thalamus on to several regions of the somatosensory cortex and also appear to connect with some regions of the brain that relate to affective responses.

Painful and other stimuli are known to trigger behavioral and involuntary responses, such as reflex reactions. Autonomic responses to painful stimuli include increased heart rate and other autonomically controlled physiologic activities. Muscle reflex responses are also affected by noxious stimulation of regional innervation. Application of noxious chemical sensitizers to cutaneous or deeper tissues in animals has been shown to generate reflex contractions of masticatory muscles and simultaneous contraction of agonist and antagonist muscles to limit movement (see Figure 28–7). These patterns of reflex response may partially explain changes of muscle and jaw activity with injury to the TMJ or other jaw structures. Chronic peripheral neural noxious stimulation in the muscles of mastication or cutaneous structures of the face appear to potentially trigger reflex and chronic adaptive responses. N-methyl-D-aspartate (NMDA) receptors and others within the spinal trigeminal tract and CNS appear to play a part in the response to noxious reflex stimulation of the trigeminal nerve.

Recently, increased attention has been given to exploration of mechanisms related to descending inhibitory control of nociceptive signals. Pain has been shown to be decreased through a variety of chemical, physical, and behavioral mechanisms that may involve descending control exerted by trigeminal nociceptive neurons of small-fiber afferents, including those stimulated through external stimuli, such as acupuncture. The location of the inhibitory control includes the substantia gelatinosa of the nucleus caudalis of the spinal tract of V, and it involves a variety of neurochemical agents, including GABA, 5-HT, noradrenaline, endogenous opioids, and other neuropeptides (Figure 28–8).

Injury to nerves at peripheral and central locations can lead to sensitization and increase in the receptive field of the nerve fiber. Deafferentation of trigeminal nerves has been shown experimentally to increase the sensitivity and receptive field of the nerve and activation of nucleus caudalis neurons. Peripheral injury associated with inflammation of tissue also generates an increase in the receptive field in the region of injury. Studies of deafferentation have led to the discovery that considerable neuroplasticity may occur in response to injury or nociceptive neurologic stimulation. It has been suggested that persistent noxious stimulation of the trigeminal system associated with deafferentation could result in plastic changes within the trigeminal system that contribute to such chronic orofacial pains as atypical facial pain, chronic myofascial pain, and trigeminal neuropathies. Deafferentation itself can occur through tooth extraction, endodontic therapy, viral infection, and other traumatic and iatrogenic injuries.

The role of behavioral factors in generation, augmentation, and modulation of pain in humans may be as important as anatomic and neurochemical patterns of pain transmission. If, as suspected, it turns out that the human nervous system is plastic, then the understanding of mechanisms and agents now thought to be associated with pain transmission and inhibition can be expected to change over time. It is likely that agents that decrease or block pain in some circumstances may actually increase pain perception under different sets of behavioral or environmental conditions. Mechanisms of pain stimulation, transmission, perception, and behavior appear to be different in patients with chronic pain syndromes, and recent behavioral research has demonstrated that measures of behavioral status are often greater predictors of pain levels and probabilities of pain persistence over time than any other physiologic, neurologic, or functional measure. These findings further suggest that plastic changes occur in some individuals and under some circumstances that result in patterns of chronic long-term pain.

Other innervation of the orofacial region

Sensory innervation

The main afferent sensory innervation of importance in orofacial pain is supplied by the trigeminal, facial, glossopharyngeal, and vagus nerves and from branches of the higher cervical nerves (Figure 28–9). The trigeminal nerve through each of its three divisions (ophthalmic, maxillary, and mandibular) supplies most of the afferent stimulation to the mouth and structures of the face to the top of the head, from the ears forward. The subcutaneous tissues are also innervated by the trigeminal nerve, including the nasal cavity, sinuses, and orbital structures. The mandibular branch provides deep proprioceptive innervation to the muscles of mastication, the anterior two-thirds of the tongue, the tympanic membrane, and the TMJ, via the auriculotemporal nerve. Some of the structures of the cranium are also innervated by branches of the trigeminal nerve.

The facial nerve has important motor functions related to the muscles of facial expression, but the facial nerve also plays a role in afferent sensory sensation through proprioceptive components of the nervus intermedius, which provides information from deep somatic tissues and the muscles of the anterior neck. Sensation to the auditory canal and tympanic membrane is also provided by the facial nerve. Most clinicians recognize that taste sensory afferents of VII in the chorda tympani supply taste sensation via the facial nerve to the anterior two-thirds of the tongue (see Figure 28–9).

The pharynx and posterior of the tongue receive sensory innervation from the glossopharyngeal nerve, along with taste sensation to the posterior of the tongue. Some posterior sensory input is also supplied by branches of the trigeminal nerve. The lower part of the pharynx is provided with afferent sensation by the vagus nerve, which also provides some sensory input to the auditory canal and the skin surface behind the ear. Minor contributions to taste are also provided by innervation of the vagus in the lower part of the oropharynx around the base of the tongue (see Figure 28–9).

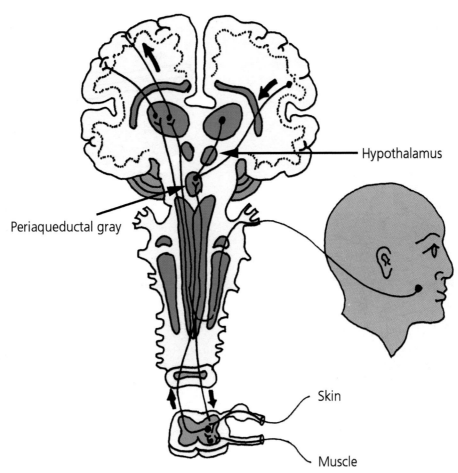

Figure 28–8 Descending inhibitory controls. Adapted from Okeson JP. Bell's orofacial pains. 5th ed. Carol Stream (IL): Quintessence Publishing Co., Inc.; 1995.

The cervical nerves primarily provide sensory input to the posterior muscles of the neck, including the cervical muscles, sternocleidomastoid, and trapezius. The skin of the neck also receives sensory innervation from the first three cervical nerves. Branches of the higher cervical nerves also provide cutaneous sensory input to the angle of the mandible and anterior of the neck just below the mandible (Figure 28–10).

Motor innervation

Important sources of motor innervation within the head and neck include the trigeminal, facial, glossopharyngeal, vagus, accessory, hypoglossal, cervical nerves, and the three cranial nerves that control movement of the eye (oculomotor, trochlear, abducens). These nerves provide motor input that controls facial expression and mastication, along with control of the tensor muscles of the middle ear. Muscles of the pharynx are controlled by the vagus and glossopharyngeal nerves, and the hypoglossal nerve controls movement of the tongue. The cervical nerves provide motor efferents to the posterior cervical muscles, whereas the trigeminal nerve

provides motor control to the anterior digastric and mylohyoids. Other muscles of the anterior neck are innervated by the facial nerve (see Figure 28–9).

Understanding of the afferent sensory and efferent motor supply to the structures of the head and neck is useful in the diagnosis of neurologic dysfunction and neuropathic pain with accompanying motor or sensory defects, and for assessment of possible sources of referred pain within the face and neck.

Autonomic innervation

The autonomic nervous system provides afferent and efferent input to the head and neck through sympathetic and parasympathetic innervation. Sympathetic fibers are found throughout the body, controlling sweat glands, blood vessels, and piloerector muscles of the skin. They reach these areas by emerging from the thoracolumbar region of the spine and traveling through sympathetic

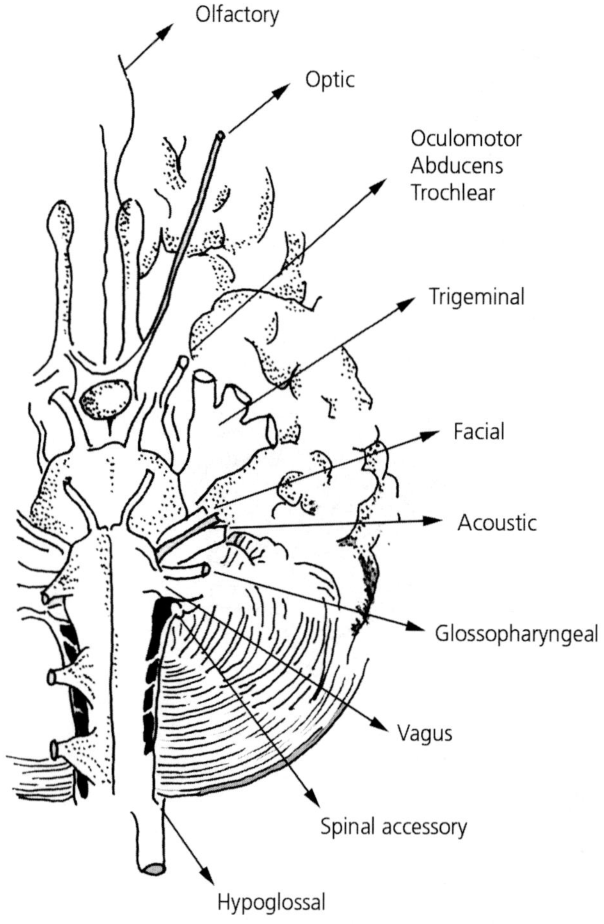

Figure 28–9   Innervation of the head and neck.

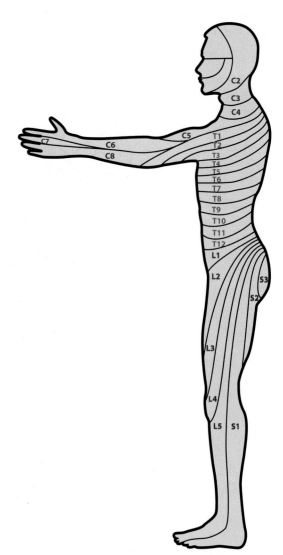

Figure 28–10   Cervical nerve and dermatone innervation of the body.

ganglions located beside the spine, including the cervical region. Parasympathetic fibers emerge via craniosacral routes, from cranial nerves III, VII, IX, and X, and from the sacral region of the spine. Sympathetic afferents follow the distribution of the trigeminal, glossopharyngeal, and facial nerves. Efferents of sympathetic origin follow the carotids (internal and external) into the neck and head, to provide control of blood vessels, salivary and cutaneous glands, and the pupil. Parasympathetic afferents provide input to the salivary and lacrimal glands, with the nerves coursing along with the trigeminal, facial, and glossopharyngeal nerves. Efferents of parasympathetic origin supply the salivary glands and the pupil and follow the distribution of the glossopharyngeal, facial, and oculomotor nerves (see Figure 28–5). The autonomic nervous system controls vascular tone by a single neuronal input, either sympathetic or parasympathetic, by a steady state of activity that maintains the vessel at a level of constriction that is normally appropriate. Stimulation or inhibition of the nerve triggers either greater vasoconstriction or vasodilation. The sympathetic nervous system is also responsible for sudden, system-wide reactions to challenge or stress, including increasing muscle strength and metabolic rate, increasing blood flow and glucose concentrations, and higher levels of alertness and attention.

Processing of pain signals through the CNS

A number of mechanisms operate within the CNS, resulting in clinical expressions of sensation and pain. Several primary sensory afferents can converge to signal a single second-order neuron, resulting in more diffuse sensations of pain and sensations of pain in sites other than the origin or source. Pain that is felt at a site other than the origin of the nociceptive stimulus is called heterotopic pain and can arise from sensations triggered within the CNS (central pain), pain that is felt at a different site along the same neurologic distribution (projected pain), and pain that is felt in a site of a different neural distribution (referred pain) (Figure 28–11). The CNS may also play a role in what appears to be referred pain through central sensitization caused by persistent stimulation of central neurons that sensitizes them through a variety of neurochemical agents, including glutamate and NMDA. The process is much like that seen with peripheral areas of injury that can be sensitized, resulting in pain from stimuli that are normally not painful. It is even thought that under some circumstances the process can become permanent, resulting in neuropathy.

Referral of pain is a common source of diagnostic error and is facilitated by convergence of primary afferents from two or more regions to second-order neurons. Painful stimulation of cervical or cranial regions can be

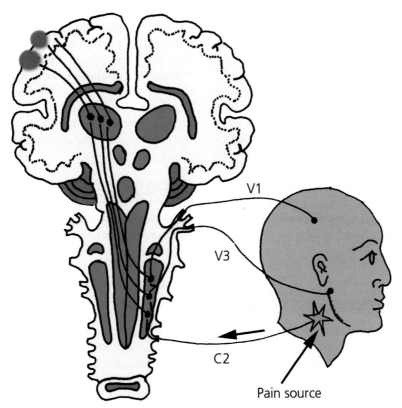

Figure 28–11 Referred pain. Adapted from Okeson JP. Bell's orofacial pains. 5th ed. Carol Stream (IL): Quintessence Publishing Co., Inc.; 1995.

felt as referred pain in other regions of the head or face. Painful stimuli can also result in reflex-style efferent stimulation of regional muscles, resulting in contraction or co-contraction of a muscle that would otherwise remain relaxed.

Gate-control theory of pain modulation and transmission

Although the innervation and neurochemical mechanisms of pain origination and modulation are similar between individuals, significant differences exist in pain affect and sensation. One model that helps to explain individual differences is the gate-control model of pain transmission. Basically the pain control theory suggests that nociceptive neurologic tissues are modulated to allow pain to be passed on to higher centers, dampened, or blocked, depending on descending control mechanisms operating within the "gate." Components of the gate include higher functions, such as affective and emotional components and specific neuronal components that react to higher-center stimulation. A recent model of the gate that focuses on local dorsal horn control of pain-signal transmission proposes that an inhibitory interneuron synapses with myelinated and unmyelinated fibers that also synapse with the major transmission neuron. The interneuron also synapses with the transmission neuron and acts upon stimulation, to dampen the transmission neuron. Stimulation of the interneuron by the myelinated fiber excites the interneuron, which in turn inhibits the transmission. Stimulation of the unmyelinated neuron dampens the interneuron, which reduces its ability to inhibit the transmission neuron, thus allowing the transmission neuron to transmit the pain signal strongly onward. If a peripheral pain impulse is carried only via unmyelinated fibers, the signal gets through. If it is carried only by myelinated fibers, it is blocked, and if it is carried by both myelinated and unmyelinated fibers, it is dampened and modulated, according to which signal is the strongest. Figure 28–12 schematically displays the components thought to be part of the pain processing system controlled by the pain gate.

Descending inhibitory pain control

Other endogenous pain control mechanisms exist besides the gate system. The function of the pain transmission system is such that some sensory signals arise in the dorsal root ganglion, resulting in continuous low-level signaling, which, if not blocked or dampened, could lead to persistent pain, if the signal is through nociceptive fibers, and arousal, if from other

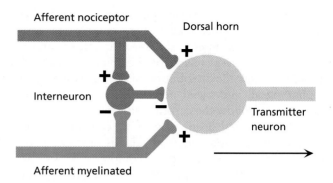

Figure 28–12   Modified gate-control theory of pain.

sensory fibers. The continuous central stimulation from these sources could also inhibit rest and sleep. Two different processes appear to be responsible for descending inhibitory control. The first is the periaqueductal gray region of the brain and the raphae magnus nucleus, which can completely suppress painful signals. The second consists of neurons that terminate in the spinal tract nucleus. Several neurotransmitters are important in descending inhibition. They include serotonin and a number of endorphins, including alpha and beta endorphins, and the enkephalins. These agents bind to opioid receptors (mu, delta, and kappa) to inhibit pain transmission. The inhibitory system can block pain transmission via release of endorphins or serotonin at different points along the neuronal distribution. Activation of the inhibitory system can occur through stimulation of peripheral structures as is seen with acupuncture, vibratory stimulation, and electrical stimulation, or through psychologic and psychoactive stimulation, as experienced with hypnosis and other behavioral techniques. The method of inhibition differs, depending on the inhibitory stimulus employed.

Summary

From this discussion, is should be clear that the neurologic and neurochemical mechanisms of pain generation and transmission are extremely complex, subject to individual modulation via physiologic and behavioral mechanisms, and not completely understood. Painful sensations arising from the mouth or orofacial region can involve more than the trigeminal nerve and may arise from autonomic and other somatic sources of innervation. Pain can be felt in or around the mouth but arise from adjacent structures, such as the cervical structures, pharyngeal tissues, or the sinuses. The complex nature of the innervation of the head and neck results in frequent pain referral and often allows poor localization of painful signals. Understanding of the neurophysiology and neuropharmacology of somatic and autonomic nerves is useful in deciding on pain management strategies, including selection of particular types of medications and pain control methods that do not include pharmacologic approaches (behavioral therapy, acupuncture, counter-irritation, etc.).

Suggested reading

Allen GV, Pronych SP. Trigeminal autonomic pathways involved in nociception-induced reflex cardiovascular responses. Brain Res 1997;754:269–78.

Cairns BE, Sessle BJ, Hu JW. Evidence that excitatory amino acid receptors with the temporomandibular joint region are involved in the reflex activation of the jaw muscles. J Neurosci 1998;18:8056–64.

Carlton SM, Coggeshall RE. Inflammation-induced changes in peripheral glutamate receptor populations. Brain Res 1999;820:63–70.

Cervero F, Meyer RS, Campbell JN. A psychophysical study of secondary hyperalgesia: evidence of increased pain input from nociceptors. Pain 1994;58:21–8.

Fristad I. Dental innervation: functions and plasticity after peripheral injury. Acta Odontol Scand 1997;55:236–54.

Hargreves KM, Roszkowski MT, Jackson DL, et al. Neuroendocrine and immune response to injury, degeneration, and repair. In: Sessle BJ, Bryant PS, Dionne RA, eds. Temporomandibular disorders and related pain conditions. Progress in pain research and management. Vol. 4. Seattle: IASP Press, 1995:273–92.

Hu JW, Tsai CM, Bakke M, et al. Deep craniofacial pain: involvement of trigeminal subnucleus caudalis and its modulation. In: Jensen TS, Turner JA, Wiesenfelf-Hallin A, eds. Proceeding of the 8th World Congress on Pain. Progress in pain research and management. Vol. 8. Seattle: IASP Press, 1997:497–506.

Jasmin L, Burkey AR, Card JP, Basbaum AI. Transneuronal labeling of a nociceptive pathway, the spino-(trigemino-) parabrachio-amygdaloid, in the rat. J Neurosci 1997; 17:3751–65.

Komorowski RC, Torneck CD, Hu JW. Neurogenic inflammation and tooth pulp innervation pattern in sympathectomized rats. J Endod 1996;22:414–7.

Maillou P, Cadden SW. Effects of remote deep somatic noxious stimuli on jaw reflex in man. Archs Oral Biol 1997; 42:323–7.

Raja SN, Meyer RA, Ringkamp M, Campbell JN. Peripheral neural mechanisms of nociception. In: Wall PD, Melzack R, eds. Textbook of pain, 4. London: Churchill Livingstone, 1999:11–57.

Sessle BJ, Hu JW, Amano N. Convergence of cutaneous, tooth pulp, visceral, neck, and muscle afferents onto nociceptive and nonnociceptive neurons in trigeminal subnucleus caudalis (medullary dorsal horn) and its implications for referred pain. Pain 1986;27:219–35.

29 Pain and Behavior

Edmond L. Truelove, DDS, MSD

Pain diagnosis and management in clinical practice can be straight forward or very complex. By its very nature, assessment, diagnosis, and treatment of pain, and especially chronic pain, requires an appreciation of the pathophysiologic processes that occur in peripheral tissues and a fundamental understanding of the processes within the central nervous system (CNS) that transmit and process signals that result in a sensation of pain. At least two additional components enter into the assessment of pain. The first of these is recognition of the significant role that behavioral status plays in augmenting or diminishing pain sensation and pain reporting. The second is the powerful influence of the understanding of the clinician managing the patient relative to views about behavioral and psychological contributors that alter treatment environment. It is essential to remember that pain is a subjective report of an unpleasant sensation, either peripherally or centrally generated, and influenced by endogenous and programmed modifiers. For pain that is peripherally triggered, the source may represent signals from progressive pathology, but persistent peripheral signals resulting in pain may also represent misinterpretation of nonnociceptive (nonpainful) signals because of neurosensory dysfunction at higher levels of the nervous system.

One of the best examples of such a process is the extremely painful signal that occurs in trigeminal neuralgia. Simple touch-evoked signals within the CNS provoke pain that is acute in nature, recurrent, and often unbearable. There is no pathology, however, at the tissue site of the neurologic stimulus that provokes the pain. Just as neurologic dysfunction centrally can alter sensations and create painful stimuli where none should exist, behavioral factors can influence central pain mechanisms, leading to exaggerated pain.

Behavioral issues important in pain management

Historically, pain has been thought to arise and be modulated by purely physical, chemical, and mechanical events. Research revealing the significant role that psychological status and the social environment play in the expression and sensation of pain has led to the emergence of the biopsychosocial model of pain. The model suggests that pain and suffering are the sum total of biologic inputs, psychological factors, and the social role of the patient. These psychosocial contributors are thought not to be conscious and explicit but operating at a subconscious level to either intensify pain and suffering or to minimize them. Family experiences, social role, and secondary gain are all components of the biopsychosocial model of pain. The net result of these components is the manifestation of pain behavior. Social factors can intensify pain if pain protects the patient from other threatening events, creates attention that is otherwise lacking, or reduces other demands upon the patient. Prior adverse social or psychological events can sensitize the patient to pain and increase fear that a terrible illness is creating their symptoms. Patients may feel pain more acutely as a means of diverting the negative effects of another stressor or as a manifestation of distress, anxiety, or depression.

Behavioral modifiers appear to have their most significant negative impact in chronic pain. They certainly do alter responses to acute nociceptive stimuli, but usually the effect is limited to anxiety and fear responses prior to real or perceived suffering from acute painful experiences. Such experiences are significant and can generate anxiety during dental or medical treatment even overriding prior experiences that have not been painful or have not triggered phobic responses in the past. The fact that a perceived risk of significant pain can generate life-long phobias and avoidance of dental care speaks powerfully to the ability of the mind to create psychological and physiologic responses even to the thought of a potentially painful experience.

Behavioral factors, such as stress generated during acute traumatic events, can actually decrease or prevent pain sensations. Numerous reports exist of complete lack of pain sensation during life-threatening events, such as gunshot wounds. If behavior and cognitive control can alter pain perception, it should be possible to program cognitive and subliminal responses in such a manner that pain is reduced or blocked and coping ability improved. Responses to painful stimuli and thoughts of pain can also include physiologic reactions, such as elevation in blood pressure and pulse, vagal reactivity, and loss of consciousness. These adverse physiologic responses are characteristically seen in acute pain, but chronic pain can also generate physiologic changes, and more importantly, behavioral stressors can generate physiologic changes, including responses that actually generate pain. The process of pain modulation occurs within the CNS and is particularly relevant in headache and chronic musculoskeletal and neuropathic orofacial pains.

The behavioral arenas that have been most associated with chronic pain are depression, somatization (nonspecific physical symptoms), and the number of other pain complaints. Many studies of chronic pain have demonstrated that high scores of depression or somatization are stronger predictors of pain severity and pain persistence than physiologic or physical measures of pathology. For example, in patients with painful temporomandibular disorders (TMD) high scores on depression or somatization scales are greater predictors of persistent pain and dysfunction than any physical measure of pathology, including temporomandibular joint (TMJ) sounds or limitation in mandibular opening. The same is true for comparisons of TMJ changes as seen on radiographs versus behavioral

measures as predictors of pain persistence. No physical measure is as accurately predictive of persistent chronic pain in TMD as scores of depression or somatization, with two possible exceptions, pain during palpation of placebo sites and the number of other pains. All four measures (depression, somatization, placebo site palpation, and number of other pain complaints) are highly correlated with one another and with persistent pain. These findings should have a powerful impact on the type of diagnostic assessment clinicians use when approaching patients with chronic orofacial pain and should trigger caution in the selection of invasive treatments.

It is essential that any assessment of patients with chronic pain, whether orofacial or in other locations, include two axes of evaluation: Axis I includes a physical structural assessment, functional evaluation, imaging, and laboratory studies; Axis II evaluation assesses behavioral, social, psychological, vegetative, and adaptive components of the patient's profile. Far more attention has been devoted to issues of physical assessment in orofacial pain than behavioral factors, partly because both patients and clinicians usually believe that pain arises predominantly from pathophysiologic processes that can be corrected by physical-mechanical-surgical interventions. They often fear, rightly, that serious progressive pathology may be overlooked. Some clinicians argue that excessive attention has been given to behavioral factors in facial pain. They fail to appreciate that most pathologic conditions are modulated by both physiologic and behavioral influences. Failure to detect specific organic causes for persistent pain suggests that behavioral factors may be contributing to the level of symptoms and need to be explored. It is inappropriate to assume that behavioral factors do not influence organic disease processes or responses to persistent illness and disease. Even in the presence of painful organic disease, there are differences in the ability of patients with the same disorder to tolerate and cope with the pain and disability that their disorder has created. Studies have found significant differences in disability and coping in patients with rheumatoid arthritis, depending on the behavioral status of the patient.

Based on the preceding discussion, it is obvious that the beginning of any evaluation of a patient presenting with pain that is not clearly caused by acute conditions (infection, trauma, etc.) must include assessment of behavioral status on a second axis that describes behavioral contributors. A number of questionnaires and examination protocols have been developed for Axis I (physical assessment and diagnosis) (see Chapters 1 and 30). Axis II status can readily be determined through use of a series of questions and subscales selected from behavioral questionnaires commonly used in behavioral and pain research, including studies of the pain in TMD. The method that has received the most attention recently in dentistry is the Axis II component of the Research

Table 29–1 Research Diagnostic Criteria Classification of Chronic Orofacial and Temporomandibular Disorder Pain

Axis I: physical diagnosis of TMD
  Muscle disorders
  Disc disorders
  Joint disorders
Axis II: behavioral and chronic pain diagnosis of TMD
  Characteristic pain intensity (CPI)
  Graded chronic pain (GCP) (I–IV)
  Depression
  Somatization
  Number of other pains

TMD = temporomandibular disorders.
Adapted from Dworkin SF, LeResche L. Research diagnostic criteria for temporomandibular disorders: review, criteria, examinations and specifications, critique. J Craniomandib Disord 1992;6:301–55.

Diagnostic Criteria (RDC) for Temporomandibular Disorders (Table 29–1). The Axis II assessment uses information gathered from a structured behavioral assessment to score the patient on several important behavioral factors, including an index of characteristic pain intensity (CPI), pain disability, depression, somatization, and number of other pains. The CPI measures the overall pain intensity over time, using three specific questions about present, average, and worst pain (Table 29–2).

Another important component of assessing pain is to determine the impact of the pain on the ability of the patient to engage in normal daily activities, such as employment, housework, and family and social duties. Since an important aspect of the impact of chronic pain is the degree of disability it causes, questions about disability are an important component of any workup of chronic orofacial pain. The RDC for TMD assesses the level of pain disability using four additional questions (Table 29–3).

Axis II scoring of CPI and pain disability are combined to arrive at a graded chronic pain (GCP) score of I through IV, with each grade of chronic pain describing the patient

Table 29–2 Characteristic Pain Intensity (CPI) Questions

On a scale of 0 to 10, 0 indicating "None" and 10 indicating "Pain as bad as it could be," answer the following questions:
1. How would you rate your facial pain at the present time, right now?_____
2. In the past 6 months how intense was your worst facial pain?_____
3. In the past 6 months, on average, how intense was your facial pain?_____

To find the CPI score, find the mean of the three answers.*

*Other sources often obtain CPI scores by multiplying the mean number by ten. However, for this book, the method has been modified, as it makes calculations easier in a practice setting.

Table 29–3 Pain Disability Questions

1. About how many days in the past 6 months have you been kept from your usual activities (employment, school, or housework) because of facial pain?* _____
2. On a scale of 0 to 10, 0 indicating "no interference" and 10 indicating "unable to carry on any activities," in the past 6 months, how much has facial pain interfered with your daily activities?† _____

On a scale of 0 to 10, 0 indicating "no change" and 10 indicating "extreme change," answer the following questions:
3. In the past 6 months, how much has facial pain changed your ability to take part in recreational social and family activities?† _____
4. In the past 6 months how much has facial pain changed your ability to work (including housework)?† _____

*To find the disability days score, award the following disability points: 0–6 days = 0 pts; 7–14 days = 1 pt; 15–30 days = 2 pts; 31+ days = 3 pts.
†To find the disability score, find the mean of the answers for questions 2, 3, and 4 then award the following disability points: 0–2.9 = 0; 3.0–4.9 = 1 pt; 5.0–6.9 = 2 pts; 7.0+ = 3 pts.
Adapted from Dworkin SF, LeResche L. Research diagnostic criteria for temporomandibular disorders: review, criteria, examinations and specifications, critique. J Craniomandib Disord 1992;6:301–55.

in terms of high or low level of pain and level of adaption or dysfunction as a result of pain (pain disability) (Table 29–4). The GCP score is strongly predictive of the chronicity of the pain. As previously stated, the levels of depression and somatization (nonspecific physical symptoms) and number of other pain complaints are important measures related to chronic pain and response to treatment. They are assessed using subscales from the Symptom Check List (SCL-90), a commonly used behavioral questionnaire. Patients who receive a GCP score of III or IV are more likely to experience pain that is persistent and chronic and

Table 29–4 Graded Chronic Pain Scoring

Grade	Effect of Chronic Pain	Scoring
0	No disability and no pain	No pain in the previous 6 months
I	Low disability with low pain intensity	CPI <5; <3 disability points*
II	Low disability with high pain intensity	CPI ≥5; <3 disability points
III	Moderately limiting	3–4 disability points regardless of CPI
IV	Severely limiting	5–6 disability points regardless of CPI

*Determine total disability points by adding together the disability days score and the disability score (see Table 29–3).
CPI = characteristic pain intensity.
Adapted from Dworkin SF, LeResche L. Research diagnostic criteria for temporomandibular disorders: review, criteria, examinations and specifications, critique. J Craniomandib Disord 1992;6:301–55.

to respond less well to usual treatment protocols. Patients in the GCP I and II groups are less likely to develop chronic pain, and they seem to respond more favorably to treatments that are straight forward.

In addition, the RDC for TMD Axis II assessment gathers information about levels of depression, and somatization (nonspecific physical symptoms) using the Symptom Check List (SCL-90) Scales for Depression and Vegetative Symptoms. Specific questions important in determining whether the patient has a high rate of somatic complaints or depression are listed in Table 29–5. Other measures of anxiety, depression, and somatization using other questionnaires and scales are available. Findings from the SCL that should alert the clinician to possible depression, somatization, and risk of suicide are identified in Table 29–6.

Scoring all components of the Axis II status provides a patient profile that is important in determining the best clinical approach to the patient. In some cases the data can alter dramatically the primary focus of treatment. Determining the Axis II characteristics of the patient does not suggest that Axis I treatments are not important. It is most useful to consider the two axes as complementary. For the more chronic and dysfunctional patient, the dual approach is more likely to result in a successful therapeutic outcome, since it promotes combined physical and behavioral management strategies.

In addition to the specific scores that are determined from use of the Axis II process, other valuable psychological and behavioral information can be derived when a dual axis approach is used in assessing patients with chronic orofacial pain, including risk of suicide, the presence of major psychological or thought disorders, loss of coping ability, and associated findings that may be critical in the management of patients with chronic pain (eg, number of other pains, sleep dysfunction).

It is important to identify the number of other pain complaints before initiating therapy for chronic facial

Table 29–5 System Check List: SCL 90 Depression and Vegetative Symptom Scales and Somatization Scale

Symptom	In the last month how much have you been distressed by?				
	Not at all	A little	Moderately	Quite	Extremely
Headache	0	1	2	3	4
Loss of sexual interest	0	1	2	3	4
Faintness or dizziness	0	1	2	3	4
Pain in heart or chest	0	1	2	3	4
Feeling low in energy or slowed down	0	1	2	3	4
Thoughts of death or dying	0	1	2	3	4
Poor appetite	0	1	2	3	4
Crying easily	0	1	2	3	4
Blaming self for things	0	1	2	3	4
Pains in the lower back	0	1	2	3	4
Feeling lonely	0	1	2	3	4
Feeling blue	0	1	2	3	4
Worrying too much about things	0	1	2	3	4
Feeling no interest in things	0	1	2	3	4
Nausea or upset stomach	0	1	2	3	4
Soreness of your muscles	0	1	2	3	4
Trouble falling asleep	0	1	2	3	4
Trouble getting your breath	0	1	2	3	4
Hot or cold spells	0	1	2	3	4
Numbness or tingling in parts of your body	0	1	2	3	4
A lump in your throat	0	1	2	3	4
Feeling hopeless about the future	0	1	2	3	4
Feeling weak in parts of your body	0	1	2	3	4
Heavy feeling in your arms or legs	0	1	2	3	4
Thought of ending your life	0	1	2	3	4
Overeating	0	1	2	3	4
Awakening in the early morning	0	1	2	3	4
Sleep that is restless or disturbed	0	1	2	3	4
Feeling everything is an effort	0	1	2	3	4
Feeling worthlessness	0	1	2	3	4
Feeling of being caught or trapped	0	1	2	3	4
Feelings of guilt	0	1	2	3	4

Table 29–6 Positive Responses Suggestive of Depression, Somatization, and Suicide Ideation

Depression	Somatization with Pain	Somatization without Pain
Loss of sexual interest	Headaches	Faintness or dizziness
Low energy	Faintness or dizziness	Trouble getting your breath
Thoughts of death or dying*	Pains in the lower back	Hot or cold spells
Poor appetite	Nausea or upset stomach	Numbness or tingling in parts of your body
Crying easily	Soreness of your muscles	Lump in your throat
Feeling lonely	Trouble getting your breath	
Feeling blue	Hot or cold spells	
Worrying too much	Numbness or tingling in parts of your body	
Feeling no interest in things	Lump in your throat	
Trouble falling asleep		
Feeling hopeless about the future		
Thought of ending your life*		
Awakening in the early morning		
Sleep that is restless or disturbed		
Feeling everything is an effort		
Feelings of worthlessness		
Feeling caught or trapped		
Feelings of guilt		

*Important suggestions that the patient may be so distressed that suicide is possible.

pain, because the number of other pains predicts significantly whether the orofacial pain will resolve or be persistent. Patients with only one painful condition are more likely to experience a remission in their pain compared to those with complaints of several other pains (headache, back pain, abdominal pain). Those with complaints of three or more other pains have approximately an 80% probability that their facial pain will persist for more than 3 years with or without treatment. For patients with serious psychological dysfunction, referral to, and comanagement with a psychologist is wise. Components of the Axis I (physical assessment) workup should also receive attention as part of the behavioral assessment, including medication history, history of abuse, psychiatric history, phobias, and other chronic illnesses.

Table 29–7 Components of the Axis II Behavioral and Psychological Interview

Impact of pain on work, personal life, attitudes
Coping methods, including use of medications, alcohol, illicit drugs
Factors that increase symptoms
Factors that decrease symptoms
Evidence of depression (sleep dysfunction, other symptoms)
Evidence of somatic focus (other nonspecific symptoms)
Other pain complaints (chest, back, headache, other)
Evidence of anxiety or panic disorder
Reports of suicide ideation
Goals from the visit

Psychological and behavioral Axis II interviewing

Axis II assessment is not complete without a behavioral interview that offers an opportunity to expand understanding of factors that modify the level of pain, trigger recurrences, or modulate the patient's ability to cope with symptoms. The interview should be structured but can follow the format most comfortable for the clini-

Table 29–8 Positive Findings from Behavioral Interview That Should Be Explored for Influence in Management of the Patient with Orofacial Pain

Sleep dysfunction (insomnia, hypersolumbulance, nonrestorative sleep)
Nonspecific physical complaints (dizziness, tingling, weakness, fatigue, etc.)
Fatigue
Depression or anhedonia (loss of interest or pleasure in life)
Anxiety
Thought disorders
Panic attacks
Mood swings
Abuse history (physical, verbal, mental, sexual)
Significant work stress
Significant family or home stress
Worry
Phobias, fears
Recent death or deaths of family members or loved ones
Suicide ideation

cian. Responses to questions in the Axis II database can be used to explore and expand upon potent contributing behavioral factors. Negative responses on a questionnaire do not necessarily mean that there are no behavioral issues significant in the case. Some patients are either reluctant to provide that data or do not appreciate that the area of questioning could be important in their diagnosis and management. A suggested format for the interview is listed in Table 29–7. Generally, it is best to initiate the behavioral component of the patient workup and scoring of behavioral findings of the psychological interview after questions about the chief complaint and medical history have been completed. Some patients are resistant to providing information about their psychosocial and behavioral status until they have developed more trust in the clinician. When it is clear that the patient is unwilling to provide an open level of communication about behavioral issues it is important to reopen the discussion at a later date.

Findings from the questionnaire or interview that indicate potentially important behavioral issues require follow-up. In some cases positive findings should trigger immediate referral to the patient's primary care physician or to a mental health professional (Table 29–8).

Behavioral management strategies in orofacial pain

Patients suffering chronic facial pain can benefit from the use of one or more self-management behavioral interventions. These interventions can be initiated in most dental offices and have been shown to improve the status of patients with pain and other neurosensory symptoms. They generally include the following methods or concepts:

- progressive relaxation
- relaxation breathing (abdominal breathing)
- imagery
- expressive writing
- identification of stressors
- general stress management
- sleep management

Together these interventions can help to reduce pain and improve coping. Each method is briefly described, and the reader is encouraged to learn more about them.

Progressive relaxation

Progressive muscular relaxation is a well established method for improving the ability of patients to achieve physical and muscular relaxation as a reflection of mental and physiologic relaxation. Several different techniques are advocated, but they all have in common the process of progressively tensing a muscle group and then releasing the tensed muscles to a state of complete relaxation. Usually, the patient is asked to start either at the top of the head or at the feet and to tense the muscles in that region for 10 to 15 seconds until they are recognized as being tense. The patient is then asked to completely relax the muscles that were deliberately tensed, with the patient noting how different the muscles feel in a relaxed state. The process is repeated in each muscle group as they move up the legs, thighs, chest, back, arms, shoulders, and neck, eventually reaching the muscles of mastication and frontalis and repeating the process of tensing and relaxing the muscles. The entire process of tensing then relaxing the major muscle groups of the body takes 5 to 15 minutes. Progressive relaxation attempts to teach the patient to know when muscles are tense and how to completely relax them and, particularly, the muscles responsible for sensations of musculoskeletal tension and pain. Another goal of progressive relaxation is to teach the patient to detect muscles that are becoming tense before pain develops. Patients are asked to repeat the progressive relaxation exercise at least once a day until they can easily notice muscle tension and relax quickly.

Imagery

Imagery is a commonly used relaxation and pain management strategy that can usually be mastered quickly by the patient. Patients are asked either to picture in their minds a real place remembered as being very relaxing and peaceful or to imagine such a place (ocean shore, mountain meadow, etc.). They are encouraged to pay particular attention to the feelings they have when they are, or they imagine themselves to be in such a peaceful place. They are asked to try to sustain the feelings of peace and relaxation for several minutes by concentrating on the images and sensations they have generated. Imagery can help patients to generate physiologic sensations associated with being in a place of mental and physical relaxation. Blood pressure and pulse rates have been shown to decrease during imagery. Patients are asked to stay in their place of imagery for 5 to 10 minutes each day and to regenerate the sensations felt during imagery periodically throughout the day. For many patients, engaging in imagery can reduce pain and improve ability to cope with it.

Expressive writing

Experimental studies have shown the value of expressive writing in helping patients to gain greater understanding of the impact of traumatic behavioral experiences on mental status, health, and chronic symptoms. Expressive writing has been shown to reduce pain and disability in asthma and rheumatoid arthritis and to reduce medical treatment-seeking behavior in otherwise health students. It is based partly on the premise that expressively writing about feelings can reduce subliminal negative stress generated by failure to openly analyze thoughts and events and personal reactions to them. The technique usually employed is to ask patients to spend 30 minutes each day for a few days (3–5 d) engaging in writing about events that have been particularly stressful or distressing in their lives (major events). They are asked to concentrate on their feelings and the impact of the stressful experience on them. In experiments using expressive writing with college students, it was found that engaging in an expressive writing exercise reduced visits to the college health center significantly over the follow-up period, which extended several years. Like other pain self-management techniques, expressive writing is simple, requires no expert knowledge of psychological assessment or management and can be done easily by most patients.

Other strategies for behavioral management of pain

Abdominal deep-breathing exercises have long been considered an effective method for enhancing relaxation. Patients are asked to slowly breath in, using abdominal rather than chest-wall muscles. Next they are asked to hold the breath for a few seconds, followed by slowly exhaling while concentrating only on the breathing activity. Patients repeat the process eight to ten times and repeat the series when they become stressed or distressed and two or three other times each day. Usually blood pressure and heart rate decrease following deep-breathing exercises, and patients report that they feel more relaxed.

Sleep problems are common in patients with chronic facial pain. Sleep can also be disturbed in patients suffering acute pain of dental etiology, but the process of sleep disruption appears to be different in chronic pain and is more destructive relative to coping ability. Sleep dysfunction can indicate that severe psychological distress is present. Addressing sleep difficulties and assisting the patient in developing a sleep-management program can result in pain reduction or improved pain coping. Development of a sleep hygiene program is wise in patients that report regular sleep difficulties whether the problem is described as difficulty in going to sleep, waking frequently throughout the night, or waking early and not being able to return to sleep. Table 29–9 identifies components of most sleep hygiene programs. Addressing them in dental patients with chronic orofacial pain should be part of chronic pain management.

If the patient has extreme sleep problems, a sleep medication may briefly be necessary, but care should be taken with sedative medications since they can produce

Table 29–9 Sleep Hygiene Recommendations

Avoid caffeine after noon each day.
Exercise daily but before the evening (brisk walking 30–60 min).
Avoid heavy meals within 3 to 4 hours of sleep.
Avoid stressful or exciting activities within 4 hours of bedtime.
Go to bed at the same time each night.
Arise at the same time each morning.
Do not read or watch television in bed (use the bed to sleep).
If you are hungry before bed have a light snack.
Avoid any food that irritates the stomach within 4 to 6 hours of bedtime.
Engage in progressive relaxation or imagery exercises before bedtime.
Avoid heavy alcohol consumption within several hours of bedtime.

dependency. If questions about their safety or value for a particular patient arise, it is important to consult with the primary health provider.

Some patients with chronic pain have a tendency to overuse pain medications and muscle relaxants. They have a similar potential for becoming dependent on sleep medications, which themselves have significant potential for abuse and should not be used, or used only with extreme care in patients with a history of drug dependency or alcoholism. On the other hand, amitriptyline, a tricyclic antidepressant, and trazodone, another antidepressant, have little potential for abuse or dependency and are better choices when the patient profile suggests risk of abuse. Unfortunately both medications have strong anticholinergic properties, including xerostomia which some patients find irritating. Generally, it is not recommended that sleep medications in the benzodiazepam family be used for more than a few days.

Psychological or psychiatric consultation or referral

A number of findings that suggest the need for consultation or referral to a psychologist or psychiatrist were previously identified. For patients with these findings, an open discussion with the patient about the value of a referral to a behavioral therapist or psychologist is warranted. Findings that particularly suggest the need for such a referral include major family or marital stress, depression, nonspecific anxiety or panic attacks, thoughts of death or suicide, and major mood swings, such as those seen in patients with bipolar disorders (mania and manic depression). Chronic orofacial pain and TMD are difficult to manage successfully in patients with any of these major psychological disorders without concurrent professional behavioral therapy.

A significant percentage of patients with major depression or other major behavioral problems may require treatment with medications in addition to behavioral therapy. Generally the medications used include a wide range of antidepressants, including the older generation tricyclic antidepressants (amitriptyline, imipramine, nortriptyline, etc.), which have been shown to have efficacy in chronic pain, or one of the newer generation selective serotonin reuptake inhibitors, such as Prozac or Zoloft. A significant risk when using some antidepressants is their effect on patients with undiagnosed bipolar disorders, in whom they can trigger manifestations of mania. If major psychopathology is diagnosed, treatment with an antipsychotic medication may be necessary. Some patients report a decrease in pain with use of medications for their behavioral disorder. Whether the effect is directly antinociceptive or associated with medication-induced improvement of their behavioral dysfunction is not well understood.

Chronic pain

All chronic pain begins as an acute painful experience. Pain becomes chronic when it lasts longer than normal healing takes to resolve the biologic process responsible for the pain. Although some chronic diseases produce chronic symptoms, patients with these disorders may or may not develop a chronic pain syndrome. For example, patients with rheumatoid arthritis are known to suffer constant pain because of joint inflammation. They are not normally thought of as chronic pain patients. The term chronic pain patient is usually reserved for someone who suffers chronic pain for which no clear and specific pathology can be detected or, if present, the pathology is not normally thought to produce the kind and severity of symptoms seen. Chronic pain in that context normally implies that the patient is disabled and made dysfunctional by the pain in excess of the physical findings of his or her condition. The level of suffering and alterations in life style are beyond those that would normally be predicted for the condition. Chronic pain often triggers major changes in life style, including increased reliance on others for support of activities of daily living, loss of employment, reduced ability to care for family members, and reliance on them. The most successful therapies for chronic pain that is not associated with progressive pathology appear to come from behavioral therapy programs, such as those offered in pain centers. The programs usually include work activation, behavioral therapy, cognitive therapy, and self-management pain protocols. Even with these interventions, many patients with chronic pain syndromes fail to be able to return to a normal life style. Patients with chronic orofacial pain who have a prior history of treatment for chronic pain should be considered for referral back to a pain center or a pain specialist for evaluation and treatment.

Psychological disorders in orofacial pain

Among patients with chronic orofacial pain are a small group that have significant psychological disorders. Much has already been discussed about depression and somatization, but other significant disorders detected in a small percentage of patients with chronic pain include serious thought disorders. They frequently present with complaints of pain caused by others who are persecuting them, including governmental agents, family members, and religious cults. Their beliefs are unshakable, and they express that something is terribly wrong and caused by others. Patients that report loss of motor function or progressive change in tissues that are visible to them but not visible to the examiner may also have major thought disorders. Their complaints may include pain accompanied by swelling which is never present when the patient is examined, discharges, loss of motor or sensory function, and the presence of parasitic or other infections that are destroying deep tissues. When the description of the condition or symptoms is not verifiable using normal physical, laboratory, or radiographic methods and the patient is agitated or unreasonable in his or her beliefs, a major thought disorder should be suspected and the patient referred for psychological evaluation. Unfortunately, under such circumstances the patient usually refuses referral and seeks another practitioner who will accept his or her model of the condition and treatment direction.

Other psychological problems encountered in patients with chronic orofacial pain are somatoform disorders and somatoform pain disorders. Patients with these disorders report physical symptoms that may include pain. They do not have organic disease but usually have many symptoms and no physical or other findings that verify the existence of organic pathology. To achieve a diagnosis of somatoform disorder, the patient must have many somatic complaints. Such patients often receive unnecessary treatments because they are demanding and express symptoms in a believable way. Hypochondriasis is another of the psychological disorders that manifest through frequent development of physical complaints in the absence of actual pathology. The hypochondriacal patient benefits from reassurance and regular clinical follow up.

Post-traumatic stress disorder (PTSD) can also trigger pain as a major symptom, but PTSD usually involves other behavioral changes, including anxiety, panic attacks, and depression. Specific criteria exist for determination of PTSD, including exposure to a significantly stressful event. The exposure can include witnessing a terribly traumatic event. Flash backs to the event occur, and the patient involuntarily relives the event daily. Often unexplained episodes of anxiety or panic occur before the stressor emerges. Involvement in, or witnessing a death, severe trauma, assault, or abuse increase the risk of developing PTSD. When a patient describes PTSD, it is important to refer him or her to a psychologist or psychiatrist with experience in managing the condition.

Occasionally patients do contrive to report symptoms that do not exist. In such cases, the patient is malingering and reports a problem for a consciously sought secondary gain, which can include money, disability compensation, litigation gain, and avoidance of other risks.

Special note about thoughts of death or suicide

Some patients suffering from depression or other psychological problems experience thoughts of death or suicide. Data suggest that major depression is a risk factor for suicide, and since depression is also a common finding in patients suffering from all forms of chronic pain, including facial pain and TMD, it is important to recognize that a professional responsibility exists to explore whether a depressed patient with pain has thoughts about ending his or her life. Most behavioral questionnaires address the issue but follow-up verbal questions are also important, since the patient may not choose to report having thoughts of suicide on the questionnaire. If the patient indicates having suicidal thoughts, the clinician must explore whether the patient has serious potential for carrying out the act. Tips that suggest the patient is at imminent risk of suicide include having an actual plan, arranging for others to care for children or pets, and prior attempts. If the clinician believes that there is a real risk of suicide, it is essential to refer the patient to a mental health professional immediately, and to persuade the patient to contact an agreed upon person if thoughts of suicide become strong or if they find themselves planning to end their life. If the patient refuses to agree, it may be necessary to contact local mental health authorities for possible involuntary commitment while the patient is evaluated to determine whether they are a risk to themselves or others.

Summary

Behavioral assessment and management is an integral part of the management of any patient with chronic orofacial pain, including TMD. Assisting patients to determine behavioral and psychological factors negatively influencing their lives can be one of the most rewarding aspects of patient management, since improvements in behavioral status can have a positive impact on many parts of a patient's life as well as the life of his or her immediate family. The application of behavioral interventions can prove a more powerful treatment intervention in chronic pain than many physical or pharmacologic alternatives.

Suggested reading

Asmundson GJ, Norton GR, Allerdings MD, et al. Post-traumatic stress disorder and work-related injury. J Anxiety Disord 1998;12:57–69.

Derogatis LR. SCL-90-R administration, scoring, and procedures manual: II. Revised version. Towson, MD: Clinical Psychometric Research, 1983.

Dworkin SF. Behavioral characteristics of chronic temporomandibular disorders: diagnosis and assessment. In: Sessle BJ, Bryant PS, Dionne RA, eds. Progress in pain research and management. Seattle: IASP Press, 1995:175–92.

Dworkin SF, LeResche L. Research diagnostic criteria for temporomandibular disorders: review, criteria, examinations and specifications, critique. J Craniomandib Disord 1992; 6:301–55.

Dworkin SF, Wilson L, Massoth DL. Somatizing as a risk factor for chronic pain. In: Grzesiak RD, Ciccone DS, eds. Psychologic vulnerability to chronic pain. New York: Springer, 1994:28–54.

Feine JS, Lavigne GJ, Dao TT, et al. Memories of chronic pain and perception of relief. Pain 1998;77:137–41.

Foreman PA, Harold PL, Hay KD. An evaluation of the diagnosis, treatment, and outcome of patients with chronic orofacial pain. N Z Dent J 1994;90:44–8.

Fricton JR, Olsen T. Predictors of outcome for treatment of temporomandibular disorders. J Orofac Pain 1996;10:54–65.

Gallagher RM. The comprehensive pain clinic: a biobehavioral approach to pain management and rehabilitation. In: Glock MH, Friedman R, Myers P, ed. Integration of behavioral and relaxation approaches into the treatment of chronic pain and insomnia. Bethesda, MD: NIH Technology Assessment Conference, NIH 1995:1–34.

Gatchel RJ, Garofalo JP, Ellis E, Holt C. Major psychological disorders in acute and chronic TMD: an initial examination. J Am Dent Assoc 1996;127:1365–70.

Korszun A, Hinderstein B, Wong M. Comorbidity of depression with chronic facial pain and temporomandibular disorders. Oral Surg Oral Med Oral Pathol Oral Radiol Endod 1996;82:496–500.

Turk DC, Rudy TE, Kubinski JA, et al. Dysfunctional patients with temporomandibular disorders: evaluating the efficacy of a tailored treatment protocol. J Consult Clin Psychol 1996;64:139–46.

National Institute of Health. National Institutes of Health Technology Assessment Conference Statement. Oral Surg Oral Med Oral Pathol Oral Radiol Endod 1997;83:177–83.

VonKorff M, Ormel J, Keefe FJ, Dworkin SF. Grading the severity of chronic pain. Pain 1992;50:133–49.

30 Temporomandibular Disorders

Edmond L. Truelove, DDS, MSD

Temporomandibular disorders (TMD) are a collection of disorders involving the temporomandibular joint, the soft-tissue structures within the joint, and the muscles of mastication. The most common type of painful TMD is myofascial pain, which is characterized by pain in the muscles of mastication, frequently along with muscle dysfunction, and tightness. The most common non-painful type of TMD is an internal derangement of the meniscus (disc) of the temporomandibular joint (TMJ), which causes clicking to occur during opening and closing movements. Less common are the degenerative arthritic types of TMD, including osteoarthritis and osteoarthrosis. These TMD conditions as a group are one of the more common chronic painful disorders of the face and jaws.

An extensive scientific literature has been developed covering virtually all aspects of TMD. For a number of years considerable controversy has existed concerning the etiology of TMD and even greater controversy has existed regarding treatment approaches. These debates have generated enough confusion that both the American Dental Association and the National Institute of Dental and Craniofacial Research have held consensus conferences for purposes of identifying the current state of scientific knowledge about TMD and to explore common beliefs about TMD and their management.

Patients with TMD have also become active in the debate, and a number of patient advocacy groups have evolved demanding that more research be initiated to find preventive strategies and better treatment options for the most common types of TMD. The vigor of this debate was increased significantly when thousands of patients with TMD who had previously received joint surgery found it necessary to undergo a second surgery for removal of a synthetic material used to replace the meniscus, because of severe foreign-body reactions to the synthetic material. The widespread adverse reaction that arose from use of the synthetic disc replacement resulted in thousands of patients developing intractable joint pain and persistent giant cell-mediated rejection reactions within the joint. Although not all of the answers about the etiology or treatment of TMD are known, enough scientific data have been accumulated in the past 10 years to provide practitioners with reasonable guidelines for the diagnosis and management of TMD. This chapter attempts to provide practical guidelines for the diagnosis and management of TMD in the primary care dental practice.

Epidemiology and etiology

Temporomandibular disorders were thought, until recently, to be far more prevalent in females than in males. Epidemiologic research completed in the 1980s, using sophisticated sampling and carefully structured, objective evaluation methods of a random sample of community populations rather than clinic patients, found that TMD were only about 1.8 to 2.0 times more prevalent in females than males. These studies discovered that females were more likely to seek treatment for their condition and, when affected, had higher levels of pain and dysfunction, and greater persistence of symptoms over a longer time. As with most other health conditions, females are more likely to seek treatment for the problem than males, leading to the erroneous assumption that females have a higher incidence of TMD. Studies have also demonstrated that certain age groups have a greater risk for developing TMD than others. The most prevalent age group for TMD are females between the ages of 20 and 40 years. The condition is extremely uncommon in males after the age of 55 years and is also uncommon in elderly females. Shortly after the onset of puberty, the rates of TMD begin to rise in both genders, and rate continues to increase in prevalence in females up to age 40 to 45 years, when the rate begins to drop. The same pattern of rising TMD risk occurs in males after puberty, but the rate is about one-half that of females at each period.

The epidemiology of TMD varies depending upon the kind of TMD that is being studied. Temporomandibular disorders involving the muscles of mastication (myofascial pain) are more common in young to middle-aged adults, and TMD involving arthritic changes are more common in the elderly.

Epidemiologic studies of TMD have determined that clicking in the TMJ is a common finding in approximately 30% of all adults; during episodes of painful TMD, the rate of clicking rises significantly. The same studies have shown a wide variation in patterns of jaw movement in normal individuals during opening and closing, in joint sounds, and in jaw relations. Table 30–1 provides a summary of major findings from recent epidemiologic studies of TMD. The data displayed in the table call into question a number of prior concepts about factors thought to be common in TMD.

Extensive scientific effort has been directed toward identifying the causative factors associated with TMD. Table 30–2 identifies known etiologic factors; however, most of these factors are also reported frequently in individuals who do not suffer TMD. Therefore, deter-

Table 30–2 Etiologic Factors in Temporomandibular Disorders

Direct trauma to the jaws from accidents or assault
Iatrogenic injury during dental or medical treatment
Developmental defects in the joint (hypoplasia, etc.)
Degenerative joint disease: osteoarthritis, arthrosis
Autoimmune disease: rheumatoid arthritis, lupus
Parafunctional jaw activities: clenching, bruxism
Orofacial movement disorders
Behavioral disorders: stress, depression, somatization
Major discrepancies in jaw relations
Major discrepancies in dental occlusion
Unknown factors

mining the exact etiology for the disorder in specific patients can prove to be challenging. In general, it is accepted that direct trauma to the jaw represents one etiologic risk factor. However, data also show that for many TMD patients no firm etiology can be identified except for behavioral factors, which include stress, tension, and somatic focus. Autoimmune disorders, such as rheumatoid arthritis and lupus erythematosus can cause significant inflammation and destruction within the TMJ, but these disorders are relatively uncommon in populations of patients with TMD studied in clinical settings. Psoriatic arthritis has also been documented to cause destructive changes within the TMJ. Jaw parafunction, as seen during bruxism and jaw clenching behaviors, has been suggested to be one of the more common causes for TMD, but clinical studies have determined that those types of jaw activity are common in patients whether they have TMD symptoms or not. Among all of the factors that have been studied as potential causes for TMD, behavioral and psychologic factors have received the most significant amounts of attention during the past few years. Those factors have also been identified as important contributors to the onset and persistence of other chronic musculoskeletal complaints, such as low back pain and tension type headache. There is now a reasonable body of scientific data suggesting that behavioral and psychologic factors are important in the development of some types of TMD, and particularly those associated with muscle pain and dysfunction. Jaw relations and dental occlusion were once thought to be the dominant etiology for TMD, but epidemiologic research during the past 20 years has shown that malocclusion and occlusal discrepancies, except in extreme circumstances, are not more prevalent in patients with TMD than in normal individuals. It is currently understood that TMD has characteristics common to tension-type headache and low back pain. Therefore, the etiology of most types of TMD that are not primarily associated with autoimmune-based inflammatory or degenerative changes is probably closely aligned with that of tension-type headache and low back pain.

Table 30–1 Epidemiology of Temporomandibular Disorders

Ratio of TMD (F:M)	1.8:1.0
Age of highest prevalence	25–44 yr
Prevalence in 18-year-olds	
Female	11%
Male	7%
Rate in 65-year-olds	
Female	2%
Male	0%
Percentage with TMJ clicking	
Cases	40%
Controls	30%
Class of occlusion in TMD	Not different than normal population

F:M = female:male ratio.

Pathophysiologic correlates of disease

The pathophysiology of TMD is complex and not well understood. Since they comprise a collection of disorders that can affect muscle function, the joints, the meniscus within the joint, and the neuromuscular system controlling the jaws, it is obvious that the pathophysiology of TMD depends upon the specific subtype that is present. Perhaps the most easily understood pathophysiologic process in TMD is the process seen in patients with inflammatory or degenerative joint disease. Patients suffering from such conditions develop inflammation within the joint or the articulating surfaces of the joint, which leads to progressive joint destruction and remodeling described as degenerative remodeling. The causes for the onset of either degenerative or inflammatory change may be system-wide as is seen with rheumatoid arthritis and other polyarthritic diseases. Isolated degenerative remodeling of the joint is often described as caused by microtrauma from occlusal disharmonies or from parafunctional patterns of excessive loading of the TMJ during nocturnal or waking jaw activities. Joint disease associated with an autoimmune dysfunction, such as rheumatoid arthritis or lupus, is associated with high concentrations of inflammatory mediators within the joint but sometimes is triggered by system-wide immune dysregulation. The pathophysiology of autoimmune-based arthritis of the TMJ is the same as that found in other joints.

The pathophysiology of TMD primarily manifesting with painful muscle dysfunction is unclear but thought to involve fatigue in the muscles of mastication, leading to spasms and inflammation in muscle tissues. Tightening in these muscles has been thought to produce both pain and reduced ability to open the jaw normally. Recent studies, however, have not been able to identify physiologic markers indicating that muscle pain is caused by actual spasm, or trismus. Thus, the reason for muscle pain in TMD is not clear from a pathophysiologic perspective.

A relatively common form of TMD, the internal derangement (disc displacement), has been studied extensively, from the standpoint of radiographic assessment of joint function in patients with disc displacements, and whereas the physical process of developing and maintaining an internal derangement is understood and well documented, the structural and pathophysiologic processes leading to the internal derangement are not clear. Obviously, direct trauma to the jaws can trigger a mechanical displacement of the meniscus (disc), but a significant percentage of patients with internal derangements report no history of direct trauma to the joint, and many who experience direct joint trauma do not develop internal derangements. Physical trauma to the jaws is considerably more common in males than in females, yet internal derangements are more common in females.

The concept of microtrauma to the joint and muscles has also been advanced as an explanation for the development of TMD in patients who do not have other clear etiologic factors. The pathophysiology proposed involves chronic low grade trauma to the muscles of mastication or the TMJ, which produces microscopic and microphysiologic changes that become additive over time, resulting in the gradual development of joint symptoms and muscle dysfunction. The kinds of microtrauma that have been proposed to lead to pathophysiologic changes in the muscles or the TMJ joint include chronic jaw posturing, shifts in occlusion, and habitual or parafunctional jaw activities, such as clenching and bruxism. Unfortunately studying microtrauma has proven to be a difficult scientific task, since it is difficult to determine when microtrauma is present and the point at which microtrauma exceeds physiologic tolerances and leads to pathologic processes.

Clinical assessment

The clinical assessment of patients suspected of having TMD may need to involve a variety of clinical and other diagnostic approaches; however, the assessment must begin with the patient's history and proceed through clinical and special diagnostic procedures based upon both history and clinical findings. In general, a standardized questionnaire is best for assessing patient characteristics of TMD, and the patient history is critical in arriving at decisions about etiologic factors and in determining a final diagnosis.

Assessment for TMD using the Research Diagnostic Criteria (RDC) evaluation process includes a group of standardized questions that are a good beginning in the history assessment of patients with facial pain suspected of having TMD. Specific data of importance include known risk factors for the onset of TMD, including direct trauma to the jaw or joint, long dental or medical procedures, and systemic diseases that commonly affect the TMJ (rheumatoid arthritis, psoriatic arthritis, osteoarthritis). Other questions important in the history include those that elicit information about traumatic events, motor vehicle accidents and sources of direct or indirect trauma to the joint or muscles of mastication. Since behavioral and stressful events have been identified as important risk factors in TMD, every patient's workup should include a set of questions regarding behaviors along with an interview that explores those issues further (see Chapter 29). The RDC assessment system includes a number of questions that provide data about possible behavioral factors and also uses a system to score the type of chronic pain and level of psychological dysfunction (see Chapter 29).

Table 30–3 lists important questions that should be asked during the assessment of patients with facial pain and suspected TMD other than those related to the behavioral profile of the patient.

Classification of temporomandibular disorders

A number of classification systems have evolved for TMD, but most of them are based on vague clinical criteria or assumed, but not proven, etiologic factors. The most extensive work done in development of a classification system for TMD supported by scientific findings, has been the work done to establish the Research Diagnostic Criteria for Temporomandibular Disorders (RDC for TMD). Development of the RDC for TMD was the product of the collaboration of scientists at a number of universities. The classification system includes a specific examination process that has been shown to be reliable and designed to collect data important in establishing TMD subtype diagnoses. It also contains a TMD classification system that uses rigid diagnostic criteria based upon the patient's history and objective findings from the structured and standardized clinical examination. The RDC for TMD is particularly useful because it ensures that calibrated examiners using the same examination technique will arrive at the same diagnosis when examining the same patient. Not all types of TMD have been included in the RDC classification system, but the most common types of TMD are included, and in the future, it is assumed that the classification system will be expanded to include disorders that are less common. Table 30–4 lists the components of the RDC examination and Table 30–5 lists the RDC diagnoses and diagnostic criteria for each of the diagnoses contained within the RDC classification. The system is useful clinically and for TMD research, because it provides for multiple simultaneous diagnoses of one or more types of TMD within the same patient. Since it is common for a patient to have both a muscle and a joint disorder, and both must be addressed during treatment, establishing a formal process for determining all diagnoses that are present allows the clinician to determine exactly which of the diagnoses to address in each component of treatment. Specifically the RDC for TMD provides for a set of muscle diagnoses (Group I), disc diagnoses (Group II), and joint diagnoses (Group III), and each with a specific set of diagnostic criteria.

Table 30–3   Questions Useful for Diagnosis of Temporomandibular Disorders

1. Have you had pain in the face, jaw, temple, around the ear, or in the ear in the past month?
2. How long have you had the facial pain?
3. Is your facial pain persistent, recurrent?
4. Have you ever seen a health care provider for your facial pain?
5. How would you rate your facial pain on a 0 to 10 scale?
6. Have you ever had your jaw lock or catch so that it would not open completely?
7. Was the limitation in jaw opening severe enough to interfere with your ability to eat?
8. Does your jaw click or pop?
9. Does your jaw make a grating noise?
10. Have you been told, or do you know that you grind your teeth or clench while asleep?
11. During the day do you grind your teeth or clench?
12. Does your jaw feel stiff in the morning?
13. Do you have ringing or tinnitus in the ears?
14. Is your bite uncomfortable?
15. Do you have systemic arthritis, rheumatoid arthritis, or other disorders?
16. Does anyone in your family have systemic arthritis?
17. Are any of your other joints swollen or painful?
18. Have you recently injured your face or jaw?
19. Did you have pain before the injury?
20. Have you recently (in the past several months) developed headaches or migraine?
21. Does your jaw problem limit any of these activities: chewing, exercising, eating hard foods, eating soft foods or drinking, smiling, oral hygiene, yawning, talking, sexual activity, normal facial appearance?

Changes in occlusion

Changes in occlusion are an important signal that structural changes are occurring within the joint. In several types of inflammatory and degenerative arthritis, joint remodeling or destruction results in either unilateral or bilateral open bite (Figure 30–1). Such changes can be slowly progressive or rapid in development with less progression. In elderly patients with degenerative osteoarthritis or arthrosis, open bite can develop with little or no pain. Patients with immune-based arthritic change normally experience significant pain during the inflammatory and remodeling process. It is difficult to determine when joint remodeling will end, and serial lateral cephalometric films are usually required over a 2- to 4-year period to monitor joint changes. Dental or other reconstructive treatments should not be initiated until remodeling has stopped. In some cases, a large open bite may close considerably and stabilize once the remodeling process is complete. A cautionary note is appropriate here: sudden changes in occlusion in adults with a history of malignant disease (breast cancer, prostate cancer, etc.) should alert the clinician to rule out metastatic disease before focusing on degenerative disease.

Dentists often assess occlusal status in patients with TMD and upon finding occlusal prematurities, shifts or slides in occlusion, reach the conclusion that the shift is responsible for the development of the pain syndrome.

Table 30–4 Research Diagnostic Criteria Examination Components, Including Pain Location Questions

Do you have pain in the right side of your face, the left side, or both sides?
Could you point to the areas where you feel pain? (right muscles, left muscles, both, right joint, left joint)
Jaw opening pattern: straight, right uncorrected deviation, right corrected deviation, left uncorrected deviation, left corrected deviation, other
Vertical range of opening unassisted without pain _____ mm
Vertical range of maximum unassisted opening _____ mm
Vertical range of maximum assisted opening _____ mm
Overbite _____ mm,
Was there pain in the muscles with maximum opening, and if so where was the pain? (right side, left side, both sides)
Was there pain in the joint with maximum opening? If so, was it the right or left or both?
Opening sounds: right and left, none, click, coarse crepitus, fine crepitus
If there was a sound, at what point in opening did it occur? right _____ mm, left _____ mm
If there was a sound on closing, at what point did it occur? right _____ mm, left _____ mm
If there was a reciprocal click during movement, is it eliminated during protrusive opening and closing? (right side, left side)
Measure right lateral excursion. _____ mm
Was there pain during the movement? If so, was it on the right or left side or both, and was it in the right or left joint or both?
Measure left lateral excursion. _____ mm
Was there pain during the movement? If so, was it on the right or left side or both, and was it in the right or left joint or both?
Measure protrusive movement. _____ mm
Was there pain during the movement? If so, was it on the right or left side or both, and was it in the right or left joint or both?
Measure midline discrepancy in alignment of the midline alignment of the upper and lower central incisor embrasures. _____ mm (right or left)
Were there joint sounds in the right joint on right excursion? (none, click, coarse crepitus, fine crepitus)
Were there joint sounds in the right joint on left excursion? (none, click, coarse crepitus, fine crepitus)
Were there joint sounds in the right joint on protrusive excursion? (none, click, coarse crepitus, fine crepitus)
Were there joint sounds in the left joint on right excursion? (none, click, coarse crepitus, fine crepitus)
Were there joint sounds in the left joint on left excursion? (none, click, coarse crepitus, fine crepitus)
Were there joint sounds in the left joint on protrusive excursion? (none, click, coarse crepitus, fine crepitus)

Muscle palpations for pain are done with 2 pounds of pressure on the extraoral muscles and 1 pound on intraoral muscles; palpations of the TMJs are done with 1 pound of pressure. Scored as 0 = no pain, 1 = mild, 2 = moderate, 3 = severe

Posterior temporalis:	right:	left:	Posterior stylohyoid region:	right:	left:
Middle temporalis:	right	left:	Anterior digastric region:	right:	left:
Anterior temporalis:	right:	left::	Lateral pole of joint:	right:	left:
Superior masseter:	right:	left:	Intermeatal joint palpation:	right:	left:
Middle masseter:	right:	left:	Lateral pterygoid:	right:	left:
Inferior masseter:	right:	left:	Tendon of temporalis:	right:	left:

Adapted from Dworkin SF, LeResche L. Research diagnostic criteria for temporomandibular disorders: review, criteria, examinations and specifications, critique. J Craniomandib Disord 1992;6:301–55.

They sometimes treat the problem by adjusting the occlusion hoping to restore balance in tooth contact. The concept of occlusal adjustment may be appropriate for long-standing major prematurities in occlusion that have become a focus of parafunctional activity by the patient, and may be of value in protecting teeth that are traumatized because they are carrying most of the occlusal load. However, recent research findings have demonstrated that changes in muscle function created by injection hypertonic saline bring about eccentric contraction and tension in jaw muscles that create transient alterations in the occlusal relation of the teeth and jaws. These findings strengthen the concept that occlusion is not normally the cause of TMD pain and dysfunction, and occlusal changes seen in TMD may be the result of muscle fatigue or dysfunction rather than the cause. Occlusal adjustment during acute TMD is not normally appropriate and can lead to persistent symptoms if the patient is occlusally focused and cannot adjust to the new bite. Changes in the occlusion of patients that have been previously treated with orthodontic or aggressive splint therapy can result in iatrogenic alterations in occlusion that are mistaken as progressive degenerative joint disease (Figure 30–2). Assessment of the patient with TMD who has previously been treated by another care provider can lead to confusion.

Diagnostic imaging

The RDC examination provides careful guidelines for the history component of the assessment process, and for the physical examination of the patient, but based upon symptoms and findings from the full RDC assessment, other diagnostic procedures may be required. For example, patients who report significant pain directly within the joint or pain in the joint during jaw function, may need joint imaging to determine whether degenerative or arthritic changes have occurred. The most com-

Table 30–5 Research Diagnostic Criteria*

RDC -TMD Diagnosis	Essential Diagnostic Criteria
Muscle diagnoses	
Myofascial Pain	1. Report of pain in muscles positive
	2. Palpation response in three or more muscles
	3. One of muscles tender on side of complaint
Myofascial pain with limited opening	1. Myofascial pain (as defined above)
	2. Pain-free unassisted opening of <40 mm
	3. Maximum assisted opening of 5 mm or more beyond unassisted opening
Disc displacements	
With reduction	1. Reciprocal click in TMJ on opening and closing that is at least 5 mm greater on opening than closing
	2. Click is eliminated during protruded opening, or click in either opening or closing and in excursive movement
Without reduction with limited opening	1. History of significant limitation in opening, plus
	2. Maximum unassisted opening ≤35 mm, plus
	3. Passive stretch increases opening by 4 mm or less, plus
	4. Contralateral excursion <7 mm and/or uncorrected deviation to the ipsilateral side on opening, plus
	5. Either absence of joint sounds or presence of joint sounds not meeting criteria for disc displacement with reduction
Without reduction	1. History of significant limitation in opening, plus
	2. Maximum unassisted opening of >35 mm, plus
	3. Passive stretch increases opening by 5 mm or more, plus
	4. Contralateral excursion ≤7mm, plus
	5. Presence of joint sounds not meeting criteria for disc displacement with reduction
	6. Imaging studies with MRI, arthrograms
Arthralgia, arthritis, arthrosis	
Arthralgia	1. Pain in one or both joints during palpation, plus
	2. One or more self-reports: pain in joint, pain in joint during maximum opening, during lateral excursion
	3. For simple arthralgia alone coarse crepitus must be absent
Arthritis	1. Arthralgia, plus
	2. Either or both of the following
	a. Coarse crepitus in the joint
	b. Imaging (tomograms showing erosions, etc.)
Arthrosis	1. Absence of all signs of arthralgia
	2. Either or both of the following
	a. Coarse crepitus in the joint
	b. Imaging (tomograms showing erosions, etc.)

*One muscle diagnosis is established for the patient, but the joint diagnoses are for each joint and can include one from the disc group and one from the joint group.

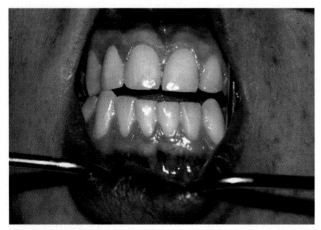

Figure 30–1 Progressive open bite caused by degenerative arthritis and remodeling of the joint.

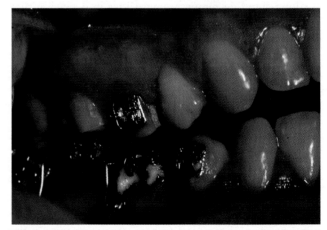

Figure 30–2 Open bite caused by repositioning splint therapy and orthodontic care.

mon type of initial TMD joint image is that provided by panoramic dental radiography (Figures 30–3). For most patients with TMD, panoramic jaw films provide adequate information for determining whether significant joint changes have occurred and whether more sophisticated radiographs are necessary. If the patient is experiencing occlusal changes, an open bite, pain localized to the joint, and joint pain with simple jaw activities and the panoramic film identifies the presence of osseous changes within the joint, more advanced imaging of the joint is required. Tomograms of the joint in open and closed positions are specific enough to detect most joint changes. Figure 30–4 shows a normal TMJ tomogram; Figure 30–5 shows early degenerative changes causing erosion of the cortical bone of the condyle. As greater amounts of degeneration and remodeling occur, the joint undergoes progressive remodeling with flattening of the condyle and condylar eminence (Figure 30–6). In advanced cases of degenerative disease, beaking of the condyle and osteophyte formation occur (Figure 30–7). The combination of a panoramic dental radiograph and tomograms usually provides ample data regarding the

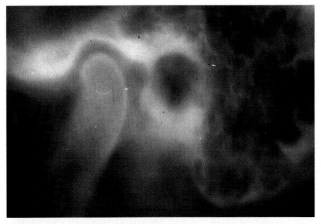

Figure 30–4 Tomogram of TMJ showing a normal condyle and fossa.

osseous status of the joint. When conventional tomographic views of the joint fail to provide enough diagnostic information computed tomography (CT) of the joint can provide a reconstructed image of the joint from almost any angle (Figures 30–8). If a diagnosis of internal derangement is suspected standard joint films are of minimal value and magnetic resonance imaging (MRI) of the joint should be considered (Figures 30–9). The MRI is now considered the gold standard for detection of derangements of the disc, even though MRI cannot detect disc perforations. The MRI provides images of the joint and disc in an open and closed position and usually clearly identifies the presence of a disc that is displaced and not reducing into a normal position during opening (Figure 30–10). If a perforation of the disc or the attachment is suspected, an arthrogram is the diagnostic procedure of choice.

In some cases, questions arise as to whether pain within the joint is caused by inflammation or referred muscle symptoms or is attributable to neuropathic pain. Such questions can usually be resolved by ordering a radioactive bone scan, which can identify areas of

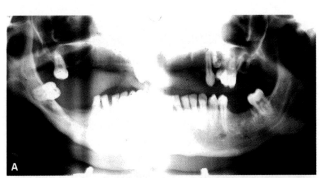

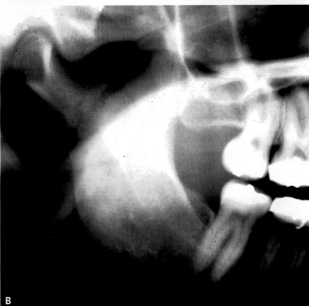

Figure 30–3 Panoramic jaw film showing, *A*, developmental changes in the jaws and TMJ; *B*, a fracture of the neck of the condyle.

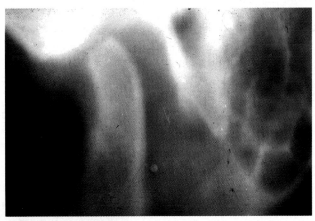

Figure 30–5 Tomogram of TMJ demonstrating early degenerative changes with erosion of the cortical plate. The fossa is intact.

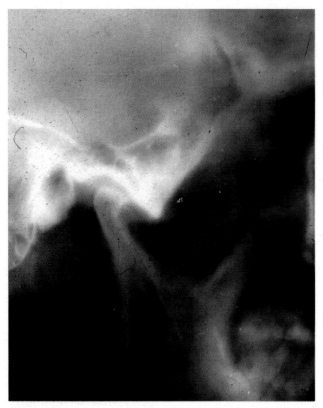

Figure 30–6 Tomogram of TMJ identifying moderately advanced degenerative changes. The condyle is significantly flattened, and the eminence of the fossa is also sclerotic and flattened.

radioactive uptake caused by inflammation (Figure 30–11). If the scan fails to show uptake, the joint is not inflamed or undergoing inflammatory degenerative damage, and the pain is either neuropathic, referred, or even possibly from malingering.

Diagnostic blocks

Another useful, but often overlooked, diagnostic technique to assist in determining whether pain is arising from the joint or is being referred from other structures is the use of diagnostic blocks. Anesthesia of the suspected referral site (muscles and dental structures) stops referred pain. Local anesthetic into the joint can also be a useful

diagnostic process and can help to differential limitations in opening and joint movement attributable to pain versus limitations caused by other structural factors.

Laboratory studies

Autoimmune diseases can affect most joints, and the presence of pain, swelling, and limitation in the TMJ should trigger a search to rule out systemic arthritic disease localized to the TMJ. Findings that should raise suspicion that an autoimmune disease is present include a family history of rheumatoid arthritis, lupus, Sjögren syndrome, or psoriatic arthritis; the presence of other dysfunctional joints in the patient; a past diagnosis of systemic arthritis; and laboratory tests results suggestive of autoimmune disease. Several hematologic tests should be ordered, including: complete blood cell count (CBC) and differential white cell count, erythrocyte sedimentation rate (ESR), antinuclear antibody (ANA), and Sjögren panel. If any of these tests is positive, the patient should be referred to his or her primary care provider or to a rheumatologist.

Special problems

Occasionally, patients present with low-grade pain in the facial region along with complaint of limited opening. Clinical evaluation fails to detect the presence of classic signs of TMD or joint pathology or an internal derangement of the disc. In such circumstances, it is important to determine whether the limitation in opening was gradual in onset or sudden. If sudden, it is likely that the disc has been displaced, but if it has been gradual over many months or years, a coronoid impingement syndrome should be ruled out. In such cases, the wing of the coronoid process continues to grow and sometimes curves medially, impinging on the lateral aspect of the maxilla and malar process, resulting in limited opening. Standard panoramic radiographs can sometimes demonstrate the elongation of the coronoid, but in some cases, special imaging is required. Pain is not a significant finding in most coronoid impingement cases.

Figure 30–7 Open and closed tomographic images of the TMJ showing severe degenerative remodeling of the condyle with cupping of the articulating surface. The fossa and eminence are also flattened, and the entire osseous lining of the fossa appears sclerotic.

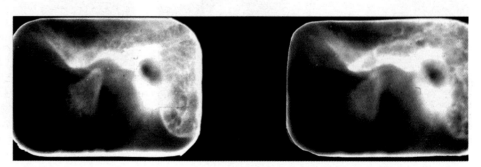

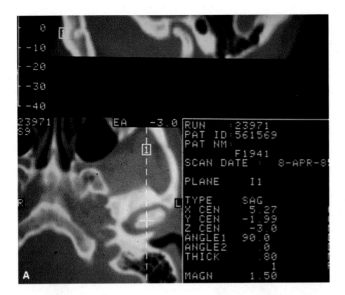

Figure 30–8 *A*, Computed tomography of TMJ with two different directions of image reconstruction. In the lateral view (*top*) the condyle appears thin and hypoplastic; *B*, from a frontal reconstruction plane, the head of the condyles show degenerative changes and fracture lines on the left condylar neck, suggesting that a fracture has occurred. On the right, significant degenerative and remodeling changes are evident.

If a reduction in mouth opening begins shortly after dental treatment that included use of local anesthetic, and opening progressively diminishes over 2 to 6 weeks, the problem may be caused by development of an injection hematoma or secondary infection from the injection site in surrounding muscles. When limited opening is caused by a hematoma, the onset of the decrease in opening usu-ally occurs shortly after the dental visit and pain levels are not high. As the hematoma organizes, scar tissue can fur-ther limit opening. Pain is also not normally high during the organizing phase of repair and healing. On the other hand, if limitation is associated with deep infection from an injection site, pain is more common and usually more intense. Low-grade fever is also common and white cell

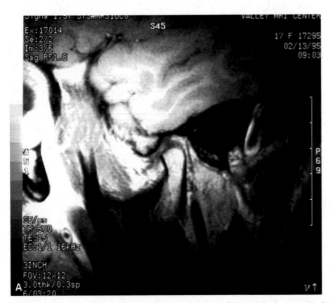

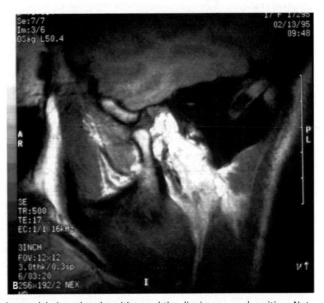

Figure 30–9 *A*, Magnetic resonance imaging of the TMJ demonstrating the condyle in a closed position and the disc in a normal position. Note that the cortex of the condyle is a black line, and the marrow space appears white. *B*, Magnetic resonance imaging of TMJ in an open mouth posi-tion showing the disc in a normal position.

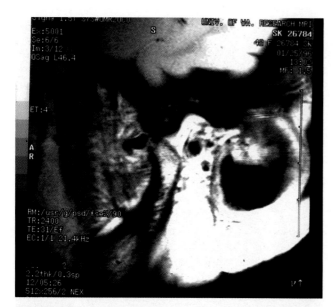

Figure 30–10 Magnetic resonance imaging of TMJ in an open mouth position demonstrating that the disc is trapped in an anterior and displaced position (anterior displacement of the disc without reduction). Note that the joint space has filled with vascular tissue as the condyle moved forward, causing the joint space to image as a light area.

count may be elevated. In severe cases, loss of opening can become extreme and mimic a complete dislocation of the disc. Diagnosis usually requires either a CT scan with contrast (Figure 30–12), or other radioactive scans that label areas of infection (white cell scan). Extended use of antibiotics are required when deep infection is present in addition to aggressive stretching to breakdown adhesions and scar tissue.

Management

The management of TMD depends on the type of disorder. General guidelines for management are possible, based on the category of the condition. The majority of patients with TMD have more than one TMD diagnosis, and it is important for the clinician to initiate treatments directed toward each one and toward known etiologic factors. For example, it is common for patients with TMD to present with a long-standing internal derangement (clicking joint) that is complicated by the presence of myofascial pain. The treating clinician must decide whether treatment should be initiated for one or both conditions. On the other hand, if an internal derangement (clicking disc) with myofascial pain is accompanied by joint pain and inflammation and a diagnosis of arthralgia, it is appropriate to initiate treatment directed toward the joint, the disc, and the muscle dysfunction.

A common protocol in patients suffering all three conditions (myofascial pain, arthralgia, disc displacement) includes prescription of a nonsteroidal anti-

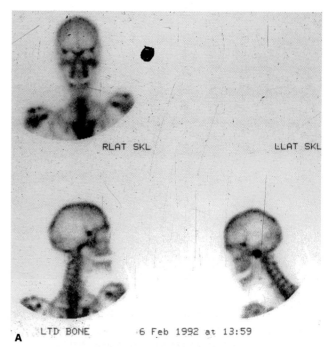

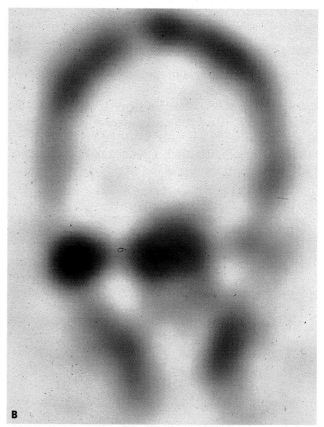

Figure 30–11 *A*, Radioactive bone scan of the head and neck in a patient reporting bilateral TMJ pain, taken to detect inflammation. Note that the region of the TMJ has taken up the dye, which provokes a strong black signal. Marrow spaces in the shoulder also image clearly (seen as dense black areas). *B*, Radioactive bone scan of the head in a patient with TMD who reported unilateral joint pain. The affected side demonstrated significant uptake of the imaging dye. The image suggests high levels of metabolic activity in the joint.

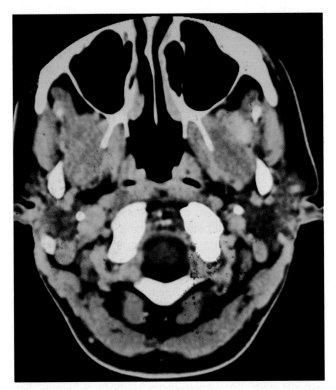

Figure 30–12 Cross-section CT with contrast media showing osseous and soft tissues. Note the presence of a light area on the right side of the image in the areas just anterior to the ramus of the mandible. There is an organizing hematoma with secondary infection.

inflammatory agent, such as diclofenac or ibuprofen, to reduce inflammation within the joint while initiating therapy to reduce muscle pain and dysfunction. Treatment of the myofascial component of the pain while assisted by the analgesic properties of diclofenac should include other therapies aimed at physical factors that cause the muscles to be tense and painful as well as functional and behavioral factors that contribute to continuation of muscle symptoms. Treatment directed at muscle pain and dysfunction usually includes a reduction in functional activities that aggravate the muscles, including chewing tough or hard foods, and reduction in some oral activities, such as singing. Passive opening exercises, use of ice or heat packs, and gentle massage can provide palliative relief of pain. Directing the patient's attention toward identifying patterns of jaw tensing and parafunction helps to find actions that contribute to prolonged symptoms. Patients with myofascial pain often develop patterns of persistent tooth contact, whether or not they engage in clinching or bruxism. Teaching the patient to keep their teeth apart and jaws relaxed often results in a significant reduction of pain within a short time. In severe cases, the use of a muscle relaxant, such as methocarbamol, cyclobenzaprine, or diazepam, has been reported to assist in symptom reduction whether they actually reduce muscle activity or simply reduce

anxiety. The combination of self-treatments practiced by the patient at home and the use of a muscle relaxant often results in a quick reduction of symptoms. If the patient has high pain or chronic pain, symptoms may persist even if local therapy is successful (see Chapter 29). In such patients a more global behavioral approach is likely to result in symptom reduction. When symptoms persist beyond the time that would normally be expected or pain severity continues to be high, alternative approaches merit consideration. Chronic persistent musculoskeletal pain resistant to other modes of therapy has shown considerable susceptibility to antidepressants, pain attributable to TMD follows that same pattern of responsiveness. A report of sleep dysfunction further supports the potential value of antidepressants for symptom control. Several different antidepressants appear to be useful, including amitriptyline, nortriptyline, desipramine, and others. They should be introduced at a low therapeutic level and gradually increased in strength over 4 to 8 weeks.

Splint therapy has been the mainstay in most methods of TMD treatment during the past 40 years. Splints have been used to treat myofascial pain, disc displacements with reduction, and disc displacements without reduction. Over all, the literature has suggested that splint therapy is highly effective and reduces parafunctional jaw activities, which in turn reduces muscle and joint pain. The most commonly used appliance has been the flat acrylic splint, which is used most often to treat myofascial pain and nocturnal bruxism (Figure 30–13). Splints have also been designed to reposition the mandible into a forward and open posture in attempts to capture and hold the displaced disc in a more favorable position.

Repositioning appliances are much less commonly used today because they can cause occlusal changes (Figure 30–14). It was noted that symptom relapse occurred when repositioning splints were discontinued. Interestingly however, several recent and some prior studies have found that a significant component of splint success appears to arise out of either a placebo response or a nonspecific response that is independent of the splint design, type of material, cost of the appliance, or the amount of time that the splint is used during a week. Studies have found that low-cost soft vinyl splints made chairside at a cost of only a few dollars have favorable outcomes equivalent to hard splints in pain reduction (Figure 30–15). Studies have also found that splints that do not affect the occlusion and splints that are worn for only a short time each week have the same effect on pain reduction as appliances worn many hours per week. These findings are important, since splint therapy can be costly and limit access to care. Studies comparing splint and nonsplint treatment protocols have also shown equivalent pain reduction without use of an appliance. Therefore, it is wise to use splints carefully and not universally in patients with TMD and to focus on factors

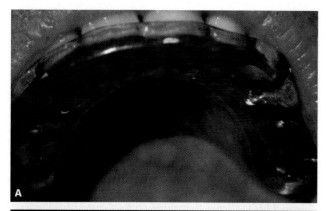

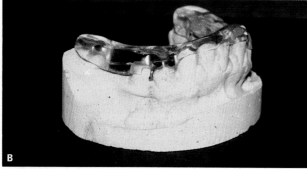

Figure 30–13 *A,* Maxillary flat acrylic splint covering the occlusion and hard palate. The appliance is used to treat myofascial pain and other forms of TMD. *B,* Mandibular flat acrylic splint used to treat myofascial pain and clenching.

associated with the development of symptoms. The patient should be encouraged to use other self-treatment strategies, such as those outlined in this chapter. Although intraoral splints are generally thought of as conservative and noninvasive, it is important to remember that some patients have developed malocclusions as a result of splint therapy. Acrylic splints that reposition the mandible in an anterior position or posture it laterally are more likely to produce a change in the occlusion that may not resolve when the appliance is withdrawn.

Treatment of an internal derangement depends upon whether the disc reduces during closing. The most common clinical finding in patients with a displacement with reduction is the presence of reciprocal clicking in the TMJ during opening and closing activities. Some patients are bothered by the sound of the clicking joint and measure treatment success more on whether the sounds persist than if pain levels decrease. This is particularly true in patients that have loud clicking and in those with low levels of initial TMD pain. Part of treatment is to advise the patient that treatment and eradication of the clicking sound may be difficult and have outcome risks that are not acceptable. If the disc displacement is without reduction and myofascial pain accompanies the disc displacement, pain often resolves as the muscle dysfunction decreases, but in some patients, as myofascial pain resolves pain becomes more localized to the joint, indicating that the disc displacement is an important contributor to overall pain scores. In such patients, anti-inflammatory agents can help reduce pain and increase function. If pain and joint limitation persist, a small percentage of patients select arthroscopic joint surgery to stabilize the joint and reduce pain. Recent studies of patients with disc displacements without reduction that were not treated surgically found that a majority improved over 2 years with resolution of pain and limited opening. Failure of a patient to respond to conservative physical, pharmacologic, and behavioral therapies for TMD does not specifically indicate that more aggressive and invasive treatments are appropriate. Consideration of more aggressive forms of therapy to correct physical defects, including joint surgery, orthodontic or orthognathic surgery, or restorative reconstruction, should be soundly based on corrective procedures that are likely to reduce or eliminate pain. Untested therapies should be avoided because of the risk of side effects; unexpected adverse effects can be difficult to correct. For example, in the case shown in Figure 30–14, the patient was treated with high crowns to prevent TMJ clicking that had not

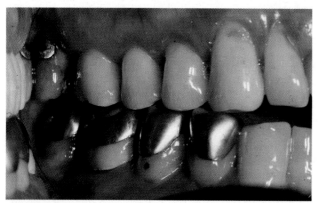

Figure 30–14 Occlusal change caused by use of a repositioning splint followed by cementation of large crowns on the posterior teeth.

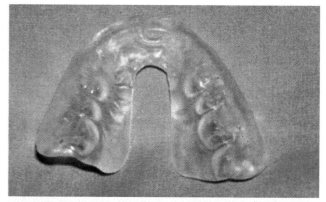

Figure 30–15 Soft vinyl splint fabricated at chairside using a thermoplastic material that conforms to the teeth when it is heated in water.

been painful. The result of the treatment was development of alteration in the occlusion, which did not correct with removal of the crowns, and the onset of chronic pain and degenerative changes around the TMJ.

Temporomandibular disorders may cause tenderness and referred pain from trigger points in cervical muscles or the muscles of mastication. These trigger points usually have not been recognized by the patient. When the trigger point is palpated or otherwise stimulated, pain develops at a distant site in the head and neck as well as around the location of the trigger point. Sites of referral include almost any structure, including the TMJ, other muscles, teeth, periorbital structures, and the sinuses. Usually the site of referral is more cephalic in location than the trigger point.

Tables 30–6 to 30–10 identify specific treatment protocols recommended for patients with different types of TMD. A treatment checklist form (Figure 30–16), can be used to establish treatment protocols

Table 30–6   Treatment of Myofascial Pain

Identify onset factors: trauma, stress, parafunction, depression.
Rule out serious local pathology.
Initiate a structured self-management program:
  Encourage jaw relaxation techniques (eg, teeth and lips apart and rested).
  Encourage passive jaw stretching exercises to loosen muscles and focus on relaxation.
  Apply thermal (ice or heat) packs to muscles twice a day.
  Identify environmental factors that increase or decrease symptoms.
  Encourage stress- and tension-releasing activities, abdominal breathing, and progressive relaxation.
  Prescribe a muscle relaxant (eg, methocarbamol, cyclobenzaprine).
  Prescribe an analgesic such as over the counter (OTC) or opioid, if pain is high.
  Provide a soft vinyl splint if patient reports constant clenching.
  If symptoms persist and resist treatment, assess psychological status and referral.
  For chronic pain, initiate treatment with an antidepressant (amitriptyline 10 mg to start, max. 75 mg).

Table 30–7   Treatment of Arthralgia

Rule out systemic arthritis, metastatic disease, traumatic injury, fracture.
Initiate structured self-management program:
  Reduce jaw function, eat soft foods, and reduce wide opening for 1 week.
  Prescribe NSAID (eg, ibuprofen, Naprosyn, etc.). If symptoms are severe, prescribe prednisone.
  Apply thermal packs (cold or heat).
  After 1 week, initiate passive opening exercises but do not force jaw opening.
  If condition does not respond within 2 weeks, consider re-imaging of joint.

NSAID = nonsteroidal anti-inflammatory drug.

Table 30–8   Treatment of Disc Displacement with Reduction

Explain the nature of the problem and treatment risks to patient.
Reduce or address presence of myofascial pain, if present.
Initiate a structured self-management program:
  Encourage jaw relaxation program similar to that for myofascial pain protocol, and encourage constant jaw relaxation, discontinuing use of chewing gum, etc.
  Encourage passive jaw opening exercises without completely closing the mouth to trigger click.
  If joint becomes tender or painful, reduce exercises and start use of NSAID.
  Observe and record parafunctional and eccentric jaw habits that may strain joint.
  Consider use of nocturnal splint if jaw is locked or hard to move in morning.

NSAID = nonsteroidal anti-inflammatory drug.

Table 30–9   Treatment of Disc Displacement without Reduction

Explain the nature of the problem and risks of aggressive therapy to the patient.
Initiate a structured self-management program:
  Encourage jaw relaxation program similar to that used for myofascial pain.
  Encourage careful and passive opening exercises, but no strained or force jaw opening.
  Prescribe NSAID (eg, ibuprofen, Naprosyn, prednisone, etc.).
  If pain is present, prescribe analgesics including opioid analgesics if needed.
  If secondary muscle tenderness and muscle recruitment has occurred, prescribe muscle relaxant: methocarbamol, cyclobenzaprine, diazepam.
  Attempt disc and joint manipulation if displacement has been recent: careful and gentle movement of the joint to see if the disc will reduce.
  Consider further disc manipulation during sedation if some clicking is episodically present.
  Consider referral to an oral surgeon for arthroscopic surgery if pain is persistent and disc does not reduce within 2 months.

NSAID = nonsteroidal anti-inflammatory drug.

Table 30–10   Treatment of Arthritis and Joint Inflammation

Rule out systemic arthritis with appropriate tests.
Obtain baseline joint films and record jaw relation.
Initiate a structured self-management program:
  Prescribe NSAID (eg, ibuprofen, Naprosyn, etc.).
  Encourage passive opening exercises to maintain joint mobility.
  Apply thermal packs daily (cold or heat).
  If joint pain causes clenching and jaw posturing, construct splint to reduce strain.
  Chew bilaterally, and do not avoid chewing on the affected side if unilateral.
  Watch for muscle recruitment, and if present, treat to myofascial pain diagnosis.
  If joint does not respond to NSAIDs, use short-term prednisone therapy (10–14 d).

NSAID = nonsteroidal anti-inflammatory drug.

TREATMENT PROTOCOL CHECKLIST
Patient:_____ Date:_____
N = New Treatment   C = Continue Treatment
M = Modify Treatment

Muscle and Jaw Relaxation: Box # 1

☐ Keep jaws relaxed, teeth separated, lips apart, & check frequently to assure the muscles are relaxed.

☐ Don't stretch muscles by opening or moving jaw side to side. Don't posture jaw forward or to the side.

☐ Relax jaw muscles by placing tip of tongue behind lower front teeth, let tongue go completely relaxed.

☐ Open mouth as wide as possible <u>without</u> pain, and hold for 5 to 10 seconds, close halfway and rest for 5 seconds; repeat 15 times, 3 to 4 times a day.

☐ Keep shoulders down (check often).

☐ Breathe deeply from abdomen, hold 3 seconds, exhale, let shoulder and jaw sag.

☐ Soft diet, avoid crunchy foods, avoid chewy foods, take small bites, and avoid wide opening.

☐ Reduce parafunctional jaw habits, don't bite finger nails or cheeks, don't hold pencils or other items in mouth.

☐ Exercise 30 minutes, 5 times/wk, walking or aerobics.

☐ Avoid caffeine to enhance relaxation.

Pain Control: Box # 2

☐ Apply heat to the area of pain with heating pad (moist heat preferred) 15 to 30 minutes.

☐ Apply cold pack to areas of pain twice a day for 10 to 15 minutes.

☐ Apply cold or heat pack to back of neck and skull for 10 to 15 minutes.

☐ Massage the areas of pain daily by hand or machine.

General and Behavioral Management: Box # 3

☐ Relaxation exercises:_____

☐ Identify stressors and make a plan to manage them.

☐ Obtain and read a book on stress management.

☐ Practice expressive writing.

☐ Improve sleep pattern and amount.

☐ Develop a pain management personal plan.

Signature:

Medications and Dosages: Box # 4

☐ NSAIDS:_____

☐ Narcotic #1:_____

☐ Narcotic #2:_____

☐ Mus. Relaxant:_____

☐ Anxiolytic:_____

☐ Antidepress: _____

☐ Sedative:_____

☐ Other #1:_____

☐ Other #2:_____

☐ Change other medication:_____

Physical Medicine & Physiotherapy: Box # 5

☐ Stretch muscles in the base of the neck by tipping head down slowly until your chin touches the chest (repeat).

☐ With chin to chest, tip head side to side & hold for 15 sec.

☐ Active jaw opening exercises:_____
_____

☐ Trigger point injection:_____

☐ Joint inject:_____

☐ Spray and stretch:_____

☐ Nerve block:_____

☐ Joint manipulation:_____

☐ Spot occlusal adjustment:_____

☐ #1: Other:_____

Splints and Appliances: Box # 6

☐ Splint impression   ☐ Provided soft splint blank

☐ Seat hard splint_____

☐ Seat soft splint_____

☐ Existing splint adjustment_____

☐ Other:_____

Referrals and Consultations: Box # 7

☐ Oral surgery:_____

☐ Psych consult:_____

☐ Medical consult for:_____

☐ Other dental consult :_____

☐ Other:_____

Figure 30–16 Treatment checklist form used to give instructions to patients and record treatment selection.

and to provide the patient with a detailed reminder of their treatment plan along with information on how to accomplish the self-treatment aspects of their care.

Treatment of severe bruxism and jaw parafunction

Some patients report that they engage in severe bruxism and parafunction that is impossible to discontinue. They report such activities during sleep and sometimes more so even during waking activities. The first concern is to address whether the jaw activity is part of or a response to anxiety, and to determine whether stressful environmental factors increase the rate of bruxism. If that is the case, a strong behavioral therapy program guided by a qualified psychologist may be beneficial. If stress or anxiety does not seem to be a factor, it may be wise to rule out an orofacial movement disorder that is either arising from endogenous changes or triggered by medications. A number of psychoactive medications can trigger facial and jaw movement disorders. Use of some illicit drugs may provoke movement disorders and bruxism. If the pattern is progressive, consultation with a neurologist is advisable as is a careful evaluation of all medications and signs of illicit drug use. If no etiology can be identified, treatment may include use of centrally acting medications and construction of upper and lower splints to protect teeth from wear.

Management of behavioral factors in temporomandibular disorders

Patients report significant benefits from simple therapies for TMD, such as home-based, self-provided physical therapies, including ice packs, passive opening exercises, and jaw relaxation. Most conservative treatments for TMD work effectively, with minimal risk of adverse side effects or negative outcomes. Only about 10% of patients who receive TMD therapy report long-term chronic persistent pain. Among the other 90%, approximately half report that their pain undergoes remission with no recurrence and the remainder report episodic recurrences over 3 to 5 years. If patients note continuing symptoms after a reasonable duration of conservative therapy, it is advisable to again address possible behavioral factors that may be causing pain and jaw dysfunction to persist (see Chapter 29). Indications that personal, psychological, or work-related factors are playing a role in causing persistence should suggest that further consultation with a psychologist could be of value. Patients often resist such suggestions at the outset of treatment but often become more receptive as they gain confidence in their dentist. In general, therapies that address functional problems and behavioral factors demonstrate success rates as high as or higher than therapies directed toward mechanical interventions alone.

Suggested reading

Dao TT, Lavigne GH, Charbonneau A, et al. The efficacy of oral splints in the treatment of myofascial pain of the jaw muscles: a controlled clinical trial. Pain 1994;56:85–94.

Dao TT, Reynolds WJ, Tenenbaum HC. Comorbidity between myofascial pain of the masticatory muscles and fibromyalgia. J Orofac Pain 1997;11:232–41.

Drangsholt M, LeResche L. Temporomandibular disorder pain. In: Crombie IK, Croft PR, Linton SJ, et al, eds. Epidemiology of pain: a report of the Task Force on Epidemiology of the International Association for Study of Pain. Seattle: IASP Press, 1999:203–34.

Dworkin SF. Behavioral characteristics of chronic temporomandibular disorders: diagnosis and assessment. In: Sessle BJ, Bryant PS, Dionne R, eds. Temporomandibular disorders and related pain conditions. Seattle: IASP Press, 1995:175–92.

Dworkin SF, Huggins KH, LeResche L, et al. Epidemiology of signs and symptoms in temporomandibular disorders: clinical signs in cases and controls. JAMA 1990;120: 273–81.

Dworkin SF, LeResche L. Research diagnostic criteria for temporomandibular disorders: review, criteria, examinations and specifications, critique. J Craniomandib Disord 1992; 6:300–55

Fricton JR, Olsen T. Predictors of outcomes for treatment of temporomandibular disorders. J Orofac Pain 1996;10: 54–65.

Korszun A, Papadopoulos E, Demitrack M, et al. The relationship between temporomandibular disorders and stress-associated syndromes. Oral Surg Oral Med Oral Pathol Oral Radiol Endod 1998;86:416–20.

Lundh H, Westesson PL, Eriksson L, Brooks SL. Temporomandibular joint disc displacement without reduction. Treatment with flat occlusal splint versus no treatment. Oral Surg Oral Med Oral Pathol 1992;73:655–8.

National Institutes of Health Technology Assessment Conference on Management of Temporomandibular Disorders. Bethesda, Maryland, April 29–May 1, 1996. Proceedings. Oral Surg Oral Med Oral Pathol Oral Radiol Endod 1997;83:149–83.

Ohrbach R, Dworkin SF. Five-year outcomes in TMD: relationship of changes in pain to changes in physical and psychological variables. Pain 1998;74:315–26.

Okeson JP, eds. Orofacial pain: guidelines for assessment, diagnosis and management. Chicago: Quintessence, 1996.

Schiffman EL. The role of randomized clinical trial in evaluation management strategies for temporomandibular disorders. In: Fricton JR, Dubner RB, eds. Orofacial pain and temporomandibular disorders. New York: Raven Press, 1995:415–63.

Stohler CS. Muscle-related temporomandibular disorders. J Orofac Pain 1999;13:273–84.

Tsuyama M, Kondoh T, Seto K, Fukuda J. Complications of temporomandibular joint arthroscopy: a retrospective analysis of 301 lysis and lavage procedures performed using the triangulation technique. J Oral Maxillofac Surg 2000;58:500–5.

Zarb GA, Carlsson GE. Temporomandibular disorders: osteoarthritis. J Orofac Pain 1999;13:295–306.

Headache is one of the most common acute and chronic pain complaints reported in adolescents and adults. Estimates of the prevalence of headache differ somewhat, but most surveys report that over 80% of adults report periodic episodes of headache. The life-time risk for migraine has been reported to be over 35%. For unexplained reasons headaches are reported much less frequently in children, but it is not known whether the lower number represents an actual lower rate of headaches in children or an error in reporting since children often underreport other pains. Studies have shown that headache in general, and migraine in particular, become more prevalent in the adolescent years, after puberty, and increase in frequency into adulthood. Dentists are often ask to determine if orofacial pain or headache is caused by local pathology, such as infection or a temporomandibular disorder (TMD). The clinical manifestations of headache syndromes overlap with dental pathology and frequently lead to unnecessary dental treatment. This chapter addresses the clinical manifestations of headaches, methods for diagnosis, and treatment recommendations appropriate to primary health care providers in medicine and dentistry. The challenge for the dental provider is to be able to distinguish symptoms and signs of headache disorders from primary dental disease and TMD, and to assist other health care providers in determining effective treatment strategies.

Many attempts have been made to establish a clear classification system for headache, and several are in active use, including the classification systems reported in the International Classification of Disease, the International Headache Society (IHS) (Table 31–1), and the International Association for the Study of Pain.

All of these classification systems are similar, and the focus recently has been to develop highly specific classifications based on reliable signs and symptoms and stable inclusion and exclusion criteria. There are no specific diagnostic tests readily available that allow a guaranteed confirmation of a headache diagnosis. The final diagnosis of headache type is usually derived from a working diagnosis that is dependent upon the persistence and reliability of the patient's report of symptoms and failure to detect other etiologic factors. Probably the most effective method of diagnosis is to combine a careful understanding of signs and symptoms common to the various headache groups and an objective analysis of responses to reversible treatments known to be specific for particular headache conditions (eg, sumatriptan success in migraine, etc.).

Diagnostic and patient management considerations

The discussion of headache in this chapter is limited to the most common and important types of headaches, and those most commonly presenting in clinical practice that can easily be confused with local orofacial pathology and odontogenic disorders. The first and most important consideration when assessing patients with complaints of facial pain and headache is to rule out potentially progressive and damaging forms of disease that present with headache or facial pain as part of their symptom complex. Severe infections, whether intracranial or systemic, commonly produce headache and, depending upon the location of inflammatory changes, can also cause facial pain. Intracranial tumors are also known to trigger gradually progressive headaches that

Table 13–1 Classification of Headache (International Headache Society Classification)

1. Migraine headache
2. Tension type headache
3. Cluster and chronic paroxysmal hemicrania
4. Miscellaneous headache associated with structural lesions
5. Headache associated with head trauma
6. Headache associated with vascular disorders
7. Headache associated with nonvascular intracranial disorders
8. Headache associated with substances or their withdrawal
9. Headache associated with noncephalic infections
10. Headache and facial pain associated with disorders of the cranium, face, mouth, etc.
11. Cranial neuralgias, nerve trunk pain, and deafferentation pain
12. Headache not classifiable

become more frequent and severe as disease progresses. Intracranial and extracranial vascular lesions, such as aneurysms, and vascular occlusions can cause pain identical to headache or provoke pain referral into the face or neck. Extracranial tumors of the head, orofacial region, and neck can also cause pain that is localized or diffuse and sometimes similar to headache. A common systemic condition known to produce headache is uncontrolled hypertension which has been shown to produce hypertensive headaches in 15% of patients.

Migraine

Migraine is considered to be one of the most painful of the headache groups. Patients usually rate episodes of migraine as moderately severe to very severe, and some rate the pain as the most severe that they have ever encountered. The life-time prevalence of migraine is approximately 35% in adults, and intractable migraine, which is a less common disorder, can be a completely disabling condition. Migraines occur in young children and become more prevalent after puberty. Genetic and familial risk is considerable, with more than 50% of those suffering migraine reporting that family members are also affected. Hormonal changes during and after puberty are thought to be an important contributor in migraine, and some women suffer severe premenstrual migraines as hormone levels change during their monthly cycle. Although migraines affect both genders, generally the ratio is 3:2, favoring females.

Etiology and pathophysiology

The exact mechanisms responsible for migraine are just now becoming more clearly understood. The process involves vascular changes triggered via trigeminovascular innervation, causing vasoconstriction and dilatation of cerebral vessels innervated by branches of the trigeminal nerve. Many factors appear to contribute to the process, including physiologic and psychophysiologic stimulation of the central nervous system (CNS). It is thought that the trigeminal innervation of cerebral vessels provides a sensory role, protecting the brain from agents that cross through the circulation during pathologic insult and from agents produced within the brain. The trigeminal innervation of cerebral vessels also has a motor component that is activated upon threat of change in normal blood flow to the brain. Response to stimuli can trigger release of vasodilator peptides or vessel hemodynamic changes through central interaction with parasympathetic innervation of the seventh cranial nerve. It is thought that stimulation of trigeminovascular fibers by electrical, chemical, and mechanical stimulation triggers plasma extravasation and inflammation of neurogenic origin in regions of the dura and other extracranial tissues. The process also fires painful signals centrally. The components of neurogenic inflammation include release of substance P, calcitonin gene-related peptide (CGRP), and neurokinin A (NKA). These agents cause vasodilation and extravasation of protein from vessels. The entire process includes trigeminal sensory stimulation, resulting in pain; vasodilation; mast cell degranulation; increased vessel permeability; and platelet aggregation. Calcitonin gene-related peptide appears to play a particularly important role and is found in higher concentrations in the jugular but not peripheral vessels during migraine. The elevation of CGRP seen in migraine is prevented by sumatriptan and other recently introduced migraine medications.

Some scientists report that hormonal changes initiated around puberty increase migraine risk, but it is obvious that all migraines are not directly hormonally triggered, since not all migraines are premenstrual and they can occur randomly. Since the condition also affects males, other hormonal and regulatory factors must also play a role in genesis of headache episodes. Migraine can onset as a postmenopausal late-life migraine disorder, which suggests multiple etiologic and neurochemical components. It is interesting to note that some migraine suffers continue to note prodromal symptoms of migraine later in life without onset of headache. Also, children who suffer pediatric migraine have attacks long before hormonal changes of puberty begin.

Signs, symptoms, and clinical diagnosis

Migraine as classified by the IHS criteria is generally divided into two distinct subtypes: migraine with aura, and migraine without aura. The former presents with a variety of symptomatic and physical changes that predict the onset of the migraine episode. Generally these predictive changes occur 5 to 20 minutes before the onset of headache and include one or more of the following: visual changes, dysphasia, other unilateral sensory changes, feelings of hopelessness, altered sense of smell or vision, stiff neck, and feelings of paresthesia or other neurologic sensations around the head and neck on the side that will become painful. Some patients continue to have these same sensations during the headache attack, and others note a decrease in the aura as pain becomes the dominant sensation. Migraine pain rarely lasts less than 4 hours and normally is gone within 24 hours, but some episodes can last for a week or longer. Historically it was thought that migraine was a unilateral pain disorder, but recent epidemiologic studies suggest that up to 40% of migraine episodes are bilateral.

Migraine without aura presents as a headache without warning. Both forms of migraine are usually rapid in onset and can move from preheadache to headache status within a few minutes. Although most attacks of migraine are unilateral and can repeat on the same side and location or move from side to side with each episode, the location of pain can encompass the entire side of the head or localize to a much small area. It can even be felt in one tissue or organ (eye, tooth, sinus, temporomandibular joint [TMJ], etc.). Once pain begins, there are few differences in the manifestation of migraine with or without aura. Most patients report that neurologic stimulation of any type increases pain and nausea if present. Neurologic stimulation that aggravates migraine includes light, sound, motion, smells, exercise, and touch. As a result, most migraineurs seek a dark quiet space during attacks and generally do not like to be disturbed. In contrast patients with tension type headaches (TTHA) often find that exercise decreases symptoms as do other activities that distract them. Most migraines do not occur more than 2 to 4 times a month, although occasionally, patients encounter migraine recurrences up to 6 to 8 times per month. Factors that provoke recurrent episodes of migraine are not clearly understood, and for some patients no specific triggering mechanism can be detected. Certain smells trigger episodes in those with olfactory sensitive migraines. The most common olfactory triggers are perfumes and cosmetic smells. Other patients report migraine triggered by alcohol, preservatives in foods, artifical sweeteners, and foods. The most commonly reported food triggers are chocolate, diary products, citrus fruits, and wine or other alcoholic drinks. Hunger and hypoglycemia have also been reported to trigger attacks, as have changed sleep patterns and sleep deprivation. Stressful life events have been reported by about 50% of migraineurs to trigger headache episodes. In some patients, exhaustive analysis of triggering factors fails to reveal any obvious patterns.

Facial migraine

Facial migraine is a clinical variant of migraine in which the major location of the migraine is within the orofacial complex, including the jaws, TMJ, dentition, salivary glands, and maxillary sinus. The pattern is usually similar to that seen in other forms of migraine and an aura may be present or the pain onset can be without warning. Facial migraine is frequently incorrectly diagnosed as dental pathology by both physicians and dentists because the severity of pain and the precise location of symptoms easily resemble odontogenic infection, sinusitis, or acute TMJ dysfunction. During attacks, the teeth in the field of pain can be hypersensitive to percussion and temperature, leading to an incorrect diagnosis of pulpitis or maxillary sinusitis. Tactile stimulation of the dentition and periodontal tissues can also trigger increased symptoms, mimicking acute periodontal infection. If the pain is located around the TMJ and ear, patients often provide a history of repeated visits to their primary care doctor to rule out ear infections. A key report by most patients with facial migraine is a report that the pain stops after sleeping. Complete resolution of symptoms after sleeping is uncommon in dental infection, TMJ dysfunction, or sinusitis. Another key clinical report that should cause the clinician to consider migraine is the report that light and sound increase symptoms, or that nausea occurs with pain episodes. Patients with facial migraine may report recurrent pain thought to be odontogenic in origin. Frequently, they report repeated endodontic treatments and even extractions. Those with less clearly localized facial migraine commonly report prior unsuccessful treatment of sinus disease. One or more of these reports should cause the clinician to consider facial migraine and pursue that diagnosis prior to engaging in additional irreversible treatments. A surprising number of patients with migraine and facial migraine report attempts at treatment through chiropractic therapy. This usually occurs in those with some level of cervical or occipital symptoms associated with migraine attacks. Although not commonly known, migraine can be preceded by neck stiffness, and during the headache episode pain can radiate throughout one side of the neck and into the head. The nature of the migraine episode with complete resolution of symptoms within 24 hours often causes the patient or treating doctor to assume that their treatment was responsible for resolution of symptoms. This error leads to repeated use of the same therapy with each recurrence.

Other migraine variants

Other symptoms and changes reported in migraine and facial migraine include weakness, indigestion, diarrhea, and visual changes, including partial blindness and tunnel vision. Ophthalmoplegic migraines are accompanied with paresis of ocular cranial nerves, and retinal migraines typically produce blindness or scotoma of one eye. The full range of generalized and systemic symptoms reported by some migraine patients is not appreciated by many clinicians. Prodromal features can extend to variation in temperature regulation; fatigue; gastrointestinal symptoms, including either constipation or diarrhea; aphasia; hypersensitivity to touch; tinnitus; phonophobia; nasal congestion; hypertension; vertigo; and even loss of consciousness. Basilar migraine often

presents with stupor and emotional changes, including aggressive behavior and swearing. Hemiplegic migraine causes unilateral changes in sensory and motor control. An interesting migraine variant seen in the orofacial region is ice pick migraine, which manifests as a severe stabbing sensation in a tissue or region. It often triggers stabbing pains through the eye, temple, TMJ, or teeth. The symptom lasts only a second or two and can recur from once or twice a day to many times. It is often confused with a cracked tooth syndrome, pulpitis, or momentary catching of the meniscus of the TMJ. The difference is that all of the other conditions require some form of jaw movement or activity to illicit the symptom, but ice pick migraine occurs at times when the mouth and jaws are completely inactive. A variety of exertional migraines have also been reported. Most common among these migraine variants are those triggered by exercise and sexual activity. They are usually of much shorter duration (20–60 min) than other migraines. Last among the migraine variants is persistent or intractable migraine, which continues for days or weeks. It is the most impairing of all the migraine variants and carries a risk of vascular accident and crisis. It can require emergency medical treatment to interrupt the episode.

Migraine management

The management of migraine can be divided into three specific strategies: prevention, abortive therapy, and symptomatic or palliative therapy (Table 31–2). For those with infrequent recurrences of less than once or twice a month the best therapy may be abortive or palliative, since neither requires continuous use of medication to prevent onset of symptoms. Patients who experience more frequent or severe episodes may desire therapy aimed at aborting an attack in the initial stage or treatment that prevents recurrence. Response to any of the three management approaches can be highly varied among individuals, and even in the same patient over time. Factors that cause widespread variation in response to interventions are not well understood.

Preventive protocols for migraine commonly employ continuous use of either a beta blocker, such as propranolol, or one of the tricyclic antidepressants, such as amitriptyline or nortriptyline. Recently, some success has been reported with use of the newer generation of selective serotonin reuptake inhibitor (SSRI) antidepressants, such as fluoxetine or sertraline, although both have also been associated with increased headaches. Membrane stabilizers, such as carbamazepine, valproic acid, and gabapentin, have also shown value in preventing migraine in some patients that have not responded to other migraine protocols. Thermal biofeedback, which trains the patient to raise the temperature of the hands and feet, has been shown to reduce headache frequency and abort headaches in some migraine patients. The mainstay of abortive therapy primarily continues to be three approaches: use of ergotamine derivatives, sumatriptan and other triptan medications, and Midrin.

Tension-type headache

The most common type of headache is tension-type headache (TTHA). Over 80% of adults experience TTHA periodically. These headaches are also common in children and adolescents. The condition is usually divided into two main categories: episodic TTHA, and chronic TTHA. Symptoms can range from mild to very severe, with the pattern of episodes varying depending on factors related to headache triggers. Most patients who suffer TTHA do not seek specific medical treatment for the condition and choose to use over-the-counter (OTC) medications to combat symptoms.

Etiology and pathophysiology

Tension-type headache has been widely studied relative to issues of both etiology and pathophysiology. It is generally considered to be triggered by psychophysiologic changes related to stress, worry, and depression. It is more common during episodes of stress and unhappiness and often becomes infrequent during times of relaxation and low stress. Some clinical scientists divide TTHA into two clinical subtypes: without tender pericranial muscles, and with tender pericranial muscles. The two conditions are distinguished by a patient response to palpation of pericranial muscles during a headache attack. The muscles involved include the frontalis, temporalis, suboccipitalis, masseter, other paravertebral and cervical muscles, and even the muscles of facial expression. The finding of muscle tenderness in some patients with TTHA leads to the assumption that TTHA and myofascial pain are related and specifically so in TTHA with tender pericranial muscles. Studies have not confirmed that patients with TTHA with tender muscles have significantly higher readings on electromyography (EMG). The pathophysiology of TTHA without tender muscles remains unresolved but generally is thought to include actions within the CNS that lead to peripheral pain without evidence of peripheral pathology.

Clinical presentation and diagnosis

Tension-type headache presents differently than migraine, yet many patients with moderate to severe TTHA believe that they have migraine. Usually, TTHA is bilateral during attacks and often includes a band-like sensation of tightening around the head. The regions of the temporalis and frontal muscles are often painful, and as the headache progresses, the entire head and upper cervical region may become painful. Some patients, however, report that their symptoms are primarily bitemporal with pounding sensations that are nonpulsating in character. Tension-type headache often begins in the late morning and persists throughout the day. Nausea and vomiting are not normally a constituent of TTHA except when pain becomes severe, which initiates sensations of nausea in a minority of patients. Most patients report that they are more likely to develop symptoms during times of stress and worry or depression. Sleep loss also increases frequency of episodes of TTHA. If pericranial muscles are tender to palpation, the diagnosis of TTHA with pericranial muscle tenderness is established. Since EMG levels in such patients are normal, it has been suggested that the process of tenderness is neurogenic and centrally controlled.

The condition most commonly confused with TTHA is myofascial pain dysfunction (MPD) of the muscles of

Table 31–2 Management of Migraine and Migraine Variants

Preventive	Abortive	Palliative
Beta blockers (propranolol)	Ergotamines (oral)	Narcotic analgesics (oral)
Calcium channel blockers	Midrin (oral)	Meperidine with promethazine (injectable)
Antidepressants: amitriptyline, nortriptyline, doxepin, fluoxetine, sertraline	Sumatriptan (oral, injectable, nasal)	DHE (dihydroergotamine mesylate) for persistent migraine
Ergotamine	Zolmitripan (oral)	Ice packs
Anticonvulsants: valproate, carbamazepine, gabapentin	Acetaminophen (oral)	Sleep
Baclofen	Lidocaine (intranasal)	Dark room and sensory deprivation
Lithium	Thermal biofeedback	
Sodium caffeine benzoate	Imagery and relaxation therapy	
Thermal biofeedback		
Stress management, cognitive behavioral therapy		

mastication. Both can present as facial pain and headache, and both have chronic durations of several days or cyclic patterns like chronic daily headache. Both exhibit pain in the region of the temporalis and other pericranial muscles and both seem to be triggered or aggravated by the same exogenous and endogenous factors, including stress and other behavioral dysfunctions. Both TTHA and MPD are common conditions, with prevalence rates that result in a significant likelihood of both occurring in the same patient. Tension-type headache with tender pericranial muscles has the potential for causing referred pain to the maxilla, mandible, TMJ, and odontogenic structures. Both conditions are associated with a tendency for increased somatic focus (expression of behavioral stressors as physical symptoms).

Subtypes of tension-type headache

Tension-type headache can have a highly varied duration, with episodes lasting longer than a week or less than 30 minutes. Current IHS criteria for TTHA diagnosis require that to establish a diagnosis of episodic TTHA requires 10 prior episodes of the same set of headache symptoms, pain that is mild to moderate, bilateral pain, lack of symptoms commonly associated with migraine (photophobia, nausea, etc.), and pain that last more than a few minutes. Episodic and other forms of TTHA also have in common a lack of symptom increase from walking or stair climbing.

A diagnosis of chronic TTHA requires that the other criteria for TTHA are met plus the presence of the headache 15 days per month over a period of 6 or more months. Such headaches are usually more difficult to manage and result in risk of rebound headache, because of chronic use of analgesics, including both non-narcotic agents, acetaminophen, ibuprofen, aspirin, and narcotic analgesics. The chronic use of any of these medications on a daily basis leads to rebound headache when medications are discontinued. As with episodic TTHA, chronic stress and other behavioral or psychological factors are thought to play a major role in the pathophysiology of chronic TTHA. Treatment is often difficult, since the triggering factors may not be evident. Some patients can experience transformation of vascular headaches, such as migraine, to chronic daily headaches, and others report symptoms of both TTHA and migraine, leading to the suggestion that they suffer from a mixed headache syndrome made up of both migraine and TTHA.

Patients may also report TTHA that arises in the posterior of the neck and sometimes spreads to encompass most of the pericranial regions. These cervicogenic headaches can be a part of TTHA or represent manifestations of myofascial pain involving the cervical muscles. Cervical dysfunction representing pain caused by cervical nerve irritation can also provoke pain in the head, neck, and shoulders, but it usually follows neurologic distributions and generates symptoms down the arm and into the hand. Cervical nerve compression headache usually is accompanied with other neurologic symptoms, including paresthesia involving the neck or arm, tingling sensations that radiate down the arm, and a significant increase in pain with neck movements or compression of the cervical vertebra. It is always wise to seek consultation in patients reporting pain in the neck with referral into the cranial or facial region, since cervical nerve compression can arise from degenerative arthritis of the cervical spine, tumors, and vascular lesions and as the result of injury to the cervical region. In cases of recent trauma, referral is particularly wise, since stress on the cervical vertebrae could cause additional neurologic symptoms and, in some cases, damage the spinal cord. Pain radiating down the arm could also suggest referred ischemic cardiovascular pain and warrants medical consultation.

Management of tension-type headache

Management of TTHA depends upon the frequency and severity of episodes. It is generally recommended that simple TTHA occurring less than twice a week be treated symptomatically with analgesics, including common OTC medications (Table 31–3). Most are not dependency-producing, but some have the potential for habituation or triggering rebound headaches if used excessively. Since TTHA appears to be associated with behavioral factors, attention should be directed toward altering psychological and behavioral issues. This may necessitate referral to a psychologist or other mental health professional for assessment and treatment. An important component of treatment should be working with the patient to identify conditions that increase headache episodes. Noting the pattern of headache recurrences and associating them with exposure to stressful social or personal events can lead to preventive interventions. Late-life tension headache is seen in depressed elderly individuals and requires exploration of endogenous sources of depression more than exploration of exogenous factors, such as worry about health issues, financial status, or loneliness. Organic degenerative brain syndromes in the elderly can cause headaches and depression.

The management of tension headache using a preventive process is usually reserved for those patients who experience more than two headaches per week or have particularly severe TTHA that persists for more than a day. Preventive protocols are also worth consideration in patients who cannot comply with the requirements of symptomatic treatment (excess use of narcotic analgesics,

Table 31–3 Management of Tension-Type Headaches (TTHA)

Symptomatic Treatments	Preventive
Episodic TTHA	
Aspirin	Behavioral management protocols relaxation training, stress management, meditation,
Caffeine (40–50 mg)	cognitive behavioral therapy biofeedback
Acetaminophen	Sleep hygiene
NSAIDS (ibuprofen, Naprosyn, meclofenamate	Exercise
Codeine, hydrocodone, oxycodone	Antidepressants (amitriptyline)
Butalbital (50 mg)	
Propoxyphene (50, 65, 100 mg)	
Chronic TTHA	
Same as for episodic TTHA with attention to possible rebound reactions to analgesics	Migraine medications: antidepressants, beta blockers, calcium channel blockers, anticonvulsants
	Cognitive behavioral therapy
	Exercise

use of multiple medications, obtaining medications from more than one source, etc.). When narcotic analgesics are used for TTHA or any chronic pain syndrome, it is wise to establish a medication compliance contract with the patient that outlines the clinician's rules for use of the medication. Most narcotic analgesic patient contracts usually include a series of statements that the patient must agree to or the medication should not be prescribed or renewed. The list of requirements varies but generally includes the items listed in Table 31–4.

Cluster headache

Cluster headache is significantly less prevalent than migraine but is confused with migraine because of its extreme pain. Cluster is more common in males and is infrequent in adolescents and young adults, although cases have occurred in individuals less than 25 years of age. Cluster, like migraine, is unilateral and is among the most painful of the headache disorders. It, in addition to pain, is frequently accompanied by a variety of autonomic changes caused by contribution of cross-signaling of trigeminal and autonomic components of the orofacial region. Cluster occurs more frequently in smokers and is sometimes related to a variant of trigeminal neuralgia.

Etiology and pathophysiology

The etiology of cluster is not understood, and it is considered to be a member of the vascular headache group, with some characteristics related to neuralgias and migraine. Abnormal function within the trigemino-vascular system has also been suggested as part of the pathophysiology. Oxygen desaturation appears to play a role and trigger serotoninergic reactions. Attacks are

often seen during periods of reduced oxygen, including high altitude and rapid eye movement (REM) sleep, and attacks have been aborted with exposure to 100% oxygen. It has been suggested that chemoreceptors in the carotid body become hypersensitive in cluster. Neurogenic inflammation is also a component of cluster, with CGRP levels elevated during attacks. Stimulation of the sphenopalatine ganglion occurs in cluster, including parasympathetic autonomic innervation in the face and sinuses. Exact mechanisms responsible for the trigeminal, trigeminovascular, and autonomic innervation that results in the pain and physical characteristics of cluster have not been resolved. Attacks can trigger pain within cranial nerves V, VII, IX, and X and cervical nerves 1, 2, and 3. Irritation of the sphenopalatine region by tobacco smoke or other irritants plays a role in recurrent episodes of cluster in some patients but not others. Blocking the trigeminal, sphenopalatine, and occipital nerves have all resulted in relief of cluster symptoms. It is evident that active cluster involves vasodilation of extracranial vessels but

Table 31–4 Component of a Medication Contract

Medications will only be received from one provider.
The patient agrees to use the medication only as prescribed.
The patient will protect the medication from loss or theft, and it will not be replaced early under those circumstances.
The medication will not be used with other agents, such as alcohol or street drugs.
The patient will not call early and request that the medication be renewed prior to the appropriate time.
The medication will be used on a time-contingent basis and not saved to be used in greater concentrations when pain is high.
Medications from others will not be used to augment the prescribed medication.
Violation of the agreement will result in the prescribed medication being discontinued.

not intracranial vessels. The release of inflammatory mediators, including CGRP, substance P, and other neuropeptides is associated with cluster episodes.

Clinical presentation and diagnosis

Cluster is an interesting and perplexing member of the orofacial pain group. Episodes are usually unilateral and last less than 60 minutes, but can persist for up to 3 hours. It is common for episodes to start and stop within a 5-minute window of activity. During the episodes patients often report pain rated as 10 on a 0 to 10 pain scale. Unlike migraine, the pain is so aversive that it makes sufferers walk the floor, pound their head, or do other physical activities to distract themselves from the pain. Between episodes they usually report no symptoms and feel completely normal. Attacks start rapidly, without warning, and stop just as suddenly. It is often impossible to function normally during attacks. Autonomic changes include facial flushing, sensations of facial swelling, rhinorrhea, lacrimation, injection of the mucosal of the eye, salivation, and even facial edema. During episodes, the structures in the region are often hyperpathic, and the dental occlusion can feel altered. Teeth can become hypersensitive to cold and percussion during pain episodes, with rapid resolution of symptoms after the pain has passed. The location of pain can vary and involve small regions of the head, neck, face, dentition, and mouth, or expand to create pain in several tissues adjacent to each other. Pain can be localized to the area around, in, or above one tooth or in the TMJ. Episodes recur from once a day up to 4 to 5 times in 24 hours. Pain can occur while awake or asleep, and it is common for patients to report that they wake during the night in extreme pain. Patients with cluster often undergo unnecessary dental and medical therapy when their symptoms are located in the region of the sinuses or dentition. Symptoms around the teeth and jaws can mimic the severe pain of pulpitis or odontogenic infection. Cluster often follows seasonal patterns or can go into remission and recur months or years later.

Diagnosis of cluster is made through clinical assessment, after ruling out serious head and neck pathology. There are no specific commonly employed laboratory or other diagnostic tests, except for administration of 100% oxygen during an attack. If administration of oxygen results in resolution of the pain more rapidly than would normally occur, the diagnosis of cluster is confirmed. Application of 4% lidocaine intranasally has also been reported to abort cluster attacks. Beyond these medication trials, diagnosis is clinical and based upon the classic nature of symptoms and signs along with response to trials of medications known to be effective in cluster.

Cluster-trignal neuralgia

Classic cluster cannot be provoked by tactile stimulation of the tissues in the head and neck, but a small percentage of patients with cluster also have symptoms of trigeminal neuralgia which is triggered by touch of the trigger zone within trigeminal innervation. The combined occurrence of these conditions causes spontaneous episodes of severe unilateral headache that cannot be provoked with tactile stimulation, along with pain triggered by light mechanical stimulation in the distribution of the trigeminal nerve. The combination of these two symptom complexes often results in confused diagnoses and inappropriate therapy. Treatment often requires joint therapy for trigeminal neuralgia and cluster. Patients with the combined condition can experience significant symptoms when the dentition is stimulated (thermal, percussion), leading to a false diagnosis of pulp pathology.

Management of cluster

Treatment of cluster usually targets prevention of recurrences, since each episode is so brief that the pain is gone by the time the medication has taken effect. There are exceptions to that rule, and abortive medications are useful in confirming the diagnosis of cluster. Abortive therapies include administration of 100% oxygen at the outset of an episode, which results in a rapid resolution of symptoms in over 70% of cases, or administration of 4% lidocaine solution sprayed intranasally, which also terminates the pain episode in approximately 40 to 50% of patients. Other abortive treatments are less effective. Preventive therapies include systemic prednisone, methysergide, and cyproheptadine. Refractory cases sometimes respond to migraine medications, such as sumatriptan, ergotamine, dihydroergotamine (DHE), lithium, or valproate (Table 31–5). Since cluster occurs as a series of episodes of pain and usually goes into remission, it is common for patients to experience months or years free of symptoms only to have them return. After several months of preventive therapy it is usually advisable to discontinue the medication to see if remission has occurred.

Chronic paroxysmal hemicrania

Chronic paroxysmal hemicrania (CPH) is another of the vascular headache syndromes that are commonly confused with odontogenic, regional pathology of the head and neck, or TMD. It has features common to migraine and may have some of the same etiologic and pathophysiologic components.

Table 31-5 Cluster Treatments

Abortive Medications	Preventive Medications
Oxygen: 100% at 7 L/min	Prednisone: oral, 20–40 mg/d
Lidocaine: 4% nasal spray	Cyproheptadine: oral, 4 mg every 8 hr
Sumatriptan:	Methysergide: oral, 2–4 mg every 12 hr
(oral, injectable, nasal)	Lithium: oral, 300 mg every 8 hr
	Valproate: oral, 250–500 mg every 12 hr
	Carbamazepine: oral, 200 mg–400 mg
	every 8 hr

Clinical presentation and diagnosis

As with cluster, CPH onsets rapidly and provokes severe pain that lasts from a few minutes up to 45 minutes. It is consistently unilateral and occurs on the same side of the head and face. The temporal area, orbital region, face, or structures of the jaws can be the sites of pain. Attacks are often more frequent than experienced in cluster, with more than five episodes occurring per day during peak periods of recurrence. Associated findings include conjunctival injection, sinus stuffiness or rhinorrhea, lacrimation, and edema of the region of pain. No specific diagnostic test is available and diagnosis is via clinical decision based on symptoms and findings of autonomic changes during attacks. In contrast to cluster, CPH is almost always responsive to indomethacin in dosages of 25 mg per day to 150 mg per day. Cluster is often unresponsive to indomethacin.

Management

Chronic paroxysmal headache usually responds well to indomethacin, but because it can have significant impact on the stomach and gastrointestinal system the lowest possible therapeutically effect dosage should be used. When patients cannot tolerate indomethacin medications, therapies effective for cluster can be administered with a positive effect.

Headaches associated with head trauma

Acute post-traumatic headache

Acute post-traumatic headaches (APTH) occur secondary to actual physical injury, edema, and irritation of extracranial and intracranial tissues. In its mild form, APTH represents the result of benign trauma and soreness in the head and neck. Symptoms are most commonly reported to be in the temporal, frontal, and occipital area, with symptoms in the face and jaw less often reported. Of primary concern in patients presenting with APTH is the potential that they are experiencing significant cranial edema or even an intracranial hematoma. In such cases, emergency assessment and management is necessary to ensure that brain damage caused by intracranial hemorrhage or edema is prevented. With that consideration, it is recommended that any patient seen in the primary care medical or dental setting who reports significant head pain following trauma be evaluated carefully, and if any evidence of diminished cognitive, reflex, or other neurologic function is detected, the patient must be referred for complete neurologic assessment and cranial imaging. Use of any medication that increases intracranial pressure, masks symptoms of progressive cranial involvement, or increases the risk of intracranial hemorrhage is contraindicated in patients with acute head trauma.

Chronic post-traumatic headache

Chronic post-traumatic headache (CPTH) is caused by organic and neurochemical alterations in the CNS following blunt trauma to the head. The onset of CPTH does not require serious injury to the brain, such as concussion, subdural hematoma, or skull fracture; CPTH can occur without direct trauma to the skull and has been reported to develop after whiplash or other acceleration-deceleration accidents. Approximately 60% of patients with documented closed head injuries develop CPTH. Symptoms vary considerably depending upon the type of trauma but often include chronic generalized headaches, neck pain, or shoulder symptoms. Many patients develop cognitive and reasoning deficits, memory changes, and significant alterations in personality and mood. It is not uncommon for family or friends to report that the patient has become argumentative, short tempered, and hostile. Vertigo is another common feature, as are migraine-like throbbing headaches that can be localized or widespread throughout the head and neck. The structures of the face and jaw can be involved in the regions of pain, although cranial and temporal symptoms are more common. Cluster-like severe episodic headaches also occur in some patients, and generalized cervical pain can occur in the absence of cervical spine or muscular damage. Postural changes are also known to aggravate headache symptoms. Most CPTH patients complain of headaches, mood changes, and memory and other cognitive dysfunctions. They have difficulty in concentrating, experience disordered thoughts, and feel depressed without reason. Some report pseudoseizures or seizure-like episodes related to, or independent of pain. Headaches are frequent and chronic, with durations that extend for days or weeks. Anhedonia and loss of sexual interest is also a common feature of CPTH. Treatment is similar to that of other vascular headache syndromes, but patients often respond better to tricyclic antidepressants, including amitriptyline. Recently, gabapentin has also been reported to be effective. Headaches and other symptoms usually slowly resolve over a period of several months to 2 years, but medications may need to be continued longer. If significant cognitive and neuromotor changes have occurred, occupational therapy and psychotherapy may be required to improve productivity and a return to pretrauma levels of function.

Headaches associated with vascular disorders

A wide range of headaches and cephalalgias occur as the result of vascular changes and disease within the CNS. Most are less common than the conditions presented thus far, but some discussion of these vascular conditions is important, since they have significant morbidity associated with their progression. Diagnosis usually requires vascular imaging along with neurologic assessment. Although headache is a common component, it is possible for these conditions to develop without headache, and the first manifestation can be other neurologic deficits including memory loss, decreased motor control, sensory changes, or pain in other regions of the body or within the cranium or head and neck. Several of the conditions require urgent care to avoid permanent brain damage or death. Since disruption of vascular supply to regions of the brain can occur, early discovery is important. Specific conditions that represent intracranial and nearby vascular pathology resulting in headache are included in Table 31–6.

Subarachnoid hemorrhage

Most of the conditions listed in Table 31–6 require immediate medical or neurosurgical intervention. Subarachnoid hemorrhage (SAH) results in paralysis, and most of the other conditions also cause serious, if not life-threatening brain damage if not managed early and effectively. Onset of head and neck pain with SAH is usually sudden and described as the most severe headache of the patient's life; it is accompanied with nausea, vomiting, and mental and emotional changes. More than half of patients with SAH experience a warning leak with headache that precedes the full hemorrhagic episode. Detection during the leak period can result in saving life, however, mortality overall is almost 50%. Cranial imaging is necessary for detection, but not all patients with SAH are detected during such examinations. Lumbar puncture is essential as part of the diagnostic approach in suspected SAH and other intracranial sources of suspected pathology.

Carotid lesions

Of all vascular disorders, the most commonly detected in dental settings are carotid lesions, since they can often be identified by direct palpation of the carotid artery, which provokes the symptom complaint of the patient. Symptoms are similar to those of giant cell arteritis with palpation-triggered pain that radiates upward into the head and face. Both are seen predominantly in the elderly and are extremely uncommon before 60 years of age. Segmental enlargement of the carotid suggests that a dissecting aneurysm or carotid body tumor is present. Final diagnosis requires magnetic resonance angiography or an angiogram.

Giant cell arteritis

Giant cell arteritis (GCA) or temporal arteritis is an inflammatory disorder of the arterial vessels of the head and neck. Coronary vessels can also be involved, but most commonly the vessels affected include the ophthalmic artery, the temporal artery, and the carotid. Symptoms include diffuse headache that is unilateral, which can also include facial, neck, and jaw pain. Symptoms are initially low-grade and gradually become more severe and persistent until they reach a constant state. Pain increases at night and when the patient reclines. Fatigue is a common feature, and patients report that they feel ill. Pain in the maxilla and maxillary teeth is often reported, and symptoms also radiate into the TMJ and ear. In later stages, the patient takes on a pale complexion and distention of the involved vessels is evident. Since the vascular system is compromised and blood flow to the region is decreased, muscle activity can result in claudication of the jaw. This manifests as jaw fatigue with eating. Long-term risks associ-

Table 31–6 Vascular Disorders Associated with Headache

Subarachnoid hemorrhage
Giant cell arteritis and other forms of arteritis
Venous thrombosis
Arterial hypertension
Intracranial hematoma
Unruptured vascular malformations
Carotid and other vertebral artery disorders
Acute ischemic cerebral vascular disease
Intracranial aneurysm

ated with GCA include blindness caused by occlusion of vessels of the eye, stroke, and myocardial infarction, if coronary vessels are involved. Diagnosis is accomplished by ordering an erythrocyte sedimentation rate (ESR), which is almost always elevated, and arterial biopsy, to confirm the presence of giant cells. Treatment requires high-dose prednisone for up to 1 year. Prompt treatment is essential to avoid ocular damage or other CNS complications.

Headaches associated with nonvascular intracranial disorders

Many other intracranial disorders besides vascular changes can trigger pain and headache. Some of these can be life-threatening and, as with vascular disorders, prompt diagnosis is critical. Most of these conditions can be associated with headache or pain within the head and neck, but the onset of pain is highly variable, and depending upon the location of the lesion, pain can develop either early or late in the course of the disorder. Most of these conditions cause other neurologic and cognitive changes in addition to sensory and pain symptoms. Table 31–7 list several of the more common disorders.

Tumors are most commonly diagnosed via brain imaging, either magnetic resonance imaging (MRI) or computed tomography (CT). The location of pain, when present (about 50% of tumor patients report no headache), is often persistent and gradually radiates out over larger areas. Headache associated with tumors is worse in the morning and can cause nausea and vomiting. Symptoms increase when the patient bends over. Aggressive tumors can lead to rapid escalation of headache and other cranial symptoms, including motor dysfunction.

Intracranial infections normally are accompanied with high fever, hematologic evidence of systemic infection, and other neurologic changes. Viral infections are the most common type of intracranial infection seen in the United States. In most cases, intracranial infections are easily identified, except in cases of chronic low-grade infections, such as seen in Lyme disease, which,

Table 31–7   Headache Associated with Nonvascular Intracranial Disease

Cerebrospinal fluid hypertension
Cerebrospinal fluid hypotension
Intracranial tumors
Headache associated with intrathecal injections
Intracranial infections
Intracranial sarcoidosis and other noninflammatory disease

by nature is usually low-grade. Mood alterations are common in chronic intracranial infections, as is chronic fatigue. Diagnosis depends on the type of infection and whether serologic tests are available. Culture of spinal fluid can be valuable in establishing the final diagnosis.

Low cerebrospinal fluid pressure headache

Low cerebrospinal fluid (CSF) headache occurs after spinal anesthesia and after some cases of cranial trauma resulting in skull fracture, with gradual loss of fluid into the ear or nasal cavity. Occasionally CSF hypotension occurs in the absence of actual fluid loss from trauma. Symptoms include onset of headache when standing, with reduction of pain when the patient reclines. The pain is often located in the frontal region and accompanied with nausea, vomiting, dizziness, and stiffness of the cervical region. Diagnosis is established by lumbar puncture and detection of very low CSF pressure (less than 30 mm).

High cerebrospinal fluid pressure headache

High CSF fluid headaches (idiopathic intracranial hypertension or pseudotumor cerebri) are idiopathic, and the etiology is unclear. They occur in young adult obese females and are persistent. Symptoms often include generalized head pain with the retrobulbar location being the most common site. Eye movement and head movement cause symptoms to increase. The high level of hypertension within the brain causes significant pain, visual changes, such as diplopia, stiffness in the neck, and dysfunction of the sixth cranial nerve. Tetracycline use has been associated with the condition. Excessive pressure causes papilledema and threatens vision. Lumbar puncture reveals excessive fluid pressure. In some patients, compression of the jugular results in decreased pulsatile tinnitus, which is common in the disorder. Treatment includes removal of spinal fluid to reduce pressure, prednisone at or above 40 mg per day, and diuretics. If pressures continue to be high, surgical implantation of a shunt may be in order.

Headaches caused by substances or withdrawal of substances

A number of medications, illicit drugs, and other agents trigger the onset of headache or facial pain when discontinued. The most commonly known example is rebound headache, which occurs when patients have continually taken headache medications over an extended period of time. Rebound can occur with almost any pain medication and is seen in headache patients after discontinuing acetaminophen, ibuprofen, and other prescription or OTC medications. The rebound process encourages patients to continue to use medications that may not be necessary or indicated, except that rebound headache occurs without the medication or agent. Coffee is another example of a potential rebound agent.

Other agents reported to trigger headaches include artificial sweeteners. Tobacco and alcohol withdrawal have been associated with onset of headaches in patients who are chronic users of narcotics and other psychoactive medications. Selective serotonin reuptake inhibitor antidepressants are known to commonly trigger headaches. Determination of which agent or medication is responsible for the headache requires removal of the medication, if possible. Rebound can occur from medications that have just been withdrawn and incorrectly suggest to the examiner that the medication should be restarted because it is providing a therapeutic effect. Obtaining a complete list of all OTC and prescribed medications is an important component in exploring headaches and their management.

Headaches caused by foods also represent a significant source of head pain. Common triggers are alcohol, pickled foods, chocolate, dairy products, nitrites, bananas, oranges, and raisins. Onions, beans, and nuts are also known to provoke headaches. An elimination diet may be required to discover the specific agent in food that triggers the headaches.

Metabolic disorders-induced headaches

A number of metabolic disorders can cause headaches that are generally diffuse and low-grade. Onset occurs when metabolic changes are significant enough to alter metabolic processes. Hypoglycemia is a common source of headache and occurs in diabetics and patients that have low blood sugar. Hyperglycemia can also trigger headaches, as can other metabolic disorders, such as hyperthyroidism. Conditions that decrease oxygen supply can provoke headaches, including respiratory disease, sleep apnea, and other functional causes of oxygen deprivation. Autoimmune diseases, such as lupus, are also known to trigger chronic severe headaches.

Suggested reading

Delcanho RE, Graff-Radford SG. Chronic paroxysmal hemicrania presenting as tooth-ache. J Orofacial Pain 1993;7:300–6.

Ekbom K, Krabbe A, Micelli G, et al. Cluster headache attack treated for up to three months with subcutaneous sumatriptan (6 mg). Sumatriptan Cluster Headache Long-Term Study Group. Cephalalgia 1995;15:230–6.

Goadsby PJ, Edvinsson L. Human in vivo evidence for trigeminovascular activation in cluster headache: neuropeptide changes and effects of acute attacks therapies. Brain 1994;117:427–34.

Headache Classification Committee of the International Headache Society. Classification and diagnosis criteria for headache disorders, cranial neuralgia, and facial pain. Cephalalgia 1988;8(Suppl 7):1–96.

Hu XH, Markson LE, Lipton RB, et al. Burden of migraine in the United States. Disability and economic costs. Arch Intern Med 1999;159:813–8

Jensen R, Rasmussen BK, Pedersen B, Olsen J. Muscle tenderness and pressure pain thresholds in headache. A population study. Pain 1995;52:193–9.

Kudrow L. The pathogenesis of cluster headache. Curr Opin Neurol 1994;7:278–82.

Lipton RB, Stewart WF, Ryan RE Jr, et al. Efficacy and safety of acetaminophen, aspirin, and caffeine in alleviating placebo-controlled trials. Arch Neurol 1998;55:210–7.

Millard H, Mason D, eds. Third World Workshop in Oral Medicine. Ann Arbor, MI: University of Michigan, School of Dentistry, Continuing Education, 2000.

Olesen J. Clinical and pathophysiological observations in migraine and tension-type headache explained by integration of vascular, supraspinal, and myofascial imputs. Pain 1991;46:125–32.

Rasmussen BK. Migraine and tension-type headache in a general population: precipitating factors, female hormones, sleep pattern, and relation of lifestyle. Pain 1993;53:65–72.

Sjaastad O. Chronic paroxysmal hemicrania and similar headaches. In: Dalessio DJ, Silberstein SD, eds. Wolff's headache and other head pain. 6th Ed. New York: Oxford University Press, 1993:198–202.

Stewart WF, Lipton RB, Simon D, et al. Reliability of an illness severity measure for headache in a population sample of migraine sufferers. Cephalalgia 1998;18:44–51.

32 Orofacial Neuralgias and Neuropathic Pain

David A. Sirois, DMD, PhD

One of the most challenging clinical issues the dentist confronts is the patient with persistent orofacial pain without obvious proximate physical cause. Patients with persistent pain often seek consultation from many clinicians and undergo multiple unnecessary procedures before receiving a correct diagnosis and appropriate treatment. Clinicians unfamiliar with neuropathic pain may become frustrated and, with the best of intentions but limited information, provide familiar but inappropriate treatment directed toward a dental or other somatic pain. The spectrum and prevalence of orofacial neuropathic pains is such that every dentist will certainly encounter patients with neuropathic pain. Therefore, to avoid unnecessary and inappropriate diagnosis and treatment, the dentist must gain familiarity with the pathophysiology, presentation, diagnosis, and treatment of orofacial neuropathic pain.

By definition, neuropathic pain is nonadaptive and does not contribute to healing, such as would be the case with pain attributable to tissue inflammation, where pain results in adaptive behaviors, such as use limitation, guarding, rest, and avoidance, which contribute to heal-ing. Neuropathic pain persists without real or potential benefit, resulting only in unnecessary suffering.

Somatic versus neuropathic pain

Somatic pain

As a first step toward understanding neuropathic pain it is important to recognize the fundamental difference between somatic and neuropathic pain. Somatic pain always results from stimulation of nociceptors, owing to tissue injury. Nociceptors are the sensory receptors specialized for detecting noxious thermal, mechanical, or chemical stimuli resulting from tissue injury. The neuroimmune interactions following tissue injury result in nociceptor sensitization such that the threshold for activation is reduced and the magnitude of response is increased. Thus, light touch in an area of inflammation or warm water in contact with burned skin or mucosa becomes painful, not because the physical energy itself is noxious but because the nervous system response is heightened. Primary hyperalgesia is the term used to describe the increased perception of a painful stimulus following receptor sensitization; it is a hallmark of somatic pain. Allodynia refers to the perception of pain in response to a non-noxious stimulus; this too is often present during primary hyperalgesia. Most somatic pains end when the underlying tissue injury and inflammation resolves.

Neuropathic pain

Neuropathic pain is fundamentally different from somatic pain in that nociceptor stimulation is not necessary. Whereas tissue and nerve injury may initiate processes that lead to pain, neuropathic pain persists once the initial injury heals. Herein lies the diagnostic challenge, since in most cases of neuropathic pain there is no evidence of ongoing tissue injury or inflammation to "substantiate" the pain, often leading to treatments directed at disease that does not exist (ie, endodontic therapy without pulpal injury, tooth extraction without odontogenic disease). Allodynia and mechanical hyperalgesia are common features of neuropathic pain: the patient experiences increased pain to noxious stimuli as well as pain to non-noxious stimulation. Two general types of neuropathic pain exist: paroxysmal pain and continuous pain. Paroxysmal pain refers to sudden, brief (seconds to minutes) but intense pain, which may be spontaneous or provoked by light touch or movement in the affected area. Continuous neuropathic pain has a constant burning or stinging quality that may have periods of greater or lesser intensity. Unlike somatic pain, paroxysmal neuropathic pain is characterized by pain-free intervals and, therefore, does not exhibit the same reliable provocation of pain upon stimulation. Furthermore, neuropathic pain does not necessarily occur in the area that evokes the pain when stimulated; that is, there can be referral of the pain sensation to areas outside the stimulation zone.

A final note regarding the origins of sensation and perception is required before discussing specific neuropathic pain illnesses. Certainly, the vast majority of sensory perceptions are evoked by and accurately represent the actual physical stimulus delivered. However, one must realize that all perception is a product of neural activity in the central nervous system (CNS). Although most times the evoked CNS neural activity appropriately encodes a physical stimulus, it is certainly the case that CNS activity in the absence of an externally applied physical stimulus can lead to a sensory experience. It is well known that electrical stimulation of the CNS can produce vivid sensory perceptions in the absence of peripheral stimulation. Pathologic processes that result in inappropriate CNS activity can produce sensory perceptions that have no physical correlate, yet they can be as real and valid as the sensory perception evoked by a physical stimulus.

A dramatic illustration of the neurogenous origin of perception is the common experience of phantom sensations and pains that follow amputation, where there no longer exists a peripheral substrate (ie, arm, leg) for experiencing the sensation. Bear in mind that the most common amputation performed is pulp extirpation and tooth extraction, both of which can result in neuropathic phantom sensation and pain in a denervated or missing tooth. The unorthodox yet undeniable fact remains that one does not need to have a body part to experience a sensation or pain from the corresponding region, and there exist neural processes that can initiate and sustain a real perception in the absence of a physical stimulus. Thus, the practitioner must accept what the patient says he or she is feeling as a real sensory experience with a physiologic, albeit not necessarily physical basis. Treating the neuropathic pain condition as though the pain originates in the structures where the pain is perceived fails to recognize the neurogenous nature of neuropathic pain and often leads to inappropriate and ineffective treatment. Instead, successful treatment is that which focuses on eliminating or controlling abnormal neural activity.

Orofacial neuralgias

Trigeminal neuralgia

Clinical features
Trigeminal neuralgia is an excruciating, debilitating orofacial pain illness largely recognized as one of the most painful human conditions. It is also known by the name *tic douloureux* owing to the facial expression or wince that often accompanies the painful episode. Trigeminal neuralgia is a rare disorder, with an overall incidence of 3 to 5 persons per 100,000 (and an increased risk in the elderly where incidence rises two- to threefold to 6 to 12 persons per 100,000). Although rare, trigeminal neuralgia assumes a place of prominence in dental medicine because many patients with trigeminal neuralgia believe the pain may be tooth-related and seek inital care from the dentist. The pain is described as stabbing, shooting, electric shock-like pain lasting seconds to minutes. Most times the patient is aware of the trigger for pain, such as light touch to an intra- or extraoral region, or facial or tongue movement. Thus, trigeminal neuralgia is the quintessential neuropathic pain, characterized by profound allodynia. The pain often radiates to areas outside the trigger zone. The frequency is variable, from several episodes daily to every few months; in rare and progressive cases the pain may become continuous. The pain is almost always unilateral and occurs nearly equally in the maxillary and mandibular trigeminal divisions, less commonly, in the

ophthalmic division. Trigeminal neuralgia occurs nearly equally among males and females, though some reports have found slightly higher rates among females.

Trigeminal neuralgia may be primary or secondary. Secondary trigeminal neuralgia occurs because of some identified abnormality, such as an intra- or extracranial tumor or other space-occupying lesion, multiple sclerosis (MS), or trauma. Primary trigeminal neuralgia occurs in the absence of an identified cause; most cases of trigeminal neuralgia are primary. Primary trigeminal neuralgia usually occurs in individuals over 50 years of age, whereas secondary trigeminal neuralgia usually occurs in younger individuals. Thus, the suspicion for an underlying illness, such as tumor or multiple sclerosis, is increased in younger patients with trigeminal neuralgia, and their evaluation must include computerized tomography (CT) or magnetic resonance imaging (MRI) of the head and brain to identify related pathology.

Etiology

Most cases of trigeminal neuralgia are primary in nature, without an identified underlying cause. Although a universal etiologic theory for trigeminal neuralgia does not exist, there is little disagreement that it is a neuropathic pain disorder resulting from altered sensory processing either in the trigeminal ganglion or the central trigeminal neuraxis. Detection and encoding of the light touch stimulus that provokes the pain is apparently normal at the sensory receptor level, with a loss of modality properties (light touch leading to pain sensation) occurring at or proximal to the trigeminal ganglion. A commonly accepted but not proven etiology is the presence of abnormal vascular anatomy, most commonly the superior cerebellar artery, which presses against the trigeminal root in the posterior cranial fossa. Neurosurgical correction by microvascular decompression has been widely used for correction of the vascular abnormality. Demyelination has often been suggested as the underlying pathology that leads to abnormal electrical excitability and pain, although sound evidence to support this theory is lacking.

Secondary trigeminal neuralgia develops as a result of an underlying disorder, such as intra- or extracranial tumor or other space-occupying lesion, MS, or trauma. Common intracranial tumors that can cause trigeminal neuralgia include pituitary adenoma, meningioma, glioma, and acoustic neuroma. In such cases, the underlying disorder presumably leads to ectopic electrical activity caused by direct pressure or demyelination. It is not clear, however, why the pain is episodic even though the underlying pathology is constant. Approximately 5 to 10% of patients with MS develop trigeminal neuralgia, which may be the initial symptom of undiagnosed MS. Whenever trigeminal neuralgia develops in a younger individual, the suspicion for underlying disease

should be increased and appropriate diagnostic imaging tests should be ordered.

Diagnosis

Trigeminal neuralgia is a clinical diagnosis based almost exclusively on the history and physical examination; imaging studies may further identify underlying disorders. Paroxysmal unilateral pain described as sharp, stabbing, or electric-like with pain-free intervals and an identified trigger are the essential features. The possibility for local somatic disease (ie, odontogenic) should be carefully evaluated, though odontogenic somatic pain is unlikely to be characterized by intermittent episodes of pain. A complete cranial nerve examination should be performed, and suspicion for trigeminal neuralgia secondary to tumor, vascular abnormality, or MS should be increased when there are other abnormalities on the neurologic examination. Because the condition is intermittent and paroxysmal, the physical examination is typically completely normal. Trigeminal sensory thresholds are generally normal and symmetric, except during a pain episode when there exists profound allodynia. There are generally no signs of somatic or inflammatory injury. Diagnostic imaging (CT or MRI) when multiple sclerosis is suspected should be performed for all patients with trigeminal neuralgia, and especially those who develop symptoms before 50 years of age.

Do not treat what has not been diagnosed. Adherence to this simple principle avoids the unfortunate but not uncommon experience of many patients with trigeminal neuralgia who receive inappropriate treatment directed toward an odontogenic source that does not exist. Although certainly there are some instances in which it is difficult to exclude the possible contribution of coexisting dental disease, bear in mind the fundamental differences between odontogenic (somatic) and neuropathic pain. If the pain is believed to be caused by an odontogenic disease, then generally speaking the pain will be more constant in nature, respond faithfully to provocation by mechanical or thermal stimulation, and be localized to the region of presumed pathology. If the pain is caused by trigeminal neuralgia, virtually none of those features of somatic pain will exist, rather the pain will be intermittent, paroxysmal, and outside the trigger or provocation zone.

Treatment

Several medical and surgical modalities of treatment exist for trigeminal neuralgia; all therapies are directed toward reducing nerve excitability. Medical therapy is the preferred initial treatment for those who can tolerate the medications. Membrane-stabilizing medications, such as carbamazepine, gabapentin, valproic acid, phenytoin, and baclofen are commonly used alone or in combination. These medications all act to reduce nerve excitability by modulating conductance of ions across the excitable nerve membrane. Medications should be prescribed only by those clinicians experienced with their use, since all have side effects and adverse reactions, and some require hematologic monitoring. Medical treatment provides complete or acceptable levels of relief for approximately 75 to 80% of patients. Some patients enjoy complete remission, and a minority may become unresponsive after prolonged medical therapy. Surgical therapies exist for those patients who cannot tolerate, become refractory to, or do not respond initially to medical therapy.

An invaluable class of medications for the treatment of neuropathic pain in general are the tricyclic and heterocyclic antidepressant drugs, most notably amitriptyline and nortriptyline. These drugs are used alone or in combination with membrane-stabilizer medications, but at doses far below those used to treat clinical depression or other mood disorders. Although their exact mechanism of action for providing relief of neuropathic pain is not known, it appears that their modulation of norepinephrine neurotransmission at segmental (spinal cord and brain stem) as well as supraspinal levels reduces neuronal excitability and pain perception. It is clear that these drugs used in the dose range for neuropathic pain are not treating a clinical depression or other primary mood disorder.

Minimally invasive treatments for trigeminal neuralgia include percutaneous glycerol or alcohol injection or radiofrequency neurolysis directed toward the affected trigeminal division. These neuroablative procedures are performed by the anesthesiologist or neurosurgeon under fluoroscopic imaging for guidance and generally aim to inactivate, for varying periods of time sensory signals from the trigger zone; a common side effect is variable levels of anesthesia in the territory supplied by the treated nerve. Most recently, preliminary results using minimally invasive stereotactic gamma radiation ("gamma knife") have demonstrated excellent relief. The percutaneous and stereotactic radiosurgery techniques provide relief for about 75% of patients, especially those who have failed medical therapy; these procedures may need to be repeated months to years later if symptoms recur. Finally, microvascular decompression is a cranial neurosurgical procedure to reposition an aberrant blood vessel, usually the anterior superior cerebellar artery. As a neurosurgical procedure, it has the risks of hearing loss, corneal anesthesia, cerebral embolism, and facial nerve injury, among others. However, for patients who have failed other forms of treatment, it also offers an approximately 75% success rate. Trigeminal neuralgia secondary to intra- or extracranial tumor or attributable to MS is treated by addressing the underlying disorder. However, many patients require the additional use of membrane-stabilizing medications or tricyclic or heterocyclic medications.

Glossopharyngeal neuralgia

Clinical features
Glossopharyngeal neuralgia is a neuropathic pain that shares many of the features of trigeminal neuralgia, with a few notable exceptions. The pain location is in the distribution of the glossopharyngeal nerve, specifically the posterior tongue and lateral oropharynx. The pain is less intense than that of trigeminal neuralgia, though still paroxysmal and episodic in nature, and is provoked by swallowing or contact with the mucosa overlying the region innervated by the glossopharyngeal nerve. Glossopharyngeal neuralgia is a rare disorder, affecting approximately 0.5 to 1 person per 100,000.

Etiology
Glossopharyngeal neuralgia, more so than trigeminal neuralgia, lacks a unifying etiologic theory. Most recognize underlying disease processes similar to those proposed for trigeminal neuralgia, namely tumors and vascular abnormalities that result in nerve compression and ectopic nerve impulses, demyelination, and trauma.

Diagnosis
The diagnosis of glossopharyngeal neuralgia, much the same as for trigeminal neuralgia, is a clinical diagnosis based on the history and examination. The possibility for an odontogenic source is less likely, owing to the anatomic region involved. A complete cranial nerve examination is essential for detecting other abnormalities that might support an underlying illness, such as MS or a tumor. Computed tomography and MRI are appropriately prescribed to detect related intra- or extracranial disease.

Treatment
Glossopharyngeal neuralgia is responsive to the same medical therapies used to treat trigeminal neuralgia. Minimally invasive and cranial neurosurgical procedures are seldom used owing to more limited accessibility to the glossopharyngeal nerve. As in trigeminal neuralgia, glossopharyngeal neuralgia secondary to intra- or extracranial tumor or attributable to MS is treated by addressing the underlying disorder. However, many patients require the additional use of membrane-stabilizing medications or tricyclic or heterocyclic medications.

Postherpetic neuralgia

Clinical features
Unlike trigeminal and glossopharyngeal neuralgia, postherpetic neuralgia (PHN) is not a paroxysmal neuropathic pain, rather it is a continuous burning or stinging neuropathic pain that persists for more than 3 months in the distribution of a previous outbreak of herpes zoster,

or shingles. Postherpetic neuralgia shares with other neuropathic pains the features of hyperalgesia and allodynia. Except in the rare case of herpes sine zoster, or zoster reactivation without associated lesions, the vast majority of patients report an antecedent episode of shingles. Since herpes zoster, like other human herpes viruses, is a neurotropic DNA virus, it remains dormant in the DNA of primary sensory ganglia following primary infection by varicella zoster (chicken pox). Subsequent viral reactivation is associated with a painful vesiculoulcerative rash on the skin or mucosa, corresponding to the sensory dermatome of the involved nerve. The condition is usually unilateral, though it may disseminate by the blood in immunocompromised hosts. Only about 20% of shingles cases affect the trigeminal nerve, involving both intra- and extraoral dermatomes; approximately 80% of cases affect the spinal nerves.

Most cases of herpes zoster affect individuals over 60 years of age, with an estimated prevalence as high as 24% in that age group. The estimated prevalence of PHN following herpes zoster among patients over 60 years of age is between 15% and 40%, an approximately 15- to 25-fold increased risk compared to patients younger than 30 years. Thus, the risk for, and need to prevent PHN increases significantly with age. Postherpetic neuralgia is more common among females.

Etiology

Following viral reactivation, the herpes zoster virus is transported through the neuronal axoplasm to the peripheral afferent terminals, where its release initiates an intense inflammatory response resulting in the clinical lesion of shingles. During the approximately 2-day period it takes for the virus to travel the distance of the trigeminal nerve, there is an intense neuritis that may be associated with a tingling or burning prodrome before lesions develop. Several reports have demonstrated neuronal degeneration of affected primary afferents in the spinal cord, resulting in a loss of primary fibers as well as degeneration of local and second-order neurons. These degenerative changes are believed to play a major role in the establishment of PHN that persists as a neuropathic pain long after the zoster lesions have healed.

Diagnosis

Postherpetic neuralgia is generally a clinical diagnosis based on the history and examination, which reveal antecedent zoster with burning, hyperalgesia, and allodynia in the affected dermatome. Since no virus exists in the painful region after the zoster lesions have healed, there is little benefit to viral culture or evaluation of serum antibody titers to herpes zoster.

Treatment

Since PHN occurs most commonly in patients over 60 years of age, this age group should receive the most aggressive treatment at the earliest opportunity. Treatment outcome is dramatically improved with early treatment: the risk for developing permanent PHN doubles when pain persists for more than 6 months. Any patient over 60 years of age who develops shingles should be treated with both antiviral medication (acyclovir, famciclovir) and a tricyclic antidepressant (amitriptyline, nortriptyline) to reduce the risk for PHN since preemptive treatment with a tricyclic antidepressant reduces by 50% the risk of developing PHN. Unfortunately, the dentist rarely has the opportunity to contribute to preemptive treatment, since patients most often seek care from their physician for shingles. Nonetheless, tricyclic antidepressant medications should be prescribed as soon as possible during the course of PHN. Corticosteroid medications have also been prescribed during the acute phase of zoster to reduce neuritis, though its efficacy in preventing PHN has been inconclusive.

Capsaicin cream (0.025% and 0.075%) has been shown to be an effective topical medication for the relief of PHN when applied to the painful region. Application 2 to 3 times daily of capsaicin depletes substance P, a neuropeptide contained in nociceptive C-fibers that contributes to neurogenic inflammation and pain. Initial application of capsaicin may result in a burning sensation, but this is diminished after repeated use during the first 48 to 72 hours.

Nerve injury and neuroma pain

Clinical features

Nerve injury associated with tissue injury results in a complex series of bidirectional events between the nervous and immune system. Whereas this response is intended to promote healing, it may also result in pathologic events that lead to persistent neuropathic pain. These events may include functional changes in CNS and peripheral sensory processing (neuroplasticity) as well as neuroma formation. A neuroma is an incomplete or failed attempt at nerve repair following injury to a peripheral nerve, resulting in a disorganized nerve fiber that is focally electrically excitable. The pathologic sensitization of the injured peripheral nerve or CNS results in both peripheral and CNS hyperexcitability, which are manifest as focal allodynia and mechanical hyperalgesia at the site of injury.

What sets nerve injury and neuroma pain apart from the neuralgias is the provocation of pain upon stimulation of a discrete region innervated by the injured nerve. Whereas the neuralgias demonstrate episodic pain, pain-free intervals, and periods of normal stimulus-response function between attacks, neuroma and nerve injury pain most often result in constant allodynia and mechanical hyperalgesia in a discrete zone supplied by the injured nerve. Rarely is there a palpable or otherwise detectable mass corresponding to the location of a neuroma. Neuroma pain is usually bright, sharp, and well localized but may also result in radiating pain sensations as well as continuous burning pain that spreads beyond the immediate injured region.

Etiology

Although knowledge of the full spectrum of events that can occur following nerve injury continues to expand at a rapid pace, several relevant events are known at this time. Within moments of tissue and nerve injury, a complex series of neuroimmune events occur that can: (1) sensitize the injured nerve, (2) lead to neurogenic inflammation and promote further leakage of proinflammatory mediators from the injured blood vessels, (3) contribute to neuroproliferative events that may contribute to neuroma formation, and (4) result in functional and phenotypic changes in primary and second-order neurons such that these neurons change their future excitability and responsiveness. Together, the pathologic events may result in CNS neuroplasticity and hyperexcitability that sustain a neuropathic pain condition. It is not clear why literally millions of patients undergo millions of invasive procedures every day yet only a small portion develop postprocedure neuropathic pain. Certainly, there are multiple factors that come to bear, none of which are sufficiently well understood to develop a working theory. It is interesting to note that there exist engineered strains of mice that predictably respond to nerve injury by developing painful neuromas. Thus, a genetic factor may contribute as the risk factor.

Diagnosis

Nerve injury and neuroma pain most often are associated with an identifiable antecedent injury. However, the nature and extent of that injury can vary. Although a rare event, even minor trauma from periodontal scaling, pulp extirpation, and minor incision can potentially lead to neuropathic pain. There must be a careful search for focal mechanical hyperalgesia and allodynia; this can be difficult and be associated with an area as small as 2 mm^2. Identification of a reliably sensitive focal area is highly suggestive of a neuroma. A small amount of local anesthesia applied to the painful focus eliminates the pain and further supports the essentially peripheral nature of the problem. However, persistence of pain after local anesthesia does not exclude the existence of a neuroma, but may indicate the coexistence of pathologic neuroplastic changes in the CNS that contribute to the pain experience.

Treatment

When the injury involves a large-caliber nerve (inferior alveolar, lingual) and the precise location of the presumed neuroma can be reasonably well determined, microsurgical repair is an option. However, such localization and involvement of a larger nerve is uncommon, making surgical repair a less effective treatment alternative. Furthermore, nerve injury and neuroma pain that persists for a long time (more than 6 mo) is less amenable to a favorable surgical outcome. Locally applied capsaicin cream can be an effective treatment for focal nerve injury pain. Use of capsaicin intraorally may require fabrication of a stent that can keep the cream in contact with the mucosal surface and minimize leakage throughout the mouth. The cream should be massaged into the painful area three times daily, then covered with a stent when possible for approximately 20 minutes. Although there exist several reports of repeated local anesthetic injection with or without corticosteroid (which has been shown to reduce neuroma excitability), definitive long-term data are lacking. Likewise, several topical formulations of membrane-stabilizer and N-methyl-D-aspartate (NMDA) antagonists have been reported in isolated cases and small case series, again without definitive long-term data. The use of tricyclic antidepressant medications as neuropathic analgesics often provides additional relief.

Phantom tooth deafferentation pain

Clinical features

Phantom tooth pain (PTP) is a condition of persistent pain in the teeth, face, or alveolar process that follows pulp extirpation, apicoectomy, or tooth extraction. Several reports have demonstrated that approximately 3 to 4% of patients undergoing endodontic therapy have persistent, unexplained pain or unpleasant sensations in the treated tooth. The term phantom tooth pain was first coined in 1978, though the condition has been recognized by different terms for many decades. The patient with PTP is the one most likely to have undergone multiple conventional and surgical endodontic treatments as well as tooth extractions in a continued attempt to relieve the phantom pain. This also is the patient most likely to be labeled by the clinician as having a psychogenic pain. Recognizing the condition as a neuropathic pain rather than a somatic or psychogenic pain should immediately prevent such treatment, since somatic pain would not move from one tooth to the next or persist after the nerve has been amputated. Patients with PTP are often diagnosed incorrectly with atypical facial pain (see Chapter 33).

The patient with PTP usually describes a constant dull, deep, aching pain with occasional spontaneous sharp pain; there is no refractory period. The pain is experienced in a tooth that is denervated by root canal therapy or has been extracted. The phantom sensation is in the missing tooth itself, rather than in the edentulous alveolar ridge, which is more accurately described as an intraoral stump pain. The patient may also experience perverted sensations of tooth size, shape, or location. As treatment is directed toward the "symptomatic" tooth, the symptoms often spread or move to adjacent teeth; subsequent treatment of adjacent teeth results in the same pattern of phantom migration. The reader is advised to recall the discussion of neuropathic pain and the origins of perception, distinct from sensation, in the introductory sections of this chapter.

Etiology

The etiology of phantom pain in general and certainly phantom tooth pain in particular is not known. However, many of the features of phantom tooth pain parallel the experiences of limb amputees. Phantom pain in general is a well recognized though poorly understood phenomenon that affects 80% of limb amputees during the immediate postoperative and healing period and remains permanently to some lesser degree for the majority of patients. Several theories exist that only partly explain some of the phantom pain phenomena, but no unifying theory exists that describes all features. These theories focus on pathologic neuroplasticity in the CNS as a result of intense nociceptive afferent activity and neural injury following amputation. The sympathetic nervous system is believed to play a role in several features of phantom pain (see Chapter 33).

Pulp amputation, more than tooth extraction, has been shown to result in peripheral neuropathology (neuroma formation) as well as CNS neuropathology (degeneration of local and projection neurons in the CNS). Ample experimental evidence exists to demonstrate that the sensory map of the periphery can be immediately and permanently altered following tissue and nerve injury. This central neuroplasticity is the physiologic substrate by which one can understand how sensations and pain can "move" or spread from one area to another. Consider the common experience of the genuine perception of a swollen lip following anterior maxillary anesthesia. While the perception of a swollen lip is very real, certainly the lip is not swollen; that is, there is no physical correlate of swelling. However, the local anesthetic immediately altered the relative amount of neural activity and led instantly to a change in perception of body size and shape. In the same way, nerve injury can lead to altered nerve activity that results in phantom pain and dysmorphic perceptions that have a very real physiologic, though not physical, basis.

Perhaps the most provocative theory to explain phantom pain sensations is Melzack's neuromatrix theory. This theory proposes a genetically determined but experience-dependent neurosignature, a person's representation of self somewhere in the brain, which once established, exists to some degree independent of the continued existence of various body parts. This neurosignature can be accessed to contribute to awareness of body size and shape by any number of neural processes, including those that are independent of any peripheral input. Thus, injury to the nervous system by removal of a body part does not eliminate awareness of that body part, rather it changes whatever neurophysiologic dynamics maintained that awareness in some healthy and accurate form. The undeniable perception of altered body size or shape, or pain from a body part that does not exist, therefore, becomes a product of altered CNS activity and how that activity relates to the neurosignature of an individual. Considerable psychophysical and physiologic experimentation is currently underway to explore this theory in more detail. There is little doubt that psychological factors contribute to phantom sensations, but little evidence to suggest that the phantom is a result of psychological illness.

Diagnosis

Phantom pain, although likely initiated by peripheral injurious events (amputation), is certainly predominantly maintained by CNS processes. The diagnosis of PTP is a clinical diagnosis based on the history and examination. The patient with PTP complains of persistent deep, dull, aching pain in a denervated tooth or at the site of an extracted tooth; not uncommonly the patient may have difficulty identifying the precise tooth that is painful. There may be occasional periods of sharp pain. The phantom may emerge days, weeks, months, and even years after the initial injury, making identification of the antecedent injury potentially difficult. There are no associated radiographic abnormalities, and pain is not worsened by mechanical or thermal stimulation. The possibility for local odontogenic pain should be considered and careful examination performed to be sure no somatic source of pain exists (fractured tooth, failed root canal therapy). However, the clinician must be cautious not to assume an odontogenic source when there is no evidence to support the diagnosis, and should not initiate treatment based on that assumption. Although potentially frustrating to both patient and doctor, initiating inappropriate treatment based on an unsupported diagnosis will not improve the condition and is more likely to worsen it. As difficult as it may be, offering no treatment is preferable to inappropriate treatment.

Treatment

Treatment of PTP is challenging and generally is based on local (injection) and oral medications, always combined with cognitive therapy and psychological counseling. The patient must be reassured that the pain is not imagined and does not represent an undiagnosed serious disorder (ie, cancer). The patient must be educated about the nature of the problem so he or she comprehends how the nervous system itself can lead to such painful perceptions.

Medical therapy includes the use of neuropathic pain analgesics, such as tricyclic antidepressant medications (amitriptyline, nortriptyline) and GABA agonists, such as baclofen and clonazepam. Some patients require fixed daily doses of oral narcotic, though this should only be pursued by clinicians familiar with the addictive and medical complications of chronic narcotic use. A trial of the anticonvulsant carbamazepine may be appropriate if other treatment fails. Although it is unlikely to relieve PTP, if the patient does experience relief, one should consider the possibility that the patient suffers from trigeminal neuralgia. A relatively new anticonvulsant medication, gabapentin, may provide relief for PTP, as it has been found to be effective in other neuropathic deafferentation pain disorders, though no study has examined its use in PTP.

Some authorities recommend the use of repeated injection with long-acting local anesthetic (without epinephrine) combined with low-dose corticosteroid (dexamethasone); both have been shown to reduce neuronal excitability at sites of nerve injury. The success of injection therapy depends on selection of the correct site for injection. A careful history and examination are essential to precisely identify the location of the phantom pain or pains. In addition to sites at the teeth, others are at the terminal points of the trigeminal divisions (ie, supraorbital, infraorbital, nasolabial, mental). Efficacy of repeated injection for PTP awaits well-designed, prospective clinical trial.

Sympathetically maintained pain

Clinical features
The role of the sympathetic nervous system in the initiation or maintenance of chronic neuropathic pain has been a topic of considerable debate and some confusion; its role in orofacial neuropathic pain is understood even less. Adding to the confusion, it has been known by other terms, such as causalgia and reflex sympathetic dystrophy. Sympathetically maintained pain (SMP) may be an independent pain disorder, or a contributing pathologic process to other orofacial neuropathic pain, most notably nerve injury and phantom tooth pain. When SMP is a major component of a neuropathic pain, the features include constant aching and burning pain with periods of exacerbation. The pain may at times be accompanied by other signs of sympathetic dysregulation in the affected region, such as altered local skin temperature, excessive sweating, and trophic changes, although none of these signs is essential in SMP. In all cases where SMP is

involved, there is a history of prior injury. The pain is worsened during periods of physiologic or psychological stress and often following injection of a solution containing epinephrine into the painful region.

Etiology
Although a single unifying, accepted theory for SMP does not exist, several well-developed models provide a theoretic basis for the disorder. In general, it is proposed that following injury, sympathetic-sensory coupling occurs in which nociceptors upregulate α-adrenergic receptors and respond to norepinephrine released from sympathetic terminals in the injured region. The sympathetically generated nociceptor activity produces a dynamically maintained state of CNS sensitization and hyperexcitability such that activity in low-threshold mechanoreceptors, which normally is not painful, results in allodynia and mechanical hyperalgesia. Regional sympathetic blockade interrupts the sympathetic-sensory coupling and resets the CNS neurons to a desensitized state, relieving spontaneous pain and allodynia. Injection of epinephrine into the affected region worsens or rekindles the pain.

Diagnosis
The features of SMP are not unique to the condition and are seen in other nonparoxysmal neuropathic pain conditions: constant burning, aching, or cramping pain, allodynia, and hyperalgesia. However, by definition SMP is abolished when sympathetic activity to the affected region is blocked. Thus, the diagnostic test for SMP requires sympathetic blockade by one of two means: local anesthetic blockade of the stellate ganglion (performed by an anesthesiologist) or intravenous administration of phentolamine, an α-adrenergic antagonist. Contrary to early suggestion that signs of autonomic dysfunction must be present for a diagnosis of SMP, it is now recognized that such signs are not required. That is, the signs of sympathetic dysregulation (altered local skin temperature, excessive sweating, and trophic changes) are dissociated from the pain condition. If sympathetic blockade is achieved yet there is no reduction in pain, then the condition is a sympathetically independent pain (SIP).

Treatment
Treatment of SMP requires chronic blockade of sympathetic activity in the affected region. This is achieved by repeat stellate ganglion blockade or sympathectomy. Several reports describe the use of clonidine, available in a slow-release patch, for SMP. Clonidine is an agonist for the presynaptic adrenergic autoreceptor, which then reduces the presynaptic release of norepinephrine. Sympathetic blockade can result in postural hypotension and bradycardia.

Suggested reading

Bonezzi C, Demartini L. Treatment options in postherpetic neuralgia. Acta Neurol Scand Suppl 1999;173:25–35.

Bowsher D. The effects of preemptive treatment of postherpetic neuralgia with amitriptyline: a randomized, double-blind, placebo-controlled trial. J Pain Symptom Manage 1997;13:327–31.

Byers MR, Narhi MV. Dental injury models: experimental tools for understanding neuroinflammatory interactions and polymodal nociceptor functions. Crit Rev Oral Biol Med 1999;10:4–39.

Degreef H, Famciclovir Herpes Zoster Clinical Study Group. Famciclovir, a new oral antiherpes drug: results of the first controlled clinical study demonstrating its efficacy and safety in the treatment of uncomplicated herpes zoster in immunocompetent patients. Int J Antimicrobial Agents 1994;4:241–6.

Fudin J, Audette CM. Gabapentin vs. amitriptyline for the treatment of peripheral neuropathy. Arch Intern Med 2000;160:1040–1.

McLaughlin MR, Jannetta PJ, Clyde BL, et al. Microvascular decompression of cranial nerves: lessons learned after 4400 operations. J Neurosurg 1999;90:1–8.

Millard HD, Mason D. Third World Workshop on Oral Medicine. Ann Arbor Michigan: University of Michigan Continuing Dental Education School of Dentistry, 2000.

Ochoa JL. Truths, errors, and lies around "reflex sympathetic dystrophy" and "complex regional pain syndrome." J Neurol 1999;246:875–9.

Sindrup SH, Jensen TS. Efficacy of pharmacological treatments of neuropathic pain: an update and effect related to mechanism of drug action. Pain 1999;83:389–400.

Woolf CJ, Mannion RJ. Neuropathic pain: etiology, symptoms, mechanisms, and management. Lancet 1999;353:1959–64.

Zakrzewsk JM, Sawsan J, Bulman JS. A prospective, longitudinal study on patients with trigeminal neuralgia who underwent radiofrequency thermocoagulation of the gasserian ganglion. Pain 1999;79:51–8.

33 Atypical Facial Pain

Bruce Blasberg, DMD, FRCD(C)

Atypical facial pain (AFP) is not as common as other diseases associated with facial pain, such as temporomandibular disorders (TMD). Its importance though is emphasized by its chronic nature, resistance to treatment, and the devastating effects it has on patients suffering from this condition. Patients with AFP often consult numerous dentists and physicians seeking an explanation and effective treatment. Their use of medical and dental services is excessive, costly, and usually unsatisfactory. A history of multiple ineffective treatments is common. Surgical treatments are often performed, including tooth extractions, endodontic procedures, exploratory surgery, sinus surgery, and temporomandibular joint (TMJ) surgery, that have no effect on the pain and often complicate the problem.

The lack of a definite etiology and positive diagnostic criteria has led some authors to recommend against using the term. This is in part a reaction to the historic association between AFP and psychological disorders. Behavioral and psychological abnormalities are often present in AFP but are likely to be a consequence of chronic pain. Behavioral and psychological abnormalities are part of chronic pain disorders regardless of the original source or site of pain. Even though AFP has yet to be explained, clinicians still apply the term to a group of patients who defy other diagnostic criteria and who share some common features. This chapter outlines the clinical features of AFP.

Etiology

Numerous theories have been proposed for the etiology of AFP, but a definite etiology has not emerged. The term was first used to describe patients with chronic facial pain who did not respond to neurosurgical procedures aimed at interrupting pain pathways in the peripheral and central nervous system (CNS). When surgical lesionmaking of somatic afferent nerve fibers and tracts was not effective, surgical procedures on the sympathetic nervous system pathways were performed and also failed. The model of pain as a sensation generated by a peripheral stimulus and relayed to the brain, and the lack of predictable effects of sectioning nerves suggested that a psychological abnormality was the likely cause. The absence of a local orofacial abnormality or ongoing injury supported this assumption. Variants of AFP, burning mouth syndrome and atypical odontalgia, have emerged as distinct conditions and are addressed in Chapters 32 and 34.

A specific psychological or behavioral disorder has not been consistently identified with AFP. Depression has been considered as the cause, but it is well established that psychological problems occur as a result of chronic pain, and depression is one of the most common consequences. Behavioral and psychological changes often dominate the clinical picture of AFP, but their role as cause or effect is not clear.

The role of peripheral trauma leading to chronic neuropathic pain has been a research focus in the recent literature. A significant percentage of patients with AFP ascribe the onset of pain to dental procedures that were of a routine nature: scaling, restorative, and endodontic procedures and dental extractions. Neuropathic pain may result from tissue injury that affects peripheral nerves, resulting in CNS changes, causing persistent pain (see Chapter 32).

The absence of a clear explanation for AFP and studies demonstrating the effectiveness of tricycle antidepressant (TCA) medication have been used to support a psychological explanation. The effectiveness of TCAs at doses lower than the antidepressant dose and their effectiveness against AFP in nondepressed patients, support the hypothesis that these drugs have analgesic effects separate from their antidepressant properties.

Chronic pain for any reason causes psychological and behavioral changes. Identifying these abnormalities in a population with AFP may only reflect the changes that have occurred as a consequence of chronic pain. It does not establish that these abnormalities were present prior to the onset of pain and that they are the cause. No one specific psychiatric diagnosis has emerged to be associated with AFP. At present there is no convincing evidence that AFP is a psychiatric disorder, however, the comorbidity of AFP and depression is clear.

Necrotizing intrabony cavitational osteonecrosis (NICO) has been proposed as a cause of AFP. Pathologic jaw bone cavities have been proposed as the cause of not only continuous or nearly continuous facial pain but also intermittent paroxysmal pain disorders. There has not emerged a characteristic clinical presentation nor are there specific imaging techniques that can be used to establish this diagnosis. The diagnosis remains controversial, especially since the treatment is surgical, which could further aggravate chronic pain.

Recently studies on brain activity indicate that pain processing in the CNS is different in patients with AFP than in control subjects. The hypothesis that AFP may be related to abnormal processing of information in the CNS is still speculation.

Classification

Atypical facial pain has been included in some classifications and not others. It remains in the International Disease Classification, 9th Edition, Clinical Modification (IDC-9-CM) in the section "Diseases of the Nervous System and Sense Organs." The term is also included in the International Headache Society's Classification of Headache and Craniofacial Pain. Atypical facial pain was replaced with the descriptor "facial pain not fulfilling criteria in groups 11 and 12." The definition provided is "persistent facial pain that does not have the characteristics of the cranial neuralgias classified and is not associated with physical signs or a demonstrable organic cause." Although the term has been associated with specific etiologies such as depression, and is subject to misinterpretation or misuse, the term still is clinically useful, and no better terminology has emerged. It is often described as a disorder characterized by what it is not rather than by positive diagnostic criteria. The most prominent features often included in classification systems are the presence of continuous or nearly continuous pain, the lack of ongoing stimulus at the site of pain even though there may have been an initiating peripheral

injury, and no physical or diagnostic imaging findings to explain the pain. Atypical facial pain has been used in classifications as a category that includes all chronic facial pain that has not been diagnosed or classified in other categories. This complicates interpreting the literature on AFP, since the populations studied are heterogeneous and often include patients with other diagnoses and causes for the pain.

Clinical features

Descriptive studies primarily from orofacial pain clinics or specialty practices indicate that the majority of patients with AFP who seek treatment are postmenopausal women between 40 and 60 years of age. The ratio of females to males is four or five to one. Published reports are primarily case series studied retrospectively in specialty clinics or by practitioners involved in the diagnosis and treatment of chronic facial pain, and no data are available of the prevalence or incidence of AFP in the general population. Whereas older women present more frequently than any other population, no correlation has yet been established with hormone physiology and AFP.

Pain is continuous or nearly continuous and usually does not have clear associations to events or activities that make it better or worse. Patients often use dramatic descriptions of pain in an attempt to convey the experience: "as if someone had poured gasoline in my mouth and set it on fire." Pain can be unilateral or bilateral or can start on one side and spread to involve the opposite side. There are characteristically no local physical or imaging findings at the site of pain. The physical examination and the results of diagnostic imaging and other special tests and consultations are negative. Local anesthetic testing to attempt to establish a peripheral source of pain is usually equivocal. Local anesthesia may alter the symptoms, but it usually fails to completely eliminate pain. This pain does not tend to prevent sleep nor does it seem to significantly affect chewing ability. Some patients experience contact sensitivity when eating and avoid the involved side or area, but this is not consistent.

Psychosocial problems and disability are part of AFP. Patients are characterized as using medical services excessively, being nonresponsive to treatments, and experiencing psychological problems. Conventional treatments, such as analgesic medication, are usually ineffective. It is also characteristic of this group of patients to frequently undergo surgical procedures that are ineffective in altering the pain. This profile often leads the patient to be seen as a "problem patient." It is not always possible to separate cause and effect with regard to these issues given the information available.

Many of the problems patients with AFP have can be explained on the basis of the difficulties they have had in attempting to obtain a diagnosis and effective treatment. Patients often are referred to a variety of medical and dental specialists and often seek out specialist consultations themselves.

Diagnosis

The application of the AFP diagnosis has narrowed since distinctions have been made for other diagnoses, such as burning mouth syndrome, glossodynia, and atypical odontalgia. These have previously been considered variants of AFP but are now more distinct entities (see Chapter 34). Diagnostic features of AFP have been listed in classifications such as that published by the International Headache Society, but these criteria have not been subjected to studies that establish their validity.

Clinical assessment

The process necessary to establish the diagnosis of AFP is complex, because there are so many possible causes of chronic facial pain. The diagnostic assessment must include investigations required to detect alternative causes before the diagnosis of AFP is established. Because there are no positive criteria that define the diagnosis of AFP, the process is directed toward eliminating other possible causes. A comprehensive assessment to rule out other conditions is critical, which implies that the detail and quality of the diagnostic process must be exhaustive. Full assessment of the physical structures of the head and neck and their functional competence should be preformed. Muscle assessment for both pain and motor quality is needed to rule out TMD and myofascial pain. Neurologic assessment of the cranial nerves should be coupled with CNS functional assessment to rule out degenerative neurologic disorders. Cognitive and memory assessment is important since dementia with CNS dysfunction is known to generate symptoms similar to AFP, either by causing abnormal neurologic sensations or reducing the ability of the patient to distinguish normal sensations from nociceptive input. Care must be taken to rule out referred pain from adjacent structures, such as the sinuses, cervical muscles, and vascular structures of the head and neck. Occasionally, atypical presentations of odontogenic pain can mimic AFP, which necessitates that pulp testing be done on all teeth in the region that could refer pain to the principle site of pain. Questionable teeth should be tested with the electric pulp tester and subjected to hyper-

stimulation with cold and heat. Periodontal sulcus areas should also be carefully examined for the presence of neuropathic periodontal triggers. These often occur around teeth that have encountered prior traumatic injury, such as tooth fracture, fractured restorations, and food impaction into the periodontal sulcus. During examination of the head and neck, careful observation is warranted to detect signs suggestive of autonomically triggered pain. Indicators include increased pain along with other autonomic changes, such as flushing, ischemia, salivation, or sweating with stimulation. Tumors of the base of the tongue and pharyngeal area are known to refer atypical pain sensations to the posterior area of the mandible, so assessment should include those tissues.

Behavioral assessment

Chronic pain may cause behavioral or psychological problems that have to be treated as part of comprehensive management. These abnormalities may be significant in the perpetuation of symptoms and may prevent other treatments from being effective. Most dental schools do not include training in psychological diagnosis, but a dentist should be able to screen the patient to determine the need for a more thorough assessment. In multidisciplinary clinics treating chronic pain, psychological assessment is one part of the comprehensive process. Psychological and behavioral techniques have become an important part of chronic pain management, regardless of the original cause of the problem.

One should inquire about recent stresses at work and at home, changes in mood, or events that are thought to contribute to the problem. A family history of chronic pain disorders or other close relationships with people suffering from chronic pain or illness should be explored. Responses to events that preceded or followed exacerbation of pain and identification of activities that have been modified (increased or decreased) since the pain began may help assess the disability associated with the pain. The presence of chronic pain in other body sites should be explored. Obtaining details about the vegetative signs of depression, disrupted sleep, loss of appetite, and libido may increase the level of suspicion that a depressive disorder is present.

Diagnostic imaging

Imaging of the dental, sinus, and osseous structures of the face and jaws is important in patients with suspected AFP. They often are suspicious that organic pathology is responsible for their pain syndrome and often resist a diagnosis of AFP until it is clear that no structural pathology exists. Imaging, therefore assumes two purposes in these patients. First and foremost, imaging is required to rule out pathology, and second, it is psychologically necessary to reassure the patient that no pathology in deeper structures has been overlooked. Radiographs of the teeth and alveolar structures are essential as are sinus films to make certain that occult sinus disease is not responsible for the symptoms. Since there is some possibility that symptoms are arising from CNS pathology, computed tomography (CT) or magnetic resonance imaging (MRI) of the head and neck may be appropriate, depending upon the presence of other signs or symptoms suggestive of CNS pathology. Occasionally a radioactive bone scan merits consideration. If the patient has had invasive treatment, exploratory or other inflammation producing procedure in the region in question within 6 to 12 months, the scan will show a false-positive response, with the area of surgery showing up brightly on the scan.

Diagnostic local anesthetic testing

Anesthetic testing can be a useful part of the workup of patients thought to have AFP. Topical anesthetics can be applied to the region of pain to rule out atypical presentations of neuropathy or neuralgias that present with active superficial nociceptors in the epithelium and skin. Infiltration anesthesia around the teeth and into soft-tissue structures can isolate local triggers and define the region of pain. Intraligament injection of the teeth can isolate individual teeth and periodontal structures that are triggering symptoms. Divisional anesthetic blocks and regional infiltration anesthesia help to determine the trigeminal division involved and whether more than one division is active. Failure of anesthesia to extinguish painful symptoms suggests that they are being generated from a more proximal point or that they are referred from adjacent tissues or arising from the CNS. In extreme cases, sympathetic and other autonomic nerve blocks are useful.

Consultation

As with most complex physical or neurologic problems, consultation is often advisable during the diagnostic and case planning phase of care. Consultation with dental specialists, such as endodontists, can provide new findings or confirm that no odontogenic pathology is present. Medical consultations usually include primary care physicians or specialists in internal medicine to rule out metabolic disease and consultations with neurologists, otolaryngologists, and behavioral specialists.

Confirming the diagnosis

If after a thorough search for a specific cause none is identified, the diagnosis of AFP can be considered and tentatively applied or used as the working diagnosis. It is necessary to perform reassessments periodically to minimize the risk of missing early local disease that is not initially detectable and to ensure that no other disease is present that changes the diagnosis or requires alternative treatment.

Other orofacial pain disorders may have specific characteristics in the history or physical, imaging, or laboratory findings to differentiate them from AFP. Because AFP has such a variable presentation in terms of pain characteristics, differential diagnosis may be difficult. The most likely disorders confused with AFP include myofascial pain, odontogenic pain, and neuropathies attributable to occult or intracranial pathology or nerve injury, temporal arteritis, and somatoform pain disorder (Table 33–1). These conditions may result in continuous vague pain in which the presenting physical findings may be minimal or not obvious.

Chronic orofacial pain may also be associated with more generalized disorders. Fibromyalgia is a chronic pain disorder associated with muscles, and may present as facial pain. A thorough history and review of systems should detect systemic symptoms that would raise the possibility that the orofacial pain is a manifestation of a systemic disorder.

Treatment

Atypical facial pain has been managed mainly as a chronic pain disorder requiring a multidisciplinary approach. Several studies have demonstrated the effectiveness of tricyclic antidepressants in pain reduction, but no treatment has been found to abolish the pain. Although amitriptyline has been shown to be effective, it may cause dry mouth, dysphoria, increased appetite, and sedation that may limit its value. Amitriptyline also has cardiovascular effects that may make it inappropriate for patients with existing cardiovascular disease.

Cognitive-behavioral therapies, relaxation techniques, pain medications, medications that promote or enhance restorative sleep, physiotherapy, conditioning and stretching programs, occupational therapy, and family counseling are treatments that are usually included in comprehensive management. No one discipline or individual is able to provide the multiple aspects of care that are required for chronic pain management. For this reason health care professionals have organized themselves into interdisciplinary clinics to provide these services.

A dentist has a role in the ongoing management of patients with AFP. The dentist should be the individual

Table 33–1 Differentiating Other Disorders from Atypical Facial Pain

Disorder	Characteristics
Myofascial pain	Tender muscles on palpation
	Altered range of mandibular movement
	Reproduction of the pain by palpation examination of the involved muscle
	Association of pain with masticatory function
Odontogenic pain	Changing pain symptoms to reflect advancing inflammatory disease
	Consistent changes in symptoms associated with thermal stimulation to teeth
	Physical findings on examination (eg, specific tooth abnormalities on diagnostic testing)
	Radiographic findings
Neuropathy	History of injury
	History of altered sensation
	Altered sensory findings on physical examination
	Loss of function
	Symptoms becoming increasingly severe over time
Temporal arteritis	Temporal pain
	Constitutional symptoms of illness
	Findings of swelling and tenderness associated with the temporal artery
	Increased erythrocyte sedimentation rate
	Positive temporal artery biopsy
Somatoform pain disorder	Pain causing significant distress or impairment in social, occupational, or other important functioning
	Psychological factors are judged to have an important role in the onset, severity, exacerbation, or maintenance of the pain
	Pain is not better accounted for by a more specific mood, anxiety, or psychotic disorder

who performs periodic examinations to identify any undetected orofacial disease that may contribute to or explain pain. Often, there is a tendency to perform dental procedures when the patient identifies a tooth or localized site in the mouth as the possible source of pain. Many patients submit to or pursue endodontic therapy, dental extractions, alveolar surgery, and occlusal adjustments when the pain is localized to the dentition or surrounding structures. The dentist should be the individual to determine whether the clinical findings indicate the presence of an odontogenic or periodontal disease that is likely to explain the pain. The dentist should counsel the patient, to prevent unnecessary procedures that may complicate the AFP problem.

Most of the medications used in the treatment of chronic pain have been originally approved for use in other conditions. Anticonvulsants, antidepressants, and antianxiety medications are often used as part of chronic pain management for their analgesic effects. These medications have effects primarily in the CNS. Newer medications, especially anticonvulsants and antidepressants, are being developed with the hope that they will be more effective without as many side effects. Gabapentin, a drug recently approved as an adjunct in treating seizure disorders, is an example. It is also being used for chronic pain disorders, especially neuropathic pain.

There has also been a renewed interest in the use of opioid medications to manage chronic nonmalignant pain. A concern that is often raised as the argument against using these drugs is the possibility of dependence, resulting in increased disability and antisocial behavior. The preliminary research that has been published suggests that dependence and psychosocial dysfunction are not significant problems. These medications may be effective in certain circumstances in chronic nonmalignant pain.

Patients with AFP pursue many alternative or holistic therapies when they do not receive satisfaction from their physicians and dentists. Most patients will have consulted numerous physicians and dentists; five to seven, according to recent studies. The lack of patient's ability to access appropriate care drives them to seek any possible method of treatment. There is little data on the use of these therapies in AFP. Acupuncture has been used, with anecdotal reports of effectiveness.

Presently the most effective method of managing AFP is the multidisciplinary pain clinic model, with the dentist participating as part of the team. The dentist is in a unique position to perform the comprehensive examination of the orofacial region, including diagnostic local anesthetic testing when indicated. Dentists are also skilled at taking and interpreting radiographs of the teeth, periodontium, and jaw bones. The dentist can be the individual who supervises the use of any medications applied directly to the oral mucosa or the construction and fitting of any oral appliances that may be part of treatment. The dentist who has advanced training and skill in managing chronic facial pain may prescribe and manage the medications and coordinate the interdisciplinary treatment.

Conclusion

The cause of AFP remains an enigma. The population seeking treatment is reported to be mainly female between the ages of 40 and 60 years. A significant percentage of patients relate a dental procedure as the initiating event related to the onset of pain, but examination reveals no abnormality. Patients have histories that usually include multiple consultations with dentists and physicians and multiple treatments including surgical procedures, that are ineffective. The diagnostic assessment to establish the diagnosis of AFP is extensive, to rule out alternative explanations. Treatment is best approached using the multidisciplinary pain clinic model that can adequately address the many problems that develop as a result of chronic pain. The dentist's role is to provide the expertise in orofacial examination and to provide and supervise local therapy that is part of comprehensive management.

Suggested reading

Glueck CJ, McMahon RE, Bouquot J, et al. Thrombophilia, hypofibrinolysis, and alveolar osteonecrosis of the jaws. Oral Surg Oral Med Oral Path Oral Radiol Endod 1996; 81:557–66.

Gruber AJ, Hudson JI, Pope HG Jr. The management of treatment-resistant depression in disorders on the interface of psychiatry and medicine. Fibromyalgia, chronic fatigue syndrome, migraine, irritable bowel syndrome, atypical facial pain, and premenstrual dysphoric disorder. Psychiatr Clin North Am 1996;19:351–69.

Merrill RL. Orofacial pain mechanisms and their clinical application. Dent Clin North Am 1997;41:167–88.

Millard H, Mason D, eds. Third World Workshop on Oral Medicine. Ann Arbor: University of Michigan Continuing Dental Education School of Dentistry, 2000.

Rosenberg JM. The effect of gabapentin on neuropathic pain. Clin J Pain 1997;13:251–5.

Truelove EL. The chemotherapeutic management of chronic and persistent orofacial pain. Dent Clin North Am 1994;38:669–88.

Truelove E. Orofacial pain. In: Millard H, Mason D, eds. Second World Workshop on Oral Medicine. Ann Arbor: University of Michigan Continuing Dental Education, 1995:187–266.

Vickers E, Cousins MJ, Walkers S, Chisholm K. Analysis of 50 patients with atypical odontalgia. A preliminary report on pharmacological procedures for diagnosis and treatment. Oral Surg Oral Med Oral Pathol Oral Radiol Endod 1998; 85:24–32.

Woda A, Pionchon P. A unified concept of idiopathic orofacial pain: clinical features. J Orofac Pain 1999;113:172–84.

Zuniga JR, Meyer RA, Gregg JM, et al. The accuracy of clinical neurosensory testing for nerve injury diagnosis. J Oral Maxillofac Surg 1998;56:2–8.

34 Burning Mouth Syndrome

*Miriam Grushka, DDS, PhD, Joel B. Epstein, DMD, MSD, FRCD(C),
and Jill S. Kawalec, PhD*

Burning mouth syndrome (BMS) is currently defined as a condition in which burning pain in the tongue or other oral mucous membranes occurs in association with normal signs and normal laboratory findings. Although there is no clear understanding of pathogenesis of BMS, recent concepts are dramatically affecting the manner in which clinicians conceptualize this disorder and the way in which these patients are managed.

In BMS, pain intensity and other symptoms commonly develop gradually over time, although in some patients, onset is sudden and precipitous. The most common sites of burning are the anterior tongue, anterior hard palate, and lower lip, but the distribution of oral sites affected does not appear to affect the natural history of the disorder or the response to treatment. Burning mouth syndrome may persist for many years.

Although the majority of patients cannot identify an apparent cause of onset, approximately one-third of patients attribute the onset of their symptoms to a previous dental procedure, illness, or a course of antibiotics. Thus, for some patients the possibility exists of neurologic change as an etiologic factor by virtue of viral infection, mechanical damage, or neurotoxic effect of local anesthetics.

Nocturnal pain is not common for most patients with BMS, rather, the pain, usually of moderate to severe intensity, gradually increases throughout the day, reaching maximum intensity by late evening. As a result, it is not uncommon for patients with BMS to report having difficulty falling asleep at night and experiencing interrupted sleep. Reported mood changes, such as irritability and decreased desire to socialize, may be related to altered sleep patterns.

Personality characteristics including depression and anxiety are commonly reported in patients with BMS and may affect the pain report or be secondary to the chronic pain. The significance of the diurnal variation is unknown but may be related to postural changes in blood flow or to central nervous system (CNS) changes during sleep. There is some support for this concept in the literature, which has demonstrated decreased tongue temperature in BMS during the day; nighttime temperature has not been measured.

Most clinical studies suggest that oral burning is frequently accompanied by dry mouth and thirst (despite lack of evidence of decreased salivary flow in most patients); altered taste (dysgeusia); and additional pain complaints, including facial pain and pain at other sites. Taste and pain are both mediated by small-diameter fibers, whereas salivary stimulation is under the control of the parasympathetic and sympathetic nervous system. Interestingly, whereas both oral burning and altered taste are decreased by stimulation with food, rinsing with a local anesthetic elixir usually increases the oral burning pain but decreases the dysgeusia.

Although BMS may persist for many years following onset, partial remissions have been found to occur in approximately two-thirds of patients within 6 to 7 years after onset. No significant differences in age, gender, duration of disease, or distribution of burning sites have been found among individuals who experience partial or full remission compared with those whose burning continues. Recent studies, however, have suggested that responsiveness to treatment in BMS may be enhanced with shorter disease duration. It is not known what effect treatment has in the long-term on the disease process itself. Further, no studies have yet investigated whether earlier intervention or earlier and better pain control also lead to earlier disease remission.

Suggested etiologies

There is a widespread belief that BMS may be the result of specific systemic diseases or nutritional deficiencies, including B vitamins and iron. However, no consistent relation has been found to support this belief. Further, even when abnormal laboratory results are identified, management and correction of these findings usually do not lessen the oral burning and other associated complaints.

The current definition of BMS excludes patients with clinical mucosal conditions. However, a higher incidence of oral soft-tissue lesions, such as gingivitis, periodontitis, ulcerative or erosive lesions, or geographic, fissured, scalloped, or erythematous tongue has been reported in patients with BMS, and the possibility that these conditions may cause irreversible neuropathic changes has not yet been fully explored. Similarly, the possibility that conditions such as Sjögren syndrome, other connective tissue diseases, and diabetes may cause neuropathic changes that result in oral burning also requires consideration.

Burning pain, the main feature in BMS, is also a characteristic feature of some post-traumatic nerve injuries. In contrast to other post-traumatic nerve injuries, alterations in perception to touch, temperature, two-point discrimination, and threshold pain have been noted infrequently in BMS. On the other hand, abnormalities in taste and heat pain tolerance have been noted, and a recent report by Lauritano and colleagues has demonstrated subclinical polyneuropathy in 50% of patients with BMS, involving a loss of function in small-diameter nerve fibers. In this study, polyneuropathy was determined by means of quantitative sensory examination, tongue and face telethermography, and selected tongue biopsy. Qualitative and quantitative differences in some sensory functions of patients with BMS have also been noted, with argon laser stimulation. Other recent studies have identified loss of taste, especially to bitter, in the taste buds subserved by the chorda tympani nerve. Abnormalities in the blink reflex of patients with BMS, associated with disease duration, also suggest a possible generalized pathologic involvement of the nervous system, leading to modification in peripheral or CNS processing in BMS.

Although there is strong evidence from clinical studies to suggest that BMS is most prevalent in postmenopausal women in their mid- to late fifties, some recent epidemiologic data suggest a more equal male to female ratio. If menopause does appear to play a role in BMS, its mechanism remains unclear, since most reports suggest that oral burning is not usually reversible with hormone replacement therapy.

It is also notable that in BMS most studies have not demonstrated a significant decrease in salivary flow rate despite subjective complaints of mouth dryness and thirst. In contrast, significant alterations in salivary pH, buffering capacity, proteins, mucin, and immunoglobulins have been documented. Changes in salivary constituents rather than overall reduction in flow rate appear to be of significance in BMS and suggest involvement of sympathetic or parasympathetic function in BMS in addition to neuropathic injury. The mechanism whereby the autonomic nervous system is involved in BMS has also gone largely unexplored.

Although current evidence clearly indicates a strong psychological component within BMS, there still exists no evidence of a close causal relation between psychogenic factors and burning mouth. Personality characteristics, such as depression and anxiety, which are common to BMS, may be secondary to the pain in accord with the types of personality changes noted in other chronic pain conditions.

Most studies have also not supported chemical irritation or allergic reaction to dental materials as a significant cause of BMS; similarly, there has been little support for galvanic currents as a causative factor. However, mechanical irritation caused by dentures may be a factor in some patients, since errors in denture design and parafunctional habits with associated myofascial pain have been reported in BMS. Whether the parafunction is secondary to pain or is part of the disorder is unknown.

Interestingly, there have recently been case reports of oral burning secondary to the use of angiotensin-converting enzyme (ACE) inhibitors, such as captopril, enalapril, and lisinopril, which has remitted following discontinuation of the medication. Loss of taste sensation has also been reported to occur with use of ACE inhibitors, suggesting an additional link between pain and taste.

Evolving concept of etiology

Continuing research suggests that BMS may represent a peripheral or centrally mediated neuropathic condition with multiple etiologies. In view of the increase in oral burning after a topical anesthetic rinse, it has been suggested that oral burning may be a centrally based neuropathic condition that results in decreased peripheral inhibition of the trigeminal nerve. This is in accord with taste studies that have shown that loss of inhibition between the central projection areas of the chorda tympani and glossopharyngeal taste nerves following peripheral injury to either nerve can result in the production of phantom tastes. Preliminary spatial taste testing in patients with BMS has provided further support for the possibility that for some patients, oral burning may result from the loss of inhibition of nociceptive trigeminal fibers secondary to injury to either the chorda tympani or the glossopharyngeal nerves.

Recent studies have demonstrated a relation between pain, taste, and alterations in the perception of oral dryness. For instance, there have been reports that taste loss, burning pain of the tongue and lips, tingling, and drooling can follow mild nerve injury after local anesthetic block (without extraction) to the inferior alveolar and lingual nerves. Similarly, paresthesias, pain, abnormal tastes, and drooling have been reported to follow damage to the inferior alveolar nerve and lingual nerve during mandibular third molar extraction. Moreover, although a male:female ratio of 30:70 in patients who have suffered injury to the trigeminal nerve during lower third molar extraction has been demonstrated, women and older patients tended to have the most severe complaints.

Management

For many years BMS has been managed with low-dose tricyclic antidepressants (TCA) based on earlier reports of their effectiveness as analgesics in alleviating oral burning in some patients with BMS. Many tricyclics have been used, including amitriptyline, desipramine, nortriptyline, imipramine, and clomipramine, although only amitriptyline has been evaluated in controlled clinical trials. In contrast, controlled trials of trazodone, a selective serotonin reuptake inhibitor (SSRI), have failed to document relief of BMS. There are no data that indicate that other SSRIs are effective in BMS.

Recently, several studies have suggested that various benzodiazepines, including clonazepam, a GABA (gamma-aminobutyric acid) receptor agonist, may be effective for various orofacial pain disorders, including BMS. Clonazepam is thought to have both peripheral and central effects and to bind more to central than to peripheral GABA receptor sites than other benzo-

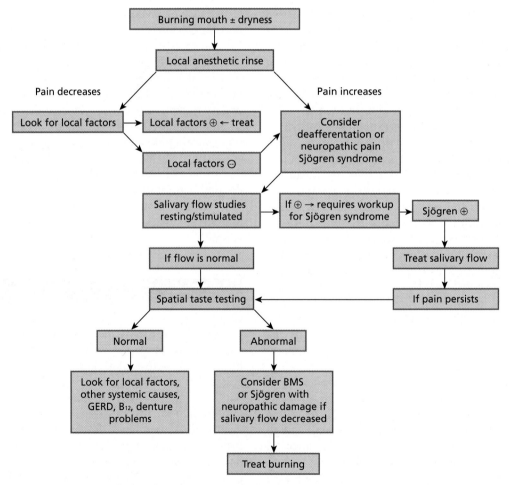

Figure 34–1 Proposed workup for the diagnosis of burning mouth syndrome. GERD = gastroesophageal reflex disease.

diazepines. Notably, the study by Grushka and colleagues showed that clonazepam was effective in relieving taste dysgeusias and oral dryness along with the oral burning.

Other medications and treatments recommended for the symptomatic relief of the burning pain include topical capsaicin; the monoamine oxidase inhibitor tranyl-cypromine sulphate in combination with diazepam, and the systemic anesthetic mexiletine, a use-dependent sodium channel blocker, all of which have been used for other neuropathic pain conditions. However, there are no controlled studies validating the effectiveness of any of these medications.

Workup and hypothetic model

A new approach to the diagnosis of BMS, based on the above review, is outlined in Figure 34–1. Based on the assumption that BMS is a neuropathic pain condition secondary to loss of inhibition of the trigeminal nociceptive fibers, this approach seeks objective evidence of oral dryness, taste disturbance, and effect of topical anesthetic. In contrast to earlier diagnostic paradigms, this diagnostic paradigm is one of inclusion and not exclusion. Hopefully, with this type of modeling, criteria for inclusion, much as for other diseases like Sjögren syndrome, will be developed.

Figure 34–2 presents a hypothetic model of the multifactorial nature of BMS. This includes burning pain as the result of increased excitatory output of the trigeminal nerve either from direct injury to the nerve, leading to increased output, or from decreased inhibition of the trigeminal nerve, leading to increased spontaneous output. Treatment depends on the mechanism of injury and helps direct investigation. This is thought to be the first easily testable model of BMS.

Summary and conclusions

It is currently believed that morphologic alterations in peripheral tissue attributable to injury or disease can cause biochemical and pathophysiologic changes in nociceptive neurons in the CNS. As a result of these changes, ongoing neuronal activity, referral of pain, and response of nociceptive-specific neurons to previously non-noxious stimuli can occur. These types of conditions may occur in BMS as a result of common systemic or local disorders in which nerve damage occurs to either the trigeminal nerve directly or other cranial nerves, which usually inhibit oral nociceptive activity. Hopefully, with further testing, further elucidation of the model will occur and universally accepted criteria for the diagnosis of BMS will be established.

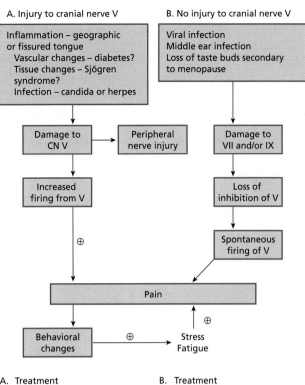

Figure 34–2 Hypothetic model for burning mouth syndrome.

Suggested reading

Bartoshuk LM, Duffy VB, Reed D, Williams A. Supertasting, earaches, and head injury: genetics and pathology alter our taste worlds. Neurosi Biobehav Rev 1996;20:79–87.

Bartoshuk LM, Grushka M, Duffy VB, et al. Burning mouth syndrome: A pain phantom in supertasters who suffer taste damage? (Abstr) Proceedings of the American Pain Society, November 1998, San Diego, California.

Basker RM, Main DMG. The cause and management of burning mouth condition. Spec Care Dentist 1991;11:89–96.

Ben Aryeh H, Gottlieb I, Ish-Shalom S, et al. Oral complaints related to menopause. Maturitas 1996;24:185–9.

Formaker BK, Mott AE, Frank ME. The effects of topical anesthesia on oral burning in burning mouth syndrome. Ann N Y Acad Sci 1998;885:776–801.

Grushka M, Epstein E, Mott A. An open-label, dose escalation pilot study of the effect of clonazepam in burning mouth syndrome. Oral Surg Oral Med Oral Pathol Oral Radiol Endod 1998;86:557–61.

Grushka M, Sessle BJ, Howley TP. Psychophysical assessment of tactile, pain, and thermal sensory functions in burning mouth syndrome. Pain 1987;28:169–84.

Haas DA , Lennon D. A 21-year retrospective study of reports of paresthesia following local anesthetic administration. J Can Dent Assoc 1995;61:319–30.

Jaaskelainen SK, Forssell H, Tenovuo O. Abnormalities of the blink reflex in burning mouth syndrome. Pain 1997;73: 455–60.

Lehman CD, Bartoshuk LM, Catalanotto FC, et al. Effect of anesthesia of the chorda tympani nerve on taste perception in humans. Physiol Behav 1995;57:943–51.

Ship J, Grushka M, Lipton JA, et al. Burning mouth syndrome: an update. J Am Dent Assoc 1995;126:842–53.

Woda A, Navez ML, Picard P, et al. A possible therapeutic solution for stomatodynia (burning mouth syndrome). J Orofac Pain 1998;12:272–8.

Zakrzewska MM, Jamlyn PJ. Facial pain. In: Crombie IK, ed. Epidemiology of pain. Seattle: IASP Press, 1999:175–82.

35 Regional and Referred Orofacial Pain

Edmond L. Truelove, DDS, MSD

The diagnosis of facial pain is often complicated by referral of pain to the face, jaws, and teeth from pathologic conditions in nearby structures. The process leading to referral of sensations is not completely understood but appears to involve a number of mechanisms, including peripheral and central neural synaptic connections as well as multiple converging ascending sensory and nociceptive paths within major nerves serving regional areas and the convergence of nerves supplying distant sites. In some cases the sensation may be attributable to the common peripheral innervation of the tissues. This is seen in referral of pain from sinus pathology to the maxillary dentition or alveolar process. A second mechanism resulting in referral is interneuronal communication in the brain stem. Regardless of the process, it is abundantly clear that pain felt in a region does not necessarily mean that the source pathology is in that tissue. The astute clinician is persistently vigilant in assessing each patient to rule out the possibility of referred orofacial pain from near or distant sources. Failure of local findings to clearly and decisively identify the source of pain should result in a systematic search for other sources rather than an assumption that the painful symptom is caused by an atypical presentation of local pathology. Endodontic treatment of sound teeth and extraction of otherwise healthy dentition frequently occurs when pain is referred to the mouth.

The greatest concern is pain referral by serious and progressive pathology, including infections, vascular disorders, and neoplastic disease. Well-known sources of pain referred to the jaws include the pain of ischemic cardiac disease, esophageal pathology, and central lesions that cause increased intracranial pressure or produce compression of one or more of the cranial nerves. Major sources of referred pain are discussed, but the reader is reminded that thorough epidemiologic research documenting all important categories and sources of pain referral to the head and neck has not been completed, and the full extent of possible sources of pain referral is yet to be documented.

Referred cardiac pain

One of the most important sources of pain referral to the jaws comes from symptoms generated during attacks of angina in ischemic heart disease. Typically, pain or other unpleasant symptoms develop in the jaws during actual ischemic episodes with remission of pain when the crisis is over. Symptoms are usually felt in the left body of the mandible or left ramus, but pain may also occur within the mandibular teeth on the left side. It has generally been suggested that the pain is located at the angle of the mandible, but pain can occur over the entire left side of the mandible or in the maxillary teeth on the left. It is relatively common for the patient to also report pain in one or more of the following areas on the left side: lateral neck, shoulder, elbow, biceps, chest, or back. Symptoms most frequently onset during periods of exertion, exposure to cold, stressful events, and shortly after meals. The duration can be brief, lasting only a few seconds, or persist for 15 minutes or longer. Symptoms are usually resolved with nitroglycerin sublingually or as a dermal patch and can be replicated with cardiac stress testing.

Whereas most clinicians are familiar with the concept of referred cardiac pain, they may not recognize that other, nonpainful, sensory symptoms can be referred during ischemic episodes. Patients may complain of cold sensitivity in the teeth on the left; a left-sided sensation of tightness in the muscles of mastication; feelings of pressure within the mandible or maxilla, neck, or the dentition of the left side; and even sensations of paresthesia and tingling that create the urge to rub or massage the site of referred sensation. Pain or tightness in the chest may accompany other referred sensations, but some patients have no direct cardiac or chest complaints. Fatigue upon exertion, however, is frequent and should be taken seriously.

When cardiac sensations are referred to the jaws it is not uncommon for the patient to report temporary resolution of symptoms after dental therapy with a return of symptoms later that are slightly different. Since dental caries and periodontal disease are both common oral diseases it is understandable that patients with referred cardiac pain would receive treatment for active dental caries or periodontal disease before the clinician would begin to search for alternative explanations. Concurrent cardiac pain and dental symptoms arising from decay, apical pathology, or active periodontal infection are easily confused, and at times, the dentist must first attend to the active dental disease before exploring other sources of pain. However, if the dental status is stable and it is not possible to provoke the painful symptoms reported by the patient using normally accepted means for challenging dental innervation (cold testing, percussion, electric pulp testing, diagnostic anesthesia), it is prudent to begin early to rule out cardiac disease in those within the risk group for ischemic cardiac disease.

Many patients with referred ischemic pain already have a history of heart disease. For those with undiagnosed ischemia, it is advisable to assess their risk factors for cardiovascular disease to determine whether further cardiac assessment is appropriate. Important history findings include family history, obesity, high-fat diet, tobacco use, hypertension, alcoholism, age, and a sedentary life style. If assessment of risk factors suggests that the potential for cardiac disease with pain referral is present, use of nitroglycerin during symptom attacks may provide additional information, but ultimately, the patient should be returned to his or her primary care physician for definitive assessment of cardiac function.

Pain referred from neoplastic disease of the pharynx, nasopharynx, base of tongue, and hypopharynx

Neoplastic disease has known and documented potential for referring pain to the face and mouth. The site of referral can vary, depending on the tissue involved and individual characteristics of the patient. Nevertheless, several patterns of referral are more common than others. Base of tongue and hypopharyngeal lesions can refer symptoms of pain, burning, and fullness to the posterior region of the mandible, the ramus, and body of the mandible. Symptoms can also be referred to the ear, preauricular region, and in the general distribution of pain from disorders of the temporomandibular joint (TMJ). These lesions can also cause pain, burning, and paresthesia unilaterally in the tongue and floor of the mouth. Typically, symptoms are ill-defined and may increase during swallowing, jaw function, and eating or speaking. If the lesion is superficial or eroded, spicy foods and acids can increase symptoms and, if deep within tissues, palpation and swallowing can be provocative, resulting in generation of pain much in the same way that tender muscles in myofascial pain provoke symptoms when subjected to palpation. Invasion of neoplastic disease into peripheral neural tissues can also initiate sensations of local or referred paresthesia and numbness. As the size of the neoplasm increases, symptoms progress and usually become more localized.

Nasopharyngeal lesions even more frequently refer pain to the ear and TMJ region and can refer pain into the posterior of the maxilla and maxillary teeth. Hearing changes are sometimes reported in cases of nasopharyngeal malignancy. As nasopharyngeal tumors advance, a number of cranial nerves can be compromised, depending on the site of the tumor, but frequently several nerves are affected, since they emerge from the cranial base in close approximation. Occasionally, the multiple involvement of cranial nerves causes confusion in establishment of a diagnosis and symptoms are mistaken as signs of hypochondriasis or somatization disorder. When symptoms include referred sensory dysfunction or pain into the face or jaws, patients may be mistaken as having TMJ pain secondary to psychologic or behavioral problems. Jaw function can be compromised because of involvement of motor innervation provided by several of the cranial nerves. The neoplastically generated neurologic dysfunction can take the form of muscle weakness, contractions, or paralysis, depending on the nature of the invasion and stage of disease. Taste can also be altered via invasion of the tongue or tumor impact on the seventh and ninth cranial nerves, which provide taste to the posterior one-third of the tongue. Facial weakness or paralysis can also occur, causing a mistaken diagnosis of simple Bell's palsy. Sensory, motor, special sensory (taste, etc.), and autonomic functions can be disturbed or extinguished along with localized pain or referral of pain into the face and jaws. The consequences of errors in diagnosis of referred pain arising from nasopharyngeal tumors can be devastating. Neoplastic disease symptoms as described here can be confused with a number of chronic oral pains, including temporomandibular disorders (TMD), myofascial pain, burning mouth syndrome, glossodynia, reflux, dysgeusia, sinusitis, and pulpal pathology. Symptoms can also mimic cranial neuralgias, with paroxysmal pain triggered by movement or swallowing. When arising from referred neoplastic peripheral lesions, symptoms are unilateral except in midbase-of-tongue lesions or other midline lesions, in which case symptoms can be bilateral but not necessarily identical. As with referred cardiac pain, it is always advisable to remember that many common findings in uninvolved patients (TMJ clicking or crepitus, deviation in jaw opening, occlusal discrepancies, etc.) can cause the clinician to associate the referred pain with findings that represent normal variation. The ability to trigger pain with provocative challenging of suspected sites of pathology, such as the joint or muscles, and prevention or elimination of pain after diagnostic anesthesia or topical application of ethyl chloride to the suspected muscle help to differentiate local jaw pathology from referred pain. Any time that pain is accompanied with paresthesia, numbness, or other signs of neuropathy, it is important to consider malignant disease as the referral mechanism. History findings that increase concern for neoplastic symptom referral to the jaws include long-standing tobacco use, chronic alcohol consumption, prior head and neck radiation or chemotherapy for non-head and neck malignancy or for leukemia or lymphoma, and bone marrow transplant or organ transplant. Studies have shown that use of chronic immunosuppressive therapy increases the risk for head and neck malignancy at a later date. The only way to confirm or rule out the presence of tumor in these peripheral regions is to seek evaluation by an otolaryngologist and to consider magnetic resonance imaging (MRI). Neurologic consultation may also be appropriate.

Pain referred from lung lesions

Lesions of the upper lobes of the lung have been reported to refer pain to the face and jaws. The pain is usually unilateral and diffuse in distribution. The referral mechanism is most likely through input of the vagus, which refers the pain to the face. Facial pain can be the first symptom of lung cancer and other inflammatory or destructive forms of lung disease. Treatment of the lung lesion results in elimination of the referred facial pain. Patients presenting with a complaint of facial pain without local pathology and a positive history of lung disease or tumor should be evaluated for recurrence.

Pain referred from intracranial lesions

Lesions of the central nervous system (CNS) located within the cranial vault can produce generalized headache and trigger more localized referred pain. The types of problems generating these pains include tumors that are either benign or malignant; vascular lesions, such as aneurysms; demyelinating diseases, including multiple sclerosis (MS); post-traumatic brain injury; and disorders of cranial fluid pressure (intracranial hypertension, hypotension, etc.). Generalized problems cause diffuse bilateral pain that is most often characterized as "headache." Isolated unilateral lesions can produce generalized head pain if they increase pressure within the cranium; pain may be unilateral or bilateral with pain dominant on one side. The pain can be felt in the temporal region, leading to an erroneous diagnosis of myofascial pain. Localized lesions can also refer pain along the distribution of the neural path affected. For example, tumor or vascular pressure on the trigeminal nerve may cause neuralgia-like (paroxysmal) or persistent pain far peripherally in the nerve and into the jaws and teeth. If neuralgia-like, the pain can be triggered by light touch and stimulation that is not usually nociceptive. Change of position (sitting, bending over, reclining) can increase or decrease some intracranial sources of referred facial pain. Diagnosis is often confused with tension-type headache (TTHA), migraine, TMD, myofascial pain, sinusitis, and trigeminal neuralgia. Diagnosis is usually made through neurologic referral, MRI of the brain, computed tomography (CT), and lumbar puncture. Symptoms that cannot be fully explained by local findings or that escalate in the face of rational treatment require assessment to rule out CNS pathology.

Pain referred from disorders of the ears, nose, throat, and sinuses

The close proximity of the ears, nose, and throat structures to the face and jaws, along with shared innervation, sets the stage for possible confusion in diagnosis, caused by referral of painful symptoms to the face. The most common source of referred pain is disease of the sinuses. It is particularly easy to mistake sinus pain for odontogenic pathology when sinus involvement is unilateral, because inflammation in the region can cause percussion and biting sensitivity in one or more teeth in the quadrant of the maxilla adjacent to the inflamed sinus and because neuronal sensitization of the second division of the trigeminal nerve can trigger hypersensitivity of dental innervation, leading to responses that mimic odontogenic pathology. In either of these situations the teeth and periodontium can be mildly to exquisitely hypersensitive to touch, palpation, percussion, and thermal stimulation. Symptoms can be restricted to as few as two teeth, but usually more than one tooth is reactive. The molars and bicuspids are the most frequently symptomatic in sinusitis. The two most common errors in diagnosis are to label the problems as arising from pulpitis or occlusal trauma. When sinus disease is bilateral (allergic, infectious) symptoms can be referred bilaterally, and since bilateral odontogenic pathology that is simultaneously painful is not a frequent occurrence, a diagnosis of pulpitis is less often entertained, and more commonly, a diagnosis of occlusal traumatism, bruxism, or myofascial pain is suggested. Findings that help to reduce the risk that sinus disease will be incorrectly diagnosed as odontogenic include a history of episodic or recent symptomatic sinus disease, respiratory allergies, nasal discharge, nasal obstruction, pain with extraoral palpation of the maxillary and or frontal sinus, and palpation tenderness with intraoral and extraoral palpation over the maxillary sinuses. Other findings that reduce the probability that odontogenic problems are generating the pain include lack of obvious periapical infection or deep caries, prolonged pain with thermal stimulation of the teeth, and a significant elevation in facial pain when bending over. The diagnosis becomes more confusing however if nonsymptomatic dental disease is present (early caries, cracked restorations, signs of tooth wear, etc.). Final diagnosis may require CT of the sinuses; ear, nose, and throat consultation; or therapeutic trial using an appropriate antibiotic, decongestant, and nasal spray. Panoramic radiographs of the jaws and sinuses, and dental radiographs of the teeth and alveolar structures can sometimes identify clouding of the sinus cavity, but if both sinuses are involved it may be difficult to distinguish the presence of sinus changes on dental films, since both sides have the same appearance. When sinus disease is suspected, CT of the region effectively identifies thickening of the sinus mucosa and fluid levels in the sinus caused by sinusitis.

Sinus tumors can produce referred pain to the teeth and alveolar tissues. As the tumor invades, it may affect regional innervation, and referred pain can be replaced by paresthesia or numbness. Also, the perception of premature occlusal contact and a high occlusion can develop. If the lesion is expanding, it can destroy osseous support or produce occlusal changes by causing expansion of the alveolar structures. Complicating the differential diagnosis of sinus versus dental infection is the common occurrence of odontogenic infection spreading into the lining of the sinus causing reactive swelling, owing to fluid retention, and overt infection of the sinus. The end result is infection in both areas with little success if only one source of infection is treated.

Allergic rhinitis can provoke headaches and migraine along with sinus stuffiness and congestion. When the pain is localized in the face rather than more cephalic, it is easy for the treating doctor to assume that odontogenic infection or sinus congestion is triggering the pain.

Referred pain from ear and eustachian tube symptoms

Disease of the external, middle, and inner ear can generate symptoms in the face and jaws. Inflammation in the external ear canal caused by allergy or local factors (trauma, foreign objects, etc.), or infection can provoke symptoms around the TMJ that are poorly localized and trigger modifications in jaw posturing (protrusive jaw thrusting) to reduce the symptoms during jaw movement and function, which in turn often initiates the onset of secondary myalgia and muscle fatigue. The pseudo bite that results from the protrusive posturing sometimes confuses the examiner, and an incorrect diagnosis of joint changes or myofascial pain secondary to occlusal factors is established. External canal inflammation can cause palpation tenderness over the joint, leading to an erroneous diagnosis of arthritic joint inflammation. The most common infectious agents in adults are bacteria and fungi, and their presence is usually easily identified by visualization of inflammatory changes in the external canal, and in more severe cases by exudation from the ear. Fungal infections result in the growth of fungal colonies along the wall of the external canal, producing a film that covers the wall. Usually patients who present with these conditions have a prior history of external otitis. As the external canal becomes more inflamed, pain develops as the condyle generates tissue distortion along one surface of the canal.

Middle ear disease can also refer pain anteriorly to the TMJ, masseter region, and posterior maxillary teeth. Pressure caused by fluid accumulation and inflammation behind the tympanic membrane causes pain to be localized to the ear (classic earache) and sometimes produces a generalized ache over the side of the head and forward to the preauricular region. Diagnosis is established through otoscopic examination of the tympanic membrane. Middle ear infection can be unilateral or bilateral. In some cases a reduction in hearing acuity or balance can occur as the condition becomes chronic. The onset of facial pain accompanied by a hearing deficit, vertigo, or a sensation of fullness within the ear should automatically trigger an assessment of the ears. Tumors of the middle ear provoke unilateral symptoms that are progressive and eventually include hearing loss, vertigo, localized pain, referral of pain to the jaws and face, and facial nerve dysfunction (loss of facial expression, drooping). When pain associated with tumors of the middle ear begins, it is often diffuse and often referred to the TMJ and midfacial region. Secondary myofascial pain often develops.

Tinnitus is another symptom of ear disease that many clinicians confuse as arising from TMD. Although studies report higher rates of tinnitus in patients with TMD, most tinnitus occurs in patients without TMD, and both tinnitus and TMD have been associated with depression and high rates of somatic complaints. Since tinnitus can be caused by a number of serious conditions, all patients with tinnitus should be referred for assessment of ear pathology and CNS and cardiovascular function. Hypertension and vascular disease can cause tinnitus and headache, so the combination of tinnitus and headache certainly requires a thorough medical evaluation to rule out both local pathology and systemic dysfunction, such as hypertension.

Eustachian tube dysfunction, as occurs in allergy and middle ear infections, can generate a sensation of fullness and plugging of the ears and discomfort in the ear, TMJ, and preauricular region. The reason for the dysfunction must be determined, since it can arise from reactions to allergins, tumors, or infections. Nasopharyngeal carcinomas and other tumors can cause eustachian tube dysfunction and often cause altered neurologic function in cranial nerves VIII, IX, and XI.

Referred pain from the esophagus

Less is known about symptom referral to the face from pathology in the esophagus than that in the nasal and ear region, but symptom referral does occur irregularly. In general, symptoms are provoked by neoplastic disease, esophagitis caused by reflux, and by esophageal muscle pain and myalgia generated by dysfunction in swallowing and by esophageal strictures. Lesions on the lateral wall of the esophagus can produce unilateral referral to the jaws and mouth, and lesions near the midline can produce bilateral symptoms. The usual region of referral is the posterior aspect of the tongue and ramus of the mandible. Symptoms can also be referred to the lateral aspect of the mandible up to the preauricular and auricular regions. Symptoms often increase after sleeping in a reclining position. Symptoms also increase with acidic and spicy foods or excessive swallowing during eating or habitual activities. Symptoms at the referred site are improved with trials of antacids, coating agents, antireflux medications, and topical anesthetic rinses or gels swallowed. Usually referred esophageal pain is low grade and persistent, with a rise in pain during swallowing. Another source of pain arising in the esophagus is glossopharyngeal neuralgia with a local trigger in the upper aerodigestive tract. Movement in the esophageal tissues or cutaneous stimulation during swallowing triggers the neuralgia pain, which can be felt in the throat but more often is referred higher into the back of the oropharyngeal region and to the base of the tongue or mandible. Topical anesthetic gel swallowed differentiates referred pain arising from the esophagus. Pain from glossopharyngeal neuralgia is usually significantly sharper and more severe than pain caused by local pathology in the esophagus. It is also of shorter durations and paroxysmal in nature. Referred esophageal pain is easily confused with burning mouth syndrome, atypical facial pain, or myofascial pain. Diagnosis is confirmed by blocking symptoms with topical or regional anesthesia and by conducting a thorough medical workup that includes endoscopy, soft-tissue MRI, and other forms of soft-tissue imaging designed to detect lesions of the esophagus. The greatest risk from referred esophageal pain is malignant disease in the wall of the esophagus, which often is not detected until significantly advanced because symptoms are subtle and usually thought to be caused by reflux or chronic indigestion.

Referred pain from cervical myofascial trigger points and degenerative disease

Perhaps one of the most common of all sites for referred pain to the oral and facial complex is cervical disease and dysfunction. Among chronic pain disorders, cervical problems are prevalent and persistent. Since several local disorders of the jaws (TMD, odontogenic infection, periodontal disease) are also prevalent, it is understandable that clinicians sometimes confuse referred cervical symptoms with local dental pathology. Most cervical pain that is referred to the face and jaws arises from cervical myalgia and myofascial pain of the anterior and posterior strap muscles of the neck. Compression of cervical nerves can cause cervical, shoulder, and arm pain. It is often accompanied by paresthesia of the fingers. Under normal circumstances referred cervical pain is located in the lateral aspect of the face, the maxilla and maxillary teeth, and the region of the TMJ. The eye and retro-orbital region are also common sites for referred cervical pain and particularly from cervical myofascial pain trigger points. Pain can arise from any of the major cervical muscles, including the paravertebral muscles along the posterior aspect of the neck and the sternocleidomastoid, located along the lateral aspect of the neck. Palpation of the affected muscle or muscle trigger provokes local pain within the muscle and refers pain to the distant site. Repeated stimulation of the muscle can provoke prolonged pain at the distant site, and desensitization of the trigger by chilling with ice or vapocoolant sprays (ethyl chloride or fluormethane) or by anesthetic infiltration (2% lidocaine, without a vasoconstrictor, or other accepted injectable local anesthetic) into the muscle trigger extinguishes the referred pain. Headaches are also frequently caused by cervical muscle dysfunction. Referral of pain to the teeth from cervical muscles is common and can result in diagnostic confusion. In many cases, neck movement does not specifically trigger the referred pain but specific localized palpation does, as does muscle fatigue. Triggers from cervical muscles to the muscles of mastication or the TMJ also occur. Referred neurologic symptoms are usually of a sharper quality than referred muscle symptoms and are more likely to be triggered by turning the head or flexing the neck. Turning the head can also provoke myofascial pain in the neck and trigger referral of pain to the face and structures of the jaws. The most commonly accepted method for diagnosis of referred pain from the cervical region is to palpate the muscles of the neck and upper shoulder region (splenius capitis, scalene, sternocleidomastoid, trapezius) while observing for the development of pain at the site of complaint (maxillary teeth, face, TMJ, muscles of mastication). Flexing and extending the neck and lateral rotations can be used to help detect referred nerve compression pain as seen in degenerative cervical pathology and pain arising from tense cervical muscles. Since muscle tension and pain in the pericranial, masticatory, and cervical muscles can occur in response to stress (anxiety, tension, depression, etc.), it is common for patients with such disorders to have symptoms arising in several regions (headaches, facial pain, neck pain) with cervical constituents triggering local and referred pain and headache. Occasionally, progressive pathology of the cervical spine causes progressively more severe pain at the distant site. Since the lateral aspect of the neck and the area from the lower lateral border of the mandible downward to the clavicle are innervated by cervical nerves, it is possible for serious pathology associated with the cervical nerves to trigger pain in the lower part of the face and anterior of the neck immediately below the mandible, causing confusion and errors, including errors in attributing submandibular pain to salivary gland and lymph node disease.

Pain referral from carotidynia

Carotidynia is an uncommon condition that is poorly understood. The epidemiology of the disorder is not well documented, but it appears to occur predominantly in females and is most common in young adult females and elderly women. It is characterized by significant pain arising from the carotid during palpation of the vessel. Referral of pain to the mandible, lateral face, and preauricular region occurs. The pathophysiology that triggers the pain is also not well understood, but patients often respond to either indomethacin or amitriptyline. The mechanism of action is not clear, and whether the condition undergoes spontaneous remission without treatment is not known.

Pain referral from giant cell arteritis

Giant cell arteritis (GCA), or temporal arteritis, affects elderly patients and often refers pain into the jaws, face, and eyes. It can mimic TMD and also creates headaches that are characterized by muscle tension except that they are often unilateral or predominantly one-sided. The facial pain of GCA is usually diffuse and mild at onset, but over a number of months, symptoms progress and become more severe. Use of the jaw becomes more difficult, and jaw fatigue is common when the condition is chronic. Visual acuity can be progressively affected as giant cell lesions involve the optic vessels. Since the only symptoms may be headaches, jaw fatigue, and jaw pain it is easy to understand why treating physicians and dentists can fail to detect giant cell arteritis early, but discovery is important, since the vascular lesions of GCA can be progressive and lead to blindness. Additionally, involvement of the carotid can increase the risk of stroke. Diagnosis is easily confirmed by detection of pain during palpation of the carotid or temporal artery, referral of pain to a distant facial or head site during palpation of the vessel, and by detection of an elevated erythrocyte sedimentation rate. Temporal artery biopsy is often used to confirm the diagnosis, and treatment with long-term systemic prednisone is the treatment of choice.

Pain referred from thyroid disease

Normally, hyperthyroid or hypothyroid disease does not cause localized pain in the neck or referred pain to the face or dental structures. One exception that occasionally occurs is pain that arises from Hashimoto thyroiditis, which is an autoimmune inflammatory disease of the thyroid gland. It can cause painful or tender enlargement of the thyroid, and in a small percentage of cases, pain can be referred into the mandible or other submandibular sites. Palpation of the thyroid can provoke the same referred symptom. Thyroid function studies should be ordered and thyroid scans completed to determine the exact nature of the thyroid dysfunction. Subacute thyroiditis has also been reported to cause referred pain to the face.

Pain referred from salivary obstruction, infection, or neoplastic disease

Normally, pain arising in the major salivary glands is localized to the region of the gland but not necessarily localized enough to distinguish that the gland is painful, rather than adjacent structures. When salivary obstruction, infection, or neoplasia is located in the parotid, it can create symptoms around the gland that are diffuse enough to be confused with myofascial pain of the masseters or even refer pain preauricularly to the area around the TMJ. Stimulation of the gland to function during the first phase of eating causes increased gland discomfort and a sensation that chewing is producing pain in the muscles or joint. The presentation of pain onset in the area of the muscle or joint with first jaw use usually results in an erroneous diagnosis of TMD. Persistent aching can occur if the lesion is caused by an infiltrating tumor, and palpation of the soft tissue over the gland leads to a diagnosis of myofascial pain rather than parotitis or parotid pain. Any suspicion that pain may be arising from parotid pathology requires that the gland be examined carefully, including assessment for purulent discharge or lack of flow, as seen in obstruction, and palpation of the gland for enlargement or a mass. Malignant salivary gland tumors, in some cases, have a predisposition for following perineural channels with resultant neurologic stimulation, pain, and paresthesias. Lesions of the submandibular gland can also trigger pain within the gland and pain referred into the tongue, laryngeal region, and the posterior of the mandible. The same types of lesions should be considered and appropriate diagnostic steps taken to rule out submandibular salivary gland pathology.

Pain referred from dental structures to other sites

It is not often thought that dental structures and the dentition commonly refer pain to adjacent or distant sites, however, such patterns of pain referral do occur with regularity and, when present, lead to delayed or incorrect diagnosis and treatment. Among the most common sources of referred odontogenic pain is pulpitis in the posterior dentition. Pulpitis can refer pain to the adjacent muscles of mastication and particularly the masseter and temporalis, creating the illusion of pain arising from myofascial pain. Odontogenic pain is also sometimes referred into the maxilla and sinus region and into the preauricular zone near the TMJ. Diagnosis can become difficult when the referred pain also stimulates muscle tension, which reduces mandibular range of movement, further mimicking TMD. As pulpitis pain progresses and becomes both more chronic and severe, adaptive motor behavior sometimes occurs, causing significant restrictions in mandibular movement, further increasing the likelihood of the pulpal condition being incorrectly diagnosed as muscular dysfunction and TMD.

Another common cause of referred odontogenic pain is pericoronitis arising around erupting third molars. The pattern of tissue pain and inflammation frequently results in musculoskeletal tightness and muscular tension and trismus. Some of the symptoms are provoked by inflammatory changes that spread to include regional fascial and muscular tissues, but neurogenic sensitization also contributes to the pattern of pain and dysfunction that spreads through the affected site. Occasionally, pulpal or periapical infection or inflammation in the anterior of the maxilla results in referred pain to the orbital region on the affected side.

Odontogenic inflammatory pain, as occurs in pulpitis, can also trigger paroxysmal pain with light to moderate cutaneous or thermal stimulation of the dentition. The pain is usually felt in the tooth with pulpitis, but the extent of pain or hypersensitivity felt in the tooth may not be as great as in the site of referral. Generally, referred odontogenic pain is felt in sites in the maxilla or mandible on the same side as the pulpal pathology. With exquisite hypersensitivity in pulpitis, even very light touch, mechanical stimulation, or thermal challenge can provoke pain that spreads and radiates throughout the entire side of the head. Pain of pulpitis or pulpal necrosis is sometimes referred to the muscles of mastication and particularly the masseter and temporalis muscles. It is provoked by the same factors that would be expected to worsen muscle pain, including chewing, cold air, tension, clenching and parafunction, and any thermal challenge to the face or dentition.

Pain arising in the periodontium can also be referred to adjacent structures, but in most circumstances, the pain is referred from the area of periodontal hypersensitivity or inflammation to dentition in the same neurologic distribution as the periodontal origin of the stimulus. The referral pattern frequently results in a misdiagnosis of pulpitis or cracked tooth. The pattern of referral is usually to a tooth more anterior in the arch. Diagnosis is best established by triggering symptoms after periodontal probing and stimulation of the peridontium followed by extinguishing the odontogenic pain by application of topical anesthetic onto the periodontal trigger or by careful infiltration of local anesthetic into the same area. These areas of periodontal hypersensitivity are usually not in regions of advanced periodontal disease and are more likely to occur in tissues in which pocket depth is less than 5 mm. The trigger is usually along the lateral soft-tissue wall of the pocket. If the tissue is inflamed, the problem can sometimes be resolved with aggressive local periodontal therapy. The triggers can also be extinguished, in some cases, with regular application of local anesthetic several times a day, combined use of a topical steroid cream and topical antibiotic therapy and systemic use of an antidepressant (amitriptyline 30–60 mg/d). Occasionally, persistent periodontal triggers respond to sclerosing injections, when other therapies have failed. Surgical excision of the triggers is not as effective, and they often return.

Another oral soft-tissue problem that results in referred pain is the development of hyperpathic scar tissue in sites of surgery or traumatic mucosal injury. These triggers are different from the periodontal triggers just discussed in that the periodontal triggers associated with periodontalgia, once stimulated, provoke continuous pain and aching. The triggers in surgical sites and scars generate sharper pain that is brief and only occurs during direct stimulation of the trigger site. These triggers sometimes respond to excision and may represent small traumatic neuromas. They also may respond to topical anesthetic protocols and topical steroids, but may not remain quiet without systemic medications, such as carbamazepine or other antiseizure agents. Ruling out a peripheral neuropathy versus a soft-tissue trigger of a true neuralgia is important in such cases.

Suggested reading

Bansevicius D, Sjaastad O. Cervicogenic headache: the influence of mental load on pain level and EM of shoulder-neck and facial muscles. Headache 1996;36:372–8.

Bindoff LA, Heseltine D. Unilateral facial pain in patients with lung cancer: A referred pain via the vagus? Lancet 1998;1:812–5.

Blume HG. Cervicogenic headaches: radiofrequency neurotomy and the cervical disc and fusion. Clin Exp Rheumatol 2000;18(Suppl 19):S53–8.

Chukwuemeka AO, John LC. An unusual cause of unilateral face pain. Int J Clin Pract 1999;53:312.

Clerico DM, Fieldman R. Referred headache of rhinogenic origin in the absence of sinusitis. Headache 1994;34:226–9.

Ellis BD, Kosmorsky GS. Referred ocular pain relieved by suboccipital injection. Headache 1995;35:101–3.

Ellrich J, Anderson OK, Messlinger K, Arendt-Nielsen L. Convergence of meningeal and facial afferents onto trigeminal brainstem neurons: an electrophysiological study in rat and man. Pain 1999;82:229–37.

Falace DA, Reid K, Rayens MK. The influence of deep (odontogenic) pain intensity, quality, and duration on the incidence and characteristics of referred orofacial pain. J Orofac Pain 1996;10:232–9.

Goldberg HL. Chest cancer refers pain to the face and jaw: a case review. Cranio 1997;15:167–9.

Kreiner M, Oekson JP. Toothache of cardiac origin. J Orofac Pain 1999;13:201–7.

McCarron MO, Gone I. Glossopharyngeal neuralgia referred from a pontine lesion. Cephalalgia 1999;19:115–7.

Smith MJ, Myall RW. Subacute thyroiditis as a cause of facial pain. Oral Surg Oral Med Oral Pathol 1977;43:59–62.

Taub E, Argoff CE, Winterkorn JM, Milhorat TH. Resolution of chronic cluster headache after resection of a tentorial meningioma: case report. Neurosurgery 1995;37:319–21.

Webb CJ, Makura ZG, McCormick MS. Glossopharyngeal neuralgia following foreign body impaction in the neck. J Laryngol Otol 2000;114:70–2.

Yanagisawa K, Kveton JF. Referred otalgia. Am J Otolaryngol 1992;13:322–7.

36 Orofacial Pain in Patients with Cancer

Joel B. Epstein, DMD, MSD, FRCD(C)

Pain attributable to cancer or cancer treatment is a major concern for patients and health care providers. Orofacial pain affects the quality of life and can complicate the course of treatment and rehabilitation following cancer therapy. Head, neck, and oral pain may arise from the primary tumor, metastases, and infiltration of tumor cells into bone (Table 36–1). Pain attributable to treatment of cancer includes acute pain due to direct toxicity damaging mucosal surfaces and surgical pain (Table 36–2). Pain associated with mucositis is the most frequently reported complication of greatest concern to patients who are receiving head and neck radiation therapy or the aggressive chemotherapy protocols associated with bone marrow transplantation. Whereas acute pain associated with cancer or its therapy is understood, chronic symptoms following cancer therapy have received less study although they certainly affect the quality of life (see Table 36–2).

Pain due to tumor

Head and neck malignant disease, primarily squamous cell carcinoma, is frequently associated with pain at patient presentation and may be present in up to 85% of patients, typically described as low-grade discomfort. Other manifestations of malignant disease involving the head and neck may present as a mass or altered mandibular function (limited opening, deviation on opening) or may not be associated with any symptoms. Systemic malignant disease may present first with orofacial symptoms that may include orofacial pain or numbness and paresthesia along neurologic distribution. Lymphoma involving the oral region may present as a mass and as discomfort, although symptoms of discomfort are typically low-grade. Orofacial discomfort and paresthesia or anesthesia may be the first manifestation of metastatic disease and, rarely, may be a manifestation in patients with leukemia. Hematologic malignancy may present with orofacial findings of tissue pallor, petechiae, ecchymoses, gingival bleeding, gingival hyperplasia, local infection, and healing of prior treatment. Manage-

Table 36–1 Orofacial Pain in Cancer Patients

Acute
Due to disease
Invasion of bone, nerve, muscle
Mucosal damage
Tumor pressure
Due to cancer therapy
Surgical
Radiation therapy
Chemotherapy
Oral or dental pain
Mucositis
Infection
Neuropathy
Unrelated conditions causing pain
Chronic
Due to persisting or progressive disease
Due to cancer therapy
Surgery, radiation therapy, chemotherapy
Mucosal atrophy or xerostomia
Mucosal infection
Neuropathy
Temporomandibular (myofascial disorders)
Dental caries
Osteoradionecrosis or mucosal necrosis
Post-herpetic neuralgia
Unrelated conditions causing pain

ment of pain due to tumor depends on the severity of the pain and the level of pain tolerance of the patient. Whereas nonsteroidal anti-inflammatory drugs (NSAIDs), such as ibuprofen, may be adequate in early disease, opioids, such as hydrocodone are often necessary. Pain must be controlled.

Acute pain during cancer therapy

Pain due to mucositis

The incidence and severity of mucositis is related to the treatment provided to patients with cancer. Oral mucositis is a therapy- and rate-limiting complication of cancer treatment in aggressive chemotherapy protocols associated with bone marrow transplantation and head and neck radiation therapy. Whereas increasing intensity of therapy in both radiation protocols and chemotherapy has been possible as the management of hematologic toxicity has improved, oral mucosal damage has been a limiting factor. Prevention of mucositis is the best means of reducing pain. There is evidence that improved oral hygiene leads to lower rates and severity of mucositis. Avoidance of physically irritating food products and removal of physical irritants from the oral environment are indicated. Oral care products that are highly flavored and contain local tissue irritants should be avoided. Various means of preventing or reducing tissue damage are actively being investigated. Approaches that include anti-inflammatory, antimicrobial agents, and other medications that affect growth factors or delivery of biologic

response modifiers and growth factors to oral tissues are actively being investigated.

Pain management should include use of topical agents, including topical anesthetics (diphenhydramine and lidocaine, 3 to 5%) and analgesic rinses and mucosa coating agents (sucralfate, etc.). Systemic analgesics are frequently required and should be provided based upon the World Health Organization (WHO) analgesic ladder with nonopioids as the first step, later combined with opioids if necessary. Although systemic analgesics are frequently indicated, use of topical agents should be considered in addition to systemic agents, to reduce the dose and duration of systemic agent that may be needed. Acute surgical pain is managed in the usual manner with oral analgesics.

Oral infection

Pain may be caused by oral infections, including those arising from preexisting dental and periodontal sources. Therefore, dental assessment is essential prior to cancer therapy. Necessary treatment may include extraction of nonrestorable teeth, particularly when infection risk is anticipated during periods of cancer therapy. In cases of radiation therapy, the risk of necrosis of the bone following treatment necessitates lifetime maintenance of the teeth within the radiation field, and if it is anticipated that dental maintenance will be inadequate, precancer therapy extractions are indicated. When appropriate, endodontic therapy can be provided. The most common reason for dental extraction prior to cancer therapy is periodontal disease.

The occurrence of infections of the mucosa may complicate oral findings, including candidiasis or reactivation of herpes viruses, most commonly herpes simplex virus (HSV). Prophylaxis to prevent oropharyngeal infection is standard in leukemia-bone marrow transplant units. This includes a pretreatment assessment of HSV serology, and if positive, prophylactic antivirals are provided. Prophylaxis for oropharyngeal candidiasis using topical therapies is provided, but systemic antifungals (amphotericin B or fluconazole) are more common treatment. The ideal prophylaxis for *Candida* infections is not yet available.

Chlorhexidine rinses may be useful in managing gingivitis and plaque, and suppressing *Candida* colonization, but it has not been documented, in most studies, to prevent mucositis. Use of broad-spectrum antibiotic lozenges that suppress *Candida* and have a specific gram-negative spectrum has been shown, in initial studies, to reduce mucositis. Systemic antibiotics and antifungals are routine in prophylaxis in patients with leukemia or undergoing bone marrow transplantation receiving aggressive treatment protocols anticipated to

Table 36–2   Frequencies of Oral Pain Associated with Cancer Therapy

Classification of Pain	Frequency (%)
Acute pain during treatment	
Oropharyngeal mucositis	
Chemotherapy	40–70
Bone marrow transplant	60–85
Radiation therapy	100
Postsurgical therapy	100
Chronic pain following cancer therapy	
Mucosal pain	up to 33
Pain associated with mucosal infection	
Candidiasis	
Post bone marrow transplant	up to 50
Post radiation therapy	20–33
Herpes simplex in seropositive BMT patients	up to 90
Neuropathy	16
TMD or myofascial pain	25–30
(patients with head and neck SCC)	

BMT = bone marrow transplant; TMD = temporomandibular disorders; SCC = squamous cell carcinoma.

produce neutropenia. These antimicrobial agents may also suppress preexisting low-grade dental infections.

Musculoskeletal pain

Musculoskeletal pain is commonly seen in patients following treatment for head and neck cancer. Etiologies include the effects of the tumor on the musculature, the effect of surgical treatment that may result in jaw discontinuity, or fibrosis within the muscles and soft tissues that may occur following surgery and radiation therapy. In addition, osteonecrosis of the jaw may affect jaw function and, if pathologic fracture occurs, may be associated with mandibular discontinuity. Stress, anxiety, and depression may magnify the pain experience and may affect habitual jaw activities that can themselves lead to symptoms of a temporomandibular disorder (TMD). Restriction in jaw opening following radiation therapy has been related to inclusion of the heads of the lateral pterygoid muscles in the radiated field.

There are no studies assessing the management of mandibular dysfunction in patients following cancer therapy. Management of pain of mandibular dysfunction may include unique approaches, such as a mandibular guidance appliance and approaches as described for management of TMD. Guidelines provided in other parts of this chapter also apply.

Management of osteoradionecrosis includes prevention by effective pre-cancer therapy dental management. In addition, maintenance of good oral hygiene and excellent fit and function of any prosthesis that may be present in the oral cavity is essential. Management of bony exposure may include hyperbaric oxygen therapy, sequestrectomy, and more complex surgery, if healing does not follow. Secondary infection must be managed and, when pain is present, it must be managed through local (topical) means and use of systemic analgesics as necessary.

Neurologic pain

Neurologically mediated pain may present as a neuralgia-like symptom or as a neuropathy, with aching and burning discomfort. Management with noninvasive protocols is important, particularly in patients who have received radiation therapy in the region of pain. Diagnostic anesthetic blocks may be useful in localizing symptoms, and anesthetic and neurolytic blocks may be helpful in localized pain due to tumor or owing to persisting pain in a nerve distribution affected by radiation or surgery. Complexity of management is increased owing to the impact of significant stress or depression, as well as the pain from recurrent disease. Neurosurgery is rarely considered. The principal approach following diagnosis of neu-

rologic-based pain is systemic medication appropriate for neuralgia or neuropathic pain states. Medical management of neuralgia and neuropathy is discussed elsewhere in this chapter. Medications to consider include anticonvulsants (carbamazepine, gabapentin), antidepressants, and other adjunctive medications and analgesics.

Chronic mucosal pain

Persisting symptoms following head and neck cancer therapy have been reported to last for more than 1 year. The symptoms of discomfort are low-grade but may relate to complications of radiation therapy that persist, including dry mouth, atrophy of mucosal tissues resulting in sensitivity, and neuropathy that may be present within radiated fields. This mucosal sensitivity may result in burning sensation with oral function. Management may include attempts at stimulating salivary flow, if reduced, ruling out the presence of *Candida*, and local or systemic management of neuropathy. Dietary changes have usually already been initiated by the patient.

Summary

Oral cancer is frequently associated with low-grade discomfort which is the principal reason patients with head and neck cancer present for diagnosis and treatment. Pain may become a significant management issue with progression of disease or with complications of current therapies. In addition, pain may be present due to other causes that require assessment and diagnosis. In patients who have previously been treated for cancer, pain in the oral region may result in considerable anxiety, with fears of recurrent disease, even years following cancer therapy. It is incumbent on the health care provider to thoroughly assess the oral environment and to identify potential sources of pain. It is also essential that the provider be fully aware of past cancer therapy and whether this could have an impact on current treatment choices, particularly those of surgical nature. New, second, primary, or recurrent cancers may occur in up to 25% of patients, and those who continue tobacco and alcohol use are at higher risk. Careful evaluation and a diagnosis of the cause of pain is mandatory along with ruling out malignant disease in those who have previously received treatment.

The majority of patients have pain at the time of diagnosis, and the vast majority experience significant pain through the course of the treatment of their disease. In head and neck cancer, whether the patient receives radiation or surgical management, pain is universal. In those who receive intensive chemotherapy and bone marrow transplant, mucositis occurs in up to 90% of patients and is associated with significant pain. When analgesics are the treatment of choice, appropriate drug selection and dosing is necessary. A number of studies have identified too limited use of adjunctive pain management medications and inadequate dosing of analgesics owing to concerns of possible drug addiction. However, in studies assessing the use of opioids by patients with cancer, addiction has not been substantiated as a serious problem. The greater concern is inadequate management of pain that is easily controlled if appropriate treatment schedules are followed. Effective pain management is possible for most patients and greatly improves their quality of life.

Suggested reading

Barasch A, Safford MM. Management of oral pain in patients with malignant diseases. Compendium 1993;14:1376, 1378–82.

Bonica JJ. Introduction to management of pain in advanced cancer. In: Bonica JJ, Ventafridda V, eds. International Symposium on Pain of Advanced Cancer. New York: Raven Press, 1979:115–30.

Du Pen SL, Du Pen AR, Polissar N, et al. Implementing guidelines for cancer pain management: results of a randomized controlled clinical trial. J Clin Oncol 1999;17:361–70.

Epstein JB, Emerton S, Lunn R, et al. Quality of life and oral function following radiotherapy for head and neck cancer. Head Neck 1999;21:1–11.

Epstein JB, Schubert MM. Management of orofacial pain in cancer patients. Oral Oncol 1993;29:243–50.

Epstein JB, Stewart KH. Radiation therapy and pain in patients with head and neck cancer. Oral Oncol 1993;29:191–9.

Epstein JB, van der Meij E, McKenzie M, et al. Postradiation osteonecrosis of the mandible. A long-term follow-up study. Oral Surg Oral Med Oral Pathol 1997;83:657–62.

McGuire DB, Yeager KA, Dudley WN, et al. Acute oral pain and mucositis in bone marrow transplant and leukemia patients: data from a pilot study. Cancer Nurs 1998;21: 385–93.

Syrjala KL, Chapko ME. Evidence for a bio-psychosocial model of cancer treatment-related pain. Pain 1995;61:69–79.

Index